# HEBREW VERSE STRUCTURE

# Hebrew Verse Structure

**M. O'Connor**

EISENBRAUNS
P.O.B. 275
Winona Lake, Indiana 46590

This essay was originally accepted in partial fulfillment of the requirements for the degree of Doctor of Philosophy (Near Eastern Studies) in The University of Michigan, 1978.


Library of Congress Catalog Card Number: 80-68370
International Standard Book Number: 0-931464-02-1

*For Anna Maria O'Connor*
*and John David O'Connor*

*mh mtwq mdbš*
*wmh ʿz mʾry*

*Judges 14:18*

# CONTENTS

## PART I: OVERVIEW

## CHAPTER ONE: HEBREW VERSE STRUCTURE

## CHAPTER TWO: THE TEXTS



# PART II: FINE STRUCTURE

## CHAPTER THREE: THE SHAPE AND STRUCTURE OF THE LINE

## CHAPTER FOUR: THE WORD-LEVEL TROPE OF REPETITION



## CHAPTER FIVE: THE WORD-LEVEL TROPES OF COLORATION: BINOMINATION, COORDINATION AND COMBINATION

## CHAPTER SIX: THE LINE-LEVEL TROPE OF MATCHING



## CHAPTER SEVEN: THE LINE-LEVEL TROPE OF GAPPING AND RELATED PHENOMENA

## CHAPTER EIGHT: THE SUPRALINEAR-LEVEL TROPE OF SYNTACTIC DEPENDENCY



## CHAPTER NINE: THE SUPRALINEAR-LEVEL TROPE OF MIXING



# PART III: GROSS STRUCTURE

## CHAPTER TEN: AN OVERVIEW

## APPENDIX: THE TEXTS



## BIBLIOGRAPHY

## INDEXES

# ABBREVIATIONS

| | | | |
|---|---|---|---|
| A | adverbial | NappN | appositional phrase |
| Akk | Akkadian | NcN | construct phrase |
| Arb | Arabic | NwN | conjunct phrase |
| Arm | Aramaic | np | nominal phrase |
| c. | common gender | O | (direct) object |
| cl | clause | occ | occurrence(s) |
| con | constituent | P | prepositional phrase |
| cstr. | construct | p.c. | personal communication |
| dec | decrease | pl. | plural |
| dep | dependent | Pred | predicate |
| ex(x) | example(s) | Q, R, T, U, V | dummy variables |
| f. | feminine | r | rise |
| f | fall | Rev. | review |
| HB | Hebrew Bible | s. | singular |
| Heb | Hebrew | S | subject |
| inc | increase | Sam | Samaritan |
| ind | independent | st. | stave |
| LXX | Septuagint | Ug | Ugaritic |
| m. | masculine | v(v) | verse(s) |
| MT | Massoretic Text | V | verb |
| N | nomen | Voc | vocative |
| n(n). | note(s) | X, Y | dummy variables |
| NadjN | adjectival phrase | | |

For abbreviations of texts, see the bibliography.

# PREFACE

In the summer of 1971 I devoted myself to the study of the psalm versions of Mary Herbert, the Countess of Pembroke. Out of my concern with her renderings of Hebrew poetry grew the work that has culminated in this essay. An earlier draft of it was read in D. N. Freedman's seminar on Hebrew poetry in November 1974. The final version was prepared in 1976 and 1977.

I am glad to have written these pages and glad to thank those who have helped me in writing them. I mention first my friends, who matched superficial diffidence with obliquity of concern; second, the members of the Department of Near Eastern Studies at The University of Michigan, especially those with whom I first read many of the texts studied here: D. R. Burton, Jr., Freedman, C. R. Krahmalkov, G. E. Mendenhall, of Ann Arbor; C. G. Libolt, of Lansing; and Allen Myers, of Grand Rapids; and third, those who read these pages or handfuls of them in draft or in passing, informally, Burton, Libolt, and Juliet Pressel, of Ann Arbor; and formally, Freedman, E. N. McCarus and G. L. Windfuhr, of Near Eastern Studies, and Lin Shuen-fu, of the Department of Far Eastern Languages and Literatures. Of the women and men from whom I have received the second life of reading, I mention here only my most perspicuous teacher, Li Chi, of the Center for Chinese Studies, who will not mind since it is her window the green fills when the grass is not cut.

*eve of Jerome's Day, 1977*
*Ann Arbor, Michigan*

I realize now more clearly than when I wrote this essay that the boundaries of my concerns as they transgress various realms may be mistaken for the landmarks I cite. Naive readers may misstep. Nothing in the writing of Semitists on poetic structure that I have seen lately will stipulate changes here; much may require review at a later date. Developments elsewhere in study and reading are more attractive and I hope to profit from them in sequels to this work.

I confine myself to an innocent example, the increased availability of the Aleppo Codex, and in particular the Codex's text of Deuteronomy 32. The Song text holds few surprises. The compression of vv 7 and 11 seems mechanical but that of v 25 confirms our general impresion of the native speaker tradition of verse writing. I am happy to report that the noun phrases in Deut 32:14b are treated in the Codex as they are here, against BFBS and both BH3 and BHS. I would be happier if I were sure what that fact reveals about grammar, in what context of manuscript integrity.

My debts have continued to grow and I must thank those who have helped me see the essay into print, notably C. G. Libolt, and J. R. Battenfield of Winona Lake, who read the whole of it in proof; and Kent Jackson, of Provo, and Kenneth L. Mathews, of Dallas, who proofread the Hebrew. To offer thanks too often for diffidence would seem like praising air or blood for circulating though surely to note that the grass is still not cut is simply blessing lithogenesis.

*eve of Jerome's Day, 1980*
*Two Tiger Book Hut*
*Ann Arbor, Michigan*

# CHAPTER ONE
# HEBREW VERSE STRUCTURE

*The Past Is the Present*

*If external action is effete*
*and rhyme is outmoded,*
*I shall revert to you,*
*Habakkuk, as when in a Bible class*
*the teacher was speaking of unrhymed verse.*
*He said — and I think I repeat his exact words —*
*"Hebrew poetry is prose*
*with a sort of heightened consciousness." Ecstasy affords*
*the occasion and expediency determines the form.*

*Marianne Moore (1967: 88)*

## *1.0 Introduction*

From a woman who claimed that she called her writings poems only because she did not know what else to call them, we borrow a poem about a vast body of literature which we call poetry often, it seems, because we do not know what else to call it. The most important and accessible feature of the heightened consciousness of Hebrew poetry is its form, its heightened self-consciousness. As a result of discoveries and reconceptualizations in linguistic study, the forms of Hebrew poetry are becoming increasingly well-known. This essay will describe the major forms, that is, the structural features basic to Hebrew verse.

The essence of the structural system has been recognized since the mid-eighteenth century, when Robert Lowth formulated the description which we shall call standard. Before undertaking to refine Lowth's description, it is good for us to observe what one of the most sensitive formalists of the twentieth century made of it. That Marianne Moore found adequate the phrase she quotes from childhood Bible class is striking testimony to the fact that descriptions of verse serve various needs, because they serve various readers. There is no single model for a description, because there is no single reason for reading.

The kind of description readers need is deictic, a description that tells them what to look for, and a deictic description can only be a distillation of a fuller and more rigorous description. The project we are essaying is a description that seeks to satisfy the demands of the closest readers of single texts, philologists, as well as those of the acutest students of speech, linguists. We cannot say whether Lowth would have recognized his description of Hebrew verse in Marianne Moore's lines. We can be sure that he would have gladly acknowledged the diversity of readership that stimulated the distillation.

The diversity in itself is an unusual feature of Hebrew verse: no one reads Classical Hebrew as a native language; all readers of the Bible are barred from the intimacy most readers have with most texts, though that intimacy is not itself a simple thing. There is a sense in which all readers of the Bible aspire to the conditions of philologists and linguists, the first because the texts are isolated and the second because they are of language stuff, which all readers are familiar with in the shape of their first languages. Hjelmslev builds the notion of comparing native and non-native speech into his idea of the linguist when he contends that "it is not the individual language alone that is the object of the linguist" (1970: viii). Reference to philology reminds us that the situation of the Bible is shared *mutatis mutandis* by all the canonical traditions of the Old World. In China, the distance between the Confucian classics and the spoken language is bridged by the writing system; in a sense every Chinese child raised on the classics, as many were until recently, became a philologist before puberty. In most other traditions the distance is greater. In the Islamic sphere and in North India, the distance stimulated philology proper, and Arab and Sanskrit ideas continue to shape modern linguistic study. In the Levantine and Euroamerican sphere, the diversification of the study of canonical texts has been more recent.

By this delay, as it were, it has profited enormously and we hope to increase this profit by proceeding in an awareness of modern intellectual history. Such history is not our main concern, however, and we use it only to take our bearings. The history of the modern study of the biblical languages remains to be undertaken; only one point is needed here. Lowth is commonly credited with discovering the notion of parallelism. This is on any reading a slight historical error. More importantly it misestimates Lowth's crucial insight, that parallelistic phenomena alone cannot suffice to describe Hebrew verse; something else is going on, which Lowth called meter. Both parts of Lowth's Standard Description need refining, but his realization that two phenomena are interacting is central. The naming of parts, which we shall undertake here, is secondary to the recognition that there are two parts to be named.

The feature of Hebrew verse structure Lowth believed hopelessly lost he called meter. We shall argue that the regularities he and his successors have regarded as phonological are in fact syntactic. Descriptions of the relation between clause and phrase distribution and line shape are more precise and account for a wider range of features of the verse than any phonological treatment proposed. The other construct of Lowth's description, parallelism, we will show to be a congeries of phenomena. Some of these admit of precise description and these, along with other syntactic phenomena, we group together as the tropes and offer as a replacement, in the description, for the broader and partly overlapping notion of parallelism. The syntactic regularities, which take the form of constraints on line shapes, along with descriptions of dominant syntactic constellations, *and* the tropes act together in structuring Hebrew verse. To be sure, there are other regularities, but these regularities and turns are more basic, more frequent, and more integral to the structure of the language.

After as full a preliminary statement of the proposal as seems necessary, we rely on demonstration: the proposed description is adequate for a diverse corpus of 1225 lines, representative of pre-exilic Hebrew poetry. We have been explicit and exhaustive in the demonstration not because we regard our description as definitive, but because on the contrary we regard it as strictly preliminary. We wish to make it possible to test the proposal at every point because only then will its weaknesses emerge. Similarly, we erect the unwieldly structure of the whole proposal at once because it needs to be considered as a unity. It is likely that the whole will need to be refined for individual texts or bodies of texts, however discriminated. Only the rudiments of such smaller-scale descriptions are visible here; in further study they will be drawn out and the whole structure be tested again for its general applicability.

We have sought to avoid some faults which nevertheless mark the essay. First, we have tried to make the exposition of linguistic matters as free of formalism as possible, but the treatment is sometimes demanding. Second, we have tried to avoid polemic, as a symptom of both *dis*ease and parochialism, but violent debate seems as integral a part of Euroamerican philological traditions as accurate citation and we have sometimes been forced to enter lists. We seek to do so while benefiting from "the healing office of time" (Lonergan 1972: 150). We wish to assure the reader that we are acquainted with the conventions for the use of number words and hyphens in English; they are sometimes ignored here in what we have taken to be the interests of readability.

## *1.1 Assumptions and axioms*

Our reexamination of the forms of Hebrew verse must begin with an assessment of how we approach the texts. Since it is the forms we are concerned with, many complex features of the verse are to be excluded. We cannot forget, however, that restrictions on language behavior are just as social as those which control other forms of action. The tradition of philological study has spared readers of Hebrew the error often committed by anthropologists, who assume that because language is social, it is uniform within a speech community. Philology has always recognized that "the patterning of language goes far beyond the laws of grammar to comprehend the use of language in social life [and that] such [patterning] inescapably involves the radical linking of the verbal and the sociocultural in the conduct of speaking" (Bauman and Sherzer 1974b: 6). Within this salutary framework, however, there is room for adjustment. Philological study has tended to mistake the study of texts in themselves for the study of their social dimensions. The task of distinguishing priorities has been aided by modern development in literary theory and we shall marshall some relevant points (1.1.1).

At the same time, philological study has concentrated on the texts in themselves, often neglecting their status as samples of language. Because of the difficulty of making claims about that status, philology has often been exhaustive in textual study and neglectful of linguistic study. Often, to be sure, linguistics has similarly shied away from literary material because of its known "deviance." There is an important part of the humanistic tradition which insists that such deviance is crucial not only to linguistic study but also to reading itself. A contemporary representative of this tradition has observed: "The poetic resources concealed in the morphological and syntactic structure of language, briefly the poetry of grammar, and its literary product, the grammar of poetry, have seldom been known to critics and mostly disregarded by linguists but skillfully mastered by creative writers" (Jakobson 1967: 319). Philologists, in part critics and linguists in part, have often been attuned to these resources. Advances in linguistic study will be cited to increase and refocus that attention (1.1.2-1.1.3).

Linguistic study can also aid in reconsidering philology's relationship to its material. Dead traditions and text corpora (if a corpus that is read can rightly be called dead) require different approaches than living languages do. The mediating discipline of historical linguistics has often been helpful in refining these postures. We shall call upon it to be of special service with regard to historical poetics (1.1.4).

### *1.1.1 Some assumptions*

Though it is impossible to make explicit all the assumptions that will govern our reading and study of Hebrew verse, there are a few which require mention. The process of reading is more easily engaged in than reflected upon. When reflection has been brought to bear on the case of Hebrew, refuge has often been sought in the contexts of reading rather than the act itself. The most superficial layers of context have been stripped off thoroughly by now, although it would be wrong to underestimate the extent to which the history of Europe since the late Middle Ages has been a function of reading past or around the sanctions of the biblical text, through to the text itself.

The next stage requires the elimination of the refuge of language mystique; Hebrew cannot be treated as if it were a different kind of language from all others. This stage, too, is past us for the most part. When the eighteenth century grammarian Lowth compared Hebrew and English in the preface to his English grammar, he confronted a dilemma posed by two old beliefs, both passing out of fashion in his time. The first is that vernacular languages do not "really" have grammars; Sidney had explained this feature of English in his *Apologie for Poetrie* (Ong 1962: 178). The second belief, to which we shall return, is that grammatical complexity is a sign of degeneration; this reading of the Babel story requires that Adam's language must be simplest. Lowth resolves these rival claims "in favor" of English.

> The *English* language is perhaps of all the present European languages by much the most simple in its form and construction. Of all the ancient languages extant that is the most simple, which is undoubtedly the most ancient; but even that language itself does not equal the *English* in simplicity (Lowth 1762: iii).

Granted that Hebrew is no longer taken to be the oldest language, it is still often referred to as possessed of more of any number of qualities than some unspecified body of other languages. Such statements are no more useful than speculation on Adam's grammar. Yet one finds that an astute Semitist and a serious literary theorist agree that Hebrew, as reflected in its verse, is "highly logical" (Kosmala 1964; Wimsatt 1972: x). We not only do not regard Hebrew (or texts written in it) as intrinsically simpler or more logical than other languages and texts; we similarly do not expect to find them freer or more vigorous.

Ideas of simplicity and sincerity as properties of literary texts are also alien to reading. Assertions that the poets composed "naturally" and "freely" without "consciously" laboring to fit their "material" into any "system" are meaningless. We may quote the report of a Russian grammarian and entomologist.

> I am aware that the specious terms 'simplicity' and 'sincerity' are constantly employed in a commendatory sense by well-meaning teachers of literature. Actually, of course, no matter how 'simple' the result looks, fine art is never simple, being always an elaborate, magical deception. . . . Art is a magical deception, as all nature is magic and deception. To speak of a 'sincere' poem or picture is about the same thing as to call 'sincere' a bird's mating dance or a caterpillar's mimetic behavior (Nabokov 1964: 53).

We could as well have quoted the even more pertinent remark of a grammarian of our own language: "The truest poetry is the most feigning" (*As You Like It* 3.3.20); the remark exactly renders an Arabic proverb: *ʾašʿar ʾaš-šiʿr akḏabuhu* (Cantarino 1975: 36).

The reading of a text requires that it be the text we are concerned with. Authorial intention in itself is not a central focus, though reference to intentionality is often a substitute for questions about the resources of the language, with which we are preoccupied. Authorial consciousness is also beyond our purview. We cite as examples two great Slavic epic poets, one a literate nineteenth-century Russian, the other an illiterate twentieth-century Serb. Just as Nabokov assures us that the master Russian prosodist Pushkin was an incompetent theorist of meter (1964: 25), so Lord reports that there were no signs about him to hint that Avdo Mededović was a poet, let alone one of the greatest modern oral epic poets (Lord 1976). It is not simply the case that poets do not consciously know what they are doing, but that first approximation is sufficient here.

The process of taking texts, rather than supposed authors and editors, seriously has been basic to literary study in this century, for "this is the age which has repudiated books about the girlhood of Shakespeare's heroines" (Ong 1962: 15). The basic considerations of New Criticism have entered biblical studies in part through the good offices of Muilenburg in America and Alonso-Schökel in Europe. The trend has been reinforced by Albright's positivist approach to the biblical text; and in the work of his student Freedman literary study has been enriched by a balance of critical and positivist perspectives. The fruits of this revaluation of readerly stance can be seen in studies like those of Lack (1973) on Isaiah and Lundbom (1975) on Jeremiah; both attend to the text, giving it the primacy it must have over questions of authorship, sources, and methods of composition.

Modern critical insistence on the text is often discussed in the terms set by the anticritical gesture of Keats's "Ode on a Grecian Urn," a supremely human artifact. In an essay on "The Jinee in the Well-Wrought Urn," Ong explains the difficulties created by this insistence, the sources of the temptation constantly to talk about a person, not a text.

> The fact is that, in the last analysis, as a matter of full, serious, protracted contemplation and love, it is unbearable for a man or a woman to be faced with anything less than a person — and thus, tragically, even part-way unbearable to be faced with only other human persons, where the personal relationship is inevitably enmeshed in material situations involving objects, and where even the human being, measurable, definable, partakes of the nature of object at the same time that he is person. In all our moves, our motivation, perhaps in secret and by indirection, bears toward the countermove, hopes to find itself really a countermove. Our great fear is that we are not being loved. Our gaze on the object, we peep anxiously from the corners of our eyes, alert for someone's response somewhere (Ong 1962: 25).

It is useful to keep these difficulties in mind, as we avoid the temptation they occasion. If we fail to keep our gaze on the object, we are liable to start out with a blinding trivialization of the effort. Insipid assertions that poetry is an art, and "artistic feel" is needed for the analysis are harmful and misleading, reducing, in a ritual castration, formal description of poetry to the "merely technical." The romantic dichotomy between the "real" thing and the "way it's done" is inspired by the false fear that reading will exhaust the object; in truth, reading begun with such an attitude will exhaust the reader, and quickly. No reading will ever exhaust a poem.

The last of our assumptions involves the material and milieu of reading; having penetrated the outermost layers of context, we turn to those that are impenetrable. We assume that the "poems are unified compositions and . . . [that] the text has been transmitted faithfully" (Freedman 1976a: 85).

### *1.1.2 Prologue to the linguistic axiom*

A basic tenet of the humanist tradition holds that "languages are to be learned before the arts." These are the words of a mid-seventeenth-century Harvard thesis, i.e., a proposition publicly defended in Latin by the teenage students of Harvard College (Ong 1962: 158). The priority grows out of a recognition of the need for a good grasp of languages in studying the arts of communicating: rhetoric, dialectic, logic, and so on. The truth behind this premise has been neglected over the past two and a half centuries, which have seen the diversification of language study, literary criticism and history, anthropology, philology, and linguistics. Only now that the divergence has grown to the point that each of these studies can be pursued separately have students sought new ways to grasp this truth.

Diversities of concern, focus, and conception are not easily overridden, however. Recent attempts to reexamine the language arts have often failed in attempting to shortcircuit the process. This is shown most clearly in references to style, a term frequently used as if it has even an ascertainable plain sense (Greenfield 1967). This error has appeared both in studies of Canaanite poetry and elsewhere, often marring the work in collections like Chatman and Levin (1967) and Freeman (1970). What is usually meant by style is a group of features which vary in a piece of discourse. Seminal advice is available here from a linguist who spent his youth in Moscow among some of the great Russian poets of the twenties and who has since devoted himself to the study of all uses of language. It is apropos of another facet of language study that Jakobson remarks: "Naive attempts to deal with variations without attacking the problem of invariants are condemned to failure" (1963: 272). There are qualifications to be made in extending this to the study of poetry, many of them implicit in Jakobson's own work. The principle is in itself strong enough to warn us off attempts to separate arbitrarily the study of invariants, grammar, from the study of variations, notably in reading poetry. (This is the principle applied in discussing putative cases of alliteration in some Phoenician and Hebrew texts in O'Connor 1977; the same point is made concerning some allegations regarding Homeric alliteration in O'Nolan 1969: 18-19).

Jakobson's warning points to the error of the work of Muilenburg and Alonso-Schökel, who tend to gather phenomena significant for literary study on a plane which they treat as isolated from "mere" grammar. The considerable gains of the approach can be seen, e.g., in the incisiveness of commentary in Muilenburg (1953, 1969), Jackson and Kessler (1974), and Kessler (1973, 1974, cf. Stek 1974). The use of the term rhetoric by Muilenburg and his students requires a comment. As a designation of argumentation, it is acceptable; but in their broader use, extended to the whole realm of style and structure, it is not. A gentle rebuke may be borrowed from a contemporary student of medieval and Renaissance rhetoric, who writes that the proper sense of the term is "the art of persuasion, which in our day is much more the province of the advertising man and marketing specialist than of the *littérateur*" (Ong 1962: 228). A firmer statement is Yeats's dictum: "Rhetoric is the will doing the work of the imagination." Insofar as we write the language of Yeats, to refer to something as rhetorical is at best constraining and at worst damning.

Alonso-Schökel (1975) urges the importance of considering "form" in the task of reading biblical literature, a task he refers to under the traditional but infelicitous term exegesis. He shows that what is called form can never be separated from what is called content: "The literary work is a revealing of meaning, and not a concealing of meaning, through the artifice of form" (1975: 10). He notes a lack of interest in and trust of formal study. Working from the premise that "a serious analysis of a poem cannot be satisfied with grammar, which in itself could be substylistic," he commits the grave error of suggesting that analysis can begin at the level of what he calls a styleme (p. 11).

This error is but a transmutation of the erroneous belief that grammar is a well-understood phenomenon with discrete boundaries. Serious theoretical linguists in this century have continually been driven back to first principles, often only to find that they were conceived on too narrow a base. Even within realms that seem discrete, like the study of grammar in general or the study of Hebrew grammar, limitations are not clear. One grammarian describes the character of his work in this way.

> Serious grammatical investigation at the moment is rather like traveling in quicksand. There are no firm supports. Every step is uncertain. Every move is questionable. There are no well-worked-out, unshakable analyses of particular portions of individual languages from which general principles of grammar can be inferred. There are few well-supported, substantively-detailed general principles of grammar that can serve as a guide in the analysis of particular cases. The linguist interested in providing a principled account of a

> significant range of actual factual details must thus stumble around trying to formulate a general principle here or there that can constrain the description of particular facts and trying to find firm analyses of factual fragments that will constrain the formulation of universal linguistic principles. Ill-considered boasts to the contrary, we are, in short, really almost at the beginning of the study of the incredibly complex and still largely unknown domain of natural language grammar. . . . It is all very well and comforting, therefore, for the layman or literary figure to believe that [even] English grammar is a well-understood and already described body of doctrine, perfectly grasped by the authorities. But it is sheer delusion . . . of the most harmful sort for linguists to accept this view, which cannot stand sixty seconds' confrontation with the facts (Postal 1971: 3-4).

We would suggest that Postal underestimates the needs of the "literary figure" and probably also those of laypeople. He continues:

> Many writers attempt to give the impression of a well-worked-out system of grammar by terminological fence building. Grammar is defined, often progressively, in a very narrow way such that more and more facts are left to other domains, "semantics," "pragmatics," and so on, that are, in general, not studied. Since a priori we do not know the bounds of grammar, this is, to say the least, a rather dangerous course of action (Postal 1971: 4).

An astute prediction is contained here: grammatical study in America since Postal wrote has concentrated on semantics and pragmatics.

It could be objected that language-particular study proceeds on bases different from those of more theoretical study and in part this is true. We are well equipped to understand Hebrew grammar, it might be suggested. A glance at the seminal monographs of Andersen (1970a, 1974) should serve to disarm the suggestion's force: he consistently shows that received descriptions of Hebrew syntax are at best incomplete and often wrong. He is conscious of the restrictions he has imposed on his own work, but even within those limits his breadth is extensive. Alonso-Schökel refers to word order as being of potential significance; until the publication of Andersen (1970a), the word orders of the simplest kind of Hebrew sentence had not been differentiated.

The dangers of relying on the distance between general grammatical study and language-particular study are pointed up in a review of Andersen (1970a) by Hoftijzer (1973). This essay systematically berates Andersen for not writing a grammar of Hebrew verbless clauses based on semantics and pragmatics, in particular on presuppositions and entailments. Hoftijzer's voluminous comments are of little help *in grammatical description* because they refer to the discourse in paraphrases of ordinary language. They do not specify the relation between the *grammatical* structure of the verbless clause and the discourse around it. (For an attempt to consider informally presuppositions and grammatical study in English and Modern Hebrew, see Keenan 1974 on relative clauses.)

Everyone has always known that sentences like *Have you stopped beating your lover?* are trick questions. The grammatical problem is to describe the trick, viz., to make explicit why beating is presupposed and cessation is queried, and why there is no limit to the number of sentences that work the same way. Hoftijzer's comments are paraphrases of the "trick" sentences; the suggestion is that the "trick" has to do with something that is not quite on the surface. Such comments do not contribute to grammatical study and the need which Hoftijzer rightly sees, to describe all the facts involved, does not obviate Andersen's description of the surface syntax.

Andersen, not surprisingly, treats rhetorical questions as questions in syntactic form. Hoftijzer insists that they be treated as assertions (1973: 46-62). Rhetorical questions are questions in form *and* assertions (or the like) by conversational implication. Both facts must be treated. The theory of grammar (as of any scientific inquiry) requires that complex facts be treated in terms of simpler ones. Thus, the interrogative shape of rhetorical questions must be accounted for before their assertive function is described. (For a more balanced treatment, see Held 1969.) Hoftijzer explicitly denies the status of rhetorical questions as questions; his proposal is indefensible.

The need to account for the kinds of problems raised by Hoftijzer is recognized in Andersen's monograph (1970a) and plays a major role in his study (1974) which deals with discourse structure. The terms for a general treatment of presupposition, however, are not agreed on by grammarians of living languages, or by philosophers of language, as the essays in Cole and Morgan (1975) show. A full treatment of the phenomenon in the grammar of a written language is not to be anticipated.

It could still be objected that the phenomena which are of greatest interest to the student of literary language are distinct from the issues involved in Andersen's work. The brunt of this essay is to allege the contrary; a few simple examples can be cited here. Andersen (1972) has shown that certain features of descriptions of births in Hebrew need to be considered in light of the grammar of the verb *yld* 'to bear.' The relationship between the use of passive verb forms and the understanding (not to say, conception) of the divinity is a similar subject. The passive in Classical Hebrew is a marginal modality; the language is losing a passive system (the *Qal* passives), while the other system (*Nipᶜal*) is being diversified. Yet, in many situations in which God acts on or for the good, the passive is an ideological hinge: the evil are not acted on or for by God; rather they are patients in passive sentences with no surface agents. The situation is not uniform. The contrast of Exodus 15 and Psalm 1 suggests that historical developments are involved. The prophetic notion of the instrumentality of the great political powers is *in nuce* a cognate grammatical idea (though only *in nuce*).

All of this is not to say that Alonso-Schökel's work is misguided, but only that it will continually be stumbling, like Postal's grammarian, and that it is healthier to have people stumbling together, instead of over each other. Some varieties of possible accidents can be seen in a reading of Psalm 1 by Lack (1977). In considering only the clauses of the psalm, Lack builds into his analysis the results of an unformalized survey of all Hebrew syntax, without noting that the regularities in Hebrew discourse in general may have special relevance to those clauses. Similarly, in considering only the vocabulary of the poem while ignoring the semantic patterning of language elsewhere in Hebrew poetry (except to dismiss, a trifle hastily, some work of Dahood's), Lack silently incorporates some of the results of traditional study, but completely loses others. Notable among these is the smallness of the image field used in the poem, which happens to be the feature that makes it readily amenable to a French structuralist reading. By taking the entire text as his object, Lack contributes to current study; but by refusing to read the poem in its tradition, he fails to do so. (This may be a good place to remind the reader that we are concerned with reading Hebrew poetry, poetry in a written tradition derived from a largely oral culture with literary forms, formats, and attitudes alien to ours. Our qualifications here have little application to reading at closer hand. Readers who are such simply, i.e., readers who read within a written tradition and in a living language, will make different demands than we do. We ask simple questions and try to eke out the rudiments of the complex answers; having answers to the simple questions, monolingual, printbound readers are free to ask complex questions.)

### *1.1.3 The linguistic axiom*

All considerations regarding grammar adduced above must be balanced by appreciation of the fact that "verse is the most idiosyncratic use of language and is subject to extreme individual manipulation" (Lotz 1972b: 119). Even with this in mind, however, it is necessary to set out certain basic facts about approaches to verse that can serve as a modern approximation of the Arab grammarians' insight that metrics is a part of grammar.

Verse is a subsystem of language. All the phenomena of a language are available for use in poetry written in that language. Not all are used; of those that are, some are used structurally, that is, determining the fine structure of the verse (line structure) and its gross structure (stanza and poem structure). Another group of those phenomena are used poetically but not structurally. The use of poetic here derives from Jakobson's definition of the poetic function as that which "projects the principle of equivalence from the axis of selection into the axis of combination" (Jakobson 1967: 303). This formulation refers to the use of repetition in poetry: items that in ordinary language are selected among are arranged in poetry in distinctive ways which amount to combining them. There must be two instantiations of a phenomenon for the poetic function to work; the instantiations of some phenomena are so frequent as to be structural. Finally, there are phenomena in a language that are used in verse and mark it as such, without contributing either to its gross or fine structure or to its poetic character; they are the elements usually gathered under the heading poetic diction.

Although the phenomena in a language are by no means entirely translucent to native speakers of it, they have a good handle on them. To the extent that this handle is usable, they can do without the linguistic axiom we have just sketched. They intuitively grasp its implications. The case is different for literatures in languages for which there are no living speakers. Again, although not all linguistic phenomena are held in common within the cultural modality of writing, there is at the core of that modality, in Europe and America, a group of languages which are closely related and of literatures which have commingled. Native speakers and readers in this core can to a certain extent move within it without use of the axiom. This is a crude attempt at explaining the difficulties of current French structuralism in dealing with non-Euroamerican literatures: beyond the charmed circle of its birthplace the fundaments of structuralism do not have room to settle. On alien soil, they are not steady enough to give structuralism the purchase it needs to do its work.

Like most critical theory our program is useless in itself; the goal of criticism is practical criticism, which is but another term for reading. The program is substantially derived from Russian formalism and Prague School linguistics, and has been taken up by Kiparsky in a number of important papers. Kiparsky has followed Jakobson in emphasizing that reading has a role to play in linguistics. Important questions can be considered or even answered by using the evidence of poetic language. The area most promising for such study is metrics.

> Perhaps the most remarkable and most disappointing aspect of many influential manuals on metrics, both ancient and modern, is the astonishing innocence of their authors in matters linguistic, even during most recent times when such a shortcoming can no longer be excused. For surely metricists ought to have realized long since that in metrics there are involved linguistic problems crying out for linguistic answers, and not only questions of aesthetics and recitation (Pulgram 1975: 180-81).

In two papers on English meter Kiparsky has fully justified the usefulness of the linguistic axiom in studying even an accessible tradition like that of English. In the conclusion to the second of these, he remarks: "Traditional poetics underestimated the formal richness of meter rather like (and perhaps in part because) traditional linguistics underestimated the formal richness of grammar" (Kiparsky 1977: 245-46).

It is with a historical example that Kiparsky begins his exposition of some consequences of the linguistic axiom for the reading of verse.

> Many . . . seemingly radical changes in poetic form are actually more or less automatic responses to linguistic change. Alliteration, for example, seems to be found as an obligatory formal element only in languages where the stress regularly falls on the same syllable. Old English was such a language, for the stress fell predictably on the root syllable. In modern English, on the other hand, words with the same root can be stressed in many different places. . . . When this kind of stress system was established in English, verse forms with fixed alliteration were abandoned (Kiparsky 1974: 233).

On the basis of such considerations Kiparsky discusses the possibilities of a theory of poetry that would refer to all poetries of the world. Such a theory would distinguish structural phenomena (which Kiparsky calls fixed elements) like Old English alliteration, from poetic phenomena (Kiparsky's free elements), like alliteration in Modern English.

Although native speakers do, as we noted above, have a great ability to recognize the linguistic phenomena involved in verse, the ability is more useful negatively than positively. "Neither poets nor students of literature have thought much about the intrinsic limits of poetry, any more than football players or spectators think much about gravity. The limits of poetic form are simply psychological givens, just as gravity is a physical given. In trying to define them we will have to make the effort . . . of not taking the 'natural' for granted" (Kiparsky 1974: 235). The native speaker of a language will more readily isolate what is not functional in a language than what is. Almost all discussions of English meter include an account of why quantitative verse and isosyllabic verse are marginal in the language and an explanation of the post-traditional character of the twentieth-century poets who use these forms. Such accounts have little to say about why most English verse is iambic, and much of it is pentameter.

The form of the theory Kiparsky sketches is interesting, though preliminary. He limits himself at the outset to recurrent elements, structural and poetic, and thus sets aside poetic diction. Given that all form, structural and poetic, involves linguistic elements, the first task is to describe the set of elements. He distinguishes phonological elements like stress, quantity and tones (used in meter), and vowels and consonants (used in rhyme, alliteration, assonance, and consonance); and syntactic phenomena. The next part of the theory refers to patterns, like *aaa* . . . , *aabb*, *abab*. All elements used structurally are fitted into a pattern, and the fit is called a schema. Thus, if *a* and *b* are rhymes, *abab* is a rhyme schema; if they are unstressed and stressed syllables, *abab* is a metrical pattern (iambic dimeter), and so on. Observing that the number of elements available for use in poetry is determined by the structure of the language ("the linguistic sames which are potentially relevant in poetry are just those which are potentially relevant in grammar," Kiparsky 1974: 237), he notes that the number is small and likely to be fairly discrete. Further, the number of patterns involved is small. He discusses some phonological examples, observing that just as in phonology, so in meter, language must be segmented into syllables but no further to describe phenomena involving stress.

A tension between grammatical studies and treatments of verse often arises because it is claimed that grammar cannot deal with the ungrammaticality of poets. In fact, the argument is reversible: only if, for example, the grammar of English sentence structures is described, can the word order deviations called poetic inversions be treated. No one would hesitate to agree that not all possible types of inversion occur in Miltonic blank verse. This use of grammaticality is even more important in "ungrammatical" phenomena like metaphor, and here, too, the continuity with ordinary language grammar is strong because metaphors are deeply involved in everyday speech.

Kiparsky makes two revealingly hedged remarks.

> At least some constants of poetic form are dependent on the structures of language itself. . . . The homologies between grammar and poetry account, at least in part, for the universality of poetic form (Kiparsky 1974: 245).

In part the anxiety behind the qualifications is due to the fact that written poetry in our time is at the end of a tradition so full that it is actively seeking to circumvent the facts we are dealing with. Although Kiparsky often prefers examples from modern written poetry, there is much in such poetry that will resist a linguistic approach, since the processes of cultural development that have led to current linguistic study are the processes that shape the lives of poets. In part, too, the anxiety reflects an awareness that linguistics will never be adequate to deal with poetry; past a certain point, most linguistic study would be wasted in elaborating what a competent reader can better deal with in a non-technical framework. Since we are well before that point in reading Canaanite verse and since it is well before our time, we need not stay long over these scruples.

There are some features of Kiparsky's notion of pattern which we should discuss. (We do so, not because Kiparsky advanced his notion as anything like a final statement, and not in order to propose a restatement, but because the difficulties will be those we shall encounter in Canaanite verse, and insofar as Kiparsky's work will aid the reader's appreciation of our argument, these points will also be helpful.) The first difficulty is that the variety of formalization he uses suggests that in the relevant patterns the items will be absolutely different, i.e., the patterns will be syntagmatic.

This is often true for rhyme schemes: when two rhymes alternate in the schema *abab*, they are almost always entirely different rhymes. Consider, however, the stanza structure of the Shakespearean sonnet, three quatrains and a couplet. The *a-b* formulation would yield, setting *a* equal to four lines and *b* to two, the shape *aaab*; this suggests wrongly that it is not important that a couplet is half a quatrain. In fact, the proper formulation must be *a-a-a-1/2a* in order to allow for the fact that stanza lengths are drawn from a unitary paradigm. A Petrarchan sonnet with a sestet written in couplets will have the pattern: *a-a-1/2a-1/2a-1/2a*; if the sestet is in triplets, the form must be *a-a-3/4a-3/4a*. The last is not elegant, but it reflects the fact that the two triplets are somewhat tighter than the two quatrains.

Another difficulty has to do with the continuity presupposed by the pattern form. There is no doubt that continuity is by far commoner than discontinuity in schemas. Further, most cases of discontinuity can be handled simply with breaks in the pattern. If, for example, only the last lines of a series of poetic units rhyme in a couplet, we could write . . .*aa* . . .*bb*. . .*cc*. This is the form of some Elizabethan and Jacobean plays in blank verse, in which rhyme is used to mark scene endings. There are more complex examples, however. Consider the tonal structure of a quatrain in the Chinese 8-line *lü shih*, Regulated Verse (Frankel 1972). There are two substructures. One governs the even-numbered syllables of the line; there are two tonal values, one level (a simple value), the other deflected (a composite of three other tones, rising, falling, and entering). This is the pattern for a seven-syllable line; *a* and *b* can be either level or deflected.

| syllable | 1 | 2 | 3 | 4 | 5 | 6 | 7 |
|---|---|---|---|---|---|---|---|
| line 1 | | a | | b | | a | |
| 2 | | b | | a | | b | |
| 3 | | b | | a | | b | |
| 4 | | a | | b | | a | |

Such discontinuity in two directions is difficult to reduce to a simple pattern. The second substructure governs the last two odd-numbered syllables. Again, we give the pattern for a seven-syllable line, using *x* and *y* for the tonal values, and repeating the *a-b* pattern above; *a* can be the same as either *x* or *y*, *b* having the opposite value.

| syllable | 1 | 2 | 3 | 4 | 5 | 6 | 7 |
|---|---|---|---|---|---|---|---|
| line 1 | | a | | b | x | a | y |
| 2 | | b | | a | y | b | x |
| 3 | | b | | a | x | b | y |
| 4 | | a | | b | y | a | x |

The domains of the patterns interlock to make the line endings much tighter than the beginnings; this is as true of Greek dactylic hexameter and of the Finnish folk epic lines as of this Chinese line. The elements in the two patterns are of the same sort but the two domains are discontinuous, and in different degrees. Such irregularity is central to some patterns we will examine.

One observation Kiparsky has made on the basis of his notion of pattern deserves attention: there are rarely more than three phenomena interacting at the same time in a pattern. Frequently, to be sure, there is only one (as in monorhyme), or two; patterns with four are known. This observation, which we shall henceforth call Kiparsky's Rule, refers only to the elements actually interacting in any given segment of a pattern. Thus although the *terza rima* schema for any substantial passage includes a large number of terms, only two are interacting at any point.

```
a b a        b c b        c d c        d e d        e f e. . .

1 2 1       ⌈2⌉
            ⌊1⌋2 1       ⌈2⌉
                         ⌊1⌋2 1       ⌈2⌉
                                      ⌊1⌋2 1        2. . .
```

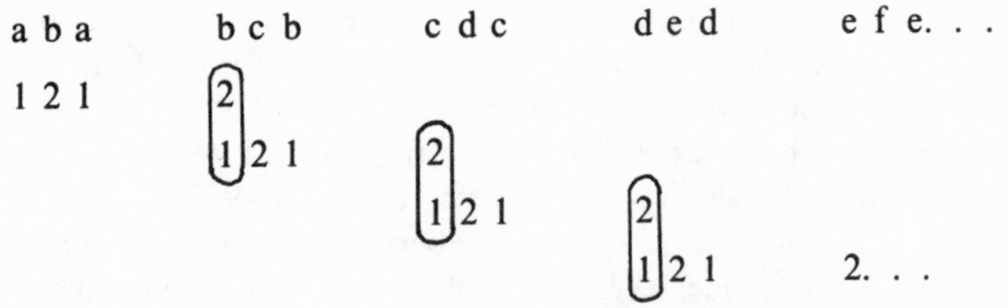

The crossing points are at the junctures circled; the forward movement of the verse form through hundreds of lines shows that these crossings are made.

The advantage of the Rule is that it covers a wide range of phenomena not usually grouped together with meters and rhyme schemas. Two of these involve syntactic deviations (Kiparsky 1973). The first is characteristic of Old Norse Skaldic verse, a poetry of almost inconceivable density. Skaldic sentence meshing intertwines groups of sentences within stanzas. That is, independent sentences are taken apart and the fragments of them are interlaced in complex and diverse patterns. The phenomenon is constrained by the fact that no more than three sentences can be meshed at once (cf. Reichardt 1928).

A similar phenomenon is related to word order in Latin, Greek, and Sanskrit verse; these "free word order" languages show regularities in the way in which parts of certain phrases are juxtaposed with others within a sentence. One of these regularities is that no more than three phrases are disassembled and intermeshed at once. One source of examples is the Golden Hexameter, a line which is also a clause; the verb is central and there are two nouns and two adjectives around it, in the order ABCAB.

| egressi | optata | potiuntur | Troes | harena |
|---|---|---|---|---|
| A | B | C | A | B |
| emerging | welcome | occupy | Trojans | sand |

The emerging Trojans occupy the welcome sand. (*Aeneid* 1.172)

Classical rhetoric refers to these rearrangements under the heading hyperbaton, leap-frog word order. (Our examples are derived from Young 1931-32, Wilkinson 1963, and Williams 1968.) Other examples of phrasal meshing can be seen alongside the Golden Hexameter in these four lines. Note that while the second line does not have plain word order, there is no phrasal meshing.

Horace *Epistola* 2.2.72 ABCB

| festinat | calidus | mulis—gerulisque | redemptor. |
|---|---|---|---|
| hastens | hurried | mules—and-porters | contractor |

2.2.73

| torquet | nunc | lapidem | nunc | ingens | machina | tignum. |
|---|---|---|---|---|---|---|
| turns | now | stone | now | huge | crane | beam |

2.2.74 ABCAB (a Golden Hexameter)

| tristia | robustis | luctantur | funera | plaustris. |
|---|---|---|---|---|
| sad | oaken | wrestle | funerals | carts |

2.2.75 ABCB. ABCB

| hac | rabiosa | fugit | canis | hac | lutulenta | ruit | sus. |
|---|---|---|---|---|---|---|---|
| here | rabid | flies | dog | here | muddy | crashes | horse |

A hurried contractor hastens by with mules and porters.
A huge crane turns now a stone, now a beam.
Sad funerals wrestle with oaken carts.
Here a rabid dog flies. There a muddy pig crashes.

The chief varieties of hyperbatonic word order are catalogued by Young (1931-32); we note only two of these, similar to the Golden Hexameter.

*Eclogues* 1.2. ABACB

| silvestrem | tenui | musam | meditans | avena |
|---|---|---|---|---|
| woody | slim | muse | you brood | pipe |

You brood on a slim pipe over a woody muse.

*Eclogues* 2.1 ABCA

| formosum | pastor | Corydon | ardebat | Alexim |
|---|---|---|---|---|
| fair | shepherd | Corydon | warmed for | Alexis |

Shepherd Corydon warmed for fair Alexis.

In these examples, line and clause boundaries coincide though line and clause do not rigidly coincide in Latin. Kiparsky's Rule can work across line boundaries, since the variation in ordering phrases is at work there, too.

We can conclude our discussion of the linguistic axiom by referring to some more general remarks of Kiparsky's (1973-74). Aesthetic theory, he suggests, is a "kind of grammar which accounts for our perceptions of aesthetically relevant features in works of art" (p. 178). Although he is not advocating the transposition of linguistic study into aesthetic and literary work, he urges that structure and interpretation not be blandly differentiated. The converse of the linguistic axiom is relevant: "Any formal property that a literary work may have that is not (consciously or unconsciously) perceptible is by definition aesthetically irrelevant" (p. 179). Observe that the question of consciousness is set aside: people talk without being conscious of grammar and so we read without being constrained by notions of what a poet could be conscious of.

The language of literature "may (though it perhaps need not) differ from ordinary language both by extending the system of standard language, and by imposing special restrictions over and above those that hold in standard language" (p. 180). The task of reading begins with the isolation of those special restrictions. To go further, by considering their aesthetic function both in general (that is, in the terms of biology) and in particular (in the terms of the work itself) is to go further than we can yet in reading poetry.

The range of linguistic study is undefined in part because of our ignorance, and in part, and much more importantly, because poetry is read and listened to for reasons. The study of poetry will ultimately avoid the isolation of purely linguistic study. No one concerned with it will freely and without qualification agree that Hjelmslev's statement at the end of his introduction to typological linguistics is adequate. He wrote that "For the scholar there is nothing more beautiful than the vision of a science still to be created" (1970: 96). It has never been true that *hoti*'s business was settled only for *hoti*'s sake. Exhaustiveness of linguistic description will never be sought as a final goal by a reader. Her or his goal is always to become a better reader, more adequate to texts sought in the first place for other reasons. Similarly, the threats of the atomistic and emergence fallacies cited by Hockett (1977), fallacies of explaining everything that can be separated out and calling that the whole, will never be succumbed to by anyone aware of the difficulty of all branches of linguistics. These fallacies are part of what Jakobson calls "the creeping empiricism of the neo-grammarians, which viewed any system, and in particular the linguistic system, as a mechanical whole (*Und-Verbindung*) and not at all as a formal unity (*Gestalteinheit*)." Insofar as the formal unity of a linguistic system derives from and reflects that of the uses of the system, we are proof against ultimate forms of misreading.

### *1.1.4 The uniformitarian axiom*

We quoted earlier from Lowth on the simplicity of English and Hebrew: he referred to Hebrew as the oldest language in the world but conceded that it need not be regarded as the simplest. Rather, it was the second simplest of the languages under discussion. This is a small concession from our perspective; in the intellectual history of Europe, it is a large one. We have reached the point in preparing to discuss Hebrew poetry at which the central role of the Bible in our culture demands attention.

The matter can be put briefly. The priority of Hebrew among the languages of the world, a basic postulate of medieval and Renaissance students of language, followed from the usual understanding that the antediluvians spoke Hebrew. Gradually, as it was realized that no such thing is hinted at in the Bible, the postulate faded. The model of linguistic history derived from it held on. This model essentially regarded the oldest stages of a language as simpler and more pure than later ones. Language change was regarded as babelization, a species of degeneration.

The earliest stages of historical linguistics were conceived within this frame, and only during the nineteenth century was its inadequacy appreciated. The reconceptualization that came about has an instructive parallel in the history of geology (Ong 1960b). Until the biblical creation account was rejected as an adequate framework for geological thinking, the history of the earth was approached as if the planet had developed into its present shape through a series of distortions of an original ideal state. The required constraint on investigation was the uniformitarian hypothesis: only developments of a sort paralleled in the earth at present can be used to explain its history. This was proposed as a preface to investigation, in order to avoid the notion of special, viz. divine, creation. The hypothesis set the boundary of science at a point chronologically later than creation. In the course of time this hypothesis has grown into an axiom. The science of geology has developed its major modern hypotheses by considering the developments attested in the geological record. Recent study of continental drift has gone hand in hand with the mapping of the ocean floor.

The development is paralleled in the history of biology (Wolsky 1960). The acrimony has been greater because after all though the biblical creation account does not presuppose the geological consistency of the planet, it does assert that the animals were created more or less all at once. It is difficult for people raised in an intellectual framework in which evolution is widely accepted to grasp the shocking nature of Darwin's proposal in 1859. Paleontology, in particular among the biological sciences, was well developed by the mid-nineteenth century. Virtually all early paleontologists saw that the fossil record witnessed a pattern of development. This development is now blandly referred to as a facet of evolution, but in 1859, almost all students rejected evolution as an explanation. They saw the development as the result of countless acts of special creation (Bowler 1977). The core of Darwinian theory is a uniformitarian axiom. It requires that biology begin by supposing that nothing has happened in the period within the purview of science of a sort different from what happens at present.

The development of historical linguistics in the nineteenth century is due to another uniformitarian hypothesis; we owe the extension of the term to linguistics to Kiparsky. In linguistics, it was required that no language be conceived which was unlike a living language. More specifically it led to the stipulation that no linguistic feature unknown in a living language be reconstructed in a dead language. Thus, since there are no living languages without vowels, no dead language can be reconstructed without vowels (cf. Halle 1970b). Further, the vowel system of Proto-Indo-European (PIE) has on various occasions been reconstructed as a one-vowel system. Such systems have been rejected on the grounds of the uniformitarian hypothesis, since, it is claimed, no living languages have one-vowel systems. The counterclaim is that there are such languages. In the most recent discussions, the languages of the Caucasus region of Georgia have been described as having a one-vowel system. If the description is correct, then the one-vowel reconstruction of PIE is acceptable (cf. Hamp 1974).

This example illustrates the weakness of the uniformitarian axiom in historical linguistics. Because not all the languages of the world have been described, and few have been described adequately, historical linguistics is dependent on descriptive studies for a major methodological check.

Despite this weakness, the uniformitarian axiom is a useful working tool. We can provide some examples of its application from a recent study of the classical languages by Pulgram (1975). The first example involves Classical Greek accentuation, which was essentially based on pitch. There is a type of syllable syncopation which is regularly associated, in stress accent languages, with basically unstressed syllables. Such syncopation is common in English, especially British English, and accounts for the bisyllabic pronunciation of *secretary*, roughly *sec'try*. It is also common in Akkadian and explains alternations like those between *šiprī* 'my work' and *šipiršu* 'his work'; *limad* 'learn (m.s.)' and *limdā* 'learn (c.pl.).' There are about three dozen examples of such syncopation in Classical Greek. These cases, a tiny number compared to those which are liable to syncopation in say, British English, led Szemerenyi to suggest that Greek pitch accent could serve as a condition for syncopation. The fact that syncopation due to accent is a phenomenon of languages with stress accent, but not of those with pitch accent, leads Pulgram to reject this suggestion (1975: 113-14 and refs.). The rejection is based on the uniformitarian axiom: if pitch accent does not condition syncopation in living languages, then the pitch accent of

Classical Greek cannot be reconstructed as conditioning the process.

Pulgram also makes use of the axiom in rejecting the more or less current account of the development of Romance accentuation from Classical Latin to the living Romance languages. This account involves several switches in the overall structure of the language, since accent is a feature of broad structural importance in a language. Pulgram rejects the account as groundless.

> There is no sense in, and no reason for, a sequence of prehistoric Latin or Proto-Latin with a pitch accent inherited from Proto-Indo-European, followed by Old Latin with predominant stress, then again by classical Latin with pitch, and then by 'Vulgar Latin' with stress, leading over to Proto-Romance, to say nothing of a period, inserted somewhere in pre-classical Latin, of a prehistoric initial stress accent (Pulgram 1975: 127).

The reason for this rejection is again the uniformitarian axiom: living languages do not undergo major changes in overall structure without motivation and without effect, yet the accent shifts posited for Romance history are largely without either motivation or effect. Pulgram substitutes a reconstruction of two different languages of different accentual type: Spoken Latin, the language of the comic playwrights, and the lower social orders, and the ancestor of "Vulgar Latin" and the Romance Languages, a language little attested in written form; and Written Latin, the language of the major poets and orators and the higher social orders (1975: 113-35, 260-61). Pulgram's hypothesis explains the accentual facts associated with Old Latin, "Vulgar Latin," and Romance by gathering them together under the rubric of Spoken Latin, in a context which makes its coexistence with Written Latin plausible. There is an abundance of sociolinguistic evidence for a split in the speech community in Rome which the hypothesis accounts for. Further, it reflects the particular bias of linguistic elitism which prevailed at Rome, the rampant Hellenism that sponsored efforts to reshape Latin in a form as much like Greek as possible.

The uniformitarian axiom in historical linguistics has a corollary in the study of the verse of dead languages. No poetic system attested only in written form can be reconstructed as possessing features unknown in a living poetic system. Just as the uniformitarian axiom in historical linguistics is weakened by the fact that not all the languages of the world have been described, so it is weakened in historical poetics by the fact that only a few of the poetic systems of the world have been described.

The usefulness of stating the axiom is largely indirect. Just as the uniformitarian axiom is not often made explicit in historical linguistics, so it is rarely made explicit in poetics. The difference in the histories of the fields is crucial. While historical linguistics could have developed only in conjunction with the axiom, historical poetics has not. Therefore, the non-explicit use of the axiom is dangerous in poetics, instead of by-the-way.

Unless the axiom is made explicit in historical poetics, its limitations will go without notice.

Those limitations are all-important, however. The number of well-described poetic systems is miniscule and of these usually only the European are studied. There is much valuable information in handbooks like the *Princeton Encyclopedia of Poetry and Poetics* (Preminger, Warnke and Hardison 1965) and Wimsatt's *Versification: Major Language Types* (1972), to be sure; we shall often refer to them and similar works of smaller scope. But our statement of the axiom reminds us pointedly of the narrow base on which historical poetics stands.

There are partial compensations. It is often true that though a poetic system has not been adequately described, features can be deduced from available comments and texts. This procedure is often necessary in dealing with material treated by anthropologists, who (perhaps correctly) regard poetic study as beyond their purview or (with justification) believe models for such study are lacking. Such material will often be important to us because, like most anthropologists, we are dealing with the literature of a partially oral culture. Whatever is made of orality in Israel, it cannot be denied; as scholars are increasingly coming to realize, reading Hebrew poetry requires some knowledge of other oral poetries. We shall sometimes, then, have to refer to raw text publications and brief comments rather than full descriptions, as we are guided by the uniformitarian axiom in seeking out other poetic systems.

One final point shall bring us back to the consideration from which we began in discussing uniformitarianism. As scholars of other poetic systems have used the axiom, they have included in their base of consultation Hebrew poetry. Though it is inadequately described, it is among the best known bodies of verse in the world and has often served students of other poetries in formulating descriptions. Though those accounts are sometimes no stronger than the analogy, they are useful in reflecting an investigator's intuitive grasp of similarities which might otherwise be statable only after intensive study.

The axiom will play a small role in our studies. It is important in part because it directs our reliance on a small group of verse systems outward to a much larger one; and in part because it cautions us to rethink all our claims about one system in the light of others. It provides a distant carrot while serving as a powerful and all-too-handy goad.

## *1.2 New evidence for the description of Hebrew verse*

Among the reasons that a reconsideration of current descriptions of Hebrew poetry is needed is the radical alteration in perspective brought about by archeological study, most of it undertaken after what we will call the Standard Description achieved its canonical form in Gray (1915). The benchmark dates are 1929, the discovery of Ras Shamra/Ugarit, and 1949, the discovery of Qumran. Each site yielded a major corpus of poetic material. Also important are numerous, smaller archeological finds, along with further textual studies in the Bible itself. Just as the language of the Bible must be seen as part of the Canaanite dialect group described by Harris (1939), so its poetry must be treated in a similar framework.

The poetic texts from Ugarit and Qumran are of complementary significance. Ever since Ginsberg's pioneering studies, scholars have recognized that the poetic traditions of Ugarit and pre-exilic and exilic Israel are largely homogeneous. The consensus that the poetry of the Qumran psalms is heterogeneous from biblical psalmody, though sharing many of its features, emerged shortly after the texts were published. These two discoveries enlarge the perspective in which Hebrew poetry is viewed. There was a Canaanite poetic tradition that retained its integrity from the Late Bronze Age through the first part of the first millennium; in the second half of that millennium, it underwent considerable diversification. In Palestine, this process culminated in Qumran psalmody; its earliest roots are to be found in post-exilic prophecy (Hanson 1975).

It is not surprising that the similarities have received more attention than the differences. The difficulties of reading Ugaritic are immense, as Ginsberg observed in the justly celebrated aphorism, "The only people who have never made mistakes in Ugaritic philology are those who have never engaged in it" (1950: 156). Nonetheless, great clarity has arisen from the joint study of the two sources of the first phase of Canaanite poetry. Important recent work includes the lexical studies of Dahood, whose early work (1952-1965), indexed in Martinez (1967), has culminated in the Hebrew-Ugaritic Lexicography series (1963b, 1964c, 1965b, 1966b, 1967a, 1968f, 1969c, 1970a, 1971b, 1972, 1973d, 1974c) and other smaller studies (e.g., 1968g, 1973a, 1973c, 1973e, 1974d, 1974e); and of Held (1959, 1965a, 1968, 1973, 1974). Other benefactions which have resulted from Ugaritic studies will concern us throughout.

The consensus that pre-exilic Hebrew and Ugaritic verse are similar leads to an important clue for further exploration. Insofar as the verse works in the same way in the two corpora, a description of Hebrew verse will have to describe Ugaritic verse. Any description capable of fulfilling this task will have to refer largely to features common to the dialects. The major differences between the dialects are the result of sound shifts and changes in morphological structure; it would seem that a description suitable for both Hebrew and Ugaritic verse will not then refer to phonological patterning, but to those features of language structure common to the dialects. These features are essentially syntactic.

Less major finds, which both antedate and follow 1915, have spread a broader canvas in which to situate the three major poetic corpora of

Ugarit, the Bible and Qumran. These finds have clarified the literary situation along with the linguistic diversity by providing examples of highly crafted prose as well as verse. The role of inscriptional study in clarifying poetic traditions has been emphasized by recent students (Cross and Freedman 1972: 419, Dahood 1960, 1975a).

Most prominent have been texts in the first-millennium Canaanite dialects described as poetic. Poetic structure has been suggested for a number of Hebrew texts, including the Gezer Calendar (Stuart 1976: 42). The Tell Siran Bronze Bottle Inscription in Ammonite of the late seventh century is treated as partially or wholly verse by Cross (1973b), Krahmalkov (1976), and Shea (1978). The Arslan-Tash Portal Plaques are treated as Phoenician poems by Cross and Saley (1970) and Cross (1974a: 486-90). The Kilamuwa Inscription, one of the most important texts in Phoenician, is read as a poem by Collins (1971), wrongly, as we have shown (O'Connor 1977). Whatever the final assessment of these cases, they have not yet made a substantial direct contribution to our knowledge of Canaanite poetry.

One study of inscriptional verse has made such a contribution, Krahmalkov's essay on two Neo-Punic poems (1975). The texts are two dedicatory lintels from Mactar. Both texts are eulogies written in a poetic form that has much in common with Ugaritic and pre-exilic Hebrew verse, and both are consistently rhymed. Text A is a eulogy in the monorhyme *-ot*, in alternating lines of three 6-line stanzas. Text B is another eulogy, in four 6-line stanzas. Each stanza has a different rhyme; here, too, the rhyme is in alternating lines. The role of Neo-Punic poetry is readily appreciable because it dovetails with that of the Qumran finds: Neo-Punic verse is another product of the diversification of the Canaanite poetic tradition that eventuated elsewhere in Qumran psalmody. The development took different forms at Qumran and Mactar; because the source tradition is well-known, its offspring are recognizable.

Close study of inscriptions has been directed not only at the recognition of poetic texts, but also at literary language in general (Gevirtz 1975). Appreciation of ornate and figurative uses in prose has enabled Gevirtz to extend the range of study to the El-Amarna letters (1973). In studying the letters of Abimilku of Tyre to Akhenaton, Gevirtz recognized (a) the fixed pairings of water and wood (if the logograms are read *mē* and *iṣū*, this is a case of Panini's Law, on which, see 1.5.2); (b) "number parallelism"; (c) verb sequencings of complex sorts; (d) changes of grammatical person, with continuity of referent; and (e) annalistic language used of reign transitions. The second, third, and fourth of these are used in Canaanite poetry, and the first is related to phenomena known there; the last is comparable to the norms of literary prose in the Bible, reflected at still greater remove in Punic texts (Krahmalkov 1974). Important work on stylistic features in Phoenician texts has been offered by Greenfield (1971), who considers the Ahiram, Tabnit, Eshmunazor, and Azitawadda (i.e., Karatepe) texts. He has also enlarged the field of consideration to include the Aramaic dialects in studies of the Old Aramaic Sefire inscriptions (Greenfield 1965a: 11-18, 1965b, cf. 1974). His venture into the Old Aramaic has been seconded by Tawil (1974). These studies demonstrate that non-poetic language could be figured and fixed, and lay the foundations for describing the resources and conventions of Levantine literary prose.

The last variety of new evidence we need to discuss involves a phenomenon with no name. It has long been recognized that the prose narratives of the Bible contain little poems, usually of two or four lines, sometimes longer. Recognition of these has increased in recent years (Dahood 1968c; Freedman 1960, 1975a; Kselman 1973; Gottwald 1962: 836) and, more importantly, reliance on them as guides to Hebrew poetic form has increased. This reliance is in part misguided and not just because such poems are hard to recognize (Andersen 1974: 43, cf. 55, 101-2, 111, 123-26). The short poems, e.g., Gen 1:27, Gen 7:11, 2 S 3:33-34, are atypical of Canaanite poetry; virtually all the poems in the Bible and from Ugarit are longer.

Let us designate poems under six lines as short: those between 7 and (about) 200 lines medium, and all longer poems as simply long; this provides a typology which can be applied to other poetries besides Canaanite. The rough results of such an application are interesting in the case of short and medium lengths. All long poems, epics and romances, we can set aside. Canaanite poetry is like Arabic, European, and Chinese poetry in assigning primary value to medium-length poems; these are the channel for most poetic expression in these poetries. The epigram in European poetry (Smith 1968: 196-210), the *chüeh chu* in Chinese, the *qiṭᶜah* in Arabic are, like the short poem form in Hebrew, always available, but tend to have restricted uses. (The split is also known in Somali, Andrzejewski and Lewis 1964: 49-51.) There are periods in which these minor forms dominate and certain poets are devoted to them, but overall they take second place. In contrast, Japanese, Turkic, and Persian literature use as their major forms, short forms: the *choka* and *haiku* (Brower 1972) and the *rubaᶜi* and *tuyug* (Fearey 1977). In these traditions, medium-length poems are created from chains (Japanese *renga*) of short forms. To be sure, as the Turkic and Persian cases suggest, the matter is complex, because Arabic forms were taken up in both Persian and Osmanli (Anatolian) Turkish, and flourished there.

While the putting in perspective of the short poems of the Bible does require that they be set aside in first considerations of Canaanite poetry, its usefulness is not only negative. What are these short forms used for elsewhere? Often, most notably in the case of *haiku* but also in that of *chüeh chu* and epigrams, they are the poems used in prose narrative. This is how they are used most often in the Bible. As Campbell (1975) and Freedman (1977: 16-17) have argued, these poems are not the wreckage of larger works that have been largely ground down into prose; they are little poems, used to stud the narrative. The poems say nothing against the integrity of the text in which they occur. (From this use of little poems we must derive the phenomenon of setting medium-length poems at major narrative boundaries.)

Another common use for short forms is riddles, proverbs, apothegms, and gnomai. There are only a few of these isolated in the Bible, but there are many in a great heap, in the Book of Proverbs. Much of Proverbs in its received form has great thematic integrity, but its component parts may well have originated in the short form. (This form is also that of the concluding lines of the first part of the Kilamuwa Inscription.) Many students of Proverbs have recognized the tendency of the book to fall into tiny units. Reference to other literary traditions allows us to bring together the bits of Proverbs and the other short poems in the Bible and recognize in them a distinct poetic form. At the same time we are cautioned not to expect that poetic form to be identical to the basic form of the poetry. (It is likely that if any short inscriptional poems do exist, they belong with these poems.)

With these bodies of new evidence, the history of Canaanite literature will eventually be written. Some of the new evidence has merely confirmed what we already knew: dense, literary prose outside the Bible is substantially of a piece with most within it, differing in being available in short units, free of editorial reshaping. Studies of such prose remind us that many of the resources of poetic composition in any language are not unique to it.

The new evidence also gives a crude periodization of Canaanite poetry: (a) the Homogeneous Period, from the mid-second millennium to the mid-first millennium, the period of the Ugaritic texts, and pre-exilic poetry in Hebrew and (b) the Heterogeneous Period, from the mid-first millennium to the end of the millennium, in which are attested the post-exilic prophets, whose verse diverges only slightly from the earlier material, and the Qumran and Neo-Punic verse, with their substantial divergences. The first of the periods was the basis for the Standard Description of Biblical Hebrew, and it encompasses the body of poetry we are seeking to describe. We have clarified its character somewhat by distinguishing two forms of verse within, which we call short and medium length. Canaanite literature is among those literatures which invest major efforts in the medium-length poem, and reserve the short form for poems in narratives and for proverbs. The largest single group of poems we are concerned with is made up of the poems in the Pentateuch and the Former Prophets, the Latter Prophets and the Psalms; it is the group of poems Gray set out to describe in his 1915 essay and nearly the group Lowth attended to in his lectures. In reading this group, we shall be aided directly at every turn by the addition of the Ugaritic texts to the large group of medium-length poems from the Homogeneous Period, and indirectly by the exclusion of short forms.

### *1.3 Previous descriptions of Hebrew verse*

The need to review the state of the study of Canaanite verse brings with it the considerable obligation to try to do justice to two and a quarter centuries of study. The project is approachable only because the fundamental terms were introduced into the discussion early and have remained in use. We owe the canonical usage of these terms to Lowth, whose formulation we shall call the Standard Description of Hebrew verse. Its two components, parallelism and meter, are at the heart of most descriptions of the verse (1.3.1). We shall briefly sketch some of these; it is important to keep in mind that so widely accepted is Lowth's treatment that scholars do not always explicitly state their adherence to it in discussing one or the other of its parts. After we review some forms of the description, we shall note objections raised to the metrical component (1.3.2) and some modified descriptions based on reconceptualization of it (1.3.3).

We shall treat briefly two issues peripheral to the linguistic description of verse, music and orality (1.3.4). After we note two programs for variant descriptions which neglect the Lowthian economy (1.3.5), we shall state some further objections to the Standard Description (1.3.6-1.3.7). We shall then be ready to recast both components of the Standard Description and reconsider their interrelation.

#### *1.3.1 The Standard Description*

Awareness in scholarly research of general difficulties can be misleading. At first glance, the following observation seems true, if rather bland: "In spite of the fact that many capable scholars have turned their attention to the problem of the poetic structure of Classical Hebrew poetry, no agreement has been reached; in fact sharp differences of opinion have arisen" (Culley 1970: 12). While it can hardly be said that harmony prevails in the field, there *is* an immense amount of agreement about the structure of Hebrew verse. The considerable common ground, so generally presumed that it has sometimes been lost sight of, is roughly what we shall call the Standard Description.

The sources of the Standard Description have not been sorted out with sufficient care. The greatest source is the tradition of writing verse in line units which appears in the Massoretic texts of the three major poetical books, Job, Psalms, and Proverbs; and a few other poems, the Song at the Sea (Exodus 15), the Song of Moses (Deuteronomy 32, but not the Testament of Moses which follows immediately in Deuteronomy 33), the Song of Deborah (Judges 5) and the Psalm of David in 2 Samuel 22. The tradition is reflected not only in medieval texts of canonical material, but also in ancient texts of both canonical and extracanonical verse. Both types of verse are represented in the Psalms Scroll of Qumran Cave 11; some Hebrew fragments of Sirach are also written in verse lines.

This "native" tradition is on the whole uniform: the verse lines are, within large bounds, similar, and the lineations are roughly consistent. Most often the lines are arranged columnarly, but Exodus 15, Judges 5, and 2 Samuel 22 (though not its duplicate Psalm 18) are arranged in a running text with large spaces separating the lines. (This "native" tradition is lost sight of as such in most modern texts; it is preserved in the BFBS text prepared by Snaith from the first hand of BM MS Or. 2626-8, a fifteenth-century Sephardic text.)

The remarkable feature of the native tradition is that it is so erratic. Only a rather unusual selection of verse is presented in lineation. There is, further, no hint (even if the selection could be explained) that the poetic character of the rest of Hebrew verse was recognized. It is plausible to suppose that a poetic tradition could endure without any marks of lineation: line divisions are not used in Chinese, for example. But why so rarely? The witness of Hebrew tradition, though it ultimately inspired the Standard Description, does not in itself inspire complete confidence.

Because the "native" tradition of verse structure was taken up as a base for the Standard Description, its intrinsic value is rarely considered. It is of limited relevance, as Lowth intuitively sensed, perhaps as a result of his knowledge of the classical sphere where a comparable tradition created not only manuscripts but manuals and descriptions. Maas summarizes the contribution these make: "Ancient metrical theory offers nothing but superficial description, mechanical classification, and unprofitable speculation" (1962: 5). He adds that the colometry of ancient manuscripts is not reliable. The same is true in general of Islamic manuscripts, Windfuhr (p.c.) informs us. Latin metrical theory is notably weakened by the bias toward describing Latin as if it were Greek, which was strong in the sphere of language (Pulgram 1975: 88-92, 125-26), and violently so in literary matters (pp. 180-83). It is not that native traditions of verse structure are useless, but rather that they only provide a rough starting point for consideration. The process of using them is exemplified in Maling's recent study of Arabic metrics (1973), based on some earlier work by Halle (1970a): she begins with the native descriptions, extending and simplifying them. Lowth saw that extension and simplification were required of him. It would be unfortunate if that segment of his accomplishment were ignored. (Incidentally, Horwitz 1973 has recently suggested that the word divider is functional in marking Ugaritic verse; if he is correct — the evidence is not clear — we can anticipate that the verse structure will be marked only in a fairly rough fashion.)

The primacy of the "native" tradition is, in most accounts of the history of Hebrew poetry, slighted in favor of a cento of 1,500 years' worth of miscellaneous remarks in a variety of languages. The purpose of the quotations is to reveal the linguistic naivete of the writers and their obtusity in confronting what moderns take to be the plain facts about Hebrew poetry. Such demonstrations do make these points, but the points in themselves are unfair. The modes of conceptualization involved in our understanding of Hebrew poetry are entirely post-Renaissance developments. Ancient and medieval writers could not possibly have availed themselves of our modes of thought. Note a fairly typical remark:

> It is astonishing that the formal structure of ancient Hebrew poetry was transmitted through the centuries largely intact in spite of the lack of poetic format [surely an overstatement], even though the older forms were no longer employed in contemporary poetry and were, in fact, largely disregarded in biblical exegesis (Gottwald 1962: 830).

It is astonishing, but only in so far as it will always be astonishing to people who are oriented to print and electronic media that there exist quite other ways of living in the world (Ong 1962: 62-87). Since we are not concerned with the history of Hebrew poetic interpretation, the only crucial point to make is that in the early Renaissance period, intimations of the Standard Description appear (Cooper 1976).

These appear in the Jewish tradition, notably in the work of Azariah de Rossi, a rabbi of sixteenth-century Ferrara. The observations of de Rossi and earlier Jewish readers are transmitted, along channels not yet described, among Jews and eventually Christians. Recent study of the prehistory of the Standard Description, the period between de Rossi and Lowth, has sidestepped real questions of intellectual history in favor of the great pseudoquestion of primacy. In preliminary work, it is useful to get basic matters straightened out and for this we may be grateful to Baker (1973) and Lundbom (1975: 121-27). The major question remains: why is it that Lowth and several other scholars, working independently across early eighteenth-century Western Europe, began to see the same thing, in places where no one had seen it before? The key word is *see*. It was in part because Lowth and his near contemporaries were *looking* and not listening that they were able to observe the crucial phenomena *and* conceive a vocabulary with which to describe them.

Further study of this seminal period, and especially of Lowth himself, is called for. This study must set Lowth in the context of early Romantic speculation on the sublime (Feldman 1972). The nature of philological study and primitivist longings elsewhere in Europe than Lowth's Oxford-London axis will have to be considered as the perspective is expanded from Lowth to his Hebraist contemporaries. The tradition of universal grammar Lowth worked in has been studied by Chomsky (1966); both Chomsky and Ong (1962: 164-76) treat James Harris, an exact contemporary of Lowth's, in some detail.

It is sufficient for us to note that the Standard Description in its received form derives from lectures delivered by Lowth during his tenure as Professor of Poetry at Oxford and published in 1753 under the title *De Sacra Poesi Hebraeorum Praelectiones Academicae.* This description was widely accepted during the late eighteenth century and became the ground of most discussion in the nineteenth and twentieth centuries. Its great advances over the "native" tradition are two: it accounts more or less for the whole body of Hebrew verse (between a quarter and a third of the Hebrew Bible), including much of the text of the Latter Prophets; and it accounts for the material in an orderly way. The first advance was canonized in 1906 when the first edition of the *Biblia Hebraica*, prepared under the direction of Rudolf Kittel, was printed with most of the verse set off in lines. It did not penetrate translations of the Bible until somewhat later, in English, for example, not until 1949, with the publication of the Revised Standard Version of the Christian Churches of North America (Gottwald 1962: 830).

Our concern is with the second advance. The point of departure for the Standard Description is the line, or colon, *and* the couplet, or bicolon, and the triplet, or tricolon: "In all Biblical poetry basic units of several words each (called 'cola' [here, lines]) combine in groups of two or three to form a verse (bicolon or tricolon) which shows an orderly semantic balance of cola" (Boling 1960: 221). The fundamental unit is variously named; Yoder (1972), for example, calls lines 'cola' with Boling, but refers to the supposed combinations of two and three cola as 'lines.'

The essential perception behind the Standard Description is that Hebrew verse has two bases, one related to features of contiguous lines, the other, referred to lines in themselves. This is unquestioned and unquestionable. Few descriptions of Hebrew verse have ever departed from this two-part structure. Lowth described the first base as parallelismus membrorum and the second he called meter. Virtually all descriptions follow him in these designations.

As a construct of the mid-eighteenth century, the Standard Description is a marvel of scientific thought. Lowth is careful and systematic in describing as much parallelism as he could, and wonderfully frank in refusing to describe the meter he regarded as irrecoverably lost. In the two and a quarter centuries since Lowth's lectures were published, scholars and students have sought to refine his typology of parallelism and to specify the nature of the metrical base. Within the Standard Description's framework, there have been countless improvements, but all of them together have not been adequate to render the Standard Description a serious instrument of study. It remains an attempt to solve one mystery (Hebrew poetic structure) by splitting it into two mysteries, one more obscure than the first (meter), the other only slightly less so (parallelism).

The major restatement of the Description in the twentieth century is Gray's *The Forms of Hebrew Poetry* (1915). The opening words of that volume attest to persistent dissatisfaction with the Description; they are still true. "The existence of formal elements [in Hebrew poetry] is now generally recognized; but there are still great differences of opinion as to the exact nature of some of these, and as to their relation to one another" (Gray 1915: 3). Despite these differences of opinion, Gray adheres to the framework of the Description and devotes himself to examining first parallelism and then meter.

Since Gray's preeminence as a student of Hebrew verse is generally acknowledged, we would do well to observe some features of his approach. He seeks first of all to enlarge the textual base from which he is working by discussing intertestamental apocalyptic literature (pp. 27-33). He prefaces his discussion of Hebrew parallelism with brief remarks on other forms of parallelism in Semitic literatures, Akkadian (pp. 38-40) and Arabic (pp. 40-47); and in non-Semitic literature. The only non-Semitic example he knew much of was the folk poetry of Karelia collected by Lönnrot, which rose to prominence in late-nineteenth-century Europe as a vehicle of Finnish nationalism (pp. 38-39). The major work of this enormous corpus, the epic *Kalevala*, is available in English, along with an antecedent work, the *Old Kalevala*, in translations by Magoun (1963, 1969). Both volumes make instructive reading for students of ancient Semitic verse. Finally, we note that Gray attends to other poetic forms, especially those of Old English and the Anglo-Saxon revival which culminated in the work of Langland, in considering metrical questions.

Gray seeks to reform the parallelism component of the Standard Description from within. He devotes particular attention to Lowth's garbagecan category, synthetic parallelism (pp. 51-64, 69-78). He introduces the notion of incomplete parallelism with and without compensation which is used to good effect (within a slightly different framework) by Gordon (1965: 130-44). The most glaring deficiency in the original statement of the Standard Description, the unspecified nature of the metrical component, had much exercised nineteenth-century European scholars, including Bellerman, Bickell, Budde, Ewald, Ley, Meier, Saalschutz, and Sievers (see Cooper 1976, Goodwin 1969, Stuart 1976). Gray sensibly insists on the existence of rhythm (pp. 87-129) while refusing simplistic approaches (pp.

135-54, 203-27), particularly the rigid schemes of Sievers (in his later work) and Duhm (pp. 227-36). Declining to see either a quantitative or rigidly accentual system, or a system which was both simultaneously or alternately (all these possibilities have been favored), Gray followed Ley and the earlier studies of Sievers in using a loosely accentual system to explain the regularity of line length. He insists on following at least roughly the received text, rejecting metrical schemes which bear no direct relation to it. Most scholars have followed Gray in referring to accentual rather than quantitative meter though current applications are inconsistent and often so tentatively offered as to be extrinsic to textual criticism and study (Kurylowicz 1972: 166-77 and Segert 1960).

Gray's final contribution is to introduce into the discussion the analysis of the structures of whole poems (pp. 81-83, 87-120, 157-97, 243-95). We shall return to such study below (1.6.1).

The program laid out by Lowth and restated by Gray has been the program of biblical scholarship in our times. There have been further restatements and reconsiderations, especially regarding the putative meter; these are by now about as numerous as the sand of the seas. One important version of the Standard Description is T. H. Robinson's (1950, 1953), because in it he seeks to strengthen the Description by polarizing the two components. "Parallelism," he contends, "is concerned solely with ideas" (1959: 439), and can thus be opposed neatly to meter, which is a matter of sound. Another device he uses is a generalization of parallelism beyond its formal reflections, so that it is said to be "the principle which controls the form which every line of Hebrew poetry takes" (p. 443). (Note the easy Platonism there.)

One final suggestion regarding meter must be mentioned. The students of metrics cited above concentrated their attention on accentual and quantitative metrical theories. There remains the possibility of iso-syllabism, as foreshadowed by a late medieval commentator who referred to eight-syllable lines as having meter (quoted apud Cooper 1976: 154), and by Moses Ibn Habib, who talked of isosyllabic units in the late 15th century (Cooper 1976: 17). Vagueness and confusion, to be expected in such early speculation, are not appropriate to scholarly work in our time.

Yet the matter of counting syllables seems to bring confusion in its train. There are three ways that syllable counts can be made part of a consideration of Hebrew verse: (a) they can be alleged to reveal the existence in Hebrew of syllabic meter; (b) they can be alleged to describe the order or structure which exists in Hebrew verse, without being associated with a metrical pattern; and (c) they can be made a part of a close consideration without any claims being made for them. The second position is the position of Freedman and Culley, which will be considered below, among the Modified Standard Descriptions; the third position is irrelevant here. The first position has been taken up firmly only by Stuart (1976); his work is discussed in Cooper (1976) but some further consideration is warranted. (Christensen 1974, 1975 and Hanson 1968, 1973 follow Stuart's approach, at a distance.)

Stuart and Cooper, as well as Goodwin (1969: 150), have confused the three positions. Neither Freedman nor Culley has ever written of syllabic meter; they use syllable counting as a way of describing features of verse structure which are intuitively recognizable but which have so far resisted descriptive efforts; Cross also refers to syllable counts as an index of symmetry, not as a measure of metrical reality (1974).

Stuart explains that it is *possible* to count syllables with an "unwavering reliance upon Masoretic vocalization and tradition," in the knowledge that the traditional phonology is not entirely accurate. Freedman, Stuart explains, "prefers this risk to that of the arduous and uncertain reconstruction of a theoretically original poetic form, as attempted in this present study [viz., his own]" (Stuart 1976: 6). Stuart continues his exposition of Freedman's method.

> Freedman's recent work has used the MT without emendation as the basis for a controlled experiment. Although highly skilled in the techniques necessary to reconstruct original vocalizations and forms, he has purposely limited himself to the received text. In this way scholars hostile to or unacquainted with reconstructive techniques are able and willing to follow his arguments for the newer syllabic scansion. While Freedman knows that using the MT uncritically involves a certain degree of error, he is also aware that a margin of error accompanies reconstructions of supposed original texts as well (Stuart 1976: 8).

The term reconstruction in both these passages might mislead the reader. What Stuart means in part is compensation for certain minor phonological rules, e.g., an epenthesis rule for the major noun class of segholates, and a contraction rule for diphthongs. With these belong some adjustments required by minor indeterminacies in the graphic system. *Pace* Stuart, *all* these features of his "reconstruction" Freedman uses, *without exception*; Culley uses the second but not the first group. The other feature of "reconstruction" is systematic emendation of the text, not often or properly considered a variety of reconstruction. By systematic emendation we mean emendation motivated not by difficulties of a particular textual locus but by a desire to establish a system extrinsic to a text as characteristic of it. Stuart uses, in justification of his emendations, supposed difficulties in text dictation and transmission. He denies that he emends for the sake of meter, adding that "no exception to this" practice of not emending need be made in the case "of the grossly unbalanced couplet where an element [the term is undefined] or two is obviously missing due to haplography or an element has obviously been added through dittography or deliberate harmonization. In such cases there exists a need to emend from the standpoint of *any* theory of meter, as well as the demands of the parallelism" (Stuart 1976: 211). Emendation would only be required *if* one had a theory of meter; many do not and read on. Stuart refuses to consider as emendation the systematic deletion of *ky*, *ᵓt*, *ᵓšr*, and other particles which "are patently prosaic and usually suspicious in a poetic context" (1976: 31); Freedman has argued that such particles should be retained in poetry because they are rare there (1977).

Stuart asserts that Freedman's non-emendation policies are designed to appeal to an audience for whom "the practice of emendation has been put on a level with drug addiction, Manicheism, and other debaucheries," to borrow a phrase from Strugnell (1974: 551). It was emendation of Koine Greek texts that Strugnell defended in a gracious pitch, and it was emendation of single difficulties, with attention to the text and not an outside system. Freedman does use emendation in Hebrew to resolve single difficulties; he never uses it systematically. (The same is true, *pace* Stuart and many others, of Dahood.) Stuart's statement that "Freedman has shown that one *can* use the MT while demonstrating the superiority of syllabic meter over stress meter" (1976:9) is erroneous (a) in that Freedman does not use the Massoretic Text as Stuart alleges he does, and (b) in stating that Freedman deals with syllabic meter.

Stuart is faithful to his declaration that "the production of good poetry by these means [viz., those of textual study] is always the highest consideration" (1976: 22). He is innocent of the thought that textual study might seek to study rather than produce poetry and innocent of any doubts about his ability to recognize "good poetry" when he produces it.

The essence of Stuart's proposal is that Hebrew verse used "a system of meter based on the quantity [i.e., number!] of syllables per colon [i.e., line]" (1976:9). The number of syllables is (allowing for "reconstruction") constant, but only within a bicolon or tricolon. The meter is not at all bound to continue for more than two or three lines, and usually does not. This "system" is not a system at all. Descriptions of isosyllabic meters are abundant and in none is there even hinted at a system that within a single medium length poem "changes meter" every two or three lines. On isosyllabic meters, see, for example, Brower (1972), Fussel (1965, 1972), Jakobson (1967), Lotz (1972a, 1972b), and Zeps (1973). In this case, the uniformitarian axiom is useful because the basis of isosyllabic verse is not clear. Surely, as Jakobson (1967) points out, much more is involved than consistent temporal spacing of units, but the syllable is a problematic concept and the uniformly negative results of psycholinguistic tests of its psychological reality, though not discomfiting, are not encouraging (Bell

1975; Ladefoged 1967, 1971). Syllabic meter exists, but how it works is hard to say.

Stuart is in fact aware of potential difficulties and indicates his awareness of them at several points. First, he contends that his description of Hebrew meter does not ignore or abandon "the possibility of internal feet" (1976: 11). This is either false or a denial of his basic claim, since although meters which are accentual or quantitative may be generally (though not invariably) isosyllabic, they are referred to as accentual or quantitative, not as isosyllabic. Meters which are simply isosyllabic do not show other organizational schemes (Lotz 1972a). Further, in order to characterize more than three lines at once, Stuart uses a scheme of grouping together lines 3 to 5 syllables in length as short and lines 8 to 13 syllables in length as long, reserving 6 and 7 as free; he then describes passages of verse as either shortlined or longlined. He does not, however, mention the relation of this form of characterization to the meter, to which it has no obvious connection. Even with these supports, however, and the stipulation of regularity as a desired result, and with the aid of frequent reference to orality and musicality, Stuart still concludes with descriptions of verse as irregular, mixed, and unbalanced. Those are distinct categories.

### *1.3.2. Objections to the Standard Description on the basis of meter*

The greatest and most obvious of the Standard Description's weaknesses is its treatment of the metrical component, the component which is intended to characterize the lines of verse in themselves. It appears that the lines should be describable in themselves, and that a metrical description would be appropriate. Just as the first of these observations is motivated by evidence of the texts, the second is not, even though it is a plausible inference from comparative poetics. The active, chiefly European advocates of a precisely defined metrical component are of no concern here because after a century of research, they have no scientifically usable conclusions, i.e., no one of them can consistently reproduce another's results.

Yoder (1972) is an acute representative of those who adhere tentatively to the Standard Description. He comments: "In contrast . . . to parallelism, the occurrence and basic nature of which are recognized by all, there is little consensus regarding meter. Its very existence is denied . . . ; among those who affirm it there is only limited agreement as to its nature" (Yoder 1972: 58). Conceding the value of the major theories about Hebrew verse, especially those which involve accentual meter, Yoder gently but firmly describes the petard with which they must be hoist.

They require numerous, often nearly systematic, emendations to work. This approach is untenable, as Freedman notes: "Strophic and metrical or rhythmic structures must be derived from the text as we have it, since it would be methodologically untenable to emend the text in the interests of a certain metrical or strophic structure or to base such a structure on an emended text" (1974: 163). Some theories allow extrametrical words or lines to accumulate in large classes that can only be defined by their metrical deviance. All theories of meter often disregard parallelism and syntax and occasionally fail to separate what is universally acknowledged as prose from poetry. Thus Sievers was, by the end of his studies, on the verge of scanning the whole of the Hebrew Bible as verse, without distinguishing clearly what is taken by all as verse within it. (Yoder notes also that most theories tend to be overly elaborate; this is an acute but crudely put objection.)

Yoder ultimately seeks to enlarge the Standard Description, contending that a loosely accentual meter follows from "colonic" and parallelistic structure. He makes the terminological crossing preliminary to some of the Modified Standard Descriptions when he writes: "Parallelism is a fundamental prosodic feature of Hebrew verse" (Yoder 1972: 62), in using the term prosodic to describe a non-phonological feature of the language subsystem.

Objections to the Standard Description on the basis of meter suggest that either the metrical component is misconceived or the relation of the parts of the Descriptions needs rethinking. The former possibility has been more widely explored.

### *1.3.3 Modified Standard Descriptions*

There are some overall substantive modifications of the Standard Description which have arisen out of the objections on the grounds of meter. The older, more audacious, and less fully described modification is due to Young (1950), following his teacher Gordon (1965). It requires only the simple clear statement toward which we have seen Yoder leaning: "That regular meter can be found in such poetry [as Hebrew, Ugaritic, and Akkadian] is an illusion" (Young 1950: 133). Both Young and Gordon eliminate the metrical component of the Standard Description.

A more nuanced Modified Description is offered by Freedman in a series of papers beginning in 1960, and by Culley (1970). Noting first of all that "no regular, fairly rigid [metrical] system will work with any large sample without extensive reshaping of individual poems and verses" (Freedman 1977: 10), Freedman offers syllable counting as a means "to achieve an adequate description of the phenomena" (1977: 11). These proposals regarding syllable counting have been widely misunderstood, as we remarked earlier. Freedman and Culley do not propose that Hebrew had a syllabic meter. They propose rather that the second component of the Standard

Description should no longer be regarded as meter, but rather as a device with which to track phonological regularity in the text.

> In analyzing the metrical evidence, scholars may reduce it to some kind of arithmetic pattern, but this does not mean that the poet consciously used a numerical process. It is not likely that the Israelites counted syllables carefully, or even accents for that matter, when composing their poetry. But it is convenient for us to do so in tabulating the evidence (Freedman 1960: 101).

Thus the second component, actual metrical description, is dismissed. Its place is taken by a device to describe the regularity, without any attempt to explain it. (There are a number of students who use syllable counts for purely descriptive purposes, e.g., Dahood 1968e, 1968h, 1969a, 1970c, 1975c, 1975e; Holladay 1968; Kselman 1973.)

Althought syllable-counting is "a more sensitive instrument for measuring the length of lines or cola" (Freedman 1974: 168) than study of other features of the text, it is not without its difficulties. Freedman and Culley both deviate in simple, systematic, and defensible ways from the received text; the details of their approaches are not crucial here.

One feature of syllable counting in the Modified Standard Description is that it produces a large amount of data. Culley set out to describe line and bicolon length in a group of poems. He found an average line length of 8 syllables in Psalms 2, 78, 96, 111, and 112; Job 6 and 9; and the Oracles of Balaam; and an average length of 10 syllables in Psalms 9, 17, 41, and 74. The average bicolon length in Psalm 119 is 17 syllables, and in Lamentations 1 it is 13 syllables. (We shall return to such considerations below.)

Freedman has sought to characterize both small poetic units (1960, 1968a, 1973a, 1975c) and whole poems in terms of the symmetries of units that can be discerned through study of syllable counts. He has studied a number of archaic poems, Psalm 29 (Freedman and Hyland 1973), Exodus 15 (Freedman 1974), and 2 Samuel 1 (Freedman 1972a), and a number which can be dated to the sixth century, including Psalms 23 (1976b) and 137 (1971a), and Lamentations (1972d). A smaller group are less clearly datable: Job 3 (1968a) and other acrostic poems (1972d).

### *1.3.4 Alleged supports for the Standard and Modified Standard Descriptions*

Students have often recognized the inadequacies of the Standard and Modified Standard Descriptions of Hebrew verse and sought to remedy them. Frequently, recourse has been had to phenomena associated with the verse, music, and orality. It is legitimate to refer to these in explaining the integrity of a performance, but they cannot be incorporated into a description of a linguistic phenomenon. Even on a level beyond language, it is difficult to bring verse together with these phenomena generally, since music and orality seem to be particular to cultural areas.

### *1.3.4.1 Musicality*

As in contemporary discos, so in contemporary descriptions of Canaanite poetry, much is done under the cover of music that is amusing but not entirely licit. Music, when used in describing poetic systems, is a way of covering over variations in verse. This is not to say that music has no place in the description of verse, merely that it can never have an integral place. Reference to music has general explanatory power, but no descriptive usefulness. To claim that variation in a language subsystem is due to music is to claim that it is unanalyzable without saying so; but if a phenomenon is unanalyzable, the analyst cannot licitly be allowed to label it as anything but that. Variations in poetic texture may result from musical variations, but they are distinct from it because music is distinct from language. This is the view expressed with great vigor by the master Russian prosodist, Sirin, in a description of his quest for a good description of English verse: "I have of course slammed shut without further ado any . . . works on English prosody in which I glimpsed a crop of musical notes or those ridiculous examples of strophic arrangements which have nothing to do with the structure of verse" (1964: 4). We may be satisfied with the more modest statement of Lotz: "Music cannot be the basis for metric analysis" (1972a: 3, cf. LaDrière 1965: 670).

The essential point is conceded even by students like Monroe Beardsley who regard the relation of verse and music as a proper field of inquiry for aesthetic theory. Beardsley observes that "metric patterns, as here defined, involve both more prominent and less prominent syllables." He must then admit that "the arrangement of [syntactically ordered] words in lines solely on the principle that each line must contain a certain [fixed] number of syllables ['syllabic meter'] is not meter at all by my definition. It is certainly a sound pattern and may constitute the organization of certain kinds of verse," but it is not amenable to correlation with music (1972: 248). Since much poetry is syllabic, Beardsley's inquiry is tangential to the general correlation of music and verse. Beyond the basic fact of isochrony of music and speech, there is no such correlation.

We may pause over the question of what ancient Near Eastern music was like. This is an active area of study at present, focused on two text groups; one includes only the Neo-Babylonian Converse Tablet published by Lambert (1971), which appears to use an entirely different musical system than the other group. This second group includes four major ancient scholarly texts (Kilmer 1971, 1974: 70) which present a vocabulary of musical intervals used in a unique text from Ugarit containing a Hurrian cult song followed by "explicit musical notation" (Kilmer 1974: 81, Dietrich and Loretz 1975). The scholarly traditions are entirely Mesopotamian, but the musical text is derived from the West Semitic sphere, though it is written in a non-Semitic language. There is potential for clarification here but since the interpretation of the text is difficult, only potential.

After the initial recognition of the musical vocabulary in the text by Güterbock (1970), three major lines of interpretation developed, those of the musicologist Wulstan (1971, 1974), of the Assyriologist Kilmer (1974, 1976), and of Duchesne-Guillemin (1975), a historian of music. The points of disagreement are the nature of the music, and the relationship of words to music. Kilmer asserts that the music was based on dyads or chords and that the music was heterophonic; Wulstan and Duchesne-Guillemin agree that Kilmer is wrong; the latter calls the music diatonic and sets it in a tradition of synagogal and Syriac and Latin Christian chanting. It is clear from this last point that Duchesne-Guillemin regards the Hurrian music as non-syllabic (1975: 163). Wulstan does, too: "All that we know of Near Eastern music suggests that purely syllabic music [i.e., music in which there is a fixed coincidence of note and syllable] would be very unusual" (1974: 127). Kilmer is absolutely clear in her contrary position: "It is my premise that the notation *must* fit the lyrics, or there is no point to the whole thing having been written down in the first place" (1974: 77).

The disagreements here are not the result of argumentation but of presuppositions. Duchesne-Guillemin and Wulstan are arguing from ethnomusicological principles and from music history and Kilmer from a need to explain the tablet. It seems clear that the former two (who do not entirely agree) are on safer grounds than Kilmer; there are any number of apparently useless texts written on more durable materials than clay that survive from the ancient world. The mysterious role of writing in itself is never to be underestimated in thinking about why anything would be recorded in writing in a preliterate world. But we need not settle the argument. The crucial facts to note are that when information about ancient music turns up, it strongly resists study, and that even the parameters of argumentation are obscure. We still know nothing about whatever music might have been associated with Canaanite poetry, so music cannot play an active role in the description of the poetry, even if such use were licit; if we ever find out about such music, it will be difficult to figure out how to talk about it.

We do not wish to deny the strong native speaker tradition which alleges that Hebrew and other Canaanite verse was sung, only that it can play a part in describing verse. It *must* be used in explaining how verse was performed. It could be used to explain how an irregular or "odd" metrical system was compensated for in the creation of integral pieces of verse production. Indeed, we will present below a strong argument that Canaanite verse was sung; but the argument will follow from our description, not be part of it.

### *1.3.4.2 Orality*

In recent years, an attempt has been made to use the supposed oral character of Canaanite verse to account for the deficiencies of the Standard Description. There has been a notable, if understandable, lack of precision in such usage. Orality, like musicality, can be used to explain how Canaanite poetry worked in its full social context, but it cannot be used to describe how it worked as a linguistic subsystem (Freedman 1977: 12).

The status of orality in Canaanite studies is unclear. There have been preliminary studies of orality in verse (Culley 1967, Whallon 1969, Watters 1976). As in the case of Homer, so with Canaanite poetry, orality is not a hypothesis, subject to falsification, but a source of analogy. Thus it can never be allowed to assume priority over the object of description. One clue regarding the limitations of any orality hypothesis can be extrapolated from a remark of Lord's: "Your model should be to some degree comparable; that is to say, you shouldn't seek a model in another genre. If you're going to talk about narrative poetry, you shouldn't seek a model in some tradition which is not narrative and come up with some formula in lyric, for example, and apply that in the area of the narrative genre" (Lord in discussion in Stolz and Shannon 1976: 66-68). This is eminently sensible advice and no one familiar with a wide range of literatures would hesitate in pronouncing it so. Canaanite poetry, however, is homogeneous across major genres: Ugaritic myths and legends, and Hebrew lyrics and historical recitations are written in a substantially uniform medium. This medium seems, then, to lack genre specificity; this is not surprising but it vastly limits the available oral analogies because the "model should be to some degree comparable" to the material under study. Even given a model or a group of models, the use of analogy must still be restrained. Robertson, in a discussion of approaches to Canaanite verse within contemporary critical frameworks, has seen this clearly: orality does not help or hinder the close reading of a text (1976: 548).

Coote puts the opposite case in offering another Modified Standard Description. He proceeds from a general assumption of orality to description based on oral compositional techniques moving into written form. He postulates that "each time a [Canaanite poetic] composition is performed, it is recomposed from a set of traditional elements whose makeup and relations continually shift" (1976: 914). He introduces the concept of the formula, suggesting that some formulas are line length, others shorter or longer; he transmutes the parallelism component of the Standard Description into a loose vocabulary of variants and multiforms. He contends that analogies can be used to discover the multiform conventions of Canaanite verse. He transforms the other component of the Standard Description in asserting that orality provides a basis for working out the non-rules of verse structure. "The verse line was not measured in stresses, beats, syllables, or words, but by some nonverbal component of oral performance such as rhythm, musical phrasing, or the poet's feeling of rightness" (p. 916).

He states that "the meaning of the line was self-contained, so that in oral performance a pause between lines did not disrupt the flow of meaning" (p. 916). This is either not true or trivially so, depending on definitions of the line and of containment, which Coote does not provide. The final stage of his argumentation is provided by the suggestion that "prosodic rules were indeterminate at the oral stage" (i.e., either they were coming into or going out of existence) and thus Hebrew poetry, which exists in a limbo between oral tradition, manuscript tradition, and memory, cannot be described in an orderly way at all.

This extreme form of an oral hypothesis cannot be defended. If the Homeric or Slavic analogies are relied on, they offer no support for non-orderly structure, since the poetries are metrical. Coote's version of the parallelism component of the Standard Description has the effect of obliterating the useful boundaries it draws by leveling all patterning to multiforms, while not providing any way of differentiating prose formulas from poetic ones, even though prose must be distinguished from verse.

A less extreme oral hypothesis has been offered by Cross (1974b), in discussing Ugaritic verse texts. He begins from the Standard Description, asserting that phenomena of parallelism derive at base from oral compositional techniques and that "usually the formulaic structure gives an extreme symmetry or regularity to Ugaritic." This symmetry can be measured by syllable counting which serves as an index of it (1974b: 1). "The symmetry and internal structure normally does [sic] not extend beyond the single bicolon or single tricolon" (p. 5). However, "alongside verse units of striking symmetry or metrical regularity are many verses [scil., sequences of words] which appear to be irregular or asymmetrical" (p. 5). Assuming that the verse had formulaic structure, Cross believes there are grounds for regularizing all the verse, i.e., "rewriting" wherever "necessary." There are three avenues for regularization. The first is variable vocalizations of proper nouns, nouns in construction (with or without case vowels), and of certain problematic verb forms. All these cases are genuinely indeterminate and if one is going to count syllables and look for symmetry in the counts, the degree of freedom represented by these cases is unquestionable.

This latitude is far from sufficient to regularize all the Ugaritic texts even in the tiny corpus Cross examines. Before introducing the other avenues of regularization, Cross remarks: "It is fair to say, I believe, that Homeric verse is less regular on the surface than Ugaritic verse; however, we know the rules of Greek metrics, and hence can perceive its full symmetry" (p. 5, n. 6). The reader might suppose that Cross intends to follow this statement with a search for the rules of Ugaritic metrics. Rather, he regards the symmetry as so nearly evident that all that is required for its perfect revelation is recognition of (a) the admissibility of systematic emendation, and (b) the fact that some lines included in the verse text are prose interpolations. These are counsels grounded firmly in an appreciation of the texts, but they are counsels of despair which cannot be seconded. (Some of our objections are discussed in Long 1976: 195-97).

The first point is based on the work of Lord, one of the major students of modern oral literature. He observes that formulaic poetry, which is usually sung, is hard to dictate without music and that because of the absence of music, the great Serbocroatian epic singers he, along with his teacher Parry, worked with, tended to confuse, reverse, or expand formulas (1965: 124-38). Cross suggests that the same process was at work in the recording of the Ugaritic texts, and that its untoward effects can be corrected (a) from "parallel passages" which may preserve the "correct text" or provide sufficient information from which to reconstruct the correct text; *or* (b) by rearrangement of words within a bicolon or tricolon or deletion of words. The desideratum of these four powerful forms of "emendation" is the "restoration" of a balanced syllable count (pp. 6-10).

The final avenue for revealing the regularity of Ugaritic verse involves recognizing that the verse text may contain prose fragments or rubrics, which have no lines parallel to them and break "a consistent metrical sequence," i.e., a pattern of regular syllable counts over two or three lines. These breaking lines are extrametrical. Cross recognizes that not all unparalleled lines are necessarily prose; occasionally these prose fragments include poetic language; and there are rubrics which are poetic, i.e., have a "poetic" syllable count.

It is not necessary to discuss the proposal's tentativeness, since Cross is conscious of this feature. We must rather address the assumptions and methodological approaches. Before doing so, however, let us take stock of the status of the two oral hypotheses we have discussed vis-à-vis the Standard Description. Coote's remarks on Hebrew verse represent the weakest version of it known to us and Cross's on Ugaritic, one of the strongest. Cross, that is, absolutizes parallelism where Coote almost loses track of it; and Cross absolutizes phonological regularity where Coote dismisses it. If Cross had gone on to defend a notion of syllabic meter, then his form of the Standard Description would be the strongest conceivable. The polarization of Coote and Cross in describing the two major corpora of Canaanite poetry is intrinsically unsatisfactory since although there are differences between the two corpora (and no one has taken these into account so well as Cross has), there are significant common features to be considered. We have noted some of the problems with Coote's approach. One of the difficulties with Cross's requires little notice: if a text is to be taken as poetic, it must be taken as entirely so unless the putative intrusions can be shown to be consistently extrinsic. Categories of rubrics and prose fragments cannot licitly be admitted into the discussion unless they can be shown to be discrete; Cross has not shown this.

Cross's other regularization tool deserves more attention. Lord, on the basis of his own extensive field work as well as study of previous workers' efforts at collecting oral epics, notes that the poets who compose the texts have trouble composing and dictating simultaneously. Lord's remarks refer explicitly to poets who *compose* orally and who compose *epics*. Often, Lord relates, a naive scribe will take down a bad text with unmetrical lines and even passages of prose. He explains the process as a result not only of simultaneity of composition and dictation, but also of the lack of music to keep the beat.

This is the process Cross envisions in the recording of texts at Ugarit. Let us consider some objections to the analogy. First, all modern students of oral poetry write with a simple alphabetic script on paper; the Ugaritic scribes wrote with a wedge-shaped alphabet on clay. If the time discrepancies involved in transcription are so great as to make it difficult for a modern to keep up with a singer, one might think it impossible for an Ugaritian, as Freedman (p.c.) observes. Indeed, if Lord is correct in insisting on the flexibility of oral epic composition, then the hypothesis of oral composition for Ugaritic (and Hebrew) verse must be abandoned. This is not to say that orality must be abandoned: other modes of oral literature are attested. Nor is this the only argument against oral composition. It would indeed be surprising if material of central, sacral significance at Ugarit were subject to variation in composition; such variation leaves open countless possibilities for ideological revisionism. Speaking of non-epic Finnish folk poetry, Kiparsky aptly remarks: "It might be expected that changes in content are avoided in a poem which tells you how the world originated and which in addition makes the corn grow" (1976: 98). Contemporary Serbocroatian epics, in contrast, derive from the private sphere and are without public significance.

Another objection to the analogy is related to the problem of song length. Lord allows that short songs can be got by heart, even by poets working in a tradition with oral composition. We have no evidence that the Ugaritic texts were performed in the great cycles scholars have made of them; the largest domain of recitation warranted by the texts would be one whole tablet. Even that may be too large. It may be that the songs were performed not by a single poet but by a panel working in alternation or rotation, each producing an episode or some other unit. Such team work of poets with other poets, with reciters, or with the audience, is common in oral literary cultures. (On the difficulty of interpreting passing references in ancient texts to oral transmission, see Hillers and McCall 1976.)

The role of literacy in modern times has restructured society so vastly that the oral poets of Europe (if not elsewhere) are marginal people of the lowest orders. The oral poets of Ugarit, in contrast, worked for the great institutions of a state apparat; their relations with one another and with the scribes they have supervised (assuming that the scribes were not themselves poets) were under none of the pressures of their medieval and especially modern counterparts. Further study in the historical sociology of literacy as well as oral poetic composition is needed.

Since Cross's proposal is the source of a potentially important tool for understanding Canaanite verse, it may be useful to dwell longer on the analogy and look at what we know of a great modern singer. "Among the singers of modern times there is none to equal Homer, but he who approaches the master most closely in our experience of epic song is Avdo Mededović of Bijelo Polje, Yugoslavia. He is our present-day Balkan Singer of Tales" (Lord 1965: iii, cf. 1976). A good deal is known about Mededović (ca. 1870-1955). Before we discuss the poet as he is revealed in Lord and Bynum (1974), we must point to the poem *The Wedding of Smailagić Meho*, which is given there in Lord's translation. *The Wedding* is a poem of such astonishing magnitude and complexity as to give the lie to any trivialization of oral literature. Even Lord, who as a theorist of oral composition has consistently emphasized that the fruitfulness is in the conventions, freely acknowledges Avdo's originality.

To learn of the resources of oral verse, we must turn to the poem; in considering the poet we can rely on Bynum's translations of taped conversations with him. Before we consider those conversations it may be apposite to note that *The Wedding*, which is 12,323 lines and is thus one of the two longest songs recorded in modern times, was taken in dictation; the other, also by Avdo, which is about a thousand lines longer, was mechanically recorded. Generalizations about the limits of dictation must take into consideration phenomena like the dictation of *The Wedding*.

Keeping in mind that the Ugaritic texts were found in the monumental buildings of a flourishing city-state and are the products of a state sponsored class of ideologues, let us review Avdo's situation as he reveals it in the taped conversations. It admits of a simple summary: he was a marginal man. He was a Muslim in a region dominated by Christians after the fall of the Ottoman Empire. Even before the fragmentation of the Balkans, he was out of the religious mainstream of much of the society he traveled in since his upbringing and behavior were more pious than those of the Turks with whom he served in the army. (He calls Turks 'Anatolians,' using 'Turks' for all Ottoman subjects.) Avdo was disciplined only once during seven years of army service, after he hit another soldier with a shoe because "he was swearing at me in a way that wasn't right. He was an

Anatolian and he said, 'Fuck your faith!' It's going too far to say a hard thing like that" (Lord and Bynum 1974: 44).

Further, Avdo was illiterate and felt inferior to his cultural compeers, though proud of having gotten on as a tradesman without writing skills. He was perhaps most marginal as a patriot of the fallen Ottoman Empire. The theme of *The Wedding* is the saving of the Empire from the threat of Christian takeover. His sorrows over the passing of such glory as belonged to Suleiman the Magnificent are central to his reverent historical, rather than mythic, approach to story telling, but the sorrows of Avdo go much further. Lord's summary is apt: "He was a quiet family man in a disturbed and brutal world" (Lord and Bynum 1974: 6).

As a poet too, he was lonely: he sang little in his later years. He always learned from other poets gratefully but with honest knowledge of his own superiority. In reading over this man's story and his remarks on his art, we note only one feature of language behavior that he may have shared with the poets of Ugaritic: he was partially bilingual, as some of them doubtless were, though his knowledge of Turkish was acquired in young adulthood and does not seem to have been active later.

Consider, then, Avdo and his fellow Eastern European epic poets giving their verse to the scholars whose experience Lord seeks to explain. Parry, under whose supervision *The Wedding* was recorded, and his Serbocroatian assistant were literate and "Christian" in culture, Western or Common European in perspective, and of higher social rank than poets like Avdo. That the oral poets were able to deliver their words to them at all is a tribute to the strength of both poets and scholars. What is, however, a great virtue in a modern scholar can be readily presupposed in an ancient Ugaritian. The freely given trust that arises from common culture, religion, and political situation, which Parry had to elicit as a response to his passion for the poetry, would have obtained freely between North Syrian scribe and poet. These factors need to be considered along with the absence of music in explaining difficulty in transmission.

We have dwelt on the case of Avdo Mededović partly to show the need for explicitness in the use of analogies, and partly to represent the sorrows of a great poet to our imagination. Even if we cannot accept Cross's conclusions based on the use of Lord's remarks, we must be grateful to him for having introduced the Serbocroatian analogy into discussion.

We hope that our remarks show that we are not beset by the second of two fears cited by Lord: "There seems to be a fear of oral literature — as far as Homer is concerned, and any of our sacred texts — a fear of its being oral, and then there is a fear of its being oral in accordance with this or that model " (Lord in discussion in Stolz and Shannon 1976: 66-68). As to the first fear, we can only say that we have never entered the realm of modern oral literature without feeling our understanding of Canaanite literature enriched. The social similarities between the Xhosa (Bantu) *imbongi* described by Opland (1975, 1976) and the Hebrew prophets, for example, are worthy of close study. Since we are concerned here only with formal literary structure, we shall not be able to acquit ourselves fully of the charge of the fear of orality here; we hope we have established grounds for a presumption of innocence. (For some recent studies of the diverse uses of oral poetic form and on the range of forms of orality, see Austerlitz 1975, 1976; Brickner 1974; Finnegan 1970, 1973, 1976a, 1976b; Fox 1971a, 1971b, 1971c, 1973, 1974; Gossen 1974; Kiparsky 1973-74, 1976; Sherzer 1974.)

### *1.3.5 Two programs for variant descriptions*

In the Standard and Modified Standard Descriptions, there are two components, one which describes the lines in themselves and the other which refers to common features of contiguous lines; both components are necessary to the description, though in any particular form of it, one may receive more attention than the other. In the Standard Description, the first component is meter. In the Modified Standard Descriptions we have discussed, this component is a descriptive device which measures a group of phenomena which control the rhythm but resist description. There are several programs for variant descriptions which actively reconsider the framework of the Standard Description.

The first is the structuralist program associated with Alonso-Schökel and his students on the Continent and with Cooper (1976) in North America, all working within the orbit of current French intellectual life ("They will get it straight one day at the Sorbonne."). Cooper, following a structuralist desire for exhaustiveness, proposes that no noticeable features of Hebrew verse texts can be ignored (1976: 72). He recognizes that the noticeability must be made a function of some unit, the line, and he extends the traditional term parallelism to cover the noticeability: "Parallelism is the one universally acknowledged prosodic feature of the Hebrew poetic line" (p. 77).

Using this enlarged sense of parallelism, Cooper puts the burden of poetic structure on what he calls structural parallelism, roughly anything not on the semantic level that serves to tie lines together: phonology, syntax, overall structure. He provides a close reading of phonological parallelism in Nah 1:10 (three lines), along with some general remarks on repetition and ambiguity. He also looks closely at the gross structure of Jer 5:26-27 (six lines), noting the use of chiasmus and inclusion. On the use of syntax, he comments: "Syntactic parallelism has not received a great deal of scholarly attention. This is probably because, with the exception of a certain amount of ellipsis and inversion, the poetic colon might just as well be a line of prose" (Cooper 1976: 46, n. 31). When he comes to treat syntactic patterning in verse, Cooper does not consider it in its own right, but as a phenomenon constrained by traditional metrical devices. He nowhere calls on these devices except in his syntactic analysis of Prov 8:22-31 (21 lines). This mixing of the bowsprit with the rudder, though hard on the navigational progress, is useful. Cooper has generalized the component of parallelism to cover the whole poetic structure of Hebrew verse, only to find that a metrical system is apparently needed to sort out parallelism on the syntactic level. This auto-da-fé of a structuralist program suggests that although there are problems in the Standard Description, they cannot be handled by eliminating its two-part structure.

A second program for a variant description, explicitly concerned with syntax, is presented in Kosmala (1964, 1966, Margalit 1975). It may be misleading to refer to Kosmala's work as a program since he denies the existence of any order to be discovered. He correctly notes the difficulty of working out metrical principles on the basis of the Massoretic text. The body of verse to be characterized Kosmala regards as including the bulk of Ugaritic and pre-exilic Hebrew, but rather eccentrically he rejects the archaic Hebrew poetry, which is the central portion of the continuum between Ugaritic and Hebrew.

Kosmala ties his description to the observations of Azariah de Rossi. Like Cooper's, Kosmala's description is based on a fusion of the two components of the Standard Description. There is, he asserts, a regularity of the number of the word units in a line; from his count he excludes most but not all particles. He finds that six is the dominant number of units although five, seven, and eight are also common.

The advantage of Kosmala's work is that it allows him to turn his attention to problems of gross poetic structure. The basic strophic units he finds to be between two and five bicola; three is most common. He shows a good sense of inclusive or circular, as well as progressive or frieze, structures. A defect of his work, especially on the Oracles of Balaam, Amos, and Second Isaiah, is that he allows for major accretions to the texts; he often but not always treats the formula *nᵓm yhwh* as intrusive. The greatest drawback of his study is that, although he isolates the core problem of the correspondence of clause and line, he avoids the difficulties of it by overstating the extent of the correspondence.

Both variant descriptions emphasize the centrality of syntax in reconsidering the Standard Description, and both grow out of a sensitivity to the tradition and uses of the Description. Their originators are not alone in showing an awareness of the need to study poetic syntax. Collins is reported by Barr (1975: 53) to be at work on the question and Hillers

(1972: xxxv-xxxvii, 1974) has attended to it. Before we examine syntactic patterning, we need to return to the Standard Description and consider further objections to it.

### *1.3.6 Objections to the Standard and Modified Standard Descriptions on the basis of parallelism*

There is an asymmetry in the array of descriptions of Canaanite verse which reflects an asymmetry in the original form of the Standard Description. The parallelistic component of Lowth's description is specifiable and therefore the stronger portion of it; few have ever suggested that there is something basically wrong with it. Numerous objections to the treatment of parallelism have been made and consideration of these objections will lead us to see the necessity of rethinking it altogether.

The most obvious objection is that there is no adequate nomenclature for parallelism (Gottwald 1962: 831). Lowth's original three-way split of synonymous, antithetical, and synthetic has frequently been restudied and supplemented. The number of types of parallelism that have been added to the system is considerable: emblematic, repetitive, climactic, and so on. The most recent addition is impressionistic parallelism which consists "of overlapping images, formally contradictory, in fact evoking a complex picture of richness and depth" (Cross 1974b: 7). Even if it were possible to define the original trio, it is clear that terms like impressionistic parallelism are themselves so impressionistic that they cannot be defined. Further, no one has attempted to account for the fact that synonymous parallelism is far more common than all other varieties combined (Boling 1960: 221).

Let us consider the term synonymous parallelism: can it be defined in itself? It seems that it cannot. Hockett has recently commented on the synonym fallacy, which he defines as "simply the belief that there can be exact synonyms in a language."

> In fact it seems that exact synonymy is always a matter of special convention — a willful suspension, not of disbelief, but of distinctiveness. Thus, in arithmetic we agree to ignore any difference in meaning between *two and three* and *three and two*, whereupon the two phrases are *arithmetically* synonymous. But *linguistically* they are not. For linguistics, the only secure working principle about such matters remains the one formulated four decades ago by Bloomfield (1933: 145): if forms differ in phonemic shape, we must assume they differ in meaning. Neglect of that guideline has led to no end of confusion (1977: 81, cf. Taber 1976).

There are occasions in contemporary linguistic and philosophical study when arguments involving synonymy and paraphrasability are used. Such arguments are the result of the original program of transformational grammar proposed by Harris and they are directed toward specifying the linguistic value of the *difference* between synonymous paraphrasable entities (cf. Postal 1971: 36-38). These are the arguments Hockett is concerned with. Reference to synonymy in descriptions of Canaanite poetry is never concerned with investigating the difference, however, but with neutralizing it. Hockett's injunctions apply all the more forcefully.

The reason that no adequate nomenclature has been developed for parallelism is because of a fundamental error committed by Lowth in innocence and perpetuated unthinkingly since. In almost all cases in which parallelism is defined, scholars define it in relation to non-verbal realities. Thus Robinson writes that "parallelism is concerned solely with ideas" (1950: 439) and Lundbom refers to the line as a "basic thought unit" (1975: 20). This would be suitable in the description of non-verbal poems; there are none. A poem is made up of words; to describe a construct of words, terminology which refers to words must be used.

This fundamental problem has not escaped the notice of students. Yoder (1971) deserves the credit for having recognized clearly that synonymy and antonymy are not explicitly relevant to the structure of what he calls parallel or fixed pairs. Yoder is working within the framework of a theory of orality and treats the pairs as formulas and refers to the cooccurrence of pairs as a formulaic system. Realizing that in Parry's conception of the formula, formulaic composition exists to make meter usable, Yoder is forced effectively to equate parallelism with meter. But we have seen above that he also regards the verse as accentual; this brings us to a further objection to the parallelistic component of the Standard Description. "The study of parallelism must lead . . . to the conclusion that parallelism is but one of the forms of Hebrew poetry" (Gray 1915: 123). Parallelism cannot cover the field of Hebrew poetry unless it is not only left undefined, but allowed to cover so many phenomena that it is undefinable. This is the defect we noted in Cooper and it is apparent behind Robinson's statement that parallelism is "the principle which controls the form which every line of Hebrew poetry takes" (1950: 443). If this statement could be grounded in a definitional apparatus, the concept of parallelism would be entirely transmuted. It cannot be so grounded.

The formalism that has been developed in the course of the study of parallelism in Hebrew verse (Gray 1915, cf. Gottwald 1962) does not provide any clarification for reading and general study, though it is occasionally useful in philological research. Further, it frequently leads to erroneous descriptions, as in a celebrated case in Judges 5.

Jdg 5:26a *ydh lytd tšlḥnh*
Jdg 5:26b *wymynh lhlmwt-ᶜmlym*

5:26a She stretches her hand to the tent peg,
5:26b Her right hand to the workers' mallet.

The misconceptions of synonymous parallelism in the Standard Description have led to the violently counter-intuitive suggestion that only one hand is being stretched and only one thing picked up. This leads to the notion that in Hebrew poetic discourse the noun phrases *ytd* 'tent-peg' and *hlmwt-ᶜmlym* 'workers' mallet' mean either the same thing or some third thing like them both, perhaps a loose screw. This is far-fetched. It is proposed because the words *yd* 'hand' and *ymyn* 'right hand' are regarded as synonymously parallel. The beginning of a correct approach is to recognize, as Dahood has on numberless occasions, that the woman being described uses two hands and that *ydh* here means 'her left hand.' (To further suppose that the women spoken of nailed the single thing described into a man's skull with one hand runs counter to strong non-linguistic intuitions.)

### *1.3.7 A final objection to previous descriptions*

We began our remarks on the "native" tradition of verse structure with reference to lineation of texts and have continued throughout to refer to lines. We have referred only once to a characterization of the line, Kosmala's; this is because no one has ever seriously set out to characterize it. The core phenomenon of the Standard Description remains undefined. It is conceivable that neither the line nor the line-pair (the bicolon) is the basic unit, but no one has ever suggested this possibility and we need not consider it.

The character of the undefined unit is not widely in doubt, since a notion of what it is can be extrapolated from a glance at the lineation provided by the "native" tradition. The first step in specifying this character would be to determine whether the smallest apparent unit (which we call the line, and others the colon or hemistich) is basic, or whether two of these (which we call a pair of lines and others a bicolon, stich, line, verse, etc.) compose the smallest working unit (Gottwald 1962: 831). It is most commonly contended that two of the smallest apparent units are needed, but it is immediately added that three of them can also serve as an instantiation of the smallest working unit. (In the past, it was sometimes customary to make sure that only two units occurred together by deleting any possible third units. Happily, such mutilation of the evidence has grown unfashionable.) There is no systematic description of the relation between working units of two apparent units and those of three: "bicola" and "tricola," in descriptions that refer to them, vary freely.

Let us inspect a description of the line. After writing that because of the stability of the line, "Hebrew poetic form remained more or less unchanged throughout the biblical period" (Cooper 1976: 7), Cooper defines the line. It is composed of one or two or three cola; if there is one colon, the line is an unsegmented short line. If there are two or three cola, the line may be segmented by one or two caesuras, or it may be unsegmented. The basis of the distinction between the cola in a line of two or three cola is *both* semantic or syntactic juncture between the lines *and* parallelism. What this means is that it can be either juncture *or* parallelism *or* both (Cooper 1976: 7-8; Yoder 1972 is similar.)

If the line (as used here) can be composed of one or more cola, then the distinction is unparsimonious, as the colon is more basic. We therefore use the term line in the sense in which colon is used here. The problem is not simply one of parsimony, however. The so-called unsegmented line is another problem. The problems are not distinct ones, since the syntax of Hebrew poetry is frequently not simple enough to keep them apart.

Without dwelling on the defects of particular descriptions, we can depict the net effect. Everyone agrees on the shape of most lines and there are some lines in virtually every poem on which everyone disagrees. It is not the case that the areas of disagreement are few and concentrated: they are everywhere. Neither is it the case that the areas of disagreement are due to idiosyncratic differences among scholars and scholarly traditions. Inconsistencies within the German scholarly tradition can be found in half the headnotes to Chapter 2. There are cases in which the problem is more acute, to be sure: the Massoretic text divides Exodus 15 into 43 lines, while the German scholarly tradition divides it into 84 lines. (We shall attempt to show that the correct lineation is in between, 56 lines.)

Another area of recent attention is the half-line unit which Dahood (1967d) refers to as "a phrase . . . suspended between the first and third cola of a verse and simultaneously modifying both of them." Dahood, it will be observed, treats the phrase as a colon and he calls the whole scheme a "metrical pattern," which he characterizes by means of syllable counting. The class of units he has recognized in this way have no standing in the context of lineation firmer than the line characterizations they are based on. (This consideration does not reflect on the modifier scope mentioned by Dahood, which raises altogether independent questions.)

Let us consider what these defects in previous descriptions mean. It is customary in traditional grammar to illustrate normal structures by vague generalities and examples, and to document fully exceptions to ordinary behavior. The received descriptions of Hebrew poetry do not distinguish normal from exceptional line forms even in this simplest way, by listing exceptions. They do not allow the formation of any conception of the line which would guide the reader, to say nothing of the scholar. Yet anyone who has read Hebrew verse has formulated conceptions of which line shapes are common, which are rare, and of which word sequences never occur as lines. A major part of our concern will be to set down those conceptions.

It may be objected that the study of Hebrew verse has proceeded ably without a definition of its basic unit. To a limited extent this is true. Recall, however, that in reviewing the work of Kosmala and Freedman we noted that they were able to turn to problems of gross structure, after having settled on an approximate way of specifying line structure. Hebrew poems are not homogeneous from top to bottom. Rather, they have shapes which are amenable to discussion and likely to be involved in a serious reading of any portion of a poem. The importance of gross structural study has long been recognized. It can only be pursued seriously if the fine structure of the verse is defined. Moreover, the extent to which gross structure can be pursued is a direct function of the precision with which fine structure is described. Further, in a study like that of Lundbom (1975) on chiasm and inclusion as features of gross structure, the failure to define the line is an augury of a failure to define the stanza and the poem. At the same time, because the linguistic nature of the basic unit is unspecified, the author sometimes garbles linguistic levels and attempts to isolate poetic features on any but linguistic grounds. All this is to say that people tend not to lean on breakable reeds. In the final chapter of this essay, we will suggest approaches to gross structural study more far-reaching than any currently available.

### *1.4 The constriction of Hebrew verse*

Any description of Hebrew verse will have to take into account the defects we have noted in the Standard Description. It will have to define the line, and it will have to delimit phenomena previously included under the headings of parallelism and meter, and demarcate relations among these phenomena. It will seek to avoid solving problems by reducing them to further problems, while trying to account for some of the properties of verse which have remained mysterious in current descriptions.

There are two groups of explicanda: those which involve the line in itself, grouped together in the Standard Description as meter; and those which involve groups of contiguous lines, gathered together previously under the rubric of parallelism. The "metrical" phenomena we shall describe, following the lead of Kosmala, as syntactic. The system which he alleged did not exist we shall describe within a syntactic framework that is only slightly more attentive to the language than his own. The "parallelistic" phenomena we shall show to be involved with much more complex linguistic phenomena than have been supposed; but we will also show that the poetically structural devices compose a small and discrete subgroup of these.

Before we discuss the syntactic system, it may be useful to introduce an analogy to the whole fine structural system we will describe, an analogy from metrics. The structure of the standard line of English verse has two parts: a frame, set up essentially on an isosyllabic base, and a modulation within that frame, of accents. Thus the line has 10 syllables, which show an alternating unstress-stress pattern. The frame is open to variations: it can be 9 or 11 syllables; the modulation is open to other variations. We shall discuss some complexities of both these features, but for the moment, we can take this description as accurate. In the poetic system we shall describe for Hebrew verse, the frame is the syntactic component and the modulation is the system of tropes to be described below. The frame corresponds to Lowth's meter and the tropes to his parallelism, though we shall include among the tropes phenomena not previously considered with parallelistic features and exclude certain "parallelisms" as non-structural.

Before we examine the frame, however, we need to consider the nature of meter and how it is perceived (1.4.1); and to reconsider the usual view that meter is independent of syntax (1.4.2). Having seen that to be heard, a piece of metrical verse must often be analyzed both phonologically and syntactically, we will be in a position to propose that a frame can be syntactic, rather than phonological (1.4.3). We will outline the frame, to be called a constriction, and consider the text of Psalm 106 (1.4.4). Then we shall examine the grammatical features of the system with some attention to the peculiarities of the language (1.4.5) and restate the constriction (1.4.6).

Both in considering Psalm 106 here and in reviewing the rest of the corpus in the full description of the constriction in Chapter 3, we will be building on the "native" tradition and on previous studies of verse structure. We will not outline our differences at every point, nor make specific claims for the usefulness of our description at every point. Neither will we point out constantly that our proposal is intended only as a first approximation of the actual systems at work.

### *1.4.1 The character of verse and meter*

There is a good reason that virtually all descriptions of Hebrew verse refer to meter: most verse systems have meter. The general view is expressed by Wimsatt: "Whatever the language, some marked phonetic or physical and immediately perceivable recurrent quality seems part of the essential device [of verse]" (1972: ix). He is immediately brought up short by Hebrew verse, "the striking intrusion from the East into our prosodic history . . . where the recurrent sameness lies very conspicuously, not in syllables, accents, or any small phonetic elements such as 'feet,' but in the syntax and the semantics of parallel clauses" (p. ix). This is the situation as Wimsatt is willing to leave it: there is, on the one hand, most verse, which is metrical; and on the other hand, there is Hebrew. This is a fair reading of the Standard Description, though it is not adequate to the poetry. We shall inquire further into the subject of verse and meter, and try to discover whether Hebrew is so anomalous as it looks.

The channel of communication between any speaker and any listener envisioned in Wimsatt's remarks is of an ordinary type. It is commonly imagined that the process of human communication is as simple as the relationship between a radio transmitter and a radio receiver. The speaker broadcasts and the listener receives. This model is entirely inadequate to account for ordinary speech and therefore for any special linguistic subsystem like meter. In noting that Lotz argues that some kinds "of metrical effects are not in the text; rather, they are added by the hearer or reader," Hockett adds quite firmly "But so, in a sense, is everything else!" (1977: 79).

There is an immense difference between what is perceived as intrinsic to language structure and the physical reality the speaker produces and the listener analyzes. Chomsky and Halle, in their description of English stress (1968), note that while there is no question that stress contours in English are a perceptual reality, there is no evidence from experimental phonetics to suggest that they are a physical reality, i.e., that they are transmitted in the acoustic signal in the often-great detail with which they are perceived. Rather, they suggest, the speaker of English uses a single basic principle which accounts for semantic, phonetic and syntactic realities (which they call the transformational cycle), in combination with a few basic rules of stress, in order to determine the stress contour of an English utterance from its syntactic structure. The speaker "need not deal with the stress contour of the utterance independent, in whole or in part, of its syntactic organization."

> A correct description of perceptual processes would be something like this. The hearer makes use of certain cues and certain expectations to determine the syntactic structure and semantic content of an utterance. Given a hypothesis as to its surface structure . . . he uses the phonological principles that he controls to determine a phonetic shape. The hypothesis will then be accepted if it is not radically at variance with the acoustic material. . . . Given acceptance of such a hypothesis, what the hearer "hears" is what is internally generated by rules. That is, he will "hear" the phonetic shape determined by the postulated syntactic structure and the internalized rules (1968: 24).

Stress then is a function of syntactic structure, which is what directly engages the attention of speaker and listener. There is no sense in which the speaker "encodes" a sentence after she or he forms it before speaking it nor is there any sense in which a listener "decodes" it after hearing it. This proposal is not only intuitively sound; it also follows from the complete failure of phoneticians to find any evidence "that perceived stress contours correspond to a physically definable property of utterances" (1968: 26). In fact, even if stress contours like those of English were real, they would probably be too complex to process. In experiments in which "complex stimuli had to be sorted along several dimensions," it is found that "more than two or three distinctions along each dimension will overload perceptual capacity" (1968: 26, cf. Pulgram 1975: 54-66, Corcoran 1971: 120-21, 147).

Despite the fact that a broadcast model of the speech chain is commonly assumed, even in studies in metrics, some have always realized the model is inadequate. Coventry Patmore opposed the notions that sound patterns can actually be heard and that perception of verse is passive. Patmore's protests coincide with the results of recent work in psycholinguistics which shows that all perception is active. "Cognitive psychology emphasizes the universality of internally constructed patterns in all perceptions" (Boomslitter, Creel and Hastings 1973: 201).

Boomslitter and his associates have shown that in unled choral readings of verse, speakers read in unison. This is simply because people "accomplish perception by using constructs. . . . The internal organization by expectation is essential for all perception including that of meter" (1973: 205), and any other sort of verse scheme. "Language, being tailored for our brain, does display a remarkable amount of regularity" and any scheme based on that regularity is available to organize verse (p. 206).

How can we show that these facts about the perception of speech must be used to qualify the standard view of meter? Given that verse is the temporal regulation of linguistic material, measured in terms of units like length or stress that are functional outside the poetic system, what difference does the speech channel model make? Most obviously it would make a difference in connection with verse systems which are indisputedly metrical, but in which the meter has some erratic features: systems, that is, recognized as such plainly but marked by noticeable irregularities. In explaining the "irregularities" of these systems, if we could show that the system was regular on a level that the hearer would have to analyze in processing the utterance, we could suggest that the regularities of the system belong to that level and not to the pronounced word. Our concern is not with proving the purity of a particular metrical system, but with clarifying the notion of meter itself, with qualifying the assumption that "the metrically relevant features of a line are phonetic, that is, audible in the recitation intended by the poet" (Kiparsky 1972: 174).

There are metrical systems of this type and in discussing them linguists have been able to show that hearers of texts in such systems do not work with what they hear acoustically but with analyses of it. A simple example is provided by the obligatory alliteration of some forms of Finnish, Germanic, and Celtic verse (Kiparsky 1970). All languages involved have strong initial stress and the use of alliteration in the verse is obligatory. The simpler and more common sort of alliteration, used in Finnish, requires that the initial stressed syllables be identical; they can be of the shape *CV* (e.g., *ta . . . ta*) or of the shape *V* (e.g., *a . . . a*). The complex variety used rarely in Finnish and generally in Germanic and Irish verse requires only that the initial consonant be identical (e.g., *ta . . . ti*), but a permissible variant allows any two vowels to alliterate (e.g., *a . . . i*). The two Finnish cases are in themselves comprehensible, as in the first Germanic-Irish case; but the second is rather odd, superficially not of a piece with the others. The alliteration of the simpler type can be described in a scheme, in which # stands for a word boundary, *m* for an upper limit, and *n* for a lower limit: each alliterating unit has the form $\# C^{m}_{n}$ V, in which $m = 1$ and $n = \emptyset$. This scheme supposes that the hearer has analyzed the syllable as initial (because stressed) and then analyzes the alliteration; this is a formalization of the description above. The second (*ta . . . ti, a . . . i*) type can be described with the scheme: each alliterating unit has the form $\# C^{m}_{n}$, in which $m = 1$ and $n = \emptyset$. This scheme expresses the fact that to perceive the alliteration, the hearer must analyze the syllable and then separate its parts. Only after she or he has performed this basic operation, can the alliteration be recognized. (We have simplified the cases slightly. The *m* specification is superfluous for Finnish, which has no initial consonant clusters; and the Germanic case has to be qualified to allow initial *s* plus stop clusters, *sp*, *st*, *sk*.) A further complexity is that in Finnish the alliteration can be heard irrespective of a rule that diphthongizes some initial vowels; that is, the vowels in a line can be said to alliterate if the effects of the rule are ignored. The hearer hears her or his way through the rule.

This approach can also be used to explain irregularities of Finnish epic meter, in which the hearer has to perform more complex analyses than in the alliteration case. The meter is trochaic octosyllables: the first syllable of a foot must be a stressed, long syllable or a monosyllable; and the second must be a stressed, short syllable; unstressed syllables can substitute in either position in a foot. This metrical scheme is applied by the hearer at a level in the analysis of the line after a rule of consonant gradation has applied but before a number of other rules have applied. (These are rules of vowel gemination, partial intervocalic *h* deletion, consonant gemination, optional final short *i* deletion, and diphthongization.) The problem here is not a historical one, since all the rules are active in the epic dialect.

There are comparable historical cases, in which the hearer must "reverse" elaborate and complex developments in order to perceive the poetic form. In the case of Chinese, the loss from many dialects of a tonal distinction basic to major metrical forms has had the effect of making certain features of poetic form audible only to an educated listener (Frankel 1972). The more drastic fate is the simpler one: the form simply becomes imperceivable. This was the fate of much Middle English verse from the

Jacobean to the Victorian periods. During this time, for example, Chaucer was read and admired as a salty but primitive poet: the orthographic system in which his work was recorded presented vocal and silent *e* in the same form and was thus impervious to scansion. With the rise of English historical phonology, the final *e* could easily be sorted out. Now Chaucer can be read in metrical form without trouble by a reader who can understand the orthography.

Even with luck, these historical cases require an educated and literate listener. The Finnish cases do not. They refer to phenomena in the ordinary language and to an oral poetic tradition in which there can be no presumption of literacy. In such cases, we can be sure that in so far as we speak of regularity, we are speaking about what the listener has analyzed. There are other cases. In the syllabic meters of Latvian folk songs discussed by Zeps (1973) there are certain variations in the syllable counting patterns that can be explained (i.e., referred to the listeners' analyses) by requiring that "syllables may be or must be counted prior to the application of a morphophonemic rule that truncates the final vowel" (p. 208); a rule that is obligatory in speech is optional in poetic scansion.

Another example occurs in Skaldic poetry. There is a peculiarity of rhyme in earlier Skaldic poetry, written in Norway from the mid-ninth century to the time of Snorri Sturluson (fl. 1225); after his time, the peculiarity was lost (Anderson 1973). It involves a variety of line-internal rhyme (*adhalhending*), in which *a* rhymes with *ö* (orthographic ǫ). The segment *ö* is derived from *a*, if *u* occurs in the next syllable by a rule of *u*-umlaut. Rhymes of *a* and *ö* can best be described if the hearer is taken as capable of analyzing the two segments as identical. A final example involves the difficulties in scansion in Rgvedic meter described as Sievers' Law (Kiparsky 1970, cf. Hock 1977). The syllabation of words with *i* and *u*, and *y* and *v* is complicated by the fact that the vowels and the semi-vowels are used as both surface and more basic, underlying forms. The scansion can use a syllabation based on either the surface form or (if it differs) the underlying form. Thus, to scan a line accurately the listener must be able not only to hear the way it is pronounced, but also to analyze the way it is shaped.

All of these examples are concerned only with phonological rules, those which change a word after it has been shaped; none is concerned with morphological rules, rules that shape a word. They suggest the relevance to poetics of a fundamental axiom of linguistics: people hear and read things that aren't there and don't hear or see things that are. Meter is not a simple but rather a complex matching of an abstract schema with a series of instances.

Having seen this principle in some exotic cases, we can discern its relevance for metrical systems which seem to have what Wimsatt calls a "physical and immediately perceptible recurrent quality" like English (1972: ix). The non-match between meter and instance of it has been the source of much theoretical discussion. Since we are concerned with the fact rather than its evaluation in a theory of meter, we can be content with a few examples of how it is dealt with. Here is Nelson's description of the Spanish case.

> Meter in Spanish, as in other languages, is a theoretical concept like the line in geometric figures and the phoneme in linguistics. It may be closely or distantly approximated in given lines of verse, but it can never be absolutely realized. . . . Any given line of verse . . . is in counterpoint to the ideal meter. . . . Empirically, if a number of verse lines written in the same meter are averaged according to stressed and unstressed positions and according to syllable count, the average should point quite closely to the absolute conditions of the ideal meter (Nelson 1972: 169).

An elegantly impressionistic account is given by Kinbote, speaking of elision in English.

> The beauty of the English elision lies neither in the brutal elimination of a syllable by an apostrophe nor in the recognition of an added semeion [i.e., syllable] by leaving the word typographically intact, but in the delicate sensation of something being physically preserved by the voice at the very instant that it is metaphysically denied by the meter. Thus, the pleasure produced by a contraction or a liaison is the simultaneous awareness of the loss of a syllable on one level and its retention on another and the state of balance achieved between meter and rhythm. It is the perfect example of the possibility of eating one's cake and having it (1964: 32).

With this aphoristic reversal, we can conclude that metrical order is not simply something heard.

### *1.4.2 The role of syntax in meter*

The plainest reason why meter is not consistently instanced in verse is that it would often be too demanding, would limit the range of expression too greatly, if it were. The demands would be made on the syntax in particular. The best known such limitation, which is accepted, is the requirement for non-enjambement in English and French neo-classical verse. The law is the one laid down by Boileau: "Que toujours dans vos vers le sens coupant les mots,/Suspende l'hemistiche, en marque le repos" (*Art poétique* 1.105-06, Flescher 1972). There is no reference here to syntactic construction, because any syntactic break that can be made to coincide with a verse break can be used. The requirement is only that there be a break at the medial caesura, i.e., at the end of the half-line, the hemistich, and at the end of the line. Another example of the syntactic consequences of meter is noted by Maling (1973). She remarks that there is only one Arabic meter, *rajaz*, the commonest, in which a 3 m.s. perfect form of a strong verb can be followed by an indefinite noun (e.g., *fa*$^{c}$*ala zaydun*), because of limitations on sequences of three short vowels such as those which appear in relevant verb forms. Further, there are no meters which allow four short vowels in a row.

In these cases, the phonological requirements of meter control certain features of the syntax. This is in harmony with the standard belief that metrical patterning is a phonological phenomenon. No matter how complex the phonological analysis necessary to get hold of the meter, it is believed, only phonological analysis is needed. This belief is untrue: in at least some metrical systems, syntactic analysis is also required. "Any attempts to confine such poetic conventions as meter, alliteration, or rhyme to the sound level are speculative reasonings without any empirical justification" (Jakobson 1967: 312).

The case examined most carefully is that of English iambic pentameter, especially Shakespeare's. Kiparsky (1975) has demonstrated that "the way stress is patterned in English verse depends on word and phrase structure, according to strict rules not accounted for by either traditional or more recent metrics" (p. 576). The phonological aspects of English stress, syllabation and pause, are not enough to describe iambic pentameter. The particular stress problem arises from the analysis of the English system of stresses as simply binary: all syllables, that is, are treated as either stressed or unstressed. This false distinction comes from the model of Greek metrics in which all syllables are correctly treated as either long or short. At the time of the earliest descriptions of English verse, the uniformitarian axiom was applied against the base of classical metrics, and it was assumed that the binarization in the verse corresponded to a binary feature of the language. Any speaker of English realizes that more than two states of stress are used in the language; the assumption that only two are used in verse is therefore suspicious.

In fact, the assumption fails the goal of traditional metrics, that of "discovering the principles that differentiate metrical and unmetrical verse" (p. 577). Although Halle and Keyser (1972) use some syntactic information to frame a more linguistically oriented description of English meter, they erroneously retain the notion of a simple binarization of stress levels. Behind most approaches is "the assumption that meter regulates just the phonological shape of verse," which Kiparsky characterizes as a mistake. "The most important, virtually unbreakable constraints on meter in English involve the grammatical structure of the verse, notably the phrase and word units of which it is made up" (p. 579). We can summarize his justifications for these claims.

Kiparsky recognizes two categories of words: those in lexical categories (nouns, including the parts of compound nouns, adjectives, verbs, adverbs); and those in nonlexical categories (viz., grammatical words, roughly pronouns and particles). We shall not be concerned now with the difference between these groups in his description, since our examples will refer to the first category; the separation will be instructive later. He uses four phrase boundaries: noun, verb, adjective, and prepositional phrases. These boundaries together make up the syntactic phrasing of an utterance, which determines its phonological phrasing. Versification must be described in terms of the syntactic phrasing.

There are four degrees of speech stress used in Kiparsky's system; they are numbered from one, the strongest, to four, the weakest. (English can be described as having more functional levels of stress; it cannot be described with fewer.) Only one stress per word is metrically relevant, and thus English meter can be stated in terms of unstress or stress. The problem of going from the range of four possibilities to the binary choice is handled by two metrical rules. The first specifies that a Metrical Stress position, the second half of an iamb, can be filled by any of the four Speech Stresses, though preference is given to stronger stresses. The second specifies that a Metrical Unstress position, the first half of an iamb, can be filled by a Speech Stress other than the weakest, only if it is a monosyllable or if it follows an intonation break. In addition to the metrical rules, there is a metrical tension index which measures the difficulty of applying the metrical rules to the utterance; it serves to formalize intuitions that, for example, Pope's and Cowper's iambic pentameter is more regular than Shakespeare's or Shelley's. The index, originated by Halle and Keyser, is quantified on the basis of the four degrees of speech stress and is only as accurate as descriptions based on the degrees; it has a relative rather than an absolute value.

The prosodic rules in Kiparsky's description handle the metrical use of stress in determining which are the metrically relevant stresses in a word; they also determine syllabation. The prosodic rules which govern compounds and their behavior vis-à-vis phrases provide some crucial evidence for the role of syntax in English meter. Let us consider three groups of words.

Two syllable compounds like *highway*, *deathbed*, *love juice*, *daylight*, and *self-love*, have a pattern of Strong Stress-Ternary Stress (1-3 on a scale of 4); they are treated as two words. The metrical rule for strong positions allows them to occur freely across iambs (i.e., with *high*, etc., as the second half of the foot) and they do so. The metrical rule for weak positions allows them to occur within iambs, but with considerable metrical tension. This reflects the fact that the Speech Pattern Strong Stress-Ternary Stress is rather different from the Metrical Pattern Unstress-Stress. In fact, according to most descriptions of iambic pentameter, such compounds do not occur within iambs; but they do. Nonetheless, they are much more common across iambs and this is accounted for by Kiparsky's description.

Similarly, phrases like *long night*, which have a pattern of Secondary Stress-Primary Stress (2-1) occur within or across iambs. These are more frequent within the foot, since the Speech Pattern Secondary Stress-Primary Stress is close to the Metrical Pattern Unstress-Stress. The phrase type can occur across iambs, i.e., *night* can fill a Metrical Unstress position, because it is a monosyllable.

Trisyllabic compounds like *housekeeping*, *bloodsucker*, and *play fellow* have a pattern of Primary Stress-Ternary Stress-Low Stress (1-3-4), and are treated as two words. These can only occur as one iamb plus a half-iamb (Unstress-Stress/Unstress), never as a half-iamb plus an iamb (Stress/Unstress-Stress), because *house*, *blood*, and *play* are counted as monosyllabic words and thus their Strong Stress in speech can be treated as a Metrical Unstress. The non-occurrence follows from the non-word status of *keep-*, *suck-*, and *fel-* in the compounds.

The monosyllable constraint also limits the use of polysyllabic non-compounds. Thus disyllabic non-compounds with non-initial stress, e.g., *weakness*, *feeling*, occur across rather than within iambs. Trochaic substitution in iambic pentameter is only consistently tolerable if the first half of the trochee is a word or if the foot follows an intonation break. The second case is the common one: most trochaic substitution is line initial.

Prosodic conventions can be derived from the prosodic rules. Metrical equivalences of polysyllabic non-compounds provide an example. Such words with speech stress pattern Ternary Stress-Strong Stress (3-1), e.g., *maintain* are equivalent to those with Low Stress-Primary Stress (4-1), e.g., *attain*; both are Metrical Unstress-Stress. Similarly, polysyllabic non-compounds with Strong Stress-Ternary Stress (1-3), e.g., *incest*, are equivalent to those with Strong Stress-Low Stress (1-4), e.g., *modest*; both are Metrical Stress-Unstress.

These examples refer to word boundary discriminations. Kiparsky shows that phrase boundaries are needed to describe the behavior of disyllabic prepositions (which varies, depending on whether they have a lexical or pronominal object, or no object). They are also used in describing intonation breaks (used in the metrical rule for weak positions), line endings and extrametrical syllables. The occurrence of a non-monosyllabic speech stress in the first half of an iamb is only permitted after an intonation break, i.e., after a sentence, clause or phrase boundary. Line endings in all of Shakespeare's plays occur at these points, except in the late plays. In these, run-on lines occur, but are still subject to the monosyllable constraint. That is, a run-on line rarely starts with a stressed syllable in a polysyllabic non-compound. Other rules create the headless lines of iambic pentameter in which the first foot is a single stressed syllable, and insert extrametrical syllables before a syntactic boundary and in line final position.

The history of English verse form can be traced in terms of the history of variation in metrical rules and prosodic conventions. The situation described above is that of the iambic pentameter line used by Shakespeare, Marlowe, and Spenser. Modifications in the system are demanded for earlier and later Renaissance poets like Wyatt and Donne, and for Milton, all of whom use a different form of the monosyllable constraint. The neo-classical verse of Pope differs in using a tighter version of the metrical rule for weak positions. Other meters can also be treated within this description's framework; Kiparsky discusses trochaic and anapestic lines. Major trends of the iambic pentameter line can be treated by using the metrical tension index. There is a tendency for the line to become dipodic, with iambic patterns of two feet appearing along with those within the foot. Thus the odd numbered feet are weak and the even numbered are strong and the line consists of two and a half superiambs. This trend is in competition, as it were, with another, the general tendency to reduce metrical tension toward the end of the line. Finally Kiparsky notes that the description of meter should refer to common features in other languages. "We must make our theory [of meter] account for metrical systems of other languages, and begin to construct 'a universal metrics' " (p. 612).

In the previous section (1.4.1), we discovered that the phonological patterning known as meter is not always immediately perceptible. Kiparsky's description of the monosyllable constraint in English verse demonstrates that meter is not always exclusively phonological, and that the syntactic involvement can be both crucial and complex.

### *1.4.3 Meter and non-meter*

The varieties of recurrence that are gathered together under the heading meter are diverse. They involve complex phonological and syntactic facts of language, yet one of the most obvious consequences of this involvement is quite simple. To comprehend one of the most specialized uses of a language, the hearer or reader must be familiar with a language. In listening to or reading verse, she or he is engaging in continual and close analysis, as at all times in listening or reading; and such engagement must often be especially trenchant for verse.

In seeking to formalize our intuitions about the regularity of Hebrew line shape, what do we have to compensate for lack of native speaker knowledge? In terms of reading in general, two and a quarter millennia. In terms of more or less formal study, two and a quarter centuries. All readers agree on the existence of regular line shapes and virtually none agree on a simple, straightforward way to describe them, let alone the irregular line shapes which are always implicitly recognized. Regular and loose accentual, quantitative, and isosyllabic verse have all been considered. The disagreement is not comparable to that prevailing in most scholarly inquiry because it has been going on for two and a quarter centuries. Schemes of the strict accentual type explicitly rejected by Lowth are advocated without substantial modification at present; proposals are still subscientific, i.e., without replicable results and unsupported by a scholarly consensus. We may therefore agree with those scholars who reject the applicability of a metrical scheme to Hebrew.

We are at the same point in our consideration as the scholars who propounded the Modified Standard Descriptions and projected the programs for variant descriptions. The position of Young and Gordon is untenable because there must be some way to account for the regularity of the lines apart from parallelism. Similarly, the position of Cooper cannot be held because it so vastly generalized the component of parallelism as to lose sight of the greatest regularities within it, without offering a direct accounting for the phenomenon of lineation. The two remaining positions are the only serious alternatives.

The proposals elaborated by Freedman and independently launched by Culley hold that, given the existence of regularities and the failure of all metrical descriptions, we must describe the system as sensitively as possible without making any direct claims about its structure. The best tool for such monitoring is syllable counting, as they have shown. Any alternative will have to account for the regularities they, and all observers, have cited.

What alternative is there? Kosmala's proposal, in explicitly denying the existence of any rules, swerves away from the possibility of adequacy. The regularities in question are not, after all, trivial. Rather, they involve most of the verse in Hebrew. We assume such regularities bespeak an order that can be described and we assume that a set of wrong or weak rules, rules that need further consideration, is better than none at all. The core of Kosmala's suggestion is the fact noted by most students: there are significant regularities on the syntactic level. What we wish to propose is that just as most poetic systems are shaped in part by a series of phonological requirements, i.e., by a system of metrical constraints, so there are poetic systems shaped in part by a series of syntactic requirements, i.e., by a system of syntactic constraints. Among them is Canaanite verse.

We can begin by discussing what this claim means. Let us consider an exposition of the activities of poets and readers, including that special sort of reader, the scholar, from Halle and Keyser. They discuss poets and readers (or listeners) first.

> When a poet composes metrical verse, he imposes certain constraints upon his choice of words and phrases that ordinary language does not normally obey. The poet and his readers may not be able to formulate explicitly the nature of the constraints that are operative in a given poem; there is little doubt, however, that neither the poet nor the experienced reader would have great difficulty in telling apart wildly unmetrical lines from lines that are straight-forwardly metrical (1972a: 217).

There is little in the description that would be altered if the word metrical were removed at its first occurrence, and changed to poetic at its second, with a corresponding change in unmetrical.

The task of the scholar, the reader concerned with formal description, is characterized as a summary of what a reader needs to know in order to be able to say if verse is metrical and if so, whether it is complex or simple.

> It is . . . the task of the metrist to provide a coherent and explicit account of this knowledge [i.e., readers' knowledge used in recognizing verse as metrical], just as it is the task of the grammarian to make explicit what it is that the fluent speaker of a language knows about it (Halle and Keyser 1972a: 218).

Again, with simple alterations, this program can extend to a system of verse without meter. The student must provide a notion of the abstract patterns in the verse and of the rules used in instantiating the patterns. The complexity of these rules will provide a measure of the complexity of lines they refer to and thus an orderly explanation of it.

The first objection to the proposal that there are non-metrical verse systems is that such systems would be indistinguishable from prose. The difference between prose and verse, though it is probably universal, is impossible to describe in any simple way. In grosso, it is clear that some English poetry is more like prose than other poetry is. Milton's verse, which would never be mistaken for prose, is yet more like prose than Pope's poetry. Similarly in Latin: Cicero says that the works of the "comic playwrights are, due to their similarity to prose, often so wretched that at times one can catch (*intellegi*) neither meter (*numerus*) nor verse (*versus*) in them" (quoted in Pulgram 1975: 225, cf. pp. 244-48). In fine, prose-verse differentiation in a work that uses both is rarely simple and often impossible; a superficial comparison of any two editions of Shakespeare will reveal that the editors often differ in distinguishing brief prose segments from poetic continuity. Aware of this situation, recent commentators have tended to say rightly that the rigid separation of prose and verse is not among the highest priorities in the study of Hebrew (Freedman 1977, Cooper 1976: 43).

The second objection is a more serious one: since such a syntactically constrained type of verse is apparently unknown, there is no source of checks on the description. We will show below that the premise of the objection, with its implicit invocation of the uniformitarian axiom, is wrong. Further, we can reply that a description, to be adequate for a subsystem of the language, must refer only to the resources of the language. Just as the description is limited by our knowledge of the grammar, so the grammar as we know it will check the description. No account of English verse that refers to vowel length as a major structural feature will be acceptable, since vowel length plays only a trivial role in the language's structure, if it plays any role at all. A proposal to describe Hebrew verse which referred to nominal compounds would be immediately suspicious, since the language has virtually none; a proposal that relied crucially on distinguishing substantives from adjectives would be rejected because the distinction is marginal in the language; and so on.

Further, a system of syntactic constraints can be limited by requiring that it not deviate from the general structure of metrical systems and that it not describe a body of texts radically unlike other bodies of verse. The second requirement will be automatically fulfilled by our proceedings since we begin under the aegis of all previous investigators and study texts conceded to be poetic by all students. It will be no surprise that we describe only "a small set of language texts characterized by numerical regularity of speech material within certain syntactic frames," to use Lotz' definition of verse (1972a: 1). The system we describe will be of the same sort as a meter, which Lotz defines as "the numerical regulation of certain properties of the linguistic form" of verse (1972a: 2). It may be that Lotz intended to allow for the description of syntactically regulated verse systems, since he was aware of the phenomenon, as we shall see below (1.7.2). Given the standard usage of meter, it seems that it would be confusing to extend the term from predominantly phonologically based systems to syntactically based systems.

Thus, although we have no usable analogous systems as yet at hand, we do have two powerful restrictions before we begin on a description of a syntactically regulated verse system. It must refer to the features of the language as we know them, and it must describe the numerical regulation of certain of the features. We have decided not to call the system a meter; we shall refer to its components as constraints and to the whole as a constriction.

### *1.4.4 A preliminary statement of Hebrew verse constriction*

In many verse systems, the boundaries of clause and line sometimes coincide; various students have claimed that this is true of Hebrew. In fact, this coincidence is an important phenomenon in poetics in general and in the poetics of oral literature in particular; Peabody (1976) extends the observations of Lord (1965) on this point. The coincidence is crucial to the characterization of Hebrew verse. Previous treatments have alluded to the coincidence as if it were characteristic of Hebrew verse consistently, and some have even claimed that it was. If it ever were, then the constriction of Hebrew verse could be described simply: every clause is a line. That would constitute a simple and elegant system; the only question remaining would be why such a simple system is non-metrical.

The syntactic structure of Hebrew verse is not so simple. If there were consistent coincidence, i.e., if a line contained only a clause, and contained it entirely, there would be no subordinate clauses, since an independent clause governing a subordinate clause could not be contained within a line, unless the line contained two clauses. There is an abundance of subordinate clauses, which can be contained in the same line as the clause governing them, or in another line. Further, there are instances in which two or three independent clauses occur within a line. The matter of coincidence will not be settled by a reanalysis of linguistic levels but by a complication of the account of coincidence. Further, there are, in addition to lines which are clausal portions of independent clauses, others which are phrases of clauses.

Let us begin by distinguishing three grammatical categories with the medieval students of Arabic and Hebrew: *ism* 'noun,' *fiᶜl* 'verb,' *ḥurūf* 'particles.' Because of the non-match between the first category in Hebrew and the noun category of Indo-European languages, we will sometimes refer to the Hebrew class as nomina, to remind the reader that substantives, pronouns, adjectives, and most adverbials are meant. The problems of separating nomina from verbs will be treated below. The particle class includes all conjunctions, markers of negation and emphasis, and prepositions. A particle is said to be dependent on the noun or verb that follows it directly.

Further, let us distinguish three grammatical levels. The first and lowest refers to individual verbs and nouns; each of these, along with the particles dependent on it, is a *unit*. (We could have said lexical word or even real word, but such usage often creates confusion.) The second level refers to verbs and nouns as they function together in the syntax. Since verbs are only used independently, it is nominal phrases that are crucially distinguished here; each verb and nominal phrase, along with the particles dependent on it, is a *constituent*. The third level refers to the basis of syntactic functioning, the clause. There are two types of clauses in Hebrew: verbal clauses, in which the verb is the predicator; the verbless clauses, in which there is no express predicator; we shall refer to a $\emptyset$ predicator. Each verb and $\emptyset$ predicator of a verbless clause is a *clause predicator*. Given the way in which these levels are distinguished here, the first and second seem redundant and the third seems independent. It will become evident that all the complexities we have omitted so far, viz., participles, infinitives, vocatives, and the focus-markers, will make the second and third as redundant as the first and second.

Using this vocabulary, we can restate two fundamental results of all previous study; neither has ever consistently been rejected. The first is that no unit can stand alone as a line. The second we shall call the principle of syntactic integrity, which can be stated thus: if a line contains one or more clause predicators, it cannot contain a nominal constituent not dependent on one of them.

In the exposition given below in Chapter 3, we will deal with a corpus of 1225 lines of verse. Any specifications for the verse system in general are based on this corpus. In this preliminary approach to the constriction it would be awkward to draw on such a large corpus. Let us consider first Psalm 106, a poem of 106 lines, few textual difficulties, and relatively infrequently disputed lineations. Before we review the poem, there is one feature of syntax which, though not crucial to the constriction of verse, does deserve a note here. That is the starting point of the native speaker grammatical traditions, the differentiation of verbal and verbless clauses. Though it does not control the constriction, i.e., the clause types are used equivalently, verbless clauses are much commoner in poems generally agreed to be older than in later poems. Like all historical differentiae, this one is beyond our purview here; we cite it here because it seems likely to be related to the origins of the constriction system, as it is fundamental to the syntax.

In the simplest line structure in Hebrew, the clause coincides with the line; a verbal clause predicator governs only one dependent nominal phrase in the line, which consists of one unit, and a verbless predicator governs two 1-unit nominal phrases. Most often, the clause predicator is a verb, as verbal sentences are commoner in general. Let us begin by considering cases in which the coincidence of clause and line is complete, viz., in which the clause is independent.

Ps 106:35a *wyt*$^{c}$*rbw bgwym*
They-intermingled with-nations.

There are 26 independent clauses of this structure: 1a, 1c, 4b, 6a, 12a, 12b, 13b, 17a, 17b, 19b, 24b, 25a, 29a, 30b, 33a, 33b, 35a, 35b, 36a, 39a, 40b, 42a, 42b, 43c, 48d.

Another common line structure is similar; it differs only in having a 2-unit dependent nominal phrase instead of a 1-unit phrase. (We will join the units of a constituent with a dash; this only occasionally coincides with the Massoretic mark of punctuation, the *maqqep*.) Again, let us look first at independent clauses.

Ps 106:43a *pʿmym-rbwt yṣylm*
He-rescued-them many-times.

There are 13 independent clauses like this one: 7b, 10a, 10b, 16b, 17c, 24a, 25b, 28a, 28b, 32a, 41a, 43a, 45b.

Let us look at a third common line structure in which the clause predicator governs two 1-unit noun constituents, if it is a verb, or three, if it is a verbless clause predicator and the predicate is discontinuous. Let us consider only independent clauses for the moment.

Ps 106:38d *wtḥnp hʾrṣ bdmym*
The-land was-polluted with-blood.

There are 17 independent clauses of this structure: 9b, 11a, 11b, 14a, 14b, 15a, 15b, 18a, 18b, 19a, 29b, 32b, 36b, 38d, 41b, 43b, 45a.

In these 56 lines, over half the poem, there occur some participles; participles constitute one of the word classes that are intermediate in linguistic behavior between nomina and verbs. Since this intermediacy and that of infinitives is reflected in the syntax, we have to consider the matter here (Kosmala 1966: 162-63). In those cases in which participles and infinitives manifest only nominal behavior, they are treated only as nomina. Consider the participle, underscored, in the following line.

Ps 106:10a *wywšyʿm myd-śwnʾ*
He-saved-them from-the-power-of-the-hater.

The participle here is such only morphologically; it has no verbal syntactic features. The same participle is used later in the poem.

Ps 106:41b *wymšlw bhm śnʾyhm*
Those-who-hate-them rule over-them.

Here, some verbal force appears in connection with the suffix. That this is not materially different from the previous case is shown by the fact that many non-participial nouns in Hebrew take a suffix (or govern a construct) which expresses an objective genitive.

Among these lines, there are cases in which aspects of phrasal structure are ignored in our treatment. In most of the lines the constituents are independent phrases of the sentence.

Ps 106:18b *lhbh tlhṭ ršʿym*
Flame consumed the-wicked.

Here, both nominal constituents are in independent construction with the verb, i.e., they are arguments of it. Rarely, both of the constituents are parts of a phrase governed by the verb.

Ps 106:44a *wyrʾ bṣr lhm*
He-saw their difficulty.

The object in Hebrew includes two constituents, *bṣr* 'the difficulty' and *lhm* 'to them.' The verb governs a single phrase here made up of two constituents. This phrasal level of analysis is not relevant here. Such phrases containing two nominal constituents are often a source of ambiguity in Hebrew verse.

Over half the lines of the poem coincide with independent clauses completely. There are further cases in which independent clauses coincide with two or more whole lines.

Ps 106:8a *wywšyᶜm lmᶜn-šmw*
106:8b *lhwdyᶜ ʾt-gbwrtw*

106:8a He-saved-them because-of-his-name
106:8b In-order-to-reveal his-strength.

The first line contains an independent clause, which is continued in the second. The clause/line behavior described suggests that the clause is a working level of constriction and that for the system of constraints it is immaterial whether the clause is complete. (In almost all cases, the clause would be complete without the other line(s).) Let us remove the relationship across lines from consideration here; we shall return to it below (1.5.8).

An independent clause which coincides with two or more lines can be associated not only with another clause in the other line(s), but with further constituents, as in this example.

Ps 106:31a *wtḥšb lw lṣdqh*
106:31b *ldr-wdr ᶜd-ᶜwlm*

106:31a It-is-credited to-him as-an-honest-deed
106:31b From-generation-to-generation for-eternity.

Sometimes both a further clause and another constituent are involved.

We can enlarge the number of independent clauses of each of the three line structures we have considered by adding the cases in which an independent clause does not coincide completely with a single line. To the first group (1 clause-2 constituents-2 units), we can add three examples: 8a, 34a, 47b. We add to the second group (1 clause-2 constituents-3 units), four examples: 2b, 21a, 38a, 47a. We add to the third group (1 clause-3 constituents-3 units), six examples: 16a, 20a, 23b, 26a, 31a, 44a.

Since it is the clause that is the working level, we can also add dependent clauses to these categories. Thus, to the first group, we add five examples: 5c, 8b, 27b, 44b, 47d. To the second group, we add four cases: 5a, 5b, 21b, 47c. And we add four to the last group: 23c, 26b, 27a, 34b.

In the 26 examples we have added, there are further nonfinite verb forms. Most of these are infinitives which have verbal force.

Ps 106:44a *wyrʾ bṣr lhm*
106:44b *bšmʿw ʾt-rntm*

106:44a He-saw their distress
106:44b When-he-heard their-cry.

The infinitive in the second line governs not only a subjective genitive suffix, but also an object. In one case, a participle has verbal force.

Ps 106:21b *ʿśh-gdlwt bmṣrym*
The-one-who-did-great-things in-Egypt.

The location of the verbal action is expressed along with its object. In all these cases, the nonfinite verb form is treated as a clause predicator, as well as a nominal constituent of the higher clause of which it is part. We account for the intermediacy of nonfinite verb forms by counting them as nomina on one level and as clause predicators on another. The only infinitive in this group of 26 lines which has no verbal force occurs with a clause predicating infinitive.

Ps 106:23b *ʿmd bprṣ lpnyw*
106:23c *lhšyb ḥmtw mhšḥyt*

106:23b He-stood in-the-breach before-him
106:23c To-turn his-anger from-destruction.

The first infinitive in the second line, *lhšyb* 'to turn,' is the clause predicator of the line; the second, *mhšḥyt* 'from destruction,' has no verbal force.

Let us consider our conclusions thus far. Of 106 lines in the poem, 81 contain one clause and two or three constituents of two or three units. Exactly two-thirds of the group, 54, contain one clause and two constituents; one-third, 27, contain one clause and three constituents. Somewhat less than two-thirds, 47, contain three units; somewhat over one-third, 34, contain two units. Of the three subgroups, the first (1 clause-2 constituents-2 units) is the largest (34 lines). The third (1 clause-3 constituents-3 units) is the next largest, with a third of the lines (27 lines). The class in which constituents do not match units (1 clause-2 constituents-3 units) is the smallest (20 lines). The class of lines we have described has some measure of internal coherence and it is easily predominant in the poem. This is the core of the constriction system.

What are we to make of these facts? First, since there are other rare types of 1-clause lines we have not yet cited, consideration of some linguistic level other than the clause is warranted. Second, the structure of the class cannot be described without citing both constituents and units. There are 1-clause, 2-constituent lines with more than three units, and there are 1-clause, 3-constituent lines with more than three units, but these are rare.

The distribution of lines in Psalm 106 is not unique; although it has more of the three groups of lines discussed than any other poem, it does not differ substantially from the other poems or the corpus overall. That is, throughout the body of 1225 lines under study, these three groups of lines are best exemplified. At every junction in the preceding paragraph at which a rare line structure was cited, the description can be taken to mean rare among 1200 lines.

The most obvious interpretation of these facts is to regard them as isolating the basic constriction in Hebrew, comparable to the basic meters of English, the iambic pentamenter, of French, the hexameter, and of Russian, the iambic tetrameter (Kinbote 1964: 52). This interpretation is essentially the one advanced by most scholars who have adverted to the syntactic patterns before; it is indefensible. It is possible that there are poems written only in such lines, to be sure. The fact that not one of the 14 substantial poems dealt with in this essay comes close to being such argues against the possibility; if there are such poems, they are probably either short poems or catenae of such poems. At any rate, such an interpretation cannot succeed for our texts.

The groups of lines we have isolated reveal the dominant constraints in the system, but they always occur with lines which are structured according to other constraints. In fact, the variety of line structures which occur is bewildering, though it is derived from a simple matrix. In elucidating all these structures, we shall continue to refer to Psalm 106, but the argument will be derived from factors involving the entire corpus. Most of the relevant points can be illustrated from the Psalm. As we move through the variety of line structure, we shall elaborate a typology which will eventually yield the matrix and the constraints themselves. The three groups of lines presented so far we take together as the first type, the lines of Class I. The string of factors describing the groups we call their constellations.

Class II lines belong to the next three commonest constellations. The first is similar to the three parts of Class I in having one clause, and to the third of them in having three constituents; it differs in having four units.

Ps 106:40a *wyḥr ʾp-yhwh bʿmw*
Yahweh's-anger was-enkindled against-his-people.

There are five examples: 2a, 7c, 37, 38c, 40a. It is important to note that on syntactic criteria only, unusually long lines are not always given special treatment. Of these five lines, the longest (37) is almost twice the length of the shortest (2a, 7c, 40a), and a third longer than the only other long line (38c).

Since we are describing a syntactic system, the difference in length is not recorded on the level we are dealing with. This is not to say that the difference is non-existent or trivial. The situation is rather that the difference is functional on a level other than the one with which we are concerned, i.e., the difference is not crucial in the syntactic structure of the poem.

The second constellation of Class II includes lines which contain two clauses. Sometimes the clauses are both independent without coordination; the first verb often verges on serving as an auxiliary to the second.

Ps 106:13a *mhrw škḥw mᶜśyw*
They-made-haste. They-forgot his-deeds.
(They quickly forgot his deeds).

In some cases, the clause predicators are coordinated.

Ps 106:9a *wygᶜr bym-swp wyḥrb*
He-rebuked the-Reed-Sea and it-dried-up.

There is another instance in Ps 106:30a. Finally, the two clauses can be interdependent.

Ps 106:1b *hwdw lyhwh ky-ṭwb*
Praise Yahweh: "He is good."

In this example, the only one in the poem, the form *ṭwb* 'good (m.s.)/he is good' is ambiguous between the adjectival and verbal readings. A clear example from Psalm 78 shows another quasi-auxiliary governing a non-finite verb.

Ps 78:38c *whrbh lhšyb ᵓpw*
He-acted-often to-bring-back his-anger.

There are four examples of this constellation in Psalm 106.

The last group of Class II lines includes lines that have no clause predicator and only one constituent, of three units.

Ps 106:38b *dm-bnyhm-wbnwtyhm*
the-blood-of-their-sons-and-their-daughters

The phrase is in apposition to the direct object of the previous line, *dm-nqy* 'innocent blood,' Ps 106:38a, and is modified by a relative clause in the following line, Ps 106:38c.

There are a dozen Class II lines in Psalm 106. Let us consider what we know so far about the constriction. We accepted from the outset that there are no 1-unit lines, so the smallest number of units allowed is two. The smallest number of constituents allowed is one, as we have seen, and the smallest number of clauses allowed is ∅. We have seen 2-clause lines, 3-constituent lines and 4-unit lines. Let us set these numbers into a matrix, putting next to them matrices marked for the two classes we have considered so far.

| | *Base* | *Class I* | *Classes I & II* |
|---|---|---|---|
| Clauses | ∅ 1 2 | 1 | ∅ 1 2 |
| Constituents | 1 2 3 | 2 3 | 1 2 3 |
| Units | 2 3 4 | 2 3 | 2 3 4 |

We have recorded the structures of 93 of the 106 lines of the Psalm and used in so doing three linguistic levels that admit of simple characterization. We must consider a baker's dozen more lines.

The matrix given above is not complete. There is a group of lines which consistently go the limits marked one better. There are no examples in Psalm 106 of lines with three clauses; indeed such lines are rare. There is, however, one unquestionable case.

Dt 32:15b *šmnt ʿbyt kśyt*
You-got-fat. You-grew-thick. You-were-gorged.

In Psalm 106, there is one 4-constituent line of four units.

Ps 106:7a *ʾbwtynw bmṣrym lʾ-hśkylw nplʾwtyk*
Our-ancestors in-Egypt did-not-remember your-wonders.

(In this line, *bmṣrym* may be part of the same verbal argument as *nplʾtwyk,* viz., 'your-wonders in-Egypt.') In this instance, too, length is not relevant: many 4-constituent lines are shorter than this one (e.g., Ps 78:24a). In Psalm 106, there is one 5-unit line, also of four constituents.

Ps 106:46 *wytn ʾwtm lrḥmym lpny-kl-šwbyhm*
He-made them compassionable before-all-their-captors.

Note that the independent object pronoun *ʾwtm* is used here instead of a suffixed form. Length again is not obviously crucial, since there are shorter 5-unit lines. There are 5-unit lines of three constituents, though this structure is rare (Ps 78:9a). Lines of four constituents and five units are sometimes shorter than the example given above (e.g., Dt 33:12c). The matrix of constriction is to be expanded by one column.

| | | | | |
|---|---|---|---|---|
| Clauses | ∅ | 1 | 2 | 3 |
| Constituents | 1 | 2 | 3 | 4 |
| Units | 2 | 3 | 4 | 5 |

The separation between Classes I and II was based on frequency; given the diversity of the remaining constellations, frequency is not an adequate criterion for a further separation. We shall separate off lines with any of the highest levels as Class IV and treat the rest as Class III.

The distinction does have a frequency base, though in the case of Psalm 106 it is not apparent; there Classes II and III are almost equally represented. In the corpus overall, however, the relation of the classes follows a simple pattern. Class I accounts for two-thirds of all lines; Class II for two-thirds of the remainder (viz., two-ninths of the whole); Class III for two-thirds of the subsequent remainder (viz., two-twenty-sevenths of the whole); and Class IV for the remainder (viz., one-twenty-seventh of the whole). In terms of the matrix, only one class distinction can be justified: I-III *v.* IV. Our inability to justify thus the first three class divisions does not eliminate their usefulness, reflected clearly in the frequencies.

We have noted above the two examples of Class IV lines in Psalm 106. We need to examine the Class III lines; only seven of the twelve Class III structures are represented. There are eleven lines, 5 with no clause predicators, 1 with one clause predicator, and 5 with two clause predicators; this distinction is typical of the class.

Of five Class III lines without a clause predicator, there are two time expressions, one of two units, and one of three, the only examples of their constellations.

Ps 106:48b *mn-hʿwlm wʿd-hʿwlm*
From-eternity to-eternity

106:31b *ldr-wdr ʿd-ʿwlm*
From-generation-to-generation for-eternity

Two adjacent lines, Ps 106:22ab, have the same constellation as the last example, with three units. There is one 4-unit example in Psalm 106.

Ps 106:3b *ʿśy-ṣdqh bkl-ʿt*
Those-who-carry-out-justice at-all-times

This line belongs to a small class of unpredicated phrases, used as introductions, exclamations, and so on; these are called independent noun phrases.

There is only one 1-clause line among the Class III lines here; it has two constituents and four units.

Ps 106:48a *brwk yhwh-ʾlhy-yśrʾl*
Blessed-be Yahweh-god-of-Israel

The rarity of the line structure is related to the distribution of long nominal phrases.

There are three 2-clause constellations. One is the simplest possible (2-clause, 2-constituent, and 2-unit).

Ps 106:6b *hʿwynw hršʿnw*
We-have-done-wrong. We-have-been-wicked.

In another, the constellation has three units; in the example, the second clause predicator is a vocative, which we treat not as part of the clause it modifies, but as a distinct clause.

Ps 106:47a *hwšyʿnw yhwh-ʾlhynw*
Save-us, Yahweh-our-god.

The three remaining Class III lines have three constituents and four units. In one, the second clause predicator is a vocative.

Ps 106:4a *zkrny yhwh brṣwn-ʿmk*
Remember-me, Yahweh, in-your-goodwill-toward-your-people.

In another, there is an embedded clause.

Ps 106:23a *wyʾmr lhšmydm lwly-mšh-bḥyrw*
He-would-have-ordered their-destruction except-for-Moses-his-chosen.

In the last example, the embedded clause is a quotation, Ps 106:48c.

There are some further features of constriction which involve the structure of nominal phrases and the number of nominal constituents which can occur in lines with more than one clause. There are three linguistic levels of examination: clause, constituent and unit. The features we have considered so far refer to each of these singly. Each group of the remaining minor features refers to two of the three levels.

The constraints that refer to the shape of nominal phrases involve the constituent and unit levels. Let us return to Psalm 106. Most of the nominal phrases there, as elsewhere, are one unit, that is, single nomina, but 2-unit phrases are common. Longer phrases are rare; in this poem, as in the corpus generally, 3-unit phrases occur only in lines with no clause predicator, or in lines with one predicator and two constituents. The following are the only relevant examples.

Ps 106:38b *dm-bnyhm-wbnwtyhm*
the-blood-of-their-sons and-their-daughters

106:48a *brwk yhwh-ʾlhy-yśrʾl*
Blessed-be Yahweh-the-god-of-Israel.

There are no examples of 4-unit nominal phrases in Psalm 106; they are rare altogether; here is an example from Psalm 78.

Ps 78:12b *bʾrṣ-mṣrym-śdh-ṣʿn*
in-the-land-of-Egypt,-the-field-of-Tanis

There are no 5-unit nominal phrases.

The final group of constraints refers to the level of clauses and constituents. Not all clause predicators have dependent nominal phrases, but if, in a 2-clause line, one has a dependent nominal phrase, the other cannot. In lines with three clause predicators, none has dependent nominal phrases.

Before we consolidate our findings, we must examine carefully the bases on which we have proceeded. We turn then to a review of the material presented here; in the following section, we shall refer back to the examples used in this one.

### *1.4.5 Major grammatical features of the constriction*

Some of the notions used in the preliminary statement of constriction require clarification, either for their use there or their extension below. This clarification shall require that we go outside the framework of notions we have used, in search of formulations precise enough to make evident points that need further study.

We shall need to refer to some notions from the mainstream of modern American grammatical study. This work, which is generally called generative (-transformational) grammar, derives from Harris's idea that "complex sentences can be thought of as being in some way 'composed' of more elementary sentences, which may only appear in a deformed shape in the complex sentence" (Ross 1967: 27, cf. Harris 1970). Harris's rules serve to relate pairs of spoken sentences, regarding one as more basic than the other. Chomsky has pointed out that the more basic sentence need not be a pronounceable entity, but can be a structure of a different order. The relationship of such a structure, called deep, to meaning has been controversial. Chomsky and some of his students have distinguished deep structure, the realm of syntactic operations, from semantic interpretation rules, which are applied to the results of the syntactic operations. This approach is variously referred to as the extended standard theory of generative grammar or interpretivist grammar. Other of Chomsky's students, and grammarians of other backgrounds, have treated syntax and semantics as conjoint realms, refusing to exclude meaning from linguistic study. More recently, such linguists have recognized that the conjoint realms must be related to a third realm, that of pragmatics (Cole and Morgan 1975). This approach is usually called generative semantics and associated with the work of Lakoff, McCawley, Postal, and Ross. It is the research of this last group that we shall cite most often, though the matters of controversy are not crucial here since we are almost entirely concerned with surface structure. (See Frantz 1974, Jacobson 1971, Lakoff 1970b, 1972, and McCawley 1972 in general.)

A device adopted by all generative grammarians is the representation of relations among elements in a sentence by bracketing of items. Bracketing schemes can be simplified by projecting them into the form of trees. Such simplified representations will be useful in isolating areas of difficulty. We will not attempt to write fully labeled trees. The bulk of the lines in our corpus have shapes like the following: *Cl* stands for clause, *V* for verb, *Q*, *R*, for nominal phrases; *X* stands for a node on the argument level (on which, see below).

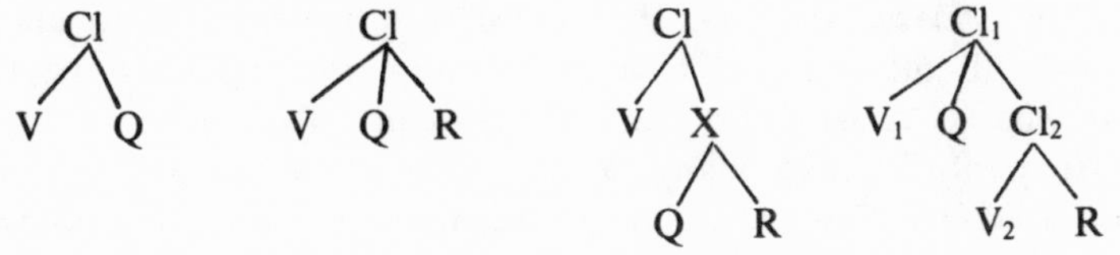


Examples of these structures given in 1.4.4 are (reading left to right): Ps 106:35a, Ps 106:38d, Ps 106:44a, Ps 106:8ab (in which 8b = $Cl_2$, 8a = the rest of $Cl_1$).

The first difficult area is the vocative/focus problem, which involves elements "extraneous" to the clause they are associated with. There are noun phrases which occur within or juxtaposed with clauses, to which they belong; but these noun phrases are not in any sense predicated by the verb of the clause or involved in the equivalence relation of the verbless clause. There are two classes of such phrases. The simpler and commoner class of vocatives was noted in regard to Ps 106:4a and 47a; let us consider these first (Zwicky 1974). The analysis of vocatives we wish to propose belongs to a large class of analyses used by generative semanticists to account for a wide variety of phenomena, called higher predicate analyses. These are based on extracting from clauses of the leftmost shape above multiple predicates, yielding structures of the rightmost shape.

Let us consider a simple example, extending the node V to include not only verbs but adjectives, which are often predicates used in English with the copula and in Hebrew in verbless clauses (Lakoff 1970a: 115-33, 142-43, 191-94; Ross 1969). We can begin with a group of English sentences.

| | |
|---|---|
| John is dead. | David caused John to die. |
| John came to be dead. | David killed John. |
| John died. | |

All these sentences are related: all but the first involve the same predication as the first, among others. We can account for the relatedness in meaning (without supposing synonymy) by treating the second and third sentences as containing two predicates, one identical to that of the first, the other, higher one, of inchoation; and by treating the last two sentences as containing three predicates, the two already noted and a still higher one, of causation (Lakoff 1970a: 91-107). This explanation does not fully describe the sentences but it does partially describe their relation. There are features of finite verbs which can be explained if they are treated as embedded under forms of *do* (Frantz 1974, Ross 1972); and about the use of declarative sentences which can be explained if they are treated as embedded under a form of a *say* predicate, with the speaker as subject and addressee as indirect object (the performative analysis, Ross 1967: 205, 270; 1970b). Many features of quantifiers (Lakoff 1970b, McCawley 1972) and modal verbs (Palacas 1971) can be treated with higher predicate analyses.

Almost all the analyses have in common the fact that the higher predicate and its constituents cannot consistently be observed in speech, though they often leave many traces; these are thus abstract higher predicate analyses (Sadock 1975). The analyses we wish to propose are non-abstract in that they refer to actual constituents of a higher predicate. In the case of the vocative, the predicate (as in the abstract analysis of declarative sentences) is one of saying, with the speaker as subject and addressee as indirect object. Before the sentence is pronounced, the non-essential parts of the higher clause are removed, viz., the predicate, the subject, and the indirect object marker. The addressee is left alone, and appears as the vocative of the clause embedded under the predicate of speaking. We will consider vocatives, then, clause predicators; this is somewhat inaccurate since they are actually the remnants of a predication. Since they occur only with another predicator, we call them minor clause predicators.

This analysis accounts for the fact that vocatives occur with predicates, but are not related to them as arguments; and it corresponds to a family of analyses which have yielded rich results in the study of spoken languages. These points alone should commend the analysis as a good way of formalizing the intuitive recognition of the greater complexity of a clause with a vocative. There is, however, some evidence from the language itself for its correctness. Hebrew regularly requires no vocative marker; although *h*, the definite article, is sometimes treated as such, its use merely marks the definiteness of the addressee. Recent studies have recognized, however, that there is a rare vocative marker, *l*, in Hebrew, also used in Ugaritic. Recall that we said that non-essential parts of the higher predicate are deleted before the clause is pronounced and among these is the preposition before the addressee, i.e., *l*. The "vocative" *l* is in fact the preposition which is not always deleted. Thus our analysis explains the usage in the following line.

Zph 3:16b *lyrwšlm ʾl-tyrʾy*
Jerusalem, do-not-be-afraid.

The double clause structure is $Cl_1$: *He says to* Jerusalem; $Cl_2$: do-not-be-afraid. Ordinarily in Hebrew, the predicate *say,* the subject *he,* and the preposition *to* (*l*) would be deleted; but in this case, the *l* has been retained. The apparent homonymy of the preposition *l* and the vocative *l* is a case of identity.

The other higher predicate analysis involves focus-markers. To set a perspective on this analysis we must distinguish the processes of copying and chopping, two processes in which constituents are moved from what can be taken to be their basic position in a clause. The process of chopping refers to moving a whole constituent within a sentence; it has been called Y-movement (Postal 1971: 142-49), referring to the fact that it is commoner among English speakers influenced by Yiddish, and topicalization (Ross 1967: 115-16, 232, Hudson 1975: 40-41). Here are some examples: the first of each pair is the non-chopped case, the second, the chopped version.

I like Harry.
Harry, I like.

I bought a book for Harry.
Harry, I bought a book for.

I'm going to ask Bill to make the old geezer take up these points later.
These points, I'm going to ask Bill to make the old geezer take up later.

To describe chopping, we would need to make claims about word order, and no such claims are part of our description of Hebrew constriction.

Copying is the term used to refer to displacement of a nominal constituent and the replacement of it by a pronominal constituent. Copying processes have been called left and right dislocation (Ross 1967: 232-36, Postal 1971: 135-37). The second example below shows right dislocation, and the fourth and sixth left dislocation; the other examples show the non-dislocated sentences.

The cops spoke to the janitor yesterday.
They spoke to the janitor yesterday, the cops.

Charley's out of his mind.
Charley, he's out of his mind.

Tony thinks Chemosh's wife was crazy.
Chemosh, Tony thinks his wife was crazy.

The many factors involved in copying processes need not concern us. There is a small group of dislocations which do concern us; the fourth and sixth examples above are apposite. In these, the dislocated element either matches an expressed constituent of the clause or does not correspond to any constituent of the clause, i.e., *Charley* matches *he* completely and

*Chemosh* matches only part of the subject of the embedded clause; each of these marks the focus of the whole clause.

The higher clause analysis of focus-markers is similar to the vocative analysis: the focus-marker is the object of a higher predicate of saying, in which the speaker is the subject (cf. Andersen 1974: 92-93). There is no crucial evidence in Hebrew to support the analysis of focus-markers as minor clause predicators. (This may be the explanation of the emphatic *l*.) Indeed, there are few examples. Here is one of the five examples of the Chemosh type.

Ps 78:56b *ʿlywn wʿdwtyw lʾ-šmrw*
Elyon: they do not observe his witness.

In this line, the focus-marker corresponds to no constituent of the clause; we therefore analyze it as part of another, higher clause and treat it as a clause predicator. There are only two examples of the other type of focus-marker.

There are some further discriminations which we can discuss with the aid of sentential trees. We have explained that the constriction of Hebrew verse only refers to certain syntactic features. It refers, in the first instance, to the highest level of trees, at which clauses are marked, distinguishing the number of clauses in a line. It also refers to a low level, which we have called the level of constituents. It refers finally to a lower level of trees, the unit level. Let us examine the constituent level first.

As we treat this level, it is somewhat different in structure than it is in most grammatical treatments, in two important respects. The term constituent is ordinarily used of the level at which the arguments (i.e., subject, object, etc.) of the clause predicator are arranged. Consider the following tree, in which *S* and *O* stand for subject and object.

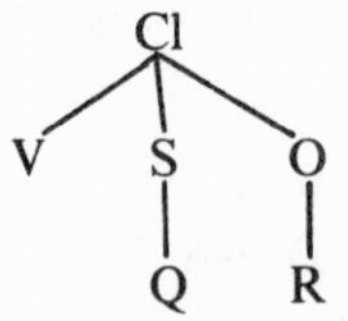


Since constituents *Q* and *R* correspond to the subject and object, the constituents match the argument level. This is the case in Ps 106:18b, a common one. If this correspondence is broken, the argument level does not agree with the constituent level. Consider the following tree, in which the subject is not independently pronominalized and thus not a constituent; *A* stands for adverbial.

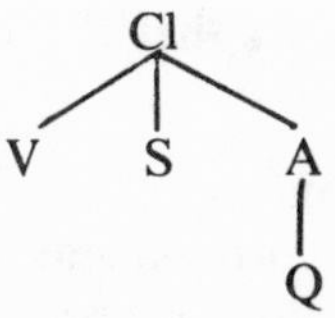


This is the case of Ps 106:43a; the adverbial node is the only argument which appears on the constituent level.

Another significant difference between the ordinary use of constituent and our use involves arguments of clause predicators which are internally complex (Hudson 1975). Consider this tree.

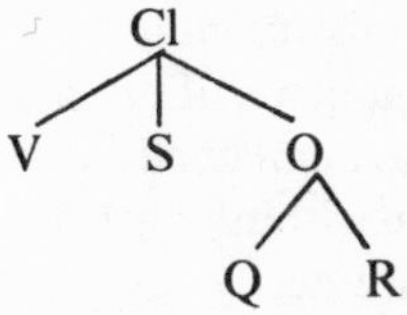


The two constituents *Q* and *R* are both parts of the object; this is the case of Ps 106:44a. Two constituents can be part of a single argument only if one (or both) is a prepositional phrase. No other arguments appear as two constituents.

Ross (1967) has described a group of constraints on sentence structure which require that certain configurations, called islands, not be divided in any way. One of these is relevant here. The complex noun phrase constraint guarantees that the two constituents of a single argument are never separated and never appear out of their underlying order. The Hebrew constriction as we have it is not sensitive to this Ross constraint.

Let us consider the complex noun phrase constraint further; in English, it is responsible for the fact that the second of the following sentences only paraphrases one meaning of the first.

I talked with a person in a suit of armor.
In a suit of armor, I talked with a person.

Roughly speaking, the island constraint would require that in Hebrew the first sentence could occur but the second could not.

Ps 106:44a *wyrʾ bṣr lhm*
He-saw the-difficulty to-them.

**wyrʾ lhm bṣr*
He-saw to-them the-difficulty.

This is apparently correct. To prove that the constriction is not sensitive to the second type of Ross island, we would need to find cases like the last, as well as account for their grammar fully. While we cannot do the latter, there are some examples which do show movement out of complex noun phrase islands. We suggested earlier that Ps 106:7a is one such. A clearer case is the following.

Dt 32:39f *wʾyn mydy mṣyl*
There-is-not from-my-hands one-who-plucks.

It is easy to see that *mydy* here has been moved out of the underlying island *mṣyl mydy* 'one who plucks from my hands.' Since examples like this are rare, and since this case can be accounted for as a poetic figure (cf. 39c and 10.5.9 on figures), we are reluctant to say that complex noun phrases are freely separable in Hebrew verse. Their internal structure, however, is not relevant to the constriction.

The examination of the constituent level obviates the need for comment on the unit level. There are arguments of the clause predicators which are not constituents, and these same arguments do not appear on the unit level. All relationships between nomina within constituents are analyzed on the unit level irrespective of their character.

In the discussion of the clause predicator level, we shall simplify the trees by not representing the syntactic features between clause and constituent which do not concern us. We shall use a convention of representing them with branching dummy variables, *X*, *Y*, etc., reserving the variables, *Q*, *R*, etc., for constituents. We shall also usually omit arguments of clause predicators which do not appear as constituents.

We can begin with the major cases. Note the following trees.

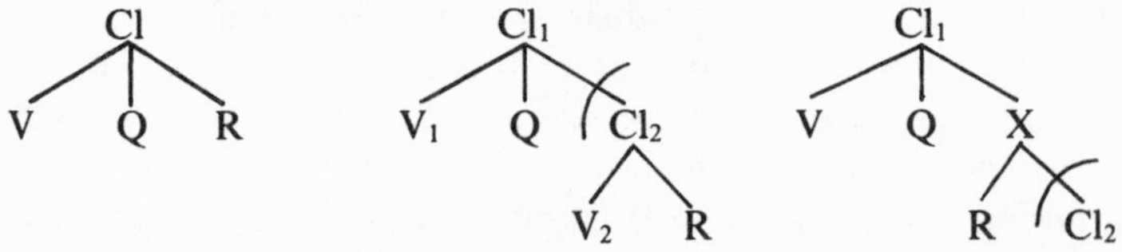


These illustrate the sources of the commonest line structures in Hebrew verse. If the first coincides with a line, there is a single clause line. In the second and third, if the whole coincides with two or more lines, and the line break fall at the arc, there are two single clause lines. The first corresponds to Ps 106:38d, and the second to Ps 106:8ab; the third corresponds to Ps 106:21ab.

Ps 106:21a *škḥw ʾl-mwšyʿm*
106:21b *ʿśh-gdlwt bmṣrym*

106:21a They-forgot El-their-savior
106:21b The-one-who-did-great-things in-Egypt.

The phrase node X includes the object in the first line, and its appositive in the second line; since the break occurs at the arc, the two lines are both single clause lines. The group of lines that fits these conditions is the largest group in the verse in general; we call these *clausal lines*, since the highest node within the line marks a clause boundary. These lines are dealt with in 3.3 and 3.4.

There are other structures we have discussed. Consider the following trees.

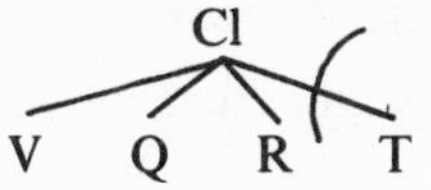


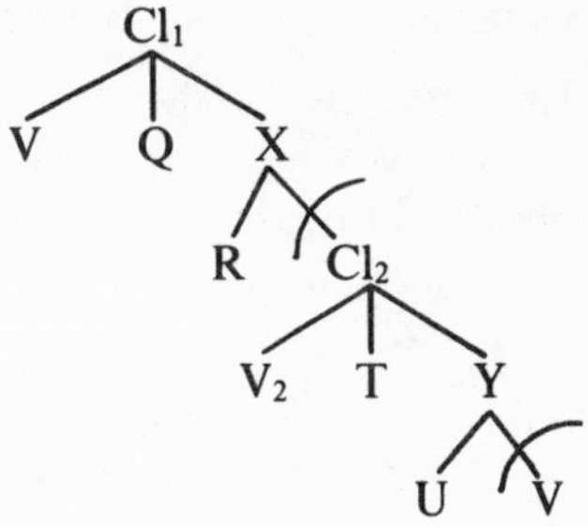


These illustrate the sources of the next largest group of lines, those with no clause predicator. If, in the first tree, the line break comes at the arc, the first line (or better, core line, since it is not always first) is a single clause line, and the other contains a phrase, or more; this illustrates Ps 106:31ab, in which the temporal expressions in the second line correspond to the node labeled *T*. In the second tree, there are two arcs; the first separates a clausal line, the second phrases of it, usually, appositives to it. This is the diagram of the whole of Ps 106:21ab 22ab, the first two lines of which we considered above. The rest of it reads as follows.

Ps 106:22a *nplʾwt bʾrṣ-ḥm*
106:22b *nwrʾwt ʿl-ym-swp*

106:22a Wonders in-the-land-of-Ham
106:22b Aweful-things by-the-Reed-Sea.

These lines are phrases in apposition to the last phrase of Ps 106:21b.

There is a third source, in which the subordinate clause line does not follow the independent clause line directly, as in this tree.

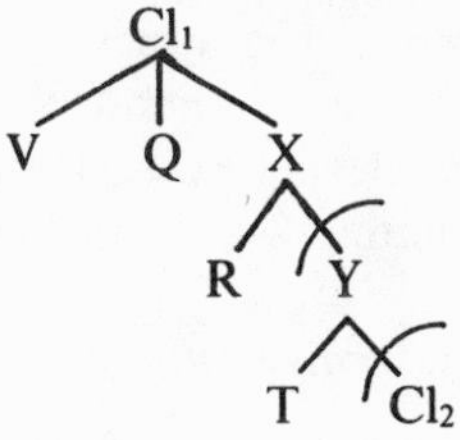


Here the second clausal line follows a line with no clause predicators. This is the structure of Ps 106:38abc.

Ps 106:38a *wyšpkw dm-nqy*
106:38b *dm-bnyhm-wbnwtyhm*
106:38c *ʾšr zbḥw lʿṣby-knʿn*

106:38a They-poured-out innocent-blood
106:38b The-blood-of-their-sons-and-daughters
106:38c Whom they-sacrificed to-the-idols-of-Canaan.

All these lines without clause predicators contained within them are *phrasal lines*. They are discussed in 3.5.

There is a small and distinctive group of phrasal lines which contain a clause predicator. These involve structures like the following one.

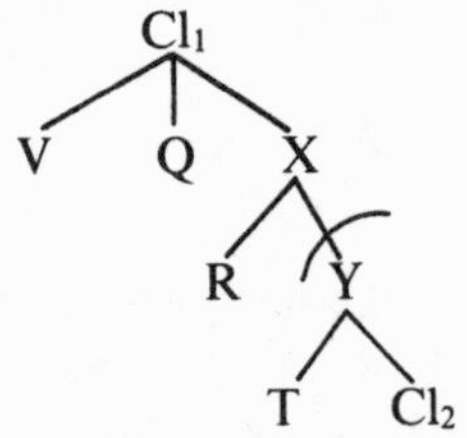


This is identical to the tree for Ps 106:38abc except that the second arc, i.e., the second line break, is missing. There are no examples of this configuration in Psalm 106; we can consider one from Psalm 78.

Ps 78:60a *wyṭš mškn-šlw*
78:60b *ʾhl škn bʾdm*

78:60a He-abandoned the-Shilo-tent
78:60b The-tent [in-which] he-tented among-people.

The asyndetic relative clause here, *skn bʾdm*, is structurally comparable to the relative clause in Ps 106:38c, except that it is contained within the same line as the nominal phrase it modifies. Thus line 60b is phrasal in relation to the larger clause of which it is a part, and yet clausal in that it contains a clause. These lines, which we call *phrase-clause* lines, are discussed in 3.5 with the other phrasal lines; in the constriction system they are reckoned as containing a clause predicator. The system of constriction refers to the presence of clause predicators rather than tree structure; it is possible that this is incorrect and that the relevant examples must be analyzed otherwise. These are 21 in number, under 2% of the corpus.

### *1.4.6 A restatement of the constriction*

*Definitions.* A clause predicator is a finite verb; an infinitive which is not used absolutely or which governs only an agent; a participle which is not used absolutely or which governs only an agent, object or possessor; or a ∅ predicator of a verbless clause (the major predicators); or a vocative or focus-marker (the minor predicators). A constituent is a verb, or an argument of a predicator which appears on the surface, unless it includes a prepositional phrase, in which case it is split. A unit is a verb or an individual nomen.

*Constraints.* 1. *On clause predicators.* No line contains more than three. 2. *On constituents.* No line contains fewer than one or more than four. 3. *On units.* No line contains fewer than two or more than five. 4. *On the units of constituents.* No constituent contains more than four units. Constituents of four units occur only in lines with no clause predicator. Constituents of three units occur either alone in lines with no clause predicator; or as one of two constituents in 1-clause lines. 5. *On the constituents of clauses.* No line of three clause predicators contains any dependent nominal phrases. In lines with two clause predicators, only one had dependent nominal phrases. 6. *On the integrity of lines.* If a line contains one or more clause predicators, it contains only nominal phrases dependent on them.

*The dominant line form.* Most lines of Hebrew verse contain one clause and either two or three constituents of two or three units. A lineation which yields lines of these constellations is preferred to other lineations.

## *1.5 The tropes of Hebrew verse*

The component of his description to which Lowth devoted most attention was the one which focused on the interrelations of small numbers of lines, usually two or three. Among the poetic systems he knew, Hebrew has an astonishing formal density, a density so great that Lowth did not try to penetrate it. Since we are familiar with more than Western European poetry, we can go further than Lowth did. If we begin by looking at other forms of parallelistic poetry, we shall see that though the Hebrew system is unique, it shares features with other systems.

This recognition will allow us to take apart the construct of parallelism and examine its parts. All of these are diverse and we shall not try to describe them exhaustively. Rather we shall suggest that among them can be found a group of phenomena which occur regularly and serve as part of the verse structure. These we shall separate from all the others, as the tropes. Syntactic regularities of large components are behind two groups of these, the line level and the supralinear level. Small component syntactic regularities are involved in the word-level tropes.

Not all the phenomena treated as tropes have been taken as parallelistic. On the word level, repetition has usually not been associated with parallelism; we shall show that it belongs to a subgroup of entities which are generally treated as parallelistic and that it is an important sector of that subgroup. The group of elliptical constructions we call constituent gappings is not generally treated as a feature of parallelism, but is proper to the level on which many such features are defined. Syntactic dependency across lines, again, is not normally regarded as a feature of parallelism, but we shall include it as a trope.

The other three tropes are among those taken up in traditional accounts of parallelism: coloration on the word level, matching on the line level, and mixing on the supralinear level. Because these three are *in nuce* parallelistic, we shall treat them as distinct from the other three. In fact, the relations are more complex. Coloration and repetition are completely distinct, but gapping and matching overlap in part and dependency includes mixing entirely. The structural difference between the latter two is plain; the separation is misleading unless we recall that the tropes are designed to account for the ordering force Lowth called parallelism. With that in mind, it seems legitimate to separate mixing as a trope in itself, though it is actually a proper subtrope of dependency. Although there are no descriptions of parallelism full enough for us to work directly from, the gestalt of phenomena called parallelism is our concern. Coloration, matching, and mixing are tropes of parallelism; and repetition, gapping, and dependency, tropes of continuity.

Our starting point lies far in advance of these specifics; we shall begin with a glance at parallelism in some other languages (1.5.1). Using recent studies of related phenomena in ordinary language, the word-level relations in parallelism will be sorted out (1.5.2), and the structural entities repetition and coloration described (1.5.3-4). Remarks on general problems of syntax related to structural parallelism (1.5.5) preface discussion of the line-level tropes of matching and gapping (1.5.6-7). The supralinear-level tropes are discussed last (1.5.8). In conclusion, we look at the reassemblage of some of what we have dismantled in the complex cooccurrences of tropes.

### *1.5.1 Parallelism*

It is surprising to learn that *parallelismus membrorum* is a coinage of Lowth's (Baker 1973), so common is the phenomenon in every realm of language use, especially poetry. The reasons which prompted Lowth to coin the term and the results of the coinage could be brought together in a fascinating chapter of European intellectual history. We do not need to examine that history in detail here; we need only consider some of its results.

The first result is the unhealthy one we have already cited: a set of phenomena are labeled without suitable definition and thereby removed from serious study. Parallelism is like any term in technical language: without restrictions, it can be extended to any phenomenon; and it has been. The situation is in fact not as bad as it sounds; the work which will undergird our reconceptualization is both extensive and valuable. The character of our objection depends on the original and more or less correct recognition by Lowth that parallelism is a structural element in Hebrew poetry. We are concerned with parallelism as a component of structural description of poetry; if there were a single feature of parallelism which is a major structuring device of the verse system, it would be available for definition and close consideration.

No such definition exists because no single feature exists. Rather, a small group of parallelistic features are central to the system and all others occur sporadically. There is no doubting Jakobson's precept:

> Pervasive parallelism inevitably activates all the levels of language — the distinctive [phonological] features, both inherent and prosodic, the morphologic and syntactic categories and forms, the lexical units and their semantic classes in both their convergences and divergences acquire an autonomous poetic value (1966: 423).

Because of this activation, the structural and non-structural features of parallelism have been confused on the syntactic and semantic level (usually called a level of thought). Phonological parallelism has been commented on only sporadically; Cooper (1976) and Schramm (1976) provide recent examples.

A central impetus to rethinking parallelism in Hebrew verse can be derived from a consideration of its importance in other poetic literatures. Some of these entered into the discussion at Lowth's time and many are still to enter for "our information about the distribution of parallelism in the folklore of the world and its character in various languages is still sparse and fragmentary" (Jakobson 1966: 403). A brief survey of the poetic systems which use parallelism as a major phenomenon will provide some idea of the breadth of the uniformitarian base we have to work with. Unfortunately not all the systems are equally known or described, but there are in most cases materials available which provide some orientation.

The best known systems are Finnish and Chinese; Finnish parallelism is discussed by Gray (1915) and, along with Chinese, by Popper (1918) and Newman (1918). Jakobson sets Finnish poetry into its Uralic family context along with Ob-Ugric (Vogul and Ostyak) (1966: 403-05); he also refers to some phenomena in the Turkic languages (which are partially contiguous with, but no longer thought to be related to, the Finno-Ugric languages). Parallelistic phenomena have been reported in Mongolian languages, which are related to the Turkic languages. The only living oral tradition in the Indo-European family which uses parallelism is Russian folk poetry, the chief concern of Jakobson (1966). The Chinese case fills in a picture of parallelism used sporadically across the northern Asian landmass from the Pacific to the Baltic.

The southern half of Asia is less well known. In Southeast Asia, parallelism is reported to be common, extending through the Austronesian language family off the continent in both directions from Madagascar to Hawaii (Fox 1974); only the Indonesian case of Rotinese has been described, and then only preliminarily. In South Asia, the case of the Dravidian language Toda, presented in Emeneau (1971), seems to be isolated; no traces of parallelism are found in the Old Tamil poetry of the first three centuries C.E. (Hart 1975), and there seem to be no modern parallels in the region or the family. The Toda texts, like the Rotinese, are somewhat beyond our grasp. *Toda Songs*, the only major text collection in the language, is entirely open to reading in translation, but resistant to study in the original: it is "virtually unanalyzed linguistically" and not "in a form in which it is of maximal utility to linguistics — either Dravidianists or general linguists interested in Toda" (Lass 1977: 251). The Semitic uses of parallelism complete the spread across southern Asia and putative non-Semitic Afroasiatic examples may extend the phenomenon into Africa.

In comparison with the heartland of Old World culture, Africa and the Americas are *terrae incognitae*. It will be a long time before the enormous body of African oral poetry treated in Finnegan (1970) becomes accessible to comparative study. In the Americas, the best known examples are Central American, largely Mayan (Brickner 1974, Gossen 1974); there is a further example, from Panama, in the Cuña language, which is unrelated to the Mayan family (Sherzer 1974).

We can refer to these poetic systems to discover ways in which notions of parallelism can be made more specific. In particular, we need to discover what are the basic phenomena which can be used in parallelism and the domains over which the resulting linkages extend. These discoveries are a crucial preliminary to examining Hebrew verse without taking its most essential features for granted and thus failing to characterize them. At the same time, we can consider the relationships of parallelism to poetic structure overall.

Let us begin with examples from the parallelistic literatures which are, next to Hebrew, best known, Chinese and Finnish, in especial Chinese Regulated Verse, *lü shih*, an 8-line lyric form, and Finnish popular epic verse. These forms have in common metrical strictness; the Chinese form is rigid and the Finnish nearly so.

Chinese Regulated Verse requires parallelism in the two central couplets. The domain is the couplet and words match in categories which refer to major grammatical features and functions (nouns with nouns, subjects with subjects, etc; verbs with verbs, adjectives with adjectives, postpositions with postpositions; there are no particles allowed). Within the classes of nouns and adjectives, the categories often have restricted semantic bases. Thus, for example, colors match colors, numerals match numerals, seasons match seasons, and compass points match compass points. Within the domain of names, the restrictions are even tighter: place names match place names and dynastic names match dynastic names. Let us consider some examples from Tu Fu, the T'ang poet; the first are seven character lines; the bracketed words are supplied in English; the numbers above the line indicate the order of the words in Chinese.

| 1 | 2 | 3 | 4 | 5 | 6-7 |
|---|---|---|---|---|---|
| river | by | small | pavilion | nest | kingfisher |
| park | in | high | tomb | lie | unicorns |

In a small pavilion by the river nest kingfisher-birds.
Close by a high tomb in the royal park lie stone unicorns.
(Liu and Lo 1975: 127)

The second example is from a five character poem.

| 1 | 2 | 3 | 4 | 5 |
|---|---|---|---|---|
| country | road | clouds | all | black |
| river | boat | sparks | only | light |

Clouds on country road, all black,
Sparks on a lantern from river boat, the only light.
(Liu and Lo 1975: 134)

In the first example, both lines match item for item. The first nominal phrase (# 1-2) is marked with a postposition for location, while the second locative phrase (# 3-4) is unmarked; the verb (# 5) is followed by the two word, unanalyzable compound subject. Similarly in the second pair, a noun phrase of one word is surrounded by two phrases of two words each, one locative, the other appositional. In addition to this item for item matching, the word order of the phrases and their parts is identical.

Further, the coherence of the lines is supported by other correspondences. In the seven character lines, the postpositions are locative (the second means more nearly 'at the edge of' than 'in'); the nouns they modify both refer to places of calm, if not luxe. The opening noun phrases denote two small pieces of monumental architecture (small, on a scale extending to, say, palaces); the difference in size between a pavilion and a tomb is reduced by the opposed adjectives: what is small in size for a pavilion approaches what is large for a tomb. The verbs both refer to abiding, as the living do (in a pavilion) and the dead do (in a tomb). The subjects of both verbs are exotic animals, drawn from the classes of living and non-living animals. The thematic structure of the lines is *not* parallelistic: the evocation of death in the second line does not "match" the reference to predation in the first in any simple way. Both the lines comport with the *carpe diem* point of the poem, but in rather different ways.

Let us turn to the five character lines. The single nouns (#3) are ephemera and the locative phrases (#1-2) describe foci of activity in otherwise unmarked territory. One relation of the single nouns is to each other (across the lines), but they are also opposed to two unspecified terms (sky and air). The heads of the locative phrases (#2) are related to each other (across the lines) as the single nouns are, and they are also opposed to further terms, which are specified (within the lines). Thus, there are four oppositions specified in six terms.

| | |
|---|---|
| clouds | [:sky] |
| fire (sparks) | [:air] |
| road: | countryside |
| boat: | river |

All four of the left-hand column's terms move in relation to those of the other column. The difference between the road/boat oppositions and the clouds/fire opposition is permanence; the former endure, the latter can only perpetuate themselves. The concluding appositives (#4-5) are opposed in both terms and the oppositions are perfect, in logic (all *v.* only) and in physics (the absence of light, black *v.* the presence of light). These two perfect oppositions (which are not definable "linguistically," but only extra-linguistically) qualify the imperfect oppositions introduced in the first part of the lines. Notice that there are no further oppositions involved, notably not a day/night opposition.

Hebrew poetry rarely shows parallelism this complete; Regulated Verse is a demanding form even in Chinese and these examples are from the work of a major poet. In addition to these parallelistic demands, further, Regulated Verse allows no repetition. The strictness of this form of parallelism is related to the fact that Classical Chinese is basically a monosyllabic language. Little morphological binding occurs; the brunt of the syntactic information in an utterance is borne by particles and word order, and in strict poetic forms there are no particles. Thus word order is crucial in such poetry. (These remarks were prepared in consultation with Li Chi.)

Finnish is another parallelistic poetry which uses strict meter (cf. 1.4.1). We shall quote from Magoun's translation, arranging each of his lines as two, to avoid drop lines (1969: 86). The following passage concerns the homecoming of one of the central figures, Ilmarinen, after his wedding.

1a. Now a noise is heard in the lane,
1b. the crack of a whip is heard there,
2a. the noise of a sled on the shore,
2b. the clatter of a shaft on the road to the spring.

The domain of the parallelism here is not two half-lines, but four. The first two half-lines have verbs, the second two do not. There is a location described in 1a, 2a, and 2b, and referred to with a deictic in 1b. The time reference appears only in 1a. The noise is not detailed in 1a, is partly evoked in 1b and 2b, and fully so in 2a. These lines are parallel by Finnish epic canons (we follow the remarks of Kiparsky 1973): noun phrases are parallel irrespective of internal structure; and verbs, adverbs and post-positions need not occur in all the lines. Further, the word order need not correspond across the lines; it is in part determined by Panini's Law, on which see 1.5.2. Let us return to the text.

3a. Ilmarinen's mother
3b. uttered a word, spoke thus.

Here is no parallelism between the parts of the line, and there is parallelism within the second half-line. This is the start of the mother's speech.

4a. "This is my son's sleigh;
4b. now he is coming from North Farm.
5a. The cuckoo bells are singing
5b. in front of the decorated basket sleigh,
6a. squirrels are roving about
6b. on the maplewood shafts,
7a. black grouse are singing
7b. on the elmwood shaft-bow.
8a. The settlement was waiting for a new moon,
8b. the community for a sunrise,
9a. the children for land grown with berries,
9b. the rollers for a tarred boat.
10a. I was waiting for my son,
10b. for my son, for my daughter-in-law."

The first and last half-line pairs are not parallel; the first two half-lines are entirely different, while 10ab involve repetition. Note that it is not half-lines but lines that are parallel in 5ab, 6ab, 7ab. The references to the decorations are complex, but not essentially parallel: the first decoration, the cuckoo, is small, squirrels are bigger, and grouse are about the same; the decorations start on the sleigh front, move forward to the shafts and then up to the bow bridging the shafts; and finally the references progress from insubstantial bells to solid maple and sturdier elm. This is not parallelism but a set of schemes that undergird it. In lines 8ab 9ab, the domain of parallelism is the half-line. The parallelism extends over all four lines, though the first two have other similarities, referring to the community and proximate time. The next two half-lines refer to two variously sectioned subparts of the community, one set off by age, the other by occupation; the last group seem to be awaiting a proximate time, while the children are holding out for spring.

In Finnish epic parallelism the parallel segments must be nearby, but they are not rigidly limited as in Chinese Regulated Verse. Word order is free and certain omissions allowed. Noun phrases correspond without regard for internal structure.

In these two cases, parallelism takes vastly different forms, involving different factors and producing entirely distinctive textures. In both these examples, parallelism uses the domain of metrical ordering for its own ends. Let us consider another parallelistic system in which there is no such use.

The basic unit in the 260 Toda songs discussed in Emeneau (1966) and recorded in Emeneau (1971) is a three syllable song unit or line. A pair of lines is parallel rarely, usually only in lists of proper names. Much more often, between two and six lines form a group of one or two sentences which is then paralleled by a sequence of the same number of lines forming the same sort of group. Emeneau's numeration is by double sentence group, not line; we supply the number of lines per group in the following section from a funeral song.

*Sentence Group 38a* (three lines). They are all through shedding tears from the right eye. What is left?

*Sentence Group 38b* (three lines). They are all through being tickled in the right nostril. What is left?

*Sentence Group 39a* (one line). O Buffalo!

*Sentence Group 39b* (one line.) O Osum!

*Sentence Group 40a* (one line). O Buffalo Nesof!

*Sentence Group 40b* (one line). O beautiful Nesof!

*Sentence Group 41a* (four lines). The old mothers are all through going across the Avalanche river. What is left?

*Sentence Group 41b* (four lines). The old fathers are all through going across the Avalanche river. What is left? (1971: 301).

Here parallelism occurs twice between line pairs, in 39ab and 40ab; it is likely that all four of these lines are parallel. In 38ab, the parallelism is suspended for a three line stretch before it begins its work, and in 41ab, the suspension is longer; still longer suspensions are not rare. It is easy to see that repetition is more important here than in the Finnish case: in 38ab, all of the third lines, most of the second, and a portion of the first are identical; in 41ab, all of the third and fourth lines, and most of the first lines are (1971: 298). The word order in the parallels is not free. Sentence breaks correspond to line breaks but not vice versa. Phrases can be broken across a line, and the vocative usage is complex (1966: 326-28).

Similar breadth of parallelistic array across pieces of verse is found in short Rotinese compositions. We include one of these here in part because we shall contend below that Rotinese verse is not metrical but uses (along with parallelism) a constriction; that point is immaterial here. The case demonstrates the variability of domain more clearly than Toda because the lines are longer (between six and twelve syllables) and thus more distinct. The following is a succession song cited by Fox (1974) as appropriate to "the installation of a new lord to continue a line of rule, or the replacement of father by his son or of a lineage member by another lineage member" (p. 74). Œ No and Kedi Poi refer to one person, and Dai and Sela, to one place.

1. The goat of Oe No from Dai
2. The goat has a yellow-necklaced beard
3. And the cock of Kedi Poi from Sela
4. The cock has gold-stranded tailfeathers.
5. Cut away the goat's beard
6. Leaving but the goat's throat
7. That throat will beard again
8. And the beard will be a yellow necklace again;
9. And pluck out the cock's tailfeathers
10. Leaving only the cock's rear
11. That rear will feather again
12. And the tailfeathers will be gold strands again.
13. Still perfect as before
14. And ordered as at first.

(Fox 1974: 74-75)

In this text, lines 13 and 14 are parallel to each other; this is not obvious, but is confirmed by Fox on the basis of other examples; here, the domain of parallelism is the line unit. In lines 1-4, the domain is twice that, i.e., two lines; in lines 5-12, the domain is double that and four lines parallel four lines. In the four succession songs Fox has published, the domain of parallelism varies. The poem we have quoted, Fox's text 1, includes a four line domain, an eight line group and a single couplet. Texts 3 and 4 are less complicated; text 3, which is 12 lines long, has four couplets with parallelism and closes with a quatrain; text 4, which is 14 lines, has three parallel couplets and closes with two quatrains. The suggestion that the domain units are systematically used within the texts, evident from text 1 and in simpler form in texts 3 and 4, is supported by text 2, the longest of Fox's succession texts.

These examples could be extended indefinitely. Mayan parallelism, like Finnish and Chinese, has a restricted domain, not often extending to triplets and rarely beyond that limitation. Zinacantan and Chamula Tzotzil parallels are more often semantic than syntactic; Yucatec parallels are rarely syntactic. In Cuña parallelism, there are usually one or two grammatical frameworks for the whole utterance and they are reused with extensive repetition of a complex sort that reflects the intricacies of Cuña verb morphology.

With these examples in mind, we can take up the task described by Jakobson: "The structure of parallelism which underlies biblical and Ugaritic poetry requires a rigorous linguistic analysis, and the seemingly infinite variety of extant parallels must yield to a precise and comprehensive typology" (1966: 400-01). We take it up, however, in the framework of a reformulation of the Standard Description of Hebrew poetry and we shall not actually provide a typology. We will contend that poetic structure is determined by certain parallelistic phenomena, which we call tropes. There are many other parallelistic phenomena which fall into two groups: (a) those which are rare and minor and belong to the realms of figuration and ornamentation and (b) those which result from the cooccurrence of tropes. In fact, previous descriptions of parallelism have failed in general because they combined in description phenomena which do not always occur together. Repetition and the extraordinary troping of single constituents does not consistently accompany correspondences of whole syntactic structures. The reason for this underanalysis is probably the one isolated by Jakobson: "the fictitious but still indelible view of parallelism as a survival of a primevally helpless, tonguetied means of expression" (1966: 422-23). Far from being remote survivals in exotic poetic systems, the phenomena behind parallelism are in the heartland of language, and there we shall venture.

### *1.5.2 "Parallel pairs," dyads, orality, and formularity*

The psychotherapeutic exercise of free association reveals, if it is not obvious, that any single word in a language can be paired with another. Irrespective of its psychological usefulness, the exercise will elicit many word complexes which are related to the structure of the world as it is perceived through the medium of language. Some of these and many other dyads, pairs of words which can be associated in some way, reveal particular facets of language behavior.

Aspects of language irregularity have traditionally been explained in terms of word pairs or dyads; such explanations, though they are often weak, give some idea of how widespread dyads are. The treatments are usually gathered under the head of analogical formation (Hjelmslev 1970: 51-56). Forms of dyading result in leveling, blend words, and morphological reanalysis.

Dyadic behavior also influences the accentuation of words which are partially similar. The enormous and ever-increasing class of words in English which serve as both nouns and verbs illustrates this phenomenon. This determination also appears in contrastive situations. The group suffix *-ese* normally bears the stress: *Portugése*, *Japanése*; but the stress shifts to the stem if the two nouns are used together: *Pórtugese*, *Jápanese*. In all these cases, dyads are only subparts of larger sets which can show accentual irregularities.

Given the generality of dyading and the erratic character of the linguistic consequences of it, is there any way that we can get a sufficient handle on it to make it useful in considering parallelism? There is and it is due in part to the ancient Sanskrit grammarian Panini and in part to Cooper and Ross (1975) who have recently studied, under the rubric of world order, a large class of fixed and semifixed phrases in English. Cooper and Ross derive from their work two sets of principles which govern the large class of freezes in English, which includes idioms like *kit and caboodle*, non-idiomatic phrases like *now and then*, and compound phrases, largely reduplicative, like *namby-pamby*. The bulk of these are two word groups (setting particles aside); some include three words. The likeness to parallel pairs in Hebrew and other poetries should be obvious from the outset.

The first set of Cooper-Ross principles is semantic and partially language particular; it is focal in their paper in part because they are interested in engaging the Whorfian postulate which asserts that the language one speaks makes a difference in how she or he sees the world. Because of this general relevance and because many of the principles are at work in the Semitic languages and Hebrew in particular, we shall summarize the Cooper-Ross semantic principles. In the following list, the italicized item describes the correlate given preference over an opposite of it in a freeze involving the two. One or two English examples follow the items and should give a good notion of the multifariousness of dyads. There are linguistic judgments involved and they refer to standard American English and in particular to the dialectal forms of it used by Cooper and Ross; we do not differ from them at all, but there may be speakers who do; such variation should not be surprising.

1. *here:* here and there
2. *now:* now and then, today and tomorrow
3. *present generation:* father and grandfather
4. *adult:* man and boy
5. *male:* man and woman
6. *positive:* positive or negative; now or never
7. *singular:* singular or plural

8. *patriotic:* cowboys and Indians
9. *animate:* people and things
10. *friendly:* friend or foe
11. *solid:* land and sea
12. *front:* front and back
13. *agentive:* subject and object
14. *power source:* bow and arrow
15. *living:* living or dead
16. *at home:* at home and abroad
17. *general:* abstract and concrete

Given a need to mention two items which can be described within a given single feature parameter, one out of the two will be favored. The range of features can be diverse; Cooper and Ross cite a partial food and drink hierarchy which determines the order of priority: fish, meat, drink, fruit, vegetables, baked goods, dairy products, spices.

There are deeper principles behind these principles. Cooper and Ross cite the *me first* principle, "First conjuncts refer to those factors which describe the prototypical speaker" of the language who is, in American English, adult (#4), male (#5), allied with his in-group (#8), animate (#9), friendly (#10), in control (#13 and #14), and alive (#15). This principle is overridden by priority of the numinous (*God and man*, never the reverse) and, in English, by certain rules of politeness (*you and I*). (Thus the Semitic languages have, e.g., *ʾny wʾth* 'I and you' because they lack certain trivial politeness conventions.) The hierarchy dictates: adult humans before non-adult humans, before animals, before inanimates.

There are freezes the ordering of which has no apparent semantic explanation, *dribs and drabs*, *spic and span*, *by hook or by crook*, *hem and haw*. Consideration of these led Cooper and Ross to work out a series of phonological rules to differentiate first and second place terms. Given the necessarily shaky state of our knowledge of Hebrew phonology, we must be cautious in applying these to Hebrew, but happily the most important principle is the simplest.

*Principle I.* Panini's Law was stated by the grammarian in his description of Sanskrit word compounding; he noted that other things being equal, the shorter of two items comes first in a compound, which Cooper and Ross observe is also true of English freezes; *vim and vigor*, *lock*, *stock and barrel*, *free and easy*.

*Principle II.* The vowel of the second place word is longer than that of the first. Since English does not use simple length distinctions, this statement is approximate but since the judgments are confined to two vowels, it is not hard to make: *stress and strain* (ɛ before e; in Hebrew *ṣere* [e] is often treated as the long counterpart of *seghol* [ɛ]); *trick or treat* (ɪ before i).

*Principle III.* The second place word has more initial consonants than the first place word: *sea and ski*, *sink or swim*, *harum-scarum*.

*Principle IV.* The second place word has a more obstruent initial consonant than the first. The scale of obstruency ranges from stops (most obstruent: Heb *p t k b d g ṭ q ʾ h*) through spirants (Heb *ḥ ʿ s z ś š ṣ*), nasals (Heb *m n*), liquids (Heb *r l*) to glides (Heb *w y*). (The proper internal ordering of the Hebrew groups is uncertain.) Examples in English in which the first word's consonant is less obstruent are *wear and tear*, *wing-ding*, *rough and tough*.

*Principle V.* The second place word has a vowel with a lower second formant, an acoustic feature (cf. Ladefoged 1967). The English vowels in order of decreasing second formants are i, ɪ, ɛ, æ, a, ə, o, u; this is a progression from high front vowels to low vowels to high back vowels. The Hebrew progression is similar: *ḥireq*, *ṣere*, *seghol*, *pataḥ*, *qameṣ*, *ḥolem*, *qibbuṣ*, and *šureq*; the place of Heb *šwa* is unclear. English examples of the principle are *this or that*, *one or two*, *fiddle-faddle*, *crisscross*, *ping-pong*.

*Principle VI.* The second place word has fewer final consonants than the first place word: *sink or swim*, *wax and wane*.

*Principle VII.* The second place word has a less obstruent final consonant than the first: *slapdash*, *kith and kin*.

The first two principles and Principle V refer to the shape of the two words in comparison; the other principles deal with the shape of the whole phrase. Consonant clusters and more obstruent consonants are kept inside the group; the start and finish of the phrase are kept as simple as possible.

These two sets of principles suggest that semantic and phonological rules sometimes work so that "in certain well-defined instances the relation between sound and meaning is not arbitrary" (p. 81). The freezing principles take over in the area between syntax and semantics; they are strongest in regulating the order of segments within a morpheme and of morphemes within a word, and of items in coordinations and disjunctions; they play some part in arranging elements in proverbs, and more generally, in English at least, in arranging adjectives before a noun and terms over a whole clause. When the two sets of principles clash, semantic principles seem stronger than phonological ones. As we mentioned earlier, the semantic principles are language particular in part; the phonological ones, Cooper and Ross suggest, may not be. They mention that they know of two semantic principles without exceptions: star before extra (*Charlton Heston and a cast of thousands*) and the principle of chronology (*wash and wear*).

In the consideration of poetry, the semantic principles tend to be less important than the phonological ones, as well as being more difficult to discuss, and among the phonological principles, the central one is the first,

Panini's Law. In the most obvious cases of Panini's Law in ordinary language, shorter items precede longer ones outside the core of the sentence (i.e., the subject and verb). In the classical Semitic languages, for example, pronominal elements, generally shorter than other substantives, tend to follow the verb directly regardless of what relation they have to it.

Panini's Law makes a striking appearance in Finnish epic verse, in which, "other things being equal, the words of a line are arranged in order of increasing length" (Kiparsky 1972: 168). This is a meaningful feature of Finnish verse in part because the language has a complex morphological system which often creates words of great length. In Hebrew poetry, Panini's Law has a small domain because word size is less subject to variation. The Law does sometimes structure parts of lines, usually within nominal phrases. A striking example in our corpus is from the *Dies irae* catalog of Zephaniah. In five lines, the word *ywm* 'day' governs two nouns and in each case, the first has two syllables and the second has three. Only three of the disyllables are masculine nouns from strong roots, the largest possible source of disyllabic nouns; the first two of them are feminine nouns from weak roots. Of the trisyllables, only two, the third and the fifth, are feminine nouns from strong roots, the largest potential source of trisyllabic nouns; the first two are feminines from weak roots; the fourth is a quadriliteral masculine. (All the nouns from weak roots are in the first two lines, and all the nouns there are feminine). This source diversity means the catalog has no major simple morphological determinant. The leading factor is Panini's Law which shapes five lines of three words each with the rising contour: 1 syllable - 2 syllables - 3 syllables.

| | | |
|---|---|---|
| Zph | 1:15b | *ywm-ṣrh-wmṣwqh* |
| | 1:15c | *ywm-šʾh-wmšwʾh* |
| | 1:15d | *ywm-ḥšk-wʾplh* |
| | 1:15e | *ywm-ʿnn-wʿrpl* |
| | 1:16a | *ywm-šwpr-wtrwʿh* |

| | | |
|---|---|---|
| Zph | 1:15b | A day of stress and distress |
| | 1:15c | A day of holocaust and devastation |
| | 1:15d | A day of gloom and darkness |
| | 1:15e | A day of clouds and storm gatherings |
| | 1:16a | A day of horns and alarums |

The coherence of this passage could be discussed at length; especially striking are the root initial *ṣ* in 15b, *š* in 15c, and ʿ in 15e.

This example suffices to show that Panini's Law is involved with the patterning of Hebrew poetry. In fact, it is crucial in fixing the shape of the words used in slots traditionally called parallel. It explains, for example, the ordering of *hrym* (2 syl.) over *gbʿt* (3 syl.) the 17 out of 18 times the words are parallel (Yoder 1972). Boling (1960) lists the 16 words and phrases used parallel to *ʾwyb* (2 syl.) in the Psalter; 13 of these are longer words. Of the three remaining cases, which have the same number of syllables, one begins with a stop like *ʾwyb*, so Principle IV does not directly apply; since the stop, *q*, is highly marked in the phonology of Hebrew, we believe that a good argument for treating ʾ as less obstruent than *q* could be formulated. The two remaining cases are both sibilants and apparent counter-examples of Principle IV. Since we are not concerned here with formulating an exact application of all the Principles to Hebrew, it is enough to say that it is likely that secondarily articulated consonants like those in both examples need special handling (*ṣ* is pharyngealized and we take *ś* as lateralized). In Ugaritic, too, the first word in parallel slots is shorter than the second: *bt* (2 syl.) is the first word to *hkl*, *ḥẓr*, and *mṯb* (all 3 syl.); and *ʾaḥ* is the first word to *bn-ʾum*, *ʾary*, and *ʿl-ʾumt* (Boling 1960).

The importance of this application of the Cooper-Ross principles is *not* to observe that first words in parallel slots are shorter than second words. Students have long recognized this. Nor does the application exhaust the relevant facts. Alongside the enormous and productive class of deverbative nouns in Hebrew, there is a tiny class of nondeverbatives, which constitute the language's core nominal vocabulary. Most of the deverbatives are disyllables and most of the nondeverbatives are monosyllables. Many references to the most basic order of reality involve a monosyllabic noun which will be followed almost of necessity by a disyllabic noun, and thus the words will fit Panini's Law, although the nondeverbative origin of one of the nouns is more "important." Recognition of Panini's Law is important because it serves to push our attention back where it belongs in reading poetry: onto the language itself. Most parallelistic usages result from ordinary facts of the language, not special poetic features.

One source of parallels unrelated to the Cooper-Ross principles is dialect diversity. Thus the Hebrew (South Canaanite) word for 'gold' is *zhb* and the North Canaanite word is *ḥrṣ*; in Hebrew poetry, the latter is used sometimes as the second word in a pair (Harris 1939: 52-53). Driver (1953) has suggested that Aramaic as well as North Canaanite served as a source for Hebrew "second words." There is justifiable confusion about what is involved here: are the other dialect words archaic in poetic usage or are they borrowings, or some of both? We suspect the last. It is more important to note than in none of the explanations are processes unknown outside the ordinary business of language involved. Every day, in ordinary conversation, speakers of English use archaic and borrowed words for purposes which have no connection with verse, to quote a legal preciosity or name a new import.

In relation to the principle of dialect scrutiny, we can report important confirmation from the Indonesian language Rotinese (Fox 1974). In all the Eastern and most of the Western dialects of this language, for example, the word for 'person' is *hataholi*; some Western dialects use *daehena*. The latter is a poetic word in the other dialects and vice versa. This usage is striking because South and North Canaanite split on the same lexical point, *ˀyš* and *ˀdm*; and the split structures the double story of the creation of people. In Genesis 1, *ˀdm* is created, while in chapters 2-3, *ˀyš* and *ˀšh* are created. (We do not mean to suggest that the stories were composed jointly, only that the final editor knew a little dialectology.)

What, then, are "parallel pairs?" The current hypothesis contends that they are entities fixed in a special "dictionary," learned by poets working in a tradition. The dictionary hypothesis is as old as the comparative study of Hebrew and Ugaritic and has descended from Ginsberg and Cassuto to Patton, Held, Boling (1960: 223), and Yoder (1972). It has never been fully elucidated because the facts are resistant: if *ˀwyb* had 16 parallels, were they all in the dictionary? The notion of the dictionary is based on pairs, but there are numerous pairings for some words. Further, are we to think of the Hebrew poet learning from commercial jargon that Phoenicians call 'gold' *ḥrṣ* (this, as an ordinary language speaker) and learning (as a poet) that in poetry, a suitable parallel for *zhb* is *ḥrṣ*? Surely these are not separate facts.

The reference to a poetic dictionary of parallel pairs reveals again the erroneous supposition that poetic language is a phenomenon entirely apart from ordinary language. The creation of the dyads used in Hebrew verse is not nearly so much the result of special poetic annexation of parts of the language as it is poetic penetration into all the resources of speech. The supposed dictionary of poetic parallels is a cover term which swerves away from the linguistic facts and the situation of poetry. It is an interesting swerve which points to an important difference between Hebrew poetic parallelism and Chinese Regulated Verse parallelism. The former is extremely loose next to the latter. The strictness of this sort of Chinese parallelism (and parallelism in other forms occurs everywhere in Chinese), might lead one to expect that in that most long-lived of literary cultures, actual dictionaries of parallels exist. They do. Such are the harsh demands of all poetry, they are scorned by serious writers as the playthings of beginners and hacks, but they exist. (We owe this information to Li Chi.)

One useful approach to poetic dyading is furnished by recent work on conspiracies and targets which derives from the early studies of Jakobson (Watkins 1974: 90). The terms refer to situations in a language which have various, distinct explanations, i.e., in which separate rules may be said to conspire. The situations themselves are sometimes targets (i.e., actual sets of phenomena in the language, like "columnar" stress) and sometimes anti-targets (i.e., phenomena avoided, like homonymy of words from different roots). Poetic dyading is less readily grasped than most of the phenomena so far put under the head of conspiracies. Nonetheless, the basic goal of having a stock of language to use in poetic forms is comparable to the goal of maintaining the general intelligibility of pronunciation associated with conspiracies.

Dyading arises from many sources which may be said to conspire together. Hebrew *zhb* and *ḥrṣ*, for example, are a dyad of native plus foreign dialect words, but one which fulfills Cooper-Ross Principles IV and VII. The Ugaritic dyad *bt* and *ḥẓr*, besides being a dyad of a non-deverbative and a deverbative noun, fulfills Panini's Law; *bt* and *hkl* does so, too, and is made up of a nondeverbative native word and a loan word. The generality and diverse structure of this treatment suggest why there are exceptions to the parallel pairs; just because there are so many factors creating dyads, there are many ways to get around them, as there are not on any serious form of the dictionary hypothesis.

The dictionary hypothesis has merged into another hypothesis, and this one also deserves our attention. It involves orality and we can begin by stating that we do not question the essential orality of Canaanite poetry. In particular, we do not wish to sever the tie students have seen between dyading and orality. We do wish to observe that the analogy of formulas in other oral poetries to dyads in Hebrew does not require the notion of a fixed stock of usages. Formulas in all oral poetries are to a large extent involved with the languages of use and it is unparsimonious to suppose that a poet in any language learns thousands of poetic collocations which can be "figured out" afresh every time they are needed. If the same solution turns up every time, it is because that best fits the requirements. If there are a number of good fits, they will all turn up.

The formula has generally been accepted as a distinctively poetic phenomenon because of the complexity of language behavior involved. Toda exhibits almost perfect formularity (Emeneau 1971) and Rotinese and Serbocroatian are close (Fox 1974, Lord 1965). In these cases, it may be that the hypothesis of distinctive formulas arising from the character of the language itself, but existing independently, will need to be considered. There are other "formular" literatures. Kiparsky has considered the master-piece of antique orality with regard to this question, contending that "a strictly grammatical characterization of the [Homeric] formula may be illuminating" (1976: 18).

Kiparsky focuses his attention on the phrasal patterns of oral poetry and those of some ordinary languages. In the latter, there is a large class of bound expressions (similar to complex words) which is characterized by arbitrarily limited distribution, frozen syntax, and non-compositional semantics (i.e., the sense of the whole does not follow from the sense of the parts, is "idiomatic"). In English, these include phrases like *foregone conclusion* (nothing else can be described with the adjective), *arrant nonsense* (only a small group of things can be described with the adjective), and so on. Bound expressions are of two types. Some are syntactically fixed. Like the examples cited, most of these show no variation; consider further *in the nick of time*. Those with variation allow only the substitution of a noun phrase in a fixed slot: *get x's goat*. Fixed bound phrases can be syntactically anomalous, as in *knight errant*, with a postposed adjective; and show a high degree of noncompositionality: *eat your heart out*. These correspond essentially to the fixed formulas of Homeric verse. (See further discussion between Kiparsky and Watkins in Stolz and Shannon 1976: 108-9, 112-13.)

A much larger class of bound phrases is syntactically flexible, i.e., based on a definable syntactic relation which can take a variety of forms: *addled eggs* (cf. *The eggs are addled*, but not *The knight is errant*), *take advantage of* (cf. *He was taken advantage of*, but not *Her heart was what she ate out*, or *Her heart was eaten out*). These syntactically flexible bound expressions correspond to the flexible formulas in Homer, formulas which can be inflected in various forms, split across a line or often across two or three lines, and modified by other words. Their grammatical structure can be accounted for by a qualification of one of their parts since they tend to be less noncompositional. The noncompositionality of these requires only the statement that, e.g., eggs can be addled, or advantage can be taken. Fixed bound phrases need to be specified *in toto*: only knights can be errant, and the adjective must follow the noun.

Kiparsky's treatment takes into account the most important fact about formulas described in all oral literatures: they are sentences or phrases of definable grammatical shape. It also brings together the Homeric formula, which in Parry's work is defined on metrical grounds, and other formulas since, as Kiparsky notes, on the basis of his description, "formulas should occur equally [i.e., as in Homer] in oral poetry that uses relatively free metrical schemata, and in oral prose" (1976: 87). This is true: O'Nolan (1969) describes formulas in Irish prose tales and Finnegan (1967) in Limba story forms; and formulas occur in poetic systems that lack Homeric metrical rigidity. Further, formulas can have diverse relations to strictly metrical systems. In Toda, for example, formula matches line; in Homer, it rarely does so.

The insistence of Kiparsky and others on the separation of the formula from metrical definition confirms an important point about intellectual history, as well as a sound intuition of previous students of Canaanite orality. The intuition is that orality is a crucial part of the poetry. All

American students of Canaanite poetry have sought to confirm this intuition within the framework of the Parry-Lord treatment of Homeric and Serbocroatian epic verse. Most have (correctly we believe) trusted their intuition and ignored the fact that, whatever the poetic structure of Hebrew and Ugaritic, it does not possess the immense rigidity of the Homeric and Serbocroatian epic verse lines. The original definition of the formula given by Parry could not conceivably be made to fit Hebrew and Ugaritic: a formula, Parry wrote, is "a group of words which is regularly employed under the same metrical conditions to express a given essential idea" (1930: 80).

Had previous students been stymied by the incomparability, their preliminary explorations would have been lost. As it is, we can see that the dyads of Hebrew verse are of the same class of phenomena as formulas in other poetries. They differ in involving much less syntactic complexity and fixity. On a scale of formularity, Hebrew and Ugaritic verse must be set low because the entities which are "formularized" are smaller. Greater precision is not possible (or, we think, desirable) because orality is not a discrete or well-defined phenomenon. One point, which we have hinted at, involves the character of a poetry's orality. The Parry-Lord model associates formulaic style in long, strictly metrical texts with oral composition; just as the metrical comparison fails, so the notion of oral *composition* fails. It has been a great benefit of Lord's strong formulation of his hypothesis about composition that it has stimulated other students to isolate other oral modes (see, e.g., Opland 1975, 1976, and generally Finnegan 1976a, 1976b).

There are some other features of Homeric formularity which need attention. We have used the term formula as if it were solid coin, still stable around the Parry standard, because that was sufficient, and we have been satisfied with a general treatment of Homeric poetry as oral. If we hope to go further in considering orality, we must be more precise. In Homeric studies there has been a broadening of the notion of formula from Parry's base that rivals the extensions of parallelism in Robinson. We need not hesitate to agree with a recent observation of a classicist: "The tradition of Homeric scholarship that concerns itself with formulary style has, by now, begun to run the risk of generating as many misconceptions as insights" (Russo 1976: 31). Parry's definition of the formula was extended by its originator and others, notably Notopoulos, to include other phenomena. Russo has articulated a full system: (1) the verbatim formula (essentially Parry's starting point); (2) the formula with one variable item; (3) the formula with two variables, "the structural formula"; (4) the single term formula, or colonic formula; and (5) the rhythmic formula. All (1) formulas have complete identity; all (2) formulas have identical syntax, meter, and some repetition, and all (3) formulas are similar with less repetition; (4) formulas have only meter and word types in common; and (5) formulas have only metrical instantiation in common. (The term colon used of a hexameter refers to a third or a quarter of a line set off by syntactic breaks; it does not correspond entirely to either Semitist usage or Lotz's usage [1972a].) Not all of these are formulas in the terms Kiparsky set out; only (1) and (2) and sometimes (3) are. Russo's (4) and (5) types should not be called formulas; they have no relation to orality since such metrical localizations are found in written verse of all types, most commonly in rigidly metrical verse (Kiparsky 1976, 1977). The formula cannot be defined in general on the grounds of meter; and further, no formulas can be defined on the grounds of meter alone, without reference to repetition and grammatical structure.

Having discriminated these formular types, Russo goes on to consider the case of Homer and in particular the formularity of the poems. He notes that the usual treatments of Homer's formularity have been based on small samples; here, as often, the seminal work has been Lord's. If we read Russo correctly, there has never been a study of the formular density of even as much as a whole book of either Homeric poem, let alone of the 28,000 lines of both. Using all the formular types above and on extremely generous readings, Russo's samples of the texts reveal less than 50% formularity; if the last two types are discarded and the range of comparison tightened, they have even less. The two most accessible corpora of living oral poetry, the Parry-Lord Serbocroatian songs and Emeneau's Toda songs, are both described as having 100% formularity, and the evidence in the latter case is entirely available for inspection. The Homeric case seems quite different.

Qualification of the Parry-Lord analogy for Homeric poetry reveals the similarity of Homeric and Canaanite cases, since not only can formularity in both be defined on non-metrical grounds; in neither is it amenable to full demonstration. The latter point cannot be related to any one fact: it is the result of limited attestation only in part. Russo prefers to designate Homer a traditional, rather than an oral, poet; this is a terminological issue. It seems better to consider Homeric verse as orally-based, without making claims about oral composition. The non-metrical definition of the formula enables us to see that the meter does not create the formula and insofar as they coincide the reverse relation may obtain. There is considerable evidence to support this notion, to which we shall return below (1.7.3). The central consideration is not at all evidentiary, however: *a priori* one would not expect an abstractly definable form like meter to lead in the shaping of segments of language.

Having readjusted the framework in which dyads of Hebrew poetry are examined, we can consider some recent treatments. The most industrious scholar of dyads has been Dahood, who in numerous articles (e.g., 1967c, 1973b, j, 1976c, d, e) has treated dyads and who has produced the major treatments of the corpus of attested dyads (Dahood and Penar 1970,

1972; Dahood 1975b). As always in his work, Dahood has taken as the first priority the texts themselves and in seeking to describe them as fully as possible has avoided making claims about the phenomena. He extends the range of the previously recognized 60 "parallel pairs" common to Hebrew and Ugaritic from the set of words that occur in parallel slots in both verse corpora to include words that are parallel in one corpus and juxtaposed or used in a single text unit (collocated) in the other. He also includes words used in parallelistic and inclusive structures over great distances in the text and he treats along with parallel pairs repetitions. Further, he includes particles and pronouns, slighted by previous students. He has thereby increased the number of "parallel pairs" over 16 fold (at last count, 1976b: 669). His reviewers have frequently proceeded from the dictionary and orality hypotheses to observe that the set of parallel pairs common to the two literatures (which describes the overlap of the "dictionaries") should only include words which are strictly parallel; these points are well made by Clifford (1977) and Pardee (1977). The difficulty of the objections is that Dahood's attention to the texts has led him to go beyond the received hypothesis, without proposing a new one, which will essentially eliminate the notion of the dictionary and replace it with something like target structures. It may also be useful to eliminate the term parallel pair and replace it with the term we have preferred, dyad, which more readily describes the juxtapositions and collocations gathered by Dahood. His preliminary work on Phoenician dyads has been rounded out by Avishur (1975); some relevant Akkadian material is cited by Watson (1975).

A new treatment of parallel pairs will also provide a framework for consideration of the facts studied by Talmon (1961, 1975: 338-78, 1976), who has shown that dyads are sometimes interchangeable across textual traditions. Further, it rejoins the study of "parallel pairs" to the active research in historical linguistics of the most incisive of Dahood's reviewers, Loewenstamm (1975a) and his student Avishur (1971-72).

Dahood's great catalogs contain a record of dyad attestations; they are not a survey of a supposed dictionary. Had we the texts, the tools and the time, we could construct an instrumentum that would include most Ugaritic and Hebrew words in all their various relations. The differences among a list of parallel pairs, a working dictionary, and a concordance are in part a function of attestation and in part of scholarly discrimination. They are *not* the result of actual language structure because we do not know how the knowledge a speaker uses is structured. Often the devices in a dictionary coincide with those which must exist in a speaker's head. This is truest of "idioms" and bound phrases. A speaker of English must know that only *eggs* and a few words for brain matter can cooccur with *addled*. In many cases, however, these devices are wrong, wrongest in the cases of, in both Hebrew and English, the "super-verbs" which express such a variety of notions that they resist any available calculus. No simple entry for verbs like *ntn* 'to give,' *śym* 'to set,' and *ᶜśy* 'to do,' will ever be adequate to all their uses. In these instances, a working dictionary has to rely on a variety of devices: lists, arbitrary categories, tangential relations, and so on. Similarly, Dahood's lists are bound by his restrictions of them and by facts of attestation.

It is a sign of vitality when research outstrips hypothesis formation as vastly as Dahood's work on dyading has done; his critics have frequently remarked that Dahood's approaches show signs of confusion. We hope to have said enough to suggest that, though they are in part right, the confusion is a token of astonishing vitality. A further approach to dyads, foreshadowed for Hebrew by Kaddari (1973), is suggested by Fox who notes that "an element or word [in Rotinese verse] may form a pair with more than one other element. Most elements are not confined to a single fixed dyadic set but rather have a variable range of other elements with which they form acceptable sets" (1974: 76). He suggests that underlying all poetic expression is "a stable network of semantic elements whose inter-relations can be formally represented." He lays out the portion of the network involving *fada* 'to speak' and refers to more networks in a forthcoming "dictionary" of ritual language. (His estimate of the number of dyadic sets needed for basic chanting is 1,000-1,500. The numerical range is not far from the lower limit of the range Dahood has treated. It may be that we have enough Hebrew and Ugaritic verse to approximate the competence of an ordinary Canaanite poet, though we cannot imagine what ordinary could mean here.)

Our subject, however, is not parallelism. The range of phenomena we have delineated characterizes the texture of Hebrew verse but not all of them contribute to its structure. Only the phenomena at the two extreme ends of the range do so; these are the word-level tropes and together they are involved in the structure of about one-third of the lines of the corpus. The range extends from words which form a dyad because of some marked similarity, to those which form a dyad despite a marked lack of similarity. Most of the range is fluid and ill-defined as to source and structure; the dyads are derived from every facet of language and are involved in all its various complexities.

The two extremes of the range are clearly definable in source and structure. At the end involving likeness, there is absolute likeness, repetition, with source and structure as elementary as language allows. At the opposite end, we find difference: the members of dyads which are not intrinsically similar but actually different parts of a single phrase. This is the phenomenon described by Melamed (1961); we shall replace Melamed's term, "the breakup of stereotyped phrases," with a term from the language of poetic description, colorations, and continue recent efforts to categorize the colors.

### *1.5.3 The word-level trope of repetition*

Students of "parallel pairs" in Canaanite verse have generally resisted considering the use of one word twice over as the same sort of phenomenon as other sorts of parallels. This reflects a general and correct intuition of the fact that simple repetition in everyday language is generally forbidden. Thus, of the following sentences, the third is not related to the first as the second is, and the similarity in sense of the last three cannot be expressed in any simple way.

John talked.
John talked and read.
John talked and talked.
John talked and talked and talked.
John talked a lot.

We need not try to describe the structure of these repetitions here; we need only note that the repetition contributes to the meaning in a special way. In cases in which no contribution can be made, repetition is forbidden.

Repetition is unusual among the dyads in drawing together two words which are identical; the importance of repetition among the Hebrew dyads has long been recognized, notably by Albright (1969); despite the essentially accurate strictures of Mendenhall (1975: 63-64), Albright's study remains important.

There are two phenomena associated with each other and with repetition we wish to distinguish. First, "it is essential to distinguish repetitive parallelism from paronomasia" (Andersen 1966: 108); we exclude the latter entirely from the realm of troping. We also separate from repetition the *figura etymologica*, viz., the use within a definable distance of two words from the same root. The difference between the two last can be made precise: repetition involves the same lexeme, performing the same syntactic function whether singular or plural, suffixed or not, if a noun, in construct or not, and if a verb, no matter how inflected within a verbal theme or form; *figura etymologica* covers all other cases, notably the use of two verbal roots in different stems (Held 1965a). The *figurae etymologicae* do not belong with the structural device of repetition. *Figurae* that involve variant themes occur in part because "synonyms of verbs [i.e., dyads of verbs] are relatively rare," as Held notes (1965a), but it is not clear that *figurae* take up any structural slack. The rarity of verb dyads results from the fact that in all languages that distinguish nouns and verbs, the noun class is larger and more flexible (Jakobson 1963: 273-74). The facts regarding the *figura* are set out in detail in Chapter 4, along with all examples of the repetition trope.

Repetition is the only trope which seems to be non-local in manifestation, i.e., to involve lines not directly contiguous, and we shall treat non-local repetitions over small distances as being of a piece with cases involving contiguous lines. There is some evidence this treatment requires further nuancing; see Chapter 10.

In considering repetition we treat first simple repetition, with regard to the relative positions of the repetitions, their extent in relation to the constituents of which they are a part, and the character of the constituents (4.1). In Psalm 106, there is an example of simple repetition in which the repetition involves parts of two identically positioned noun phrases.

Ps 106:10a *wywšyᶜm myd-śwnᵓ*
106:10b *wygᵓlm myd-ᵓwyb*

106:10a He-saved-them from-the-power-of-the-one-who-hated-[them].
106:10b He-redeemed-them from-the-power-of-the-enemy.

In the other case of simple repetition, the constituents are clause predicator infinitives.

Ps 106:26b *lhpyl ᵓwtm bmdbr*
106:27a *wlhpyl zrᶜm bgwym*

106:26b To-fell them in-the-steppe
106:27a To-fell their-seed among-the-nations

There are cases in which simple repetitions cooccur in the same lines, and a few in which they interlock across a group of lines (viz., a repetition occurs in lines 1 and 2 of 3 lines; another occurs in lines 2 and 3). Cases of the *figura etymologica* are treated along with a few cases in which the repetition trope is blocked by the fact that the repeated words have different grammatical functions; these are mostly proper nouns (4.2).

Repetitions which extend over non-contiguous lines are usually founded on the common ground of other, local repetitions (4.3). Several complex examples appear in Psalm 106:37-38d.

Ps 106:37 *wyzbḥw ᵓt-bnyhm-wᵓt-bnwtyhm lšdym*
106:38a *wyšpkw dm-nqy*
106:38b *dm-bnyhm-wbnwtyhm*
106:38c *ᵓšr zbḥw lᶜṣby-knᶜn*
106:38d *wtḥnp hᵓrṣ bdmym*

106:37 They-sacrificed their-sons-and-their daughters to-demons.
106:38a They-poured-out innocent-blood,

106:38b The-blood-of-their-sons-and-their-daughters,
106:38c Whom they-sacrificed to Canaanite-idols.
106:38d The-land was-polluted with-blood.

There is a simple repetition of *dm* 'blood' in 38a and 38b; 38a is the common ground which supports the repetition in 37 and 38b of (ʾ*t*)-*bnyhm-w*(ʾ*t*)-*bnwtyhm* 'their sons and their daughters.' Together 38ab are the common ground for the repetition of the forms of *zbḥ* 'to sacrifice' in 37 and 38c; and 38c is the common ground for the repetition of *dm* in 38b and 38d. The noun *dm* in 38ab refers to the children's living blood, so it is singular (for the "natural" state of a mass noun); in 38d, it is no longer their blood at all but the land's pollution, so the noun is plural (the "unnatural" state of a mass noun, "spilt blood"). The scheme of repetitions is as follows, using *bn* 'son,' for the long noun phrase.

| | | | |
|---|---|---|---|
| 37 | | *bn* | *zbḥ* |
| 38a | *dm* | | |
| b | *dm* | *bn* | |
| c | | | *zbḥ* |
| d | *dm* | | |

The reader will have noticed the unusual length of 37; there are examples below in which this apparent problem does not arise. This particular passage is often emended, not only for reasons of grammar; ample examples below show it is not anomalous in usage.

There are repetitions separated by no more than two lines neither of which contains a repetition itself: these are repetitions without common ground (4.4). There is an example in Psalm 106.

Ps 106:7c *wymrw ʿly-m bym-swp*
106:8a *wywšyʿm lmʿn-šmw*
106:8b *lhwdyʿ ʾt-gbwrtw*
106:9a *wygʿr bym-swp wyḥrb*

106:7c They-rebelled against-ʿEly at-the-Reed-Sea.
106:8a He-saved-them for-the-sake-of-his-name
106:8b To-reveal his-strength.
106:9a He-rebuked the-Reed-Sea and-it-dried-up.

Here the repetitions are separated by two lines; more often only one line separates them.

In summing up Chapter 4, we report on patterns in which repetitions are grouped together (4.5) and on the overall usage of repetitions in the texts (4.6).

### *1.5.4 The word-level tropes of coloration: binomination, coordination, and combination*

At the opposite extreme of the range of dyading from repetition is a group of phenomena first recognized by Melamed (1961) under the title the breakup of stereotyped phrases and since discussed widely (see, e.g., Auffret 1977, Dahood 1976b, Dahood and Penar 1970, 1972, Freedman 1970, 1971c, 1973, Gefter 1977, Gevirtz 1975, Kselman 1977; the work is negatively treated in Whitley 1975). These we shall group together as the tropes of coloration; we shall distinguish three subgroups (Chapter 5). In each trope, words which constitute a single phrase in ordinary language are split apart and the parts are set in "parallel" slots. In binomination, the phrase is a single name; in coordination, it is a pair of words; and in combination, it is a phrase with construct or adjectival modification. There are some cases in which there are not enough attestations of the putative phrase to allow us to be sure about the trope; nonetheless, there are more than enough certain cases for us to proceed. (These usages could be illumined further by the study of polar pairs in other languages.)

An interesting feature of the color tropes is that they correspond to a group of rhetorical figures known in Chinese as *hu wen*. These are structurally more complex and diverse than the Hebrew examples, although binomination is not among them. A good exposition of *hu wen* is given by Frankel (1976: 144-85). (The Greek figure of enallage, the transfer of an adjective from a genitive to its noun, may also be related.)

The most readily comprehensible cases of coloration involve the binomination of numina, as we call minor deities, in Ugaritic. Among these deities is *qdš-wamrr*, 'Holy-and-Strong,' who like other numina is sometimes one and sometimes two, *qdš* and *amrr*, according to the grammar of the texts. Grammar is not a reliable guide to problems of divine identity and we can welcome iconic confirmation of the numen's multiple identity. If Pope's identification of the scene on the El-Ašerah Drinking Mug excavated in the twenty-fourth campaign at Ras Shamra with an epical passage is correct (1971), then we have evidence that the representation of the numen, like his name, could be split in half. The phenomenon of binomination is much more general, but confirmations in the Levantine sphere are not likely to be common. Gathering cases of similar phenomena from traditions richer in the visual arts seems necessary. We have found only one. The Chinese charioteer of the sun god, Hsi Ho, 'Brightness-Harmony,' often a unitary figure (Hawkes 1959: 28, 49), is sometimes represented as two gods, Hsi and Ho (Needham and Wang 1965: 572, pl. 704a); we do not know why Hsi Ho split in two or fused into one (cf. Legge 1960: 18-22, 162-66; Needham and Wang 1959: 168-88), although there are grounds to suspect binomination. For a Russian example, see Jakobson (1966: 427).

At Ugarit, only one of the high gods has a binome, *kṯʿr-wḫss* 'Clever-and-Wise,' which is overwhelmingly preferred to his unitary name *hyn* 'Skillful.' All these names are taken by scholars to be transparent etymologically, but they are not clearly separable from opaque names. The high god of Israel has a great variety of names, epithets, and binomes (5.1.1). We shall sidestep the issue of discriminating among these as much as possible, taking most binomes of the god of Israel as consisting of a name and an epithet. There are no cases of divine binomination in Psalm 106; the Oracles of Balaam furnish a convenient example.

Num 23:8a *mh-ʾqb lʾ-qbh-ʾl*
23:8b *wmh-ʾzʿm lʾ-zʿm-yhwh*

23:8a I-cannot-curse what-the-god-has-not-cursed.
23:8b I-cannot-damn what-Yahweh-has-not-damned.

The binome here is *ʾl-yhwh* 'the god Yahweh.' Numinous binomination is so infrequent in Hebrew we need not dwell on it (5.1.2).

Other namables can have binomes, too: people, places and social groups. Personal binomination generally involves either titles or patronymics (which we suspect are often titles) (5.1.3). Thus in Num 23:7ab, Balaam addresses his patron as *blq mlk-mwʾb* 'Balaq, King of Moab,' splitting name and title across the lines; later on, in Num 23:18ab, Balaam invokes *blq bnw-ṣpr* 'Balaq, Sippor's child,' splitting name and patronymic. The personal binome par excellence in Hebrew is the eponym, Jacob-Israel, which is transmuted into the commonest binome for a social organization. Balaam calls Moses' followers *yʿqb-yśrʾl* half-a-dozen times, as in this example.

Num 23:23a *ky-lʾ-nḥš byʿqb*
23:23b *wlʾ-qsm byśrʾl*

23:23a No-one-can-curse Jacob.
23:23b No-one-can-hex Israel.

Other organizational binomes occur (5.1.4) and the not dissimilar phenomenon of geographical binomination (5.1.5) is exemplified along with what may be an organizational binome in these lines.

Zph 2:9d *ky-mwʾb ksdm thyh*
2:9e *wbny-ʿmwn kʿmrh*

2:9d Moab will be like Sodom.
2:9e The Ammonites will be like Gomorrah.

The two organizations mentioned may be meant here as a common transjordanian enemy. At any rate, the two cities of the plain are not meant in particular; rather the common fate of both and of the pentapolis they were leading parts of is alluded to.

The trope of coordination (5.2) can involve names, too. In these cases, the names designate not one individual but the two parts of a basic pair. In the theological framework of Psalm 106, for example, the two founders of Israelite religion are treated as such a pair.

Ps 106:16a *wyqnʾw lmšh bmḥnh*
106:16b *lʾhrn qdwš-yhwh*

106:16a They-vexed Moses in-the-camp.
106:16b [They-vexed] Aaron. . . .

(We shall discuss the omitted words presently.) The pair Moses and Aaron constitute a particularly clear case in which coloration must be distinguished from "parallelism." No matter how strenuously it might be argued that it is meaningful to say that *mwʾb* 'Moab' and *bny-ʿmwn* 'the-Ammonites' are "really" "synonymous," no one will argue that Moses is "really" Aaron. It may be that the *yd-ymyn* '[left] hand-right hand' dyad belongs in this group (see the essays of Needham 1973, especially Chelhod 1973); for the moment we include only names among simple pairs (5.2.1).

Other pairs can be separated from simple ones in that they do not exhaust the class of phenomena they refer to. When Moses and Aaron are mentioned, that is, they form a simple pair and Miriam is nowhere lurking nearby. When *hšmym* 'heavens' and *hʾrṣ* 'earth' are invoked, they stand for all that is between by merismus; there are other such pairs (5.2.2). Related pairs serve as emblems of a class, as *ṣʾn* 'small livestock' and *bqr* 'large livestock' stand for the class of domesticated animals (5.2.3). The phenomenon of "numerical parallelism," in which 'one' parallels 'two,' 'seven' parallels 'eight' and so on, is treated as a variety of coordination (5.2.4).

The largest class of color tropes is combination (5.3) and of these most examples involve the rupture of the construct relation. A simple construct combination occurs in Psalm 106.

Ps 106:5a *lrʾwt bṭwbt-bḥyryk*
106:5b *lśmḥ bśmḥt-gwyk*

106:5a To-enjoy the-goodness-of . . .
106:5b To-rejoice in-the-rejoicing-of . . .

The combination is *bḥyry-gwyk* 'the chosen of your people'; the terms are not "synonymous" in any sense, although they have, in defiance of much evidence, been treated as such. A comparable case occurs later in the poem.

Ps 106:43b *whmh ymrw bʿṣtm*
106:43c *wymkw bʿwnm*

106:43b They rebelled . . .
106:43c They-grew-low . . .

Here the circumstances of the action are unitary: *bʿṣt-ʿwnm* 'in-their-counsel-of-iniquity.' It is not that the rebellion is the result of counsel and the sinking, the result of iniquity; or, *horribile contemplatu*, that the nomina are "synonymous" and that all counsel is iniquity. (In these cases we seek to be clear in glossing the examples but nothing more; we do not wish to discuss how these aspects of grammar should be represented in translation.)

A more complex combination occurs in two lines of Psalm 106 already cited.

Ps 106:16a *wyqnʾw lmšh bmḥnh*
106:16b *lʾhrn qdwš-yhwh*

106:16a They-vexed Moses . . .
106:16b They-vexed Aaron . . .

The locale of the vexing is *bmḥnt-qdwš-yhwh* 'in the camp of the shrine of Yahweh'; traditionally *qdwš-yhwh* has been taken as a title for Aaron 'the-holy-one-of-Yahweh' but this is improbably exalted. On the failure to mark the second part of the locale, see below (1.5.7). The varieties of construct combination are fully described below (5.3.1-5.3.5).

There are other syntactic relations which can be violated by combination. An example of adjectival combination (5.3.6) occurs in 2 Samuel 1.

2 S 1:20c *pn-tśmḥnh bnwt-plštym*
1:20d *pn-tʿlznh bnwt-hʿrlym*

1:20c lest-the-women-of . . . rejoice,
1:20d lest-the-women-of . . . exult.

The women meant are not the "daughters" of all uncircumcised, viz., foreign males, but of *[h]plštym-hʿrlym* 'the uncircumcised Philistines.' Appositional combination most closely approximates ordinary dyading (5.3.7). Appositional and adjectival combination can interlock (5.3.8). After a survey of the occurrences of all combinations (5.3.9), in which we show that Kiparsky's Rule holds true of the more complex examples, we consider all color troping patterns of interlocking and cooccurrence (5.4). Finally, we summarize the extent of the color tropes and the word-level tropes (5.6).

### *1.5.5 Syntax, word order, harmonics, and iconics*

The next level of troping involves whole lines and study of it requires that we attend not to individual constituents but to their interrelation. Unlike word-level troping, the materia of this troping level have long been associated with artful use of language. We noted earlier that not only was phrasal mixing important in Latin verse, but that classical rhetoric recognized the phenomenon under the term hyperbaton. Indeed, ancient rhetorical study recognized many nuances of word order regulation and they were a particular concern of Latin prose writers, notably Cicero. The loose word order of languages like Latin is a basic element of style because it is so available for authorial control (Friedrich 1975: 52-58). The best known joke on such preoccupations occurs in the love letter scene of Molière's *Le Bourgeois gentilhomme* (2.6; 1856: 553).

Since we are not concerned with love letters and are unencumbered by *Latinitas*, we can turn to recent study, which has evolved from a postulate stated by Jakobson.

> There is an inventory of simple relations common to all tongues of the world. . . . [There also exist] implicational rules which set a compulsory connection between two different relational properties of languages (1963: 265).

Current study of these relations and implications derives from a paper by Greenberg (1963b), which distinguishes the factors associated with the traditional separation of *regens-rectus* and *rectus-regens* languages. In describing the effort, we will draw on some of the enormous amount of work done since, especially Lehmann (1972) and Friedrich (1975); the last named provides a thorough and exemplary study of Homeric Greek while attending to theoretical considerations.

In *regens-rectus* languages, the governing or modifying element comes before the governed or modified element; among these languages are most Western Indo-European and West Semitic languages. In these languages basically verbs precede objects, nouns precede descriptive adjectives, possessed things precede their possessors (or "genitives"; English *the book of Kathy*), the particles of relation precede the things related (and are thus prepositions), the verb or adjective precedes the pivot and standard in comparative constructions, the noun stands before its relative clause; and in general complements and embeddings follow the verb or noun they accompany.

The modified-modifier languages include most of the Eastern Indo-European languages (Iranian and Indian languages, Armenian), Turkish, and Japanese. In these, basically the opposite relations hold: objects precede verbs, descriptive adjectives precede nouns, possessors ("genitives") precede the things possessed (English *Kathy's book*), the things related are followed by the relators (which are thus postpositions), the standard precedes the pivot and the adjective (or verb) in comparatives, relative clauses stand before the nouns they modify; and in general complements and embeddings precede the verb or noun they modify.

These two trends are only trends; it is not the case that the languages of the world simply run in opposite directions. We noted above, for example, that English uses both possessive constructions. (On English, see further McCawley 1970.) Classical Latin and Greek are in general ambivalent (Friedrich 1975: 52-58). Although most Western Indo-European languages are basically *regens-rectus* or verb-object languages, the three northern European families (Baltic, Slavic, and Germanic) all have some object-verb characteristics (witness the verb in Modern German relative clauses). Despite the complexities, the various factors involved can be separated and correlated with other linguistic features: modifier-modified languages tend to have prefixing morphology, for example, while suffixing morphology is associated with modified-modifier languages.

Sorting out the intermediate types of languages involves distinguishing harmonic and iconic relations (Jakobson 1963: 269-70). Harmonic relations involve the elements of syntax and most relations listed above are harmonic to varying degrees. Iconic relations involve the perception of the whole syntactic unit in relation to the rest of discourse; although there are two basic harmonic sets, there is only one basic and clear iconic relation: an utterance proceeds from topic to comment. Greenberg conceived of iconics more broadly, as related to the fact that "the order of elements in language parallels that in physical experience or the order of knowledge" (1963b: 103) and, while Friedrich is right in urging the need for a larger conception of syntactic gestalt (1975: 71), topic-comment order is the chief phenomenon involved.

The distinction between harmonic and iconic relations is difficult to be precise about. One feature of grammatical structure that seems largely iconic is subject position. Insofar as subject corresponds to topic and the rest of an utterance to comment on that topic, subject priority is an iconic universal. This can be combined with the harmonic order verb-object in two ways: subject priority can cede to verb priority (within the comment), yielding VSO languages; or it can usurp verb priority, yielding SVO languages, by far the larger of the two groups. Greenberg suggested that relator particles are in part tied to harmonic factors and in part to iconic factors. In *regens-rectus* languages, the particle's priority as iconic topic agrees with its priority as modifier and so most of these languages have prepositions. In *rectus-regens* languages, the orderings conflict and so some verb final languages have prepositions (agreeing with the iconic order) and some have postpositions (agreeing with the harmonic order).

We are largely concerned with harmonic factors. Greenberg studied in his original sample a wide variety of languages with regard to a few harmonic factors. He characterized a language type with regard to verb-subject-object positions (since he treated subject position as a harmonic feature); the positions of relator-particles; genitives; and descriptive adjectives (i.e., most adjectives, except for articles, numerals and quantifiers). There is a fairly small group of languages which are simply *regens-rectus* on these terms, i.e., which are VSO, with prepositions, nouns before genitives, and nouns before descriptive adjectives. It includes most of the northern Afroasiatic languages, Celtic, and some languages of Central and

East Africa, Northwest America, Mexico and Polynesia (Friedrich 1975: 58-59). These languages cluster together in more discrete groups than most of Greenberg's other types, which tend to scatter geographically and genetically (Friedrich 1975: 66, n. 36).

Since we shall refer below to the Afroasiatic family, we can review the relevant, northern branches; Egyptian, Berber and most of the West Semitic languages fit the pattern cited. East Semitic, viz., Akkadian, while it shares prepositions, genitive-second and adjective-second constructions, has the order SOV. This is traditionally associated with the presence of Sumerian, an SOV language, in the region. While it is true that languages can change word order through contact, the base of the traditional explanation is probably smaller than it need be. Iraq should be conceived of as an interface between the great VSO region of the Levant and North Africa and the equally large SOV region of Iran and India. Not only is Sumerian an SOV language; so are the other ancient languages of the region: those to the East, Elamite and the Persian languages; and those to the North, Hurrian and Urartian. The region has not changed: essentially all the Persian languages and the languages of India, whether Indo-European (Hindi and Urdu), Mon-Khymer (the Munda group), or Dravidian (and thus descendants of ancient Elamite's parent language), are SOV. The pressures involved in Akkadian's switch away from the "family" pattern are strong; we cite them here as preliminaries to an argument regarding greater strength below.

The other Semitic "family" exceptions are geographically marginal. Neo-Syriac, which has moved east and north out of the region, differs in being an SVO language. The Ethiopic languages are prepositional but SOV with variations within the group and within the individual languages with regard to genitive and descriptive adjective constructions (see Hopper 1971).

Having considered these preliminaries to syntactic generalization, we can turn again to the welter of phenomena traditionally called parallelism. In particular we will consider features common to whole lines, primarily those determined by harmonic behavior. We shall not be directly concerned with variations from harmonic order; we have no simple explicit treatment of Hebrew word order.

### *1.5.6 The line-level trope of matching*

Like dyading, the use of syntactically corresponding units pervades language. The commonest examples involve simple question and answer discourse, in which answers are constructed in the same shape as the question, and then simplified before pronunciation by the deletion of all the duplicate material. The character of simplification appears whenever it is forbidden. Answers are often not simplified for "extra-linguistic" reasons; thus the question *Have you read the works of Harris?* can be appropriately answered *Yes, I have read the works of Harris* in addressing a child or a foreigner, or to express anger or pretension. Otherwise, the answer is simplified to *Yes*. If the answer is *Yes, I have read the works of Harris, completely, twice*, it is simplified to *Yes, completely, twice*. Simplification can also be avoided for purely syntactic reasons, to avoid confusion over the scope of quantifiers and negatives (*Yes, we have no bananas*), and over presuppositions (*No, I do not now nor have I ever beaten my lover*, to continue with an earlier example). There are intermediate cases, in which part of the simplification is blocked, while what is left of the matching part of the answer is stressed differently from the question.

Matching of this sort is crucial in many other realms of language use, notably poetry; this is the phenomenon most widely referred to as parallelism. The fact that it is not consistently distinguished from dyadic behavior has led to great confusion which obscures the nature of both phenomena. The implicit contention of received treatments is that the two always cooccur. On the laxest conceivable definitions this is false for Hebrew. The contention that the two *tend* to cooccur is true. In the parallelism of Chinese Regulated Verse they must cooccur, but absolute cooccurence is required only in Regulated Verse even in Chinese; other verse forms that use parallelism are not so consistently restrained. Recall, too, that Classical Chinese is a largely monosyllabic language in which token for token correspondence is liable to be plain, especially in verse, which largely forbids the use of particles. On the other hand, Kiparsky (1974) discusses parallelism in some modern English language poetry; there is rather little dyadic behavior in the examples. Between the limits of Chinese Regulated Verse, in which dyading and matching must cooccur, and that of modern written European verse, in which the two rarely do so, there is great latitude.

The Regulated Verse matching involves the lowest level of the syntactic tree: all the bottommost nodes must be identical and in the same order. In much looser parallelistic systems, the level of the tree can be higher, or the identity factors can be more broadly defined. In Finnish, the constituents (but not units) must correspond; their order is free, and certain elements can be omitted. The trope of matching in Hebrew is similar. Matching does not involve all lines which could be regarded as "parallelistic," but only a subgroup, just as repetition and coloration involve only some varieties of dyading. Lines match in Hebrew if their syntactic structures are identical: that is, if they are embedded to the same degree and they contain the same constituents. (We shall qualify the definition in 1.5.7.)

This trope is similar to the trope of repetition on an abstract level. Because of the degree of abstraction, the trope is harder to distinguish from the line-level equivalent of other dyads. Only Gordon has systematically commented on matches (1965: 138-44).

Most matching line groups are independent clauses. Word order is freest in these and most liable to manipulation. These facts are corollaries of a general syntactic principle called by Ross the Penthouse Principle: "Any rule that can operate in embedded contexts can also operate in unembedded ones, but not conversely" (1975: 248 and refs.). Of the nine sets of matching lines in Psalm 106, five involve independent clauses, three embedded clauses and only one involves phrases. None involves double clause lines.

Independent matching lines are usually two in number (6.1); they can involve two or three constituents, rarely more, showing that Kiparsky's Rule is at work here, too. We have already cited the 2-constituent line match of Ps 106:10ab, in which both lines have the order VP; in that case, the units as well as constituents match. A similar case is the following, in which the order is VO.

Ps 106:35b *wylmdw mʿśyhm*
106:36a *wyʿbdw ʾt-ʿṣbyhm*

106:35b They-learned their-customs.
106:36a They-worshipped their-idols.

These two lines do not match the previous line, Ps 106:35a, or the following line, Ps 106:36b. The first has the order VP and the last, VPP. The four lines have in common that they are all Class I lines, but the middle two of the four differ from the others in having identical constituent structures. These examples are similar in line length and unit structure. In some cases, e.g., Ps 106:23ab, the second factor varies and the first consequently does so, too; nonetheless the lines match.

There are matches of more than two lines (6.2-6.4). In one of the two 4-line matches in Psalm 106, the constituent order is constant, and the unit makeup varies.

Ps 106:24a *wymʾsw bʾrṣ-ḥmdh*
106:24b *lʾ-hʾmynw ldbrw*
106:25a *wyrgnw bʾhlyhm*
106:25b *lʾ-šmʿw bqwl-yhwh*

106:24a They-spurned-[him] in-the-desirable-land.
106:24b They-did-not-believe in-his-word.
106:25a They-murmured in-their-tents.
106:25b They-did-not-listen to-Yahweh's-voice.

All the lines have the structure VP; variety is created by the use of different prepositions (*b* in all the lines except 24b) and of different unit structures (2-unit object in 24a and 25b, 1-unit object in 24b and 25a). Greater variety is shown in the other 4-line match, in which constituent order varies.

Ps 106:14a *wytʾww tʾwh bmdbr*
106:14b *wynsw ʾl byšymwn*
106:15a *wytn lhm šʾltm*
106:15b *wyšlḥ rzwn bnpšm*

106:14a They-lusted a-desire in-the-steppe
106:14b They-tested El in-the-waste.
106:15a He-gave them what-they-asked for.
106:15b He-sent the-gnawing from-their-throats.

Here the use of the order VOP is broken by the third line, which is VPO; the match is continuous.

The three matches of embedded clauses in Psalm 106 all involve infinitive clauses; one example, 5ab, we have cited for its combination, and the other, 26bc, we have noted for its repetition. The last has two different unit structures.

Ps 106:47c *lhdwt lšm-qdšk*
106:47d *lhštbḥ bthltk*

106:47c To-give-praise to-your-holy-name
106:47b To-laud-[you] for-your-triumphs

There are other types of embedded clauses in matches. The only phrasal lines in Psalm 106 that match contain two constituents.

Ps 106:22a *nplʾwt bʾrṣ-ḥm*
106:22b *nwrʾwt ʿl-ym-swp*

106:22a Wonders in-the-land-of-Ham
106:22b Terrors near-the-Reed-Sea

There are lines of one constituent arranged so that matching is possible, but we have not treated all of them as matching. We suppose rather that 1-constituent lines match only if their unit structures match; this covers the bulk of relevant examples, but may be too strong a treatment. It requires effectively that matching is a cyclical process, which if it fails to find any tree structure above the constituent level within the lines, reapplies on the lower, unit level.

Another difficulty with matching involves the tiny class of words which serve adverbial roles. We distinguish these from direct objects and this procedure accords with our data; no matches involving only a difference of A and O are possible. The approach violates the canons of traditional Semitic grammar (i.e., of Arabic and Akkadian grammar), according to which all unmediated non-subject roles are grouped together with the prime unmediated non-subject role, the direct object.

## *1.5.7 The line-level trope of gapping*

One important consequence of matching which we only hinted at above is the fact that simplification (like that associated with questions and answers) can take place within a single utterance. The variety of simplification allowed is enormous, and traditional treatments which gather all the types under the single heading of ellipsis rarely do justice to them.

One variety of ellipsis, which we shall call blitz, removes the common term of a comparison at its second occurrence; it changes the first of the following sentences to the second.

May my future be like his future.
May my future be like his.

Blitz is a feature of ordinary Hebrew grammar; it is because the preposition *k* so often governs blitz that nineteenth-century grammarians, attributing the properties that result from the syntactic operation to the particle itself, regarded *k* as a noun of relation. Consider these sentences, glosses of the English sentences above.

**thy* ʾḥryty kʾḥrytw*
**thy* ʾḥryty kmw*

Neither is attested but both are entirely grammatical; the second is, in fact, identical to the poetic line Num 23:10d, except that the poetic version uses the pronominal form *kmhw*. The fact that this is a poetic line is irrelevant; *k* works the same way in prose.

Other varieties of ellipsis are known and many involve major segments of clauses. Consider these sentences.

The alarm rings at 6:00 and we wake up at 6:00.
The alarm rings at 6:00 and we wake up.
The alarm rings and we wake up at 6:00.

This sort of ellipsis, involving the arguments of predicates, called conjunction reduction, is not only ordinary in English (Hudson 1974), but in Hebrew. Arguments other than time expressions can be involved in English, e.g., subjects.

Hannah sang and Hannah prayed.
Hannah sang and prayed.

Conjunction reduction of this sort is largely unknown in Hebrew because verb forms are intrinsically marked for person, and the deletion of the subject in the comparable Hebrew second clause would not leave an ungrammatical unit (like **prayed* in English), but a complete clause, *ttpll*, marked for subject.

The occurrence of these varieties of ellipsis in English and Hebrew is not surprising. Further, "all languages have coordination of full sentences or clauses and . . . all have SOME type of reduced, or elliptical coordinations as well" (Sanders 1976: 1). There is another variety of ellipsis which does concern us in poetic study; it can be seen in the following sentences.

> Balaq brought me from Aram; the king of Moab brought me from the Eastern Hills.
>
> Balaq brought me from Aram, the king of Moab from the Eastern Hills.

This process, dubbed gapping by Ross (1970a, Thráinsson 1975), involves the removal of the verb of the second clause, provided it is identical to that of the first. It is an ordinary operation of English grammar; it reflects the character of English as a *regens-rectus* language: the gapping goes in the direction away from the *regens*. Verb gapping in *rectus-regens* languages like Japanese goes in the opposite direction. The English direction is called (in blithely chauvinist fashion) rightward; the Japanese direction is leftward.

Ross (1970a) has made some strong predictions about the varieties of gapping found in the languages of the world and thus stimulated a diversity of research. Sanders (1976) has summarized and extended these studies in a general typology of conjunction reduction and gapping. Given two 3-unit matching sentences containing a predicator and two arguments, there are six possible reductions; the verb and arguments occur in the basic order for the language and for the sake of comparison can be given arbitrary labels, A-F; the reduced term is in lower case.

| | |
|---|---|
| a BC and DEF | reduction A |
| AbC and DEF | reduction B |
| ABc and DEF | reduction C |
| ABC and d EF | reduction D |
| ABC and DeF | reduction E |
| ABC and DEf | reduction F |

There are six language types. Type I, to which we shall return, allows only reductions D and C.

Type II allows reductions D, C, and E; among the languages of this type is English. Thus, the first four of the following sentences are good constructions in English and the last three are not; to simplify, we will use a single basic example and thus not preserve identity of sense in both conjuncts throughout.

| | |
|---|---|
| unreduced: | I saw John and you heard Kathy. |
| D reduced: | I saw John and heard Kathy. |
| C reduced: | I saw and you heard Kathy. |

E reduced: I saw John and you Kathy.
A reduced: *Saw John and you heard Kathy.
B reduced: *I John and you heard Kathy.
F reduced: *I saw John and you heard.

The reductions in Japanese, which is an SOV language, are similar; from basic SOV + SOV, three reduction types are permitted (SOV + OV, SO + SOV, and SOV + SV) and the other three are not (OV + SOV, SV + SOV, and SOV + SO). Thus in English, the scheme yields the correct prediction that the verb can be gapped on the right (*regens-rectus*) and in Japanese that it can be gapped on the left (*rectus-regens*), the E reduction in English and the C reduction in Japanese.

Type III languages, which include Quechua, allow reductions D, E, and F, but not C (cf. Pulte 1973). Type IV languages, which include Russian, allow reductions C, D, E, and F. Only the A reduction is forbidden in Type V languages, including Hindi and Urdu, and Zapotec. In the rarest type, Type VI, all reductions are permitted; the only known example of the type is Tojolabal, a Mayan language.

Before we return to Sanders Type I, let us note some features of this typology. It is not tied to the harmonics of syntax, as we have noted. Further, there seem to be "no correlating characteristics for any of the types that are independent of the given facts about elliptical coordinations in each type" (Sanders 1976: 15). Sanders is correct in remarking, "What one might . . . expect to find here, of course, is some correlation between freedom in ellipsis and rigidity in other aspects of syntax — highly-restricted word-order, well-developed systems of agreement and case-marking, etc." (p. 15); he is also correct in recognizing that the Type II cases alone are discomfiting and there is other evidence of complexities. Sanders provides a convenient summary of ellipsis types in the form of a scheme of resistance to reduction; ∅ is the least resistant, 4 the most:

ABC + DEF
4 3 1 ∅ 1 2

In general, following conjuncts are more easily ellipted than preceding ones; and reduction is easier close to the site of conjunction.

There are several features of Type I languages which reveal some further facts about the typology. Sanders cites three Type I languages: Chinese, Thai (perhaps wrongly), and Lebanese Arabic; Type I actually includes all Asiatic Semitic languages and Egyptian, with a qualification. These are Type I languages except in *Kunstsprachen*, in which they may acquire some Type II characteristics. The language particular restatement of this for Hebrew is simple: verb gapping only occurs in poetry.

Let us return to the first case of the verb gapping we noted above; the Hebrew examples render the English cases there.

**ynḥny blq mn-ʾrm wynḥny mlk-mwʾb mhrry-qdm*
Balaq brought-me from-Aram and-the-king-of-Moab brought-me from-the-Eastern-Hills.

*mn-ʾrm ynḥny blq*
*mlk-mwʾb mhrry-qdm*

Balaq brought me from Aram
The-king-of-Moab from-the-Eastern-Hills.

The first pair of sentences, though unattested, is entirely grammatical. The second would be unacceptable in prose, but it is exemplary in verse; the lines open the Oracles of Balaam.

Before we discuss the details of verb gapping in Hebrew, let us remark on some general points. Gapping does occur in other poetries but we know of no detailed studies. Kiparsky mentions it in connection with Finnish folk poetry and we noted it in the *Kalevala* example cited above. It is not common in the classical languages, despite (or perhaps because of) their free word order. Almost every clause in Homer has an overt verb (Friedrich 1975: 21-22) and the same is roughly true of later Greek and high Roman verse, to the best of our knowledge. We are not familiar with early Roman verse (before the domination of Greek models), but there is a case of gapping in one of the oldest Spoken Latin poems, a soldier's ditty which Suetonius reports was sung (quietly, one assumes) at one of Caesar's triumphs.

*Gallias Caesar subegit,*
*Nicomedes Caesarem.*

Caesar conquered the Gauls,
Nicomedes [IV of Bithynia], Caesar.

(The catch is quoted with metrical discussion in Pulgram 1975: 282-83.)

Our reference to the literary uses of gapping above may be glossed. Egyptian, Akkadian, and the Canaanite dialects use gapping in highly formal language; we suspect that all cases will turn out to be poetry but Egyptian and Akkadian verse systems are so little known that we need to qualify the claim. Some of the Egyptian facts of gapping and conjunction reduction are cited in Gardiner (1957: 397-98, 409-10), and Gordon (1965: 130) notices the similarities of Egyptian and Canaanite in this matter. There may be further discussion of gapping in the Egyptological literature; we have not been able to search it thoroughly. The Akkadian use seems not to have been treated, but is especially interesting because while all the other languages involved are VSO, Akkadian is SOV, but uses gapping along what we believe are family lines. We can quote from Akkadian a passage from a poetic text, the *Erra Epic*, which includes the longest gap we have ever seen (or heard). The hero of the poem, Erra, decrees the destruction of Akkad's enemies, in a curse which begins thus:

*tâmtim tâmtim, subartā subartū, aššurā aššurū,*
*elamā elamū, kaššā kaššū,*
*sutā sutū, gutā gutū,*
*lullubā lullubū, mātu māta, ālu āla,*
*bītu bīta, amēlum amēlum, aḫu aḫa la igammilūma.*

Sealander shall not spare Sealander, nor Subartian Subartian, nor Assyrian Assyrian,
Nor Elamite Elamite, nor Kassite Kassite,
Nor Sutian Sutian, nor Gutian Gutian,
Nor Lullubean Lullubean, nor land land, nor city city,
Nor house house, nor man man, nor brother brother.

(On the translation of *tâmtim* see Cagni 1977: 57, n. 150; for the text, *Erra* 4:131-35, see Cagni 1969: 118 and Roberts 1971-72: 15. The erratic lineation here is typical of the Akkadian "native" tradition.) Any view of the Akkadian situation will need to consider as well the situation in the other SOV "cuneiform" languages, viz., Sumerian, Elamite, Old Persian, Hurrian, Urartian; Hittite, which is also SOV, has no gapping (Friedrich 1975: 22).

There have been previous studies of gapping in Canaanite poetry, Greenstein (1974), and Sinclair (1976), which we have not seen. Greenstein notes the phenomenon of verb gapping in both Canaanite and Akkadian, though he discusses only the former. He limits his consideration to rightward gapping (1974: 91-94), though he rejects the possibility of leftward gapping too strongly, and to verb gapping, though we shall see that the term gapping can be extended. The misleading portions of his paper involve his attempt to associate the syntactic phenomenon of gapping with psycholinguistic studies. It is a fact about *regens-rectus* languages that they gap rightward but it is misleading to suggest that the human brain cannot handle gapping in the other direction. Speakers of *rectus-regens* languages gap "backwards," just as they talk "backwards," without any trouble. Greenstein has confounded facts about harmonics, which are describable grammatical phenomena, with facts about iconics, which seem to involve the grammatical implications of the human perceptual apparatus.

The mutual delimitation of gapping and conjunction reduction is difficult. Kiparsky describes Finnish gapping as covering verbs and adverbs (1974), but it seems that the latter sort of elliptical construction is better considered a type of conjunction reduction. Gapping we shall limit to ellipses which obscure the structure of one of the clauses involved (cf. Hudson 1975), creating a structure which can only be analyzed in comparison with another. There is only one variety of gapping in Hebrew which clearly fits this description on the level of clausal structure besides verb gapping. It involves the relative pronouns which introduce in prose each relative clause (save for asyndetic relative clauses which are set off by word order rearrangements); these can be gapped in poetry, creating a structure which is only recognizable as a relative clause by comparison with the previous ungapped clause (cf. Andersen 1974: 116). In other words, Hebrew only stacks relative clauses in verse (Friedrich 1975: 29).

In addition to these clausal level gappings, there are phrase level gappings which have been discussed extensively in recent literature. They have not been sorted out from examples of conjunction reduction on the clausal level. Buttenweiser (1938) calls virtually all ellipses brachyologies, recognizing the difficult particle usages among them; Dahood, who with great assiduity has tracked these usages, refers to them as double-duty particles (in e.g., Dahood and Penar 1970). Among the double-duty usages that are the result of gapping are prepositions and suffixes. Others are better considered examples of conjunction reduction. The double-duty particles which are the result of conjunction reduction are those which modify whole clauses, viz., clausal negations and emphatics.

The range of verb gapping is a problem for idiosyncratic judgments even in English. Verbs usually cannot gap over one another in English unless a clause boundary is also gapped (Ross 1967: 193). Thus the first and third sentences are grammatical (at least in some forms of American English), but the second is not.

> Tom ordered bacon, and Dick ordered lettuce, and I think Harry ordered tomatoes.
>
> *Tom ordered bacon, and Dick, lettuce, and I think that Harry tomatoes.
>
> Tom ordered bacon, and Dick, lettuce, and I think Harry tomatoes.

There are cases in Hebrew of verb gapping which cross clause boundaries, but they are few and probably as idiosyncratic in their distribution as corresponding English cases.

How are we to connect these facts about gapping with poetic structure? The gapping of constituents, chiefly verbs, is a basic feature of it; particle gapping and reductions are not. The trope of gapping involves only constituents, being of a piece with the other tropes we have discussed. Its relation to the other line-level trope, of matching, may be considered. The tropes of repetition and coloration form an opposition over the range of dyading; repetition is based on relatedness with absolute sameness and coloration on relatedness with absolute difference. On the level of lines, the equivalent of repetition is matching, which involves relatedness with absolute sameness of grammatical structure. Matching sentences are structural repetitions on the line level. Gapping is related to matching as coloration is related to repetition. The structures involved are related, i.e., largely identical, except in one facet, in which they differ in terms of absence and presence. This opposition on the descriptive level is complicated because the relatedness of gapping structures is usually complete except for the gapped item, i.e., gapped lines usually almost match. We can now amend our definition of matching: two lines match if they are identical in constituent structure except for gapped items.

On the word level, the total opposition of sameness and difference leads to totally exclusive tropes. On the line level, the same opposition leads to frequently overlapping tropes. Our treatment of the tropes as distinct requires some attention, then. It suggests first of all that matching and gapping need not cooccur; this is true. All the examples cited so far from Psalm 106 are matching but show no gapping; we shall see cases of gapping without matching below. Our treatment also suggests that the two tropes, insofar as they pattern the verse texts overall, do so independently. This is suggested by the two poems with the least gapping: Numbers 23-24, which contains only one case of gapping, in its opening lines; and Psalm 106, which also has only one case; on both these, see Chapter 10.

We may begin a brief survey of Hebrew constituent gapping by completing our treatment of matching in Psalm 106 and picking up a loose thread left behind twice above. For the fourth time, consider these lines.

Ps 106:16a *wyqnʾw lmšh bmḥnh*
106:16b *lʾhrn qdwš-yhwh*

106:16a They-vexed Moses . . .₁ in-the-camp . . . ₂
106:16b ₁. . . [and]-Aaron ₂. . . of the shrine of Yahweh.

The coordination of 'Moses and Aaron,' and the combination of 'in-the-camp-of-the-shrine-of-Yahweh,' we have noted before; *qdwš-yhwh* has lost the preposition *b* by gapping. The lines have constituent structure VPP-PP; the verb of the first line has been gapped from the second. Since matching exists irrespective of gapping, the lines match. These lines are a concise, if incomplete, guide to the first two troping levels. An example which shows no troping on the word level can be drawn from Psalm 78.

Ps 78:51a *wyk kl-bkwr bmṣrym*
78:51b *rʾšyt-ʾwnym bʾhly-ḥm*

78:51a He-killed every-first-born-child in-Egypt.
78:51b [He-killed] the-first-fruits-of-their-strength in-the-tents-of-Ham.

Here the lines have the structure VOP-OP and, because the verb is gapped from the second, they match. Constituent order in gapped matches is variable, as the next example shows.

Ps 78:47a *yhrg bbrd gpnm*
78:47b *wšqmwtm bḥnml*

78:47a He-wiped-out with-hail their-vines.
78:47b [He-wiped-out] their-sycamores with-frost.

The first line has the constituent structure VPO, while the second has OP.

An example of gapping over verbs will serve also to illustrate cases in which gapping lines do not match.

Dt 32:7c *šʾl ʾbyk wygdk*
32:7d *zqnyk wyʾmrw lk*

32:7c Ask your-father and-he-will-tell-you.
32:7d [Ask] your-elders and-they-will-speak to-you.

The imperative verb is gapped over the first narrative verb and out of the second line. The first line has the order $V_1OV_2$, while the second the order $OV_2P$. The lines have the same two clause structure and the same number of constituents and units. The second line could have read **zqnyk wyʾmrw* '[Ask] your-elders and-they-will-speak,' and still have been (as far as we can tell) idiomatic.

Compared to rightward verb gapping over two lines, other varieties of gapping are rare. Verb gapping over three lines occurs. There are two 2-line groups in which leftward verb gapping may occur; given the linguistic nature of the phenomena, Greenstein (1974) is correct in advocating rightward leanings, but since verb gapping is entrenched in the realm of art language, we allow for a slight sinistrograde tilt. Relative pronoun gapping is also infrequent; and a few cases of what may be left dislocation are recorded below under the term object gapping. The gapping and conjunction reduction of particles and suffixes is surveyed below, though these are not regarded as aspects of the trope of gapping, since particle behavior is nowhere else crucial to poetic structure.

### *1.5.8 The supralinear-level tropes*

We remarked earlier that although an immense variety of syntactic structures occurs in Hebrew verse, the clause/line correspondence dominates the verse. We took this correspondence, and the implicit correspondence of line break and syntactic break, not as absolutes, but as working bases. We effectively neutralized syntactic relations outside the line in describing the constriction. These relations play a role in verse structure, but their role is subordinate to the constriction.

The syntactic relations which we separate here are grouped under the heading of syntactic dependencies; an independent clause line and any lines dependent on it, be they clause or phrase lines, are said to be interdependent. Considering dependency as a trope suggests that syntactic relations beyond the line are less important in Hebrew verse than those that coincide with the line; this is true. The reader may find it helpful to read again the

Rotinese text quoted above, side by side with any Hebrew poem. In the Rotinese text, the units of parallelism often go beyond the line, and they do so systematically. There is only one group of similar Hebrew usages which can be characterized simply and which occurs regularly, the cases of the trope of mixing.

The two tropes of dependency and mixing involve troping on the supralinear level, i.e., they involve relations of larger scope than line-level tropes do. The opposition of sameness and difference will help us in clarifying the level and the link of the tropes on it. On the word level, repetition is the trope of sameness and is instantiated as complete identity. On the line level, matching is the trope of sameness and is instantiated as complete identity of syntactic structure in the lines. On the supralinear level, dependency is the trope of sameness and is instantiated as identity of syntactic structure beyond the line.

Thus far, the system of levels is simple; difficulties arise with the realm of related difference. On the word level, the tropes of related difference are the colors, which are polar opposites of repetition. On the line level, the trope of related difference is gapping, which overlaps significantly with matching. On the supralinear level, the trope of related difference, mixing, is a proper subtrope of dependency; that is, all cases of mixing are also cases of dependency.

Most cases of dependency involve an independent clause line and a dependent clause line. Usually they occur in that order, as in Ps 106:8ab, quoted above, or this case.

Ps 106:23b *ʿmd bprṣ lpnyw*
106:23c *lhšyb ḥmtw mhšḥyt*

106:23b He-stood in-the-breach before-him
106:23c To-turn his-anger from-destruction.

Similar constructions occur in 34ab and 44ab. Some types of dependent clauses precede: note this case with a nominal relative clause.

Ps 106:2a *my ymll gbwrwt-yhwh*
106:2b *yšmyʿ kl-thltw*

106:2a Whoever can-recite the-strengths-of-Yahweh
106:2b Let-him-make-known all-his-praise.

Longer dependent groups occur which involve dependent clauses, like the following example.

Ps 106:26a *wyśʾ ydw lhm*
106:26b *lhpyl ʾwtm bmdbr*
106:27a *wlhpyl zrʿm bgwym*
106:27b *wlzrwtm bʾrṣwt*

106:26a He-raised his-hand against-them
106:26b To-fell them in-the-steppe,
106:27a To-fell their-seed among the nations,
106:27b To-scatter-them among-the-lands.

In this example (and in the similar case of 4b 5abc), three infinitive clauses follow one independent clause line. The middle two lines in the group match; the last three lines of the other group, 5abc, also match. Within the latter match, there is a combination, in 5ab.

Phrase lines are often dependent on independent clause lines, as in Ps 106:31ab and 48ab, both two line groups with temporal expressions in the second line. In other examples, the phrase line is in apposition to the clause, as in this case.

Ps 106:20a *wymyrw ʾt-kbwdm btbnyt*
106:20b *šwr-ʾkl-ʿśb*

106:20a They-exchanged their-glory for-an-ikon,
106:20b An-ox,-an-eater-of-herbage.

In 3ab, the first line involved is an independent phrase line, and the second a phrase line dependent on it. Both phrase and clause lines can be dependent on one independent clause. In Ps 106:38abc, 38b is a noun phrase in apposition to the object of 38a and 38c is a relative clause modifying the appositive. Lines occur in the order independent clause—dependent clause—phrase in another passage from Psalm 106.

Ps 106:21a *škḥw ʾl-mwšyʿm*
106:21b *ʿśh-gdlwt bmṣrym*
106:22a *nplʾwt bʾrṣ-ḥm*
106:22b *nwrʾwt ʿl-ym-swp*

106:21a They-forgot the-god-who-saved-them,
106:21b Who-performed-great-deeds in-Egypt,
106:22a Wonders in-the-land-of-Ham
106:22b Terrors by-the-Reed-Sea.

The participial clause of 21b is in apposition to the object of 21a, and its object has two appositives, 22ab.

A vexed problem that is usually ignored is the nature of quotation in Hebrew verse; the most troublesome aspects we also ignore by not treating unmarked quotations. Explicitly marked quotations we take as a variety of syntactic dependency, as in the enemy speech of the Song at the Sea.

Ex 15:9a *ʾmr ʾwyb*
15:9b *ʾrdp ʾśyg*
15:9c *ʾḥlq šll*
15:9d *tmlʾmw npšy*

15:9e *ʾryq ḥrby*
15:9f *twryšmw ydy*

15:9a The-enemy said:
15:9b I-will-pursue. I-will-overtake.
15:9c I-will-possess spoil.
15:9d My-throat shall-be-full-of-them.
15:9e I-will-clean-off my-sword.
15:9f My-hand shall-dispossess-them.

All six lines are interdependent: 9b-f are the words of the quotation embedded under 9a. The distinguishing of signaled and unsignaled quotations is not an easy task; we shall consider some relevant criteria in Chapter 8 below. As will be seen, double embeddings under quotations are fairly common; they are otherwise unknown.

The trope of mixing involves two dependent and two independent lines which occur in sequence, in which both dependent lines depend on both independent clauses. This is the densest structural feature of Hebrew verse and it is rare. There is an example in Psalm 106.

Ps 106:47a *hwšyʿnw yhwh-ʾlhynw*
106:47b *wqbṣnw mn-hgwym*
106:47c *lhdwt lšm-qdšk*
106:47d *lhštbḥ bthltk*

106:47a Save-us, Yahweh-our-god,
106:47b Gather-us from-the-nations,
106:47c To-praise your-holy-name,
106:47d To-laud-[you] for-your-triumphs.

The infinitive clauses in 47cd modify both 47a and 47b; in other examples of mixing, the dependent lines are phrases which modify the independent clauses.

### *1.5.9 The system of tropes, the bicolon, the tricolon, and related phenomena*

The three tiered system of tropes refers to three linguistic levels: the word level, the line level, and the supralinear level. The middle level is the basic one, on which the constriction is based. The lower level refers to the domain in terms of which the line level is described and the higher level to the domain from which the line level is partitioned. The coherence of the system of levels is revealed by the fact that each level involves slightly more than one-third of the lines of the corpus, while the percentage of lines troped overall is approximately twice that. The exact statistics are presented in Chapter 10.

The coherence of the system is not only statistically but also internally evident. Conceive of two axes. Along the ordinate, we can arrange the parameters of sameness and difference over the poem as a whole. At one end of it are the features of the poem which are related to difference, which do nothing to support the coherence of the text. At the opposite end are the features that tie the whole poem together, under the aspect of which the poem is an unfragmentary organic whole. Between these extremes are the troping levels; the word level, which involves the least amounts of the text, appears toward one end of the ordinate; the supralinear level, which involves the greatest amounts, appears at the other. Thus the ordinate looks like this.

*difference over text*

word level

line level

supralinear level

*sameness over text*

The abscissa measures sameness and difference within a trope: close to the left, we record tropes that rely on sameness, and to the right those that rely on difference.

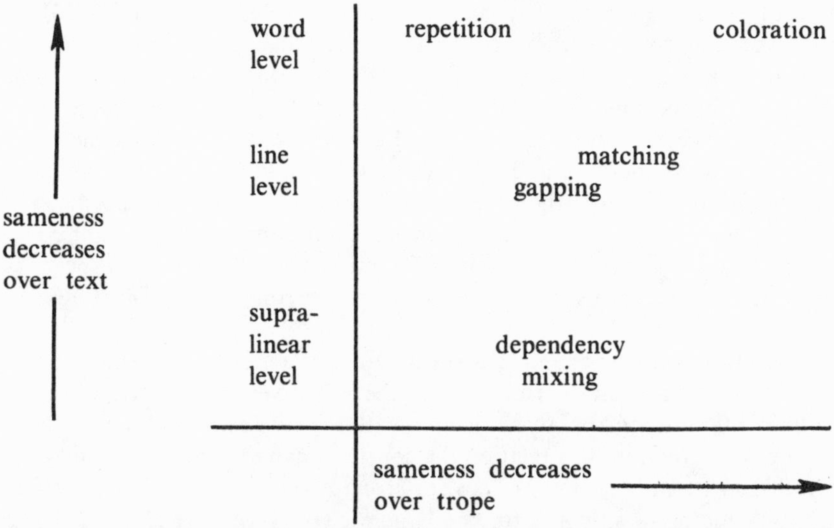


The difference in sameness of the tropes within a level is greatest on the word level: repetition and coloration stand at opposite ends of a complex range of dyads. The difference is neutralized on the supralinear level: mixing is distinguished only structurally from dependency. In the middle, there is the line level: matching and gapping overlap partially. The polarization of sameness and difference is greatest on the level of troping which involves the least amount of text.

The systemic features which we have not considered here fall into two classes: those which are derivative of the tropes, and those which are less important than the tropes. Of the structural features traditionally ascribed to Hebrew verse, the most noticeable by its absence in our description are the bicolon, and its associate, the tricolon. Our examples will have suggested the relation of the bicolon to the troping system: two line units have been regarded as basic in Hebrew because although all the tropes can extend over more than two lines, most of them extend over two lines, most of the time. The reality of the bicolon is indisputable but it has resisted characterization because it is a secondary reality and as such is not uniform. The tricolon's reality is similar: it is a byproduct of the fact that tropes extend over three lines in most cases in which they do not extend over two. We discussed above the lines Ps 106:16ab, which contain a coordination, a combination, and match, and are gapped. In cases like this one, the two line unit is plainly a focus of poetic order. Such four-fold convergence of tropes is rare. Because, however, troping is common and because it most commonly covers two lines, the bicolon emerges from the text.

The bicolon could be considered a phenomenon like a target structure, "a superficial structure in a language . . . which has distinct underlying structures mapped onto it by rules of a grammar" (Johnson 1974: 63), in this case the "poetic grammar." We can consider the notion of target structures again and in some detail. Target structures appear in all realms of language; the English indefinite article provides a simple example. This marking represents two distinct logical structures, one in which the noun phrase is both indefinite and nonspecific (*I'm looking for a tractor, but I can't find one/any*) and the other in which it is indefinite and specific (*I'm looking for a tractor but I can't find it*). To account for the grammar of *a/an*, the basic structures must be differentiated; the "collapse" in speech is the result of the status of *a/an* as a target structure in English (Peterson 1974).

A more complex example is furnished by the noun-noun relations of a number of languages. In Hebrew and the other Semitic languages, noun-noun relations are primarily associated with the construct, and there is little limitation to the kinds of relation the construct can express. The genitive in Greek and Latin is a similar focus for structure collapsing; Friedrich refers to a scheme of 78 subtypes for the Homeric Greek genitive (1975: 13) and one can easily imagine as many subtypes of the Hebrew construct. Greek and English often use descriptive adjectives where Semitic languages (as well as other Indo-European languages like Old Armenian) use descriptive noun-noun relations, e.g., *hr-qdšk* 'your holy hill.' Other target structures exist in phonology and morphology; they tend to involve fewer phenomena in more complex ways than syntactic targets. (On target structures in general, see Green 1970, Johnson 1974; in Hebrew syntax, see Andersen 1974, who calls them "deep relations.")

The "bicolon" could, then, be regarded as a target structure of poetic "grammar," with the stricture that the two line unit is a dependent and not an independent phenomenon. Armed with this qualified view of the unit, major historical and genre patterns could be studied; there are potent connections to be made in these realms.

(It would be an interesting exercise in Euroamerican intellectual history to determine the extent to which descriptions of Hebrew poetry have been influenced by notions of "Islamic" verse, i.e., the quantitative verse which originated in Arabic and spread to the principal Islamic languages, Turkish, Persian, and Urdu. There are two distinct points at issue. The first is the correct notion that every two line unit, Arb *bayt*, is entirely self-enclosed; this would support the notion of the bicolon since a *bayt* is "bicolonic." The second is the false notion that poems composed of *ᵓabyāt* are without any unity. Recent students have shown that this notion fails for Arabic, Turkish, and Persian; about Urdu, we do not know. See Abu-Deeb 1975, Andrews 1973, 1976, and Bencheikh 1975. This would require tracking what seems once to have been the most technical description deemed fitting for Oriental poetry, the cliché which when used of Arabic takes the form "orient pearls at random strung," and which for Hebrew was phrased by Herder, "pearls from the depths of the ocean loosely arranged." See Lundbom 1975: 135.)

A large category of phenomena are those which result from the cooccurrence of various tropes, or of peculiarities among the tropes. Among the latter, chiasm is most under current study (Dahood 1976a, Welch 1974). Line-level chiasm is only common among lines that match by criteria set out here; further study of it can build on the study of tropes. We consider chiasm below in classifying the examples of matching and note some features which are amenable to closer description in the context of the troping. A cognate topic is the interaction of identical roots and chiasm (Boadt 1975, Ceresko 1975, 1976); in most cases, the examples involve the cooccurrence of the tropes of repetition and matching, along with the added element of chiasm. Consideration of all these phenomena in relation to poetic structure will further study of Hebrew prose style by differentiating the structural resources and conventions of prose and verse; on the uses of chiasm in prose, see the remarks of Andersen (1974: 119-40).

We have already hinted at the treatment of compensatory or ballast variation implicit in our description (cf. Jakobson 1966: 426). Consider these lines from the Testament of Jacob.

Gen 49:10a *lʾ-yswr šbṭ myhwdh*
49:10b *wmḥqq mbyn-rglyw*
49:10c *ʿd-ky-ybʾ šy lh*
49:10d *wlw yqht-ʿmym*

The verb in 10a is gapped from 10b and the verb in 10c is gapped from 10d. The subjects of 10ab are a combination: *šbṭ mḥqq* 'the commander's rod'; and the prepositional phrases form another: *mbyn-rgly-yhwdh* 'from between Judah's feet.' (On the prepositions *m* and *mbyn*, see below.) The subjects of 10cd are a combination with coordination: *šy-ʿmym wyqht-ʿmym* 'the-tribute-of-peoples and-the-obedience-of-peoples.' The prepositional phrases in 10cd are the same. All four lines form a mix, which we can gloss: 'The-commander's-rod shall-not-depart from-between-Judah's-feet, as-long-as-there-comes-to-him the-tribute-and-obedience-of-peoples.' Lines 10ab are troped together fourfold, as are 10cd, and all four are troped together a fifth time. This is, roughly, how the lines are put together.

Consider the results if we apply a syllable counting approach. Lines 10ab are about the same length: if we delete the *w* in 10b, they are both nine syllables. But each line has a different structure and in the terms of compensatory parallelism the "lack" of a verb in 10b is ballasted by the greater length of the nominal phrases. Both these observations are descriptively accurate. In 10cd, the uniformity of length appears again: if we do not delete the *w* in 10d (or if we do, but count the *medium šwa* in *yqht*), both lines are six syllables. Again, the lines have different structures, but the length of *yqht-ʿmym* is a ballast to the shortness of *šy*, used "because" the second line is verbless. Again, the syllable counting observations describe the lines. In a stress counting system, all four lines would have a stress count of three.

Uniformity of syllable count over any considerable domain remains systemically undescribed and ballast variants do not occur with any regularity. Thus the observations describe the facts but not in a generalizable framework. In contrast, reference to the tropes describes the system of the lines entire and the operation of its parts, in a context which refers to features of the poetic structure. Perhaps most important of all, such reference does not claim to explain the structure. A basic premise of descriptions of "compensatory parallelism" is either that all lines tend to be the same length, which is so far from being true that it is useless; or that all lines tend to be the same length by pairs, which is not much more accurate. The only "explanation" that a troping description allows would refer the structure of the line group to the structure of the language. There, for example, the *regens-rectus* structure of Hebrew would dictate rightward as the prime direction of verb gapping and Panini's Law would give preference to putting the shorter part of a combination before the longer. These two features of Hebrew essentially cover the phenomena of compensatory parallelism. There is no question of anything like scientific explanation; rather we are tracing poetic forms of language features back to their origins in the language, the only possible source for them.

We need to note here that troping levels do not systematically cooccur. Aside from those cases which are inherent parts of the system, the interlocking and conjoining of tropes are not determinate features of fine structure. The richness of ballasting which we have considered, or of climactic parallelism, another variety of cooccurrence (Loewenstamm 1969, 1975b, Greenstein 1974, Avishur 1972), belong to other realms.

## *1.6 The structure, system, and texture of Hebrew verse*

In discussing the Standard Description of Hebrew, we referred rather loosely to its focus as structural. The two components of it, meter and parallelism, have generally been regarded as constituting the principal structural elements of Hebrew verse. This is meant in roughly the same sense in which we say that the principal structural element of Racinian verse is a 12-13 syllable line. The vagueness of this usage will aid us in reconsidering the vagueness of the Standard Description. Plainly, not every group of 12 or 13 syllables of French qualifies as a Racinian line. There must be certain other elements: a medial caesura, after the sixth syllable, marked by at least a word break and usually a syntactic break; and a word break and usually a syntactic break finally. Further the 12 or 13 syllables cannot be counted as ordinary units of the language, but must be reckoned on the basis of their basic phonology. Having specified these features, we can refer to the alexandrine as the principal structural element in Racine.

The sense in which the Standard Description refers to the structure of Hebrew verse is apparently this, then: there are elements which shape all of the verse, as the isosyllabism of French neo-classical verse shapes it. The next stage in the argument is crucial: insofar as it makes sense to refer only to the isosyllabism of French neo-classical lines and assume that all other features will fall in line, so it is appropriate to refer only to the major features of the Standard Description and assume that all attendant features will fall in line. This is what Lowth thought he was doing. The difficulty is that the attendant features have not fallen in line after two and a quarter centuries.

There is an apparent difference between the isosyllabic description of the French line and the Standard Description; the first contains only one component while the latter contains two. There are many two component descriptions of poetic systems; the standard line of the English poetic tradition is a good example. The term iambic pentameter stipulates a frame of 10 syllables and a modulation of unstress/stress within the frame. The frame and modulation here occur on top of one another; in Hebrew, however, the putative components of meter and parallelism occur "separately." Meter is a feature of lines and parallelism of small groups of lines, so it seems that the English analogy is imprecise.

Let us consider the alexandrine again. Is the description worked out earlier adequate? Most discussions add, with due respect for the facts, that rhyme is obligatory (e.g., Nabokov 1964: 12-13): because "a syllabic structure based on a fixed number of syllables is in itself a weaker framework than the [e.g., Germanic] stress patterns. Hence the importance in French verse of rhyme as a basic element strengthening the syllabic framework, in contrast to the auxiliary function of rhyme in English, where the stress pattern provides a sufficient framework in itself" (Flescher 1972: 177). The Racinian alexandrine is then to be defined both in terms of isosyllabism (and caesura, final break, predictable stress positions, mute *e* rules) *and* rhyme. The description contains two components, one which refers to single lines and another which refers to small numbers (in fact, usually pairs) of lines. This is the sort of description the Standard Description is meant to be.

Let us specify again the ways in which it fails, remembering that we are considering here the *shape* of the description. It fails in three ways: it does not describe the metrical component; it does not describe the parallelistic component (which corresponds to rhyme in the French example); and it does not deal with the relation of the components.

In our reformulation of the Standard Description, or more strictly, in our description of the fine structural elements of verse, we have proposed that no consensus had ever been reached in the matter of Hebrew meter because there is none. Instead, we suggest, there is a group of syntactic constraints which shape the lines of Hebrew verse. These constraints refer to three linguistic levels: the unit, the constituent, and the clause predicator. As the linguistic levels interlock, so the constraints overlap, as the following matrix shows; there are no lines of fewer than the leftmost or more than the rightmost number on any level.

| | | | | |
|---|---|---|---|---|
| Clause predicators | ∅ | 1 | 2 | 3 |
| Constituents | 1 | 2 | 3 | 4 |
| Units | 2 | 3 | 4 | 5 |

The lines of Hebrew verse do not use the resources of the matrix exhaustively. Lines which contain the rightmost number of elements on any level are extremely rare (Class IV). Further, the majority of the lines contain 1 clause predicator, and either 2 constituents (of 2 or 3 units) *or* constituents (of 3 units); these are Class I lines. All other lines fall into definable groups within the framework of the constriction. Since the constriction refers to syntactic phenomena, it can further account systematically for other syntactic features of Hebrew verse. The *sort* of description that this constitutes will be discussed further below (1.7); for the moment, it is sufficient to record that in reworking the Lowthian first component we have, as will be seen in Chapter 3, taken into account the major trends of the "native" tradition and modern research, and described a dozen hundred lines with as much explication of procedure as possible and without making non-verifiable claims about the language.

Thus far, we have the "meter" part of the Standard Description. In our recasting of the second part of the Standard Description we noted that some features usually associated with parallelism, and others related to them, admit of precise definition; we shall see, in Chapters 4-9, that the tropes occur generally in Hebrew verse. The extent of the use of the three levels varies from text to text, but overall each troping level involves one-third of the corpus and all three levels involve two-thirds of the corpus.

The two components of the Standard Description can be recast in precise terms and they will jointly describe the 1225 lines of our corpus, as the rhyming alexandrine describes Racine. The difference is that the second structural component in neo-classical verse is predictable in its occurrence, while the second component of the proposed description is not. This is not to say that the first component, the constriction, is adequate in itself; it is not. There are no appreciable segments of any of the texts treated here which are without troping; the longest untroped passage is eight lines. For Hebrew verse of the period under consideration, the two components must both be specified and they cannot be related in any simple fashion.

Let us return to the pentameter and the alexandrine, not separately, but in their union, in the Spenserian stanza. In contrast to the unending continuities of Shakespeare's blank verse and Racine's alexandrines, which can be described with regard to a single unit, a Spenserian stanza must be described with regard to a number of units. The use of pentameter and hexameter lines in a ratio of 8:1 must be described; the nonarbitrary nature of the hexameter's position in the stanza and the general correlation of rhymes need specification. Finally, the twist away from a basic three line segmentation of a nine line group merits attention; each three line segment of the stanza contains only two rhymes, but the rhyme varies across the groups and no rhyme is used the same number of times. The *a* word occurs twice, the *c* word three times, the *b* word four times: *ababbcbcc*. How are we to compare our description of the Spenserian stanza with the features of iambic pentameter or Racine's alexandrine?

Let us try to distinguish in it fine and gross structural elements. Fine elements include line lengths and rhyme. Gross elements include the position of the long line and the overall rhyme schema. Fine and gross structural elements cannot be absolutely distinguished, yet they function independently; the distinction is necessary to describe the verse, but cannot be pressed too far. It is conceivable that there exist unit forms which are less clearly defined than the Spenserian stanza but which, like it, are made up of patterned arrays of fine structural elements. Such a unit would have, say, one hexameter line to every eight pentameter lines and it would have some rhymes, but set out erratically, without the elegant schema of Spenser. We will argue in Part III that Hebrew was written in such blocks, of slightly variable length. We shall suggest that a large unit, of about 28 lines, encompasses a number of smaller units of about 7 lines.

The account of fine structural elements given in Part II is based on defined features of the language; its adequacy in treating 1225 lines of verse is offered in its support. The elements treated can be taken as constituting a verse system like that of any endlessly extensible verse. We will not take this option, however; rather we shall argue that the system of structural elements extends into the realm of gross structure and that Hebrew verse is written in larger units. Some features of previous study of gross structure are discussed below (1.6.1).

The syntax of lines in themselves and certain features of small groups of lines in juxtaposition: these constitute the fine structure of Hebrew verse. The relevant group of constraints and tropes is far from exhausting the systemic features of the verse; what about everything else? Let us again consider the Spenserian stanza, but from a different point of view.

In most stanzas of *The Faerie Queene*, there is at least one alliteration. What are we to make of these alliterations? Their position in the stanza is unpredictable, as indeed is their occurrence. The amount of text involved is tiny: 2 out of 92 syllables. Further, as we saw earlier, alliteration in Modern English is not a function of any distinctive feature of the language. Alliteration in Old English is predictable because it is related to initial stress. By Spenser's time, however, Early Modern English had essentially the stress system we use and alliteration was relegated to the status of a non-structural element in verse. The alliterations in his verse contribute to its order and coherence; because they are unpredictable and marginal, they are non-structural. The origins of alliteration in the English tradition are not relevant to its non-structural status. Alliteration is frequent because it is, as it were, a recent loss from the structural system; Smith refers to this and related phenomena as resources of the tradition (1968: 29-33).

Alliteration is most often line internal, but other devices of larger domain occur. It is not remarkable, for example, to come across in Spenser and many of his contemporaries, all speakers of English during the period in which the English Bible was being shaped, examples of matching. We may suspect the shaping influence of the pre-Jacobean versions of the Bible as well as of the classics, and certain predispositions of English syntax. Though matching lends coherence to the text, in English verse it is never structural, except in "biblical" poets like Smart.

These features have in common the fact they are poetic in the Jakobsonian sense discussed earlier, that is, they involve repetitions: there must be at least two alliterating syllables, two matching syntactic units. We shall somewhat arbitrarily separate poetic elements involving one line or two and those that involve more than a few lines. The former we shall call ornaments and the latter, figures. Briefly we shall review previous study of these realms (1.6.2-3); and in Part III we shall consider a number of figures. The following chart may help in placing the phenomena.

| | *structural elements* | *non-structural elements* |
|---|---|---|
| ↑ | gross structure | |
| amount of text involved increases | | figures |
| | fine structure | |
| | | ornaments |

The phenomena involved in each column are often the same; they differ in disposition. The domain of each rank is continuous with its immediate neighbor(s). Many phenomena referred to as parallelistic belong in the domain of figures.

This large body of systemic features covers structural and non-structural poetic elements. There are other sorts of peculiarities in poetic usage and of these Spenser provides a host of examples. We know the language Spenser used, the Early Modern English of London, where he lived with his younger contemporaries, Shakespeare and the editors of the Authorized Version of the Bible. Spenser frequently uses words and morphological processes rare or unknown in contemporary texts; these constitute a large source of his poetic diction. The ultimate source of the features should not be confused with their use: they are *derived* from older poetic texts but they are *used* to mark the text as poetic. They show that it is a special variety of discourse; in Spenser's case, the source of the features is both identifiable and functional: we are meant to read *The Faerie Queene* as an old-time romance narrative. Poetic diction can be obscure in origin and explicit function, and still mark discourse as special. Contrariwise, it is possible to write verse that is largely free of dictional restrictions, though such verse tends to be incoherent. As in Spenser, so in Hebrew most features of poetic diction are archaic (1.6.4).

### *1.6.1 Gross structural features*

There is no commonly accepted understanding of poetic units larger than the line in Canaanite poetry, since the basic unit, the line, has remained undefined. We are concerned here with features that set off whole poems or major classes of them. This group of features is not widely believed to exist.

Only one group of biblical poems has been consistently scrutinized in terms of gross structure, the acrostics (Gray 1915: 87-120, 243-95; Freedman 1972d; Paul 1976; Schramm 1976: 175-78; Skehan 1971:9, 46-51). Two bases for extrapolating information about gross structure in other poems are available: the acrostics themselves, and the basic unit of verse, the line. The latter is vastly more convenient, but lacking a definition of it, students have not been able to use it; we hope to make good this lack in Part III. Skehan had made notable progress on the basis of the acrostic length in studies of Proverbs, Job, some Psalms, and Deuteronomy 32 (1971: 9-14, 67-77, 81, 96-123). Another gross structural feature is repetition of whole lines; this too, will be studied in Part III.

### *1.6.2 Ornamentation*

The largest group of non-structural devices of Canaanite poetry has the smallest domain, equal to and smaller than that of troping. The ornaments are diverse; their central common feature is their marginal status in creating poetic structure (Gottwald 1962: 835). The only point at which this description conflicts with current practice is a minor one, since no scholar has ever suggested that any of the ornaments are definitional or necessary. Some, in the heat of argument, have come close: they propose that the existence of an ornament can be used to defend either the received or an emended text. Since the ornaments are never necessary and do not constitute a closed, definite class of phenomena, such a proposal must be rejected. In fact, since ornamentation must participate in the basic structure of the language, it seems that the class approaches definiteness, and insofar as it does, the argument gains strength.

The most commonly mentioned ornament is rhyme; in fact, we have never read a description of Hebrew verse that neglected to mention this entirely marginal phenomenon. (See in addition to the standard treatments, Freedman 1955, Stuart 1976: 19, 46, 93, 106, and Thompson 1974: 63-65.) An example of the dangers of linguistic prejudices here is provided by this remark: "Rhyme . . . would be too easy [to be useful as a structural device] in a language with case endings such as Ugaritic, or a language with as many repetitions of common final sounds as has Hebrew" (Stuart 1976: 19). This statement is objectionable on the grounds that (a) it presumes the character of rhyme is a language universal, which it is not (Lotz 1972a); (b) it neglects the evidence of other poetry: case endings are admissible, though not prized, rhymes of Russian (Veen 1964: 84, 91); (c) it neglects the evidence of Semitic versecraft: grammatical endings are frequently used as rhymes in Arabic; and (d) it predicts that no dialect of the same cluster as

Hebrew and Ugaritic will turn out to use rhyme in verse; an erroneous prediction, as Krahmalkov (1975) shows. Although rhyme is universally mentioned and is about as common in Hebrew verse as in Old English (*Beowulf* has 18 rhymes in about 3,000 lines, ca. 0.5%, according to Adams 1973: 10), there is no comprehensive study, because there has been no suitable definition of a line to provide a base for such a study. Under the heading of rhyme we may also mention an odd ornament alleged to occur in Akkadian verse. Kinnier Wilson (1968) gathers examples of what he calls "desonance . . . , the purposeful avoiding of assonance. . . . Unfortunate rhymes or jingles may be avoided by the simple device of changing an offending element or omitting it altogether." This is a commonplace phenomenon in everyday language. Kinnier Wilson's observation that it is an ornament of Akkadian verse is suggestive and any future study of Canaanite rhyme should consider the possibility of such systematic exclusions of rhyme.

The ornaments of assonance and alliteration are also known in Hebrew verse. There is a certain vagueness about the terms and their interrelations. If we restrict assonance to "the repetition of a stressed vowel but not of a following consonant or consonant cluster in syllables near enough to each other for the echo to be discernible to the ear" (Adams 1973: 8), the phenomenon is rare in Hebrew and almost impossible to discuss.

The case of alliteration is more difficult. There are three senses of the term. One, which have already used, refers to the phenomenon in literatures which use alliteration as a structural element and need not concern us. Another refers to "only the repetition of initial consonants, preferably stressed, in syllables near enough to each other for the echo to affect the ear" (Adams 1973: 8). Such alliteration does occur in Hebrew, but is rare; Ex 15:9 is an example. The third sense is any repetition of "the same sound(s) or syllable in two or more words of a line (or line group), which produces a noticeable artistic effect" (Goldsmith 1965: 15). In this sense, alliteration is rather common in Hebrew; it is to be judged within terms we have laid out elsewhere (O'Connor 1977), and along these lines it may be extended to include the use of related sounds (see the examples of Skehan 1971: 83-84 and Cross 1974b: 2-3).

Related ornaments are paronomasia and ambiguity. Paronomasia is easily discernible and is as common in certain varieties of prose as it is in verse; most cases in prose involve false etymologies of proper names (Gevirtz 1975: 33-35, Glück 1970, Guillaume 1964, Kselman 1973, Sasson 1976, Schramm 1976, Thompson 1974: 63-65). The complex morphology of the Canaanite languages makes it easy to create forms which are ambiguous as to root, and it has been alleged that such ambiguity is a genuine poetic ornament. (The repetition in such cases is collapsed: the ornament does not have two parts, but two readings.) Some examples are treated in Schramm (1976: 178-91), Jongeling (1971), and Payne (1967).

### *1.6.3 Figuration*

The realm of non-structural poetic devices used in the domain which overlaps those of gross and fine structural features is figuration. Much attention has been paid in recent study to inclusive, repetitive, and chiastic usages (e.g., Dahood 1966a, 1968a, 1970a, 1974a, 1976b, Freedman 1972b, Paul 1976, and Riding 1976). The structures these studies reveal are generally based on word dyads used in lines separated from each other by considerable distance; often the dyads are like those involved in troping, though since they are not used in contiguous lines, they are not tropes. The relation of tropes and these figurative structures deserves further study. The work might take advantage of traditional rhetorical vocabulary and thus distinguish anaphora (units with the same start), epiphora (units with the same close), ploke (units the first of which starts as the second ends), anadiplosis (the opposite of ploke: units the first of which ends as the second begins), and palindromy, continuous or discontinuous, though these terms are variously defined and difficult to sort out.

### *1.6.4 Poetic diction*

The discovery of the Ugaritic texts has been most productive in increasing recognition of features of Canaanite poetic diction, those features which distinguish poetic discourse from prose but are both non-structural and non-poetic. Diction features, that is, do not order poetic texts (and are thus non-structural) and do not involve significant sameness (and are thus non-poetic). They are peculiarities of the language of poetry which are often historically conditioned: they are usually archaic features preserved in use longer in poetic language than elsewhere. These phenomena have been among the special concerns of Dahood (e.g., 1967e, 1968b, j, 1969e, 1971a, 1973b, and Dahood and Penar 1970); another valuable study is that of Robertson (1972).

Some features of poetic diction are morphological: use of the older 3 m. pl. suffix *-mw* for later *-hm*; preservation of case endings in certain positions; the use of energic verbal endings; the maintenance of syllable-opening semivowels in final semivowel roots. Others are syntactic, involving variation in use of the three series of relative pronouns, the "Semitic" relative *š*, the deictic relative series in *z*, and the distinctively Hebrew relative *ʾšr*; and in the particle system. Some features of poetic diction are closely related to the trope of gapping, others to phenomena recognized in traditional rhetoric, like the use of an abstract for a concrete noun.

The most complex segment of poetic diction involves the verbal system (Blommerde 1969: 14-18, Dahood and Penar 1970: 384-90, 414-26, Held 1965b). The most ambitious attempt to describe the essential complexity, the variation between prefixing and suffixing finite verb forms, is due to Robertson (1972: 9-55). The basic fact is clear: prefixing verb forms can have past tense reference in poetry; but the system is obscure. Robertson's exposition serves his purpose of crudely characterizing the time reference of some passages of verse, but since it relies crucially on reconstructions of relevant narrative sequences on the basis of sources outside the poems, it cannot help to characterize the system within the poems. This is not to speak of the problem that it is rarely possible to create such reconstructions.

The materials are available for a full scale sorting out of the aspects of the poetic finite verbal system, after which the other features of the poetic verbal system, special precative uses of suffixing forms, finitiary uses of nonfinite forms, etc., will fall in line. Chief among these are the cautions that the complexity in usage is not solely the result of temporal narrative complexity, but is related to features of aspect and non-narrative (i.e., generic) reference; and the fact that at least two dialects closely related to Ugaritic and Biblical Hebrew have major differences in verb systems, Mishnaic Hebrew (Gordon 1976) and Phoenician with its rare but crucial pluperfect (cf. Arabic use of *kāna*).

Aspect, as is clear from two recent studies of Semitic aspect, McCarus (1976) on Arabic and Kurylowicz (1973) on Semitic in general, is a problematic area even when the system is fairly obvious. Kurylowicz observes that in a system with two finite verb forms, the opposition must be between simultaneity and anteriority (Latin *imperfectum* and *perfectum*). This is the basic structure of the Arabic system, and it is distinct from the three-way opposition in Slavic and Classical Greek which opposes both imperfective and perfective, and linear and punctual categories. Kurylowicz reserves the term aspect for systems with both these oppositions; McCarus uses it in the distinct sense of the type of action predicated by the verb. In Arabic there is no aspectual (in Kurylowicz's sense) or temporal marking of verb forms; the relevant information is conveyed on the syntactic level.

The poetic system of finite verbal usage in Canaanite can only be explained if the system is treated as having *either* two *or* three finite verb forms. The present approach, which involves building a grammar with two and a half forms, by incorporating the historical information that there were originally two prefixing verb forms, will never explain the system. Diachronic considerations have been used in this regard to get around the problem of synchronic description. It is conceivable that there is no possible synchronic description, but that seems unlikely; it is *likely* that a single synchronic description will not be generally suitable. As the prose system from which the poetic usage derived grew more archaic, it is probable that the poetic usage grew more fixed.

### *1.7 The fine structure of Hebrew verse*

Having set in perspective the features of Hebrew verse we are describing, we need to consider those fine structural details as a system. The burden of our description is on the demonstration, but we must show that the described phenomena are of a coherent sort. The arguments about the character of meter (1.4.1-3) must be taken up again and set alongside the fuller treatment we can now give constriction (1.7.1). The notion of constriction can be extended to other poetic systems in a variety of languages (1.7.2). Thus we shall suggest that a constriction is a coherent and fairly ordinary type of poetic system. At the last, we shall return to native ground and observe that syntactic constraints shape not only lines of Canaanite verse but also Northwest Semitic personal names (1.7.3).

### *1.7.1 Meter and constriction in general and the Hebrew constriction*

The uniformitarian axiom in historical linguistics requires that we reconstruct no feature in a dead language not attested in a living language. The reference to feature must be left rather vague, since the organic unity of a language cannot readily be dissected. The axiom steers a broad course between the individual words in a reconstruction, which will often be largely unknown in living languages, and the whole language, since there the application is trivial. The features of a language the axiom concerns are, as is plain from our examples above, systemic. The extension of the axiom in historical poetics must be similarly concerned with systemic features. The uniformitarian axiom in poetics will not be applicable to entities that are without major consequences.

It is an interesting question as to whether the uniformitarian system allows the reconstruction of identical poetic systems in dead languages. Moreover, it is not an academic one, since Latin verse is meant to be poetically identical to Greek, and the Persian and Turkish Islamic verse systems are meant to be entirely in the Arabic mode. It is generally agreed that none of the designed copies are successful imitations. The uniformitarian axiom, then, not only requires that no feature unknown in a living poetry be reconstructed in a dead one but also cautions against expecting identical poetic systems in different languages. With this caution in mind, we can consider the proposed reconstruction of the fine structure system of Hebrew, the system of constraints and tropes. We have hinted that other constrictions do exist, but before we examine them we need to return to the question of meter and non-meter.

Meter is in general taken to be immediately perceptible, purely phonological patterning of language. We saw above that both adverbs must be rejected. Meter is not immediately perceptible in some languages with essentially regular meter; in Finnish, Old Norse, Latvian, and Sanskrit, we noted instances in which the meter is entirely perceptible only as the speech is analyzed phonologically. By regular, we describe systems with little tolerance for deviation in any component of the system. These cases are distinct from essentially complex meters like the Greek dactylic hexameter which allows as many as five syllables to be lacking from the isosyllabic frame of 17 syllables; 12-syllable lines (i.e., with substitution in the fifth foot) are rare, but all the line types from 13 to 17 syllables are common. The processes of scansion are known and Homer's regularity is unquestioned. The regularity of the source poem of the English tradition, also written in a complex meter, is also unquestioned but *Beowulf* has been less thoroughly studied than Homer and the complexity of a recent description is worthy of note. The Creed-Foley scansion, which accounts for 94% of the text, is based on a metrical template which uses four measures in a line; the measures, defined with reference to three grades of stress, are of seven types (Foley 1976: 207-20). There are 83 line configurations in 94% of the text. If it is true that regular meter can often require phonological analysis, then it is *a fortiori* true that complex meters like those of Homer and *Beowulf* require analysis. So much for the adverb immediately; meter is perceptible patterning of sound.

Further, it is not patterning only of sound. The invariant requirement of a word break at line's end is only the most obvious non-phonological feature of meter. Many others are nearly but not quite invariable: there is a caesura after the sixth or seventh syllable in 99% of Homeric hexameters (the penthemimeral and trochaic caesuras; Nagy 1974: 56). We have examined a case in which not only is the patterning invariable, but in which the instantiation of the meter *in globo* is implicated. The monosyllable constraint in English iambic pentameter requires that no Speech Stress appear in a Metrical Unstress position except on a monosyllable (Kiparsky 1975). This evidence allows us to modify the notion of meter in the direction urged by careful students of metrics: meter is perceptible, phonological patterning of language. The perception may require analysis and the phonological patterning may involve features of syntax.

A point made by LaDrière in discussing the complex intertwinings of phonological patterns in a language's verse will help in focusing on the importance of syntactic involvement in meter.

> It is at times difficult to distinguish in a verse system between elements essential to a metrical scheme and redundant concomitant elements whose cooccurrence with the more primary rhythmic structure is not adverted to in production or attended to in native perception of the rhythm as such (1965: 673).

If it is difficult to separate the phonological elements involved with meter, it is even more difficult to separate phonological from syntactic elements, once the point is made that meter is not just what one hears. Let us for the moment turn away from LaDrière's criteria and consider not production or perception but description of Shakespearean iambic pentameter. To capture the meter's base, it is sufficient to use the traditional title, but so general has Kiparsky shown the monosyllable constraint to be that it must be included in a serious description. Let us call it a concomitant feature (though not a redundant one) and suggest that blank verse is a poetic system with primary phonological features (the meter in an abstract sense) and concomitant syntactic features (crucially, the monosyllable constraint). With this notion of meter in mind, let us consider what a constriction, like the one we have described in Hebrew, is. The features we have described as primary are syntactic. The features most generally studied in Hebrew verse have been phonological and though no single satisfactory statement of the palpable regularities exists, all phonological studies have turned up some undeniable quasi-systemic features. The ease of syntactic treatment combined with the obtusity of phonological treatments suggests that Hebrew verse uses a constriction, a poetic system with primary syntactic features and concomitant phonological features.

There is a terminological crossing which we should make explicit; consider this chart.

| *poetic system* | 1. meter | 2. constriction |
|---|---|---|
| A. primary feature | phonological patterning (meter) -frame -modulation | syntactic patterning (constriction) -frame -modulation |
| B. concomitant feature | syntactic patterning | phonological patterning |

The standard notion of meter is 1A, which is not adequate to describe the entire poetic system, so we generalize the term meter to the whole system; the entire system *and* 1A in English are called iambic pentameter, but a great many iambic lines of 10 English syllables (fitting 1A) will not be accepted in the system, because they violate 1B. In other words, in 1A the term iambic pentameter has a purely analytic sense, while as a system designation, it refers to how English blank verse is actually written, which involves chiefly iambic pentameter units. The reason for not separating the system and the primary patterning is simply that much of the time the latter is an adequate paraphrase of the former.

The frame in English verse is pentameter, the modulation is iambic; this is a case in which the two are superimposed. In Racinian verse, the frame, the 12-13 syllable line, and the modulation, the rhyme, are not superimposed. The 1B section in English involves the line break and the monosyllable constraint; in French it refers to the line break and the caesura, both of which feed into the 1A feature. Now recall that in our first reference to the Racinian line, we treated the alexandrine in itself as the meter. Keeping an eye on standard usage, we can say that the term alexandrine can describe three things: (1) the frame of the meter, (2) the meter, and (3) the poetic system. This collapsing of the phenomena is not unjust to any of them, though it can be confusing. The most important entity in the system is the meter and the most important entity related to the meter is the frame.

Let us turn to the constriction column in the chart. Section 2A, the syntactic patterning, has the same name as the overall system and the same name as the frame; this interlocking nomenclature reflects the analogy of meter. The frame in our proposal is the sum of the rules stated in 1.4.6 as the constriction; the modulation, i.e., the tropes, combined with the constrictional frame to make up the constriction in the sense of primary feature, the fine structure of Hebrew verse. The final point, the phonological patterning, we have not treated at all; we shall do so after we have discussed the concept of the line and some other constrictional systems.

We mentioned above that in treating English we could turn away from LaDrière's criteria of judging essence in terms of perception or production and cleave to description. Whether these are serious options in treating English, we need not discuss, since perception and production are forbidden zones in considering Hebrew. We *must* describe. We have only the criteria of scrutiny to aid us in evaluating the results. We argue that the constriction of Hebrew verse (the frame of syntactic constraints and the modulation of tropes) is a good description because it works for 1225 lines. Up to this point, we have urged the inadequacy of phonological treatments on heuristic grounds: there are no prospects for clarity. We have set up a framework which will allow us to go further and suggest that phonological patterns are not primary, not simply because of the vagaries of study, but because they are concomitant to the constrictional system.

To consider this point, we need to examine a fact of such generality that it has not been tied down: poetry is generally written in units of characterizable extent. There is a distinct limit to what can pass for a line of verse, and lines are used in describing all poetry. From the viewpoint of any single language's system, there are a plethora of possible line lengths, most of them irrelevant to the language. In English, for example, 10 syllables is the basic length; 8 and 12 syllables are interesting variants. Lines longer than 13 syllables collapse in two; lines shorter than 7 are usable chiefly in songs. Lines of 1-6 syllables and those of 14 syllables and up are marginal in the language. In the metrical systems of Europe and

Asia, the most frequently used lines of verse are between 5 and 15 syllables. The extremes of the range, as far as we know, are provided by Toda, in which the line is 3 syllables long (Emeneau 1966, 1971); and by the Greek dactylic hexameter, which is 17 syllables in basic shape. We suspect that a safer statement of the range is 3 to 21 syllables.

Since it is reasonable to suppose that line structure is related to basic phenomena in other spheres, and since the general range is based on diverse languages, let us consider the notion of line and the problem of metrical and constrictional systems, both of which describe lines. If a poetic system is structured in discernible lines, they will range between 3 and 21 syllables in length; if the range of line lengths is small and they possess a fairly consistent phonological pattern, the system is metrical. If the range is wide and no consistent phonological pattern emerges, the system is constrictional. It is not sufficient to note that the lines are of moderately uniform length to describe the system as underlyingly metrical, nor that the lines tend to be phonologically characterizable. These are features of composition in lines which occur in both metrical and constrictional systems. If constrictional regularities yield a more readily described system, then the poetic system is constrictional. There will be phonological regularities, but they will be of a more diffuse sort.

We have suggested that a coherent description of Hebrew verse in constrictional terms is possible. Now we need to show that the phonological regularities are of the diffuse sort alluded to. The argument is simply that within the constrictional framework only lines of certain lengths or accentual structures will occur. Specifically, no line of less than two units (and one constituent) occurs, and no line of more than five units (and four constituents) occurs, so the accentual structure of the lines will range between two and five accents, if every unit is allowed one accent. Statements of accentual systems usually refer to the constituent level, so the range will be between one and four accents in a line. All accentual systems of Hebrew verse allow lines of that range. Further, we argued that the basic line contains two or three constituents and all accentual systems regard two and three accent lines as basic. Since none of these systems describes the other syntactic regularities we have discussed and since none differentiates systematically between two and three accent lines, the constrictional description is to be preferred.

Accentual descriptions are necessarily crude and a closer test comes with closer measures of regularity. Consonant counting systems are not particularly adaptable; Loretz (1975) suggests 9-12 consonants in a line as basic. Syllable counting provides more accessible data. The basic range of the line noted earlier is 3-21 syllables; if our claim that Hebrew verse shows regularities of line length only because it is written in lines is correct, we should find that lines of the constriction cover a large part of the range of lengths, and that they cluster, like metrical line types, around or below the middle of the range.

This is what we do find: the lines of the corpus range between 3 and approximately 15 syllables and they cluster in the middle. Let us consider some short lines.

Jdg 5:12d *qwm brq*
5:12e *wšbh šbyk bn-ʾbynʿm*

5:12d Arise, Baraq.
5:12e Capture your-captives, Abinoam's-child.

The first line is 3 syllables and the second is 11 syllables. The segmentation of the lines is assured by the presence of a binomination, *brq-bn-ʾbynʿm*; we have no examples of this trope across a line, the situation that would result if 12e were split. In the native tradition (BFBS), 12de is treated as a single line; in the German tradition (BH3 and BHS), the lines are segmented as we have them. While another treatment is conceivable in a description that does not recognize tropes, the segmentation we have proposed is fairly secure. There are 7 other lines of the syntactic structure of 12d, a 2-constituent independent verbal clause with a vocative (3.4.18); they range in length from 5 to 11 syllables. The short line in Jdg 5:12d is not unique in length but it is more complex than other short lines.

If we consider the line paired with it, Jdg 5:12e, in the context of syntactically similar lines (3-constituent independent verbal clauses with vocatives, 3.4.6), a smaller range appears. The first class (Jdg 5:12d) ranges from 3 to 11 syllables in length, 9 possibilities, of which 6 are used in 7 lines. In the Jdg 5:12e group, there are 19 lines, between 6 syllables and 12 syllables; all but one of 7 possibilities is used. If the 19 lines are a sample of lines of this structure, we would expect most of the lines to be of intermediate length, 9 syllables. This is the case: 7 lines are 9 syllables, 7 are shorter and 5 are longer.

It is difficult to discuss long lines since such lines are often either split or emended on the grounds of "meter." If we consider the eight 4-constituent verbal lines with vocatives (3.4.20), we find lengths ranging from 7 to 13 syllables; the commonest lengths are 10 syllables (2 examples) and 11 syllables (3 examples). This and the other line groups noted are arbitrary; they are interesting because similarity of structure might lead to expectations of uniformity of length, which are disappointed. The demonstration could be continued indefinitely for syntactic groups, and for the corpus as a whole.

The task is not necessary. Freedman has already demonstrated that the kind of diversity in line length we are proposing is characteristic of Hebrew verse. Freedman (1974) treated Exodus 15, using an entirely different lineation than we do, and his results may be cited. We divide the poem into 56 lines, while he uses 78 divisions; his lines tend to be shorter than ours. The 78 lines range over 9 lengths, from 3 to 11 syllables; the differences between his counts and the Massoretic text are, as he shows, negligible. The nine lengths are not equally represented: there is only one 3-syllable line, and one 10-syllable line, and one 11-syllable line. There are two 9-syllable lines, half-a-dozen 8-syllable lines, and five 7-syllable lines. The dominant lengths are 6 syllables (21 lines), 5 syllables (23 lines), and 4 syllables (18 lines). In his acrostic study, Freedman (1972d) reports the following distribution for bicola (line-pairs) in Lamentations 1-3:

| *Syllables* | *Number of line-pairs* |
|---|---|
| 7 | 1 |
| 10 | 12 |
| 11 | 32 |
| 12 | 50 |
| 13 | 46 |
| 14 | 36 |
| 15 | 13 |
| 16 | 7 |
| 17 | 1 |
| 18 | 1 |
| 19 | 1 |

The range for these 200 pairs of lines (400 lines) is roughly 3-1/2 to 9-1/2 syllables per line (halving 7 and 19 to get a figure for individual lines). The bulk of the examples again fall around the middle of the range.

The statistical convergences which Freedman has shown over a larger body of Hebrew verse than we can report on here are the major available indications of the phonological regularities in Hebrew verse. The data are amenable to the treatment he has given them; i.e., they can be taken as an index of overall regularity and as a guide to particular loci of regularity, as he has shown clearly in his studies of various figures, notably of dyadic lines separated over long distances. Without influencing the latter use, the data can also be evaluated in the framework of a constrictional poetic system. There is a diversity of lengths because line length is not a primary patterning feature. The diversity converges around its midpoint because certain syntactic structures are favored and these tend to have mean lengths.

### *1.7.2 Constriction in other languages*

The possibility of constrictional verse systems is implicit in Lotz's definition of verse, which we quoted earlier: "a small set of language texts characterized by numerical regularity of speech material within certain syntactic frames" (1972a: 1); and in his definition of meter: "the numerical regulation of certain properties of the linguistic form of verse" (1972a: 2).

Many constrictional systems remain undescribed. Students of verse generally expect to encounter a metrical system and when they do not find one, they describe the verse as ametrical or they leave the matter open for further study. In many cases, one is stymied without knowledge of the language; cf., e.g., Andrzejewski and Lewis (1964: 46-47).

There are two types of constrictional systems: (1) those in which the concomitant patterning is loose, and refers only to a range of line lengths, and (2) those in which the concomitant patterning is reflected in line length and in line break marking. Hebrew is of the first type, and in discussing similar cases, we must refer to the modulation involved. In treating the second type it will be sufficient to refer to line marking devices. In only one case can we describe the syntactic frame in anything like the detail we have used in the case of Hebrew. The character of the phenomena will have to suffice in considering each case, and the generality of the cases in supporting the whole argument.

Constrictional systems can be composed of (a) a series of constraints regulating the syntactic complexity of lines, (b) modulations of those lines, and (c) concomitant phonological patterns which generally limit line lengths and which mark line breaks. If the breaks are signaled by the use of rhyme, this is the rhyming constriction type. We remarked earlier that Lotz's definition of meter seemed designed to allow for constriction; in fact, he refers to a rhyming constriction system. In Ghê, an African language, poetic texts consist of lines of "five or three syntactic phrases," the lines being "bound together by rhyme" (Lotz 1972a: 6). The frame of the constriction is specified, a simpler form of the sort of constraints we have seen in Hebrew. There is no reference to line length; the line breaks are patterned, by rhyme. Presumably a full investigation of Ghê would reveal modulations of a syntactic type across lines and general line length limits, and the system would coincide with what we have projected for rhyming constrictions; since we know nothing else about the language, we can rest with Lotz's notes, which fit our projection in its major points.

Another rhyming constriction may be suspected in the medieval Spanish epic, the *Poema del mío Cíd* of the mid-twelfth century (Nelson 1972: 169-70). This text is generally referred to as ametrical, since its 3,625 two stich lines range in length from 10 to 20 syllables; most lines fall slightly below the mean in length, at 13-15 syllables. The poem is not consistently rhymed, but assonantal rhymes are frequent (notably frequent enough to support the received text). The looseness of length and rhyme are the result of their position as elements of the system secondary to the constriction. The *Poema* is a useful example for several reasons. First, it is available in an English version in which the fundamental character of the constriction can be seen (Merwin 1959). Moreover, it returns us to the problem of orality: the *Poema* is a text taken from an oral base and its ametricality is sometimes explained as the result of defective recording. This has led some scholars to repair the poem, i.e., rewrite it. Others merely dismiss the bad text as fixedly ametrical. Both of these options need to be supplemented by a study of the syntax of the poem, which we suspect will reveal considerable regularities. Finally, it is a poem written on the border between Christian and Islamic spheres and we shall below discuss constriction in Arabic. Whether the form of the *Poema* is Arabizing we cannot say, but that seems possible for a poem about a man with an Arabic honorific (*Mío Cid* from Arb *sayyidī* 'my lord') and an Arabic title (*alférez* from Arb *al-fāris* 'horseman').

Satisfactory treatment of rhyming constrictions requires that we consider some texts and fortunately we can do so in the case of Arabic. Our use of the terms poetry and verse for highly regulated language materials conflicts with the highly developed literary tradition in Arabic, since Arb *ši$^{c}$r* 'poetry' is only used of quantitatively metrical material (as opposed to *naṯ$^{c}$r* 'prose,' lit., what is scattered). Further, there is no single designation of material based on the rhyming constriction. We shall go against the native tradition and apply the terms poetry and verse to material not in quantitative meter, and we shall follow Orientalist procedure in generalizing one of the native designations for constrained material, *saj$^{c}$*.

The complex Arabic regard for *saj$^{c}$* is adequately reflected in the standard gloss 'rhymed prose,' but we should not allow prejudices to confuse treatment of the material. The Arabic term has nothing to do with prose; it is derived from the root *saja$^{c}$a* 'to coo (of a male pigeon), to utter a long whinny (of a camel),' which denominatively means 'to speak in rhymed prose.' The Hebrew cognate *šg$^{c}$*, is rare and is generally glossed 'to be mad'; since it is used of prophets, both for better and worse, some take it to mean 'to mutter, rave.' We need not consider here the possibility that it sometimes means simply 'to speak in rhymed prose.' (It is in the madness sense that the root has entered English, via Yiddish, in *meshugge*, etc.)

*Saj$^{c}$* is "a peculiar mode of rhetoric in which at short intervals words occur which rhyme, though it is distinguished from poetry (*ši$^{c}$r*) by not being bound by regular rhythm or metre" (Krenkow 1934: 43). There are three uses of *saj$^{c}$*: (a) in the short proclamations and shrine shouts (*talbiyāt*) of pre-Islamic religion associated with the figure of the *kāhin* 'diviner' (the only non-Canaanite cognate of Hebrew and Phoenician *khn*); (b) in a bellelettristic essay form known as *maqāma*, literally 'session, meeting,' but oddly cognate in etymology to English 'thesis'; this discursive form flourished in the early centuries A.H., eventually degenerating into purely ornamental use in diplomatic correspondence and the like; and (c) in the Qurʾān. It is our impression that because of the doctrine of the incomparability of the Qurʾān, the last usage of the term is improper; but the formal differentiae of the "rhyme prose" suras of the Qurʾān are not of the sort that have led Arabists to separate the third usage from the other two. In view of these uses of *sajʿ*, we can understand the mixed native esteem of the form; *sajʿ* is a marginal poetic form used in forbidden religious practices, or for discursive purposes; or it is used by the Prophet and is therefore by definition not like anything else.

Important features of Qurʾānic *sajʿ* are its extremely rapid development and eventual abandonment. Before the Hijra, many suras are short and written in *sajʿ*; thereafter, they are longer and in ordinary prose. This development is in part responsible for the separation of the suras into four rather than two groups; scholars supplement the pre- and post-Hijran division of Islamic tradition with a threefold division of the pre-Hijran corpus. Only in the first two of these divisions is phonological patterning important and only in those suras is a constrictional system to be looked for. By the third Meccan period, sura cuts have lost their basis in rhyme and the constrictional system has also been lost.

In the oldest suras and in some Hadith (Blachère 1947-51, I: 179), *sajʿ* is clearly used. Scholars have noted that the lines of Qurʾānic *sajʿ* tend to be syntactically discrete, but because the rhyme does not match obvious syntactic breaks, the subject has not, to our knowledge, been investigated. Since, of the three bodies of *sajʿ*, the Qurʾān is the best known and most accessible, we can examine some early suras. We follow the dating system of Blachère.

The final sura of the Qurʾān, Q.114, is dated to the first Meccan period and is rhymed consistently in *-(n)ās*. The lines range in length from 4 to 11 syllables. The sura contains no constructions different from those we have considered for Hebrew, and in fact the matrix for Classes I-III describes the sura. The text (ʿAysa 1385) follows, with Arberry's translation (1970). We use the same marking system here as in Hebrew; we omit the first line of the sura, which is the formulaic opening prayer.

1. *qul: ʾaʿūḏu bi-rabbi-nnās*
2. *maliki-nnās*
3. *ilāhi-nnās*
4. *min-šarri-lwaswāsi-lxannās*
5. *ʾallaḏi yuwaswisu fi-ṣudūri-nnās*
6. *min-ʾal-jinnati-wannās*

1. Say: I-take-refuge with-the-Lord-of-men,
2. the-king-of-men,
3. the-god-of-men,

4. from-the-evil-of-the-slinking-whisperer,
5. who whispers in-the-breasts-of-men,
6. of-jinn-and-men. (Arberry 1970, II: 354)

There are three 2-unit lines (2, 3, 6); two 4-unit lines (1, 5); and there is one 3-unit line (4). There are four 1-constituent lines (2, 3, 4, 6) and two 3-constituent lines (1 and 5). There are four lines with no clause predicator (2, 3, 4, 6), one 1-clause line (5), and one 2-clause line (1). The constrictional matrix is the following:

| | | | |
|---|---|---|---|
| Clause predicators | ∅ | 1 | 2 |
| Constituents | 1 | | 3 |
| Units | 2 | 3 | 4 |

We are not seeking to show that *saj*ᶜ obeyed the same constraints as Hebrew, only that they are of the same sort. The syntactic constraints to be generalized over even the suras of the first Meccan period will probably present a more complex system than we have seen in Hebrew. One-unit lines are rare, but they are tolerated, as at the opening of Q.52, *waṭṭūr*, 'And the mountain,' which stands as a single line because it contains the major rhyme, *ūr*. Similarly, extremely long lines are rare in the first period, but do occur. We are not concerned with describing the exact character of Qurʾānic *saj*ᶜ, but only with the point that the dominant regularities in it are syntactic. In this connection, it is worth remarking that the regularity of rhyme in Q.114 is unusual. Many suras employ more than one rhyme, and rhymes can be supplemented with assonances.

There is much other relevant material in the Qurʾān; it should be possible to trace the gradual elaboration of the constrictional system of the suras through the first two Meccan periods up to the abandonment of rhyme in the third Meccan period. Further, it should also be possible to describe the presumably more stable syntactic systems of pre-Islamic *saj*ᶜ and *maqāmāt*. Our point can be made without these descriptions. The early Qurʾānic form is constrictional: its primary regularities are syntactic. These are supported by a general limitation on line lengths and by complex schemes of rhymes and other line break markers. The possibility of other syntactic patterns modulating within the frame we have not considered, but matching in the Qurʾān does occur.

There is another body of poetry conventionally called in English "rhymed prose," Chinese *fu*. Here again we encounter a conflict with native designations, since *fu* is not "real poetry" in the Chinese tradition, i.e., is given less regard than poetic forms which have tonal patterning, *shih* (conventionally, ode or poetry), *tzʾu* (lyric), and *chʾü* (dramatic song). The system of *fu* tends to have even greater regularity than *saj*ᶜ, since the phonological patterning extends to the point of favoring a single line length in a piece. *Fu* verse is used, like *saj*ᶜ, in *maqāmat*, for discursive purposes, and, like *saj*ᶜ, seems particularly apt for ornamental use. The Chinese example is instructive because the modulations within the syntactic frame of *fu* are parallelistic, as in Hebrew. *Fu* parallelism is much more various than the parallelism in Regulated Verse discussed earlier, but it is still plain. Both constriction and parallelism can be observed in the translations given by Frankel (1972, 1976), Bishop (1966: 3-106), Watson (1971), and Liu and Lo (1975).

The Chinese example is also revealing because the genre of *fu* merges with another type of writing which lacks rhyme but is otherwise similar. Parallel Prose uses a syntactic constriction (which tends to give it an isosyllabic base because of the isolating character of Classical Chinese), and within the framework, various modulations are deployed. The types of parallelism used in Parallel Prose have been studied in Hightower (1966), who provides several examples of Parallel Prose in translation.

Chinese Parallel Prose is an example of the Hebrew type of constrictional system, in which the syntactic constraints and modulations are not associated with the phonological marking of line breaks. There are a number of examples from other literatures and they have in common syntactic constraints, modulations within the constraints, and lines of irregular lengths, which resist metrical description. Moreover, the modulations are parallelistic, at least in part. These poetic systems seem to be fully analogous to Hebrew. In most cases, the descriptions are incomplete, so the analogy remains incomplete; it is important to record it, not only to encourage further study, but also because the available materials are in themselves illuminating.

Let us consider the contemporary oral poetry of the Xhosa Bantu (Opland 1975, 1976), and its highest form, the praise-poetry of male tradents, who were attached until recently to tribal chiefs. These tradents are *imbongi* 'praise poets' and the genre of their work is the *izibongo* 'praise poem.' "The lines of the *imbongi's* oral *izibongo* do not display either syllabic or quantitative meter . . . though there is some reason to believe that one may be able to determine certain recurrent intonational patterns that function as meter" (Opland 1975: 194). Opland notes that breath groups tend to be sense groups (p. 196); this is the core of a constrictional system. The modulations across related groups of lines involve parallelism, chiasm, linking, and repetition. The analogy to Hebrew does not escape Opland: "Poems strikingly similar in spirit and technique to Xhosa *izibongo* can be found in the Old Testament, like Moses' song of triumph in Exodus xv, and Deborah's song in Judges v" (p. 207). The accuracy of the observation on the spirit of the texts can be evaluated by an inspection of Opland's translations. We are concerned here only with the similarities in technique. We may add that Xhosa praise poetry is comparable to Canaanite as an oral literature since techniques of recurrence ("themes," "formulas") are used without the impetus of a strict meter in poems of medium length which can not only be composed orally, but also recited from memory.

Other constrictional systems tend to be described more simply as parallelistic. The Rotinese texts treated by Fox display constrictional patterns of syntax, and exhibit complex modulations, as we noted earlier. The 62 lines cited in Fox (1974) range in length from 6 to 12 syllables; a majority of lines fall in the middle range, at 8 and 9 syllables. The primacy of single clause lines in the texts can be seen in the renderings, though again a full statement on the syntax must await further study. The archaic Tzotzil prayer quoted by Brickner (1974: 369-70) has diverse syntax within the lines, but the patterns seem to be constrictional; the lines vary between 2 and 11 syllables in length. In a modern Tzotzil prayer she quotes (p. 377), the range of syntactic structures is the same, though the lines vary slightly less in length, from 3 to 6 syllables.

There is one constrictional system which has been analyzed semantically, that of the folk poetry of the Ostyaks and Voguls, treated in Austerlitz's masterly study, *Ob-Ugric Metrics* (1958). The phonological regularities involve line lengths which vary between 3 and 12 syllables; lengths of 8, 9, and 10 syllables are commonest (pp. 89-90). The constriction is based on the division into verbal lines and phrasal lines; in contrast to Hebrew, Ob-Ugric relies more on phrasal than verbal lines. Of the central corpus of 2,557 lines, 920 lines (36%) are verbal; these contain only one verb, and usually one other constituent; these lines do not generally occur in sequence. The parallelistic burden of structure is associated with phrasal lines. The largest group of phrasal lines are parallel lines, Austerlitz's term for phrase lines of identical syntactic structure and with almost complete repetition; the difference between parallel lines is usually one word; 1,160 lines in the main corpus (45%) are parallel. Some other phrasal lines are involved in more complex modulations, and some are not so involved. Because of the distinctive morphological features of Hebrew and Ob-Ugric, it is impossible to compare the lower levels of constriction. The systems are otherwise closely comparable, having (a) constraints on the number of clause predicators per line; (b) extensive use of parallelistic devices, including repetition and matching; (c) concomitant, but not controlling, phonological patterns, limiting line lengths. Parallelism and repetition in Ob-Ugric texts tend to extend over greater domains than in Hebrew, but the fine structural differences caused by this are slight; such greater extension, here as in Rotinese, probably has more gross structural effect.

The Uralic parallelistic literature most closely related to Ob-Ugric is Finnish folk poetry, which is metrical. A more distantly related language seems to have had a constriction: the now nearly extinct Samoyedic language, Kamassian. There is a single Kamassian poem known and it is discussed by Lotz (1972b: 105-14). He analyzes the text closely and describes the syntactic constriction which requires that each line contain one clause with two or three phrase units.

The range of constrictional systems which we have surveyed here shows that our reconstruction of Hebrew verse as showing predominantly syntactic patterns is plausible on uniformitarian grounds. The occurrence of parallelism in a large number of constrictional systems is striking, but its import should not be exaggerated. Metrical and constrictional poetic systems use a variety of parallelistic devices and there is no necessary tie between the occurrence of constriction and that of parallelism, though they are both semantic-syntactic phenomena, and thus distinct from the phonological regularities of meter. It seems obvious that constrictional systems are "looser" than metrical systems, but the fact that all examples of constriction are from either marginal sectors of written traditions (Arabic and Chinese) or from oral traditions should not mislead us. There may be circumstances in which it is licit to value descriptions of "real poetry" versus "junk"; within a tradition, that is probably unavoidable. That style of description cannot be extended across tradition boundaries, however, and no valuation of written over oral language can be taken seriously (Finnegan 1973).

### *1.7.3 The origins of constrictional verse, orality, and a word on music*

We have alluded in passing to an important contemporary reconsideration of a major feature of theories of orality. If we return to this reconsideration, we can set the constrictional system of Hebrew verse not only in the vast constellation of oral literature, but also in the context of other features of the language. The Parry-Lord hypothesis suggests that it is the demands of meter that create formulas. As we noted above, there are formulas in poetic systems which have no strict meter and in prose.

O'Nolan carried out a study of the Irish prose narratives which tell of the hero Finn (from the period 1200-1700 C.E.) (1969). In these narratives, the heroes' names are consistently coupled with personal epithets, in the shapes which occur so frequently in Homer that Parry postulated a metrical explanation for them. O'Nolan reverses the priority in explanation and contends that it is not that meter comes first, but that epithets personal to heroes are primitive. The epithets are then fitted into the line endings, the most metrically rigid position, as appears from the fact that the oldest epithet-name combinations in Homer are line final. "The fact seems to be that epithet formulas are a feature of heroic storytelling, not simply of epic hexameter. It must be obvious that these formulas of their nature have a slow organic growth and to assume that this slow growth took place in the context of an established hexameter verse is unreasonable" (1969: 14).

There is much independent evidence that the Greek dactylic hexameter is the endpoint of a complex development. The study of comparative Indo-European metrics, begun by Meillet in his work on Greek and Sanskrit, has been extended to Slavic by Jakobson and to Celtic by Watkins (1963). The main burden of these studies has been to show that the metrical line in all these languages has essential common features. The closing structure of the Greek hexameter is at base the paroemiac unit (short-short-long-anceps), and this is also the core of certain Slavic, Indic, and Celtic lines. O'Nolan suggests that the rhythm of line final, epithet-name groups, which correlates with the closing structure, is in fact its source.

Nagy (1976) has enlarged on the reversal of meter and formula priority. He observes that theme and episode lead in the creation of formula, which in turn leads to meter. The ensemble has reached its gelled state in Homer as a result of a long process of streamlining. The gelled state is epitomized in the situation of thrift: there is only one formula which is metrically and thematically appropriate in any narrative situation. The theme is "the key to all other levels of fixity in oral poetry — including both the formulaic and metrical levels" (1976: 247). This leads to a redefinition of the formula as "a fixed phrase conditioned by the traditional themes of oral poetry," with which is joined the notion of meter as "diachronically generated by formula rather than vice versa" (p. 251).

The argument is not based solely on the use of Homeric epithets in line final position. Nagy has shown that there are formulas in Greek and Rg-Vedic Sanskrit which are not only cognate linguistically but also metrically (1974). In Greek, the metrical context regularly matches the formula; in Vedic Sanskrit, in which there is greater metrical freedom, the formula is regular even when the meter is not strictly controlled. Thus the Sanskrit cases show the leading edge of the formula. The direct driving force behind the formula must be the syntax, but although verse lines tend to be syntactically contained, the greater regularity of meter overrides such containment in Indo-European verse forms.

The core of the Nagy-O'Nolan hypothesis has been discussed by Russo (1976) and given an important extension by Watkins (in discussion in Stolz and Shannon 1976: 107-11). Watkins conjectures that out of the factors of oral tradition which shape theme and formula emerge two varieties of poetic tradition: those with meter, in which the burden of coherence falls on the meter, and those without meter, in which it falls on grammatical parallelism. He cites as examples of the latter Semitic and Vogul-Ostyak. We can second Watkins, modifying his descriptions: in one of the two varieties, the regularities are phonological, while in the other, they are syntactic.

It seems reasonable to ask whether Hebrew verse has a core from which it might be thought to have grown, as Indo-European verse grew from the line final cadence. The Indo-European case rests on the correlation of a major class of formulas, name-epithet groups, with the most fixed position in the line, the final slots. Is there a language subsystem in Hebrew, other than verse, in which syntactic constraints occur?

There is and here, too, names appear, although the correlation with poetry cannot be made directly. West Semitic names are shaped in the same ways as lines of verse are, even if they cannot be treated as a growing point of the verse. Names in all the Northwest Semitic languages have been extensively studied in recent years and in all the corpora, the same set of constraints appear. A personal name can contain either one clause predicator or none and no more than one or two units; longer names are limited to sacred contexts.

The existence of the constraints is shown by the fact that when clausal names contain a verb which normally governs an object, if the subject occurs in the name, the object is not specified. Thus in the clause name *yhwntn* 'Jonathan,' 'Yahweh gives/has given,' the gift is not specified. The pattern is consistent. Consider *yśmᶜˀl* 'Ishmael,' 'God will hear/has heard [the parents?]'; and *ybnyh* 'Ibnijah,' 'Yahweh builds up [the family?].' There are syntactically less complex names, both 2-unit phrases like *ᶜbdyh* 'Obadiah,' 'Servant of Yahweh,' and 1-unit phrases, *ḥnh* 'Anna,' 'favor,' *brwk* 'Baruch,' 'blessed', *šˀwl* 'Saul,' 'asked-for.' There is no restriction on the kind of clause used in a name: nominal sentences are common, *ˀlyhw* 'Elijah,' 'Yahweh [is] my-god,' *ywˀl* 'Joel,' 'Yahweh [is] god'; interrogative sentences occur, *mykˀl* 'Michael,' 'Who [is] like-El?'; imperative names, though rare, are known, *śwbˀl* 'Shubaˀel,' 'Return [your people], El' (so Huffmon 1976).

We need not here review the other Northwest Semitic onomastica in detail. The Ugaritic names show the same restrictions; we shall quote vocalized examples from Akkadian texts, after Gröndahl (1967). A verb occurs with its subject but without an object in, for example, *ia-qub-ᵈIM* 'Hadad protects' (p. 11) and *ia-ab-ni-AN* 'Ilu has built' (p. 119). The Amorite name *ḫa-am-mu-pa-ta-a* 'ᶜAmmu has opened [the womb]' (Huffmon 1965: 256) also shows the constraint. The Punic name *brkbᶜl* 'Baᶜal will bless', attested in Latin orthography as *berecbal*, also shows the constraint (Benz 1972: 291).

There is a curious group of Amorite names including *ma-na-na-a*, viz., *manna ˀanā* 'Who [am] I?' and *ma-na-ba-al-te-ˀel*, viz., *manna balti-ˀil* 'Who without-El?' Krahmalkov has suggested the sense of these names appears most clearly if they are conflated: *manna ˀanā balti-ˀil* 'Who [am] I without-El?' (1965: 97). The full form is, however, too syntactically dense to stand as a name. A full survey of the onomastica would reveal other patterns like this one and probably a fuller list of exceptions than we have gathered. The latter are, as far as we can tell, limited to royal and divine names and the special names of prophets' children. One of each class occurs in the first part of Isaiah. The royal name, if such it is, is *plʾ-ywʿṣ-ʾl-gbwr-ʾby-ʿd-śr-šlwm* 'Warrior-El [is] a-wonder-counsellor. The-Eternal-Father [is] a-Prince-of-Peace' (Isa 9:5); the translation is difficult, but the name contains two clauses, four constituents and eight units on any parsing, and is both the longest and most complex name in Northwest Semitic. Isaiah's own son's name is simpler: *mhr-šll-ḥš-bz* 'The-spoil speeds. The-prey makes-haste' (Isa 8:3). Again, the name has two clauses and four constituents, but it has only four units. Another apparent counterexample may be the Punic name Hierombal which is probably Punic *ʾḥyrmbʿl* with loss of the initial glottal stop; this name, and there are probably others like it, is derived from an older personal name *ʾḥyrm* 'Ahiram, Hiram,' 'The Brother exalts,' which is here equated with Baʿal, thus 'Baʿal is Hiram.' (The name could also be rendered 'Baʿal, my Brother is exalted,' a 2-clause royal name.) This encapsulation of an older name is common in the Akkadian onomasticon, which observes similar but slightly more complex constraints in general. There, too, the most complex names are royal or otherwise sacred, as in one of Esarhaddon's ritual names, *aššur-eṭil-ilāni-kīn-aplu* 'Aššur-eṭil-ilāni sets-up an-heir,' in which the older royal name *aššur-eṭil-ilāni* 'Aššur [is] the hero-of-the-gods' is enclosed. The Akkadian onomasticon, with royal and sacred exceptions, is limited to single clause names with three constituents and phrase names.

Thus the notion of a core of a verse system can be extended from a metrical system and a rhythmic base to a constrictional system and an onomastic core. The extension is loose. Although the phenomena in the Northwest Semitic case are of the same sort, they are not, as in the Indo-European case, directly related. It is, as far as we have argued, a coincidence that names are involved in both cases, because there is no reason to suppose that names were at all crucial to the development of Canaanite verse. Our argument is only that constraints like those in verse appear in personal names; if the two long names cited, both of which have matching constituents, are any sign, troping was not foreign to names. The appearance of the constraints in the two realms is related, but how we cannot say. It is a major coincidence that proper names appear in both O'Nolan's arguments and ours, but it remains only a coincidence.

Without taking a firm position on the character of Canaanite orality, we have drawn heavily on the suggestiveness of oral analogies. Musicality does not seem so helpful, but the constriction we have proposed for Hebrew verse is amenable to musical understanding. The relevant argument derives from Emeneau (1966) who suggests that because the syntax of Toda song units is predictable, "phrase and sentence intonation patterns . . . are probably completely wiped out by the patterns, melodic or other, of song renditions" (1966: 324-25). If this argument carries, we may adapt it to Canaanite verse. Insofar as syntactic structure was predictable from the constrictional frame of the verse, intonation patterns would be predictable without being used. To that extent, at least, it is likely that Canaanite verse was sung.

### *1.8 The plan of the essay*

Before we undertake the demonstration of the workability of the proposed description of Hebrew verse, we need to review the general situation of Canaanite verse sketched in 1.2 and place Hebrew verse and our corpus of verse in particular in a broader context (1.8.1). The generality of our description is a matter for further study which will only be possible after consideration of these preliminary results. A note on the plan of the chapters concludes this chapter (1.8.2).

#### *1.8.1 The corpus*

Canaanite poetry is attested in Ugaritic and various dialects of Phoenician and South Canaanite over a span of a millennium and a half. The latest attestations, the Mactar Inscriptions, represent a system different in overall structure from the earliest, the Ugaritic myths, legends, and rituals. Poetry written in later Hebrew (i.e., from late antiquity and after) belongs to a different realm, a product of educated bilingual speakers who adapted resources and conventions from other traditions to their own language. It is an open question whether poetic texts will be found which antedate those from Ugarit; the recent discoveries at Tell Mardikh (ancient Ebla) make this likely.

Within the realm of Canaanite poetry, the Neo-Punic texts are not alone in deviating from the earliest system. Both of the major bodies of verse from the second half of the first millennium B.C.E. are also different: the post-exilic Israelite prophets and the Qumran psalmists are recognized to be writing a different sort of verse than pre-exilic poets. On the other hand, uniformity of fine structural features has been recognized in Ugaritic (14th c.) and pre-exilic Biblical Hebrew (ca. 1200-587). Within this enormous body of verse, there are some texts which are more amenable to treatment than others. Since part of our goal is to describe the gross structure of whole texts, virtually all of Ugaritic verse must be excluded from the outset because so many texts are fragmentary or of disputed structure. Much biblical poetry is thereby excluded also: the description of books which are entirely poetic would require extending our scope enormously, and we study only one such book, the Poem of Zephaniah.

The poems best suited to intensive study of fine structure and cursory review of gross structure are those with an overall shape guaranteed by the tradition, the isolated poems of the Pentateuch and the Former Prophets, and the Psalms. To a selection from these groups, we add one poem of an integrity undoubted by moderns, the Psalm of Habaqquq, appended to the prophecy in the third and last chapter of the book.

Since none of our descriptive features is unique to any poem, that is, since the features of the oldest poems treated here are essentially the features of the latest, the selection of the poems to be studied is not crucial to our description. Any group of poems reliably dated to the six centuries between 1200 and 600 would yield basically the same description. Our argument in the following chapters will be difficult because we are treating some of the most difficult texts in Hebrew; recent and intensive study of these texts in part compensates for the difficulties. Our linguistic argumentation will refer only to the parsing of the texts given in Chapter 2. There are some points at which we are dissatisfied with our reading of the text, and not only in the oldest texts.

The corpus is drawn in roughly equal portions from the three sections of the Bible. There are five poems from the Pentateuch: the Testaments of Jacob (Genesis 49) and of Moses (Deuteronomy 33); the Songs at the Sea (Exodus 15) and of Moses (Deuteronomy 32); and the Oracles of Balaam (Numbers 23-24): these include 453 lines, 37% of the corpus of 1,225 lines. Four poems are drawn from the Prophets: from the Former Prophets, the Song of Deborah (Judges 5) and David's Lament over Saul and Jonathan (2 Samuel 1); and from the Latter Prophets, the Psalm of Habaqquq (Habaqquq 3) and the Book of Zephaniah. There are 414 lines in these poems, 34% of the corpus. From the Writings, three psalms are studied: Psalms 78, 106, 107; a total of 358 lines, 29% of the corpus.

In still rougher terms, the corpus is chronologically distributed over the six centuries involved. The dating of poetic texts is problematic, but the study of the oldest poems in recent years has used enough diversity of argumentation to inspire confidence in a tentative scheme (Albright 1969, Cross and Freedman 1948, 1955, 1972, 1975, Cross 1973a, Freedman 1975b, 1976a, Robertson 1972).

The scheme proposed in Freedman (1976a) covers the period from the twelfth through the tenth and ninth centuries, recognizing three periods. (With the exceptions discussed below, the dates assigned by Robertson agree, although Robertson treats fewer poems.) In the first period of Militant Mosaic Yahwism (12th century), Freedman dates Exodus 15, Judges 5, and Psalm 29. (The first two of these are discussed in their historical context in Freedman 1975a.) The Patriarchal Revival period (11th century) he associates with the tribal testaments of Genesis 49 and Deuteronomy 33, and the Oracles of Balaam. In the last of his periods, that of Monarchic Syncretism (10th century and later), he dates, with varying degrees of firmness, the four poems of the Book of Samuel (The Song of Hannah, 1 S 2; The Lament of David, 2 S 1; The Psalm of David, 2 S 22 =

Ps 18; and The Last Words of David, 2 S 23), the Song of Moses (Dt 32), and Psalms 68, 78, 72.

The dates of two of these, Deuteronomy 32 and Psalm 78, are fairly controversial, but the arguments vary generally over the range staked out by Freedman. Substantive discussion refers to the historical situation of the Song and the Psalm. Current opinion, as Robertson (1972: 231) notes, assigns the Song to *either* the eleventh or tenth century (Eissfeldt, Albright, Robertson, and more recently Mendenhall 1975); *or* the tenth or ninth century (Wright, Cross, Freedman, and more recently Shafer 1977: 40-42). (Some support for the higher date can be found in Freedman's discussion; see 1976a: 71, 93, contra the final verdict on p. 79.) Psalm 78 is almost always dated after Deuteronomy 32, for reasons most recently summarized by Mendenhall (1975), whose proposal for dating the Song of Moses is tied in part to his suggestion that it was composed by Samuel (thus, late in the 11th century). The Psalm is also often treated as a product of the Divided Monarchy (so, e.g., Robertson 1972, cf. Carroll 1971).

This proposal covers all but four of the texts in our corpus. Two of these must on other grounds be regarded as later. Zephaniah is dated to the last half of the seventh century, perhaps the last years of its third quarter (Murphy 1968, Fensham 1976, *pace* Williams 1963). Robertson (1972) has argued that the Psalm of Habaqquq should be dated earlier than the rest of the book; while the suggestion is tempting, it violates the rule of thumb that accretions to a text are usually later than its body, and ignores the convincing evidence for the widespread use of poetic archaizing in the late seventh and sixth centuries (Freedman 1976a: 65, 76). The two remaining psalms, Pss 106 and 107, may be dated to the late pre-exilic period on general grounds: there is nothing distinctively exilic or post-exilic in them, and there are no signs of archaic composition. Such dating is not entirely satisfactory, but it is the best available.

Using these dates, our corpus falls roughly into chronological thirds. Five poems are dated to the pre-monarchic period (12th-11th centuries). Genesis 49, Exodus 15, Numbers 23-24, Deuteronomy 33, and Judges 5; 419 lines all told, 34% of the corpus. In the first two centuries of Monarchy (10th-9th centuries), we situate Deuteronomy 32, 2 Samuel 1, and Psalm 78; 333 lines, 27% of the corpus. The last two pre-exilic centuries (8th-7th centuries) we associate with Habaqquq 3, Zephaniah, and Psalms 106 and 107; 473 lines, 39% of the corpus.

### *1.8.2 The study*

In Part II we present the major features of our descriptions of the fine structure of Hebrew verse. The texts under examination are cited in full with gloss and philological discussion in Chapter 2. Only the preferred segmentation is presented but points of conflict with other treatments are cited to aid the reader's pinpointing problem areas. Along with gloss and discussion, each line entry in Chapter 2 contains an index to the line's occurrence in Part II. In Chapter 3, the lines are parsed after a presentation of difficult points not treated in 1.4. The sections of Chapter 3 are not based simply on the constriction; unit arrays in each clause and constituent group in Chapter 3 are specified. The lines are also sorted by constituent order there, and verbal and verbless and dependent and independent clauses are separated. The sorting procedures are open to dispute since the classification, especially of dependent clauses, is difficult (cf. Friedrich 1975: 17-20), but none of the disputable points is involved crucially in our treatment. The detailed classification allows the reader to check across fairly discrete groups of syntactic phenomena.

The six tropes are treated in the next six chapters. The word-level trope of repetition is described in Chapter 4 and coloration in Chapter 5. The line-level tropes of matching and gapping are treated separately in Chapters 6 and 7; the overlap between the tropes is not given special treatment, but serves to structure both discussions. All cases of syntactic dependency are discussed in Chapter 8, except for the structurally distinct subtrope of mixing, which occupies Chapter 9. All examples of the tropes are cited in Part II.

Part III departs from the major argument, which concerns fine structural features, and launches a secondary argument, that fine structural features interact to create gross structures of a sort not previously recognized. Representative as the bulk of our corpus may be considered, the number of poems involved is small. The argument in Part III is not only secondary to the major argument but much more tentative. It is also unfortunately lapidary as a result of the enormous amount of material to be treated.

Finally, it seems necessary to discuss the question of the relation of the emendations adopted to the proposal: are any of them motivated solely by the desire to carry through the proposal? We believe that none are, but there is one point at which such motivation could be alleged. We have five times, at Gen 49:14b; Dt 33:12c, 24d, and 26b; and Zph 3:5e, emended participles to finite verb forms and it could be suggested that the resulting simplification of the grammar of participles is unnecessary. We believe the simplification is worth the emendations, but if our treatment is regarded as merely simplistic, the necessary changes in the treatment of participles can be made without systemic alterations of the description of the other 1220 lines.

# CHAPTER TWO
# THE TEXTS

## *2.0 Introduction*

The corpus of texts consists of 1225 lines of Classical Hebrew verse. The text is established below and accompanied by brief annotation, which does not pretend to exhaust or even sample recent study; it does not hint at the extent of our indebtedness. Generally only proposals accepted, regarded with favor, or of special reference to our argument are cited, and then only cursorily, although sometimes the originator of a suggestion is noted and remarks on difficult etymologies are provided. Substantive deviation from the vocalization and word division of the Massoretic text and from received views of Hebrew syntax and word study are the matter of the notes; discussion of many grammatical points is deferred to Part II of the essay; some areas cannot be treated here at all. The notes to the corpus also provide a proleptic summary of Part II in the form of an index of each line's appearances in them; the references only encompass discussion of the constraints and the poetic tropes. A partial summary is also provided by the gloss which accompanies each line.

The glosses are so called to beg some interesting questions which are not proper to our discussion (cf. Newman 1976). Chief among these is, How are the tropes to be represented adequately in translation? Also important is the problem posed by the suggestion that translations of Hebrew verbs should reflect the degree of their transitivity as directly as possible; that in many cases this is impossible is an indication of the wrongheadedness of the idea. Further, hendiadyses are not consistently resolved; words required by English idiom are silently supplied; the temporal references of the verb forms are often left unspecified, notably in the older verse (cf. Freedman 1976b and Gevirtz 1973), through use of that odd tense, the English present (Wright 1974); emphatic particles are often not represented at all in the glosses (rendering them gracefully into English seems to be impossible).

The orthography used is an eclectic one. In some recent work which takes into account the development of the system of Hebrew orthography, an effort has been made to reproduce a base line orthography, i.e., the archaic texts have been set out without vowel letters. It is simpler to maintain the Massoretic spelling as often as possible; this procedure accurately reflects the state of the MT itself, which is, despite much regularization, also eclectic. Similarly, not only do we not reconstruct a pre-Massoretic vocalization; we avoid the use of vocalization as much as possible. For our purposes, a morphological note is just as clear as a vocalized form and avoids giving undue weight to what is finally in large part a complex and sinuous reconstruction, rich with indeterminacies distinct from those of the consonantal text. On the special problems of the orthography of repeated units, see Andersen (1970b).

Diacritics here are used to reflect our text parsing. All emphatic particles not recognized in the Massoretic Text are set off by a hyphen, as are all particles recognized there and treated as words. Hyphens also connect nomina in the same nominal phrase; they only coincidentally reproduce *maqqep*'s, the 'dashes' of the Massoretes. Phrases connected by hyphens correspond to constituents. Items that stand alone or, with the exception of particles, are linked by hyphens correspond to units; with one exception, this matches the Massoretes' treatment. The exception is the relative pronoun *š*, the only nomen always bound in the MT to what follows it; it here stands alone when it serves as a nomen, though not when it is used as a conjunction.

The emendations made here of the deepest level of the MT, the consonantal text without vowel letters, are few and generally well accepted. Occasionally use is made of the principle of haplographic loss; in such cases reference to the principle of *scriptio continua* would have served as well (Watson 1967, 1971), given that either way defects in the consonantal text are recognized, as Andersen (1976) notes. The vowel letters and word division of the MT are respected but some of the lines discussed here are among the most difficult in the dialect and wherever necessary the text has been reconsidered. The siglum for an emended text, ET, refers to emendation of the consonantal text. It is used whenever a dash marking an emphatic particle is introduced, although no emendation need be involved; and it is not used in cases in which the orthography of MT is not altered, even though an emendation is proposed.

Duplicate lines are handled as distinct if they occur across texts and identical if within. There are only three lines that occur twice in the corpus beyond individual text boundaries; no account is taken of these duplications. They are Gen 49:9d = Num 24:9b, Gen 49:26e = Dt 33:16d, and Ps 106:1b = Ps 107:1a. The 19 lines which occur more than once within texts are treated alone, without their 25 copies, in Part II; both copy and original are discussed in Chapters 2 and 10. The working corpus of Part II is 1200 lines. The once only duplicates are the following:

| | | |
|---|---|---|
| Ex 15:1b | = | 21b |
| Ex 15:1c | = | 21c |
| Num 23:22b | = | 24:8b |
| Num 24:3a | = | 24:15a |
| Num 24:3b | = | 24:15b |
| Num 24:3c | = | 24:15c |
| Num 24:4a | = | 24:16a |

| | | |
|---|---|---|
| Num 24:4a* | = | 24:16b |
| Num 24:4b | = | 24:16c |
| Num 24:4c | = | 24:16d |
| 2 S 1:19b | = | 27a |
| Zph 2:2c | = | 2:2e |
| Ps 106:1a | = | 48d |
| Ps 107:6a | = | 28a |
| Ps 107:13a | = | 19a |
| Ps 107:13b | = | 19b |

(Num 23:22a and 24:8a are not emended. The asterisk in Num 24:4a* indicates a complete restoration.) Zph 1:2c has three duplicates, 1:3f, 1:10b and 3:8b. Ps 107:8a and 8b are identical to 15a, 21a, and 31a, and 15b, 21b, and 31b, respectively.

The headnotes to the poems provide information about overall treatments of the poems and the boundaries and length of the texts. Further, they compare the stichometry of the text here and in BH3 and sometimes BHS. These comparisons should provide a general orientation to difficult areas in lineation according to the canons of modern study; it is only a general one because the editors of those volumes had at their command resources not at ours, viz., large scale deletion and emendation, and because they were more willing to treat as prose material within poems than we are. Major differences are seen in connection with Exodus 15, Judges 5, and 2 Samuel 1; setting these poems aside, we may say that the differences across the two or three lineations balance out. Also cited in the headnotes is the result of collation with the Massoretic text of BFBS in those cases in which it preserves lines of verse, viz., Exodus 15, Deuteronomy 32, Judges 5, and the Psalms. The Massoretic tradition of divisions has never received the same attention as the other accidents of the text; it goes unmentioned, e.g., in the otherwise voluminous study of Ginsburg (1897). The BFBS text is based primarily on the first hand of the Lisbon manuscript BM MS Or 2626-8 and in it "the Masoretic traditions as to spacing, &c., have been followed as closely as possible." That statement of editorial policy does not give perfect assurance and the text is known to have typographical errors.

## *2.1 Genesis 49. The Testament of Jacob*

The basic treatment is Speiser (1964); more recent work has concentrated on individual sections of the poem. Gen 49:1 is excluded as prose with Speiser (1964: 361, 370). The poem is 80 lines long.

The lineation of the text in BH3 and BHS is not generally distinct from the one used here. BH3 divides vv 3ab and 26ab differently, joins together vv 3cd and 22ab, and treats v 1b as verse; in the portion in which the texts overlap (i.e., after v 1b), our text is two line divisions longer. BHS reads the same text as BH3 except that vv 22ab are split; our text is only one line division fuller than theirs and differs further in excluding v 1b.

2a *hqbṣw wšmʿw bny-yʿqb*
Gather and listen, children of Jacob.
[3.4.21 4.1.4]

2b *wšmʿw ʾl-yśrʾl-ʾbykm*
Listen to Israel, your father.
[3.3.4 4.1.4]

3a *rʾwbn-bkry*
Reuben, my first born,
[3.5.5 8.3]

3b *ʾth kḥy-wrʾšyt-ʾwny*
You are my strength and the first fruit of my vigor,
[3.3.24 8.3]

3c *ytr-śʾt*
Overweening in arrogance,
For other treatments of this line, see Gevirtz (1971: 90) and Dahood (1974b: 81).
[3.5.5 4.1.1 6.1.8 8.3]

3d *wytr-ʿz*
Overweening in force.
[3.5.5 4.1.1 6.1.8 8.3]

4a *pḥz kmym ʾl-twtr*
You are as unsteady as water. You shall not excel.
The infinitive *pḥz* is used here as a finite verb.
[3.4.2]

4b *ky-ʿlyt mškby-ʾbyk*
You took over the bed of your father's beloved.
[3.3.3 5.3.2 6.1.1]

4c *ʾz ḥllt yṣwʿy ʿlh* ET *ʾz-ḥllt yṣwʿ-yʿlh*
You profaned the couch of your father's beloved.
Redividing the consonantal text, read *yʿlh* 'female mountaingoat, concubine,' after Dahood (1964b: 282, 1965b: 319, 1974b: 81). Gevirtz (1971: 98) suggests parsing *ʿlh* as a f. participle of *ʿwl* 'to suckle,' thus 'suckler, nursemaid.'
[3.3.3 5.3.2 6.1.1]

5a *šmᶜwn-wlwy ᵓḥym*
Simeon and Levi are brothers.
[3.3.24 6.1.3]

5b *kly-ḥms mkrtyhm*
Their knives are tools of violence.
On the etymology of *mkrtyhm*, see Dahood (1961, 1966b: 418, 1969b: 74).
[3.3.25 6.1.3]

6a *bsdm ᵓl-tbᵓ npšy*
O my person, do not enter the council of their congregation.
The form *tbᵓ* is a defectively spelt f. imperative.
[3.4.6 5.3.2 6.1.4]

6b *bqhlm ᵓl-tḥd kbdy*
O my glory, be not joined to the council of their congregation.
[3.4.6 5.3.2 6.1.4]

6c *ky-bᵓpm hrgw ᵓyš*
They murdered a powerful man in their anger.
[3.3.48 5.3.2 6.1.2]

6d *wbrṣnm ᶜqrw šwr*
They hamstrung a powerful man at their whim.
The sense of *šwr* 'ox, strong one' here was first observed by F. I. Andersen (p.c.).
[3.3.48 5.3.2 6.1.2]

7a *ᵓrwr ᵓpm-ky-ᶜz*
Cursed be their strong anger,
The *ky* in this line and the next are emphatic.
[3.3.25 8.3]

7b *wᶜbrtm-ky-qšth*
Their cruel wrath.
[3.5.5 8.3]

7c *ᵓḥlqm byᶜqb*
I will apportion them throughout Jacob-Israel.
Reevaluating the sense of *b* here, Freedman (1975b: 17) translates this line and the next, 'I will divide them from Jacob, / and I will banish them from Israel.'
[3.3.4 5.1.4 6.1.1]

7d *wᵓpyṣm byśrᵓl*
I will scatter them throughout Jacob-Israel.
[3.3.4 5.1.4 6.1.1]

8a *yhwdh ᵓth ywdwk ᵓḥyk*
Judah, you: your brothers praise you.
[3.4.22]

8b *ydk bᶜrp-ᵓybyk*
Your hand is on your enemy's nape.
[3.3.24]

8c *yštḥww lk bny-ᵓbyk*
Your father's children bow to you.
[3.3.31]

9a *gwr-ᵓryh yhwdh*
Judah is a lion whelp.
[3.3.25]

9b *mṭrp bny ᶜlyt*
My son, you have grown up on prey.
[3.4.6]

9c *krᶜ rbṣ kᵓryh*
He crouches. He reclines like a lion.
[3.4.2]

9d *wklbyᵓ my yqymnw* = Num 24:9b
Like a lion, who will rouse him?
[3.3.57 6.2.2]

10a *lᵓ-yswr šbṭ myhwdh*
The commander's staff shall not depart from between Judah's feet,
[3.3.28 5.3.2 bis 6.2.2 7.1.1 9.1]

10b *wmḥqq mbyn-rglyw*
The commander's staff shall not depart from between Judah's feet,
[3.3.10 5.3.2 bis 6.2.2 7.1.1 9.1]

10c *ᶜd ky ybᵓ šylh* ET *ᶜd-ky-ybᵓ šy lh*
As long as the tribute and obedience of peoples come to him,

On the emendation to *šay lōh*, see Moran (1958: 412), Speiser (1964: 366), Brockington (1973: 8), and NAB.
[3.3.66 4.1.2 5.3.5 6.1.7 7.1.1 9.1]

10d *wlw yqht-ᶜmym*
As long as the tribute and obedience of peoples come to him.
[3.3.21 4.1.2 5.3.5 6.1.7 7.1.1 9.1]

11a *ᵓsry lgpn ᶜyrh*
He ties his ass to the vine.
*ᵓsry* is an infinitive used as a finite verb.
[3.3.36 6.3.2 7.1.1]

11b *wlśrqh bny-ᵓtnw*
He ties his she-ass's foal to the stock.
[3.3.13 6.3.2 7.1.1]

11c *kbs byyn lbšw*
He washes his robe in wine.
Dahood's suggestion (1974b: 81; cf. 1970b: 392, 1971b: 355-56) that the idiom here and in v 11d means 'to wash clean of,' has much to recommend it, but the figure depicted is not so well delineated that we can be too precise about his domestic habits. D. N. and C. Freedman (p.c.) suggest that he is dyeing his clothes the color of wine, a rich, if not royal, red.
[3.3.36 6.3.2 7.1.1]

11d *wbdm-ᶜnbym swth*
He washes his mantle in grape's blood.
[3.3.13 6.3.2 7.1.1]

12a *ḥklyly ᶜynym myyn*
His eyes are brighter than wine.
[3.3.68 6.1.3]

12b *wlbn šnym mḥlb*
His teeth are whiter than milk.
[3.3.68 6.1.3]

13a *zbwln lḥwp-ymym yškn*
Zebulon lives on the seashore.
[3.3.54 4.1.1 6.2.2 7.1.1]

13b *whwᵓ lḥwp-ᵓnywt*
He lives on the harbor front.
[3.3.10 4.1.1 6.2.2 7.1.1]

13c *wyrktw ᶜl-ṣydn*
His flank lives near Sidon.
[3.3.10 6.2.2 7.1.1]

14a *yśśkr ḥmr-grm*
Issachar is a bony ass.
[3.3.24]

14b *rbṣ byn-hmšptym*
He reclines amid the hearths.

Read for MT's participle a suffixing finite verb form. On *mšptym*, see Albright (1969: 275, n. ee), and Boling (1975: 112); for further consideration of 14ab, see Andersen (1970a: 123, n.6, but cf. 55 at #33).
[3.3.4]

15a *wyrᵓ mnḥh-ky-ṭwb*
He sees the good land of rest,

Dahood (1967a: 427-28) treats the *ky*'s in this and the next line as emphatics; see Hoftijzer (1973: 478). The f. adjective *ṭwbh* is defectively spelt.
[3.3.3 5.3.2 8.2.1]

15b *wᵓt-hᵓrṣ-ky-nᶜmh*
The sweet land of rest.
[3.5.5 5.3.2 8.2.1]

15c *wyṭ škmw lsbl*
He sets his shoulder to bearing.
[3.3.34]

15d *wyhy lms-ᶜbd*
He becomes a corvée force.
[3.3.4]

16a *dn ydyn ᶜmw*
He governs his people Israel according to one judgment.

The subject here is Yahweh, not Dan, whose testament follows. The idiom *dyn ᶜmw* is reserved for the deity, as in fact are most other absolute uses of the term *dyn*. The form *dn* is a defective spelling of *dyn* 'judgment'; the preposition of *kᵓḥd* does double duty. For further discussion of the separation between 16ab and 17a, see 10.1.1.
[3.3.48 5.3.6 5.3.7 6.1.2]

16b *kᵓḥd šbṭy yśrᵓl* ET *kᵓḥd šbṭ yśrᵓl*
He rules his people Israel according to one judgment.

Read a finite verb form of *šbṭ*, for usual *špṭ* 'to rule, judge' deleting the *y* of *šbṭy* as a dittograph; cf. Dahood (1969d: 394) and Reid (1975).
[3.3.48 5.3.6 5.3.7 6.1.2]

17a *yhy dn nḥš ᶜly-drk*
Dan is a snake by the path,
[3.4.19 7.1.1 8.2.2]

17b *špypn ᶜly-ᵓrḥ*
A serpent by the road,
[3.3.10 7.1.1 8.2.2]

17c *hnšk ᶜqby-sws*
Who bites the horse's heels.
[3.3.18 8.2.2]

17d *wypl rkbw ᵓḥwr*
He makes the rider fall off backwards.

Read *ypl* as a *Hipᶜil* form; cf. Cross and Freedman (1975: 87 n. 62).
[3.3.35]

18 *lyšwᶜtk qwyty yhwh*
Yahweh, I await your saving action.

Most moderns regard this line as extrinsic in some sense or other: Speiser comments, "In all likelihood, a marginal gloss or a misplaced general invocation" (1964: 367, cf. 370); cf. Freedman (1976a: 102, n. 72). We disagree; see 10.1.1.
[3.4.6]

19a *gd gdwd ygwdnw*
A troop trounces Gad.

Andersen (1970a: 42-44), among others, takes the tribal names here and in several other oracles as "titles," comparing Deuteronomy 33; the "title" formulary there is clearly distinct.
[3.3.56]

19b *whwᵓ ygd ᶜqb* ET *whwᵓ ygd ᶜqb-m*
He tramples from behind.

The *m* of *ᶜqb-m* is taken from the MT of the following word, on which the preposition is otiose; Speiser (1964: 363) rearranges the consonantal text similarly, reading the *-m* as a 3 m. pl. suffix, thus 'at their heels,' as do some versions and, among moderns, BH3, BHS, and NAB.
[3.3.42]

20a *m'šr šmnh lḥmw* ET *'šr šmnh lḥmw*
Asher: his food is rich.
[3.4.10]

20b *whw' ytn mᶜdny-mlk*
He supplies royal dainties.
[3.3.40]

21a *nptly 'ylh-šlḥh*
Naphtali is a released hind,
[3.3.24 8.3]

21b *hntn 'mry-špr*
Who bears beautiful fawns.

The f. ending of *hntn(h)* is defectively spelt, cf. Dahood (1974b: 81). On *'mry* 'fawns,' see Speiser (1964: 367), and on *špr* 'beauty,' see Dahood (1974c: 383).
[3.3.18 8.3]

22a *bn-prt ywsp*
Joseph is a wild colt,

On *prt*, from *pr'* 'wild ass,' see Speiser (1964: 367-68) and Dahood (1970b: 401).
[3.3.25 4.1.1 8.3]

22b *bn-prt ᶜly-ᶜyn*
A wild colt by the spring of Shur,
[3.5.4 4.1.1 5.3.2 5.3.3 8.3]

22c *bnwt-ṣᶜdh ᶜly-šwr*
A wild ass colt by the spring of Shur.

On *bnwt-ṣᶜdh*, and the Arb cognate *banāt ṣaᶜdat* 'wild asses,' see Speiser (1964: 368). The combinations here were recognized by Gevirtz (1975: 37-49).
[3.5.4 5.3.2 5.3.3 8.3]

23a *wymrrhw wrbw* ET *wymrrhw wyrbhw*
They harry and contend with him.

The second verb is emended after Sam and LXX; see Speiser (1964: 368), BH3, and BHS.
[3.4.15]

23b *wyśṭmhw bᶜly-ḥṣym*
The archers harass him.
[3.3.2]

24a *wtšb bʾytn qštw*
His bow was broken permanently.

The referent of the suffix of *qštw* is unclear; Speiser renders 'each one's [scil, each of the archers'] bow' (1964: 368-69); Dahood's approach is similar (1959c: 1007). Dahood recognized the *Qal* passive of the verb *šbb* 'to break' here on the basis of Ug cognates (1959c: 1003-5); on the same root, see further Blommerde (1969: 133); cf. Brockington (1973: 8).
[3.3.31]

24b *wypzw zrʿy-ydyw*
His powerful arms trembled.
[3.3.2]

24c *mydy-ʾbyr-yʿqb*
From the power of Jacob-Israel's Champion,
[3.5.5 5.1.4 8.2.3]

24d *mšm-rʿh-ʾbn-yśrʾl*
From the strength of the Shepherd of Jacob-Israel's children,

Read *miššēm*, literally, 'from the name,' with Onkelos; see Speiser (1964: 369), Brockington (1973: 8), BH3, BHS, and NAB. Read *ʾbn* as a plural of *bn*; cf. Freedman (1976a: 65) and Stuart (1976: 150, n. 43).
[3.5.5 5.1.4 8.2.3]

25a *mʾl-ʾbyk wyʿzrk*
From the god of your father, El-Shaddai, who helps you,
[3.5.2 5.1.1 6.1.8 8.2.3]

25b *wʾt šdy wybrkk* ET *wʾl-šdy wybrkk*
From the god of your father, El-Shaddai, who blesses you,

This emendation is accepted in Cross (1973a: 9, n. 23), Brockington (1973: 8), BH3, BHS, and NAB.
[3.5.2 5.1.1 6.1.8 8.2.3]

25c *brkt-šmym mʿl*
May the blessings of Heavens, from above,
[3.5.4 4.1.1 8.2.3]

25d *brkt-thwm rbṣt tḥt*
The blessings of the Deep, crouched below,
[3.5.1 4.1.1 8.2.3]

25e *brkt-šdym-wrḥm*
The blessings of Breasts-and-Womb,
[3.5.5 4.1.1 8.2.3]

26a *brkt ᵓbyk gbrw ᶜl* ET *brkt-ᵓbyk gbr-wᶜl*
The blessings of your father, Hero and Almighty,
Read *gbr* 'warrior, hero' for MT *gbrw*; the divine name ᶜEli is spelt defectively.
[3.5.5 4.1.1 8.2.3]

26b *brkt hwry ᶜd* ET *brkt-hrry-ᶜd*
The blessings of the eternal heights,
Read *hrry*, after Hab 3:6; cf. BH3, BHS, and Speiser (1964: 269).
[3.5.5 4.1.1 6.1.8 8.2.3]

26c *tᵓwt-gbᶜt-ᶜwlm*
The delights of the everlasting hills,
On the root of *tᵓwt*, see Dahood (1963a: 42).
[3.5.5 6.1.8 8.2.3]

26d *thyyn lrᵓš-ywsp*
Be on the head of Joseph, Nazir of his Brothers,
[3.3.4 5.1.3 8.2.3]

26e *wlqdqd-nzyr-ᵓḥyw* = Dt 33:16d
On the skull of Joseph, Nazir of his Brothers.
[3.5.5 5.1.3 8.2.3]

27a *bnymyn zᵓb yṭrp*
Benjamin is a wolf that ravens.
[3.4.8]

27b *bbqr yᵓkl ᶜd*
From morning to evening he eats booty.
On the coordination here, see Dahood (1964b: 282, 1965b: 27, 1970b: 392).
[3.3.48 5.2.2 6.1.2]

27c *wlᶜrb yḥlq šll*
From morning to evening he divides spoil.
[3.3.48 5.2.2 6.1.2]

## *2.2 Exodus 15. The Song at the Sea*

The basic treatments are Cross and Freedman (1975), which substantially reprints Cross and Freedman (1955); Albright (1969); Cross (1973a);

and Freedman (1974, 1975b). We exclude the opening words of the chapter with all and include v 21 in the text after Freedman (1974: 170-71, 175). The poem is 56 lines long. On the lineation, see Coats (1969) and Muilenburg (1966).

The text of BH3 has 18 more lines than ours; this difference is the result of its tendency to make the lines as short as possible. BH3 divides vv 13ab in a different way than we do; joins together vv 16de; and splits 19 of our lines: vv 1c, 4c, 6a, 6b, 8a, 10c, 11a, 11b, 11c, 13c, 15a, 15b, 16a, 16b, 17a, 17b, 17c, 18, and 21c.

The tradition exemplified in BFBS is skewed in the opposite direction; that text has 13 fewer divisions than ours, and does not recognize 21abc as verse. The joins are at vv 1ab, 2ab, 3ab, 4ab, 5ab, 7bc, 9ab, 9cd, 9ef, 10ab, 12ab, 13ab, and 16de.

1a *ʾšyrh lyhwh*
I will sing of Yahweh.
[3.3.4]

1b *ky-gʾh gʾh* = v 21b
He is highly exalted.
[3.3.7]

1c *sws-wrkbw rmh bym* = v 21c ET *sws-wrkb rmh bym*
He threw horse and chariotry into the sea.

For MT *rkbw* 'his rider,' read *rekeb* 'chariotry,' with Cross and Freedman (1975: 54, n. 2), Cross (1973a: 127, n. 48), and NAB. A possible rendering of MT is 'his charioteer,' with Freedman (1974: 171, 175); cf. Stuart (1976: 88, n. 12).
[3.3.47]

2a *ʿzy-wzmrt yh*
Yah is my strength and my defense.

Read a form of *zmrh* 'defense'; see Cross and Freedman (1975: 55, n. b). Van Dijk (1968: 41) suggests that the suffix of *ʿzy* does double duty. Cross and Freedman (1975: 54-56) regard v 2 as extrinsic to the poem since it "does not conform to the metrical structure [sic] which prevails throughout the remainder of the song. It also seems to be out of context at this point in the poem": they allow that "the antiquity of the couplet is not at all affected by these considerations." The view is appreciably modified in Freedman (1974: 191), while Cross (1973a: 127, n. 49) regards only vv 2ab as interpolated. Stuart (1976: 89, n. 13) regards the whole of v 2 as extrinsic.
[3.3.25]

2b *wyhy ly lyšwʿh*
He has become salvation for me.

[3.3.38]

2c *zh ʾly wʾnwhw*
This is my god, whom I admire.

The verbs of vv 2c and d are flipped in Cross and Freedman (1975: 55, n. e) to remedy a supposed "metrical imbalance" on the grounds that "the transposition of words is not an uncommon phenomenon in the transmission of a text, especially in a case where both words begin and end with the same letters": cf. Cross (1973a: 127, n. 50), and Stuart (1976: 89, n. 13). On the sense of *nwy*, see Cross and Freedman (1975: 56, n. e). Freedman (1974: 176) notes that *w* here and in v 2d is used emphatically; cf. Andersen (1970a: 40).
[3.4.8 8.3]

2d *ʾlhy-ʾby wʾrmmnhw*
My father's god, whom I extol.

[3.5.2 8.3]

3a *yhwh ʾyš-mlḥmh*
Yahweh is a warrior.

[3.3.24 4.1.1 6.1.3]

3b *yhwh šmw*
Yahweh is his name.

On the word order, see Andersen (1970a: 41, 55, 63).
[3.3.24 4.1.1 6.1.3]

4a *mrkbt-prʿh-wḥylw*
Pharaoh's chariots and his soldiery

The sense of *mrkbt-prʿh-wḥylw* may be 'Pharaoh's chariots, which are his strength,' as opposed to Israel's, which is Yahweh; Freedman (1974: 171, 179) renders the phrase as a resolved hendiadys, 'Pharaoh's chariot army.'
[3.5.5 8.2.1]

4b *yrh bym*
He throws into the sea.

[3.3.4 4.1.1 8.2.1]

4c *wmbḥr-šlšyw ṭbʿw bym-swp*
His chosen troops are drowned in the Reed Sea.

[3.3.41 4.1.1]

5a *thmt yksymw*
The abyss covers them.
[3.3.6]

5b *yrdw bmṣwlt kmw-ʾbn*
They go through the deeps like a stone.
[3.3.38]

6a *ymynk yhwh nʾdry bkḥ*
Yahweh, your right hand prevails in power.

The infinitive *nʾdry* is used for a finite verb. Dahood (1972: 394) and Freedman (1974: 164) render *nʾdry bkḥ* as an epithet, 'resplendent among the powerful,' and take all of v 6a as appositive to v 6b. The phrase *bkḥ* could be rendered 'against the powerful.'
[3.4.20 4.1.1 bis 4.1.5]

6b *ymynk yhwh trʿṣ ʾwyb*
Yahweh, your right hand smashes the enemy.

Dahood (1972: 394) and Freedman (1974: 164, 203, n. 4) take Yahweh as the subject: 'By your right hand, Yahweh / you have shattered the enemy.'
[3.4.20 4.1.1 bis 4.1.5]

7a *wbrb-gʾwnk thrs qmyk*
In your great majesty, you smash your foes.
[3.3.48]

7b *tšlḥ ḥrnk*
You send forth your anger.
[3.3.3]

7c *yʾklmw kqš*
It consumes them like stubble.
[3.3.4]

8a *wbrwḥ-ʾpyk nʿrmw mym*
At the blast of your nostrils, streams of water pile up.
[3.3.44 5.3.2 6.2.2]

8b *nṣbw kmw-nd nzlym*
Streams of water gather like a dyke.
[3.3.31 5.3.2 6.2.2]

8c *qpʾw thmt blb-ym*
Deeps foam up from the sea's heart.

The sense of *b* here is indicated by the fact that the text is describing a scene and what goes on 'in the midst of the sea' (as moderns render *blb-ym*) can hardly be seen; our understanding complements the suggestion of Clifford (1972: 170) that "the cosmic sea beneath the earth is meant" here.
[3.3.28 6.2.2]

9a *ᵓmr ᵓwyb*
The enemy says:
[3.3.2 8.1.1]

9b *ᵓrdp ᵓśyg*
I will pursue and overtake.
[3.4.15 8.1.1]

9c *ᵓḥlq šll*
I will divide the spoil.
[3.3.3 8.1.1]

9d *tmlᵓmw npšy*
My gullet will be full of them.

The use of the suffix on *tmlᵓmw*, an object of material with which, hardly demands alteration; Cross and Freedman (1975: 60, n. 25), Freedman (1960: 105), Cross (1973a: 129, n. 60), and Stuart (1976: 89, n. 21) read an emphatic *m* here; Freedman (1974: 172, 183) reads the suffix, as does van Dijk (1968: 11).
[3.3.2 8.1.1]

9e *ᵓryq ḥrby*
I will draw out my sword.
[3.3.3 8.1.1]

9f *twryšmw ydy*
My hand will dispossess them.

The suffix of *twryšmw*, like that in 9d, expresses an object and need not be read as an emphatic *m*.
[3.3.2 8.1.1]

10a *nšpt brwḥk*
You blow with your wind.
[3.3.4]

10b *ksmw ym*
The sea covers them.
[3.3.2]

10c *ṣllw kᶜwprt bmym-ᵓdyrym*
They sink like lead through the dreadful waters.

The hapax *ṣll* may be better rendered 'to perish'; see Cross and Freedman (1975: 61, n. 28).
[3.3.38]

11a *my kmkh bᵓlm yhwh*
Yahweh, who is like you among the holy gods?

[3.4.20 4.1.1 bis 4.1.5 5.3.2 6.1.4]

11b *my kmkh nᵓdr bqdš*
Glorious One, who is like you among the holy gods

Read *nᵓdr* as a vocative.
[3.4.20 4.1.1 bis 4.1.5 5.3.2 6.1.4 8.3]

11c *nwrᵓ-thlt-ᶜśh-plᵓ*
Revered with praises, performer of wonders?

[3.5.5 8.3]

12a *nṭyt ymynk*
You stretch out your right hand.

[3.3.3]

12b *tblᶜmw ᵓrṣ*
Earth swallows them up.

The referent of *ᵓrṣ* 'earth' here is probably chthonian, as noted in Cross (1973a: 129, n. 62), in Freedman (1974: 172, 186), and, with some discussion of the implications of the reference for the rest of the poem, in Tromp (1969: 23, 25-26).
[3.3.2]

13a *nḥyt bḥsdk ᶜm*
You lead in your love the people

[3.3.36 8.2.2]

13b *zw gᵓlt*
Which you redeemed.

[3.3.19 8.2.2]

13c *nhlt bᶜzk ᵓl-nwh-qdšk*
You guide them in your strength to your holy enclosure.

[3.3.38]

14a *šmᶜw ᶜmym yrgzwn*
The peoples hear. They tremble.

[3.4.2]

14b *ḥyl ʾḥz yšby-plšt*
Terror seizes the Philistine rulers.

The royal sense of *yšb* 'to sit; sit on a throne, rule' is probably, though not necessarily, apposite here. Freedman (1974: 172) renders 'inhabitants,' but in v 15c, 'kings,' and Cross (1973a: 130) is similarly divided in his rendering. In Freedman (1975b: 9-10), both occurrences of *yšby* are glossed 'enthroned ones.'
[3.3.40]

15a *ʾz-nbhlw ʾlwpy-ʾdwm*
The Edomite chiefs are dismayed.
[3.3.2]

15b *ʾyly-mwʾb yʾḥzmw rʿd*
Panic grips the Moabite lords.

On *ʾyly* 'rams,' see Cross and Freedman (1975: 62, n. 44).
[3.3.43]

15c *nmgw kl-yšby-knʿn*
All the Canaanite rulers collapse.
[3.3.2]

16a *tpl ʿlyhm ʾymth-wpḥd*
Terror and fear fall upon them.

Cross (1973a: 130) and Freedman (1974: 173) emend *tpl* to a *Hipʿil*, and render 'you brought down.' The form *ʾymth*, presumably case-inflected, is difficult.
[3.3.31]

16b *bgdl-zrwʿk ydmw kʾbn*
They are as silent as a stone in the greatness of your arm,

For another parsing of the verb, see Dahood (1962b).
[3.3.50 8.2.2]

16c *ʿd-yʿbr ʿmk yhwh*
While your people crosses over, Yahweh,
[3.4.13 4.1.1 4.1.3 4.1.5 8.2.2]

16d *ʿd-yʿbr ʿm*
While the people crosses over
[3.3.21 4.1.1 4.1.3 4.1.5 8.2.2]

16e *zw qnyt*
Which you purchased.

On *qny* 'to create' see Cross and Freedman (1975: 64, n. 54); Freedman (1974: 165) retains the traditional gloss, 'to purchase.' [3.3.19 8.2.2]

17a *tbᵓmw wtṭᶜmw bhr-nḥltk*
You bring them in and set them up on your hereditary height.
[3.4.2]

17b *mkwn lšbtk pᶜlt yhwh*
Yahweh, you made a sanctuary site for your reign.
[3.4.20 5.1.1 5.3.2]

17c *mqdš ᵓdny kwnnw ydyk*
Lord, your hands made a sanctuary site.
Many moderns, e.g., Cross (1973a: 131, n. 70) and Freedman (1974: 191), emend *ᵓdny* to *yhwh.*
[3.4.20 5.1.1 5.3.2]

18 *yhwh ymlk lᶜlm-wᶜd*
Yahweh rules forever.
[3.3.41]

21a *šyrw lyhwh*
Sing to Yahweh.
[3.3.4]

21b *ky-gᵓh gᵓh* = v 1b

21c *sws wrkbw rmh bym* = v 1c ET *sws-wrkb rmh bym*

## *2.3 Numbers 23-24. The Oracles of Balaam*

The basic treatment is Albright (1944, cf. 1969); we follow Mowinckel (1930) and Stuart (1976) in separating the little oracles of Num 24:20-24, which pose a problem we shall return to in 10.1.3. The text is 80 lines long.

Our text division is essentially that of BH3 and BHS, which break vv 23:24bc in a way other than ours; and join together vv 24:3bc and 24:15bc; our text is two lines longer.

23:7a *mn-ᵓrm ynḥny blq*
Balaq, King of Moab, brought me from Aram.
[3.3.44 5.1.3 6.1.2 7.1.1]

7b *mlk-mwᵓb mhrry-qdm*
Balaq, King of Moab, brought me from the eastern hills.
[3.3.10 5.1.3 6.1.2 7.1.1]

23:7c *lkh ʾrh ly yʿqb*
Come, curse Jacob-Israel for me.
[3.4.20 4.1.3 5.1.4]

7d *wlkh zʿmh yśrʾl*
Come, denounce Jacob-Israel.
[3.4.2 4.1.3 5.1.4]

8a *mh-ʾqb lʾ-qbh-ʾl*
I cannot damn what the god Yahweh does not damn.
Albright (1969: 16) renders vv 8ab as questions: 'How shall I curse whom El hath not cursed, / How shall I doom whom Yahweh hath not doomed?'
[3.3.3 5.1.1 6.1.1]

8b *wmh-ʾzʿm lʾ-zʿm-yhwh*
I cannot denounce what the god Yahweh does not denounce.
[3.3.3 5.1.1 6.1.1]

9a *ky-mrʾš-ṣrym ʾrʾnw*
I see him from rocks' peaks.
[3.3.8 5.3.5 6.1.1]

9b *wmgbʿwt ʾšwrnw*
I spy him from hilltops.
[3.3.8 5.3.5 6.1.1]

9c *hn-ʿm lbdd yškn*
This people lodges alone.
[3.3.54]

9d *wbgwym lʾ-ytḥšb*
It does not count itself among the nations.
[3.3.8]

10a *my mnh ʿpr-yʿqb*
Who can count the loose dirt corrals of Jacob-Israel?
[3.3.40 4.1.1 5.1.4 5.3.2 6.2.2]

10b *wmspr ʾt rbʿ yśrʾl* ET *wm spr ʾtrbʿ-yśrʾl*
Who can stake out the loose dirt corrals of Jacob-Israel?
The emendation of *mspr* is virtually universal; see, e.g., Albright (1944: 213, n. 27), Brockington (1973: 21), BH3, BHS, and NAB. The form *ʾtrbʿ* may be a bastard but we leave it unemended. The root of the word is Arb *rbḍ*, Heb and Akk *rbṣ*, Arm *rbʿ* 'to lie

down,' usually used of animals, and the noun here refers to the place of lying down, Arb *marbiḍ*, Heb *marbēṣ*, Arm *mrbʿtʾ*. There are three treatments of the form available: (a) emend to the reading of Sam, *mrbʿt*; (b) emend to *trbʿ*, a nomen locis with a *t*- preformative instead of the usual *m*- preformative; the Ug form of the noun is *trbṣ* (Gordon 1965: 482); (c) retain the consonantal text and take the ʾ as a sign of a plural form; we diffidently adopt the third course. Albright (1944: 213, n. 28) realized the correct solution but rejected it as Aramaizing; in the years since he wrote, it has been realized that some variability in the notation of secondarily articulated consonants is to be expected in early Hebrew. The advantage of this explanation over the one originated by Delitzsch and supported by Landsberger and Albright (1944: 213, n. 28), which refers to Akk *turbuʾtu* 'dust-cloud,' is that by it the reference of the questions is clarified. The multitudes of animals, Israel's livestock holdings, are alluded to as a gloss on the group's independence. The usual explanation, that Israel is marching and kicking up dust, is contradicted by the situation of the poem (Balaq commissions the curse because they are *not* marching) and by the text (Israel is tenting according to 23:9c).
[3.3.40 4.1.1 5.1.4 5.3.2 6.2.2]

10c *tmt npšy mwt yšrym* ET *tmt npšy mwt-yšr-m*
May I die the death of an honest person.

The emphatic *m* was first recognized in Albright (1944: 213, n. 28a), cf. Freedman (1960: 104), and Dahood (1968b: 147, n. 76).
[3.3.27 6.2.2]

10d *wthy ʾḥryty kmhw*
May my fate be like such a one's.

[3.3.28]

18a *qwm blq wšmʿ*
Rise, Balaq, Sippor's child, and listen.

[3.4.21 5.1.3]

18b *hʾzynh ʿdy bnw-ṣpr*
Hear my witness, Balaq, Sippor's child.

Read *ʿēdî* 'my witness' with some of the versions; see Albright (1944: 214, n. 31), Stuart (1976: 117, n. 9), and NAB.
[3.4.6 5.1.3]

19a *lʾ-ʾyš ʾl wykzb*
El is not a human who lies,

[3.4.8 8.3]

23:19b *wbn-ʾdm wytnḥm*
Nor a mortal who changes his story.
[3.5.2 8.3]

19c *hhwʾ ʾmr wlʾ-yʿśh*
Does he talk and not act?
[3.4.2]

19d *wdbr wlʾ-yqymnh* ET *wdbrw lʾ-yqymnh*
He fulfills his word.

The suffix on the verb is resumptive of the suffixed object, *dbrw*, the suffix of which is obscured by misdivision in the MT and *lʾ* is emphatic.
[3.3.7 6.2.1]

20a *hnh-brk lqḥty*
I have taken up a blessing.

The object *brkh* is spelt defectively.
[3.3.7 4.1.1 6.2.1]

20b *wbrk wlʾ-ʾšybnh*
I cannot turn back a blessing.

The suffix on the verb is resumptive and not an energic ending, as Albright (1944: 214, n. 39) contends; *w*(*lʾ*) here is emphatic.
[3.3.7 4.1.1 6.2.1]

21a *lʾ-hbyṭ ʾwn byʿqb*
No one sees evil in Jacob-Israel.

Since the impersonal passive sense of *Qal* active forms is usually associated with the plural, plurals should be read here and in v 21b; Albright (1944: 214, nn. 40, 42) reads passive verb forms.
[3.3.34 5.1.4 6.1.2]

21b *wlʾ-rʾh ʿml byśrʾl*
No one spots wickedness in Jacob-Israel.
[3.3.34 5.1.4 6.1.2]

21c *yhwh-ʾlhyw ʿmw*
Yahweh, its god, is with it.
[3.3.24 6.1.3]

21d *wtrwʿt mlk bw* ET *wtrʿt-mlk bw*
Royal majesty is amidst it.

On *trʿt* 'terror-producing, majesty,' see Albright (1944: 215, n. 43) and BHS.
[3.3.24 6.1.3]

22a *ʾl mwṣyʾm mmṣrym*
El is the one who brought them from Egypt.
[3.4.8]

22b *ktwʿpt rʾm lw* = v 24:8b ET *k-twʿpt-rʾm lw*
The Bull's power is his.
For the preposition *k* of the MT, read an emphatic *k(y)*.
[3.3.24]

23a *ky-lʾ-nḥš byʿqb*
No one can curse Jacob-Israel.
For the noun *nḥš* of the MT, read a 3 m. pl. suffixing verb form; read a similar form of *qsm* in 23b.
[3.3.4 5.1.4 6.1.1]

23b *wlʾ-qsm byśrʾl*
No one can hex Jacob-Israel.
[3.3.4 5.1.4 6.1.1]

23c *kʿt yʾmr lyʿqb*
Let it now be said to Jacob-Israel,
[3.3.50 5.1.4 8.1.1]

23d *wlyśrʾl mh pʿl ʾl*
To Jacob-Israel, What has El done?
[3.4.20 5.1.4 8.1.1]

24a *hn-ʿm klbyʾ yqwm*
This people rises like a lion,
[3.3.54 9.1]

24b *wkʾry ytnśʾ lʾ-yškb*
Like a lion, it raises itself and does not relax
[3.4.2 9.1]

24c *ʿd-yʾkl ṭrp*
Until it has eaten the prey
[3.3.21 6.1.1 9.1]

24d *wdm-ḥllym yšth*
And drunk the blood of the slain.
[3.3.21 6.1.1 9.1]

24:3a *nʾm-blʿm-bnw-bʿr* = 24:15a
Oracle of Balaam, son of Beor.
[3.5.5 4.1.1 4.4]

24:3b *wnᵓm hgbr* = 24:15b
Oracle of the man

[3.5.5 4.1.1 4.4 8.4]

3c *š tm hᶜyn* = 24:15c
Whose eye is perfect.

Read *tm* as a 3 f.s. finite verb form defectively spelt; there seems to be Qumranic support for this, Wellhausen's parsing of this verse, but the note in Brockington (1973: 21) is not clear.
[3.3.64 4.4 8.4]

4a *nᵓm-šmᶜ-ᵓmry-ᵓl* = 24:16a
Oracle of one who hears the words of knowledge of El Elyon,

[3.5.5 4.4 5.1.1 5.3.2 8.4]

4a* vacat ET *wydᶜ-dᶜt-ᶜlywn* = 24:16b
One who knows the words of the knowledge of El Elyon.

Restore the line from v 16, with most commentators, e.g., Albright (1944: 217, n. 59), BH3, BHS, and NAB.
[3.5.5 5.1.1 5.3.2 8.4]

4b *ᵓšr mḥzh šdy yḥzh* ET *mḥzh-šdy yḥzh* = 24:16c
He has seen the vision of Shadday,

Delete *ᵓšr* with v 16.
[3.3.7 8.2.1]

4c *npl-wglwy-ᶜynym* = 24:16d
Prostrate and open-eyed.

[3.5.5 8.2.1]

5a *mh-ṭbw ᵓhlyk yᶜqb*
Jacob-Israel, how beautiful are your tents,

[3.4.9 5.1.4 8.3]

5b *mškntyk yśrᵓl*
Jacob-Israel, your tabernacles.

[3.5.2 5.1.4 8.3]

6a *knḥlym nṭyw*
They are stretched out like enclosured date palms,

[3.3.8 5.3.2 8.2.1]

6b *kgnt ᶜly-nhr*
Like enclosured date palms by the River.

[3.5.4 5.3.2 8.2.1]

6c *kʾhlym nṭʿ yhwh*
Yahweh plants them like aloes,
[3.3.44 8.2.1]

6d *kʾrzym ʿly-mym*
Like cedars by the water.
[3.5.4 8.2.1]

7a *yzl mym mdlyw* ET *yzl mym mmdlyw*
Water flows from his thunder strokes.

The noun *mdl*, cognate to Ug *mdl* 'thunder bolt,' also occurs in Hab 3:4b; for a bibliography of discussions of the Ug word see de Moor (1971: 109) and note especially Dahood (1966b: 414-16; 1969e: 35), who renders it differently.
[3.3.28 4.1.2]

7b *wzrʿw bmym rbym* ET *wzr ʿwb mym-rbym*
He wrings clouds of many waters.

The verb is *zwr* 'to press down and out, wring'; redivision of words clarifies the rest of the line.
[3.3.33 4.1.2]

7c *wyrm mʾgg mlkw*
May his king be higher than Agag.
[3.3.31]

7d *wtnśʾ mlktw*
May his kingdom raise itself up.
[3.3.2]

8a *ʾl mwṣyʾw mmṣrym*
El is the one who led him from Egypt.

Cf. Num 23:22a
[3.4.8]

8b *ktwʿpt rʾm lw* ET *k-twʿpt-rʾm lw* = 23:22b

8c *yʾkl gwym ṣryw* ET *yʾkl gwy-m-ṣryw*
He eats his enemies' corpses.

Read *gawē*, with emphatic *m*, after Dahood (1962c: 65, 1964c: 398).
[3.3.3 6.2.1]

8d *wʿṣmtyhm ygrm*
He crushes their bones.
[3.3.7 6.2.1]

24:8e *wḥṣyw ymḥṣ*
He strikes them with his arrows.
[3.3.7 6.2.1]

9a *krʿ škb kʾry*
He crouches. He rests like a lion.
[3.4.2]

9b *wklbyʾ my yqymnw* = Gen 49:9d
Like a lion, who will rouse him?
[3.3.57]

9c *mbrkyk brwk*
May those who bless you be blessed.
[3.3.24 6.1.3]

9d *wʾrryk ʾrwr*
May those who curse you be cursed.
[3.3.24 6.1.3]

15a *nʾm-blʿm-bnw-bʿr* = 24:3a

15b *wnʾm-hgbr* = 24:3b

15c *š tm hʿyn* = 24:3c

16a *nʾm-šmʿ-ʾmry-ʾl* = 24:4a

16b *wydʿ-dʿt-ʿlywn* = 24:4a*

16c *mḥzh-šdy yḥzy* = 24:4b ET

16d *npl-wglwy-ʿynym* = 24:4c

17a *ʾrʾnw wlʾ-ʿth*
I cannot see him now.
The *w* in this and the following line are emphatic.
[3.3.5 6.1.1]

17b *ʾšwrnw wlʾ-qrwb*
I cannot spy him at this time.
[3.3.5 6.1.1]

17c *drk kwkb myʿqb*
A tribal leader rules from Jacob-Israel.
On *drk* 'to tread; rule,' see Albright (1944: 219 n. 82), and Dahood (1954, 1964c: 404). The term *kwkb šbṭ* 'tribal leader,' literally, 'star of the tribe' is illumined by the use of the cognate Akkadian

*kakkabu* 'star' in the West Semitic milieu of the Mari correspondence as a term of respect for the king, used by intimates; see Moran (1969: 33) and Batto (1974: 93).
[3.3.28 5.1.4 5.3.2 6.1.2]

17d *wqm šbṭ myśrʾl*
A tribal leader rises out of Jacob-Israel.

[3.3.28 5.1.4 5.3.2 6.1.2]

17e *wmḥṣ pʾty-mwʾb*
He strikes the Moabites' foreheads,

[3.3.3 8.2.1]

17f *wqrqr kl bny št* ET *wqdqd-kl-bny-št*
And the heads of all Bene-Shut.

The emendation follows Sam and a parallel text in Jer 48:45 and is accepted by all moderns.
[3.5.5 8.2.1]

18a *whyh ʾdwm yršh*
Edom is his possession.

[3.3.27 4.1.2 4.1.3 4.1.5 6.2.2]

18b *whyh yršh śʿyr-ʾybyw*
Seir, his enemy, is his possession.

[3.3.30 4.1.2 4.1.3 4.1.5 6.2.2]

18c *wyśrʾl ʿśh ḥyl*
Israel does valiantly.

Read the verb form as a perfect with Albright (1944: 221, n. 95). Van Dijk (1968: 104-5), in discussing *ʿśy* 'to acquire,' suggests translating 'Israel shall acquire wealth,' i.e., spoil.
[3.3.40 5.1.4 6.2.2]

19a *wyrd myʿqb* ET *wyrdm yʿqb*
Jacob rules over them.

Albright (1944: 221, n. 93) redivides as we do, but takes the *m* as an emphatic; on the order of the terms *yʿqb* and *yśrʾl*, which Albright regards as a fault to be remedied by reversing vv 18c and 19a, see 5.1.4.
[3.3.2 5.1.4]

19b *whʾbyd śryd mʿyr*
He destroys the survivor from the city.

Perhaps with Albright (1944: 220, n. 91), *ʿyr* should be read as *ʿr* Ar, the toponym of Num 21:28, 22:36; cf. Brockington (1973: 22).
[3.3.34]

## *2.4 Deuteronomy 32. The Song of Moses*

Basic treatments include Skehan (1971), which reprints his 1951 paper, Eissfeldt (1958), and Albright (1959). A Qumran text siglaed 4QDt$^{q}$ was published by Skehan (1954). The poem is 140 lines long.

BH3 and BHS divide the text identically. Loci at which we differ from them in dividing lines are vv 14bc, 24bc. Further, they split vv 24a and 32b and join together vv 39ab. Overall, their text has one more line division than ours. Our text has the same number of lines as that of BFBS; the differences in division are among those mentioned above: the text splits v 32b and joins 39ab.

1a *hʾzynw hšmym wʾdbrh*
Listen, heaven and earth, and I will speak.
[3.4.21 5.2.2]

1b *wtšmʿ hʾrṣ ʾmry-py*
Let heaven and earth hear the words of my mouth.
[3.4.6 5.2.2]

2a *yʿrp kmṭr lqḥy*
May my teaching drip like rain,
[3.3.31 6.1.2 9.2]

2b *tzl kṭl ʾmrty*
May my speech distill like dew,
[3.3.31 6.1.2 9.2]

2c *kśʿyrm ʿly dšʾ* ET *kśrʿm ʿly-dšʾ*
Like spray upon the grass,
On *ś/šrʿ*, cognate to Ug *šrʿ*, see Moran (1962: 320-22), who translates 'wellings.'
[3.5.4 6.1.8 9.2]

2d *wkrbybym ʿly-ʿśb*
Like showers on the herbage.
[3.5.4 6.1.8 9.2]

3a *ky-šm-yhwh ʾqrʾ*
I will invoke the name of Yahweh.
[3.3.7]

3b *hbw gdl lʾlhynw*
Give greatness to our god.
[3.3.34]

4a *hṣwr tmym pʿlw*
The Rock: his work is perfect.
[3.4.10]

4b *ky-kl-drkyw mšpṭ*
All his ways are just.
[3.3.24]

4c *ʾl-ʾmwnh-wʾyn-ʿwl*
A god of faith and no-deceit,
[3.5.5 8.3]

4d *ṣdyq-wyšr hwʾ*
He is the Just and Honest One.
[3.3.25 8.3]

5a *šḥt lw lʾ-bnyw mwmm*
His not-children deal corruptly with him in their turpitude,
[3.4.19 8.2.1]

5b *dwr-ʿqš-wptltl*
A perverse and warped generation.
[3.5.5 8.2.1]

6a *h-lyhwh tgmlw zʾt*
Do you recompense Yahweh with this,
On the possibility of reading supposed *zʾt* 'indignity,' see van Dijk (1968: 19-20).
[3.3.48 8.2.1]

6b *ʿm-nbl-wlʾ-ḥkm*
Foolish and not-wise people?
[3.5.5 8.2.1]

6c *hlwʾ-hwʾ ʾbyk qnk*
Is he not your parent who created you?
[3.4.8 4.1.1 6.1.6]

6d *hwʾ ʿśk wyknnk*
Is he not your maker who shaped you?
[3.4.8 4.1.1 6.1.6]

7a *zkr ymwt-ʿwlm*
Remember the days of old.
[3.3.3 6.1.1]

7b *bynw šnwt-dwr-wdwr*
Think on the long gone years.
[3.3.3 6.1.1]

7c *šʾl ʾbyk wygdk*
Ask your father and let him tell you.
[3.4.2 7.1.1]

7d *zqnyk wyʾmrw lk*
Ask your elders and let them speak to you.
[3.4.2 7.1.1]

8a *bhnḥl-ʿlywn gwym*
When Elyon apportioned the nations,
[3.3.17 6.1.7 8.2.3]

8b *bhprydw bny-ʾdm*
When he divided up humankind,
[3.3.17 6.1.7 8.2.3]

8c *yṣb gblt-ʿmym*
He established the boundaries of peoples
[3.3.3 8.2.3]

8d *lmspr-bny-yśrʾl* ET *lmspr-bny-ʾlhym*
According to the number of God's children.

The emendation follows LXX, Vetus Latina, and Symmachus and was accepted in 1951 on that basis by Skehan (1971: 67, cf. 68-70, 76-77); a Qumran manuscript has made it more certain (Skehan 1954: 12, 1959: 21; Eissfeldt 1958: 9; Albright 1959: 343, cf. Clifford 1972: 46; Brockington 1973: 29; BHS; and NAB).
[3.5.5 8.2.3]

9a *ky-ḥlq-yhwh ʿmw*
The portion of Yahweh's grant is Jacob, his people.
[3.3.24 5.3.2 5.3.7 6.1.3]

9b *yʿqb ḥbl-nḥltw*
The territory of Yahweh's grant is Jacob, his people.
[3.3.25 5.3.2 5.3.7 6.1.3]

10a *ymṣʾhw bʾrṣ-mdbr*
He found them in the steppe,
[3.3.4 8.2.1]

10b *wbthw-yll-yšmn*
In the blankness of howling Jeshimon.
[3.5.5 8.2.1]

10c *ysbbnhw ybwnnhw*
He encircled them. He cared for them.
[3.4.15]

10d *yṣrnhw kʾyšwn-ʿynw*
He guarded them like the apple of his eye.
[3.3.4]

11a *knšr yʿyr qnw*
Like an eagle, he protected his nest.

On the Hebrew cognate to Ug *ǵry* 'to protect,' known from the formulaic conclusions of letters, see Dahood (1966a: 56, 1969c: 348), Hartmann (1967: 102-5), and Kuhnigk (1974: 36, 151).
[3.3.48]

11b *ʿl-gwzlyw yrḥp*
He hovered over his young.
[3.3.8]

11c *yprś knpyw yqḥhw*
He spread his wings and took them up.
[3.4.2]

11d *yśʾhw ʿl-ʾbrtw*
He raised them on his pinions.
[3.3.4]

12a *yhwh bdd ynḥnw*
Yahweh guided them alone.
[3.3.55]

12b *wʾyn ʿmw ʾl-nkr*
There was no other god with him.
[3.3.31]

13a *yrkbhw ʿl-bmwty-ʾrṣ*
He made them mount the land's heights.

On *rkb* 'to mount' here, see Moran (1962: 323-27).
[3.3.4]

13b *wyʾkl tnwbt śdy* ET *wyʾkylhw tnwbt-śdy*
He fed them the fields' produce.

Read the verb as a *Hipʿil* with Sam and LXX, with Eissfeldt (1958: 10), Brockington (1973: 28), BH3, BHS, and NAB. On the possibility of glossing *śdy* 'mountains' see Moran (1962: 326, n. 2).
[3.3.3]

13c *wynqhw dbš mslʿ*
He suckled them with honey from rocks,

[3.3.34 6.1.2 7.1.1 8.2.1]

13d *wšmn mḥlmyš-ṣwr*
Oil from the flinty rocks,

[3.3.12 6.1.2 7.1.1 8.2.1]

14a *ḥmʾt-bqr-wḥlb-ṣʾn*
Cattle butter, sheep and goat milk,

[3.5.5 8.2.1]

14b *ʿm-ḥlb-krym-wʾylym*
Along with the fat of lambs and rams,

[3.5.5 6.2.5 8.2.1]

14c *bny-bšn-wʿtwdym*
Bashans and he-goats,

[3.5.5 6.2.5 8.2.1]

14d *ʿm-ḥlb-klywt-ḥṭh*
Along with the fat of kidney wheat.

[3.5.5 6.2.5 8.2.1]

14e *wdm-ʿnb tšth ḥmr*
You drank the blood of grapes by the jug.

On *ḥmr* 'jug, jar' here, see van der Weiden (1970: 87), Tromp (1969: 86, n. 34), and Dahood (1964c: 408); the counterarguments of Dietrich and Loretz (1972: 28) are not apposite.
[3.3.46]

15a *wyšmn yšrwn wybʿṭ*
Yeshurun got fat and kicked.

[3.4.2 4.1.3]

15b *šmnt ʿbyt kśyt*
You got fat, grew thick, were gorged.

[3.4.21 4.1.3]

15c *wyṭš ᵓlwh ᶜśhw*
He forsook the god, the rock of his salvation, who made him.
[3.4.4 5.1.1]

15d *wynbl ṣwr-yšᶜtw*
He reviled the god, the rock of his salvation.
[3.3.3 5.1.1]

16a *yqnᵓhw bzrym*
They made him jealous with the horrors of strange ones.
[3.3.4 5.3.2 6.2.1]

16b *btwᶜbt ykᶜyshw*
With the horrors of strange ones they provoked him.
[3.3.8 5.3.2 6.2.1]

17a *yzbḥw lšdym-lᵓ-ᵓlh*
They sacrificed to no-god shades.
[3.3.4 6.2.1]

17b *ᵓlhym lᵓ-ydᶜwm*
They had not known the new gods.
[3.3.7 5.3.6]

17c *ḥdšym mqrb bᵓw*
The new gods had come recently.
[3.3.54 5.3.6]

17d *lᵓ-śᶜrwm ᵓbtykm*
Your fathers had not served them.
On the *śᶜr/šᶜr* 'to serve,' see Dahood (1963a: 47).
[3.3.2]

18a *ṣwr yldk tšy*
You forgot the Rock, the god, who bore you.
On the root *nšy* 'to forsake, forget,' see Dahood (1973: 356).
[3.4.4 5.1.1 6.1.6]

18b *wtškḥ ᵓl-mḥllk*
You neglected the Rock, the god, who labored to bear you.
[3.3.3 5.1.1 6.1.6]

19a *wyrᵓ yhwh wynᵓṣ*
Yahweh saw and spurned them.
[3.4.2]

19b *mkʿs-bnyw-wbntyw wyʾmr*
Out of anger for his sons and daughters he spoke.
[3.3.8 8.1.1]

20a *ʾstyrh pny mhm*
Let me hide my face from them.
[3.3.34 8.1.1]

20b *ʾrʾh mh ʾḥrytm*
I will see what their fate will be.
For another treatment of vv 20b-d, see Dahood (1973f).
[3.4.5 8.1.1]

20c *ky-dwr-thpkt hmh*
They are a perverse generation.
[3.3.25 8.1.1]

20d *bnym lʾ-ʾmn bm*
Children: there is no faithfulness in them.
[3.4.10 8.1.1]

21a *hm qnʾwny blʾ-ʾl*
They trouble me with a no-god.
Albright (1959: 344) renders, on the basis of *qnʾ* 'to set up as a rival,' 'they set up a no-god as my rival.'
[3.3.41 4.3 8.1.1]

21b *kʿswny bhblyhm*
They grieve me with their ikons.
[3.3.4 4.3 8.1.1]

21c *wʾny ʾqnyʾm blʾ-ʿm*
I will trouble them with a no-people.
[3.3.41 4.3 8.1.1]

21d *bgwy-nbl ʾkʿysm*
I will grieve them with a foolish people.
[3.3.8 4.3 8.1.1]

22a *ky-ʾš qdḥh bʾpy*
A fire is kindled in my nostrils.
The phrase *bʾpy* could also be rendered 'by my wrath' (Skehan 1971: 72), or 'from my nostrils' (Dahood 1964b: 283).
[3.3.41 8.1.1]

22b *wtyqd ʿd-šʾwl-tḥtyt*
It flames as far as lower hell.
[3.3.4 8.1.1]

22c *wtʾkl ʾrṣ-wyblh*
It consumes the earth and its produce.
[3.3.3 6.1.1 8.1.1]

22d *wtlhṭ mwsdy-hrym*
It ignites the foundations of hills.
[3.3.3 6.1.1 8.1.1]

23a *ʾsph ʿlymw rʿwt*
I will gather my arrows' evils against them.
For the MT's *Hipʿil* of *spy* 'to sweep away,' read a *Qal* of *ʾsp* 'to gather' with BH3, BHS, and versional support.
[3.3.36 5.3.2 6.1.2 8.1.1]

23b *ḥṣy ʾklh bm*
I will expend my arrows' evils upon them.
[3.3.47 4.4 5.3.2 6.1.2 8.1.1]

24a *mzy-rʿb-wlḥmy-ršp*
The wasting of Hunger and the devouring of Fire Bolt
Dahood (1966: 203) and Tromp (1969: 107-10) treat *rʿb* 'Hunger, the Hungry One' as a figure for Death. On the associates of Death, Deber, Reshep, Qeteb, and so on, see Tromp (1969: 162-66); on *mzy* see Cross (1974a: 488).
[3.5.5 4.4 6.1.8 8.1.1 8.2.1]

24b *wqṭb-mryry-wšn-bhmwt*
And Destruction the Bitter One and the teeth of Behemoth
[3.5.5 4.4 6.1.8 8.1.1 8.2.1]

24c *ʾšlḥ bm*
I will send against them
[3.3.4 4.4 8.1.1 8.2.1]

24d *ʿm-ḥmt-zḥly-ʿpr*
Along with the venom of dust crawlers.
[3.5.5 8.1.1 8.2.1]

25a *mḥwṣ tškl ḥrb*
The sword of terror bereaves in the streets and bedrooms,
[3.3.44 5.2.2 5.3.2 6.1.2 7.1.1 8.1.1 9.2]

25b *wmḥdrym ʾymh*
The sword of terror bereaves in the streets and bedrooms,
[3.3.11 5.2.2 5.3.2 6.1.2 7.1.1 8.1.1 9.2]

25c *gm-bḥwr-gm-btwlh*
Young man and young woman,
[3.5.5 8.1.1 9.2]

25d *ywnq ʿm-ʾyš-śybh*
Breastfeeding baby and greyhead.
[3.5.4 8.1.1 9.2]

26a *ʾmrty ʾpʾyhm*
I said I would wipe them out.
[3.4.16 8.1.1]

26b *ʾšbyth mʾnwš zkrm*
I would obliterate their memory from humankind.
[3.3.36 8.1.1 8.2.2]

27a *lwly-kʿs-ʾwyb ʾgwr*
Save that I fear their enemy's provocation,
[3.3.22 8.1.1 8.2.2]

27b *pn-ynkrw ṣrymw*
Lest their foes misconstrue,
[3.3.22 8.1.1 8.2.2]

27c *pn-yʾmrw ydynw rmh*
Lest they say Our hands are high,
[3.4.12 7.1.1 8.1.1 8.2.2]

27d *wlʾ-yhwh pʿl kl-zʾt*
Lest they fail to say Yahweh did all this.
[3.4.12 7.1.1 8.1.1 8.2.2]

28a *ky-gwy-ʾbd-ʿṣwt hmh*
They are a people of fatal counsel.
[3.3.25]

28b *wʾyn bhm tbwnh*
There is no understanding in them.
[3.3.31]

29a *lw-ḥkmw yśkylw zʾt*
If they were wise, they would figure this out,
[3.4.4 8.2.2]

29b *ybynw lʾḥrytm*
They would understand their fate.
[3.3.4 8.2.2]

30a *ʾykh-yrdp ʾḥd ʾlp*
How can one, not to speak of two, pursue a company, not to speak of a battalion,
[3.3.27 5.2.4 bis 6.1.2 9.1]

30b *wšnym ynysw rbbh*
How can one, not to speak of two, put a company, not to speak of a battalion, to flight,
[3.3.40 5.2.4 bis 6.1.2 9.1]

30c *ʾm-lʾ-ky-ṣwrm mkrm*
Unless their Rock, Yahweh, sell them out,
[3.3.22 5.1.1 6.1.1 9.1]

30d *wyhwh hsgyrm*
Unless their Rock, Yahweh, deliver them up?
[3.3.22 5.1.1 6.1.1 9.1]

31a *ky-lʾ-kṣwrnw ṣwrm*
Their rock is not like our Rock.
[3.3.25 6.4]

31b *wʾybynw plylym*
Our enemies are judges.
This sense of *plylym* is maintained by Albright (1959: 345), *contra* Speiser (1963: 303).
[3.3.24 6.4]

32a *ky-mgpn-sdm gpnm*
Their vine is from the vine of Sodom-Gomorrah.
[3.3.25 5.1.5 6.4]

32b *wmšdmt-ʿmrh ʿnbmw-ʿnby-rwš*
Their grapes, grapes of poison, are from the fields of Sodom-Gomorrah.
[3.3.25 5.1.5 6.4]

32c *ʾšklt-mrrt lmw*
Bitter clusters are theirs.
[3.3.24 6.4]

33a *ḥmt-tnynm yynm*
Their cruel wine is monster venom.
[3.3.25 5.3.6 6.4]

33b *wrʾš-ptnym ʾkzr*
Their cruel wine is snake poison.
[3.3.25 5.3.6 6.4]

34a *hlʾ-hwʾ kms ʿmdy*
Isn't this stored up with me,
[3.3.68 8.3]

34b *ḥtm bʾwṣrty*
Sealed within my treasuries?
[3.5.4 8.3]

35a *ly nqm-wšlm*
Vindication and retribution are mine.
On the meaning of *nqm*, see Mendenhall (1973: 60-104).
[3.3.25 4.1.1 6.2.3]

35b *lʿt tmwṭ rglm* ET *ly ʿt-tmwṭ-rglm*
Mine is the time of their feet's sliding.
For MT's finite verb *tmwṭ*, read a *t*-preformative noun of the same stem.
[3.3.25 4.1.1 6.2.3]

35c *ky-qrwb ywm-ʾydm*
The day of their terror is near.
[3.3.25 6.2.3]

35d *wḥš ʿtdt lmw*
The future is speeding towards them.
[3.3.28]

36a *ky-ydyn yhwh ʿmw*
Yahweh rules over his people.
[3.3.27]

36b *wʿl-ʿbdyw ytnḥm*
He has compassion on his servants.
[3.3.8]

36c *ky-yrʾh ky-ʾzlt yd*
He sees that the hand has gone slack.

A *-t* 3 f.s. suffix occurs on the verb of the subordinate clause; cf. Dahood (1967a: 422).
[3.4.4]

36d *wʾps ʿṣwr-wʿzwb*
No one is held back or let loose.

[3.3.24]

37a *wʾmr ʾy ʾlhymw*
He says Where is their god, the rock,

[3.4.3 5.1.1 8.1.1 8.3]

37b *ṣwr ḥsyw bw*
Their god, the rock in whom they seek refuge,

[3.5.1 5.1.1 8.1.1 8.3]

38a *ʾšr ḥlb-zbḥymw yʾklw*
Who eats the flesh of their sacrifices

[3.3.64 6.1.7 7.2.1 8.1.1 8.3]

38b *yštw yyn-nsykm*
And who drinks the wine of their libation?

[3.3.19 6.1.7 7.2.1 8.1.1 8.3]

38c *yqwmw wyʿzrkm*
Let them get up and help you.

[3.4.15 8.1.1]

38d *yhy ʿlykm strh* ET *yhyw ʿlykm strh*
Let them be a refuge for you.

The emendation to a plural form of the verb has versional support; cf. BH3 and BHS.
[3.3.36 8.1.1]

39a *rʾw ʿth*
Look now.

The lines vv 39ab are not separated in the Qumran text (Skehan 1954: 13).
[3.3.5 8.1.1]

39b *ky-ʾny ʾny hwʾ*
I: I am the one.

[3.4.10 8.1.1]

39c *wʾyn ʾlhym ʿmdy*
There are no gods with me.
[3.3.28 8.1.1]

39d *ʾny ʾmyt wʾḥyh*
I kill and quicken.
[3.4.2 4.1.2 6.1.5 8.1.1]

39e *mḥṣty wʾny ʾrpʾ*
I smite and heal.
[3.4.2 4.1.2 6.1.5 8.1.1]

39f *wʾyn mydy mṣyl*
There is no one who rescues from my power.
[3.4.4 8.1.1]

40a *ky-ʾśʾ ʾl-šmym ydy*
I lift my hands to heaven.
[3.3.36 8.1.1]

40b *wʾmrty ḥy ʾnky lʿwlm*
I say as I live forever,
[3.4.20 8.1.1]

41a *ʾm-šnwty brq-ḥrby*
I shall whet my sword's edge.
[3.3.3 8.1.1]

41b *wtʾḥz bmšpṭ ydy*
My hand shall hold fast to justice.
[3.3.31 8.1.1]

41c *ʾšyb nqm lṣry*
I will take up dominion over my enemies.
[3.3.34 8.1.1]

41d *wlmśnʾy ʾšlm*
I will recompense those who hate me.
[3.3.8 8.1.1]

42a *ʾškyr ḥṣy mdm*
I will make my arrows and sword drunk on blood,
[3.3.34 5.2.3 8.1.1 9.2]

42b *wḥrby tʾkl bśr*
My arrows and sword shall consume flesh,
[3.3.40 5.2.3 8.1.1 9.2]

42c *mdm-ḥll-wšbyh*
From the blood of wounded and captive,
[3.5.5 6.1.8 8.1.1 9.2]

42d *mrʾš-prʿwt-ʾwyb*
From the head of the enemy's leadership.
[3.5.5 6.1.8 8.1.1 9.2]

43a *hrnynw gwym ʿmw*
Nations, sing of his people.

Dahood (1964c: 398, 1964b: 283) emends the last two words to read *gw-m-ʿmym* 'corpses of his people,' seeing here a reference to large-scale popular regeneration. The reconstruction of a supposed original coda to the poem is undertaken by Skehan (1971: 67, 70), on the basis of LXX evidence; and Skehan (1954: 15), Eissfeldt (1958: 13-14), Albright (1959: 340, 1969: 3), and Cross (1961: 182-84, n. 30), on the further base of Qumranic witness. Skehan (1957: 150, 1971: 214) comments that "in my judgment the secondary and conflate character of verse 43 in these witnesses is . . . patent." See also Talmon (1976: 171).
[3.4.6 4.4]

43b *ky-dm-ʿbdyw yqwm*
He vindicates his servants' blood.
[3.3.7 4.4]

43c *wnqm yšyb lṣryw*
He takes up dominion over his enemies.
[3.3.47 4.4]

43d *wkpr ʾdmtw ʿmw* ET *wkpr ʾdmt-wʿmw*
He atones for the land and his people.

The emendation has versional support; cf. BHS.
[3.3.3 4.4]

## *2.5 Deuteronomy 33. The Testament of Moses*

The basic treatment is given in Cross and Freedman (1975), which reprints their 1948 paper. Excluded from the corpus are the rubrics; they are not so treated on the basis of any conclusions of our study but as a result of a prior decision, based on the consensus that the material is extrinsic. (On vv 4-5, see Freedman 1976a: 69.)

| | |
|---|---|
| Dt 33:7a | *wzʾt lyhwdh wyʾmr* |
| Dt 33:8a | *wllwy ʾmr* |
| Dt 33:12a | *lbnymn ʾmr* |
| Dt 33:13a | *wlywsp ʾmr* |
| Dt 33:18a | *wlzbwln ʾmr* |
| Dt 33:20a | *wlgd ʾmr* |
| Dt 33:22a | *wldn ʾmr* |
| Dt 33:23a | *wlnptly ʾmr* |
| Dt 33:24a | *wlʾšr ʾmr* |

The text of the poem is 97 lines long.

BH3 and BHS treat vv 3bc as three lines; they break vv 12bc, 17ab, and 28bc in a different way than we do; they split v 29d and join vv 8bc and 29ab. BH3 has the same number of line breaks we do. BHS also splits v 9a and has one more line break.

2a *yhwh msyny bʾ*
Yahweh comes from Sinai.
[3.3.54]

2b *wzrḥ mśʿyr lmw*
He dawns from his Seir.

The prepositional phrase *lmw* is a periphrastic genitive, modifying a proper noun which cannot take a suffix; the sense is 'the Seir which belongs to, is proper to, Yahweh.'
[3.3.38 4.4]

2c *hwpyʿ mhr-pʾrn*
He appears refulgent from the Paran hills.

Clifford (1972: 115, n. 16) discusses the rendering 'the mountain country of Paran,' which we approximate.
[3.3.4 4.4 6.1.1]

2d *wʾth mrbbt qdš* ET *wʾth mrbt-qdš*
He arrives from Meribat-Qadesh,

The emendation is noted in Brown, Driver, and Briggs (1907: 872); cf. NAB, BH3, and BHS. The preposition of 2c serves double-duty.
[3.3.4 4.4 6.1.1 8.2.1]

2e *mymynw-ʾšdt lmw*
From his Southland, the slopes, which are his.
[3.5.4 4.4 8.2.1]

3a *ʾp ḥbb-ʿmym*
He gathers the peoples' pure ones.

The reading substantially derives from Cross and Freedman (1975: 107, nn. 12-13). The verb is from ᵓ*pp* 'to gather round'; *ḥbb* is a m. pl. participle, as Dillmann first recognized; the root is discussed in Milik (1957: 254, n. 2), Dahood (1969e: 28), and Cross (1973a: 101-2, n. 38).
[3.3.3]

3b *kl qdšyw bydk whm tkw* ET *kl-qdšyw bydk whmtkw*
All their holy ones bow down at your hand.

The antecedent of the suffix of *qdšyw* is ᶜ*mym*. The verb is a *t*-infixed *Qal* of *mwk/mkk* 'to bend,' as Cross and Freedman (1975: 108, n. 16) note; this suggestion is also offered in BHS; Milik (1957: 252-54) preserves the consonants of MT and derives *tkw* from *tkk* 'to fall to one's feet.' On the root *mkk*, see Dahood (1967a: 425-26).
[3.3.54]

3c *lrglk yś*ᵓ *mdbrtyk* ET *lrglk yś*ᵓ*-m dbrtyk*
At your step they honor your commands.

The emphatic *m* is discussed in Cross and Freedman (1975: 109, n. 17).
[3.3.48]

4a *twrh ṣwh lnw mšh*
Moses taught us an instruction.
[3.4.19]

4b *mwršh qhlt-y*ᶜ*qb*
A royal possessor is in Jacob-Yeshurun's congregation,
[3.3.10 5.1.4 5.3.6 6.1.2 7.1.2 9.1]

5a *wyhy byšrwn mlk*
A royal possessor is in Jacob-Yeshurun's congregation,
[3.3.31 5.1.4 5.3.6 6.1.2 7.1.2 9.1]

5b *bht*ᵓ*sp-r*ᵓ*šy-*ᶜ*m*
When the heads of the people Israel foregather,
[3.5.5 5.3.7 6.1.8 9.1]

5c *yḥd-šbṭy-yśr*ᵓ*l*
When the tribes of the people Israel unite.
[3.5.5 5.3.7 6.1.8 9.1]

6a *yḥy r*ᵓ*wbn w*ᵓ*l-ymt*
May Reuben live and never die.
[3.4.2]

6b *wyhy mtyw mspr*

May his men be beyond counting.

We follow Dahood (1967a: 429), who emends MT's *mspr* to a prepositional phrase, 'beyond counting.'
[3.3.28]

7b *šmʿ yhwh qwl-yhwdh*

Yahweh, hear the voice of Judah.

[3.4.6]

7c *wʾl-ʿmw tbyʾnw*

Bring him to his people.

[3.3.8]

7d *ydyw rb lw*

May you fight for him at his enemies' hands.

The infinitive *rb* is used here for a finite verb.
[3.3.50 5.3.2]

7e *wʿzr mṣryw thyh*

May you be a liberator from his enemies' hands.

On the nuance of *ʿzr* here, see Baisas (1973: 44-45).
[3.3.58 5.3.2 6.2.2]

8b *tmyk* ET *hbw llwy tmyk*

Give your Urim and Tummim to Levi.

A longer text is apparently preserved in 4QDt$^{h}$, an unpublished manuscript mentioned in Cross (1973a: 197 and n. 13), which provides the basis for his reconstruction, which is also that of Stuart (1976: 156) and BHS. Cf. Brockington (1973: 29) and BH3.
[3.3.36 5.2.1 6.2.2 7.1.1]

8c *wʾwryk lʾyš-ḥsydk*

Give your Urim and Tummim to your faithful one,

[3.3.12 5.2.1 6.2.2 7.1.1 8.2.2]

8d *ʾšr nsytw bmsh*

Whom you tested at Massah,

[3.3.64 6.1.7 7.2.1 8.2.2]

8e *trybhw ʿl-my-mrybh*

Whom you tried at the Waters of Meribah,

[3.3.19 6.1.7 7.2.1 8.2.2]

9a *hʾmr lʾbyw wlʾmw lʾ rʾytyw*
ET *hʾmr lʾbyw-wlʾmw lʾ-rʾyty*
Who says to his father and mother, I can't see you.
Delete the final *w* as a dittograph.
[3.4.12 8.2.2]

9b *wʾt-ʾḥyw lʾ-hkyr*
He does not recognize his sibs and children.
[3.3.7 5.2.2 6.3.1]

9c *wʾt-bnw lʾ-ydᶜ*
He is not devoted to his sibs and children.
[3.3.7 5.2.2 6.3.1]

9d *ky-šmrw ʾmrtk*
They observe the words of your covenant.
[3.3.3 5.3.2 6.3.1]

9e *wbrytk ynṣrw*
They guard the words of your covenant.
[3.3.7 5.3.2 6.3.1]

10a *ywrw mšpṭyk lyᶜqb*
They teach the judgments of your instruction to Jacob-Israel.
For a variant from 4QTestimonia, see Cross (1973a: 337); cf. BHS.
[3.3.34 5.1.4 5.3.2 6.3.2 7.1.1]

10b *wtwrtk lyśrʾl*
They teach the judgments of your instruction to Jacob-Israel.
[3.3.12 5.1.4 5.3.2 6.3.2 7.1.1]

10c *yśymw qṭwrh bʾpk*
They put the smoke of a holocaust in your nostrils.
[3.3.34 5.3.2 6.3.2 7.1.1]

10d *wklyl ᶜl-mzbḥk*
They put the smoke of a holocaust on your altar.
[3.3.12 5.3.2 6.3.2 7.1.1]

11a *brk yhwh ḥylw*
Yahweh, bless his strength.
[3.4.6]

11b *wpᶜl-ydyw trṣh*
May you favor the work of his hands.
[3.3.7 6.1.1]

11c *mḥṣ mtnym qmyw* ET *mḥṣ mtny-m-qmyw*
Strike the loins of his enemies.

The emphatic *m* was recognized by Albright; see Cross and Freedman (1975: 113, n. 33) and Freedman (1960: 103-4).
[3.3.3 6.1.1]

11d *wmśnᵓyw mn yqwmwn*
Who will arise of those who hate him?

For the preposition *mn* of MT, read the pronoun *mn* 'who.'
[3.3.57]

12b *ydyd-yhwh yškn lbṭḥ*
The beloved of Yahweh tents secure.

[3.3.41 4.4 4.5]

12c *ᶜlyw ḥpp ᶜlyw kl hywm* ET *ᶜly ḥpp ᶜlyw kl-hywm*
Eli hovers over him all day.

The divine name *ᶜly* 'Eli' was recognized by Nyberg; see Cross and Freedman (1975: 113, n. 38). Read *ḥpp* as a finite verb form.
[3.4.19 4.4 4.5]

12d *wbyn-ktypyw škn*
He tents between his blades.

[3.3.8 4.4 4.5]

13b *mbrkt-yhwh ᵓrṣw*
His land is blessed by Yahweh.

[3.3.25 4.5]

13c *mmgd šmym mṭl* ET *mmgd-šmym mᶜl*
From the favor of heavens above,

For the emendation, see Gen 49:25c.
[3.5.4 4.4 4.5 8.2.3]

13d *wmthwm rbṣt tḥt*
From the deep crouched below,

[3.5.1 4.4 4.5 8.2.3]

14a *wmmgd-tbwᵓt-šmš*
From the favor of Sun's produce,

[3.5.5 4.1.1 4.4 4.5 6.4 8.2.3]

14b *wmmgd grš yrḥym* ET *wmmgd-grš-yrḥ-m*
From the favor of Moon's yield,

The *m* is probably emphatic and need not be deleted as a dittograph, as Cross and Freedman (1975: 116, n. 49) urge.
[3.5.5 4.1.1 4.4 4.5 6.4 8.2.3]

15a *wmrʾš-hrry-qdm*
From the peaks of the ancient hills,
[3.5.5 4.4 4.5 6.4 8.2.3]

15b *wmmgd-gbʿwt-ʿwlm*
From the favor of the eternal heights,
[3.5.5 4.1.1 4.4 4.5 6.4 8.2.3]

16a *wmmgd-ʾrṣ-wmlʾh*
From the favor of the earth and its fullness,
[3.5.5 4.1.1 4.4 4.5 6.4 8.2.3]

16b *wrṣwn-škny-snh*
From the pleasure of the seneh-bush Tenter,
[3.5.5 6.4 8.2.3]

16c *tbwʾth lrʾš ywsp* ET *tbwʾ-th lrʾš-ywsp*
May [blessings] come on the head of Joseph, Nazir of his Brothers,

The *t(h)* termination of the verb is the emphatic particle; see Krahmalkov (1969, 1970).
[3.3.4 5.1.3 8.2.3]

16d *wlqdqd-nzyr-ʾḥyw* = Gen 49:26e
On the skull of Joseph, Nazir of his Brothers.
[3.5.5 5.1.3 8.2.3]

17a *bkwr šwrw hdr* ET *bkwr-šwr whdr*
Splendid are the horns of an ox's first-born and an aurochs.
[3.3.25 5.3.5 6.1.3]

17b *lw-wqrny-rʾm qrnyw*
His horns are the horns of an ox's first-born and an aurochs.
[3.3.25 5.3.5 6.1.3]

17c *bhm ʿmym yngḥ*
He gores with them the peoples of earth's ends.
[3.3.59 5.3.3]

17d *yḥdw ʾpsy ʾrṣ* ET *yḥd ʾpsy-ʾrṣ*
He incites the peoples of earth's ends.

The finite verb-form is derived from a cognate of Arb *ḥadā* 'to urge, spur on, instigate.'
[3.3.3 5.3.3]

17e *whm rbbwt-ʾprym*
These are the companies of the battalions of Ephraim-Manasseh.

[3.3.24 4.1.1 5.1.4 5.3.2 6.1.3]

17f *whm ʾlpy-mnšh*
These are the companies of the battalions of Ephraim-Manasseh.

[3.3.24 4.1.1 5.1.4 5.3.2 6.1.3]

18b *śmḥ zbwln bṣʾtk*
Rejoice, Zebulon and Issachar, when you go out.

[3.4.6 5.2.1 6.1.4 7.1.1]

18c *wyśśkr bʾhlyk*
Rejoice, Zebulon and Issachar, in your tents.

[3.4.18 5.2.1 6.1.4 7.1.1]

19a *ʿmym hr yqrʾw*
The peoples call out in the hills.

[3.3.53]

19b *šm yzbḥw zbḥy-ṣdq*
There they offer legitimate offerings.

[3.3.49]

19c *ky-špʿ-ymym yynqw*
They suck the sea's abundance,

[3.3.7 8.2.1]

19d *wśpwny-ṭmwny-ḥwl*
The hidden part of the sand's treasure.

[3.5.5 8.2.1]

20b *brwk mrḥyb-gd*
Blessed is the Enlarger, Gad.

For another treatment, see Freedman (1976a: 69).
[3.3.25]

20c *klbyʾ škn*
Like a lion he reclines.

[3.3.8]

20d *wṭrp zrwᶜ-ᵓp-qdqd*
He rives arm and skull.
[3.3.3]

21a *wyrᵓ rᵓšyt lw*
He seeks the best for himself.
Read a simple prefixing form of *rᵓy* for MT's jussive with Cross and Freedman (1975: 118, n. 70).
[3.3.34 5.3.3]

21b *ky šm ḥlqt mḥqq spwn* ET *k-yšm ḥlqt-mḥqq*
He pants after a share of a commander.
Read *k*(*y*) followed by *yiššom* from *nšm*, 'to pant after,' with Cross and Freedman (1975: 118-19, n. 71), and BHS, with whom the next line is emended, after v 5b.
[3.3.3 5.3.3]

21c *wytᵓ rᵓšy-ᶜm* ET *wytᵓspwn rᵓšy-ᶜm*
The people's leaders came together.
[3.3.2]

21d *ṣdqt-yhwh ᶜśh*
He carried out the rightness of Yahweh's judgments,
[3.3.7 5.3.3 8.2.1]

21e *wmšpṭyw ᶜm-yśrᵓl*
The rightness of Yahweh's judgments with Israel.
[3.5.4 5.3.3 8.2.1]

22b *dn gwr-ᵓryh*
Dan is a lion cub.
[3.3.24]

22c *yznq mn-hbšn*
He springs away from the serpent.
On *bšn* 'serpent,' cognate to Ug and Arb *b̲ṯn* 'serpent, viper,' see Cross and Freedman (1975: 119, n. 74), Tromp (1969: 57, n. 162), and BHS.
[3.3.4]

23b *nptly śbᶜ rṣwn*
Naphtali is sated with favor.
[3.3.40]

23c *wmlʾ brkt-yhwh*
He is full of the blessing of Yahweh.
[3.3.3]

23d *ym-wdrwm yršh*
He takes possession west and south.
Read *yršh* as a finite verb form, with versional support after Cross and Freedman (1975: 119, n. 76), Stuart (1976: 168, n. 47), and BHS. Dahood (1958: 66, n. 2) has suggested that *ym* here stands for Lake Galilee and that *drwm* contains a 3 m.s. suffixed form of *dōr* 'environs,' with an emphatic *m*.
[3.3.9]

24b *brwk mbnym ʾšr*
Asher is blessed among the children.
[3.3.68]

24c *yhy rṣwy-ʾḥyw*
He is his siblings' favorite.
[3.3.3]

24d *wṭbl bšmn rglw*
He dips his foot in oil.
Read a finite verb form *ṭbl* with Stuart (1976: 168, n. 49). Cross and Freedman (1975: 119, n. 79) read *rglw* as plural, perhaps correctly.
[3.3.36]

25a *brzl-wnḥšt mnʿlyk*
Your bolts are of iron and bronze,
[3.3.25]

25b *wkymyk dbʾk* ET *wk-ymyk-dbʾk*
Your lifetime and your glory.
The *k*(*y*) is emphatic.
[3.5.5]

26a *ʾyn kʾl yšrwn*
There is no one like El, Yeshurun.
Read *kĕʾēl* with the versions; cf. BH3 and BHS.
[3.4.6]

26b *rkb šmym bʿzrk* ET *rkb šmym bʿz*
He rides the heavens in the strength of his majesty.
For the emendation, see Cross and Freedman (1975: 120, n. 82). Read finite forms of *rkb* in vv 26b and 26c.
[3.3.34 4.1.3 5.3.2 bis 6.1.2]

26c *wbgʾwtw šḥqym* ET *rkb gʾwtw šḥqym*
He rides the clouds in the strength of his majesty.
[3.3.36 4.1.3 5.3.2 bis 6.1.2]

27a *mʿnh ʾlhy-qdm*
The ancient god, the Eternal One, is his refuge.
On the reading of *mʿnh* with a suffix, see Cross (1973: 48, n. 18) and BHS.
[3.3.25 5.1.1 6.1.3]

27b *wmtḥt zrʿt-ʿwlm*
The arms of the Eternal One, the ancient god, are spread out.
For MT's compound preposition, read *mtḥt* as a f.s. participle of *mtḥ* 'to spread out.' See also Dahood (1966a: 115, 235). On the divine title *ʿwlm* here, see Cross (1973a: 48, n. 18), and BHS.
[3.3.25 5.1.1 6.1.3]

27c *wygrš mpnyk ʾwyb*
He drives out the enemy before you.
[3.3.36]

27d *wyʾmr hšmd*
He says Destroy.
[3.4.16]

28a *wyškn yśrʾl bṭḥ*
Israel-Jacob-El dwells secure.
[3.3.29 5.1.4 6.1.2]

28b *bdd ʿyn yʿqb ʾl* ET *bdd ʿwn yʿqb-ʾl*
Israel-Jacob-El lives alone,
Read for MT's *ʿyn* a finite form of *ʿwn* 'to dwell,' with Cross and Freedman (1975: 121, n. 87), Freedman (1973: 126), Cross (1973a: 157), Dahood (1969b: 77), Stuart (1976: 169, n. 54), and BHS. On the name, see Freedman (1963).
[3.3.45 5.1.4 6.1.2 8.2.1]

28c *ʾrṣ-dgn-wtyrwš*
In a land of corn and must.
[3.5.5 8.2.1]

28d *ʾp-šmyw yʿrpw ṭl*
Its skies drip down dew.
[3.3.40]

29a ʾšryk yśrʾl
Your joys, O Israel.
[3.5.2]

29b my kmwk
Who is like you,
[3.3.24 8.3]

29c ʿm nwšʿ byhwh
O people saved by Yahweh,
[3.5.1 8.3]

29d mgn ʿzrk wʾšr ḥrb gʾwtk ET mgn-ʿzrk-wḥrb-gʾwtk
The shield of your strength and the sword of your glory?
[3.5.5 8.3]

29e wykḥšw ʾybyk lk
Your enemies cringe before you.
[3.3.28 6.1.2]

29f wʾth ʿl-bmwtymw tdrk
You shall march on their backs.
On the idiom *drk ʿl-bmh* 'to walk on the back,' see Cross (1973a: 158) and Penar (1975: 27-28).
[3.3.54 6.1.2]

## *2.6 Judges 5. The Song of Deborah*

Major treatments include Albright (1969), Boling (1975), and Chaney (1976b, a paper based on 1976a); we apologize if we have been led to misconstrue Chaney's work as a result of considering a paper in private circulation, which we cite without permission. The poem is 106 lines long.

The state of uncertainty about the structure of the poetic line in Hebrew reaches disturbing proportions in the study of this poem. BH3 reads 17 more line divisions than we do, while BHS reads nearly the same number as we do; they are hardly in the same places. BH3 splits the following lines: vv 2b, 3e, 5b, 5c, 6c, 9b, 12e, 15d, 16c, 17a, 17c, 23d, 28c, 28d, 30a, and 30b. It joins vv 12bc, 21ab, and 31ab. Vv 7abc, 10c 11a, 13ab, and 22abc are segmented differently in the texts. At vv 25abc, we read 3 lines and BH3 reads four; at vv 28ab, we read 2 lines and BH3 reads 4 lines; and at vv 30de, we read 2 lines and BH3 reads 3 lines.

BHS splits far fewer lines: vv 3e, 6c, 9b, 15d, and 16c. It joins more: vv 3ab, 3cd, 4cd, 12bc, 15bc, 18ab, 23ab, 27ab, and 31ab. BHS and our text use different breaks in vv 5ab, 7ab, 10c 11a, and 13ab. At vv 25abc, we read 3 lines and BHS 4 lines; and at both vv 28ab and 30de, we read 2 lines against BHS's 3 lines. Thus, we have one more line break than BHS.

The text of BFBS is intermediate, reading 11 fewer line divisions. It splits v 15d and joins vv 3ab, 3cd, 4cd, 12bc, 12de, 18ab, 23ab, 26cd, 27ab, and 27de; at vv 7abc, 10c 11a, 13ab, 20ab, 25abc, and 28ab, the texts are divided differently. At vv 5abc and 22abc, BFBS reads two lines.

2a *bprʿ-prʿwt byśrʾl*
When locks were long, in Israel,

On the sense of *prʿ*, see Boling (1975: 107) and references; Boling renders *bprʿ-prʿwt* 'when they cast off restraint'; we retain an older translation.
[3.5.4 8.2.1]

2b *bhtndb-ʿm brkw yhwh*
When people vowed themselves, they blessed Yahweh.

Read *brkw* as finite verb, not an imperative. Most translations of vv 2ab 3a consist of a double aposiopesis, which though possible would seem at least to call for some notice that the construction is extremely rare.
[3.3.48 8.2.1]

3a *šmʿw mlkym*
Listen, kings.
[3.4.18 6.1.4]

3b *hʾzynw rznym*
Give ear, potentates.
[3.4.18 6.1.4]

3c *ʾnky lyhwh*
I will sing of Yahweh,
[3.3.10 4.1.1 4.3 7.1.2]

3d *ʾnky ʾšyrh*
I will sing.
[3.3.6 4.1.1 4.3 7.1.2]

3e *ʾzmr lyhwh-ʾlhy-yśrʾl*
I will chant of Yahweh, Israel's god.
[3.3.4 4.3]

4a *yhwh bṣʾtk mśʿyr*
Yahweh, when you emerged from Seir,
[3.4.13 8.2.2]

4b *bṣᶜdk mśdh-ˀdwm*
When you marched from the fields of Edom,
[3.3.17 8.2.2]

4c *ˀrṣ rᶜšh*
Earth shook.
[3.3.6 6.1.1 8.2.2]

4d *gm-šmym nṭpw*
The clouds of heaven dripped.

For the rendering of *gm* 'aloud; with sound; with thunder' here, see Boling (1975: 108), and Chaney (1976b: 3). The verb form *nṭpw*, usually linked with *nṭp* 'to drip,' has also been associated with *ṭpp* 'to shake,' e.g., by Cross (1973a: 101, n. 35). Chaney (1976b: 3) reads a form of *nṭp* in 4e and a form of *ṭpp* here; this effectively eliminates an instance of the repetition universally acknowledged to be an important feature of this poem; and represents a kind of paronomasia which is at best rare, probably unknown, in Hebrew; it also seems like a good try at having your cake and eating it, too, a project also essayed by Globe (1974: 175-77) in an otherwise sound discussion.
[3.3.6 4.1.3 5.3.2 6.1.1 7.2.2]

4e *gm-ᶜbym nṭpw mym*
The clouds of heaven dripped down water.
[3.3.40 4.1.3 5.3.2 7.2.2]

5a *hrym nzlw*
Hills shuddered

On the root *zll* 'to shake,' which lies behind *nzlw*, see Boling (1975: 108), Globe (1974: 174), BH3, BHS, and Brockington (1973: 36).
[3.3.6 8.2.1]

5b *mpny-yhwh-zh-syny*
Before Yahweh of Sinai,

The determinative pronoun *zh* is widely recognized (Cross 1973a: 20, n. 44, Globe 1974: 169-71), although its syntax has been somewhat obscured by overreliance on Ug analogy; the discussion of Gordon (1965: 126) is confused in general; see rather Loewenstamm (1975: 118). The Amorite usage discussed by Moran (1961: 69) also deserves study.
[3.5.5 4.1.1 4.5 6.1.8 8.2.1]

5c *mpny-yhwh-ˀlhy-yśrˀl*
Before Yahweh, Israel's god.
[3.5.5 4.1.1 4.5 6.1.8 8.2.1]

6a *bymy-šmgr-bn-ʿnt*
In the days of Shamgar, Anat's child,
[3.5.5 4.1.1 4.1.5 4.5 8.2.1]

6b *bymy-yʿl ḥdlw ʾrḥwt*
In the days of Yael, caravan routes prospered.

Chaney (1976b: 6-7), Boling (1975: 109), and Freedman and Lundbom (1975: 755) render *ḥdlw* in v 6 as 'ceased' and in vv 7ab 'grew plump,' arguing from archaeological and historical evidence. Whatever the external evidence, the word means the same thing in all three occurrences; the kind of paronomasia presupposed here by Chaney and the others (and it is well to note they differ immensely on other crucial aspects of these lines) is unknown in Biblical Hebrew. Borowski (1973) renders the verse consistently, as does Freedman (1975a: 13-14); both refer all occurrences here to *ḥdl* 'to prosper, batten.'
[3.3.44 4.1.1 bis 4.1.5 4.3 4.5 8.2.1]

6c *whlky-ntybwt ylkw ʾrḥwt-ʿqlqlwt*
Path followers followed circuitous caravan routes.
[3.3.40 4.1.1 4.1.5 4.3 4.5]

7a *ḥdlw przwn byśrʾl*
Warriors prospered in Israel,

On *przwn* 'warrior(s),' see Albright (1969: 49, n. 101); Boling (1975: 109) renders the word so here and, without a note, in v 11c renders the same word 'prowess,' presumably following Rabin (1955: 127) or Driver (1962: 8-9). Chaney (1976b: 3) returns to the traditional 'peasantry.' Freedman (1975b: 13) renders 'yeomanry.'
[3.3.28 4.1.3 4.3 4.5 9.1]

7b *ḥdlw ʿd*
They prospered on booty,
[3.3.3 4.1.3 4.3 4.5 9.1]

7c *šqmty dbwrh*
When you arose, Deborah,

We read the verb as a second person form, with most moderns, against MT, which reads a first person and against Chaney (1976b: 8), who reads a third person.
[3.3.21 4.1.3 4.5 9.1]

7d *šqmty ʾm byśrʾl*
When you arose as a mother, in Israel.
[3.3.66 4.1.3 4.5 9.1]

8a *ybḥr ʾlhym-ḥdšym*
He chose new gods.

The antecedent of *ybḥr* is Israel; it is possible that a plural verb should be read with Hillers (1965). Cross (1973a: 122-23, n. 34) emends *ʾlhym* to *ʾlym* 'rams, leaders.'
[3.3.3 6.1.1]

8b *ʾz lḥm šʿrym* ET *ʾz-lḥm śʿrm*
He served them food.

On *śʿr* 'to serve,' see the notes on Dt 32:17d.
[3.3.7 6.1.1]

8c *mgn ʾm-yrʾh wrmḥ*
Neither shield nor sword was seen

[3.3.46 8.2.1]

8d *bʾrbʿym-ʾlp byśrʾl*
In the forty companies of Israel.

[3.5.4 4.1.1 8.2.1]

9a *lby lḥwqqy-yśrʾl*
My heart belongs to Israel's leaders.

[3.3.24 4.1.1]

9b *hmtndbym bʿm brkw yhwh*
Those who volunteer themselves for the people bless Yahweh.

Read *brkw* as a finite verb, not an imperative.
[3.4.19]

10a *rkby-ʾtnwt-ṣḥrwt*
You who ride on tawny she-asses.

[3.5.5]

10b *yšby ʿl mdyn* ET *yšby ʿl-mdwn*
You who rule over the Madon realm.

On Madon, see Josh 11:1, 12:19; cf. Jdg 4:2, etc. Heb *drk* 'dominion' is discussed in Dahood (1964c: 404).
[3.5.4 5.3.2 6.1.8]

10c *whlky ʿl-drk*
You who travel through the Madon realm.

[3.5.4 5.3.2 6.1.8]

11a *śyḥw mqwl mḥṣṣym byn mšʾbym*
ET *śyḥw-m qwl-mḥṣṣym byn-mšʾbym*
Let the voices of recruiters resound amid waterholes.

The verse redivision and recognition of the emphatic *m* were suggested by Freedman apud Boling (1975: 110). On *mḥṣṣ*, see Chaney (1976b: 12-13).
[3.3.34]

11b *šm ytnw ṣdqwt-yhwh*
There let them repeat the victories of Yahweh's warriors,
[3.3.49 4.1.2 5.3.4 8.2.1]

11c *ṣdqt-prznw byśrʾl*
The victories of Yahweh's warriors on behalf of Israel.
[3.5.4 4.1.2 5.3.4 8.2.1]

11d *ʾz-yrdw lšʿrym ʿm-yhwh*
The army of Yahweh went down to the gates.
[3.3.31]

12a *ʿwry ʿwry dbwrh*
Get up, get up, Deborah.
[3.4.21 4.1.3 bis 4.1.5]

12b *ʿwry ʿwry*
Get up, get up.
[3.4.15 4.1.3 bis 4.1.5]

12c *dbry šyr*
Sing the song.
[3.3.3]

12d *qwm brq*
Arise, Baraq, Abinoam's child.
[3.4.18 5.1.3]

12e *wšbh šbyk bn-ʾbynʿm*
Capture your captives, Baraq, Abinoam's child.
[3.4.6 5.1.3]

13a *ʾz-yrd śryd lʾdyrym ʿm-yhwh*
The army of Yahweh went down to Sarid, against the mighty.

On Sarid, a city in Zebulon, see Chaney (1976b: 14-15). Forms of *yrd* 'to go down' are read here and in v 13b by BH3 and BHS. For another treatment of vv 13-18, see Globe (1975b).
[3.4.19 4.1.3 4.4]

13b *yrd ly bgbwrym*
It went down against the strong for me.
[3.3.38 4.1.3 4.4 6.1.2]

14a *mny-ʾprym šršm bʿmlq*
From Ephraim they root them out of Amaleq.
For the noun *šršm* of MT, read a *Piʿel* verb form.
[3.3.50 4.4 6.1.2]

14b *ʾḥryk bnymyn bʿmmyk* ET *ʾḥrk bnymyn bʿmmyk*
Benjamin delays you among the people.
For the preposition *ʾḥryk* of MT, read a *Piʿel* verb form.
[3.3.28 4.4 6.1.2]

14c *mny-mkyr yrdw mḥqqym*
Out of Machir, commanders go down.
[3.3.44 4.4 6.1.2]

14d *wmzbwln mškym bšbṭ-spr*
Those who march with scribal rod are from Zebulon.
[3.4.8 6.1.3]

15a *wśry byśśkr ʿm-dbrh*
The princes are in Issachar with Deborah.
The form *śry* is not a 1 c.s. suffixed form, but a cstr. pl. form used in a case in which Classical Hebrew would use an absolute; cf. similar forms in 10b and 10c.
[3.3.68 6.1.3]

15b *wyśśkr kn-brq*
Issachar is Baraq's support.
On *kn* 'base, support,' see Driver (1962: 11).
[3.3.24]

15c *bʿmq šlḥ brglyw*
It is sent through the valley at his feet.
[3.3.50]

15d *bplgwt-rʾwbn gdlym ḥqqy-lb*
In Reuben's divisions, great are the stouthearted.
[3.3.68 4.4]

16a *lmh yšbt byn-hmšptym*
Why do you sit among hearths
[3.3.50 4.4 8.2.2]

16b *lšmᶜ šrqwt-ᶜdrym*
Listening to herds hissing?
[3.3.17 4.4 8.2.2]

16c *lplgwt-rᵓwbn gdwlym ḥqry-lb*
Great are the heartsearchings about Reuben's divisions.
[3.3.68 4.4]

17a *glᶜd bᶜbr-hyrdn škn*
Gilead dwells on the Jordan's far shore.
[3.3.54]

17b *wdn lmh ygwr ᵓnywt*
Dan: why does he dwell on shipboard?

The punctuation of the gloss indicates that *dn* is a focus-marker, not that it falls outside the text as a heading. Chaney (1976b: 4) reads all the tribal names in vv 17-18 as headings, following Cross and Freedman (1975: 13-20). Stuart (1976: 125, 135, n. 22) correctly regards them as integral. Cross (1973a: 235, n. 74) reads *lmh* as an emphatic particle.
[3.4.20]

17c *ᵓšr yšb lḥwp-ymym*
Asher lives on the seashore.
[3.3.41]

17d *wᶜl-mprṣyw yškwn*
He encamps by his harbors.
[3.3.8]

18a *zblwn ᶜm-ḥrp*
Zebulon is a people of scorn.
[3.3.24 6.1.3]

18b *npšw lmwt*
His appetite is for death.
[3.3.24 6.1.3]

18c *wnptly ᶜl mrwmy-śdh*
Naphtali surmounts the highest hills.

On the phrase *mrwmy-śdh* see Freedman (1972a: 122); he suggests that the reference is to an "elevated plain, or plateau" and is used in a "battle context"; see also Boling (1975: 113). On the emendation to read a finite verb-form *ʿālâ*, see Cross and Freedman (1975: 17, n. 3). [3.3.40]

19a *bʾw mlkym nlḥmw*
The kings came. They fought.
[3.4.2 4.1.1 4.1.4 4.1.5]

19b *ʾz-nlḥmw mlky-knʿn*
The kings of Canaan fought
[3.3.2 4.1.1 4.1.4 4.1.5 8.2.1]

19c *btʿnk ʿl-my-mgdw*
In Taanach, near Megiddo Waters.
[3.5.4 8.2.1]

19d *bṣʿ-ksp lʾ-lqḥw*
They did not take silver booty.
[3.3.7]

20a *mn-šmym nlḥmw hkwkbym*
The stars fought from their heavenly paths.
[3.3.44 4.1.3 4.5 5.3.2]

20b *mmslwtm nlḥmw ʿm-sysrʾ*
They fought with Sisera from their heavenly paths.
[3.3.50 4.1.3 4.5 5.3.2]

21a *nḥl-qyšwn grpm*
Wadi Qishon swept them away.
[3.3.6 4.1.1 4.1.2 4.1.5 4.5]

21b *nḥl-qdwmym nḥl-qyšwn*
Wadi Qishon is an ancient wadi.
[3.3.25 4.1.1 4.1.2 4.1.5 4.5]

21c *tdrky npšy ʿz*
O my soul, tread down the mighty.
[3.4.6]

22a *ʾz-hlmw ʿqby*
The horses' heels hammered.
[3.3.2 5.3.2 6.2.1]

22b *sws mdhrwt* ET *swsm dhrwt*
The horses' heels thundered.

The infinitive *dhrwt* is used here as a finite verb, as it is in v 22c. On the redivision of words and the root *dhr*, see Driver (1962: 11) and Boling (1975: 113); and further on *dhr*, see Cathcart (1973: 126). The breaking of a construct chain across lines is problematic.
[3.3.6 4.1.4 4.5 5.3.2 6.2.1]

22c *dhrwt ᵓbyryw*
His stallions thundered.
[3.3.2 4.1.4 4.5 6.2.1]

23a *ᵓwrw mrwz*
Curse Meroz,

Chaney (1976b: 18-19), with versional support, emends *mrwz* to *mzr*, which he reads *mûzār* 'estranged.'
[3.3.3 4.4 4.5 8.1.1]

23b *ᵓmr mlᵓk-yhwh*
The messenger of Yahweh says,
[3.3.2 4.4 4.5 8.1.1]

23c *ᵓrw ᵓrwr yšbyh*
Curse vehemently her inhabitants.
[3.3.33 4.4 4.5 8.1.1]

23d *ky-lᵓ-bᵓw lᶜzrt-yhwh*
They did not come to Yahweh's help,

On *ᶜzrt* 'war,' see Dahood (1965b: 68) and Miller (1970: 168).
[3.3.4 4.1.2 4.5 8.1.1 8.2.1]

23e *lᶜzrt-yhwh bgbwrym*
To Yahweh's help, against the warriors.
[3.5.4 4.1.2 4.5 8.1.1 8.2.1]

24a *tbrk mnšym yᶜl*
Most blessed among women is Yael,
[3.3.31 4.4 4.5 8.2.1]

24b *ᵓšt-ḥbr-hqyny*
The wife of the Qenite Heber.
[3.5.5 4.4 4.5 8.2.1]

24c *mnšym bᵓhl tbrk*
She is most blessed among women in the tent.
[3.3.60 4.4 4.5]

25a *mym š'l*
He asks for water.
[3.3.7]

25b *ḥlb ntnh bspl*
She gives milk in a bowl.
[3.3.47 6.3.2]

25c *'dyrym hqrybh ḥm'h* ET *l'dyr-m hqrybh ḥm'h*
She brings the mighty one butter.
The *m* is emphatic; the preposition was lost by haplography.
[3.3.48 6.3.2]

26a *ydh lytd tšlḥnh*
She extends her left hand to the tentpeg.
On the energic verbal form, see Cross and Freedman (1975: 19, n. r), Freedman (1960: 102), Dahood (1962a: 63, 1965b: 21, 1969b: 71), Boling (1975: 114) and BHS. On *yd* 'left-hand,' see Melamed (1961: 145), Dahood (1965: 315), and Boling (1975: 104, 114).
[3.3.58 6.3.2 7.1.1]

26b *wymynh lhlmwt-ʿmlym*
She extends her right hand to the workers' mallet.
[3.3.12 6.3.2 7.1.1]

26c *whlmh sysr'*
She pounds Sisera's skull.
[3.3.3 5.3.2 6.1.1]

26d *mḥqh r'šw*
She smashes Sisera's skull.
[3.3.3 5.3.2 6.1.1]

26e *wmḥṣh wḥlph rqtw*
She smashes and pierces his temple.
[3.4.2]

27a *byn-rglyh krʿ*
Between her legs he crouches.
On this verse, see Globe (1975a).
[3.3.8 4.3]

27b *npl škb*
He falls. He lies prone.
[3.4.15 4.1.4 4.3]

27c *byn-rglyh krᶜ npl*
Between her legs he crouches. He falls.
[3.4.2 4.1.3 4.1.4 4.3]

27d *bʾšr krᶜ*
In that place he crouches.
The use of *ʾšr* 'place' is noted in Boling (1975: 115).
[3.3.8 4.1.3 4.3]

27e *šm npl šdwd*
There the oppressed one falls.
[3.3.45 4.3]

28a *bᶜd-hḥlwn nšqph*
Through the window lattice she looks out.
On the *femme à la fenêtre* motif here, see van der Weiden (1970: 69).
[3.3.8 5.3.2]

28b *wtybb ʾm-sysrʾ bᶜd-hʾšnb*
Sisera's mother wails through the window lattice.
[3.3.28 5.3.2 8.1.1]

28c *mdwᶜ bšš rkbw lbwʾ*
Why does his chariot tarry in coming?
[3.4.20 4.1.3 8.1.1]

28d *mdwᶜ ʾḥrw pᶜmy-mrkbwtyw*
Why does his chariotry's clatter delay?
[3.4.4 4.1.3 8.1.1]

29a *ḥkmwt-śrwtyh tᶜnynh*
The wisest of her princesses answers her.
[3.3.6]

29b *ʾp-hyʾ tšyb ʾmryh lh*
She gives her words back to her:
[3.4.19 8.1.1]

30a *hlʾ-ymṣʾw yḥlqw šll*
Haven't they found, aren't they dividing the spoil?
[3.4.2 4.4 8.1.1]

30b *rḥm-rḥmtym lrʾš-gbr*
One woman, or two, goes for each man.
[3.3.24 4.4 6.3.3 8.1.1]

30c *šll-ṣbᶜym lsysrᵓ*
Booty of dyed stuff goes to Sisera.
[3.3.24 4.1.1 4.4 6.3.3 8.1.1]

30d *šll-ṣbᶜym rqmh*
The booty of dyed stuff is embroidered.
[3.3.24 4.1.1 bis 4.1.2 bis 4.1.5 4.4 6.3.3 8.1.1]

30e *ṣbᶜ-rqmtym lṣwᵓry-šll*
The booty of embroidered stuff belongs on plunderers' necks.
[3.3.24 4.1.1 4.1.2 bis 4.1.5 4.4 6.3.3 8.1.1]

31a *kn yᵓbdw kl-ᵓwybyk yhwh*
Thus perish all your enemies, Yahweh.
Reading (*ᵓwyby)k* as an emphatic particle, van Dijk (1968: 71) renders 'all the enemies of Yahweh.'
[3.4.20]

31b *wᵓhbyw kṣᵓt-hšmš bgbrtw*
Those who love him are like sunrise in his strength.
[3.3.68]

*2.7 2 Samuel 1. The Lament of David*

The basic treatment is that of Freedman (1972a), with whom we exclude v 18 from the text. The poem is 30 lines long.

BH3 reads a text with 11 more line divisions than ours, reflecting a propensity to split lines: vv 19a, 21c, 21d, 22c, 22d, 23a, 24a, 24b, 24c, and 25a. It joins vv 26cd. At vv 21ab and 26ab, we read two lines and it reads three.

19a *hṣby yśrᵓl ᶜl-bmwtyk ḥll*
The Gazelle, Israel, was pierced on your heights.
Freedman (1972a: 116) identifies *hṣby* with Jonathan. Cross (1973a: 122, n. 34) identifies the Gazelle as Saul, as do Stuart (1976: 193, n. 3) and NAB. On the term, see Dahood (1975h). Read *ḥll* as a *Qal* passive.
[3.4.20]

19b *ᵓyk-nplw gbwrym* = v 27a
The warriors have fallen.
[3.3.2]

20a *ᵓl-tgydw bgt*
Do not say so in Gath-Ashqelon,
[3.3.4 5.1.5 6.1.1 9.1]

20b *ʾl-tbśrw bḥwṣt-ʾšqlwn*
Do not give out the news in Gath-Ashqelon's streets,
[3.3.4 5.1.5 6.1.1 9.1]

20c *pn-tśmḥnh bnwt-plštym*
Lest pagan Philistine women rejoice,
[3.3.22 5.3.6 6.1.7 9.1]

20d *pn-tʿlznh bnwt-hʿrlym*
Lest pagan Philistine women exult.
[3.3.22 5.3.6 6.1.7 9.1]

21a *hry bglbʿ ʾl-ṭl*
Hills, no dew in Gilboa.

On the syntax of *ʾl*, see Gordon's remarks on the comparable use of *bl* in an Aqhat parallel to vv 21abc (1965: 108); see further Dahood (1965a: 36-37). The form *hry* is a cstr. form used in a place in which Classical Hebrew would use an absolute.
[3.4.9 6.1.4]

21b *wʾl-mṭr ʿlykm wśdy-trwmt*
No rain on you, lofty fields.

The Ug parallel referred to above was used by Ginsberg as the basis for a proposed emendation *šrʿy-thwmwt* 'upsurging of the deep,' accepted by, e.g., Stuart (1976: 193, n. 6). Freedman (1972a: 122) argues against the suggestion on the grounds that the deep is out of place here, as a plateau battlefield is not; and that *trwmt* need not be regarded as a peculiarly cultic word; he is followed by Dahood (1972: 398-99; 1974c: 392). The second *w* is emphatic.
[3.4.9 6.1.4]

21c *ky-šm ngʿl mgn-gbwrym*
There the warriors' leader was disgraced.

On *mgn* 'benefactor, suzerain, leader' in this poem, see Freedman (1972a: 122-23).
[3.3.45 4.1.2]

21d *mgn-šʾwl bly-mšyḥ bšmn*
Leader Saul was anointed with oil.
[3.3.68 4.1.2]

22a *mdm-ḥllym*
From the blood of wounded warriors,
[3.5.5 5.3.2 6.1.8 9.2]

22b *mḥlb-gbwrym*
From the flesh of wounded warriors,
[3.5.5 5.3.2 6.1.8 9.2]

22c *qšt-yhwntn lʾ-nśwg ʾḥwr*
Jonathan-Saul's bow did not turn back,
[3.3.42 4.3 5.2.1 6.1.2 9.2]

22d *wḥrb-šʾwl lʾ-tšwb ryqm*
Jonathan-Saul's sword was not set up clean.
[3.3.42 4.1.1 4.3 5.2.1 6.1.2 9.2]

23a *šʾwl-wyhwntn hnʾhbym-whnʿymm*
Saul and Jonathan were loved and lovely.
[3.3.24 4.1.1 4.3]

23b *bḥyyhm-wbmwtm lʾ-nprdw*
In their lives and deaths they were not divided.
[3.3.8 6.2.1]

23c *mnšrym qlw*
They were faster than eagles.
[3.3.8 6.2.1]

23d *mʾrywt gbrw*
They were stronger than lions.
[3.3.8 6.2.1]

24a *bnwt-yśrʾl ʾl-šʾwl bkynh*
Israelite women, weep for Saul,
[3.4.6 8.2.2]

24b *hmlbškm šny ʿm-ʿdnym*
Who dressed you in scarlet with woven jewelry,
[3.3.63 6.1.7 8.2.2]

24c *hmʿlh ʿdy-zhb ʿl-lbwškn*
Who set gold woven jewelry on your dresses.
[3.3.63 6.1.7 8.2.2]

25a *ʾyk-nplw gbrym btwk-hmlḥmh*
The warriors have fallen in war.
[3.3.28 6.1.2]

25b *yhwntn ʿl-bmwtyk ḥll*
Jonathan was pierced on your heights.
[3.3.54 6.1.2]

26a *ṣr ly ʿlyk ʾḥy*
It is hard for me because of you, my Brother Jonathan.
[3.4.20 4.1.2 5.1.3]

26b *yhwntn nʿmt ly mʾd*
My Brother Jonathan, you were very good for me.
[3.4.20 4.1.2 5.1.3]

26c *nplʾth* ET *nplʾ ʾth*
You were a wonder.

The emendation of MT's cancerous form, by supplying a ʾ lost through haplography and redividing, originated in Cross and Freedman (1975: 26); cf. Freedman (1972a: 123), and Stuart (1976: 189).
[3.3.25 6.2.3]

26d *ʾhbtk ly*
Your love was mine.
[3.3.24 4.1.2 6.2.3]

26e *mʾhbt nšym* ET *m ʾhbt-nšym*
What is the love of women?

The usual, joint rendering of this line and the previous one is syntactically difficult. The simple redivision proposed resolves what previous commentators have taken as a tortured whole into two simple verbless clauses.
[3.3.25 4.1.2 6.2.3]

27a *ʾyk nplw gbwrym* = v 19b

27b *wyʾbdw kly-mlḥmh*
The instruments of war have vanished.

Freedman (1972a: 123-24) may be correct in taking the nominal phrase as object rather than subject, i.e., 'along with/by means of the instruments of war.'
[3.3.2 6.1.1 (with 27a)]

## *2.8 Habaqquq 3. The Psalm of Habaqquq*

The standard reading is that of Albright (1950); we have profited from some personal communications from D. N. Freedman and A. Myers. The poem is 65 lines long. The lineation of BH3's text is the same as ours, except in vv 14abcd and 16de, which are segmented differently in the two versions.

2a *yhwh šmᶜty šmᶜk*
Yahweh, I have heard report of your work.
[3.4.6 4.1.2 4.5 5.3.2 6.1.4]

2b *yrᵓty yhwh pᶜlk*
Yahweh, I have seen report of your work.
[3.4.6 4.1.2 4.5 5.3.2 6.1.4]

2c *bqrb šnym ḥyyhw* ET *bqrb-šnym ḥy yhw*
As Yahweh lives, in the upheaval of years,
[3.3.44 4.1.1 4.5]

2d *bqrb-šnym twdyᶜ*
May you reveal compassion in the upheaval of years.
[3.3.8 4.1.1 4.5 5.3.2]

2e *brgz rḥm tzkwr*
May you remember compassion in the upheaval of years.
[3.3.59 5.3.2]

3a *ᵓlwh mtymn ybwᵓ*
The Holy God comes from Teman.
[3.3.54 5.1.1 6.1.2 7.1.1]

3b *wqdwš mhr pᵓrn slh* ET *wqdwš mhr-pᵓrn*
The Holy God comes from the hill country of Paran.
[3.3.10 5.1.1 6.1.2 7.1.1]

3c *ksh šmym hwdw*
Praise of his majesty covers the heavens and earth.
[3.3.30 5.2.2 5.3.2 6.1.2]

3d *wthltw mlᵓh hᵓrṣ*
Praise of his majesty fills the heavens and earth.
[3.3.40 5.2.2 5.3.2 6.1.2]

4a *wngh kᵓwr thyh* ET *wnghh kᵓwr thyh*
The radiance of his lightning is like beams of the Light.
The referent of *ᵓwr* here and in vv 11bc is the sun, the great light; see Blommerde (1969: 131) and Dahood (1970b: 127-28).
[3.3.54 5.3.2 bis 6.1.2 7.1.1]

4b *qrnym mydw lw* ET *qrnym mdlw*
The radiance of his lightning is like the beams of the Light.

The shearing of two vowel letters from MT and redivision of words reveals the Heb cognate of Ug *mdl* 'lightning-bolt,' which also occurs in Num 24:7a, q.v.
[3.3.10 5.3.2 bis 6.1.2 7.1.1]

4c *wšm-ḥbywn ʿzh*
The name of the covering is His Strength.

For the adverb *šm* of MT, read *šm* 'name.'
[3.3.24]

5a *lpnyw ylk dbr*
Deber-Reshep goes at his face.

On the troops of the deity here, see Tromp (1969: 66, 204).
[3.3.44 5.1.2 6.1.2]

5b *wyṣʾ ršp lrglyw*
Deber-Reshep goes out at his feet.

[3.3.28 5.1.2 6.1.2]

6a *ʿmd wymdd ʾrṣ*
He stands and convulses the peoples of the earth.

[3.4.2 5.3.2 6.1.5]

6b *rʾh wytr gwym*
He looks and sets trembling the peoples of the earth.

For the suggestion to render *ytr* here as 'scanned,' from the supposed basic sense *twr* 'to explore, roam,' see Dahood (1974c: 385-86); the Ug cognate remains problematic.
[3.4.2 5.3.2 6.1.5]

6c *wytpṣṣw hrry-ʿd*
The hills of the Eternal One are shattered.

[3.3.2 6.1.1]

6d *šḥw gbʿwt-ʿwlm*
The heights of the Everlasting One bow down,

[3.3.2 4.1.2 6.1.1 8.2.1]

6e *hlykwt-ʿwlm lw*
Along the course of the Everlasting One, for him.

[3.5.4 4.1.2 8.2.1]

7a *tḥt ʾwn rʾyty ʾhly kwšn* ET *tḥtʾwn rʾyty ʾhly-kwšn*
I see that the tents of Kushan are broken.

The emendation of MT's prepositional phrase to a form of *ḥtʾ* 'to shatter' was suggested by Albright (1950: 15, n. n), and taken up by Brockington (1973: 261) and NAB.
[3.4.4]

7b *yrgzwn yryʿwt-ʾrṣ-mdyn*
The curtains of the land of Midian tremble.
[3.3.2]

8a *hbnhrym ḥrh yhwh* ET *hbnhr-m ḥrh yhwh*
Is it kindled against River, Yahweh?
The *m* in both 8a and 8b are emphatic.
[3.4.6 4.1.1 7.1.1]

8b *ʾm bnhrym ʾpk* ET *ʾm-bnhr-m ʾpk*
Is your anger kindled against River?
[3.3.11 4.1.1 6.1.1 7.1.1]

8c *ʾm-bym ʿbrtk*
Is your wrath kindled against Sea?
[3.3.11 6.1.1 7.1.1]

8d *ky-trkb ʿl-swsyk*
You mount the chariots of your horses,
[3.3.4 5.3.2]

8e *mrkbtyk yšwʿh*
The chariots of your horses, Savior.
Van Dijk (1968: 69) reads the *k* as a suffix within a construct chain, glossing 'your chariot of victory,' cf. Freedman (1972c: 535).
[3.5.2 5.3.2]

9a *ʿryh tʿwr qštk*
Nakedly your bow is laid bare.
[3.3.43]

9b *šbʿwt mṭwt ʾmr slh* ET *šbʿt-mṭwt ʾmr*
I see your seven staffs.
Dahood (1970b: 21) suggests deriving *ʾmr* from the root *mrr* 'to strengthen' with a prothetic *ʾ*. The difficult form *šbʿwt* in the MT is best emended slightly to yield a number. On Hebrew *ʾmr* 'to see,' consult Dahood (1963b: 295-96).
[3.3.7]

9c *nhrwt tbqʿ ʾrṣ*
You split the earth with rivers.
[3.3.46]

10a *rʾwk yḥylw hrym*
Hills see you and tremble.
[3.4.2]

10b *zrm-mym ʿbr*
A flood of rainwater passes by.
[3.3.6]

10c *ntn thwm qwlw*
The deep utters its noise.
Dahood (1968b: 140) reads *rwm* with v 10c and renders 'The abyss gave forth its haughty voice.'
[3.3.27]

10d *rwm ydyhw nśʾ šmš*
Sun lifts its hands on high.
[3.4.19 5.1.2]

11a *yrḥ ʿmd zblh*
Moon stands in its elevation.
Albright (1950: 16) renders *zblh* 'on his lordly dais.' On the suffix, to be read 3 m.s., see BH3.
[3.3.40 5.1.2]

11b *lʾwr ḥṣyk yhlkw*
The flash of your arrows and spear travels toward the radiance of the Light.
[3.3.57 5.3.2 5.3.5 6.1.2 7.1.1]

11c *lngh brq-ḥnytk*
The flash of your arrow and spear travels toward the radiance of the Light.
[3.3.11 5.3.2 5.3.5 6.1.2 7.1.1]

12a *bzʿm tṣʿd ʾrṣ*
In rage you stomp the nations of the earth.
[3.3.48 5.3.2 6.1.2]

12b *bʾp tdwš gwym*
In anger you trample the nations of the earth.
[3.3.48 5.3.2 6.1.2]

13a *yṣʾt lyšᶜ-ᶜmk*
You sally forth for the salvation of your anointed's people,
[3.3.4 4.1.2 5.3.2 7.1.1]

13b *lyšᶜ ʾt mšyḥk*
You sally forth for the salvation of your anointed's people.
The pronoun *ʾt* here interrupts a construct chain, as noted by Freedman (1972c: 535).
[3.3.11 4.1.2 5.3.2 7.1.1]

13c *mḥṣt rʾš mbyt ršᶜ*
You smash in the head of the wicked.
[3.4.19]

13d *ᶜrwt yswd ᶜd ṣwʾr slh* ET *ᶜrt yswd ᶜd-ṣwʾr*
You lay bare backside to neck.
Read *ᶜērôtā* for MT's *ᶜārôt*, with NAB and Brockington (1973: 261).
[3.3.34 6.1.2]

14a *nqbt bmṭyw rʾš-przw*
You pierce his warrior chief with his own shafts.
[3.3.36 6.1.2]

14b *ysᶜrw lhpyṣny* ET *ysᶜrw l-hpyṣn*
They storm. They scatter.
The preposition *l* of MT is to be read as an emphatic particle; the second verb is a *Hipᶜil* suffixing form with the durative *-ûn* termination which in Hebrew is proper only to the prefixing verb form, an "error" of the sort expected in "archaizing" verse.
[3.4.15 6.1.5]

14c *ᶜlyṣtm kmw* ET *yᶜlṣw tmk-m*
They exult. They grab out.
The prefix of the first verb appears after reparsing of v 14b. The exceedingly awkward comparative particle of MT is best read with the suffix of *ᶜlyṣtm*, as a form of *tmk*. The verb sequence is prefixing-suffixing, as in the previous line.
[3.4.15 6.1.5]

14d *lʾkl ᶜny bmstr* ET *l-ʾklw ᶜny bmstr*
They consume the poor in secret.
The *l* here is emphatic introducing a suffixing form of the verb, as in v 14b.
[3.3.34 6.2.2]

15a *drkt bym swsyk*
You trample the sea with your horses.
[3.3.36 6.2.2 7.1.1]

15b *ḥmr mym-rbym*
You trample the mighty waters with your ass.
The pronominal suffix of *swsyk* in v 15a does double duty in v 15b. This is the first time that this beast, elsewhere much dignified, has been noted as a divine vehicle in the Bible.
[3.3.12 6.2.2 7.1.1]

16a *šmᶜty wtrgz bṭny*
I hear and my belly trembles.
[3.4.2]

16b *lqwl ṣllw śpty*
My lips quiver at the sound.
[3.3.44 6.1.2]

16c *ybwᵓ rqb bᶜṣmy*
Decay enters my bones.
[3.3.28 6.1.2]

16d *wtḥty ᵓrgz*
I shake in my terror,
Freedman (p.c.) suggests that *tḥt* is a noun from the root *ḥtt*.
[3.3.7 8.2.2]

16e *ᵓšr-ᵓnwḥ lywm-ṣrh*
As I wait for the day of oppression.
[3.3.21 8.2.2]

16f *lᶜlwt lᶜm ygwdnw* ET *lᶜlwt l-ᶜm ygwdnw*
During the rising, a people will attack us.
The second *l* is an emphatic particle.
[3.3.57]

17a *ky-tᵓnh lᵓ-tprḥ*
The fig tree does not bud.
[3.3.6]

17b *wᵓyn ybwl bgpnym*
There is no yield on the vines.
[3.3.28]

17c *kḥš mʿśh-zyt*
The olive's product fails.
[3.3.2]

17d *wšdmwt lʾ-ʿśh ʾkl*
The fields produce no food.
[3.3.40]

17e *gzr mmklh ṣʾn*
Small and large livestock are cut off from the fold.
Read *gzr* as a *Qal* passive with Albright (1950: 18), Dahood (1965b: 21), and Brockington (1973: 261).
[3.3.31 5.2.3 6.2.2]

17f *wʾyn bqr brptym*
There are no small and large livestock in the stables.
[3.3.28 5.2.3 6.2.2]

18a *wʾny byhwh ʾʿlwzh*
I will exult in Yahweh, the god of my salvation.
[3.3.54 5.1.1 6.2.2]

18b *ʾgylh bʾlhy-yšʿy*
I will rejoice in Yahweh, the god of my salvation.
[3.3.4 5.1.1]

19a *yhwh-ʾdny ḥyly*
Yahweh, my lord, is my strength.
[3.3.24]

19b *wyśm rgly kʾylwt*
He makes my feet like hinds'.
[3.3.34]

19c *wʿl-bmwty ydrkny*
He makes me walk on my heights.
[3.3.8]

### *2.9 Zephaniah 1*

Basic to the discussion of Zephaniah presented here are Powis Smith (1911), Sabottka (1972), and Kapelrud (1975); cf. Loretz (1973), Olmo Lete (1973), and Pardee (1974) on Sabottka. We exclude only the first verse of the book as prose; other putative prose accretions in the text we do not believe exist. The "purification" of the text of these is a major concern of most commentators; the work of Sabottka and Kapelrud does not accord that impossible task first priority, although Kapelrud does make some exclusions. Zephaniah 1 is 69 lines long.

BH3 reads one less line division than we do. It splits vv 8b, 8c, 9c, 16b, and 18a; it joins vv 3de, 6bc, 13de, and 18bc. At vv 5bcd, and 18de, the text is broken variously; further, we read vv 12def as three lines, against BH3, which reads one.

2a *ʾsp ʾsp kl*
I will remove everything

The MT here reads *ʾāsop*, a *Qal* infinitive absolute of *ʾsp* 'to gather, remove' plus *ʾāsēp*, a *Hipʿil* 1 c.s. form of *swp* 'to come to an end.' We follow most moderns who emend to yield two forms of *ʾsp*, *ʾāsop ʾōsēp*; so, e.g., BH3, Gesenius, Kautzsch, Cowley (1910: 200-1, at 72aa; 344, n. 3), Brockington (1973: 262), NAB, RSV, BJ, and Powis Smith (1911: 191). Kapelrud (1975: 21-22) emends to read *ʾāsop ʾeʾĕsop*. Sabottka (1972: 5-7) emends to *ʾōsēp ʾasōp*, following MT in referring to forms to different roots, but preferring *ʾsp* and *ysp*; he renders 'I will again sweep away.'
[3.3.33 4.4 8.2.1]

2b *mʿl-pny-hʾdmh*
From the face of the earth.

[3.5.5 4.4 8.2.1]

2c *nʾm-yhwh* = 1:3f, 1:10b, 3:8b
Oracle of Yahweh.

[3.5.5 4.4]

3a *ʾsp ʾdm-wbhmh*
I will sweep off people and animals.

Read *ʾōsēp*; see ad v 2a.
[3.3.3 4.1.3 4.4 6.1.1]

3b *ʾsp ʿwp-hšmym*
I will sweep away heaven's birds,

[3.3.3 4.1.3 4.4 6.1.1 8.2.1]

3c *wdgy-hym*
And fish of the sea,

[3.5.5 8.2.1]

3d *whmkšlwt ʾt-hršʿym*
Scandals, along with the wicked.

With Kapelrud (1975: 22, 24), we assume *mkšlwt* is impersonal in form and personal in reference.
[3.5.4 8.2.1]

3e *whkrty ᵓt-hᵓdm mᶜl-pny-hᵓdmh*
I will cut off people from the face of the earth.
[3.3.34]

3f *nᵓm-yhwh* = 1:2c, 1:10b, 3:8b

4a *nṭyty ydy ᶜl-yhwdh*
I stretch out my hand against Judah,
[3.3.34 8.2.1]

4b *wᶜl-kl-ywšby-yrwšlm*
Against all Jerusalem's inhabitants.
[3.5.5 8.2.1]

4c *whkrty mn-hmqwm-hzh ᵓt-šᵓr-hbᶜl*
I will cut off from that place what's left of Baal,

The import of the final phrase is much discussed; see Williams (1963), Cogan (1974: 94-95 and n. 164), and Powis Smith (1911: 169, 187); for another suggestion, see Sabottka (1972: 15-18), Dahood (1972: 402), and Watson (1977: 270).
[3.3.36 8.2.3]

4d *ᵓt-šm-hkmrym ᶜm-hkhnym*
The name of komerim along with the priests,

The phrase *šm-hkmrym* may mean 'the name/theophanic presence revered by the komerim.'
[3.5.4 8.2.3]

5a *wᵓt-hmšthwym ᶜl-hggwt*
Those who worship, on rooftops,
[3.3.18 4.1.2 4.5 6.4 8.2.3]

5b *lṣbᵓ-hšmym wᵓt-hmšthwym*
Those who worship the host of heaven,
[3.3.18 4.1.2 4.5 6.4 8.2.3]

5c *hnšbᶜym lyhwh*
Those who swear to Yahweh,

Sabottka (1972: 21-23), reasoning from the variance in prepositional usage, assigns the *hnšbᶜym* of v 5c to the root *šbᶜ* 'to be satisfied,' a by-form of *śbᶜ*, while that of v 5d he parses in the usual way; we follow Kapelrud (1975: 23) in his reticence about the suggestion.
[3.3.18 4.1.1 4.5 6.4 8.2.3]

5d *whnšbᶜym bmlkm*
Those who swear by their king,

The versional understanding of MT *mlkm* 'their king' as Milcom is accepted by Brockington (1973: 262) and Kapelrud (1975: 23-24, 69); and rejected by Cogan (1974: 94-95 and n. 166), Sabottka (1972: 24-25) and Weinfeld (1972: 149); Sabottka presents evidence that *mlk* was a Baal title and suggests that the deity in question was Baal-shamem, whom he identifies with the Morning Star.
[3.3.18 4.1.1 4.5 6.4 8.2.3]

6a *wᵓt-hnswgym mᵓḥry-yhwh*
Those who slide away from Yahweh,

[3.3.18 6.4 8.2.3]

6b *wᵓšr lᵓ-bqšw ᵓt-yhwh wlᵓ-dršhw*
Who do not search for Yahweh and do not seek him.

[3.4.20 8.2.3]

7a *hs mpny-ᵓdny-yhwh*
Hush before Lord Yahweh.

[3.3.4]

7b *ky-qrwb ywm-yhwh*
Yahweh's day is near.

[3.3.25]

7c *ky-hkyn yhwh zbḥ*
Yahweh establishes a sacrifice.

[3.3.27]

7d *hqdyš qrᵓyw*
He consecrates those he has called.

[3.3.3]

8a *whyh bywm-zbḥ-yhwh*
It will happen on the day of Yahweh's sacrifice.

[3.3.4 6.1.1]

8b *wpqdty ᶜl-hśrym-wᶜl-bny-hmlk*
I will call to account princes and royal scions,

Sabottka (1972: 36) associates *bny-hmlk* with *šᵓr-hbᶜl* 'the family of Baal [sic],' and similarly renders *śrym* as cultic officers, as does Weinfeld (1972: 151).
[3.3.4 6.1.1 8.2.1]

8c *wʿl-kl-hlbšym mlbwš-nkry*
All who wear foreign dress.
[3.5.2 8.2.1]

9a *wpqdty ʿl-kl-hdwlg*
I will call to account every leaper

The supposed idiom *dlg ʿl-hmptn*, associated with 1 S 5:5, has never been satisfactorily explained and there is no plausible reason not to separate the prepositional phrases; on the idiom, see Powis Smith (1911: 208-9), and Cogan (1974: 94 and n. 165). The situation is not materially improved by trying to regloss *mptn* (although that may be necessary). Kapelrud (1975: 104) renders 'all who leap up to the pedestal' and NEB glosses *mptn* 'temple terrace.' Sabottka (1972: 30, 39) avoids the problem by rendering 'all who mount up to the Miptan.' In a cultic context, in which boundaries are granted special force, the *mptn*, understood in the traditional sense (see Watson 1977: 271), could well have been a focus of peculiar concern.
[3.3.4 8.2.3]

9b *ʿl-hmptn bywm-hhwʾ*
On the threshold, on that day,
[3.5.4 4.4 8.2.3]

9c *hmmlʾym byt-ʾdnyhm ḥms-wmrmh*
Those who fill their Lord's house with violence and deceit.
[3.3.63 4.4 8.2.3]

10a *whyh bywm-hhwʾ*
It will happen on that day.
[3.3.4 4.4]

10b *nʾm-yhwh* = 1:2c, 1:3f, 3:8b

10c *qwl-ṣʿqh mšʿr-hdgym*
The sound of a cry from Fishes Gate.

No verb need be supplied here, *contra*, e.g., RSV and BJ, nor does *qwl* need to be understood as an exclamation, *pace* Sabottka (1972: 45).
[3.5.4 6.2.5]

10d *wyllh mn-hmšnh*
The howling of great destruction from the hills of Mishneh.
[3.5.4 5.3.2 5.3.8 6.2.5]

10e *wšbr-gdwl mhgbᶜwt*
The howling of great destruction from the hills of Mishneh.
[3.5.4 5.3.2 5.3.8 6.2.5]

11a *hylylw yšby-hmktš*
The inhabitants of the Mortar howl.
[3.3.2 6.2.1]

11b *ky-ndmh kl-ᶜm-knᶜn*
All the people of Canaan are destroyed.
[3.3.2 6.2.1]

11c *nkrtw kl-nṭyly-ksp*
All those laden with silver are cut off.
[3.3.2 6.2.1]

12a *whyh bᶜt-hhyʾ*
It will happen at that time.
[3.3.4]

12b *ʾḥpś ʾt-yrwšlm bnrwt*
I will search Jerusalem with lamps.
[3.3.34]

12c *wpqdty ᶜl-hʾnšym*
I will call to account people
[3.3.4 8.1.2 8.2.3]

12d *hqpʾym ᶜl-šmryhm*
Who thicken on their lees
[3.3.18 6.1.7 8.1.2 8.2.3]

12e *hʾmrym blbbm*
Who say in their hearts,
[3.3.18 6.1.7 8.1.2 8.2.3]

12f *lʾ-yyṭyb yhwh wlʾ-yrᶜ*
Yahweh does neither good nor evil.
[3.4.2 8.1.2 8.2.3]

13a *whyh ḥylm lmšsh*
Their wealth will become booty.
[3.3.28 6.1.2 7.1.1]

13b *wbtyhm lšmmh*
Their estates will be desolate.
[3.3.10 6.1.2 7.1.1]

13c *wbnw btym wlʾ-yšbw*
They will build houses and not settle down.
[3.4.2]

13d *wnṭʿw krmym*
They will plant vineyards.
[3.3.3 6.1.1]

13e *wlʾ-yštw ʾt-yynm*
They will not drink their wine.
[3.3.3 6.1.1]

14a *qrwb ywm-yhwh-hgdwl*
Yahweh's great day is near.
[3.3.25 4.1.1 4.3 4.4]

14b *qrwb wmhr mʾd*
It approaches very swiftly.
[3.3.52 4.1.1 4.3 4.4]

14c *qwl-ywm-yhwh mr*
The sound of Yahweh's day is bitter.
[3.3.24 4.3 4.4]

14d *ṣrḥ šm gbwr*
The Warrior cries out there.

The Warrior is Yahweh, as Sabottka (1972: 52-54) observes. For another treatment, see Whitley (1974: 396-98).
[3.3.32 4.4]

15a *ywm-ʿbrh hywm-hhwʾ*
That day is a day of wrath,
[3.3.25 4.1.1 4.4 8.3]

15b *ywm-ṣrh-wmṣwqh*
A day of stress and distress
[3.5.5 4.1.1 4.4 6.4 8.3]

15c *ywm-šʾh-wmšwʾh*
A day of holocaust and desolation,
[3.5.5 4.1.1 4.4 6.4 8.3]

15d *ywm-ḥšk-wʾplh*
A day of gloom and darkness,
[3.5.5 4.1.1 4.4 6.4 8.3]

15e *ywm-ʿnn-wʿrpl*
A day of clouds and storm gatherings,
[3.5.5 4.1.1 4.4 6.4 8.3]

16a *ywm-šwpr-wtrwʿh*
A day of horn and alarm.
[3.5.5 4.1.1 4.4 6.4 8.3]

16b *ʿl-hʿrym-hbṣrwt-wʿl-hpnwt-hgbhwt*
Over fortified cities and high walltowers,
[3.5.5 8.2.1]

17a *whṣrty lʾdm*
I will press hard on people.
[3.3.4 6.2.1 8.2.1]

17b *whlkw kʿwrym*
They will walk like the blind.
[3.3.4 6.2.1]

17c *ky-lyhwh ḥṭʾw*
They rebel against Yahweh.
[3.3.8 6.2.1]

17d *wšpk dmm kʿpr*
Their bloody guts are poured out like dung in dust.
The *Qal* passive *špk* is discussed in Williams (1970: 47), and Sabottka (1972: 55).
[3.3.28 5.3.2 bis 6.2.2 7.1.1]

17e *wlḥmm kgllym* ET *wlḥm-m kgllym*
Their bloody guts are poured out like dung in dust.
Read with Sabottka (1972: 56-58) a form of *lḥ* 'sap, strength, Lebenssaft,' although there may be a byform of that word, *lḥm*, cf. BH3; the *(lḥm-)m* is emphatic.
[3.3.10 5.3.2 bis 6.2.2 7.1.1]

18a *gm-kspm-gm-zhbm lʾ-ywkl lhṣylm*
Neither their silver nor gold can rescue them
[3.4.4 6.2.2 8.2.1]

18b *bywm-ᶜbrt-yhwh*
On the day of Yahweh's wrath.
[3.5.5 8.2.1]

18c *wbʾš-qnʾtw tʾkl kl-hʾrṣ*
In the fire of his zeal the whole earth will be consumed.
[3.3.44 4.4]

18d *ky-klh-ʾk-nbhlh*
Destruction and fear
[3.5.5 4.4 8.2.1]

18e *yᶜśh ʾt-kl-yšby-hʾrṣ*
He inflicts on all earth's inhabitants.
[3.3.4 4.4 8.2.1]

### *2.10 Zephaniah 2*

The poem is 65 lines long.

BH3 reads 7 more line breaks than we do. It splits vv 1, 5b, 7b, 10a, 13c, 14c, 14e, and 15e; and it joins vv 3de, 9ab, and 10bc. At vv 6ab, 15cd, and 15fg, the text is segmented differently; and at vv 11abcd, BH3 reads 6 lines against our 4.

1 *htqwššw wqwšw hgwy-lʾ-nksp*
Make yourselves into stubble and become stubble, O worthless nation.
[3.4.21]

2a *bṭrm-ldt-ḥq*
Before the womb comes to term,
The form *ḥq* is cognate to Arb *ḥuqq* 'hollow, cavity;' see Sabottka (1972: 64). The line refers to a natural term for the prophet's threat; another prophecy with a natural term is the one in Isa 7:14.
[3.5.5 8.3]

2b *kmṣ ᶜbr ywm* ET *k-mṣ-ᶜbr ywm*
The day will be passing chaff.
The *k* is emphatic; *ᶜbr* is a participle used adjectivally.
[3.3.25 8.3]

2c *bṭrm-lʾ-ybwʾ ᶜlykm* = 2:2e
Before it comes upon you,
[3.3.21 4.3 4.5 8.2.3]

2d *ḥrwn-ʾp-yhwh*
The wrath of Yahweh's anger,
[3.5.5 4.3 4.5 8.2.3]

2e *bṭrm-lʾ-ybwʾ ʿlykm* = 2:2c

2f *ywm-ʾp-yhwh*
The day of Yahweh's anger,
[3.5.5 4.3 4.5 8.2.3]

3a *bqšw ʾt-yhwh*
Seek Yahweh,
[3.3.3 4.4 4.5 8.2.3]

3b *kl-ʿnwy-hʾrṣ*
All you poor of the earth,
[3.5.5 4.4 4.5 8.2.3]

3c *ʾšr mšpṭw pʿlw*
You who practice his justice.
[3.3.64 4.4 4.5 8.2.3]

3d *bqšw ṣdq*
Seek honesty.
[3.3.3 4.1.3 4.4 4.5 5.3.2 6.1.1]

3e *bqšw ʿnwh*
Seek poverty.
[3.3.3 4.1.3 4.4 4.5 5.3.2 6.1.1]

3f *ʾwly tstrw*
Perhaps you will be hidden
[3.3.9 8.2.1]

3g *bywm-ʾp-yhwh*
On the day of Yahweh's anger.
[3.5.5 8.2.1]

4a *ky-ʿzh ʿzwbh thyh*
Gaza-Ashqelon shall be a forsaken waste.
[3.3.54 5.1.5 5.3.6 7.1.1]

4b *wʾšqlwn lšmmh*
Gaza-Ashqelon shall be a forsaken waste.
[3.3.10 5.1.5 5.3.6 7.1.1]

4c *ʾšdwd bṣhrym ygršwh*
They will drive Ashdod out at noon.
[3.3.54]

4d *wʿqrwn tʿqr*
Eqron will be uprooted.
[3.3.6]

5a *hwy yšby-ḥbl-hym*
Woe to those who live on the seaboard.
[3.5.4]

5b *gwy-krtym dbr-yhwh ʿlykm*
Nation of Cretans, Yahweh's word is against you.
[3.4.9]

5c *knʿn-ʾrṣ-plštym*
Canaan, the land of the Philistines,
[3.5.5 8.2.1]

5d *whʾbdtyk mʾyn-ywšb*
I will make you perish with no inhabitant.
[3.3.4 8.2.1]

6a *whyth ḥbl-hym-nwt*
It will be seaboard and pastureland,
Another treatment of this verse is given in Kselman (1970).
[3.3.3 4.4 8.2.1]

6b *krt-rʿym-wgdrwt-ṣʾn*
Shepherds' cisterns, and folds for flocks.
[3.5.5 4.4 8.2.1]

7a *whyh ḥbl lšʾryt*
The territory will belong to the remnant.
[3.3.28 4.4 6.1.2]

7b *byt-yhwdh ʿlyhm yrʿwn*
The house of Judah will pasture on them [the estates].
[3.3.54 6.1.2]

7c *bbty-ʾšqlwn bʿrb yrbṣwn*
They will recline at night on the estates of Ashqelon.
[3.3.60]

7d *ky-ypqdm yhwh-ʾlhyhm*
Yahweh their god will visit them.
[3.3.2]

7e *wšb šbwtm*
He will restore their fortunes.
See Greenfield (1965a: 4).
[3.3.3 6.1.1]

8a *šmʿty ḥrpt-mwʾb*
I have heard the reproach of Moab
[3.3.3 6.1.1 8.2.3]

8b *wgdwpy-bny-ʿmwn*
And the tauntings of the Ammonites
[3.5.5 8.2.3]

8c *ʾšr ḥrpw ʾt-ʿmy*
With which they reproach my people,
[3.3.64 7.2.1 8.2.3]

8d *wygdylw ʿl-gbwlm*
Through which they expand against their territory.
On *hgdyl ʿl-gbwl*, which could also be rendered 'to boast against, make claims or threats against,' see Powis Smith (1911: 226); Dahood (1965b: 31) renders 'who . . . aggrandized themselves at the expense of its boundary.' He has since suggested the existence of a root *gdl* 'to weave, spin (i.e., tales); calumniate,' in Dahood (1966b: 73, 1968a: 34); in the latter, he renders vv 8cd as 'They taunted my people and slandered my territory.' Sabottka (1972: 84-85) retains the boasting sense.
[3.3.19 7.2.1 8.2.3]

9a *lkn ḥy ʾny*
Thus, as I am alive!
[3.3.44]

9b *nʾm-yhwh-ṣbʾwt*
Oracle of Yahweh Sabaot,
[3.5.5 8.4]

9c *ʾlhy-yśrʾl*
God of Israel.
[3.5.5 8.4]

9d *ky-mwʾb ksdm thyh*
Moab and the Ammonites will be like Sodom-Gomorrah,
[3.3.54 5.1.4 5.1.5 6.1.2 7.1.1 9.2]

9e *wbny-ʿmwn kʿmrh*
Moab and the Ammonites will be like Sodom-Gomorrah,
[3.3.10 5.1.4 5.1.5 6.1.2 7.1.1 9.2]

9f *mmšq-ḥrwl-wmkrh-mlḥ*
A field of nettles, a pit of salt,
On the morphology of *mkrh*, see Sabottka (1972: 87).
[3.5.5 9.2]

9g *wšmmh ʿd-ʿwlm*
A desolation for eternity.
[3.5.4 9.2]

9h *šʾryt-ʿmy ybzwm*
The remnant of my people will despoil them.
[3.3.6 6.1.1]

9i *wytr gwy ynḥlwm* ET *wytr-gwyy ynḥlwm*
The rest of my nation will disposses them.
[3.3.6 6.1.1]

10a *zʾt lhm tḥt-gʾwnm*
This is theirs in place of their pride.
On supposed *zʾt* 'shame, indignity,' see Sabottka (1972: 88).
[3.3.68]

10b *ky-ḥrpw wygdlw*
They have reviled and expanded
[3.4.15 8.2.1]

10c *ʿl-ʿm-yhwh-ṣbʾwt*
Against the people of Yahweh Sabaot.
[3.5.5 8.2.1]

11a *nwrʾ yhwh ʿlyhm*
Yahweh is aweful before them.
On *ʿl* 'before, in the presence of,' see Suarez (1964) and Sabottka (1972: 90).
[3.3.68]

11b *ky-rzh ʾt-kl-ʾlhy-hʾrṣ*
He destroys all the gods of the earth.

Sabottka (1972: 90-91) associates *rzh* with the root of *rāzôn* 'prince,' glossing 'he rules over.'
[3.3.3]

11c *wyšṭḥww lw ʾyš mmqwmw*
Each worships him from his own temple,

The relevance of Arb *maqām* 'holy place, shrine,' was appreciated by G. A. Smith, whose comment is unfavorably quoted by Powis Smith (1911: 229).
[3.4.19 8.2.1]

11d *kl-ʾyy-hgwym*
On every island of the nations.

[3.5.5 8.2.1]

12 *gm-ʾtm kwšym ḥlly-ḥrby hmh*
Cushites, you are wounded by my sword.

It may be that *ḥrby* should be expanded to *ḥrb yhwh*, taking *y* as an abbreviation; the role of such conventions as abbreviations in the text of the HB is not clear; see Driver (1960, 1964) in general; he does not cite this passage, but the emendation is accepted in Brockington (1973: 263); cf. BH3 and NAB. The pronoun *hmh* is a copula.
[3.4.20]

13a *wyṭ ydw ʿl-ṣpwn*
He stretches his hand over the north.

Read a simple prefixing, not a jussive, verb form; see Powis Smith (1911: 236).
[3.3.34]

13b *wyʾbd ʾt-ʾšwr*
He makes Assur perish.

[3.3.3]

13c *wyśm ʾt-nynwh lšmmh-ṣyh kmdbr*
He makes Nineveh a dry wasteland, like a steppe.

[3.4.19]

14a *wrbṣw btwkh ʿdrym*
Herds lie down in its midst,

[3.3.31 8.2.1]

14b *kl-ḥytw-gwy*
All the nation's wildlife.

[3.5.5 8.2.1]

14c *gm-qʾt-gm-qpd bkptryh ylynw*
Owls great and small overnight on its capitals.
[3.3.54 6.1.2]

14d *qwl yšwrr bḥlwn*
A voice sings at the window.
[3.3.41 6.1.2]

14e *ḥrb bsp ky-ʾrzh ʿrh*
A sword on the sill strips the cedarwork.
For MT's *ḥoreb*, read *ḥereb* 'sword,' with Aquila and Symmachus and, among moderns, Sabottka (1972:97).
[3.4.19]

15a *zʾt hʿyr-hʿlyzh*
This is the exultant city
[3.3.24 8.1.2 8.3]

15b *hywšbt lbṭḥ*
Which dwelt secure,
[3.3.18 6.1.7 8.1.2 8.3]

15c *hʾmrh blbbh*
Which said in its heart,
[3.3.18 6.1.7 8.1.2 8.3]

15d *ʾny wʾpsy ʿwd*
Me and nobody else.
[3.5.3 8.1.2 8.3]

15e *ʾyk-hyth lšmh-mrbṣ lḥyh*
It has become a wasteland, a resting place for beasts.
[3.3.38]

15f *kl-ʿwbr ʿlyh yšrq*
All who pass by hiss at it.
[3.3.54]

15g *ynyʿ ydw*
They wag their hands.
[3.3.3]

## *2.11 Zephaniah 3*

The poem is 79 lines long.

The text of BH3 allows for 11 more line divisions than ours. It splits vv 1, 3a, 6c, 6d, 7e, 8h, 9a, 10b, 11a, 11c, 11d, 13c, 18a, and 20a; and it joins vv 8ab, 12c and 13a. At vv 5bc, 7cd, 12ab, and 14cd, the same number of lines is differently divided. At vv 16abc, BH3 reads our 3 lines as 4; at vv 19ab, BH3 reads 3 lines against our 2; and at vv 20cdef, BH3 arranges as 1 line our 4.

1 *hwy mrʾh-wngʾlh hʿyr-hywnh*
Woe! Fat and polluted is the Oppressing City.

The root of *mrʾh*, as Sabottka (1972: 102) notes, is *mrʾ* 'to be fat.'
[3.4.10]

2a *lʾ-šmʿh bqwl*
It heard no voice.

[3.3.4]

2b *lʾ-lqḥh mwsr*
It took no instruction.

[3.3.3]

2c *byhwh lʾ-bṭḥh*
It did not trust in Yahweh.

[3.3.8 6.1.1]

2d *ʾl-ʾlhyh lʾ-qrbh*
It did not draw near to its god.

[3.3.8 6.1.1]

3a *śryh bqrbh ʾrywt-šʾgym*
Its princes are roaring lions within it.

[3.3.68 5.2.2]

3b *špṭyh zʾby-ʿrb*
Its magistrates are evening wolves.

[3.3.24 5.2.2]

3c *lʾ-grmw lbqr*
They gnaw at morning.

The *lʾ* is emphatic.
[3.3.4]

4a *nbyʾyh pḥzym-ʾnšy-bgdwt*
Its prophets are wantons, people of deception.
[3.3.24]

4b *khnyh ḥllw qdš*
Its priests profane the holy instruction.
[3.3.40 5.3.2]

4c *ḥmsw twrh*
They do violence to the holy instruction.
[3.3.3 5.3.2]

5a *yhwh-ṣdyq bqrbh*
Yahweh the Just in its midst.
[3.3.24]

5b *lʾ-yʿśh ʿwlh bbqr*
The evil one does not act in the morning.
The abstract noun here designates an individual.
[3.3.28 4.1.2]

5c *bbqr mšpṭw ytn*
In the morning he is given his judgment.
The verb is a *Qal* passive.
[3.3.59 4.1.2]

5d *lʾwr lʾ-nʿdr*
He is not missing at dawn.
[3.3.8]

5e *wlʾ ywdʿ ʿwl bšt* ET *wlʾ-ydʿ ʿwl bšt*
The unjust one knows no shame.
Read a finite verb form for MT's participle. If Dahood and Sabottka (1972: 108-9) are correct in supposing that here as elsewhere *bšt* is a *Schimpfname* for Baal, then we must with them render 'The Shame (god) does not recognize the evil-doer,' which sounds too much like 'There is no honor among thieves' to pass as an effective description of Baal's powerlessness.
[3.3.27]

6a *hkrty gwym*
I cut off nations
[3.3.3]

6b *nšmw pnwtm*
Their towers are desolated.
[3.3.2]

6c *hḥrbty ḥwṣwtm mbly-ᶜwbr*
I will destroy their streets, travellerless.
[3.3.34]

6d *nṣdw ᶜryhm mbly-ᵓyš mᵓyn-ywšb*
Their cities are laid waste, no people, no inhabitants.
[3.4.19]

7a *ᵓmrty ᵓk-tyrᵓy ᵓwty*
I said You shall fear me.
[3.4.3 8.1.1]

7b *tqḥy mwsr*
You shall receive discipline.
[3.3.3 8.1.1]

7c *wlᵓ-ykrt mᶜwnh kl*
Nothing shall be cut off from her dwelling
[3.3.31 8.2.2]

7d *ᵓšr-pqdty ᶜlyh*
When I take notice of her.
[3.3.21 8.2.2]

7e *ᵓkn-hškymw hšḥytw kl-ᶜlylwtm*
They quickly ruin all their acts.
[3.4.2]

8a *lkn ḥkw ly*
Wait for me, then.
[3.3.50]

8b *nᵓm-yhwh* = 1:2c, 1:3f, 1:10b

8c *lywm-qwmy lᶜd*
On the day of my rising as a witness,

There is some evidence for *ᶜd* 'throne,' and Dahood (1959a: 276-78) renders the phrase *lᶜd* 'from the throne,' and is followed by Sabottka (1972: 113-14, cf. 98-100); cf. Dahood (1968b: 81-82; 1969c: 347). We follow here the usual emendation to *ᶜēd* 'witness'; see, e.g., Powis Smith (1911: 246-47, 253), Brockington (1973: 263), BH3, and NAB.
[3.5.2 8.3]

8d *ky-mšpṭy lʾsp gwym*
My decision is to gather nations,
[3.4.8 8.3]

8e *lqbṣy mmlkwt*
To gather in kingdoms,
Sabottka (1972: 114) parses the suffix of *qbṣy* as a "dative" and renders *mmlkwt* 'kings,' as elsewhere; both suggestions are plausible.
[3.3.17 8.3]

8f *lšpk ʿlyhm zʿmy*
To pour out upon them my rage,
[3.3.62 8.3]

8g *kl-ḥrwn-ʾpy*
All the wrath of my anger.
[3.5.5 8.3]

8h *ky-bʾš-qnʾty tʾkl kl-hʾrṣ*
In the fire of my zeal, the whole earth will be consumed.
[3.3.44]

9a *ky-ʾz-ʾhpk ʾl-ʿmym śph-brwrh*
I will turn back to the peoples purified lips,
[3.3.36 8.2.2]

9b *lqrʾ-klm bšm-yhwh*
So all of them will invoke the name of Yahweh,
[3.3.17 8.2.2]

9c *lʿbdw škm-ʾḥd*
And worship him jointly.
[3.3.17 8.2.2]

10a *mʿbr lnhry-kwš ʿtry*
From the far side, over Cushite Rivers, my supplicants
[3.5.3 8.2.1]

10b *bt-pwṣy ywblwn mnḥty*
My beloved scattered ones yield my tribute.
On the root of *mnḥty*, *nḥy*, see Dahood (1968b: 357).
[3.3.40 8.2.1]

11a *bywm-hhwʾ lʾ-tbwšy mkl-ʿlyltyk*
On that day, you shall be ashamed of all your deeds

The *lʾ* is emphatic.
[3.3.50 8.2.2]

11b *ʾšr pšʿt by*
Through which you rebelled against me.
[3.3.64 8.2.2]

11c *ky-ʾz-ʾsyr mqrbk ʿlyzy-gʾwtk*
I shall remove from your midst your proudly exultant ones.
[3.3.36]

11d *wlʾ-twspy lgbhh ʿwd bhr-qdšy*
You will no more go haughtily about my holy mountain.
[3.4.19]

12a *whšʾrty bqrbk*
I will leave in your midst
[3.3.4 8.2.1]

12b *ʿm-ʿny-wdl*
A poor and humble people.
[3.5.5 8.2.1]

12c *wḥsw bšm-yhwh šʾryt-yśrʾl*
The remnant of Israel will seek refuge in Yahweh's name.
[3.3.31]

13a *lʾ-yʿśw ʿwlh*
They will not do evil.
[3.3.3 6.1.1]

13b *wlʾ-ydbrw kzb*
They will not tell lies.
[3.3.3 6.1.1]

13c *wlʾ-ymṣʾ bpyhm lšwn-trmyt*
A deceitful tongue will not be found in their mouth.
[3.3.31]

13d *ky-hmh yrʿw wrbṣw*
They will graze and recline.
[3.4.2]

13e *wʾyn mḥryd*
There will be no terrorists.
[3.3.2]

14a *rny bt-ṣywn*
Give a shout, Beloved Zion.
[3.4.18 6.1.4]

14b *hryʿw yśrʾl*
Shout, Israel.
[3.4.18 6.1.4]

14c *śmḥy wʿlzy*
Rejoice and exult,
[3.4.15 8.2.1]

14d *bkl-lb bt-yrwšlm*
With your whole heart, Beloved Jerusalem.
[3.5.2 8.2.1]

15a *hsyr yhwh mšpṭyk*
Yahweh turns away the judgments of your enemies.
[3.3.27 5.3.2]

15b *pnh ʾybk* ET *pnh ʾybyk*
He clears away the judgments of your enemies.
The Murabbaʿat 88 text (cited *apud* Sabottka 1972: 125) reads *ʾybyk*, as do LXX, Targum and Peshiṭta.
[3.3.3 5.3.2]

15c *mlk-yśrʾl-yhwh bqrbk*
The king of Israel, Yahweh, is in your midst.
[3.3.24]

15d *lʾ-tyrʾy rʿ ʿwd*
You shall no more fear evil.
Sabottka (1972: 125-29) finds in v 15 four *Schimpfnamen* of Baal, *mšpṭyk* (intensive plural), *ʾybk*, and *mlk*, as well as *rʿ*.
[3.3.35 4.4]

16a *bywm-hhwʾ yʾmr*
On that day it will be said:
[3.3.8 4.4 8.1.1]

16b *lyrwšlm ʾl-tyrʾy*
Don't be afraid, Jerusalem.

The *l* is the emphatic, used as a vocative marker.
[3.4.18 4.4 8.1.1]

16c *ṣywn ʾl-yrpw ydyk*
Don't drop your hands, Zion.

[3.4.6 8.1.1]

17a *yhwh-ʾlhyk bqrbk*
Yahweh, your god, is in your midst.

[3.3.24 8.1.1]

17b *gbwr ywšyʿ*
The Warrior saves.

[3.3.6 8.1.1]

17c *yśyś ʿlyk bśmḥh*
He rejoices over you in the joy of his loving.

[3.3.38 5.3.2 8.1.1]

17d *yḥryš bʾhbtw*
He sings in the joy of his loving.

On *ḥrš* 'to devise artfully; to improvise; to compose,' see Dahood *apud* Sabottka (1972: 132-34).
[3.3.4 5.3.2 8.1.1]

17e *ygyl ʿlyk brnh*
He delights over you with a shout.

[3.3.38 8.1.1]

18a *nwgy mmwʿd ʾspty mmk*
Those grieved in the assembly I will gather from you.

The cstr. plural stands here where an absolute would be expected.
[3.4.19 8.1.1]

18b *hyw mśʾt ʿlyh ḥrph*
They were a burden upon it, a reproach.

[3.4.19 8.1.1]

19a *hnny ʿśh ʾt-kl-mʿnyk*
I will deal with all your afflictors.

[3.4.8 8.1.1]

19b *bᶜt-hhyᵓ whwšᶜty ᵓt-hṣlᶜh*
At that time I will save the lame.
[3.3.48 8.1.1]

19c *whndḥh ᵓqbṣ*
I will gather in the outcast.
[3.3.7 8.1.1]

19d *wśmtym lthlh wlšm* ET *wśmty-m lthlh-wlšm*
I will change to praise and renown
On the emphatic *m*, see Sabottka (1972: 139); the syntax of vv 19de was first elucidated by Nöldeke; cf. Dahood (1972a: 399-400).
[3.3.4 8.1.1 8.2.1]

19e *bkl-hᵓrṣ bštm*
Throughout all the earth their shame.
[3.5.4 8.1.1 8.2.1]

20a *bᶜt-hhyᵓ ᵓbyᵓ ᵓtkm*
At that time I will bring you back
[3.3.48 4.1.1 4.1.2 4.1.5 8.1.1 8.2.2]

20b *wbᶜt-qbṣy ᵓtkm*
When I gather you up.
[3.5.2 4.1.1 4.1.2 4.1.5 8.1.1 8.2.2]

20c *ky-ᵓtn ᵓtkm lšm-wlthlh*
I will give you renown and praise
[3.3.34 4.1.2 4.1.5 8.1.1 8.2.3]

20d *bkl-ᶜmy-hᵓrṣ*
Among all the peoples of the earth
Watson (1977: 21) suggests that the *b* is comparative: 'I will give you more praise and renown than all the peoples of the earth.'
[3.5.5 4.1.5 8.1.1 8.2.3]

20e *bšwby ᵓt-šbwtykm lᶜynykm*
When I restore your fortunes before your eyes.
[3.3.62 4.1.5 8.1.1 8.2.3]

20f *ᵓmr yhwh*
Yahweh speaks.
[3.3.2 8.1.1]

*2.12 Psalm 78*

In addition to the treatment of Dahood (1968a), we have used notes from A. Myers. The poem is 163 lines long.

BH3 reads 5 fewer line breaks than we do and BHS 4 more. BH3 splits v 28 and joins vv 38ab. At vv 6abc, we read 3 lines against its 2; at both vv 19abc and 20abc, we split into 3 lines what it arranges as 1. At vv 11ab and 42ab, the lines are divided differently.

BHS also splits v 28. At vv 6abc, it reads 4 lines against our 3; and at vv 38ab and 56ab, it reads 3 lines against our 2. At vv 11ab, 19ab, and 42ab, the lines are divided differently.

BFBS has 3 fewer breaks than we do; it splits v 28 and joins v 38ab and v 20abc. At v 4abcd, it reads 3 lines. At vv 6abc, 11ab, 19ab, and 56ab, the lines are broken differently. We drop the superscription of the poem, *mśkyl lʾsp* 'a maskil of Asaph.'

1a *hʾzynh ʿmy twrty*
Give ear, my people, to my instruction.
[3.4.6]

1b *hṭw ʾznkm lʾmry-py*
Incline your ear to the words of my mouth.
[3.3.34 4.1.1 6.2.2]

2a *ʾptḥh bmšl py*
I will open my mouth in a parable.
[3.3.36 4.1.1 6.2.2]

2b *ʾbyʿh ḥydwt mny-qdm*
I will pronounce riddles from antiquity.
[3.3.34 6.2.2]

3a *ʾšr šmʿnw wndʿm*
Those things which we heard and know,
[3.4.11 7.2.1 8.2.3]

3b *wʾbwtynw sprw lnw*
That which our parents told us
[3.3.65 7.2.1 8.2.3]

4a *lʾ-nkḥd mbnyhm*
We do not hide from their descendants,
[3.3.4 8.2.3]

4b *ldwr-ʾḥrwn-msprym*
For the next generation, the reciters,
[3.5.5 8.2.3]

4c *thlwt-yhwh-wʿzwzw*
The praise of Yahweh and his triumph,
[3.5.5 8.2.3]

4d *wnplʾwtyw ʾšr ʿśh*
And the wonders which he has performed.
[3.5.1 8.2.3]

5a *wyqm ʿdwt byʿqb*
He sets up a covenant of instruction in Jacob-Israel.
[3.3.34 5.1.4 5.3.2 6.1.2]

5b *wtwrh śm byśrʾl*
He puts a covenant of instruction in Jacob-Israel,
[3.3.47 5.1.4 5.3.2 6.1.2 8.2.2]

5c *ʾšr ṣwh ʾt-ʾbwtynw*
Which he commanded our parents
[3.3.64 8.2.2]

5d *lhwdyʿm lbnyhm*
So they would reveal it to their children
[3.3.17 8.2.2]

6a *lmʿn-ydʿw dwr-ʾḥrwn*
So that the next generation would know.
[3.3.22 8.2.2]

6b *bnym ywldw yqmw*
May the children to be born arise.
[3.4.4]

6c *wysprw lbnyhm*
May they tell their children.
[3.3.4]

7a *wyśymw bʾlhym kslm*
May they put their trust in God.
[3.3.36]

7b *wlʾ-yškḥw mʿlly-ʾl*
May they not forget the deeds of El.
[3.3.3 6.1.1]

7c *wmṣwtyw ynṣrw*
May they guard his commandments.
[3.3.7 6.1.1]

8a *wlʾ-yhyw kʾbwtm*
May they not be like their parents,
[3.3.4 8.2.3]

8b *dwr-swrr-wmrh*
A contentious and rebellious generation,
[3.5.5 4.1.1 8.2.3]

8c *dwr lʾ-hkyn lbw*
A generation which did not set its mind.
[3.5.1 4.1.1 8.2.3]

8d *wlʾ-nʾmnh ʾt-ʾl rwḥw*
Its spirit was not trued with El.
[3.3.31]

9a *bny-ʾprym nwšqy-rwmy-qšt*
The Ephraimites were handlers and raisers of the bow.
The double cstr. chain is recognized by Eissfeldt (1958: 27).
[3.3.24]

9b *hpkw bywm-qrb*
They turned tail on the day of battle.
[3.3.4]

10a *lʾ-šmrw bryt-ʾlhym*
They did not observe God's covenant.
[3.3.3]

10b *wbtwrtw mʾnw llkt*
They refused to walk according to his instruction.
[3.3.50]

11a *wyškḥw ʿlylwtyw-wnplʾwtyw*
They forgot the deeds and wonders
[3.3.3 8.2.2]

11b *ʾšr hrʾm*
Which he revealed to them.

The verbal suffix is not resumptive but has a "dative" force.
[3.3.19 8.2.2]

12a *ngd-ʾbwtm ʿśh plʾ*
Before their parents, he did a marvel,

[3.3.48 8.2.1]

12b *bʾrṣ-mṣrym-śdh-ṣʿn*
In the land of Egypt, Tanis field.

[3.5.5 8.2.1]

13a *bqʿ ym wyʿbyrm*
He split the sea. He brought them across.

[3.4.2]

13b *wyṣb mym kmw-nd*
He made the waters stand like a dyke.

[3.3.34]

14a *wynḥm bʿnn ywmm*
He led them by day by a cloud.

[3.3.39 6.1.2 7.1.1]

14b *wkl-hlylh bʾwr-ʾš*
He led them all night by firelight.

[3.3.15 6.1.2 7.1.1]

15a *ybqʿ ṣrym bmdbr* ET *ybqʿ ṣr-m bmdbr*
He smote a rock in the steppe.

The emphatic particle *m* is recognized by Dahood (1968a: 240).
[3.3.34]

15b *wyšq kthmwt-rbh*
He made them drink as from the mighty deeps.

Without discussing the merits of the suggestion that *thmwt* refers to the desert, we may note that Dahood's remark (1968a: 240) that "for the desert Arabs, *tīhāmatu* denotes 'sandy desert'" is misleading; the word denotes only the Peninsular desert and is by way of a proper name.
[3.3.4]

16a *wywṣʾ nwzlym mslʿ*
He ran streams of water out of the cliff.

[3.3.34 5.3.2 6.1.2]

16b *wywrd knhrwt mym*
He made streams of water run down like rivers.
[3.3.36 5.3.2 6.1.2]

17a *wywsypw ʿwd lḥṭʾ lw*
They continued to err against him further,
[3.4.19 8.2.2]

17b *lmrwt ʿlywn bṣyh*
By rebelling against Elyon in the dry lands.
[3.3.62 8.2.2]

18a *wynsw ʾl blbbm*
They tested El deliberately,
[3.3.34 8.2.2]

18b *lšʾl ʾkl lnpšm*
By asking for food for their gorges.
[3.3.62 8.2.2]

19a *wydbrw bʾlhym ʾmrw*
They spoke against God. They said,
[3.4.2 8.1.1]

19b *hywkl ʾl*
Is El able
[3.3.2 8.1.1 8.2.2]

19c *lʿrk šlḥn bmdbr*
To array a table in the steppe?
[3.3.62 8.1.1 8.2.2]

20a *hn-hkh ṣwr*
He smote a rock.
[3.3.3 8.1.1]

20b *wyzwbw mym*
Arroyos of water gushed out.
[3.3.2 5.3.2 6.1.1 8.1.1]

20c *wnḥlym yšṭpw*
Arroyos of water overflowed.
[3.3.6 5.3.2 6.1.1 8.1.1]

20d *hgm-lḥm ywkl tt*
Is he able to give bread and meat?
[3.4.4 5.2.3 8.1.1]

20e *ʾm-ykyn šʾr lʿmw*
Can he produce bread and meat for his people?
[3.3.34 5.2.3 8.1.1]

21a *lkn šmʿ yhwh wytʿbr*
Then Yahweh heard and got angry.
[3.4.20]

21b *wʾš nśqh byʿqb*
An angry fire was kindled against Jacob-Israel.
[3.3.41 5.1.4 5.3.2 6.1.2]

21c *wgm-ʾp ʿlh byśrʾl*
An angry fire mounted up against Jacob-Israel.
[3.3.41 5.1.4 5.3.2 6.1.2]

22a *ky-lʾ-hʾmynw bʾlhym*
They did not believe in God, His Salvation.
[3.3.4 5.1.1 6.1.1]

22b *wlʾ-bṭḥw byšwʿtw*
They did not trust in God, His Salvation.
[3.3.4 5.1.1 6.1.1]

23a *wyṣw šḥqym mmʿl*
He commanded the clouds above.
[3.3.34]

23b *wdlty-šmym ptḥ*
He opened heavens' gates.
[3.3.7]

24a *wymṭr ʿlyhm mn lʾkl*
He made manna rain on them for eating,
[3.4.19]

24b *wdgn-šmym ntn lmw*
He gave them heavens' produce.
[3.3.47]

25a *lḥm-ʾbyrym ʾkl ʾyš*
Each ate the food of the mighty.
[3.3.43]

25b *ṣydh šlḥ lhm lśbᶜ*
He sent them provisions to satiety.
[3.4.19]

26a *ysᶜ qdym bšmym*
He led Sirocco-and-Khamsin from heaven, his fortress.
On *b* 'from' here, see Dahood (1968a: 242), and cf. BHS.
[3.3.34 5.1.2 5.3.7 6.1.2]

26b *wynhg bᶜzw tymn*
He guided Sirocco-and-Khamsin from heaven, his fortress.
[3.3.36 5.1.2 5.3.7 6.1.2]

27a *wymṭr ᶜlyhm kᶜpr šʾr*
He made the flesh of winged birds rain like dust upon them.
[3.4.19 5.3.3 7.1.1]

27b *wkḥwl-ymym ᶜwp-knp*
He made the flesh of winged birds rain like sand on the seashore.
[3.3.13 5.3.3 7.1.1]

28 *wypl bqrb-mḥnhw sbyb lmškntyw*
He made it fall in their camp, all around, near their tents.
[3.4.19]

29a *wyʾklw wyśbᶜw mʾd*
They ate and were vastly sated.
[3.4.2]

29b *wtʾwtm ybʾ lhm*
He brought them what they craved.
[3.3.47]

30a *lʾ-zrw mtʾwtm*
They were not estranged from their cravings.
[3.3.4]

30b *ᶜwd ʾklm bpyhm*
Their food was still in their mouths.
[3.3.68]

31a *wʾp-ʾlhym ʿlh bhm*
God's anger mounted against them.
[3.3.41]

31b *wyhrg bmšmnyhm*
He killed their noblest.
[3.3.4]

31c *wbḥwry-yśrʾl hkryʿ*
He laid low Israel's elect.
[3.3.7]

32a *bkl-zʾt ḥṭʾw ʿwd*
Through all this, they still sinned.
[3.3.51]

32b *wlʾ-hʾmynw bnplʾwtyw*
They did not believe in his wonders.
[3.3.4]

33a *wykl bhbl ymyhm*
He finished their days in a vapor of dismay.
[3.3.36 5.3.2 6.1.2 7.1.1]

33b *wšnwtm bbhlh*
He finished their years in a vapor of dismay.
[3.3.12 5.3.2 6.1.2 7.1.1]

34a *ʾm-hrgm wdršwhw*
When he killed them, they searched him out.
[3.4.17]

34b *wšbw wšḥrw ʾl*
They turned and sought El early.
[3.4.2]

35a *wyzkrw ky-ʾlhym ṣwrm*
They remembered that the god, El Elyon, is their rock,
[3.4.5 5.1.1 8.2.2]

35b *wʾl-ʿlywn gʾlm*
That the god, El Elyon, is their redeemer.
[3.3.24 5.1.1 8.2.2]

36a *wyptwhw bpyhm*
They deceived him with the tongues of their mouths.
[3.3.4 5.3.2]

36b *wblšwnm ykzbw lw*
They lied to him with the tongues of their mouths.
[3.3.50 5.3.2]

37a *wlbm lʾ-nkwn ʿmw*
Their hearts were not set toward him.
On *ʿm* 'toward,' see Dahood (1968a: 243).
[3.3.41]

37b *wlʾ-nʾmnw bbrytw*
They did not trust in his covenant.
[3.3.4]

38a *whwʾ rḥwm*
He is compassionate.
[3.3.24]

38b *ykpr ʿwn wlʾ-yšḥyt*
He covers over evil and does not destroy.
[3.4.2]

38c *whrbh lhšyb ʾpw*
He frequently reverses his anger.
[3.4.4]

38d *wlʾ-yʿyr kl-ḥmtw*
He stirs up none of his wrath.
[3.3.3]

39a *wyzkr ky-bśr hmh*
He remembers that they are flesh,
[3.4.5 8.2.2]

39b *rwḥ-hwlk wlʾ-yšwb*
A passing wind that does not return.
[3.5.2 8.2.2]

40a *kmh ymrwhw bmdbr*
They often rebelled against him in the steppe of Jeshimon.
[3.3.50 5.3.2]

40b *yᶜṣybwhw byšymwn*
They caused him pain in the steppe of Jeshimon.
[3.3.4 5.3.2]

41a *wyšwbw wynsw ᵓl*
They repeatedly tested God, the Holy One of Israel.
[3.4.2 5.1.1]

41b *wqdwš-yśrᵓl htww*
They pained God, the Holy One of Israel.
[3.3.7 5.1.1]

42a *lᵓ-zkrw ᵓt-ydw ywm*
They did not remember his power on the day
[3.3.35 8.2.2]

42b *ᵓšr-pdm mny-ṣr*
When he redeemed them from the adversary,
[3.3.21 8.2.2]

43a *ᵓšr-śm bmṣrym ᵓtwtyw*
When he set signs in Egypt,
[3.3.66 6.1.7 7.1.1 8.2.2]

43b *wmwptyw bśdh-ṣᶜn*
When he set portents in Tanis field.
[3.3.21 6.1.7 7.1.1 8.2.2]

44a *wyhpk ldm yᵓryhm*
He turned the streams of their river to blood.
[3.3.36 5.3.2]

44b *wnzlyhm bl-yštywn*
They could not drink the streams of their river.
[3.3.7 5.3.2]

45a *yšlḥ bhm ᶜrb wyᵓklm*
He sent a swarm against them and it consumed them.
[3.4.20 7.1.1]

45b *wṣprdᶜ wtšḥytm*
He sent frogs and they destroyed them.
[3.4.15 7.1.1]

46a *wytn lḥsyl ybwlm*
He gave the product of their toil to young locusts.
[3.3.36 5.3.2 6.4 7.1.1]

46b *wygyʿm lʾrbh*
He gave the product of their toil to locusts.
[3.3.12 5.3.2 6.4 7.1.1]

47a *yhrg bbrd gpnm*
He killed their vines with hail.
[3.3.36 6.4 7.1.1]

47b *wšqmwtm bḥnml*
He killed their sycamores with frost.
[3.3.12 6.4 7.1.1]

48a *wysgr lbrd bʿyrm* ET *wysgr ldbr bʿyrm*
He delivered their cattle up to Deber and Reshef.
The emendation follows Symmachus, and is accepted in, e.g., Brockington (1973: 141) and BH3.
[3.3.36 5.1.2 6.4 7.1.1]

48b *wmqnyhm lršpym* ET *wmqnyhm lršp-m*
He delivered their livestock to Deber and Reshef.
The *m* is emphatic.
[3.3.12 5.1.2 6.4 7.1.1]

49a *yšlḥ bm ḥrwn-ʾpw*
He sent against them his fury's anger,
[3.3.36 6.4 8.2.1]

49b *ʿbrh-wzʿm-wṣrh*
Wrath, rage, and oppression,
[3.5.5 6.1.8 8.2.1]

49c *mšlḥt-mlʾky-rʿym*
A posse of messengers of evil.
[3.5.5 6.1.8 8.2.1]

50a *ypls ntyb lʾpw*
He leveled a path for his anger.
[3.3.34 6.4]

50b *lʾ-ḥśk mmwt npšm*
He did not withhold their animals' lives from death.
[3.3.36 5.3.2 6.4]

50c *wḥytm ldbr hsgyr*
He delivered their animals' lives over to Deber.
[3.3.58 5.3.2 6.4]

51a *wyk kl-bkwr bmṣrym*
He smote all the first-born in Egypt,
[3.3.34 6.4 7.1.1]

51b *rʾšyt-ʾwnym bʾhly-ḥm*
First fruits of vigor, in the tents of Ham.
[3.3.12 6.4 7.1.1]

52a *wysʿ kṣʾn ʿmw*
He led his people like a herd of sheep.
[3.3.36 5.3.2 6.4]

52b *wynhgm kʿdr bmdbr*
He drove them like a herd of sheep through the steppe.
[3.3.38 5.3.2]

53a *wynḥm lbṭḥ wlʾ-pḥdw*
He guided them to safety. They were not afraid.
[3.4.2]

53b *wʾt-ʾwybyhm ksh hym*
He made the sea cover their enemies.
[3.3.46]

54a *wybyʾm ʾl-gbwl-qdšw*
He brought them to his holy territory.
[3.3.4]

54b *hr-zh qnth ymynw*
His right hand purchased this mountain.
[3.3.43]

55a *wygrš mpnyhm gwym*
He drove out nations before them.
[3.3.36 6.2.2]

55b *wypylm bḥbl nḥlh*
He distributed to them the inheritance by lot.
[3.3.36 6.2.2]

55c *wyškn bʾhlyhm šbṭy-yśrʾl*
He set the tribes of Israel in their tents.
[3.3.36 6.2.2]

56a *wynsw wymrw ʾt-ʾlhym*
They tested and rebelled against God.
[3.4.2]

56b *ʿlywn wʿdwtyw lʾ-šmrw*
Elyon: they did not observe his covenant terms.
[3.4.7]

57a *wysgw wybgdw kʾbwtm*
They backslid and lied like their parents.
[3.4.2]

57b *nhpkw kqšt-rmyh*
They turned like a treacherous bow.
[3.3.4 6.2.1]

58a *wykʿyswhw bbmwtm*
They angered him with the ikons of their high places.
[3.3.4 5.3.2 6.2.1]

58b *wbpsylyhm yqnyʾwhw*
They provoked him with the ikons of their high places.
[3.3.8 5.3.2 6.2.1]

59a *šmʿ ʾlhym wytʿbr*
God Almighty heard and raged.
[3.4.2 5.1.1]

59b *wymʾs mʾd byśrʾl*
God Almighty rejected Israel.
On *mʾd* 'the Almighty' here and the binomination, see Freedman (1973) and Penar (1975: 74, n. 1); cf. Dahood (1968a: 246; 1969b: 79).
[3.3.28 5.1.1]

60a *wyṭš mškn-šlw*
He left the Shilo tabernacle,
[3.3.3 8.2.2]

60b *ʾhl škn bʾdm*
The tent in which he dwells among people.
Freedman (p.c.) suggests reading *ʾdm* as a toponym.
[3.5.1 8.2.2]

61a *wytn lšby ᶜzw*
He gave the fortress of his glory into captivity.

On ᶜ*z* 'fortress,' here referring to the Ark of the Covenant, see Dahood (1968a: 246).
[3.3.36 5.3.2 6.2.2 7.1.1]

61b *wtpᵓrtw byd-ṣr*
He gave the fortress of his glory into the enemy's power.

[3.3.12 5.3.2 6.2.2 7.1.1]

62a *wysgr lḥrb ᶜmw*
He delivered his people over to the sword.

[3.3.36 6.2.2]

62b *wbnḥltw htᶜbr*
He raged against his inheritance.

[3.3.8]

63a *bḥwryw ᵓklh ᵓš*
Fire consumed its choice ones.

[3.3.43]

63b *wbtwltyw lᵓ hwllw* ET *wbtwltyw lᵓ-hlylw*
Its young women wail.

Read the verb with LXX; the *l*ᵓ here and in v 64b are emphatic.
[3.3.6]

64a *khnyw bḥrb nplw*
Its priests fall by the sword.

[3.3.54]

64b *wᵓlmntyw lᵓ-tbkynh*
Its widows weep.

[3.3.6]

65a *wyqṣ kyšn ᵓdny*
My lord awakens like a sleeper.

[3.3.31]

65b *kgbwr mtrwnn myyn*
One who roars from wine is like the Warrior.

[3.4.8]

66a *wyk ṣryw ᵓḥwr*
He smote his enemies on the backside.

[3.3.35]

66b *ḥrpt-ʿwlm ntn lmw*
He gave them a permanent reproach.
[3.3.47]

67a *wymʾs bʾhl-ywsp*
He rejected the tent of the tribe of Ephraim-Joseph.
[3.3.4 5.3.8 6.1.1]

67b *wbšbṭ-ʾprym lʾ-bḥr*
He did not choose from the tent of the tribe of Ephraim-Joseph.
[3.3.8 4.1.4 5.3.8 6.1.1]

68a *wybḥr ʾt-šbṭ-yhwdh*
He chose Judah's tribe,
[3.3.3 4.1.4 8.2.2]

68b *ʾt-hr-ṣywn ʾšr ʾhb*
Mount Sion, which he loves.
[3.5.1 8.2.2]

69a *wybn kmw-rmym mqdšw*
He built his shrine like the heights.
Eissfeldt (1958: 31) and NAB read *mrmym* 'the heights, Heaven,' and Dahood (1968a: 247) glosses *rmym* similarly, without emendation; cf. Cross (1973a: 142, n. 104), BH3, and BHS.
[3.3.36]

69b *kʾrṣ ysdh lʿwlm*
He founded it like the earth, forever.
[3.3.50]

70a *wybḥr bdwd-ʿbdw*
He chose David, his servant.
[3.3.4 6.2.1]

70b *wyqḥhw mmklʾt-ṣʾn*
He took him from the sheep folds.
[3.3.4 6.2.1]

71a *mʾḥr-ʿlwt hbyʾw*
He brought him away from the ewes,
[3.3.8 6.2.1 8.2.3]

71b *lrʿwt byʿqb-ʿmw*
To be a shepherd among Jacob-Israel, the people of his inheritance,
[3.3.17 5.1.4 5.3.2 8.2.3]

71c *wbyśrʾl-nḥltw*
Among Jacob-Israel, the people of his inheritance.
[3.5.5 5.1.4 5.3.2 8.2.3]

72a *wyrʿm ktm-lbbw*
He shepherds them according to the integrity of his heart.
[3.3.4 6.1.1]

72b *wbtbwnwt-kpyw ynḥm*
He leads them with his skillful hands.
[3.3.8 6.1.1]

### *2.13 Psalm 106*

The treatment of Dahood (1970a) is basic. The poem is, *mirabile scriptu*, 106 lines long.

The lineation of BH3 is 2 lines less than ours and that of BHS 2 lines more. BH3 splits vv 7a, 23a, 37, and 46, and joins vv 4ab, 17ab, 39ab, and 48ab. Vv 20ab are differently broken, and at vv 38bcd, BH3 reads our 3 lines as 1.

BHS splits the same verses as BH3 and joins vv 17ab and 38bc. In it, too, vv 20ab are broken differently than in our text.

BFBS reads the same number of line divisions we do. Vv 1ab, 6ab, and 7ab are joined; vv 23a, 37, and 46 are split; v 20ab is divided differently.

1a *hllwyh* = v 48d ET *hllw yh*
Praise Yah.
[3.3.3]

1b *hwdw lyhwh ky-ṭwb* = Ps 107:1a
Praise Yahweh: "He is good."
[3.4.3]

1c *ky-lʿwlm ḥsdw*
His great love is eternal.
[3.3.25]

2a *my ymll gbwrwt-yhwh*
Whoever can describe the mighty deeds of Yahweh,

If vv 2a and 2b are read as questions, i.e., if *my* has been conjunction reduced across them, there may be a combination, *kl-gbwrwt*, and, as Freedman (p.c.) suggests, a binomination, *thltw-yhwh* 'His Majesty Yahweh.'
[3.3.65 8.2.2]

2b *yšmyᶜ kl-thltw*
Let him make all his praise heard.
[3.3.3 8.2.2]

3a *ʾšry-šmry-mšpṭ*
The joys of those who keep to honesty,
[3.5.5 8.4]

3b *ᶜśh ṣdqh bkl ᶜt* ET *ᶜśy-ṣdqh bkl-ᶜt*
The joys of those who act justly at all times.
The emendation is common; cf., e.g., BH3 and NAB.
[3.5.4 8.4]

4a *zkrny yhwh brṣwn-ᶜmk*
Remember me, Yahweh, in your goodwill toward the people.
[3.4.6]

4b *pqdny byšwᶜtk*
Attend to me in your salvation,
[3.3.4 8.2.2]

5a *lrʾwt bṭwbt-bḥyryk*
So that I may enjoy the prosperity of the chosen of your people.
On *rʾy b* 'to enjoy,' see Dahood (1970a: 68; 1971b: 351).
[3.3.17 5.3.2 6.2.4 8.2.2]

5b *lśmḥ bśmḥt-gwyk*
So that I may rejoice in the joy of the chosen of your people,
[3.3.17 5.3.2 6.2.4 8.2.2]

5c *lhthll ᶜm-nḥltk*
So that I may give praise along with your inheritance.
[3.3.17 6.2.4 8.2.2]

6a *ḥṭʾnw ᶜm-ʾbwtynw*
We have sinned, along with our parents.
[3.3.4]

6b *hʿwynw hršʿnw*
We have done evil, acted wickedly.
[3.4.15]

7a *ʾbwtynw bmṣrym lʾ-hśkylw nplʾwtyk*
Our parents in Egypt did not attend to your wonders.
[3.4.19]

7b *lʾ-zkrw ʾt-rb-ḥsdyk*
They did not recall the abundance of your great love.
[3.3.3]

7c *wymrw ʿl ym bym swp* ET *wymrw ʿly-m bym-swp*
They rebelled against the Most High at the Reed Sea.
On the reading see Dahood (1970c: 69).
[3.3.34 4.4]

8a *wywšyʿm lmʿn-šmw*
He saved them because of his name,
[3.3.4 4.4 8.2.2]

8b *lhwdyʿ ʾt-gbwrtw*
To reveal his strength.
[3.3.17 4.4 8.2.2]

9a *wygʿr bym-swp wyḥrb*
He rebuked the Reed Sea and it dried up.
[3.4.2 4.4]

9b *wywlykm bthmwt kmdbr*
He made them cross an abyss like a steppe.
[3.3.38]

10a *wywšyʿm myd-śwnʾ*
He saved them from the power of those who hate them.
[3.3.4 4.1.1 6.1.1]

10b *wygʾlm myd-ʾwyb*
He redeemed them from the enemy's power.
[3.3.4 4.1.1 6.1.1]

11a *wyksw mym ṣryhm*
Water covered their enemies.
[3.3.27]

11b *ʾḥd mhm lʾ-nwtr*
Not one of them was left.
[3.3.54]

12a *wyʾmynw bdbryw*
They trusted his words.
[3.3.4]

12b *yšyrw thltw*
They sang his praises.
[3.3.3]

13a *mhrw škḥw mʿśyw*
They quickly forgot his actions.
[3.4.2]

13b *lʾ-ḥkw lʿṣtw*
They did not wait for his counsel.
[3.3.4]

14a *wytʾww tʾwh bmdbr*
They expressed incessant desire in the steppe of Jeshimon.
Dahood (1970a: 70-71) derives the verb and its cognate object from *ʾwy* 'to sigh, complain,' rendering 'they complained bitterly.'
[3.3.34 5.3.2 6.3.2]

14b *wynsw ʾl byšymwn*
They tested El in the steppe of Jeshimon.
[3.3.34 5.3.2 6.3.2]

15a *wytn lhm šʾltm*
He gave them what they asked for.
[3.3.36 6.3.2]

15b *wyšlḥ rzwn bnpšm*
He sent a rotting from their throats.
[3.3.34 6.3.2]

16a *wyqnʾw lmšh bmḥnh*
They vexed Moses and Aaron in the camp of Yahweh's shrine.
[3.3.38 5.2.1 5.3.3 6.1.2 7.1.1]

16b *lʾhrn qdwš-yhwh*
They vexed Moses and Aaron in the camp of Yahweh's shrine.
[3.3.14 5.2.1 5.3.3 6.1.2 7.1.1]

17a *tpṯḥ ʾrṣ*
Earth opened.
On the chthonian allusion, see Tromp (1969: 39).
[3.3.2]

17b *wtblʿ dtn*
It swallowed Dathan.
[3.3.3]

17c *wtks ʿl-ʿdt-ʾbyrm*
It covered over Abiram's company.
[3.3.4]

18a *wtbʿr ʾš bʿdtm*
Fire burned their company.
[3.3.28]

18b *lhbh tlhṭ ršʿym*
Flame set the wicked ablaze.
[3.3.40]

19a *yʿśw ʿgl bḥrb*
They made a calf at Horeb.
[3.3.34]

19b *wyštḥww lmskh*
They worshipped molten metal.
[3.3.4]

20a *wymyrw ʾt-kbwdm btbnyt*
They traded their glory for an image,
[3.3.34 8.2.1]

20b *šwr-ʾkl-ʿśb*
An ox that eats herbage.
[3.5.5 8.2.1]

21a *škḥw ʾl-mwšyʿm*
They forgot El, the one who saved them,
[3.3.3 8.2.3]

21b *ʿśh-gdlwt bmṣrym*
The one who did great things in Egypt,
[3.3.18 8.2.3]

22a *npl*ʾ*wt b*ʾ*rṣ-ḥm*
Wonders in the land of Ham,
[3.5.4 6.1.8 8.2.3]

22b *nwr*ʾ*wt* ʿ*l-ym-swp*
Aweful things near the Reed Sea.
[3.5.4 6.1.8 8.2.3]

23a *wy*ʾ*mr lhšmydm lwly-mšh-bḥyrw*
He would have ordered their destruction but for Moses his chosen.
[3.4.4 6.1.2]

23b ʿ*md bprṣ lpnyw*
He stood in the breach before him,
[3.3.38 6.1.2 8.2.2]

23c *lhšyb ḥmtw mhšḥyt*
To draw his wrath away from destruction.
[3.3.62 8.2.2]

24a *wym*ʾ*sw b*ʾ*rṣ-ḥmdh*
They rejected him in the desirable land.
[3.3.4 6.3.1]

24b *l*ʾ*-h*ʾ*mynw ldbrw*
They did not trust in his word.
[3.3.4 6.3.1]

25a *wyrgnw b*ʾ*hlyhm*
They murmured in their tents.
[3.3.4 6.3.1]

25b *l*ʾ*-šm*ʿ*w bqwl-yhwh*
They did not listen to Yahweh's voice.
[3.3.4 6.3.1]

26a *wyś*ʾ *ydw lhm*
He raised his hand against them,
[3.3.34 8.2.2]

26b *lhpyl* ʾ*wtm bmdbr*
To fell them in the steppe,
[3.3.62 4.1.1 6.1.7 8.2.2]

27a *wlhpyl zrᶜm bgwym*
To fell their seed among nations,
[3.3.62 4.1.1 6.1.7 8.2.2]

27b *wlzrwtm bᵓrṣwt*
To scatter them throughout lands.
[3.3.17 8.2.2]

28a *wyṣmdw lbᶜl-pᶜwr*
They teamed up with Baal Peor.
[3.3.4]

28b *wyᵓklw zbḥy-mtym*
They ate human sacrifices.
[3.3.3]

29a *wykᶜysw bmᶜllyhm*
They provoked him through their actions.
[3.3.4]

29b *wtprṣ bm mgph*
A plague broke out against them.
[3.3.31]

30a *wyᶜmd pynḥs wypll*
Phineas stood up and interposed himself.
[3.4.2]

30b *wtᶜṣr hmgph*
The plague was restrained.
[3.3.2]

31a *wtḥšb lw lṣdqh*
It was reckoned to his credit as an honest act
[3.3.38 8.2.1]

31b *ldr-wdr ᶜd-ᶜwlm*
Forever and eternally.
[3.5.4 8.2.1]

32a *wyqṣypw ᶜl-my-mrybh*
They provoked him by the waters of Meriba.
[3.3.4]

32b *wyrᶜ lmšh bᶜbwrm*
It went ill with Moses because of them.
[3.3.38]

33a *ky-hmrw ʾt-rwḥw*
They rebelled against his spirit.
Dahood (1970a: 74) observes that the antecedent of *rwḥw* is Yahweh; Moses is the antecedent of the following line.
[3.3.3]

33b *wybṭʾ bśptyw*
He spoke rashly with his lips.
[3.3.4]

34a *lʾ-hšmydw ʾt-hᶜmym*
They did not destroy the peoples
[3.3.3 8.2.2]

34b *ʾšr-ʾmr yhwh lhm*
As Yahweh had ordered them.
[3.3.66 8.2.2]

35a *wytᶜrbw bgwym*
They intermingled with the nations.
Dahood (1970a: 74) renders *ytᶜrbw* 'they intermarried,' from *ᶜrb* 'to enter.'
[3.3.4]

35b *wylmdw mᶜśyhm*
They learned their customs.
[3.3.3 6.1.1]

36a *wyᶜbdw ʾt-ᶜṣbyhm*
They worshipped their idols.
[3.3.3 6.1.1]

36b *wyhyw lhm lmwqš*
They were a trap for them.
[3.3.38]

37 *wyzbḥw ʾt-bnyhm-wʾt-bnwtyhm lšdym*
They sacrificed their sons and daughters to demons.
[3.3.34 4.3]

38a *wyšpkw dm-nqy*
They poured out innocent blood,
[3.3.3 4.1.2 4.3 8.2.3]

38b *dm-bnyhm-wbnwtyhm*
The blood of their sons and daughters
[3.5.5 4.1.2 4.3 8.2.3]

38c *ʾšr zbḥw lʿṣby-knʿn*
Whom they sacrificed to Canaan's idols.
[3.3.64 4.3 8.2.3]

38d *wtḥnp hʾrṣ bdmym*
The land was polluted with blood.
[3.3.28 4.3]

39a *wyṭmʾw bmʿśyhm*
They grew unclean through their deeds.
[3.3.4 6.1.1]

39b *wyznw bmʿllyhm*
They were promiscuous in their actions.
[3.3.4 6.1.1]

40a *wyḥr ʾp-yhwh bʿmw*
Yahweh's anger burned against his people.
[3.3.28]

40b *wytʿb ʾt-nḥltw*
He abominated his inheritance.
[3.3.3]

41a *wytnm byd-gwym*
He gave them into the power of nations.
[3.3.4 4.4]

41b *wymšlw bhm śnʾyhm*
Those who hate them ruled them.
[3.3.31 4.4]

42a *wylḥṣwm ʾwybyhm*
Their enemies oppressed them.
[3.3.2 4.4]

42b *wykn<sup>c</sup>w tḥt-ydm*
They were crushed under their paws.
[3.3.4 4.4]

43a *pᶜmym-rbwt yṣylm*
He delivered them many times.
[3.3.9]

43b *whmh ymrw bᶜṣtm*
They rebelled through their iniquitous counsel.
[3.3.41 5.3.2]

43c *wymkw bᶜwnm*
They were humiliated in their iniquitous counsel.
[3.3.4 5.3.2]

44a *wyrʾ bṣr lhm*
He looked at their distress
[3.3.38 8.2.2]

44b *bšmᶜw ʾt-rntm*
When he heard their cry.
[3.3.17 8.2.2]

45a *wyzkr lhm brytw*
He remembered for their sake his covenant.
[3.3.36]

45b *wynḥm krb-ḥsdw*
He repented because of the abundance of his great love.
[3.3.4]

46 *wytn ʾwtm lrḥmym lpny-kl-šwbyhm*
He made them compassionable before all their captors.
[3.4.19]

47a *hwšyᶜnw yhwh-ʾlhynw*
Yahweh, our god, save us,
[3.4.18 9.1]

47b *wqbṣnw mn-hgwym*
Gather us from the nations
[3.3.4 9.1]

47c *lhdwt lšm-qdšk*
To praise your holy name,
[3.3.17 6.1.7 9.1]

47d *lhštbḥ bthltk*
To give laud with your praises.
[3.3.17 6.1.7 9.1]

48a *brwk yhwh-ʾlhy-yśrʾl*
Blessed be Yahweh, the God of Israel,
[3.3.25 8.3]

48b *mn-hʿwlm wʿd-hʿwlm*
From eternity to eternity.
[3.5.4 8.3]

48c *wʾmr kl-hʿm ʾmn*
Let all the people say So be it.
[3.4.3]

48d *hllw yh* = v 1a

## *2.14 Psalm 107*

A basic treatment is that of Dahood (1970a). The poem is 89 lines long.

The lineations of BH3 and BHS are both a line less than ours. BH3 splits vv 3b and 5, and joins vv 39ab, 41ab, and 43ab. It reads vv 4abc as 2 lines for our 3 and vv 25ab as 3 for our 2. At vv 8ab, 15ab, 21ab, and 31ab, the refrain, it uses different breaks than we do. The lineation of BHS is the same as that of BH3 save that it does not join vv 39ab and 41ab, but does join vv 26ab and 37ab.

BFBS also has one line division less than our text. The refrain at vv 8ab and duplicates is also differently divided. Vv 3b and 5 are split and vv 4ab, 26ab, and 37ab are joined. V 25ab is divided differently.

1a *hdw lyhwh ky-ṭwb* = Ps 106:1b
"Praise Yahweh: 'He is good.'
[3.4.3 8.1.1 8.2.3]

1b *ky-lʿwlm ḥsdw*
His great love is eternal."
[3.3.25 8.1.1 8.2.3]

2a *yʾmrw gʾwly-yhwh*
Let Yahweh's redeemed speak out,
[3.3.2 8.1.1 8.2.3]

2b *ʾšr gʾlm myd-ṣr*
Those whom he redeemed from the enemy's power,
[3.3.64 6.1.7 8.1.1 8.2.3]

3a *wmʾrṣwt qbṣm*
Those whom he gathered from the lands,
[3.3.19 6.1.7 8.1.1 8.2.3]

3b *mmzrḥ-wmmʿrb-mṣpwn-wmym*
From east, west, north, and south.
On *ym* 'southern sea, south,' see Dahood (1970a: 81).
[3.5.5 8.1.1 8.2.3]

4a *tʿw bmdbr*
They wandered in the steppe of Jeshimon.
[3.3.4 5.3.2 6.1.1]

4b *byšymwn drk*
They walked in the steppe of Jeshimon.
The infinitive absolute *drk* is here used for a finite verb, as Dahood (1970a: 82) notes.
[3.3.8 5.3.2 6.1.1]

4c *ʿyr-mwšb lʾ-mṣʾw*
They found no habitable city.
[3.3.7]

5 *rʿbym-gm-ṣmʾym npšm bhm ttʿṭp*
Hungry and thirsty people: their throats collapsed within them.
[3.4.20]

6a *wyṣʿqw ʾl-yhwh bṣr lhm* = v 28a
They cried to Yahweh in their distress.
[3.4.19]

6b *mmṣwqwtyhm yṣylm*
He rescued them from their straits.
[3.3.8 6.1.1]

7a *wydrykm bdrk-yšrh*
He set them to walk a straight road,
[3.3.4 6.1.1 8.2.2]

7b *llkt ʾl-ʿyr-mwšb*
To travel to a habitable city.
[3.3.17 8.2.2]

8a *ywdw lyhwh* = vv 15a, 21a, 31a
They praise Yahweh
[3.3.4 8.2.1]

8b *ḥsdw-wnplʾwtyw lbny-ʾdm* = vv 15b, 21b, 31b
For his great love and wonders, for human beings.
On the ambiguity of *l*(*bny-ʾdm*), note Dahood (1970a: 83) who understands *ydy l* 'to confess to, before,' in contrast to most moderns, who understand *nplʾwtyw l* 'his wonders (done) for, on behalf of.'
[3.5.4 8.2.1]

9a *ky-hśbyʿ npš-šqqh*
He sated the longing throat.
[3.3.3 4.1.2]

9b *wnpš-rʿbh mlʾ ṭwb*
He filled the ravenous throat with good things.
[3.3.46 4.1.2]

10a *yšby-ḥšk-wṣlmwt*
Those who dwell in darkness and deep gloom,
On the chthonian vocabulary here and in vv 10b and 16, see Tromp (1969: 143, 155).
[3.5.5 6.1.8 8.2.1]

10b *ʾsyry-ʿny-wbrzl*
Those who are bound in torturous irons,
[3.5.5 6.1.8 8.2.1]

11a *ky-hmrw ʾmry-ʾl*
They rebelled against the words of the god Elyon's counsel.
[3.3.3 5.1.1 5.3.2 6.1.1 8.2.1]

11b *wʿṣt-ʿlywn nʾṣw*
They spurned the words of the god Elyon's counsel.
[3.3.7 5.1.1 5.3.2 6.1.1]

12a *wykn<sup>c</sup> b<sup>c</sup>ml lbm*
He humbled their hearts with affliction.
[3.3.36]

12b *kšlw w<sup>ↄ</sup>yn <sup>c</sup>zr*
They stumbled and there was no helper.
[3.4.2]

13a *wyz<sup>c</sup>qw <sup>ↄ</sup>l-yhwh bṣr lhm* = v 19a
They cried to Yahweh in their distress.
[3.4.19]

13b *mmṣqwtyhm ywšy<sup>c</sup>m* = v 19b
He saved them from their straits.
[3.3.8 6.1.1]

14a *ywṣy<sup>ↄ</sup>m mḥšk-wṣlmwt*
He led them out of darkness and deep gloom.
[3.3.4 6.1.1]

14b *wmwsrwtyhm yntq*
He tore off their bonds.
[3.3.7]

15a *ywdw lyhwh* = vv 8a, 21a, 31a

15b *ḥsdw-wnpl<sup>ↄ</sup>wtyw lbny-<sup>ↄ</sup>dm* = vv 8b, 21b, 31b

16a *ky-šbr dltwt-nḥšt*
He burst the bronze gates.
[3.3.3 6.1.1]

16b *wbryḥy-brzl gd<sup>c</sup>*
He hewed down the iron doorbolts.
[3.3.7 6.1.1]

17a *<sup>ↄ</sup>wlym mdrk-pš<sup>c</sup>m*
The foolish, in the path of their transgressions,
[3.5.4 8.2.1]

17b *wm<sup>c</sup>wntyhm yt<sup>c</sup>nw*
Were afflicted for their iniquities.
[3.3.8 8.2.1]

18a *kl-ʾkl ttʿb npšm*
Their throats rejected all food.
[3.3.43]

18b *wygyʿw ʿd-šʿry-mwt*
They approached the gates of death.
[3.3.4]

19a *wyzʿqw ʾl-yhwh bṣr lhm* = v 13a

19b *mmṣqwtyhm ywšyʿm* = v 13b

20a *yšlḥ dbrw wyrpʾm*
He sent his word and he healed them.
[3.4.2]

20b *wymlṭ mšḥytwtm*
He delivered them of their boils.

On *šḥn-šḥnt-šḥt* 'boil,' see Dahood (1970a: 86), who also discusses the double-duty suffix of *wyrpʾm*, which is in force on *wymlṭ*; it was first identified by Franz Delitzsch, as Sabottka (1972: 112, n. 37) reminds us; it is at best ungracious of van der Weiden (1970: 57, n. 141) to point out that Delitzsch's remarks take no account of the Ugaritic finds.
[3.3.4 6.1.1]

21a *ywdw lyhwh* = vv 8a, 15a, 31a

21b *ḥsdw-wnplʾwtyw lbny-ʾdm* = vv 8b, 15b, 31b

22a *wyzbḥw zbḥy-twdh*
They sacrificed thanksgiving sacrifices.
[3.3.3]

22b *wysprw mʿśyw brnh*
They told of his actions in song.
[3.3.34]

23a *ywrdy-hym bʾnywt*
Those who go down to the sea, in ships,
[3.5.4 6.1.8 8.2.1]

23b *ʿśy-mlʾkh bmym-rbym*
Those who do business, on the great waters,
[3.5.4 6.1.8 8.2.1]

24a *hmh rʾw mʿśy-yhwh*
They saw Yahweh's actions,
[3.3.40 8.2.1]

24b *wnplʾwtyw bmṣwlh*
And his triumphs over the deeps.
Freedman *apud* Dahood (1970a: 87) regards *mṣwlh* as a personified abyss, a counterpart to *thwmwt* elsewhere.
[3.5.4 8.2.1]

25a *wyʾmr wyʿmd rwḥ*
He spoke and raised the wind of a storm.
[3.4.2 5.3.2]

25b *sʿrh wtrwmm glyw*
The wind of a storm that lifted high its billows.
On the emphatic *w*, see Dahood (1970a: 87).
[3.3.40 5.3.2]

26a *yʿlw šmym*
They went up to the heavens.
[3.3.3 6.1.1]

26b *yrdw thwmwt*
They went down to the deeps.
[3.3.3 6.1.1]

26c *npšm brʿh ttmwgg*
Their throats liquefied in distress.
[3.3.54]

27a *yḥwgw wynwʿw kškwr*
They reeled and shook like a drunk.
Read *yāḥûgû* with Dahood (1970a: 88) and BH3.
[3.4.2]

27b *wkl-ḥkmtm ttblʿ*
All their common sense was swallowed up.
[3.3.6]

28a *wyṣʿqw ʾl-yhwh bṣr lhm* = v 6a

28b *wmmṣwqtyhm ywṣyʾm*
He led them out of their straits.
[3.3.8]

29a *yqm sᶜrh ldmmh*
He made the storm a whisper.
[3.3.34]

29b *wyḥšw glyhm*
Their waves were hushed.
[3.3.2]

30a *wyśmḥw ky-yštqw*
They rejoiced. They were silent.
[3.4.15]

30b *wynḥm ᵓl-mḥwz-ḥpṣm*
He led them to their port of ease.
[3.3.4 6.1.1]

31a *ywdw lyhwh* = vv 8a, 15a, 21a

31b *ḥsdw-wnplᵓwtyw lbny-ᵓdm* = vv 8b, 15b, 21b

32a *wyrmmwhw bqhl-ᶜm*
They exalted him in the popular congregation.
[3.3.4 6.1.1]

32b *wbmwšb-zqnym yhllwhw*
In the assembly of elders they praised him.
[3.3.8 6.1.1]

33a *yśm nhrwt lmdbr*
He turned rivers into thirsty steppeland.
[3.3.34 5.3.6 6.1.2 7.1.1]

33b *wmṣᵓy-mym lṣmᵓwn*
He turned springs into thirsty steppeland.
[3.3.12 5.3.6 6.1.2 7.1.1]

34a *ᵓrṣ-pry lmlḥh*
He turned fruitful land into salt flats,
[3.3.12 7.1.1 8.2.1]

34b *mrᶜt-yšby bh*
Because of the evil of those who live in it.
[3.5.2 8.2.1]

35a *yśm mdbr lᵓgm-mym*
He made the steppe a pool of water.
[3.3.34 6.1.2 7.1.1]

35b *wʾrṣ-ṣyh lmṣʾy-mym*
He turned dry ground into springs.
[3.3.12 6.1.2 7.1.1]

36a *wywšb šm rʿbym*
He settled the starving there.
[3.3.37]

36b *wykwnnw ʿyr-mwšb*
They established a habitable city.
[3.3.3 6.3.1]

37a *wyzrʿw śdwt*
They seeded fields.
[3.3.3 6.3.1]

37b *wyṭʿw krmym*
They planted vineyards.
[3.3.3 6.3.1]

37c *wyʿśw pry-tbwʾh*
They harvested the fruit of produce.
[3.3.3 6.3.1]

38a *wybrkm wyrbw mʾd*
He blessed them and they were very numerous.
[3.4.2]

38b *wbhmtm lʾ-ymʿyṭ*
He did not diminish their cattle.
[3.3.7]

39a *wymʿṭw wyšḥw* ET *wymʿṭw wyšḥwm*
He diminished and declined from them
The preposition *m* in MT should be attached as a suffix to *wyšḥw*; the suffix expresses an "ethical dative," as Dahood (1970a: 90) notes. [3.4.15 8.2.1]

39b *ʿṣr-rʿh-wygwn*
Restraint, evil and sorrow.
[3.5.5 8.2.1]

40a *špk-bwz ʿl-ndybym*
He who pours abuse on leaders
[3.3.18 8.2.2]

40b *wytʿm bthw-lʾ-drk*
Set them to wander in a trackless void.
[3.3.4 8.2.2]

41a *wyśgb ʾbywn mʿwny*
He set the humble safe from sorrow.
[3.3.34 5.3.2 6.1.2]

41b *wyśm kṣʾn mšpḥwt*
He made the clans like sheep.
[3.3.36 5.3.2 6.1.2]

42a *yrʾw yšrym wyśmḥw*
Honest folk saw and rejoiced.
[3.4.2]

42b *wkl-ʿwlh qpṣh pyh*
Every wicked person shuts his mouth.
The abstract *ʿwlh* here designates a possessor of the quality; see Dahood (1970a: 90-91).
[3.3.40]

43a *my ḥkm*
Whoever is wise
Read a finite verb form.
[3.3.20 8.2.2]

43b *wyšmr ʾlh*
Will guard these things.
[3.3.3 8.2.2]

43c *wytbwnnw ḥsdy-yhwh*
Let them contemplate Yahweh's great love.
[3.3.3]

# CHAPTER THREE

# THE SHAPE AND STRUCTURE OF THE LINE

## *3.0 Introduction*

The usefulness of the line as the fundamental analytic tool in operating on the tissues of Hebrew verse is as unquestioned as the shape of the tool is unexamined. Even its genre is unknown, or rather, it is allowed that it has a character which transcends genre, apparently obscuring through sheer brilliance the difference between the phonological and syntactic organization of language. To be sure, the tool has some sort of luminosity since all told there is little disagreement about what the lines of verse actually are. This luminosity notwithstanding, the notion of lineation can be approached with rigor, even if the audacity of the attempt requires that demonstration be exhaustive. The bulk of this chapter is taken up with catalogs of the lines in the corpus at hand.

The starting point is syntactic; since the line is set out here as a syntactic unit, the parameters used in refining and defining the concept are syntactic. Major boundaries in the territory can be discovered with some ease because of the firm base of traditional Semitic grammar laid by the Arab grammarians. The insights of this "native speaker" analysis (if some flexibility be tolerated in the use of the term), marshaled in terms generalized from Arabic to describe all West Semitic languages, provide a protocol in seeking out difficult loci as well as a route among major linguistic realities.

From the parts of speech continuum borrowed from the grammarians, we elaborate the rudiments of syntactic analysis. The differentiation of what particles, nouns and verbs do in grammar leads to a differentiation of what they do in poetry. With basic navigational points fixed, we assemble a system of four constraints which together define the line in Hebrew poetry. The recognition of the covariance of clause, phrase and line lengths and shapes is complemented by a precise statement of the limits of the covariance. Major patterns in the behavior of the four constraints are assembled both for inspection here and further study in Chapter 10. From these patterns the scheme of line catalogs is abstracted.

## *3.1 The parts of speech*

The heritage of the Arab grammarians, the traditional and convenient division of the parts of speech in the West Semitic languages into nouns, verbs and particles, is not consistently workable. To be entirely useful in grammatical analysis it requires the undergirding of class specifications at the interfaces of the categories. The problematic areas, those that require specification, can be seen most readily in light of the linguistic good sense that the division is based on.

The continuum among the parts of speech is plain: particles and verbs are the extreme categories and nomina are intermediate between them. The variables along the continuum are three. The first is degree of independence: basically, particles do not stand alone, verbs do so freely, and nomina can stand alone, although they do so rarely. Or again, well-formed utterances ordinarily have a verb, often nomina, but frequently lack particles, especially particles that function below the discourse level, within the domain of a single clause. The second variable is the range of size: most particles are small, and indeed the most commonly used particles have the syllable structure *CV*; in contrast, most verbs have a triconsonantal base; nouns are again intermediate, since along with the class of deverbative, triconsonantal nouns, the classes of mono- and biconsonantal nouns are prime. The third variable is the range of inflection: particles are least often inflected, while verbs have strictly speaking no uninflected form; nouns have an uninflected form but are often inflected.

Having established the structure of the continuum, we can localize the two problematic areas: between particles and nouns, on the one hand, and, on the other, between nouns and verbs. The factors used in groping for the continuum's shape—range of government, size and inflection—will be useful further in tightening the boundaries among the continuum's three categories.

The interface between particles and noun is more complex than the one between nouns and verbs and requires more specification. The difficult classes of particles are specified below. Among the more or less functional categories used in the enumeration, three present few difficulties: conjunctions, negations and emphatics. The fourth category, prepositions, presents in itself every state of progression from the smallest possible unit to polymorphemic entities; this is the range, with examples:

| I | II | III | IV |
|---|---|---|---|
| CV | CVC | CVCVC | CV+CVCVC |
| *b* | *ʿl* | *tḥt* | *bqrb* |

There is no question that members of Class IV are to be analyzed as composed of Class I forms plus a noun, which is sometimes patient of inflection (cf. *lpny*); this analysis stands, irrespective of the fact that not all the nouns used in Class IV members occur in other shapes. Similarly, Class III members could be treated as nouns, although they are only used in prepositional frames. In fact, Class II members could also be so taken and, unjustifiable as it seems in light of recent research, Class I members have sometimes been regarded as nouns in construction with their objects. Rejecting, as we must in light of greatly increased knowledge of West Semitic particles in general, the treatment of Class I and Class II prepositions as nouns, we may go further and, according complete priority to syntactic over morphological criteria, analyze all members of Classes III and IV as prepositions plain, because they form a coherent category with, i.e., are substitutable for members of Class I and II. (As noted *sub* 3.1.1, there are a few cases in which Class II and III members must be taken as nouns.) An important argument for this analysis is the use of *m* and *mbyn*, and *b* and *bqrb* as equivalent in Gen 49:10ab and Hab 3:2de, respectively.

The division of nomina and noun phrases used below is also, coincidentally, fourfold and also functional. The three largest classes, subjects, direct objects and prepositional objects, present no difficulty. The smallest group, which we call adverbials, is the result of grammatical chaos. It ranges from what are ordinarily called adverbs through nouns bearing the so-called adverbial *-m* inflection to nouns that are saddled in most grammars of Hebrew with the name adverbial accusative, in imitation of the similar, multiform class in Classical Arabic. When in doubt regarding the particle/noun continuum, we have preferred to err on the side of nomina, seeking to compensate for the necessary faults by exhaustive specification.

The difficulties in separating nouns from verbs are fewer and chiefly involve the so-called existentials, the existential verb *hyy* and the negative existential pseudoverb *ʾyn*; the existential pseudoverb *yš* does not occur in our corpus. These we treat as verbs, despite the fact that *ʾyn* has a trivial inflectional range and neither *hyy* nor *ʾyn* can stand alone; neither is in fact anything like a true existential. In these cases, we have taken all forms (with one minor exception) as verbal, again tending to err toward the extremes rather than the middle of the continuum.

Several important points deserve note. A quick glance over the particle system will reveal it as the core of an "etymologically" interrelated network which includes the pronominal series and many morphological elements. This network should not be mistaken for the particle system, its chief progeny, although the two need to be reexamined together in the context of the entire West Semitic particle system and of certain relevant, Mediterranean areal features. In fact, in a quick graph of the class of Hebrew nomina on a morphological basis (adverbials . . . pronouns . . . "monoradical nouns" . . . biradical nouns . . . triradical nouns . . . etc.), the first four categories clearly belong with the particles and most of the inflections. We intend to undertake elsewhere a closer scrutiny of this system, a triumph of linguistic economy and a valuable key to what is loosely conceived of as the Nostratic problem (O'Connor 1977).

An area which might be thought a source of difficulty is the interrogative series. In actuality, its several members fit our categories for the most part neatly. The exception, *mdwᶜ*, is dealt with below, *sub* 3.1.3.

The problem of verbal nouns, or infinitives, and participles is of a different order than those dealt with here and is treated in 3.2.4.

Since we have shunted problem cases to the extremes, the discussion of the class of nouns is limited in this section to adverbials; the first and third paragraphs, on particles and verbs respectively, are more general in scope.

### *3.1.1 Particles*

A medley of polymorphy and polysemy as diverse as is found among the Hebrew particles is not conducive to simple harmonics. Even the most elementary survey tends spontaneously to grant itself a two-dimensional character, and the ideal presentation would be matrical. Because, however, the classification of parts of speech is here an instrumental endeavor, not an end in itself, we will restrain the drift toward clarity out of devotion to utility and let redundancies and gaps appear as the more or less traditional categories create them. For recent partial considerations of the Northwest Semitic particle system, see the work of Aartun (1974), Andersen (1974), and Pardee (1975).

The most important redundacies are those involving the categories of particles and nouns. In a few cases, a preposition is used as an adverbial; those involved here are *ᶜl* and *tḥt*; the pattern of usage validates classification of these as prepositions. Correspondingly, two members of the class of nomina, the relative pronouns *ᵓšr* and *š*, are used, rarely, as conjunctions. These four words are here granted independent membership in both classes.

We have not the space here for a full catalog of the particles and their usage. Rather, we will have to settle for a catalog of the difficult cases, those which may need to be reexamined in further study. The *CVCVC* prepositions are *bᶜd*, *lwly*, *ngd*, and *tḥt*; the compound prepositions are *bqrb*, *bᶜbr*, and *btwk*; *lmᶜn* and *lpny*; and *mᵓḥr*, *mᵓḥry*, *mᵓyn*, *mbyn*, *mbly*, *mᶜl*, *mpny*, and *mqrb*. All told, these are used under three dozen times.

### *3.1.2 Adverbials*

The class of adverbials used in our corpus is small: 23 adverbials, used a total of 41 times; it is not smaller than the class in general in Hebrew. All adverbials refer to time, place, or manner; about half are easily paraphrased with a prepositional phrase.

There are four subgroups which can be delineated with the help of traditional grammar and which will form the basis of our classification. Only one of these is morphologically marked: memized adverbials, that is, those inflected with the adverbial *-m*. The largest subgroup, including 13 of the 23 class members, includes what are called adverbial accusatives, because they are nomina which in a Semitic language with a fully articulated case system would stand in the accusative. The separation of this subgroup is predicated on the fact that its members are used as nomina non-adverbially. There are a few cases in which this criterion is difficult; certainly the best evidence for including *mʾd* in this grouping is not furnished by its simple nominal uses, rare as they are, but by its occurrence in the expression *ʿd mʾd*. The third class of adverbials includes two prepositions in their eccentric uses as modifiers of participles. The remaining adverbials form the class of simple adverbials. Some claim of being prime could be made for the notions expressed by these adverbials: now, still, (locative) there, and thus. They are morphologically diverse: *šm* and *kn* belong to the affixional-particle network, while *ʿwd* and *ʿth* are deverbative.

The class described here is located, we suggested earlier, at the upper edge of the noun category in the speech continuum, thus.

particles

nouns { adverbials / non-adverbials }

verbs

The breakdown of the particle system and of the noun system supports an ordering among the adverbial subgroups we have described. First (i.e., highest in the above diagram) are arrayed the prepositional adverbials, and last the "adverbial accusatives," which are most clearly active otherwise in the noun category. The third rank from the top belongs to the memized adverbials, since they are more like other nouns in bearing an inflection than the remaining classes. This leaves the second rung to be filled by simple adverbials, a just assignment in light of the morphological diversity. This yields the following tentative continuum.

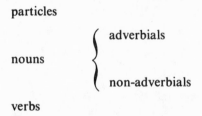

| | | |
|---|---|---|
| particles | emphatics<br>negations<br>conjunctions<br>prepositions | |
| nouns | adverbials | prepositional<br>simple<br>memized<br>"accusative" |
| | non-adverbials | |
| verbs | | |

In the lists that follow, we use this ordering of the adverbial subgroups. Compounds formed with negations are listed with their bases; other compounds are cited under separate heads.

*Prepositional adverbs*

-of place: *ʿl* Gen 49:26a; *tḥt* Gen 49:25d; Dt 33:13d.

*Simple adverbials*

-of time: *ʿwd* Zph 3:11d, 15d; Ps 78:17a, 30b, 32a; *ʿth* Dt 32:39a; in the compound *lʾ-ʿth*, Num 24:17a.

-of place: *šm* Dt 33:19b; Jdg 5:11b, 27e; 2 S 1:21c; Ps 107:36a.

-of manner: *ʾwly* Zph 2:3f; *kn* Jdg 5:31a.

*Memized adverbials*

-of time: *ywmm* Ps 78:14a.

-of place: *ʿqbm* Gen 49:19b.

-of manner: *ryqm* 2 S 1:22d.

*Simple "adverbial accusatives"*

-of time: *ywm* Ps 78:42a.

-of place: *ʾḥwr* Gen 49:17d; 2 S 1:22c; Ps 78:66a; *sbyb* Ps 78:28; *qrwb* Zph 1:14b; in the compound *lʾ-qrwb* Num 24:17b; *rwm* Hab 3:10d.

-of manner: *bdd* Dt 32:12a; Dt 33:28b; *bṭḥ* Dt 33:28a; *mʾd* 2 S 1:26b; Zph 1:14b; Ps 78:29a; Ps 107:38a.

*Compound "adverbial accusatives"*

-of time: *kl-hywm* Dt 33:12c; *kl-hlylh* Ps 78:14b; *pʿmym-rbwt* Ps 106:43a.

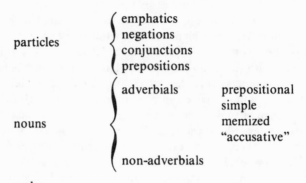

-of place: *ym-wdrwm* Dt 33:23d.

-of manner: *škm-ʾḥd* Zph 3:9c.

*3.1.3 Verbs*

Leaving aside the question of verbal nouns and participles, we face two major problems in categorizing the Hebrew verbal system: verbs which must govern noun phrases, so-called existentials, and verbs which must govern verbs, so-called auxiliaries.

The latter can be handled most simply here, since we do not single them out for special treatment (Andersen 1974: 56-57, 111). Hebrew never developed the kind of closely bound auxiliary system known from Phoenician and Arabic, in which tense valuation and sequencing are managed with the cognate verbs *kn* and *kāna*, and shows no rudiments of this development. There is a class made up of verbs that are often used, with or without explicit coordination, to modify a following verb; among those attested here are *mhr*, which predicates speed, *škm*, which predicates promptness (and more originally, earliness), and *hlk* and *qwm*, which predicate inchoation. Since this usage has no syntactic consequences which are obvious in our study, we treat auxiliaries as ordinary verbs. We do not wish to claim that the usage has no syntactic consequences, as it seems possible that it does.

Hebrew has three "existential" and "pseudoexistential" forms; the pseudoexistential *yš* is not attested in our corpus. Since there are no absolute uses of these forms, i.e., none which predicate existence, the designations are inaccurate; we retain them for the sake of convenience only.

The verb *hyy* is used most often with prepositional phrases, to indicate possession, service, comparison or transformation (with *l*: Gen 49:15d, 26d; Ex 15:2b; Zph 1:13a, 2:7a; Ps 106:36b; with *k*: Num 23:10d; Hab 3:4a; Zph 2:9d; Ps 78:8a; with *ʿly*: Dt 32:38d; similarly, without prepositions: Gen 49:17a; Num 24:18a, 18b; Dt 33:6b, 7e, 24c; Zph 2:4a, 6a, 15e); it is used once to predicate futurity (Dt 33:5a). In these cases it is used as discretely as any other verb in the language, differing only in that it cannot stand alone. It also is used with a dummy antecedent to indicate marking on the highest discourse level; these uses, confined in our corpus to Zephaniah (Zph 1:8a, 10a, 12a), we do not differentiate from the others because of the preliminary state of discourse analysis in Hebrew. It may turn out that *hyy* in poetry is sometimes a cataphoric tense marker, like the Phoenician and Arabic auxiliaries, but word on this must await further study. We list the occurrences of *hyy* by verb form and particle distribution; there are two dozen uses.

line initial forms with *w*

*whyh:* Num 24:18a, 18b; Zph 1:8a, 10a, 12a, 13a; 2:7a. *whyth:* Zph 2:6a. *wyhy*: Gen 49:15d; Ex 15:2b; Dt 33:5a, 6b. *wthy*: Num 23:10d. *wyhyw*: Ps 106:36b. *wl*ᵓ*-yhyw*: Ps 78:8a.

other line initial forms

ᵓ*yk-hyth*: Zph 2:15e. *yhy*: Gen 49:17a; Dt 33:24c. *yhyw*: Dt 32:38d. *thyyn*: Gen 49:26d.

line final forms

*thyh*: Dt 33:7e; Hab 3:4a; Zph 2:4a, 9d.

The negative pseudoexistential ᵓ*yn* serves predominantly in our corpus as a verb; despite traditional treatment of it as a noun in the construct state, it is best taken as such (cf. Andersen 1974: 82-83). Comparative evidence for this position comes from its usage in El-Amarna glosses as a verbal governing the accusative. One occurrence here is problematic: in Dt 32:4c, ᵓ*yn* is part of a noun compound, the first of the six such compounds that occur in the poem. This we regard as a deviation from regular usage on the analogy of the use of *l*ᵓ in such compounds. The nine verbal uses of ᵓ*yn* occur at Dt 32:12b, 28b, 39c, 39f; Dt 33:26a; Hab 3:17b, 17f; Zph 3:13e; and Ps 107:12b.

A final difficulty in apportioning out the parts of speech is a minor one: the only interrogative form which resists our classification, *mdw*ᶜ 'why.' Its categorization here as a verb is based in large part on its obscure but indubitable connection with the verb *yd*ᶜ 'to know.' The syntactic frame in which it is employed in creating a clause-governing clause ('why is it the case that') makes it clear that it is either a particle or a verb; the preference for the latter classification here is based on no grounds other than the etymological one, save its length.

### *3.2 Grammatical analysis*

In all current analyses of Hebrew poetry, spurious or at best ill-defined parameters are used in characterizing the units which make up a line and naturally the line itself is described with multiply compounded vagueness. Seeking to reduce the diversity of Hebrew verse lines to describable phenomena requires recognition of the need for a standing point, a level on which conceptual tools can be assembled and from which they can be used to operate on the verse. The level proposed here is syntactic. The primes of syntactic analysis derive from the great native Semitic grammatical tradition, the threefold division of the parts of speech, and the threefold division of nomina by case; these primes we have defined, with a view to our corpus, through description and specification.

In approaching the question, what counts in Hebrew poetry, that is, what units must we count up in order to be able to recount the structure and texture of the verse, its lines and sentences, we may reconsider the bases of the continuum of the parts of speech. The range from particles through nouns to verbs spans from most dependent to most independent, from least inflected to most inflected, from shortest to longest. Although we have seen that the lines among the categories are not intrinsically precise, we have also been able to clear up sources of difficulties and settle on the hard and fast boundaries suitable for our work, with no more than a pair of fugitive boundary crossers.

We have in our sights three regions and two boundaries separating them. We must apply this geography to the question of counting since we are working on a syntactic base and must work from syntactic primes. To ignore syntactic primes at this juncture would be to dismiss the strong intuitive claims, supported by the native grammatical tradition, of the parts of speech continuum. Particles, nomina, and verbs do different things in ordinary language and we may expect them to do different things in verse.

### *3.2.1 Particles*

The class of particles does not count in the fine structure of the verse. This suggestion we can borrow as a heuristic nudge from any account of Hebrew poetry since in virtually all such accounts virtually all the particles are ignored. Since the syntactic level of bookkeeping is not invoked in such accounts, principled definitions are avoided and so are the complexities of the particle system. This nudge is in fact a translation into working terms (or a lack of them) of one of the discriminatory bases of the continuum: length. Particles are taken as too small to count for much. Following this nudge in the direction of discounting particles comes a shove, also heuristic: the behavior of the particle system is so complex that we could not describe it if we wanted to. From the vantage point reached after a nudge and a shove, an argument takes shape. The particles which are active on the clause and phrase level are accounted for in considering the clauses and phrases they modify: subordinators and subordinate clauses, negations and the verbs they negate, prepositions and prepositional phrases. Since the boundary between the compound sentence and discourse is largely invisible in our texts, we are left in the position of leaving out only the emphatic particles and the non-coordinating sentential conjunctions. These are operative on precisely the level of grammatical enmeshing which, since it comprehends the outermost limits of a text, must override the shape of our starting point, the line. To reckon with the emphatics and the non-subordinating conjunctions we must be able to reckon up everything else.

Thus we find that, without considering the particles in themselves, we will take care of them by the way or let them take care of the way.

### *3.2.2 Clause predicators*

The two remaining parts of the continuum, nomina and verbs, are the building blocks of the poetic line and all our concretizations of it involve them. The intrinsic diversity of the categories must be rendered into our framework and the clue to that rendering is provided by the bases of the parts of speech continuum, specifically the criterion of independence. Any finite verb constitutes an integral utterance and predicates a clause; with a few exceptions no noun does. The first parameter in describing the lines of Hebrew poetry is the verb or, more properly, because those exceptions are important, the clause predicator. We must also reckon with the Ø clause predicator of verbless clauses. One clause predicator and its dependencies make up one clause. The use of the larger term allows us to extend this working concept across the morphological domain of the verb and into that of the noun, since some clause predicators are nomina.

The largest class of predicators is finite verbs and these require no comment. The nonfinite verbs which serve as clause predicators, some infinitives and participles, are discussed below (3.2.4). These two groups, and the Ø of verbless clauses, are the major clause predicators, capable of governing more than themselves. In the case of finite verbs, further, they are bound to govern more than themselves if they are the only clause predicators in the lines they occur in. There are two classes of minor clause predicators, remnants of clauses which are uniformly reduced before they appear in an utterance. These are vocatives and focus-markers; we call them minor because they directly govern only themselves and because they serve as clause predicators only if they occur in the same line as a major clause predicator. The arguments that vocatives and focus-markers are remnants of whole clauses under which the rest of the sentence in which they appear is embedded have been discussed (see 1.4.5). Vocatives occur in lines with all types of clauses and vary freely in position across the line. All vocatives are one constituent, as we noted above. There is only one possible counterexample, 2 S 1:21a, *hry bglbᶜ ʾl-ṭl*, in which we read only *hry* as the vocative. The consensus, which has it that *hry bglbᶜ* must be taken as a single phrase, is the result of making the best of a supposed grammatical solecism and trying to understand the phrase as a cross between *hrym bglbᶜ* and *hry glbᶜ*; since *hry* as a plural absolute is better taken as unusual than solecistic, the pattern of vocative usage becomes decisive in reading the line.

Focus-marking is a more difficult area. We do not mean by the term the operation of a movement rule which fronts a focused subject in a clause, but rather the positioning of an element before a clause in which it does not appear as an argument. Focus-markers only occur with independent clauses and with one exception they are line intial; in Gen 49:8a, the only line with both a vocative and a focus-marker, they occur in that order.

Four of the five classes of clause predicators, finite and nonfinite verbs, and vocatives and focus-markers, exhibit similarities other than the basis of the major-minor split. Finite verbs and vocatives are positionally free within the line; nonfinite verbs and focus-markers are much more limited, although it would not be accurate to say that either class must be line or clause initial. When minor clause predicators do not occur in obvious relation to a verb, their status in the discourse is obscured; we group these few cases with title formulas in a marginal category, independent noun phrases.

There are lines which contain no clause predicators, portions of superordinate clauses the main verbs of which are located in another line. Most lines contain one clause predicator only, although there is a sizable body of lines with two clause predicators and a much smaller group of lines with three. The first parameter of Hebrew verse line structure, clause predication, is governed by the clause constraint, which requires that no line of poetry contain more than three clause predicators. For reasons that will become apparent shortly, we restate this as the requirement that any line contain between zero and three clause predicators.

There are further restrictions on major clause predicators. We noted above, in passing, a trivial one: a finite verb must govern a nominal phrase if it is the only clause predicator of the line that it occurs in; this restriction is trivial here because it is agreed that there are no one word lines in Hebrew verse.

There are some important, related restrictions on the opposite end of the scale. To describe them best, we should speak in terms of major clause predicators rather than simply finite verbs. It will readily be admitted that the restriction just mentioned can be extended with no difficulty, since if an infinitive or participle does not govern one or more nominal phrases, it is not considered a clause predicator, as we shall argue in 3.2.4; and a $\emptyset$ verbless clause predicator must govern at least two nominal phrases.

The two further restrictions are related. The first is that if a line contains three major clause predicators, none have dependent nominal phrases. The predicators would have to be finite verbs, for the reasons noted above. The second restriction is that if a line has two major clause predicators, only one has nominal dependents. There are two relevant situations. First, a line can have two verbs; only one of these can have dependent nominal phrases. Second, a line can have a verbal and a verbless clause; since the verbless clause predicator $\emptyset$ must have at least two nominal phrases to govern, the verb cannot govern any.

### *3.2.3 Nominal phrase structure*

The second parameter is noun phrase structure, an element of greater variability than clause predication. The class of nomina is itself diverse, including suffixal and independent pronouns; common and proper nouns and adjectives; adverbials; two varieties of deverbative forms, participles and infinitives, the special problems of which we will return to below; and vocatives and focus-markers. Aside from the class of adverbials, there are three states of syntactic markedness for Hebrew nomina. In one state are nomina which are never marked, subjects (and with these belong vocatives and focus-markers). In another are those which are always marked, prepositional objects. In the last are those which are sometimes marked, direct or unmediated objects. In poetry, because prepositions can be gapped across adjacent lines, the marking of the second category is sometimes lost.

To accord all line-internal nominal phrases equal status as sentential constituents is a superficial procedure: since it is the surface we wish to describe it will be ours. The apparent loss in descriptive accuracy results, in verbal clauses, from the availability of prepositional phrases to qualify not only clauses but also other nomina, as we have noted.

The barriers of heterogeneity are afforded by categories relating nominal phrases to verbs. The criteria of homogeneity within noun phrases correspond in large part to the ways nouns can be tied to one another: nomina related by modification or conjunction make up a single nominal phrase. The largest class of nominal phrases consists of those made up of a single nomen (first degree nominal phrase, henceforth 1° np). Of the 1,937 line internal nominal phrases, 1,393, 72%, are 1° np. There are two kinds of exception to the homogeneity criteria. One is created by gapping, such that two nomina seem to belong to a single nominal phrase but do not. The other is created by override failure, such that nomina seem to be separated but in fact belong together. We shall return to these.

There are three kinds of modification: construction, adjection, and apposition. All are commonest among 2-unit nominal phrases (2° np). The first of these relations, construction, is easily dominant and represents the strongest bond. Of the 442 2° np, 327, 17% of the phrases, are two-member construct chains. Examples are not necessary. The 1° and 2° NcN np account for almost 89% of the np in the corpus.

The other 2-unit phrases number 115. The noun-adjective bond is much less common than construction and weaker: the first item could stand in the stead of the unit. There are 44 nominal phrases of two units with adjectival modification. The interaction of appositives is somewhat less frequent than that of nouns and their adjectives and is based on the weakest of the modification ties, since either member of the pair could stand for the unit. The 2-unit appositional nominal phrases number 25.

There are a few classical cases in which modification relations are hard to distinguish and any decision is more or less arbitrary. Two important cases are *bt-ṣywn*, which we treat as appositional, and *yhwh-ṣbʾwt*, which we treat as a construct chain.

Conjunction is the most distant nomen-nomen relation. The strongest evidence for treating it with other relations characteristic of homogeneous noun phrases comes from a tendency to ignore the strict rule that demands in prose that each item in a list be explicitly conjoined, and to allow direct juxtaposition of such items, i.e., to permit the w of NwN (the conjunct marker, not necessarily identical with *w*) to be represented as ∅, as in Ex 15:11c, Dt 33:25b, Jdg 5:30b, Zph 2:6a, Ps 107:3b and 39b. There may be another example in Jdg 5:19d. Given the multiplicity of ways in which directly juxtaposed nouns can be read, it is surprising to find that ∅ conjunction ever occurs. There are, to be sure, cases in which an appositional may be preferable to a conjunctional analysis, and vice versa. The commonest conjunct is *w*, but *ʾp* and *gm* both also serve to yoke two nomina and so do *ʾk* and ∅. The 2-unit phrases based on conjunction use *w* 37 times, *gm* 4 times, ∅ twice, and *ʾp* and *ʾk* once each. We also note the name *yʿqb-ʾl* in Dt 33:28b among the 2° np.

These four relations can be combined and varied in 3- and 4-unit noun phrases (3° and 4° np). There are 89 3° np (over 4% of the np) and 15 4° np (less than 1%). The most frequent combination is of the two most distinct types of relation, construction and conjunction. In some cases, conjunction is the dominant relation, in the forms Nw(NcN) (3 np), e.g., Zph 1:8b *ʿl-hśrym-wʿl-bny-hmlk*; (NcN)wN (5 np), e.g., Ex 15:4a *mrkbt-prʿh-wḥylw*; and 4° np (NcN)w(NcN) (5 np), e.g., Dt 32:14a *ḥmʾt-bqr-wḥlb-ṣʾn*. More often, construction is dominant in a noun phrase structure impossible in ordinary language. The use of the construction relation, that is, allows a first term to govern not only the nomen following it, but also, overriding that nomen, the one following it. The common form is Nc(NwN) (16 np), e.g., Gen 49:25e, *brkt-šdym-wrḥm*. The form (NwN)cN occurs only once, Ps 78:9a, *nwšqy-rwmy-qšt*. This contrasts with the situation in a few cases in which there is no override, e.g., Ex 15:4a *mrkbt-prʿh-wḥylw*.

Also common is use of both appositional modification and conjunction. In 3-unit phrases and sometimes in 4-unit phrases, apposition is the dominant relation, in the forms Napp(NcN) (8 np), e.g., Jdg 5:3e, *lyhwh-ʾlhy-yśrʾl*; (NcN)appN, once, at Zph 3:15c; and (NcN)app(NcN), once, at Ps 78:12b. In two similar 4-unit examples, the construct relation appears both on top and on the bottom, in the structure Nc(Napp[NcN]), at Num 24:3a and Jdg 5:6a. Less frequently are adjection and conjunction used together. Among 3-unit phrases, adjectival modification dominates, i.e., Nadj(NwN) (4 np), e.g., Zph 3:12b, *ʿm-ʿny-wdl*. The situation is reversed among 4-unit phrases, i.e., (NadjN)w(NadjN) (1 np) at Zph 1:16b. Similarly adjection and construction are rarely used together; dominant adjection is slightly more common. The forms are Nadj(NcN) (1 np); (NcN)adjN (1 np); and Nc(NadjN) (2 np). The remaining combination, adjectival and appositional modification, occurs once, in the form (NadjN)appN. There are only two noun phrases in which three different relation types appear: (NadjN)w(NcN) at Dt 32:24b; and Nc(Napp[NwN]) at Gen 49:26a.

Nominal phrases of three units involve a triple construct chain in 44 cases and a triple conjunct twice. There are three examples of a 4-member construct chain, and one of a 4-member conjunct chain.

There are four lengths of line internal nominal phrases; longer phrases are never line internal. The commonest length is the shortest, 1° (72% of the np); the rarest is the longest, 4° (less than 1% of the np). There is a great mass of 1° np, and of 2° np of the shape NcN. All other configurations are comparatively rare.

Of the two classes of exceptions to the rules of functional homogeneity, one is almost trivial. (We do not regard word orders like verb-object-object as affected by homogeneity; see 3.3.33.) This exception is the result of prepositional gapping which leaves unmarked a prepositional object, which is juxtaposed to another noun to which it is not directly related. This happens only rarely, e.g., in Hab 3:15b and Ps 106:16b. In the first case, the received text has never been understood; the second line of the second example has been taken as the appositional modification it resembles.

The second class of exceptions is larger and more complex and involves an override argument. In the lists of nominal phrases given above, we counted as single prepositional phrases both Dt 33:9a, *lʾbyw-wlʾmw* and Dt 33:16a, *mmgd-ʾrṣ-wmlʾh.* The first of these contains two prepositional phrases both governed by *l*, and the second, one prepositional phrase, with two objects, governed by the single, initial *m*. The ordinary rules of prepositional government require that every prepositional object be governed *in se*; this requirement is met by Dt 33:9a, but not by Dt 33:16a. There are 10 cases in which a preposition governs conjunct nomina. Six of these conform to the prose rule; they are Dt 33:9a; 2 S 1:23b; Zph 1:8b, 16b; and Zph 3:19d and 20c. In the other four cases, the preposition rides over the conjunction and governs more than the nomen it is attached to; these are Ex 15:18; Dt 33:16a; Ps 106:31b; and Ps 107:14a. There are two ways to deal with this split in the data. The obvious approach would treat the two groups differently in accordance with their differences. The other approach, adopted here, posits that the split reflects a tendency away from the prose rule toward a rule of prepositional override, a rule which manifests itself fully in later stages of the language; and that that tendency itself reflects a basic recognition of the homogeneity of all these phrases. In view of that recognition, we take the step of, as it were, absolutizing the tendency except in cases in which a preposition, though used twice, serves distinct functions. In some of these, *l* serves once to mark possession and once to mark service (Ex 15:2b; Ps 106:31a, 36b, 47c; cf. Zph 3:18a); and in others, *b* is used locatively and temporally (Jdg 5:2a and 15c). The sign of the direct object follows the prose rule in Ps 106:37, the only relevant example; we treat it here like the prepositions.

Nominal phrases have four possible lengths and a limited number of structures, based on four available relations among nomina, and combinations of them. It is conceivable that some important basic regularities involving nominal phrase *structure* are at work in Hebrew poetry; if so, we have not recognized them. The length limitation is a regularity of obvious relevance; in it we recognize the nominal phrase constraint: no line of Hebrew verse contains nominal phrases of more than four units. Other distributional regularities will be treated below.

### *3.2.4 Participles and infinitives*

We posed earlier the problem of discrimination among the uses of the productive categories of deverbative nouns, infinitives, and participles. As all treatments of Hebrew grammar recognize, these occupy the border ground between nouns and verbs and accordingly, we divide them between the two sections of the parts of speech continuum. Since infinitives and participles are by form nouns they are always reckoned among nominal constituents.

An infinitive is reckoned *only* as a nominal constituent

a) if it is used absolutely, as in Gen 49:3c, 15c; Ex 15:1b; Num 23:20a, 23:30b; Jdg 5:18b, 28c; Hab 3:16f; Zph 3:11d; Ps 78:10b, 17a; Ps 106:23c.

b) if it governs an agential suffix, as in Ex 15:17b; Dt 33:18b.

c) if it governs an agential construct, as in Num 23:8a, 23:8b, 24:4a*; Dt 33:5b, 5c; Jdg 5:2a, 2b, 31b; Zph 2:2a.

An infinitive is reckoned a clause-predicator, in line with the classical formulation that the object after the infinitive construct must always be regarded as in "the accusative," (a) if it governs a direct object, which may be a suffixed pronoun, alone or with a prepositional phrase following; (b) if it governs a prepositional phrase alone or with a direct object following; (c) if it governs an agential suffix or construct followed by an object, or a prepositional phrase; or (d) if it governs an agential suffix, an object and a prepositional phrase.

Participles are more nominal than infinitives. In the following, we omit a few nouns of participial form which are not deverbative, e.g., *khn*, which appears only absolutely or with possessive suffixes (Zph 1:4d; 3:4b;

Ps 78:64a). The examples are grouped according to the following scheme: (1) *Qal* active, (2) *Qal* passive, (3) *Nipᶜal*, and (4) memized participles. The chief difference between infinitives and participles with regard to clause predication is that whereas infinitives can govern in the construct only agents, participles can also govern in the construct objects and possessors.

A participle is reckoned *only as* a nominal constituent

a) if it is used absolutely or adjectivally

(1) *Qal* active—Gen 49:15d; Ex 15:6b, 8b, 9a; Num 24:4c; Dt 32:25d, 27a, 42d; 33:27c; Zph 1:9a; 2:2b, 5d, 6b, 15f; 3:1, 3a, 4a, 6c, 6d; Ps 78:8b bis, 16a, 39b, 71a; 106:10a, 10b; 107:12b.

(2) *Qal* passive—Gen 49:7a, 21a; Num 24:9c, 9d; Dt 32:25c, 34a, 36d bis; 33:20b, 24b; Jdg 5:27e; Zph 1:16b; 2:4a; 3:9a; Ps 106:48a.

(3) *Nipᶜal*—Ex 15:6a, 11b; 2 S 1:23a, 26c; Zph 2:1, 11a; 3:1, 19c; Ps 106:22a, 22b.

(4) memized—Gen 49:10b; Dt 33:21b; Jdg 5:9b, 14c; Zph 3:13e; Ps 78:4b.

b) if it is used with an object suffix (only active participles are so used)

(1) *Qal* active—Gen 49:8b; Ex 15:7a; Num 24:9d, 18b; Dt 32:6c, 31b; 33:11c, 11d, 29f; Jdg 5:31a, 31b; Zph 3:3b, 15b; Ps 78:35b, 53b; 106:41b, 42a.

(4) memized—Num 24:9c; Dt 32:18b, 41d; Ps 106:21a.

c) if it is used with an object construct

(1) *Qal* active—Gen 49:24d; Ex 15:11c; Num 24:4a, 4a*; Dt 32:24d, 28a; 33:3a, 16b; Jdg 5:6c, 9a, 10a, 10b, 10c; Zph 3:18a; Ps 78:9a bis; 106:3b, 20b; 107:23a, 23b.

d) if it is used with an agent suffix (only passive participles are so used)

(2) *Qal* passive—Zph 1:7d.

e) if it is used with an agent construct

(2) *Qal* passive—Num 24:4c; Dt 33:24c; Ps 107:2a.

(3) *Nipᶜal*—Ex 15:11c.

f) if it is used with a possessive suffix

(1) *Qal* active—Jdg 5:23c; Ps 78:44b.

(2) *Qal* passive—Ps 78:63a.

(3) *Nipᶜal*—Ps 78:11a, 32b; 106:7a; 107:8b, 24b.

g) if it is used with a possessive construct

(1) *Qal* active—Ex 15:14b, 15c; Zph 1:4b, 11a, 18e; 2:5a; Ps 107:10a.

(2) *Qal* passive—Dt 33:19d bis; Ps 78:31c.

(4) memized—Ex 15:4c; Dt 33:21b.

A participle is reckoned as a clause predicator if it governs anything not suffixed to it or in construction with it, i.e., (a) if it governs adverbials, (b) if it is governed by a *h* in a relative clause, (c) if it governs a prepositional phrase, or (d) if it governs an object not in construction with it.

### *3.2.5 Constituents*

We have discussed two variables in the Hebrew poetic line: clause predicators and nominal phrases. Each has a variation pitch of four. Clauses may number between zero and three in a line. Similarly, nominal phrases may include between one and four units, although three- and four-unit nominal phrases are uncommon and restricted in distribution. There are two further variables in Hebrew verse and both also have a limited range of variation. They represent intermediate stages between the clause level and the nominal phrase level.

Although all clause predicators are in themselves unitary, the number of nominal phrases associated with a clause predicator is variable, as is their structure. The level of analysis which includes both clause predicators and associated nominal phrases is the constituent. If the clause constraint operated alone, it is conceivable, say, that given three independent verbs in a line, each with three dependent nominal phrases, we would find lines of poetry with twelve constituents. This is not at all the case. In fact, the number of constituents is restricted independently; to the clause constraint, we must add the constituent constraint: no line of poetry contains fewer than one constituent or more than four constituents; examples follow.

*1-constituent line*

Zph 1:15e *ywm-ᶜnn-wᶜrpl*

*2-constituent line*

Ps 107:9a *ky-hśbyᶜ npš-šqqh*

*3-constituent line*

Dt 33:10c *yśymw qṭwrh bᵓpk*

*4-constituent line*

Hab 3:10d *rwm ydyhw nśᵓ šmš*

The constituents are determined on the basis of the surface structure of the clause. Nominal phrases in clauses with an expressed major clause predicator, e.g., a finite verb, are treated as dependencies of the verb. In verbless clauses, which lack an expressed clause predicator, the predicate can be composed of more than one nominal phrase. The distinction between 3-constituent and 2-constituent verbless clauses reflects the fact that nominal phrases which make up the predicate of verbless clauses can be split apart and appear discontinuously, as Andersen (1970a) points out. (See further Hoftijzer 1973: 447, 454; and more generally Greenberg 1963b: 104.)

A major difference in the level of reference of the clause and constituent constraints is the result of verb gapping, deletion of the verb on condition of identity in a group of associated lines (see 1.5.7). The clause constraint in cases in which gapping has occurred refers to the form of the sentence to which gapping applied; the constituent constraint refers to the surface form of the sentence. Both examples below have one clause predicator and two constituents.

Dt 32:10d *yṣrnhw kᵓyšwn-ᶜynw*

Dt 32:13d *wšmn mḥlmyš-ṣwr*

In the first, however, the verb is present, while in the second it has been gapped from the previous, 3-constituent line, Dt 32:13c, *wynqhw dbš mslᶜ*. The analysis, which treats both Dt 32:10d and Dt 32:13d as fulfilling both constraints, is complemented by the recognition of gapping.

### *3.2.6 Units*

There is a further level between clauses and noun phrases, closer in reference to the latter than the constituent level, the level of units, individual verbs and nomina. While finite verbs are unitary, all other clause predicators and other nominal phrases can vary in size between one and four units. If a constituent can be composed of between one and four units, and a line of between one and four constituents, we might expect to find lines of, say, four 4-unit constituents, i.e., of 16 units. Similarly, if a 1-constituent line is allowed by the constraints, we might anticipate coming upon a 1-unit nominal phrase coextensive with a line. We find nothing of either sort, but rather yet a third constraint, the unit constraint: no line of Hebrew verse contains fewer than two or more than five units; some examples follow.

*2-unit line*

Dt 32:21b *kᶜswny bhblyhm*

*3-unit line*

Dt 33:16c *tbwᵓ-th lrᵓš-ywsp*

*4-unit line*

Zph 1:18e *yᶜśh ᵓt-kl-yšby-hᵓrṣ*

*5-unit line*

Zph 1:4c *whkrty mn-hmqwm-hzh ᵓt-šᵓr-hbᶜl*

The range of variation is again four; this constraint is similar to but independent of the clause and constituent constraints. It could be enchained to them, by proposing a series of restrictions smaller in scope, e.g., in lines of two nominal phrases, if one is a 3° nominal phrase, the other can only be a 1° or 2° nominal phrase. Such a series would miss the larger generalization given here.

### *3.2.7 A definition of the line*

A small number of constraints determine the shape of the line in Hebrew verse. The first refers to the interrelations of clauses, the second to their components, and the third to their components' components. These three are the clause, constituent, and unit constraints. All three have the same range of variation, a range of four.

| | | | | |
|---|---|---|---|---|
| clause constraint | ∅ | 1 | 2 | 3 |
| constituent constraint | 1 | 2 | 3 | 4 |
| unit constraint | 2 | 3 | 4 | 5 |

This group of constraints refers to the line entire and we call these the overall constraints. They are complemented by the nominal phrase constraints which require that no nominal phrase of more than four units be line internal, and that no nominal phrase of more than three units occur in a line unless the line contains either only one clause and two constituents, or no clauses and one constituent. The overall constraints are further supplemented by the major clause predicator constraints, which require that no line contain three major clause predicators unless it contains nothing else; and that no line contain two major clause predicators unless only one of the predicators has dependent nominal phrases.

A line of Hebrew poetry is a passage of poetic discourse which obeys the overall constraints, i.e., which contains no fewer than no clause predicators and no more than three in its base structure, no fewer than one constituent and no more than four constituents in its surface structure, and no fewer than two units and no more than five in its surface structure; and which obeys the nominal phrase constraints and the major clause predicator constraints. There are examples of all the major classes of phenomena predicted by this definition in our corpus. Some have hundreds of exemplars and some are uniquely exemplified. There are no lines not described by these constraints, though there remain obscure and difficult points. There are other, important characteristics of the lines of our corpus but none that are relevant to all of them, save some implicational derivatives of the definition. The most striking of the former is the fact that 3° np occur in 1-clause lines usually only if the clause is verbless or verb initial; Dt 32:19b is the only exception.

### *3.2.8 Line types*

The four constraints which together define the Hebrew verse line correctly suggest the availability of a great diversity of line structures. Not all actualizations of the three overall constraints are equally common, just as we saw above that 1° nominal phrases are vastly more numerous than 2° phrases, in their turn more frequent than 3° and 4° phrases (3.2.3). The clause constraint allows between zero and three clauses in a line, but 898 lines (75%) have one clause; the other three possibilities are much less frequently used. One hundred and thirty eight lines (11%) have no clauses, 157 lines (13%) have two, and 7 have three.

Of the range of constituent groupings, two dominate: there are 571 2-constituent lines (48%) and 485 3-constituent lines (40%). There are, in contrast, 98 1-constituent lines (8%) and only 46 with 4 constituents (4%). A majority of lines, 690 (57%) have three units; 298 (25%) have two units, 190 (16%) have four, while only 22 (2%) have five.

Four instantiations of four constraints produces a three-dimensional matrix (not shown here) of 64 structures. Since each constituent must be represented by a unit, a dozen of these are excluded as logically impossible; further, since each clause must be represented by a constituent (though it need not be the verb, because of verb gapping), another dozen are excluded, and since single-clause lines must contain more than one constituent, four more are excluded. The nominal phrase constraint makes impossible a 1-constituent, 5-unit line. Of the 35 structures remaining, eight are not exemplified, presumably as a result of inadequate data, though other, partial explanations will present themselves below. Three are uniquely exhibited. These 35 structures may be listed with examples and number of occurrences.

1. ∅ clause-1 constituent-2 units/17 cases
Zph 1:2b *mʿl-pny-hʾdmh*
2. ∅ clause-1 constituent-3 units/65 cases
Gen 49:24c *mydy-ʾbyr-yʿqb*
3. ∅ clause-1 constituent-4 units/16 cases
Dt 32:24a *mzy-rʿb-wlḥmy-ršp*
4. ∅ clause-2 constituents-2 units/13 cases
Gen 49:17b *špypn ʿly-ʾrḥ*
5. ∅ clause-2 constituents-3 units/21 cases
Zph 1:10e *wšbr-gdwl mhgbʿwt*
6. ∅ clause-2 constituents-4 units/5 cases
Ps 107:23b *ʿšy-mlʾkh bmym-rbym*
7. ∅ clause-2 constituents-5 units/∅ cases
8. ∅ clause-3 constituents-3 units/1 case
Zph 2:15d *ʾny wʾpsy ʿwd*
9. ∅ clause-3 constituents-4 units/1 case
Zph 3:10a *mʿbr lnhry-kwš ʿtry*
10. ∅ clause-3 constituents-5 units/∅ cases
11. ∅ clause-4 constituents-4 units/∅ cases
12. ∅ clause-4 constituents-5 units/∅ cases
13. 1 clause-2 constituents-2 units/245 cases
Ex 15:7b *tšlḥ ḥrnk*
14. 1 clause-2 constituents-3 units/229 cases
Zph 2:8a *šmʿty ḥrpt-mwʾb*
15. 1 clause-2 constituents-4 units/31 cases
Ex 15:15c *nmgw kl-yšby-knʿn*
16. 1 clause-2 constituents-5 units/2 cases
Ps 78:9a *bny-ʾprym nwšqy-rwmy-qšt*
17. 1 clause-3 constituents-3 units/275 cases
Dt 32:36a *ky-ydyn yhwh ʿmw*

18. 1 clause-3 constituents-4 units/79 cases
Num 23:10c *tmt npšy mwt-yšr-m*
19. 1 clause-3 constituents-5 units/10 cases
Ex 15:4c *wmbḥr-šlšyw ṭbᶜw bym-swp*
20. 1 clause-4 constituents-4 units/20 cases
Ps 107:6a *wyṣᶜqw ᵓl-yhwh bṣr lhm*
21. 1 clause-4 constituents-5 units/5 cases
Zph 3:11d *wlᵓ-twspy lgbhh ᶜwd bhr-qdšy*
22. 2 clauses-2 constituents-2 units/23 cases
Dt 33:27d *wyᵓmr hšmd*
23. 2 clauses-2 constituents-3 units/2 cases
Zph 3:14a *rny bt-ṣywn*
24. 2 clauses-2 constituents-4 units/∅ cases
25. 2 clauses-2 constituents-5 units/∅ cases
26. 2 clauses-3 constituents-3 units/92 cases
Ps 107:42a *yrᵓw yšrym wyśmḥw*
27. 2 clauses-3 constituents-4 units/19 cases
Ps 106:9a *wygᶜr bym-swp wyḥrb*
28. 2 clauses-3 constituents-5 units/2 cases
Zph 2:5b *gwy-krtym dbr-yhwh ᶜlykm*
29. 2 clauses-4 constituents-4 units/17 cases
Num 23:7c *lkh ᵓrh ly yᶜqb*
30. 2 clauses-4 constituents-5 units/3 cases
Jdg 5:31a *kn yᵓbdw kl-ᵓwybyk yhwh*
31. 3 clauses-3 constituents-3 units/4 cases
Jdg 5:12a *ᶜwry ᶜwry dbwrh*
32. 3 clauses-3 constituents-4 units/2 cases
Gen 49:2a *hqbṣw wšmᶜw bny-yᶜqb*
33. 3 clauses-3 constituents-5 units/∅ cases
34. 3 clauses-4 constituents-4 units/1 case
Gen 49:8a *yhwdh ᵓth ywdwk ᵓḥyk*
35. 3 clauses-4 constituents-5 units/∅ cases

Of the configurations exemplified in our corpus, three are *facile principes*, ##13, 14 and 17; together they describe 749 lines, 63% of our texts. No other configuration is even half as frequent as any of these; they constitute the major approaches to satisfying the constraints.

The next most common constellations are ##2, 18, and 26, a group with a diversity to match the uniformity of the first trio. The second trio ranges over 236 lines, a further 20% of the corpus. Between the six structures which are used in 83% of the texts, and the 11 used once or not at all, there are 18 others, ranging in frequency between 31 and 2 uses.

The six dominant line constellations have some interesting features. Of the range of nominal phrase structures, they use only the lower half: only 1° and 2° nominal phrases occur in them. Each of the overall constraints offers four actualizations and in each case, the top six constellations utilize only the three lowest actualizations: zero, single, and double clause lines occur among them, but not triple clause lines; 1-, 2-, and 3-constituent lines, but not 4-constituent lines; and 2-, 3-, and 4-unit lines, but not 5-unit lines. This avoidance of the upper ranges suggests that the 17 configurations which involve one, two, or (in one case) three of the high limits for a constraint make up a distinct group. This group of 17 includes seven of the eight unexemplified constellations (##7, 10, 11, 12, 25, 33, 35) and one of the three which are uniquely shown (#34). This one and the remaining constellations describe 66 lines.

These facts together point the way to a system of classifying the line configurations based on rough acknowledgements of frequency. Class I includes the three commonest configurations, Class II the three next commonest, and Class IV, the configurations involving high constraint limits, triple clause lines, 4-constituent lines, and 5-unit lines. Class III is the remainder.

| | | | |
|---|---|---|---|
| I. | #13 | 1 clause-2 constituents-2 units | |
| | #14 | 1 clause-2 constituents-3 units | |
| | #17 | 1 clause-3 constituents-3 units | 749 uses |
| II. | #2 | Ø clause-1 constituent-3 units | |
| | #18 | 1 clause-3 constituents-4 units | |
| | #26 | 2 clauses-3 constituents-3 units | 236 uses |
| III. | #1 | Ø clause-1 constituent-2 units | |
| | #3 | Ø clause-1 constituent-4 units | |
| | #4 | Ø clause-2 constituents-2 units | |
| | #5 | Ø clause-2 constituents-3 units | |
| | #6 | Ø clause-2 constituents-4 units | |
| | #8 | Ø clause-3 constituents-3 units | |
| | #9 | Ø clause-3 constituents-4 units | |

| | | | |
|---|---|---|---|
| | #15 | 1 clause-2 constituents-4 units | |
| | #22 | 2 clauses-2 constituents-2 units | |
| | #23 | 2 clauses-2 constituents-3 units | |
| | #24 | 2 clauses-2 constituents-4 units | |
| | #27 | 2 clauses-3 constituents-4 units | 149 uses |
| IV. | #7 | ∅ clauses-2 constituents-5 units | |
| | #10 | ∅ clauses-3 constituents-5 units | |
| | #11 | ∅ clauses-4 constituents-4 units | |
| | #12 | ∅ clauses-4 constituents-5 units | |
| | #16 | 1 clause-2 constituents-5 units | |
| | #19 | 1 clause-3 constituents-5 units | |
| | #20 | 1 clause-4 constituents-4 units | |
| | #21 | 1 clause-4 constituents-5 units | |
| | #25 | 2 clauses-2 constituents-5 units | |
| | #28 | 2 clauses-3 constituents-5 units | |
| | #29 | 2 clauses-4 constituents-4 units | |
| | #30 | 2 clauses-4 constituents-5 units | |
| | #31 | 3 clauses-3 constituents-3 units | |
| | #32 | 3 clauses-3 constituents-4 units | |
| | #33 | 3 clauses-3 constituents-5 units | |
| | #34 | 3 clauses-4 constituents-4 units | |
| | #35 | 3 clauses-4 constituents-5 units | 66 uses |

As noted above, Class I includes 63% of the corpus and Class II, 20%; the two smaller classes divide the remaining 17% between them, 12% in Class III and 5% in Class IV. The usefulness of this system in commenting on the texture of the verse is in part predictable: the stuff of it will be Class I lines and the most high-marked junctures will be tied to Class IV lines. In part, it is unpredictable and must await concrete examination in Chapter 10.

### *3.2.9 The structure of the lines of the corpus*

The regularities crystallized in the four constraints that form the definition of the line refer to features shared by every line; other, important patterns have less than universal scope. Because these patterns deserve our attention and because the configurations groupings are of such different dimensions, the lines of our corpus as it is laid out in 3.3-3.5 are not ordered by configurations, but with a view to exposing other regularities. Sometimes the groups used there correspond directly to configurations, but more often a group of paragraphs in 3.3, 3.4 and 3.5 matches a group of configurations; a list of the correspondences is given at the end of this paragraph.

The most basic differentiation within the corpus refers to the highest governing element in the lines. Most lines have as their highest element a clause predicator and are called predicated (3.3-3.4); there are 1,040 predicated lines. The remaining lines, called nominal, have as their highest element a nomen not serving as a clause predicator (3.5). The reason this split does not coincide with the split between zero clause lines and others is that the latter split refers to the presence of a clause anywhere in the line, while the former issues from the hierarchy of the line's structure. The small group of lines which contain, e.g., a nominal phrase governing a relative clause, are single clause lines, but not predicated lines (3.5.1-3.5.2). The special features of nominal lines are discussed in 3.5.

Predicated lines most often contain a single clause and either two or three constituents. The 850 lines with these features make up a large enough corpus to warrant observations concerning word order and predicator interrelations. This group, which corresponds to constellations ## 13-19, is treated in 3.3. The listing of the constellations given there are not exhaustive; the further cases are given in 3.5.1 and 3.5.2. Predicated lines which contain one clause and four constituents, or two or three clauses, are grouped together in 3.4. The categorization of independent verbal and verbless lines is straightforward, but the subgroups of dependent clauses are neither standardized nor obvious; a guide to those used here is given in 3.2.10.

A crude guide to matching the constellations of 3.2.8 to the sections of 3.3-3.5 is the following. Zero clause lines, constellations ## 1-9, are given in 3.5.3-3.5.5. One clause predicated lines, with two or three constituents, constellations ## 13-19, are given in 3.3. One clause nominal lines, with two or three constituents, which display the same constellations, are given in 3.5.1-3.5.2. Finally, one clause, four constituent lines, and two and three clause lines, constellations ## 20-34, are given in 3.4. A more detailed matching is given below.

| *constellation* | *corpus paragraphs* |
|---|---|
| ## 1-3 | 3.5.5 |
| ## 4-6 | 3.5.4 |
| ## 8-9 | 3.5.3 |
| # 13 | 3.3.2-12, 17-22, 24-25; 3.5.2 |
| # 14 | 3.3.2-4, 6-14, 17-19, 21-22, 24-25; 3.5.2 |
| # 15 | 3.3.2-4, 10, 12-13, 15, 17, 24-25; 3.5.2 |
| # 16 | 3.3.24-25 |
| # 17 | 3.3.27-48, 50, 52-60, 62-66, 68; 3.5.1 |
| # 18 | 3.3.27-28, 30-31, 33-34, 36, 38, 40-51, 54, 60, 63-65, 68; 3.5.1 |
| # 19 | 3.3.31, 36, 40-41, 44, 50, 63, 68 |
| # 20 | 3.4.19 |

| | |
|---|---|
| # 21 | 3.4.19 |
| # 22 | 3.4.15-18 |
| # 23 | 3.4.18 |
| # 26 | 3.4.2-13 |
| # 27 | 3.4.2-4, 6, 8-9, 12 |
| # 28 | 3.4.9-10 |
| # 29 | 3.4.20 |
| # 30 | 3.4.20 |
| # 31 | 3.4.21 |
| # 32 | 3.4.21 |
| # 34 | 3.4.22 |

### *3.2.10 Dependent clauses*

There are two types of clauses in Hebrew, independent and dependent; quotational clauses are properly a variety of dependent nominal clauses, but for our purposes, they receive a separate analysis. Clauses in direct discourse, when they coincide with the lines they occur in, are treated as independent clauses, irrespective of their subordination to the verb introducing the direct discourse. In case a clause of direct discourse and the verb introducing it occur within the same line, the discourse is taken as dependent on the main verb. Thus, a category intermediate between independent and subordinate clauses is recognized, in an attempt to incorporate into the analysis certain features of direct discourse discussed below (Chapter 8). The results of this split analysis can be seen in the following example.

Zph 3:7a *ᵓmrty ᵓk-tyrᵓy ᵓwty*

Zph 3:7b *tqḥy mwsr*

Both clauses of direct discourse, *ᵓk-tyrᵓy ᵓwty* and *tqḥy mwsr*, are introduced by the verb *ᵓmrty*. Only the first is treated as dependent on it here (3.4.3); the second is taken as independent (3.3.3). The whole quotation is treated as a unit elsewhere. Quotational dependent clauses can be verbal, as in Zph 3:7a, or verbless.

The larger class of dependent clauses includes subordinate clauses, verbless or verbal, finite or nonfinite. The categorization of subordinate clauses is not fully noted below, for fear of needlessly expanding the rubrics of classification; the clause typology is not noteworthily difficult. In most of the examples, the clauses coincide with the lines they appear in.

Nonfinite verbal subordinate clauses are formed with infinitives and participles. There are simple infinitive clauses, like Zph 3:8e. Infinitive clauses in *l* describe purpose, e.g., Ps 106:26b; in *m*, negative purpose, e.g., Ps 107:20b; the latter is rare. Infinitive clauses of concomitant circumstances are marked with *b*, e.g., Zph 3:20e, or *bṭrm*, e.g., Zph 2:2a. Participial relative clauses are formed either with the *h* relative marker, e.g., 2 S 1:24b, or asyndetically, e.g., Ps 106:21b. Nominal relative clauses can also contain a participle, as in Dt 32:39f.

Hebrew relative clauses can also be formed with finite verbs, marked with ∅, *zw*, *š*, and *ʾšr*, as in the examples cited: ∅ in Gen 49:27a, *zw* in Ex 15:13b, *š* in Num 24:3c, *ʾšr* in Ps 106:38c. Nominal relative clauses are sometimes formed with finite verbs, e.g., Ps 106:2a, as are nominal clauses, e.g., Dt 32:36c, and interrogative clauses (clauses subordinate to *mdwʿ*), e.g., Jdg 5:28d. Temporal clauses with finite verbs (not to be too sharply distinguished from clauses of concomitant circumstance) are signed by the subordinators *ʿd*, e.g., Gen 49:10c; *bṭrm*, e.g., Zph 2:2c; *š*, e.g., Jdg 5:7d; and *ʾšr*, e.g., Ps 78:43a. Other adverbial clauses with finite verbs indicate purpose, exception, condition, and concession. Negative purpose clauses, marked with *pn*, e.g., 2 S 1:20c, outnumber their positive counterparts, in *lmʿn*, e.g., Ps 78:6a. Exceptive clauses are governed by *lwly*, e.g., Dt 32:27a. The particles *ʾm* (alone or in the negative combination *ʾm-lʾ-ky*) and *lw* introduce conditional clauses, e.g., Ps 78:34a, Dt 32:30c, Dt 32:29a. The concessive clause in the corpus is marked with *ʾšr*, at Ps 106:34b.

Subordinate verbless clauses are limited to nominal clauses. A verbless nominal clause can be seen in Ps 78:35a.

### 3.3 *Single clause predicated lines of two or three constituents*

The basic fulfillments of the two higher level overall constraints, which result in lines of one or two nominal phrases governed by a clause predicator, are the structural bases of 850 lines. Beyond the basic split in the group, between 2-constituent lines (494 lines) and 3-constituent lines (356 lines), there are categories based on the type of predication involved. Clauses may be independent or dependent. Independent clauses may be verbal or verbless. There are only two verbless dependent clauses, Gen 49:15b and Ps 78:35b, and they are not set off here from other 2-constituent clauses; there are no dependent 3-constituent verbless clause lines.

There are six classes to be treated here: (1) independent verbal clause lines of two constituents (361 lines; 3.3.1-15); (2) dependent verbal clause lines of two constituents (56 lines; 3.3.16-22); (3) verbless clause lines of two constituents (77 lines; 3.3.23-25); (4) independent verbal clause lines of three constituents (317 lines; 3.3.26-60); (5) dependent verbal clause lines of three constituents (26 lines; 3.3.61-66); (6) verbless clause lines of three constituents (13 lines, all independent; 3.3.67-68); the first paragraph of each group is a summary of the group. The independent clause lines show considerable freedom of word order and are here sorted on that basis; the dependent clauses are sorted by type (see 3.2.10). Some groups are further sorted.

The 2-constituent independent clause lines are the only predicated lines in which 3° nominal phrases occur. They occur as either subject or predicate and in either position in verbless independent clauses. They are further restricted in verbal clauses: they occur largely in verb initial lines in second position (3.3.2-4). Otherwise, 3° nominal phrases occur only in nominal lines, just as 4° nominal phrases are entirely restricted to nominal lines. This constraint is independent of other limitations, though it serves to explain one of the void constellations, viz., #24 (2 clauses-2 constituents-4 units), which could only be satisfied if a 3° nominal phrase were permitted in a two clause line. This restriction does not explain the other two void constellations among the non-zero clause lines. The nullity of #25 (2 clauses-2 constituents-5 units) is the result of the independent restriction on 4° nominal phrases and the nullity of #33 (3 clauses-3 constituents-5 units) is unexplained.

Both classes of verbal independent lines fall into three major subclasses. Lines of 2 constituents can be verb initial (232 lines), verb final (91 lines), or, as a result of verb gapping, free of a verb (38 lines). Lines of 3 constituents can be verb initial (174 lines), verb medial (106 lines), or verb final (37 lines).

There are seven constellations represented in this section. A list of them follows, with notes on their distribution in the six classes of lines dealt with.

Constellation #13: 1 clause-2 constituents-2 units

independent verbal clauses: 199
dependent verbal clauses: 30
verbless clauses: 13
*total: 242*

Constellation #14: 1 clause-2 constituents-3 units

independent verbal clauses: 146
dependent verbal clauses: 25
verbless clauses: 50
*total: 221*

Constellation #15: 1 clause-2 constituents-4 units

independent verbal clauses: 16
dependent verbal clauses: 1
verbless clauses: 12
*total: 29*

Constellation #16: 1 clause-2 constituents-5 units

verbless clauses: 2
*total: 2*

Constellation #17: 1 clause-3 constituents-3 units

independent verbal clauses: 241
dependent verbal clauses: 20
independent verbless clauses: 8
*total: 269*

Constellation #18: 1 clause-3 constituents-4 units

independent verbal clauses: 69
dependent verbal clauses: 5
independent verbless clauses: 3
*total: 77*

Constellation #19: 1 clause-3 constituents-5 units

independent verbal clauses: 7
dependent verbal clauses: 1
independent verbless clauses: 2
*total: 10*

An overview of the nominal phrase structures used in the lines of this section is given below.

*two constituent lines*

| | *1st con np* | | | *2nd con np* | | |
|---|---|---|---|---|---|---|
| | *1°* | *2°* | *3°* | *1°* | *2°* | *3°* |
| ind verbal | 90 | 39 | ∅ | 142 | 117 | 11 |
| dep verbal | 35 | 7 | ∅ | 27 | 20 | ∅ |
| verbless | 40 | 34 | 3 | 42 | 28 | 7 |
| *total* | *165* | *80* | *3* | *211* | *165* | *18* |
| *total np* | *642* | | | | | |

*three constituent lines*

| | *1st con np* | | *2nd con np* | | *3rd con np* | |
|---|---|---|---|---|---|---|
| | *1°* | *2°* | *1°* | *2°* | *1°* | *2°* |
| ind verbal | 110 | 33 | 201 | 10 | 239 | 40 |
| dep verbal | 22 | ∅ | 14 | 3 | 19 | 6 |
| verbless | 10 | 3 | 12 | 1 | 10 | 3 |
| *total* | *142* | *36* | *227* | *14* | *268* | *49* |
| *total np* | *736* | | | | | |

### *3.3.1 Single independent verbal clause lines of two constituents*

The independent verbal clause lines which consist of two constituents make up about 30% of our corpus. They are classified below on the basis first of whether the verb is present in the surface structure (lines with the verb in 3.3.2-3.3.9, lines without in 3.3.10-3.3.15) and second on the basis of word order. The ranking gives priority to the verb: verb first clauses (3.3.2-3.3.5) are followed by verb second clauses (3.3.6-3.3.9), which are followed by clauses from which the verb has been gapped (3.3.10-3.3.15). Nominal elements are ranked in the order S-O-P-A, so that first of all, VS precedes VO; and second, among clauses with two nominal elements, those with a subject precede those with an object but no subject, etc.

The commonest word orders are verb initial; about two thirds of the clauses have such orders. The least frequent orders are those from which the verb has been gapped; most sentences in this category follow single independent verbal clause lines of three constituents.

A conspectus of 3.3.2-3.3.15 is given below. The constellations are #13 (1 clause-2 constituents-2 units), #14 (1 clause-2 constituents-3 units), #15 (1 clause-2 constituents-4 units).

*Constellation conspectus*

| | *total* | *# 13* | *# 14* | *# 15* |
|---|---|---|---|---|
| 3.3.2 VS | 37 | 20 | 13 | 4 |
| 3.3.3 VO | 88 | 40 | 45 | 3 |
| 3.3.4 VP | 104 | 57 | 43 | 4 |
| 3.3.5 VA | 3 | 3 | ∅ | ∅ |
| *Verb initial* | *232* | *120* | *101* | *11* |
| 3.3.6 SV | 18 | 12 | 6 | ∅ |
| 3.3.7 OV | 32 | 18 | 14 | ∅ |
| 3.3.8 PV | 38 | 31 | 7 | ∅ |
| 3.3.9 AV | 3 | 1 | 2 | ∅ |
| *Verb final* | *91* | *62* | *29* | *∅* |

| | | | | |
|---|---|---|---|---|
| 3.3.10 SP | 13 | 8 | 4 | 1 |
| 3.3.11 PS | 5 | 3 | 2 | ∅ |
| 3.3.12 OP | 15 | 6 | 7 | 2 |
| 3.3.13 PO | 3 | ∅ | 2 | 1 |
| 3.3.14 PP | 1 | ∅ | 1 | ∅ |
| 3.3.15 AP | 1 | ∅ | ∅ | 1 |
| *Verb gapped* | *38* | *17* | *16* | *5* |
| *Total* | *361* | *199* | *146* | *16* |

*Nominal phrase structure conspectus*

| | | *1st con np* | | *2nd con np* | | |
|---|---|---|---|---|---|---|
| | *total* | *1°* | *2°* | *1°* | *2°* | *3°* |
| 3.3.2 VS | 37 | | | 20 | 13 | 4 |
| 3.3.3 VO | 88 | | | 40 | 45 | 3 |
| 3.3.4 VP | 104 | | | 57 | 43 | 4 |
| 3.3.5 VA | 3 | | | 3 | ∅ | ∅ |
| *Verb initial* | *232* | | | *120* | *101* | *11* |
| 3.3.6 SV | 18 | 12 | 6 | | | |
| 3.3.7 OV | 32 | 18 | 14 | | | |
| 3.3.8 PV | 38 | 31 | 7 | | | |
| 3.3.9 AV | 3 | 1 | 2 | | | |
| *Verb final* | *91* | *62* | *29* | | | |
| 3.3.10 SP | 13 | 11 | 2 | 9 | 4 | |
| 3.3.11 PS | 5 | 4 | 1 | 4 | 1 | |
| 3.3.12 OP | 15 | 11 | 4 | 8 | 7 | |
| 3.3.13 PO | 3 | 1 | 2 | 1 | 2 | |
| 3.3.14 PP | 1 | 1 | ∅ | ∅ | 1 | |
| 3.3.15 AP | 1 | ∅ | 1 | ∅ | 1 | |
| *Verb gapped* | *38* | *28* | *10* | *22* | *16* | |
| *Total* | *361* | *90* | *39* | *142* | *117* | *11* |

*Total np 399 (232 1°/156 2°/11 3°)*

### *3.3.2 Single independent verbal clause lines of two constituents. VS*

Number of lines: 37.
Constellation #13:20/#14:13/#15:4.
2nd con np 1°:20/2°:13/3°:4.

Ex 15:9a *ʾmr ʾwyb*

Gen 49:23b, 24b; Ex 15:9d, 9f, 10b, 12b, 15a, 15c; Num 24:7d, 19a; Dt 32:17d; 33:21c; Jdg 5:19b, 22a, 22c, 23b; 2 S 1:19b, 27b; Hab 3:6c, 6d, 7b, 17c; Zph 1:11a, 11b, 11c; 2:7d; 3:6b, 13e, 20f; Ps 78:19b, 20b; 106:17a, 30b, 42a; 107:2a, 29b.

### *3.3.3 Single independent verbal clause lines of two constituents. VO*

Number of lines: 88.
Constellation #13:40/#14:45/#15:3.
2nd con np 1°:40/2°:45/3°:3.

Gen 49:4b *ky-ᶜlyt mškby-ᵓbyk*

Gen 49:4c, 15a; Ex 15:7b, 9c, 9e, 12a; Num 23:8a, 8b; 24:8c, 17e; Dt 32:7a, 7b, 8c, 13b, 15d, 18b, 22c, 22d, 41a, 43d; 33:3a, 9d, 11c, 17d, 20d, 21b, 23c, 24c; Jdg 5:7b, 8a, 12c, 23a, 26c, 26d; Zph 1:3a, 3b, 7d, 13d, 13e; 2:3a, 3d, 3e, 6a, 7e, 8a, 11b, 13b, 15g; 3:2b, 4c, 6a, 7b, 13a, 13b, 15b; Ps 78:7b, 10a, 11a, 20a, 38d, 60a, 68a; 106:1a, 2b, 7b, 12b, 17b, 21a, 28b, 33a, 34a, 35b, 36a, 38a, 40b; 107:9a, 11a, 16a, 22a, 26a, 26b, 36b, 37a, 37b, 37c, 43b, 43c.

### *3.3.4 Single independent verbal clause lines of two constituents. VP*

Number of lines: 104.
Constellation #13:57/#14:43/#15:4.
2nd con np 1°:57/2°:43/3°:4.

Num 23:23a *ky-lᵓ-nḥš byᶜqb*

Gen 49:2b, 7c, 7d, 14b, 15d, 26d; Ex 15:1a, 4b, 7c, 10a, 21a; Num 23:23b; Dt 32:10a, 10d, 11d, 13a, 16a, 17a, 21b, 22b, 24c, 29b; 33:2c, 2d, 16c, 22c; Jdg 5:3e, 23d; 2 S 1:20a, 20b; Hab 3:8d, 13a, 18b; Zph 1:7a, 8a, 8b, 9a, 10a, 12a, 12c, 17a, 17b, 18e; 2:5d; 3:2a, 3c, 12a, 17d, 19d; Ps 78:4a, 6c, 8a, 9b, 15b, 22a, 22b, 30a, 31b, 32b, 36a, 37b, 40b, 54a, 57b, 58a, 67a, 70a, 70b, 72a; 106:4b, 6a, 8a, 10a, 10b, 12a, 13b, 17c, 19b, 24a, 24b, 25a, 25b, 28a, 29a, 32a, 33b, 35a, 39a, 39b, 41a, 42b, 43c, 45b, 47b; 107:4a, 7a, 8a, 14a, 18b, 20b, 30b, 32a, 40b.

### *3.3.5 Single independent verbal clause lines of two constituents. VA*

Number of lines: 3.
Constellation #13:3.
2nd con np 1°:3.

Dt 32:39a *rᵓw ᶜth*

Num 24:17a, 17b.

### *3.3.6 Single independent verbal clause lines of two constituents. SV*

Number of lines: 18.
Constellation #13:12/#14:6.
1st con np 1°:12/2°:6.

Jdg 5:4c *ʾrṣ rʿšh*

Ex 15:5a; Jdg 5:3d, 4d, 5a, 21a, 22b, 29a; Hab 3:10b, 17a; Zph 2:4d, 9h, 9i; 3:17b; Ps 78:20c, 63b, 64b; 107:27b.

*3.3.7 Single independent verbal clause lines of two constituents. OV*

Number of lines: 32.
Constellation #13:18/#14:14.
1st con np 1°:18/2°:14.

Dt 33:9e *wbrytk ynṣrw*

Ex 15:1b; Num 23:19d, 20a, 20b; 24:4b, 8d, 8e; Dt 32:3a, 17b, 43b; 33:9b, 9c, 11b, 19c, 21d; Jdg 5:8b, 19d, 25a; Hab 3:9b, 16d; Zph 3:19c; Ps 78:7c, 23b, 31c, 41b, 44b; 107:4c, 11b, 14b, 16b, 38b.

*3.3.8 Single independent verbal clause lines of two constituents. PV*

Number of lines: 38.
Constellation #13:31/#14:7.
1st con np 1°:31/2°:7.

2 S 1:23b *bḥyyhm-wbmwtm lʾ-nprdw*

Num 23:9a, 9b, 9d; 24:6a; Dt 32:11b, 16b, 19b, 21d, 36b, 41d; 33:7c, 12d, 20c; Jdg 5:17d, 27a, 27d, 28a; 2 S 1:23c, 23d; Hab 3:2d, 19c; Zph 1:17c; 3:2c, 2d, 5d, 16a; Ps 78:58b, 62b, 67b, 71a, 72b; 107:4b, 6b, 13b, 17b, 28b, 32b.

*3.3.9 Single independent verbal clause lines of two constituents. AV*

Number of lines: 3.
Constellation #13:1/#14:2.
1st con np 1°:1/2°:2.

Ps 106:43a *pʿmym-rbwt yṣylm*

Dt 33:23d; Zph 2:3f.

*3.3.10 Single independent verbal clause lines of two constituents. SP*

Number of lines: 13.
Constellation #13:8/#14:4/#15:1.
1st con np 1°:11/2°:2.
2nd con np 1°:9/2°:4.

Hab 3:3b *wqdwš mhr-pʾrn*

Gen 49:10b, 13b, 13c, 17b; Num 23:7b; Dt 33:4b; Jdg 5:3c; Hab 3:4b; Zph 1:13b, 17e; 2:4b, 9e.

*3.3.11 Single independent verbal clause lines of two constituents. PS*

Number of lines: 5.
Constellation #13:3/#14:2.
1st con np 1°:4/2°:1.
2nd con np 1°:4/2°:1.

Hab 3:11c *lngh brq-ḥnytk*

Dt 32:25b; Hab 3:8b, 8c, 13b.

*3.3.12 Single independent verbal clause lines of two constituents. OP*

Number of lines: 15.
Constellation #13:6/#14:7/#15:2.
1st con np 1°:11/2°:4.
2nd con np 1°:8/2°:7.

Ps 78:47b *wšqmwtm bḥnml*

Dt 32:13d; 33:8c, 10b, 10d; Jdg 5:26b; Hab 3:15b; Ps 78:33b, 46b, 48b, 51b, 61b; 107:33b, 34a, 35b.

*3.3.13 Single independent verbal clause lines of two constituents. PO*

Number of lines: 3.
Constellation #14:2/#15:1.
1st con np 1°:1/2°:2.
2nd con np 1°:1/2°:2.

Gen 49:11d *wbdm-ᶜnbym swth*

Gen 49:11b; Ps 78:27b.

*3.3.14 Single independent verbal clause lines of two constituents. PP*

Number of lines: 1.
Constellation #14:1.
1st con np 1°:1.
2nd con np 2°:1.

Ps 106:16b *lʾhrn qdwš-yhwh*

*3.3.15 Single independent verbal clause lines of two constituents. AP*

Number of lines: 1.
Constellation #15:1.

1st con np 2°:1.
2nd con np 2°:1.

Ps 78:14b *wkl-hlylh b˒wr-˒š*

### *3.3.16 Single dependent verbal clause lines of two constituents*

The small group of dependent verbal clause lines of two constituents makes up under 5% of our corpus. They are divided between those formed with nonfinite verb forms (3.3.17-3.3.18) and those with finite verb forms (3.3.19-3.3.22) into two equal groups and are further categorized roughly on the basis of function. In the first large group, the clause predicator, since it is a noun form, infinitive or participle, counts as a noun constituent; in the second, the predicator is a verb form. No note is taken here of word order since little freedom from prose order is exhibited; the rule of verb first applies except when contravened by the rule of relative fronting.

A conspectus of 3.3.17-3.3.22 follows.

*Constellation conspectus*

| | *total* | *# 13* | *# 14* | *# 15* |
|---|---|---|---|---|
| 3.3.17 | 18 | 7 | 10 | 1 |
| 3.3.18 | 13 | 8 | 5 | ∅ |
| 3.3.19 | 7 | 5 | 2 | ∅ |
| 3.3.20 | 1 | 1 | ∅ | ∅ |
| 3.3.21 | 10 | 6 | 4 | ∅ |
| 3.3.22 | 7 | 3 | 4 | ∅ |
| *Total* | *56* | *30* | *25* | *1* |

*Nominal phrase structure conspectus*

| | | *1st con np* | | *2nd con np* | |
|---|---|---|---|---|---|
| | *total* | *1°* | *2°* | *1°* | *2°* |
| 3.3.17 | 18 | 16 | 2 | 8 | 10 |
| 3.3.18 | 13 | 10 | 3 | 11 | 2 |
| 3.3.19 | 7 | 4 | ∅ | 1 | 2 |
| 3.3.20 | 1 | 1 | ∅ | ∅ | ∅ |
| 3.3.21 | 10 | 2 | 1 | 6 | 3 |
| 3.3.22 | 7 | 2 | 1 | 1 | 3 |
| *Total* | *56* | *35* | *7* | *27* | *20* |

*Total np 89 (62 1°/27 2°)*

### 3.3.17 *Single dependent verbal clause lines of two constituents. Nonfinite clauses, infinitives*

Number of lines: 18.
Constellation #13:7/#14:10/#15:1.
1st con np 1°:16/2°:2.
2nd con np 1°:8/2°:10.

Ps 107:7b *llkt ʾl-ʿyr-mwšb*

Dt 32:8a, 8b; Jdg 5:4b, 16b; Zph 3:8e, 9b, 9c; Ps 78:5d, 71b; 106:5a, 5b, 5c, 8b, 27b, 44b, 47c, 47d.

### 3.3.18 *Single dependent verbal clause lines of two constituents. Nonfinite clauses, participial relative clauses*

Number of lines: 13.
Constellation #13:8/#14:5.
1st con np 1°:10/2°:3.
2nd con np 1°:11/2°:2.

Zph 1:12e *hʾmrym blbbm*

Gen 49:17c, 21b; Zph 1:5a, 5b, 5c, 5d, 6a, 12d; 2:15b, 15c; Ps 106:21b; 107:40a.

### 3.3.19 *Single dependent verbal clause lines of two constituents. Finite clauses, relative clauses*

Number of lines: 7.
Constellation #13:5/#14:2.
1st con np 1°:4.
2nd con np 1°:1/2°:2.

Zph 2:8d *wygdylw ʿl-gbwlm*

Ex 15:13b, 16e; Dt 32:38b; 33:8e; Ps 78:11b; 107:3a.

### 3.3.20 *Single dependent verbal clause lines of two constituents. Finite clauses, nominal relative clauses*

Number of lines: 1.
Constellation #13:1.
1st con np 1°:1.

Ps 107:43a *my ḥkm*

### *3.3.21 Single dependent verbal clause lines of two constituents. Finite clauses, temporal clauses*

Number of lines: 10.
Constellation # 13:6/# 14:4.
1st con np 1°:2/2°:1.
2nd con np 1°:6/2°:3.

Num 23:24c *ᶜd-yᵓkl ṭrp*

Gen 49:10d; Ex 15:16d; Num 23:24d; Jdg 5:7c; Hab 3:16e; Zph 2:2c; 3:7d; Ps 78:42b, 43b.

### *3.3.22 Single dependent verbal clause lines of two constituents. Finite clauses, purpose, exceptive and conditional clauses*

Number of lines: 7.
Constellation # 13:3/# 14:4.
1st con np 1°:2/2°:1.
2nd con np 1°:1/2°:3.

Dt 32:27b *pn-ynkrw ṣrymw*

Dt 32:27a, 30c, 30d; 2 S 1:20c, 20d; Ps 78:6a.

### *3.3.23 Single verbless clause lines of two constituents*

Verbless clauses in which both subject and predicate are limited to one constituent each form under 1/12 of our corpus. A conspectus of 3.3.24 and 3.3.25 follows. The relevant patterns are ## 13 (1 clause-2 constituents-2 units), 14 (1 clause-2 constituents-3 units), 15 (1 clause-2 constituents-4 units), and 16 (1 clause-2 constituents-5 units).

*Constellation conspectus*

| | *total* | # 13 | # 14 | # 15 | # 16 |
|---|---|---|---|---|---|
| 3.3.24 SPred | 43 | 8 | 27 | 7 | 1 |
| 3.3.25 PredS | 34 | 5 | 23 | 5 | 1 |
| *Total* | *77* | *13* | *50* | *12* | *2* |

*Nominal phrase structure conspectus*

| | | *1st con np* | | | *2nd con np* | | |
|---|---|---|---|---|---|---|---|
| | | *1°* | *2°* | *3°* | *1°* | *2°* | *3°* |
| 3.3.24 SPred | 43 | 24 | 17 | 2 | 23 | 17 | 3 |
| 3.3.25 PredS | 34 | 16 | 17 | 1 | 19 | 11 | 4 |
| *Total* | *77* | *40* | *34* | *3* | *42* | *28* | *7* |

*Total np 154 (82 1°/62 2°/10 3°)*

*3.3.24 Single verbless clause lines of two constituents. Subject-Predicate*

Number of lines: 43.
Constellation #13:8/#14:27/#15:7/#16:1.
1st con np 1°:24/2°:17/3°:2.
2nd con np 1°:23/2°:17/3°:3.

Dt 33:22b *dn gwr-ʾryh*

Gen 49:3b, 5a, 8b, 14a, 21a; Ex 15:3a, 3b; Num 23:21c, 21d, 22b; 24:9c, 9d; Dt 32:4b, 9a, 31b, 32c, 36d; 33:17e, 17f, 29b; Jdg 5:9a, 15b, 18a, 18b, 30b, 30c, 30d, 30e; 2 S 1:23a, 26d; Hab 3:4c, 19a; Zph 1:14c; 2:15a; 3:3b, 4a, 5a, 15c, 17a; Ps 78:9a, 35b, 38a.

*3.3.25 Single verbless clause lines of two constituents. Predicate-Subject*

Number of lines: 34.
Constellation #13:5/#14:23/#15:5/#16:1.
1st con np 1°:16/2°:17/3°:1.
2nd con np 1°:19/2°:11/3°:4.

Jdg 5:21b *nḥl-qdwmym nḥl-qyšwn*

Gen 49:5b, 7a, 9a, 22a; Ex 15:2a; Dt 32:4d, 9b, 20c, 28a, 31a, 32a, 32b, 33a, 33b, 35a, 35b, 35c; 33:13b, 17a, 17b, 20b, 25a, 27a, 27b; 2 S 1:26c, 26e; Zph 1:7b, 14a, 15a; 2:2b; Ps 106:1c, 48a; 107:1b.

*3.3.26 Single independent verbal clause lines of three constituents*

Over half of our corpus is composed of single independent verbal clause lines; well over 300 of these have three constituents, one quarter of the corpus, as opposed to the third made up of 2 constituent lines. The 34 attested word orders are arranged on the basis of verb position: verb first orders (3.3.27-3.3.39); verb medial orders (3.3.40-3.3.52); and verb final orders (3.3.53-3.3.60); within these groups, the arrangement is based on the S-O-P-A ranking. Of these 34 orders, the four commonest are verb initial with prepositional phrases: VOP (3.3.34), VPO (3.3.36), VSP (3.3.28) and VPS (3.3.31), in order of frequency. Among the rarest orders are those containing an adverbial and those that are verb final; indeed, only one verb final order, SPV (3.3.54), has more than a dozen examples; word orders with two direct objects are also rare.

A conspectus of 3.3.27-3.3.60 follows. The patterns involved are ## 17 (1 clause-3 constituents-3 units), 18 (1 clause-3 constituents-4 units), and 19 (1 clause-3 constituents-5 units).

*Constellation conspectus*

| | *total* | *#17* | *#18* | *#19* |
|---|---|---|---|---|
| 3.3.27 VSO | 9 | 8 | 1 | ∅ |
| 3.3.28 VSP | 26 | 23 | 3 | ∅ |
| 3.3.29 VSA | 1 | 1 | ∅ | ∅ |
| 3.3.30 VOS | 2 | 1 | 1 | ∅ |
| 3.3.31 VPS | 22 | 16 | 5 | 1 |
| 3.3.32 VAS | 1 | 1 | ∅ | ∅ |
| 3.3.33 VOO | 3 | 2 | 1 | ∅ |
| 3.3.34 VOP | 48 | 40 | 8 | ∅ |
| 3.3.35 VOA | 4 | 4 | ∅ | ∅ |
| 3.3.36 VPO | 38 | 32 | 5 | 1 |
| 3.3.37 VAO | 1 | 1 | ∅ | ∅ |
| 3.3.38 VPP | 17 | 14 | 3 | ∅ |
| 3.3.39 VPA | 1 | 1 | ∅ | ∅ |
| *Verb initial* | *174* | *145* | *27* | *2* |
| 3.3.40 SVO | 21 | 12 | 8 | 1 |
| 3.3.41 SVP | 13 | 8 | 4 | 1 |
| 3.3.42 SVA | 3 | 1 | 2 | ∅ |
| 3.3.43 OVS | 6 | 2 | 4 | ∅ |
| 3.3.44 PVS | 13 | 9 | 2 | 2 |
| 3.3.45 AVS | 3 | 1 | 2 | ∅ |
| 3.3.46 OVO | 5 | 3 | 2 | ∅ |
| 3.3.47 OVP | 8 | 5 | 3 | ∅ |
| 3.3.48 PVO | 17 | 13 | 4 | ∅ |
| 3.3.49 AVO | 2 | ∅ | 2 | ∅ |
| 3.3.50 PVP | 13 | 11 | 1 | 1 |
| 3.3.51 PVA | 1 | ∅ | 1 | ∅ |
| 3.3.52 AVA | 1 | 1 | ∅ | ∅ |
| *Verb medial* | *106* | *66* | *35* | *5* |
| 3.3.53 SOV | 1 | 1 | ∅ | ∅ |
| 3.3.54 SPV | 21 | 15 | 6 | ∅ |
| 3.3.55 SAV | 1 | 1 | ∅ | ∅ |
| 3.3.56 OSV | 1 | 1 | ∅ | ∅ |
| 3.3.57 PSV | 5 | 5 | ∅ | ∅ |
| 3.3.58 OPV | 3 | 3 | ∅ | ∅ |
| 3.3.59 POV | 3 | 3 | ∅ | ∅ |
| 3.3.60 PPV | 2 | 1 | 1 | ∅ |
| *Verb final* | *37* | *30* | *7* | *∅* |
| *Total* | *317* | *241* | *69* | *7* |

*Nominal phrase structure conspectus*

| | total | *1st con np* 1° | 2° | *2nd con np* 1° | 2° | *3rd con np* 1° | 2° |
|---|---|---|---|---|---|---|---|
| 3.3.27 VSO | 9 | | | 9 | ∅ | 8 | 1 |
| 3.3.28 VSP | 26 | | | 24 | 2 | 25 | 1 |
| 3.3.29 VSA | 1 | | | 1 | ∅ | 1 | ∅ |
| 3.3.30 VOS | 2 | | | 2 | ∅ | 1 | 1 |
| 3.3.31 VPS | 22 | | | 21 | 1 | 16 | 6 |
| 3.3.32 VAS | 1 | | | 1 | ∅ | 1 | ∅ |
| 3.3.33 VOO | 3 | | | 3 | ∅ | 2 | 1 |
| 3.3.34 VOP | 48 | | | 45 | 3 | 43 | 5 |
| 3.3.35 VOA | 4 | | | 4 | ∅ | 4 | ∅ |
| 3.3.36 VPO | 38 | | | 37 | 1 | 32 | 6 |
| 3.3.37 VAO | 1 | | | 1 | ∅ | 1 | ∅ |
| 3.3.38 VPP | 17 | | | 16 | 1 | 15 | 2 |
| 3.3.39 VPA | 1 | | | 1 | ∅ | 1 | ∅ |
| *Verb initial* | *174* | | | *166* | *8* | *151* | *23* |
| 3.3.40 SVO | 21 | 18 | 3 | | | 14 | 7 |
| 3.3.41 SVP | 13 | 10 | 3 | | | 10 | 3 |
| 3.3.42 SVA | 3 | 1 | 2 | | | 3 | ∅ |
| 3.3.43 OVS | 6 | 2 | 4 | | | 6 | ∅ |
| 3.3.44 PVS | 13 | 9 | 4 | | | 11 | 2 |
| 3.3.45 AVS | 3 | 3 | ∅ | | | 1 | 2 |
| 3.3.46 OVO | 5 | 3 | 2 | | | 5 | ∅ |
| 3.3.47 OVP | 8 | 5 | 3 | | | 8 | ∅ |
| 3.3.48 PVO | 17 | 13 | 4 | | | 17 | ∅ |
| 3.3.49 AVO | 2 | 2 | ∅ | | | ∅ | 2 |
| 3.3.50 PVP | 13 | 11 | 2 | | | 12 | 1 |
| 3.3.51 PVA | 1 | ∅ | 1 | | | 1 | ∅ |
| 3.3.52 AVA | 1 | 1 | ∅ | | | 1 | ∅ |
| *Verb medial* | *106* | *78* | *28* | | | *89* | *17* |
| 3.3.53 SOV | 1 | 1 | ∅ | 1 | ∅ | | |
| 3.3.54 SPV | 21 | 17 | 4 | 19 | 2 | | |
| 3.3.55 SAV | 1 | 1 | ∅ | 1 | ∅ | | |
| 3.3.56 OSV | 1 | 1 | ∅ | 1 | ∅ | | |
| 3.3.57 PSV | 5 | 5 | ∅ | 5 | ∅ | | |
| 3.3.58 OPV | 3 | 3 | ∅ | 3 | ∅ | | |
| 3.3.59 POV | 3 | 3 | ∅ | 3 | ∅ | | |
| 3.3.60 PPV | 2 | 1 | 1 | 2 | ∅ | | |
| *Verb final* | *37* | *32* | *5* | *35* | *2* | | |
| *Total* | *317* | *110* | *33* | *201* | *10* | *239* | *40* |

*Total np 633 (550 1°/83 2°)*

### *3.3.27 Single independent verbal clause lines of three constituents. VSO*

Number of lines: 9.
Constellation #17:8/#18:1.
2nd con np 1°:9.
3rd con np 1°:8/2°:1.

Hab 3:10c *ntn thwm qwlw*

Num 23:10c; 24:18a; Dt 32:30a, 36a; Zph 1:7c; 3:5e, 15a; Ps 106:11a.

### *3.3.28 Single independent verbal clause lines of three constituents. VSP*

Number of lines: 26.
Constellation #17:23/#18:3.
2nd con np 1°:24/2°:2.
3rd con np 1°:25/2°:1.

2 S 1:25a *ʾyk-nplw gbrym btwk-hmlḥmh*

Gen 49:10a; Ex 15:8c; Num 23:10d; 24:7a, 17c, 17d; Dt 32:35d, 39c; 33:6b, 29e; Jdg 5:7a, 14b, 28b; Hab 3:5b, 16c, 17b, 17f; Zph 1:13a, 17d; 2:7a; 3:5b; Ps 78:59b; 106:18a, 38d, 40a.

### *3.3.29 Single independent verbal clause lines of three constituents. VSA*

Number of lines: 1.
Constellation #17:1.
2nd con np 1°:1.
3rd con np 1°:1.

Dt 33:28a *wyškn yśrʾl bṭḥ*

### *3.3.30 Single independent verbal clause lines of three constituents. VOS*

Number of lines: 2.
Constellation #17:1/#18:1.
2nd con np 1°:2.
3rd con np 1°:1/2°:1.

Hab 3:3c *ksh šmym hwdw*

Num 24:18b.

### *3.3.31 Single independent verbal clause lines of three constituents. VPS*

Number of lines: 22.
Constellation #17:16/#18:5/#19:1.
2nd con np 1°:21/2°:1.
3rd con np 1°:16/2°:6.

Zph 3:7c *wlʾ-ykrt mʿwnh kl*

Gen 49:8c, 24a; Ex 15:8b, 16a; Num 24:7c; Dt 32:2a, 2b, 12b, 28b, 41b; 33:5a; Jdg 5:11d, 24a; Hab 3:17e; Zph 2:14a; 3:12c, 13c; Ps 78:8d, 65a; 106:29b, 41b.

*3.3.32 Single independent verbal clause lines of three constituents. VAS*

Number of lines: 1.
Constellation #17:1.
2nd con np 1°:1.
3rd con np 1°:1.

Zph 1:14d *ṣrḥ šm gbwr*

*3.3.33 Single independent verbal clause lines of three constituents. VOO*

Number of lines: 3.
Constellation #17:2/#18:1.
2nd con np 1°:3.
3rd con np 1°:2/2°:1.

Jdg 5:23c *ʾrw ʾrwr yšbyh*

Num 24:7b; Zph 1:2a.

*3.3.34 Single independent verbal clause lines of three constituents. VOP*

Number of lines: 48.
Constellation #17:40/#18:8.
2nd con np 1°:45/2°:3.
3rd con np 1°:43/2°:5.

Zph 2:13a *wyṭ ydw ʿl-ṣpwn*

Gen 49:15c; Num 23:21a, 21b; 24:19b; Dt 32:3b, 13c, 20a, 41c, 42a; 33:10a, 10c, 21a, 26b; Jdg 5:11a; Hab 3:13d, 14d, 19b; Zph 1:3e, 4a, 12b; 3:6c, 20c; Ps 78:1b, 2b, 5a, 13b, 15a, 16a, 18a, 20e, 23a, 26a, 50a, 51a; 106:7c, 14a, 14b, 15b, 19a, 20a, 26a, 37; 107:22b, 29a, 33a, 35a, 41a.

*3.3.35 Single independent verbal clause lines of three constituents. VOA*

Number of lines: 4.
Constellation #17:4.
2nd con np 1°:4.
3rd con np 1°:4.

Gen 49:17d *wypl rkbw ʾḥwr*

Zph 3:15d; Ps 78:42a, 66a.

*3.3.36 Single independent verbal clause lines of three constituents. VPO*

Number of lines: 38.
Constellation #17:32/#18:5/#19:1.
2nd con np 1°:37/2°:1.
3rd con np 1°:32/2°:6.

Gen 49:11c *kbs byyn lbšw*

Gen 49:11a; Ex 15:13a; Dt 32:23a, 26b, 38d, 40a; 33:8b, 24d, 26c, 27c; Hab 3:14a, 15a; Zph 1:4c; 3:9a, 11c; Ps 78:2a, 7a, 16b, 26b, 33a, 44a, 46a, 47a, 48a, 49a, 50b, 52a, 55a, 55b, 55c, 61a, 62a, 69a; 106:15a, 45a; 107:12a, 41b.

*3.3.37 Single independent verbal clause lines of three constituents. VAO*

Number of lines: 1.
Constellation #17:1.
2nd con np 1°:1.
3rd con np 1°:1.

Ps 107:36a *wywšb šm r*ᶜ*bym*

*3.3.38 Single independent verbal clause lines of three constituents. VPP*

Number of lines: 17.
Constellation #17:14/#18:3.
2nd con np 1°:16/2°:1.
3rd con np 1°:15/2°:2.

Ex 15:13c *nḥlt b*ᶜ*zk* ᵓ*l-nwh-qdšk*

Ex 15:2b, 5b, 10c; Dt 33:2b; Jdg 5:13b; Zph 2:15e; 3:17c, 17e; Ps 78:52b; 106:9b, 16a, 23b, 31a, 32b, 36b, 44a.

*3.3.39 Single independent verbal clause lines of three constituents. VPA*

Number of lines: 1.
Constellation #17:1.
2nd con np 1°:1.
3rd con np 1°:1.

Ps 78:14a *wynḥm b*ᶜ*nn ywmm*

*3.3.40 Single independent verbal clause lines of three constituents. SVO*

Number of lines: 21.
Constellation #17:12/#18:8/#19:1.
1st con np 1°:18/2°:3.
3rd con np 1°:14/2°:7.

Num 23:10a *my mnh* ᶜ*pr-y*ᶜ*qb*

Gen 49:20b; Ex 15:14b; Num 23:10b; 24:18c; Dt 32:30b, 42b; 33:23b, 28d; Jdg 5:4e, 6c, 18c; Hab 3:3d, 11a, 17d; Zph 3:4b, 10b; Ps 106:18b; 107:24a, 25b, 42b.

### *3.3.41 Single independent verbal clause lines of three constituents. SVP*

Number of lines: 13.
Constellation #17:8/#18:4/#19:1.
1st con np 1°:10/2°:3.
3rd con np 1°:10/2°:3.

Dt 32:21a *hm qnᵓwny blᵓ-ᵓl*

Ex 15:4c, 18; Dt 32:21c, 22a; 33:12b; Jdg 5:17c; Zph 2:14d; Ps 78:21b, 21c, 31a, 37a; 106:43b.

### *3.3.42 Single independent verbal clause lines of three constituents. SVA*

Number of lines: 3.
Constellation #17:1/#18:2.
1st con np 1°:1/2°:2.
3rd con np 1°:3.

2 S 1:22c *qšt-yhwntn lᵓ-nśwg ᵓḥwr*

Gen 49:19b; 2 S 1:22d.

### *3.3.43 Single independent verbal clause lines of three constituents. OVS*

Number of lines: 6.
Constellation #17:2/#18:4.
1st con np 1°:2/2°:4.
3rd con np 1°:6.

Ps 78.63a *bḥwryw ᵓklh ᵓš*

Ex 15:15b; Hab 3:9a; Ps 78:25a, 54b; 107:18a.

### *3.3.44 Single independent verbal clause lines of three constituents. PVS*

Number of lines: 13.
Constellation #17:9/#18:2/#19:2.
1st con np 1°:9/2°:4.
3rd con np 1°:11/2°:2.

Dt 32:25a *mḥwṣ tškl ḥrb*

Ex 15:8a; Num 23:7a; 24:6c; Jdg 5:6b, 14c, 20a; Hab 3:2c, 5a, 16b; Zph 1:18c, 2:9a; 3:8h.

*3.3.45 Single independent verbal clause lines of three constituents. AVS*

Number of lines: 3.
Constellation #17:1/#18:2.
1st con np 1°:3.
3rd con np 1°:1/2°:2.

Dt 33:28b *bdd ᶜwn yᶜqb-ᵓl*

Jdg 5:27e; 2 S 1:21c.

*3.3.46 Single independent verbal clause lines of three constituents. OVO*

Number of lines: 5.
Constellation #17:3/#18:2.
1st con np 1°:3/2°:2.
3rd con np 1°:5.

Ps 107:9b *wnpš-rᶜbh mlᵓ ṭwb*

Dt 32:14e; Jdg 5:8c; Hab 3:9c; Ps 78:53b.

*3.3.47 Single independent verbal clause lines of three constituents. OVP*

Number of lines: 8.
Constellation #17:5/#18:3.
1st con np 1°:5/2°:3.
3rd con np 1°:8.

Jdg 5:25b *ḥlb ntnh bspl*

Ex 15:1c; Dt 32:23b, 43c; Ps 78:5b, 24b, 29b, 66b.

*3.3.48 Single independent verbal clause lines of three constituents. PVO*

Number of lines: 17.
Constellation #17:13/#18:4.
1st con np 1°:13/2°:4.
3rd con np 1°:17.

Zph 3:20a *bᶜt-hhyᵓ ᵓbyᵓ ᵓtkm*

Gen 49:6c, 6d, 16a, 16b, 27b, 27c; Ex 15:7a; Dt 32:6a, 11a; 33:3c; Jdg 5:2b, 25c; Hab 3:12a, 12b; Zph 3:19b; Ps 78:12a.

*3.3.49 Single independent verbal clause lines of three constituents. AVO*

Number of lines: 2.
Constellation #18:2.
1st con np 1°:2.
3rd con np 1°:2.

Jdg 5.11b *šm ytnw ṣdqwt-yhwh*

Dt 33:19b.

*3.3.50 Single independent verbal clause lines of three constituents. PVP*

Number of lines: 13.
Constellation #17:11/#18:1/#19:1.
1st con np 1°:11/2°:2.
3rd con np 1°:12/2°:1.

Zph 3:8a *lkn ḥkw ly*

Ex 15:16b; Num 23:23c; Dt 33:7d; Jdg 5:14a, 15c, 16a, 20b; Zph 3:11a; Ps 78:10b, 36b, 40a, 69b.

*3.3.51 Single independent verbal clause lines of three constituents. PVA*

Number of lines: 1.
Constellation #18:1.
1st con np 2°:1.
3rd con np 1°:1.

Ps 78:32a *bkl-zʾt ḥṭʾw ʿwd*

*3.3.52 Single independent verbal clause lines of three constituents. AVA*

Number of lines: 1.
Constellation #17:1.
1st con np 1°:1.
3rd con np 1°:1.

Zph 1:14b *qrwb wmhr mʾd*

*3.3.53 Single independent verbal clause lines of three constituents. SOV*

Number of lines: 1.
Constellation #17:1.
1st con np 1°:1.
2nd con np 1°:1.

Dt 33:19a *ʿmym hr yqrʾw*

*3.3.54 Single independent verbal clause lines of three constituents. SPV*

Number of lines: 21.
Constellation #17:15/#18:6.
1st con np 1°:17/2°:4.
2nd con np 1°:19/2°:2.

Zph 2:4a *ky-ʿzh ʿzwbh thyh*

Gen 49:13a; Num 23:9c, 24a; Dt 32:17c; 33:2a, 3b, 29f; Jdg 5:17a; 2 S 1:25b; Hab 3:3a, 4a, 18a; Zph 2:4c, 7b, 9d, 14c, a5f; Ps 78:64a; 106:11b; 107:26c.

### *3.3.55 Single independent verbal clause lines of three constituents. SAV*

Number of lines: 1.
Constellation #17:1.
1st con np 1°:1.
2nd con np 1°:1

Dt 32:12a *yhwh bdd ynḥnw*

### *3.3.56 Single independent verbal clause lines of three constituents. OSV*

Number of lines: 1.
Constellation #17:1.
1st con np 1°:1.
2nd con np 1°:1.

Gen 49:19a *gd gdwd ygwdnw*

### *3.3.57 Single independent verbal clause lines of three constituents. PSV*

Number of lines: 5.
Constellation #17:5.
1st con np 1°:5.
2nd con np 1°:5.

Num 24:9b *wklbyʾ my yqymnw*

Gen 49:9d; Dt 33:11d; Hab 3:11b, 16f.

### *3.3.58 Single independent verbal clause lines of three constituents. OPV*

Number of lines: 3.
Constellation #17:3.
1st con np 1°:3.
2nd con np 1°:3.

Jdg 5:26a *ydh lytd tšlḥnh*

Dt 33:7e; Ps 78:50c.

### *3.3.59 Single independent verbal clause lines of three constituents. POV*

Number of lines: 3.
Constellation #17:3.

1st con np 1°:3.
2nd con np 1°:3.

Hab 3:2e *brgz rḥm tzkwr*

Dt 33:17c; Zph 3:5c.

*3.3.60 Single independent verbal clause lines of three constituents. PPV*

Number of lines: 2.
Constellation #17:1/#18:1.
1st con np 1°:1/2°:1.
2nd con np 1°:2.

Zph 2:7c *bbty-ʾšqlwn bʿrb yrbṣwn*

Jdg 5:24c.

*3.3.61 Single dependent verbal clause lines of three constituents*

There are fewer 3-constituent dependent verbal clause lines than 2 constituent examples. Nonfinite clauses (3.3.62-3.3.63) are outnumbered by finite clauses (3.3.64-3.3.66).

A conspectus of 3.3.62-3.3.66 follows. The constellations involved are ##17 (1 clause-3 constituents-3 units), 18 (1 clause-3 constituents-4 units), and 19 (1 clause-3 constituents-5 units).

*Constellation conspectus*

| | *total* | *#17* | *#18* | *#19* |
|---|---|---|---|---|
| 3.3.62 | 8 | 8 | ø | ø |
| 3.3.63 | 3 | 1 | 1 | 1 |
| 3.3.64 | 9 | 6 | 3 | ø |
| 3.3.65 | 2 | 1 | 1 | ø |
| 3.3.66 | 4 | 4 | ø | ø |
| *Total* | *26* | *20* | *5* | *1* |

*Nominal phrase structure conspectus*

| | | *1st con np* | | *2nd con np* | | *3rd con np* | |
|---|---|---|---|---|---|---|---|
| | *total* | *1°* | *2°* | *1°* | *2°* | *1°* | *2°* |
| 3.3.62 | 8 | 8 | ø | 8 | ø | 8 | ø |
| 3.3.63 | 3 | 3 | ø | 1 | 2 | 1 | 2 |
| 3.3.64 | 9 | 9 | ø | 1 | 1 | 5 | 2 |
| 3.3.65 | 2 | 2 | ø | ø | ø | 1 | 1 |
| 3.3.66 | 4 | ø | ø | 4 | ø | 4 | ø |
| *Total* | *26* | *22* | *ø* | *14* | *3* | *19* | *6* |

*Total np 64 (55 1°/9 2°)*

### *3.3.62 Single dependent verbal clause lines of three constituents. Nonfinite clauses, infinitives*

Number of lines: 8.
Constellation #17:8.

1st con np 1°:8.
2nd con np 1°:8.
3rd con np 1°:8.

Zph 3:8f *lšpk* $^{c}$*lyhm z*$^{c}$*my*

Zph 3:20e; Ps 78:17b, 18b, 19c; 106:23c, 26b, 27a.

### *3.3.63 Single dependent verbal clause lines of three constituents. Nonfinite clauses, participial relative clauses*

Number of lines: 3.
Constellation #17:1/#18:1/#19:1.
1st con np 1°:3.
2nd con np 1°:1/2°:2.
3rd con np 1°:1/2°:2.

2 S 1:24b *hmlbškm šny* $^{c}$*m-*$^{c}$*dnym*

2 S 1:24c; Zph 1:9c.

### *3.3.64 Single dependent verbal clause lines of three constituents. Finite clauses, relative clauses*

Number of lines: 9.
Constellation #17:6/#18:3.
1st con np 1°:9.
2nd con np 1°:1/2°:1.
3rd con np 1°:5/2°:2.

Ps 106:38c $^{\supset}$*šr zbḥw l*$^{c}$*ṣby-kn*$^{c}$*n*

Num 24:3c; Dt 32:38a; 33:8d; Zph 2:3c, 8c; 3:11b; Ps 78:5c; 107:2b.

### *3.3.65 Single dependent verbal clause lines of three constituents. Finite clauses, nominal relative clauses*

Number of lines: 2.
Constellation #17:1/#18:1.
1st con np 1°:2.
3rd con np 1°:1/2°:1.

Ps 106:2a *my ymll gbwrwt-yhwh*

Ps 78:3b.

### *3.3.66 Single dependent verbal clause lines of three constituents. Finite clauses, temporal and concessive clauses*

Number of lines: 4.
Constellation #17:4.
2nd con np 1°:4.
3rd con np 1°:4.

Gen 49:10c *ᶜd ky-ybᵓ šy lh*

Jdg 5:7d; Ps 78:43a; 106:34b.

### *3.3.67 Single verbless clause lines of three constituents*

In verbless clauses of 3 constituents, the predicate has 2 constituents. Discontinuity occurs sometimes. A conspectus of 3.3.68 follows. The overall constellations involved are ##17 (1 clause-3 constituents-3 units), 18 (1 clause-3 constituents-4 units), and 19 (1 clause-3 constituents-5 units).

*Constellation conspectus*

| | *total* | *#17* | *#18* | *#19* |
|---|---|---|---|---|
| 3.3.68 | 13 | 8 | 3 | 2 |

*Nominal phrase structure conspectus*

| | | *1st con np* | | *2nd con np* | | *3rd con np* | |
|---|---|---|---|---|---|---|---|
| | | *1°* | *2°* | *1°* | *2°* | *1°* | *2°* |
| 3.3.68 | 13 | 10 | 3 | 12 | 1 | 10 | 3 |

*Total np 39 (32 1°/7 2°)*

### *3.3.68 Single verbless clause lines of three constituents. Predicate of two constituents*

Number of lines: 13.
Constellation #17:8/#18:3/#19:2.
1st con np 1°:10/2°:3.
2nd con np 1°:12/2°:1
3rd con np 1°:10/2°:3

*Word order: SPred²*

Zph 2:10a *zᵓt lhm tḥt-gᵓwnm*

Dt 32:34; Jdg 5:15a, 31b; 2 S 1:21d; Zph 3:3a.

*Word order: Pred²S*

Dt 33:24b *brwk mbnym ᵓšr*

Jdg 5:15d, 16c.

*Word order: PredSPred*

Gen 49:12a *ḥklyly ᶜynym myyn*

Gen 49:12b; Zph 2:11a; Ps 78:30b.

### *3.4 Other predicated lines*

The remaining types of predicated lines are not well enough represented in our corpus for us to characterize their word order. Nominal phrases are restricted in them to 1° and 2°. The largest categories are double clause lines of two or three constituents, i.e., lines with two clauses, independent or dependent, verbal or verbless, or with one clause and a vocative or focus-marker; these categories are treated in some detail. The larger group, lines with three constituents (3.4.2-3.4.13), is treated before the smaller (3.4.15-3.4.18). Four constituent lines of one, two or three clauses, and 3 constituent lines of three clauses are rare (3.4.19-3.4.22). There are 12 overall constellations treated; a list coordinating them with the paragraphs of this section and providing notes on their distribution follows.

| | | |
|---|---|---|
| #20 | 1 clause-4 constituents-4 units. 20 cases. | 3.4.19. |
| #21 | 1 clause-4 constituents-5 units. 5 cases. | 3.4.19. |
| #22 | 2 clauses-2 constituents-2 units. 23 cases. | 3.4.15-18. |
| #23 | 2 clauses-2 constituents-3 units. 2 cases. | 3.4.18. |
| #26 | 2 clauses-3 constituents-3 units. 92 cases. | 3.4.12-13. |
| #27 | 2 clauses-3 constituents-4 units. 19 cases. | 3.4.2-4, 6, 8-9, 12. |
| #28 | 2 clauses-3 constituents-5 units. 2 cases. | 3.4.9-10. |
| #29 | 2 clauses-4 constituents-4 units. 17 cases. | 3.4.20. |
| #30 | 2 clauses-4 constituents-5 units. 3 cases. | 3.4.20. |
| #31 | 3 clauses-3 constituents-3 units. 4 cases. | 3.4.21. |
| #32 | 3 clauses-3 constituents-4 units. 2 cases. | 3.4.21. |
| #34 | 3 clauses-4 constituents-4 units. 1 case. | 3.4.22. |

The distribution of nominal phrase structures in these 190 lines among the major groups of constellations is as follows.

| | *1st con np* | | *2nd con np* | | *3rd con np* | | *4th con np* | |
|---|---|---|---|---|---|---|---|---|
| *constellations* | *1°* | *2°* | *1°* | *2°* | *1°* | *2°* | *1°* | *2°* |
| ## 20-21 | 9 | ∅ | 21 | ∅ | 20 | 1 | 20 | 4 |
| ## 22-23 | 3 | ∅ | 5 | 2 | --- | --- | --- | --- |
| ## 26-28 | 41 | 3 | 64 | 5 | 61 | 15 | --- | --- |
| ## 29-30 | 13 | 1 | 14 | ∅ | 12 | 2 | 15 | ∅ |
| ## 31-32 | ∅ | ∅ | 2 | ∅ | 1 | 2 | --- | --- |
| # 34 | 1 | ∅ | 1 | ∅ | ∅ | ∅ | 1 | ∅ |

The totals for the major structures follow.

| *constellations* | *1°* | *2°* | *Total* |
|---|---|---|---|
| ## 20-21 | 70 | 5 | 75 |
| ## 22-23 | 8 | 2 | 10 |
| ## 26-28 | 166 | 23 | 189 |
| ## 29-30 | 54 | 3 | 57 |
| ## 31-32 | 3 | 2 | 5 |
| # 34 | 3 | ∅ | 3 |
| *Total* | *304* | *35* | *339* |

### *3.4.1 Double clause lines of three constituents*

Slightly more than a twelfth of the lines in the corpus contain two clauses and three constituents. Of these, half are made up of two coordinate independent verbal clauses (3.4.2); coordinate subordinate verbal clauses are rare (3.4.11); and no line contains coordinate verbless clauses. There are six categories of clauses: independent and quotational clauses, verbal and verbless subordinate clauses, vocatives and focus-markers. All but the first type occur under independent verbal clauses (3.4.3-3.4.7); fewer under independent verbless clauses (3.4.8-3.4.10); and only quotations and vocatives are themselves embedded under subordinate verbal clauses (3.4.12-3.4.13). The non-independent clauses are generally bound to follow the independent or higher non-independent clauses, except for (a) focus-markers and conditional clauses which are always line initial, (b) vocatives, which are positionally free, and the positions of which are noted, and (c) the nominal clause in Hab 3:7a, in which the verb introducing the clause appears after the verb of the clause.

A conspectus of 3.4.2-3.4.13 follows. The patterns involved are ## 26 (2 clauses-3 constituents-3 units), 27 (2 clauses-3 constituents-4 units), and 28 (2 clauses-3 constituents-5 units).

*Constellation conspectus*

| | *total* | *#26* | *#27* | *#28* |
|---|---|---|---|---|
| 3.4.2 | 47 | 44 | 3 | ∅ |
| 3.4.3 | 5 | 4 | 1 | ∅ |
| 3.4.4 | 12 | 8 | 4 | ∅ |
| 3.4.5 | 3 | 3 | ∅ | ∅ |
| 3.4.6 | 20 | 14 | 6 | ∅ |
| 3.4.7 | 1 | 1 | ∅ | ∅ |
| 3.4.8 | 11 | 9 | 2 | ∅ |
| 3.4.9 | 4 | 2 | 1 | 1 |
| 3.4.10 | 5 | 4 | ∅ | 1 |
| 3.4.11 | 1 | 1 | ∅ | ∅ |
| 3.4.12 | 3 | 1 | 2 | ∅ |
| 3.4.13 | 2 | 2 | ∅ | ∅ |
| *Total* | *114* | *93* | *19* | *2* |

*Nominal phrase structure conspectus*

| | | *1st con np* | | *2nd con np* | | *3rd con np* | |
|---|---|---|---|---|---|---|---|
| | *total* | *1°* | *2°* | *1°* | *2°* | *1°* | *2°* |
| 3.4.2 | 47 | 6 | ∅ | 18 | 1 | 20 | 2 |
| 3.4.3 | 5 | ∅ | ∅ | 3 | 1 | 5 | ∅ |
| 3.4.4 | 12 | 4 | 1 | 4 | ∅ | 6 | 3 |
| 3.4.5 | 3 | ∅ | ∅ | 3 | ∅ | 3 | ∅ |
| 3.4.6 | 20 | 7 | 1 | 14 | ∅ | 13 | 5 |
| 3.4.7 | 1 | 1 | ∅ | 1 | ∅ | ∅ | ∅ |
| 3.4.8 | 11 | 11 | ∅ | 11 | ∅ | 4 | 2 |
| 3.4.9 | 4 | 3 | 1 | 3 | 1 | 3 | 1 |
| 3.4.10 | 5 | 5 | ∅ | 4 | 1 | 4 | 1 |
| 3.4.11 | 1 | 1 | ∅ | ∅ | ∅ | ∅ | ∅ |
| 3.4.12 | 3 | 2 | ∅ | 1 | 1 | 1 | 1 |
| 3.4.13 | 2 | 1 | ∅ | 2 | ∅ | 2 | ∅ |
| *Total* | *114* | *41* | *3* | *64* | *5* | *61* | *15* |

*Total np 189 (166 1°/23 2°)*

## *3.4.2 Double clause lines of three constituents. Coordinate independent verbal clauses*

Number of lines: 47.
Constellation #26:44/#27:3.

1st con np 1°:6.
2nd con np 1°:18/2°:1.
3rd con np 1°:20/2°:2.

*Coordination without explicit conjunction*

Ex 15:14a *šmᶜw ᶜmym yrgzwn*

Gen 49:4a, 9c; Num 23:7d, 24b; 24:9a; Dt 32:11c; Jdg 5:19a, 27c, 30a; Hab 3:10a; Zph 3:7e; Ps 78:19a; 106:13a.

*Coordination with explicit conjunction*

Zph 1:13c *wbnw btym wlᵓ-yšbw*

Ex 15:17a; Num 23:19c; Dt 32:7c, 7d, 15a, 19a, 39d, 39e; 33:6a; Jdg 5:26e; Hab 3:6a, 6b, 16a; Zph 1:12f; 3:13d; Ps 78:13a, 29a, 34b, 38b, 41a, 53a, 56a, 57a, 59a; 106:9a, 30a; 107:12b, 20a, 25a, 27a, 38a, 42a.

### *3.4.3 Double clause lines of three constituents. Independent verbal clauses with quotational clauses*

Number of lines: 5.
Constellation #26:4/#27:1.
2nd con np 1°:3/2°:1.
3rd con np 1°:5.

Ps 106:1b *hwdw lyhwh ky-ṭwb*

Dt 32:37a; Zph 3:7a; Ps 106:48c; 107:1a.

### *3.4.4 Double clause lines of three constituents. Independent verbal clauses with verbal subordinate clauses*

Number of lines: 12.
Constellation #26:8/#27:4.
1st con np 1°:4/2°:1.
2nd con np 1°:4.
3rd con np 1°:6/2°:3.

Ps 78:38c *whrbh lhšyb ᵓpw*

Dt 32:15c, 18a, 29a, 36c, 39f; Jdg 5:28d; Hab 3:7a; Zph 1:18a; Ps 78:6b, 20d; 106:23a.

### *3.4.5 Double clause lines of three constituents. Independent verbal clauses with verbless subordinate clauses*

Number of lines: 3.
Constellation #26:3.

2nd con np 1°:3.
3rd con np 1°:3.

Dt 32:20b *ʾrʾh mh ʾḥrytm*

Ps 78:35a, 39a.

### *3.4.6 Double clause lines of three constituents. Independent verbal clauses with vocatives*

Number of lines: 20.
Constellation #26:14/#27:6.
1st con np 1°:7/2°:1.
2nd con np 1°:14.
3rd con np 1°:13/2°:5.
Position of vocative 1st:3/2nd:10/3rd:7.

Hab 3:2a *yhwh šmᶜty šmᶜk*

Gen 49:6a, 6b, 9b, 18; Num 23:18b; Dt 32:1b, 43a; 33:7b, 11a, 18b, 26a; Jdg 5:12e, 21c; 2 S 1:24a; Hab 3:2b, 8a; Zph 3:16c; Ps 78:1a; 106:4a.

### *3.4.7 Double clause lines of three constituents. Independent verbal clauses with focus-markers*

Number of lines: 1.
Constellation #26:1.
1st con np 1°:1.
2nd con np 1°:1.

Ps 78:56b *ᶜlywn wᶜdwtyw lʾ-šmrw*

### *3.4.8 Double clause lines of three constituents. Independent verbless clauses with verbal subordinate clauses*

Number of lines: 11.
Constellation #26:9/#27:2.
1st con np 1°:11.
2nd con np 1°:11.
3rd con np 1°:4/2°:2.

Zph 3:8d *ky-mšpṭy lʾsp gwym*

Gen 49:27a; Ex 15:2c; Num 23:19a, 22a; 24:8a; Dt 32:6c, 6d; Jdg 5:14d; Zph 3:19a; Ps 78:65b.

### *3.4.9 Double clause lines of three constituents. Independent verbless clauses with vocatives*

Number of lines: 4.
Constellation #26:2/#27:1/#28:1.
1st con np 1°:3/2°:1.
2nd con np 1°:3/2°:1.
3rd con np 1°:3/2°:1.
Position of vocative 1st:2/3rd:2.

Num 24:5a *mh-ṭbw ᵓhlyk yᶜqb*

2 S 1:21a, 21b; Zph 2:5b.

### *3.4.10 Double clause lines of three constituents. Independent verbless clauses with focus-markers*

Number of lines: 5.
Constellation #26:4/#28:1.
1st con np 1°:5.
2nd con np 1°:4/2°:1.
3rd con np 1°:4/2°:1.

Dt 32:4a *hṣwr tmym pᶜlw*

Gen 49:20a; Dt 32:20d, 39b; Zph 3:1.

### *3.4.11 Double clause lines of three constituents. Coordinate subordinate verbal clauses*

Number of lines: 1.
Constellation #26:1.
1st con np 1°:1.

Ps 78:3a *ᵓšr šmᶜnw wndᶜm*

### *3.4.12 Double clause lines of three constituents. Subordinate verbal clauses with quotational clauses*

Number of lines: 3.
Constellation #26:1/#27:2.
1st con np 1°:2.
2nd con np 1°:1/2°:1.
3rd con np 1°:1/2°:1.

Dt 33:9a *hᵓmr lᵓbyw-wlᵓmw lᵓ-rᵓyty*

Dt 32:27c, 27d.

### *3.4.13 Double clause lines of three constituents. Subordinate verbal clauses with vocatives*

Number of lines: 2.
Constellation #26:2.
1st con np 1°:1.
2nd con np 1°:2.
3rd con np 1°:2.
Position of vocative 1st:1/3rd:1.

Ex 15:16c *ᶜd-yᶜbr ᶜmk yhwh*

Jdg 5:4a.

### *3.4.14 Double clause lines of two constituents*

The rarest of the major line types, two constituent double clause lines display a slightly smaller range of variation than their three constituent counterparts. Coordinate independent verbal clause lines occur (3.4.15), but coordinate subordinate clause lines do not. Only three varieties of non-independent clauses combine with independent verbal clauses (3.4.16-3.4.18); none combines with independent verbless clauses. Many of the lines in the following paragraphs are the result of gapping across lines contained in the preceding ones.

A conspectus of 3.4.15-20 follows. The patterns involved are ##22 (2 clauses-2 constituents-2 units) and 23 (2 clauses-2 constituents-3 units).

*Constellation conspectus*

| | *total* | *#22* | *#23* |
|---|---|---|---|
| 3.4.15 | 14 | 14 | ∅ |
| 3.4.16 | 2 | 2 | ∅ |
| 3.4.17 | 1 | 1 | ∅ |
| 3.4.18 | 8 | 6 | 2 |
| *Total* | *25* | *23* | *2* |

*Nominal phrase structure conspectus*

| | | *1st con np* | | *2nd con np* | |
|---|---|---|---|---|---|
| | *total* | *1°* | *2°* | *1°* | *2°* |
| 3.4.15 | 14 | 1 | ∅ | ∅ | ∅ |
| 3.4.16 | 2 | ∅ | ∅ | ∅ | ∅ |
| 3.4.17 | 1 | ∅ | ∅ | ∅ | ∅ |
| 3.4.18 | 8 | 2 | ∅ | 5 | 2 |
| *Total* | *25* | *3* | *∅* | *5* | *2* |

*Total np 10 (8 1°/2 2°)*

### *3.4.15 Double clause lines of two constituents. Coordinate independent verbal clauses*

Number of lines: 14.
Constellation #22:14.
1st con np 1°:1.

*Coordination without explicit conjunction*

Ps 106:6b *h$^{c}$wynw hrš$^{c}$nw*

Ex 15:9b; Dt 32:10c; Jdg 5:12b, 27b; Hab 3:14b, 14c.

*Coordination with explicit coordination*

Gen 49:23a *wymrrhw wyrbhw*

Dt 32:38c; Zph 2:10b; 3:14c; Ps 78:45b; 107:30a, 39a.

### *3.4.16 Double clause lines of two constituents. Independent verbal clauses with quotational clauses*

Number of lines: 2.
Constellation #22:2.

Dt 33:27d *wy$^{\supset}$mr hšmd*

Dt 32:26a.

### *3.4.17 Double clause lines of two constituents. Independent verbal clauses with subordinate verbal clauses*

Number of lines: 1.
Constellation #22:1.

Ps 78:34a *$^{\supset}$m-hrgm wdršwhw*

### *3.4.18 Double clause lines of two constituents. Independent verbal clauses with vocatives*

Number of lines: 8.
Constellation #22:6/#23:2.
1st con np 1°:2.
2nd con np 1°:5/2°:2.

Jdg 5:3a *šm$^{c}$w mlkym*

Dt 33:18c; Jdg 5:3b, 12d; Zph 3:14a, 14b, 16b; Ps 106:47a.

### *3.4.19 Single clause lines of four constituents*

Number of lines: 25.
Constellation #20:20/#21:5.
1st con np 1°:9.
2nd con np 1°:21.
3rd con np 1°:20/2°:1.
4th con np 1°:20/2°:4.

Hab 3:10d *rwm ydyhw nś˒ šmš*

Gen 49:17a; Dt 32:5a; 33:4a, 12c; Jdg 5:9b, 13a, 29b; Hab 3:13c; Zph 2:11c, 13c, 14e; 3:6d, 11d, 18a, 18b; Ps 78:17a, 24a, 25b, 27a, 28; 106:7a, 46; 107:6a, 13a.

### *3.4.20 Double clause lines of four constituents*

Number of lines: 20.
Constellation #29:17/#30:3.
1st con np 1°:13/2°:1.
2nd con np 1°:14.
3rd con np 1°:12/2°:2.
4th con np 1°:15.

2 S 1:26b *yhwntn n˓mt ly m˒d*

Ex 15:6a, 6b, 11a, 11b, 17b, 17c; Num 23:7c, 23d; Dt 32:40b; Jdg 5:17b, 28c, 31a; 2 S 1:19a, 26a; Zph 1:6b; 2:12; Ps 78:21a, 45a; 107:5.

### *3.4.21 Triple clause lines of three constituents*

Number of lines: 6.
Constellation #31:4/#32:2.
2nd con np 1°:2.
3rd con np 1°:1/2°:2.

Num 23:18a *qwm blq wšm˓*

Gen 49:2a; Dt 32:1a, 15b; Jdg 5:12a; Zph 2:1.

### *3.4.22 Triple clause lines of four constituents*

Number of lines: 1.
Constellation #34:1.
1st con np 1°:1.
2nd con np 1°:1.
4th con np 1°:1.

Gen 49:8a *yhwdh ˒th ywdwk ˒ḥyk*

### *3.5 Nominal lines*

In the 90% of the corpus's lines dealt with in 3.3 and 3.4, the highest node realized as a constituent was a verbal node or the remnant of a higher clause analyzed as a clause predicator. In the 10% remaining, the highest node represented in the line is nominal. The majority of these lines are dependent on verbal clauses in other lines; a small group are dependent on verbless clauses; and a smaller group are independent of other clauses. A phrase-clause line contains a noun and a clause dependent on it, and may have either two or three constituents (3.5.1-3.5.2). A phrase line contains only nominal elements and may have one or two or rarely three constituents (3.5.3-3.5.5). Three constituent phrase-clause lines (3.5.1) are twice as common as their two constituent counterparts (3.5.2): all these together are half as numerous as 2 constituent phrase lines (3.5.4), which always have a prepositional phrase as the second constituent. The 1 constituent phrase line is by far the best exemplified line type discussed here (3.5.5).

The category of independent phrase lines (there are no independent phrase-clause lines) is a mixed one: most lines in it are vocatives and focus-markers on the discourse level. Thus the triple vocative in Jdg 5:10, which is not bound to either what follows or precedes it, is treated here, as are the discourse level focus-markings like woe (*hwy*) cries, happiness (*ʾšry*) pronunciamentoes, and oracle titles (*nʾm*). The traditional treatment of *hwy* as an independent particle is somewhat vague: here, *hwy* is treated as in construction with a following nominal phrase or as a focus-marker with a following clause; the only example of the first is Zph 2:5a (3.5.5) and of the second, Zph 3:1 (3.4.10). A few independent phrase lines are not formally similar to the three categories named, but also function as discourse level focus-markers.

Dependent phrase-clause and phrase lines are often appositives to phrases in the clauses on which the lines depend. In Ps 78:8abc, both 8b and 8c are in apposition to *kʾbwtm*: the first is a 1 constituent phrase line and the second a phrase-clause line in which the appositive governs an asyndetic relative clause. Sometimes nominal lines are items in a catalog, as in the Testaments of Jacob and Moses over Joseph, or are otherwise directly dependent on the verb of the main clause. Nominal lines associated with verbless clauses are further extensions of the predicate, or qualify the predication relation.

There are a dozen constellations attested in this group of lines. A list of them follows, with indications of their locations within the corpus.

| | | | |
|---|---|---|---|
| #1. | ∅ clause-1 constituent-2 units. | 17 cases. | 3.5.5 |
| #2. | ∅ clause-1 constituent-3 units. | 65 cases. | 3.5.5 |
| #3. | ∅ clause-1 constituent-4 units. | 16 cases. | 3.5.5 |

| | | | |
|---|---|---|---|
| #4. ∅ clause-2 constituents-2 units. | 13 cases. | 3.5.4 |
| #5. ∅ clause-2 constituents-3 units. | 21 cases. | 3.5.4 |
| #6. ∅ clause-2 constituents-4 units. | 5 cases. | 3.5.4 |
| #8. ∅ clause-3 constituents-3 units. | 1 case. | 3.5.3 |
| #9. ∅ clause-3 constituents-4 units. | 1 case. | 3.5.3 |
| #13. 1 clause-2 constituents-2 units. | 3 cases. | 3.5.2 |
| #14. 1 clause-2 constituents-3 units. | 8 cases. | 3.5.2 |
| #15. 1 clause-2 constituents-4 units. | 2 cases. | 3.5.2 |
| #17. 1 clause-3 constituents-3 units. | 6 cases. | 3.5.1 |
| #18. 1 clause-3 constituents-4 units. | 2 cases. | 3.5.1 |

The distribution of nominal phrase shapes in the major constellation groupings follows.

| | | *1st con np* | | | | *2nd con np* | | *3rd con np* | |
|---|---|---|---|---|---|---|---|---|---|
| *constellations* | *total* | *1°* | *2°* | *3°* | *4°* | *1°* | *2°* | *1°* | *2°* |
| ##1-3 | 98 | ∅ | 17 | 65 | 16 | --- | --- | --- | --- |
| ##4-6 | 39 | 20 | 19 | ∅ | ∅ | 28 | 11 | --- | --- |
| ##8-9 | 2 | 2 | ∅ | ∅ | ∅ | 1 | 1 | 2 | ∅ |
| ##13-15 | 13 | 3 | 10 | ∅ | ∅ | 6 | 2 | --- | --- |
| ##17-18 | 10 | 6 | 2 | ∅ | ∅ | 4 | ∅ | 6 | ∅ |
| *Total* | *162* | *31* | *48* | *65* | *16* | *39* | *14* | *8* | *∅* |

There are 78 1° nominal phrases, 62 2°, 65 3°, and 16 4°, a total of 221 nominal phrases.

### *3.5.1 Three constituent phrase-clause lines*

Number of lines: 8.
Constellation #17:6/#18:2.
1st con np 1°:6/2°:2.
2nd con np 1°:4.
3rd con np 1°:6.

Gen 49:25d *brkt-thwm rbṣt tḥt*

Dt 32:37b; 33:13d, 29c; Ps 78:4d, 8c, 60b, 68b.

### *3.5.2 Two constituent phrase-clause lines*

Number of lines: 13.
Constellation #13:3/#14:8/#15:2.
1st con np 1°:3/2°:10.
2nd con np 1°:6/2°:2.

Ex 15:2d *ʾlhy-ʾby wʾrmmnhw*

Gen 49:25a, 25b; Num 23:19b; 24:5b; Dt 33:29a; Hab 3:8e; Zph 1:8c; 3:8c, 14d, 20b; Ps 78:39b; 107:34b.

### *3.5.3 Three constituent phrase lines*

Number of lines: 2.
Constellation #8:1/#9:1.
1st con np 1°:2.
2nd con np 1°:1/2°:1.
3rd con np 1°:2.

Zph 2:15d *ʾny wʾpsy ʿwd*

Zph 3:10a.

### *3.5.4 Two constituent phrase lines*

Number of lines: 39.
Constellation #4:13/#5:21/#6:5.
1st con np 1°:20/2°:19.
2nd con np 1°:28/2°:11.

*Dependent on verbal clauses*

Zph 1:3d *whmkšlwt ʾt-hršʿym*

Gen 49:25c; Num 24:6b, 6d; Dt 32:2c, 2d, 25d; 33:2e, 13c, 21e; Jdg 5:2a, 8d, 11c, 19c, 23e; Hab 3:6e; Zph 1:4d, 9b; 2:9g; 3:19e; Ps 106:22a, 22b, 31b; 107:8b, 17a, 23a, 23b, 24b.

*Dependent on verbless clauses*

Gen 49:22b *bn-prt ʿly-ʿyn*

Gen 49:22c; Dt 32:34b; Ps 106:48b.

*Independent*

Zph 1:10c *qwl-ṣʿqh mšʿr-hdgym*

Jdg 5:10b, 10c; Zph 1:10d, 10e; 2:5a; Ps 106:3b.

### *3.5.5 One constituent phrase lines*

Number of lines: 98.
Constellation #1:17/#2:65/#3:16.

2° np: #17.
3° np: #65.
4° np: #16.

*Dependent on verbal clauses/2°*

Zph 1:2b *mᶜl-pny-hᵓdmh*

Gen 49:15b; Dt 32:25c; 2 S 1:22a, 22b; Zph 1:3c, 18d; 3:20d; Ps 78:71c.

*Dependent on verbal clauses/3°*

Ex 15:4a *mrkbt-prᶜh-wḥylw*

Gen 49:24c, 25e, 26b, 26c, 26e; Num 24:4c; Dt 32:5b, 6b, 8d, 10b, 14b, 14c, 14d, 24d, 42c, 42d; 33:5b, 5c, 14a, 14b, 15a, 15b, 16a, 16b, 16d, 19d, 28c; Jdg 5:5b, 5c, 24b; Zph 1:4b, 18b; 2:2d, 2f, 3b, 3g, 5c, 8b, 10c, 11d, 14b; 3:8g, 12b, 20d; Ps 78:4b, 4c, 8b, 49b, 49c; 106:20b, 38b; 107:10a, 10b, 39b.

*Dependent on verbal clauses/4°*

Jdg 5:6a *bymy-šmgr-bn-ᶜnt*

Gen 49:24d, 26a; Ex 15:11c; Num 24:17f; Dt 32:14a, 24a, 24b; Zph 1:16b; 2:6b, 9f; Ps 78:12b; 107:3b.

*Dependent on verbless clauses/2°*

Gen 49:3a *rᵓwbn-bkry*

Gen 49:3c, 3d, 7b; Dt 33:25b; Zph 2:2a.

*Dependent on verbless clauses/3°*

Dt 32:4c *ᵓl-ᵓmwnh-wᵓyn-ᶜwl*

Zph 1:15b, 15c, 15d, 15e, 16a.

*Dependent on a verbless clause/4°*

Dt 33:29d *mgn-ᶜzrk-wḥrb-gᵓwtk*

*Independent/2°*

Num 24:3b *wnʾm-hgbr*

Zph 1:2c; 2:9c.

*Independent/3°*

Num 24:4a* *wydʿ-dʿt-ʿlywn*

Jdg 5:10a; Zph 2:9b; Ps 106:3a.

*Independent/4°*

Num 24:3a *nʾm-blʿm-bnw-bʿr*

Num 24:4a.

# CHAPTER FOUR
# THE WORD-LEVEL TROPE OF REPETITION

## *4.0 Introduction*

The simplest verbal turn in any rhetoric is verbatim repetition and it is the most patently devious turn since its necessary effect is to advance the text's progress while reserving its diversity. Repetition translates easily and so it has always been recognized as an important feature of Northwest Semitic poetry. For some introductory remarks on the trope of repetition, see 1.5.3.

Because they are at once obvious and elusive, the varieties of repetition in Hebrew poetry have never been studied systematically. A phenomenon sometimes wrongly alleged to be common is the *figura etymologica*, i.e., proximate use of words derived from the same root, but not the same lexeme; it appears rarely in our corpus. The range of types of repetition is limited. The core phenomena, which make up the trope, involve words constant in signification and formal category.

The plainness of repetition gives it the status of being the only trope of Hebrew verse which is instantiated on not only local ground (within the compass of between two and half-a-dozen continuous lines) and on the total ground of the text, but also on intermediate territory of small extension but without continuity. (Line-internal repetition, as in Dt 32:31a, 32a, 32b, 39b; Dt 33:17b; Ps 106:7c, 31b, 48b, is not considered here.) Non-local repetition operates over small sections of discourse which are not entirely continuous or which have peculiar sorts of continuity. Most examples of repetition do involve contiguous lines, in the form referred to here as simple; and in most of these, the repeated words have the same form and grammatical function. If either of these features is lacking, the repetition is buried by the discontinuity in the texture of the discourse; we group below with buried repetition some cases of the *figura etymologica*.

## *4.1 Simple repetition*

Identity of morphological profile and grammatical function mark most examples of repetition in Hebrew poetry, both nominal and verbal. The chief variable factor is the continuity of the position of the constituent which contains the repeated word or phrase. The figure of *repetitio*, in which the repetitions are positioned at the start of the units in which they are found, is the dominant type among the cases in which the position is continuous. There are, however, some cases of continuity in the second and third constituent positions. If the constituent positions of the repetitions are different, the commonest strategy positions the repeated element late in the first line and early in the next. In the case of nominal constituents, the extent of coincidence between the repeated element and the constituent varies. Most often, the repeated words are identical, but occasionally there is variation in inflection. We take as identical but variously inflected, nomina that differ only in number, state or suffixation (but not definiteness); and verbs that differ in person and affixation.

*4.1.1 Nomina with continuity in constituent position*

The figure of *repetitio* is the commonest configuration for the repetition of nominal elements in the same constituent positions across lines. The repeated elements are often coextensive with the constituent. Common as well as proper nouns may be the repeated terms.

Ex 15:6a *ymynk* yhwh nʾdry bkḥ
Ex 15:6b *ymynk* yhwh trʿṣ ʾwyb

There are other examples in Gen 49:22ab; Ex 15:3ab; Num 23:20ab; Jdg 5:30cd; Hab 3:2cd, 8ab; Zph 1:5cd, 1:14ab; Ps 78:8bc; and 106:26b 27a. With a frequency that is remarkable in view of their overall rarity in Northwest Semitic poetic discourse, pronouns appear as the repeated elements.

Num 23:10a *my* mnh ʿpr-yʿqb
Num 23:10b *wm* spr ʾtrbʿ-yśrʾl

There are other examples in Ex 15:11ab; Dt 32:6cd, 35ab; 33:17ef; and Jdg 5:3cd.

The repeated elements may only be a portion of the constituents in which they appear.

Dt 33:14a *wmmgd*-tbwʾt-šmš
Dt 33:14b *wmmgd*-grš-yrḥ-m

There are other examples in Gen 49:3cd, 13ab; Num 24:3ab; Dt 33:15b 16a; Jdg 5:5bc, 6ab, 21ab; 2 S 1:22d 23a; and Zph 3:20ab. This kind of repetition is a basic feature of catalog making, and can be extended beyond the usual pitch of two lines, as in Gen 49:25cde 26ab, and in Zph 1:15abcde 16a. The repeated elements show variant inflection rarely, as in Jdg 5:30de.

Repetition is not bound to occur in the first position, even if it is positionally consistent. In later positions, most commonly second position, whole constituents can be repeated.

Ex 15:6a ymynk *yhwh* nʾdry bkḥ
Ex 15:6b ymynk *yhwh* trʿṣ ʾwyb

There is another case in Ex 15:11ab. The repeated elements are also on occasion parts of constituents, as in Ex 15:4bc; Jdg 5:6bc, 8d 9a; Ps 78.1b

2a; and 106:10ab. Variation in inflection characterizes the repeated elements in Ex 15:16cd; and Jdg 5:19ab.

*4.1.2 Nomina with discontinuity in constituent position*

The simplest form of repetition with discontinuity in constituent position is line internal; this ornamentation is outside our ken. Across lines, the commonest disposition arranges the first repeated element late in the first line and the second early in the second. The repeated elements are sometimes whole constituents.

Jdg 5:23d ky-lʾ-bʾw *lʿzrt-yhwh*
Jdg 5:23e *lʿzrt-yhwh* bgbwrym

There are other cases in Gen 49:10cd; Num 24:18ab; Zph 3:5bc; Ps 106:38ab; and 107:9ab. Rarely this scheme extends beyond two lines, as in Zph 3:20abc. Sometimes, only parts of constituents are repeated.

2 S 1:21c ky-šm ngʿl *mgn*-gbwrym
2 S 1:21d *mgn*-šʾwl bly-mšyḥ bšmn

There are other examples in Jdg 5:11bc; and Hab 3:6de, and 13ab.

The opposite disposition is also attested: the first token of repetition occurs early, most often in first position, in the first line, and the second, later in the second line. Generally, whole constituents are involved.

Dt 32:39d *ʾny* ʾmyt wʾḥyh
Dt 32:39e mḥṣty *wʾny* ʾrpʾ

There are other cases in Jdg 5:21ab; 2 S 1:26ab; Hab 3:2ab; and Zph 1:5ab. It may also be the case that only a portion of a constituent is repeated, as in Num 24:7ab (cf. 24:6d), and Jdg 5:30de (bis). The inflection may vary, as in 2 S 1:26de.

*4.1.3 Verbs with continuity in constituent position*

As in the case of simple nominal repetition, simple verbal repetition is most often based on *repetitio*: the repeated term appears in first position in the lines; all examples are limited to two lines.

Zph 1:3a *ʾsp* ʾdm-wbhmh
Zph 1:3b *ʾsp* ʿwp-hšmym

There are further examples in Ex 15:16cd; Num 23:7cd; 24:18ab; Dt 33:26bc; Jdg 5:7ab, 7cd, 12ab, 13ab, 28cd; and Zph 2:3de. The inflection of the forms involved may vary, as in Dt 32:15ab.

In a few cases, the continuity is in the second constituent position.

Jdg 5:20a mn-šmym *nlḥmw* hkwkbym
Jdg 5:20b mmslwtm *nlḥmw* ʿm-sysrʾ

Other cases, all drawn from Deborah's Song, include Jdg 5:4de, 12ab, and 27cd. Not only are all the instances drawn from a single text; further they are uniformly distributed in it.

[Start] } 12 lines
4de
} 25 lines
12ab
} 29 lines
20ab
} 26 lines
27cd
} 14 lines
[Finish]

The average of the intervals within the poem is 26 lines; the average of the starting and finishing intervals is half that number, 13.

*4.1.4 Verbs with discontinuity in constituent position*

The dominant pattern of repetition which is discontinuous in constituent position, noted above for nomina, is less clearly basic here. Sometimes the repeated constituent appears late in the first line and early in the second.

Gen 49:2a hqbṣw *wšmʿw* bny-yʿqb
Gen 49:2b *wšmʿw* ʾl-yśrʾl-ʾbykm

For further cases, see Jdg 5:19ab, and 22bc. Variation in inflection is attested in Ps 78:67b 68a.

The reverse pattern, early repetition followed by late, is also exemplified, in Jdg 5:27bc. The predominance of examples from Judges 5 here, and the manner in which they are regularly distributed throughout the poem, along lines entirely distinct from those noted in 4.1.3, suggest that the phenomena need to be separated as we have separated them.

*4.1.5 Cooccurrence and interlocking of simple repetition*

Repetition begets repetition. Instances of repetition cooccurrence are frequent in the examples discussed above. Two cases of nominal repetition occur in Ex 15:6ab, 11ab; Jdg 5:21ab; and Zph 3:20ab. Three occur in Jdg 5:30de. Verbal repetition is noted twice only in Jdg 5:12ab. Nominal and verbal repetition occur together in Ex 15:16cd; Num 24:18ab; and Jdg 5:19ab.

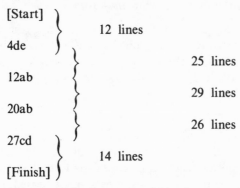

Only one pattern of repetition cooccurrence is canonically recognized in the scholarly literature, one in which the repeated words occur in proximate constituents (with which they are coextensive) in the same order in all the lines involved; all the examples are limited to two lines.

Ex 15:6a *ymynk yhwh* nʾdry bkḥ
Ex 15:6b *ymynk yhwh* trᶜṣ ʾwyb

This pattern is also found in Ex 15:11ab, 16cd; and Jdg 5:12ab, and 30de. This pattern is modified, in that the constituents are not adjacent, in Zph 3:20abc.

Another pattern is chiastic; the constituents with the repeated elements occur in crossed positions in the lines.

Jdg 5:19a bʾw *mlkym nlḥmw*
Jdg 5:19b ʾ*z-nlḥmw mlky*-knᶜn

A variant of this, in which the repetition is in part chiastic and in part not, is attested in Num 24:18ab, and Jdg 5:21ab.

In one case, simple repetitions interlock: the central line of three contains two repeated words, one repeated from the previous line and the other repeated in the next line. This example is involved in more complex figurative patterns discussed below.

Jdg 5:6a *bymy*-šmgr-bn-ᶜnt
Jdg 5:6b *bymy*-yᶜl ḥdlw ʾ*rḥwt*
Jdg 5:6c whlky-ntybwt ylkw ʾ*rḥwt*-ᶜqlqlwt

### *4.2 Buried simple repetition and the* figura etymologica

Repetition in sequent lines, to fulfill our conception of contributing materially to the local texture of poetic discourse, must be upfront, i.e., the repeated elements must be the same in form and function. If they fail these criteria, the repetition is buried. There are relatively few cases of buried simple repetition and most of them belong together in a class which can be accounted for on a non-syntactic basis.

In all examples, the repeated elements are nomina of the same form, differing only in grammatical function. Only rarely are the nomina common nouns, as in Zph 2:7bc (cf. Zph 3:11cd 12a); and Ps 78:29b 30a, and 67b 68a (cf. Ps 106:29b 30ab). Even more rarely does the inflection vary, as in Ps 78:6bc. Most often the nouns involved are proper and the repetition is as much a function of continuity of anaphora as a purely grammatical phenomena.

Zph 1:7a hs mpny-ʾdny-*yhwh*
Zph 1:7b ky-qrwb ywm-*yhwh*
Zph 1:7c ky-hkyn *yhwh* zbḥ

There are other examples in Ex 15:18 21a; Jdg 5:15ab; and Zph 2:2f 3a, and 10c 11a.

Similar are the few examples of the *figura etymologica sensu vero* arrayed over pairs of lines; the derivatives of the roots are of different parts of speech or different verbal stems; these occur in Dt 32:43bc; 2 S 1:24bc; Zph 3:2d 3a; Ps 78:60ab; and 107:2ab, 36ab, and 38b 39a. Note also Jdg 5:17ad, 30acde and Zph 2:8ac. The *figura etymologica* also occurs line-internally; see Ex 15:1b; Dt 33:19b; Jdg 5:2a, 12e; Hab 3:9a; Zph 1:8c, 1:15c; 3:20e; Ps 106:5b, 14a; and 107:7a, and 22a. The alternation of *ʾl* and *ʾlhym* in Ex 15:2cd; and Ps 78:7ab, 19ab, 34b 35a; and of *yh* and *yhwh* in Ps 106:1ab is similar.

## *4.3 Non-local repetition on common ground*

The singularity of repetition as an organizational factor which operates both locally and on small, non-continuous segments of discourse is a complex phenomenon. Non-continuous repetitions with identity of grammatical form and function may be separated by lines which are themselves joined together by repetition; there may be, that is, common territory between the parts of a repetition.

The simplest lay assumed by common ground is found in the repetition split. One line contains two terms available for repetition, one of which is repeated in an adjacent line and the other of which is repeated one line further away. The middle of these three is the common ground for the repetition contained in the first and the third lines.

Jdg 5:3c *ʾnky lyhwh*
Jdg 5:3d *ʾnky* ʾšyrh
Jdg 5:3e ʾzmr *lyhwh*-ʾlhy-yśrʾl

There are other cases in 2 S 1:22cd 23a; and Zph 1:14abc.

The repetition alternation is a similar device.

Zph 2:2c *bṭrm-lʾ-ybwʾ ʿlykm*
Zph 2:2d ḥrwn-*ʾp-yhwh*
Zph 2:2e *bṭrm-lʾ-ybwʾ ʿlykm*
Zph 2:2f ywm-*ʾp-yhwh*

There is another example in Dt 32:21abcd, a simpler case than the example cited, since there is only one repetition token per line.

In a more complex scheme, the repetition cluster, the repetition split mushrooms; the basic structure of the split is preserved but the second occurrence of one member is multiplied by simple repetition, so that the repetition cluster involves a trope within a trope.

line 1 a b
line 2 a
line 3   b
line 4   b

The only example of the cluster occurs at Jdg 5:6bc 7ab; 6ab contains a simple repetition which interlocks with the cluster, and the simple repetitions of 5bc and 7cd frame the whole.

Although this is the most extensive figuration of common-ground repetition, it is not the most complex. In the repetition tangle, three repetition splits coalesce in a single five line passage.

| | |
|---|---|
| Jdg 5:27a | *byn-rglyh krʿ* |
| Jdg 5:27b | *npl* škb |
| Jdg 5:27c | *byn-rglyh krʿ npl* |
| Jdg 5:27d | bʾšr *krʿ* |
| Jdg 5:27e | šm *npl* šdwd |

Taking *byn-rglyh* as *a*, *krʿ* as *b*, and *npl* as *c*, this factors out to the following series of repetition splits.

| | I | II | III |
|---|---|---|---|
| Jdg 5:27a | a | b | |
| Jdg 5:27b | c | c | |
| Jdg 5:27c | a c | b c | b c |
| Jdg 5:27d | | | b |
| Jdg 5:27e | | | c |

Another complex form is the repetition triangle. Like the repetition tangle, the triangle brings together splits; two are involved here, as in the first scheme below. Further, two constituents are involved in one of the repetition factors, yielding the second scheme.

| | | |
|---|---|---|
| line 1 | a | a b |
| line 2 | c | c |
| line 3 | a c | b c |
| line 4 | a | a |
| line 5 | c | c |

There is only one example, Ps 106:37 38abcd.

## *4.4 Non-local repetition without common ground*

There are cases in which repetition of functionally identical elements occurs in lines which are not immediately contiguous, but which do occupy a small segment of the discourse. The distances separating the members in these cases, split repetitions, are no greater than those taken as common ground above. Splits are usually one and no more than two lines. Most other possible cases of the trope are separated by seven or more lines and are not counted; there are only two intermediate cases: Dt 32:26ab 27abc, in which two occurrences of *ʾmr* are separated by three lines; and Hab 3:17bcdef, in which two occurrences of *ʾyn* are separated by three lines.

Simple split repetition encompasses a group of lines, the outer members of which contain a repeated term.

Jdg 5:24a *tbrk mnšym* y^c^l
Jdg 5:24b ^ʾ^št-ḥbr-hqyny
Jdg 5:24c *mnšym* b^ʾ^hl *tbrk*

There are other cases in Dt 32:23b 24abc, 43abcd; 33:2bcde, 12bcd; Jdg 5:23abc; Zph 1:9bc 10a, 18cde; 3:15d 16ab; and Ps 106:7c 8ab 9a, and 41ab 42ab. Compare the unemended text of Ps 78:47ab 48a. A double split repetition occurs in Zph 2:6ab 7a. A triple occurrence of split repetitions is known from Jdg 5:15d 16abc.

Split repetition can serve to pick up a simple repetition, or sometimes to be picked up by a simple repetition, for the isolated occurrence can precede the repetition. There are examples in Num 24:3abc 4a; Jdg 5:13ab 14abc; and Zph 1:2abc 3ab, and 2:3abcde. Pick-up split repetition can be tied to a simple repetition which itself cooccurs with other simple repetitions.

Jdg 5:30a hlʾ-ymṣʾw yḥlqw *šll*
Jdg 5:30b rḥm-rḥmtym lrʾš-gbr
Jdg 5:30c *šll-ṣbᶜym* lsysrʾ
Jdg 5:30d *šll-ṣbᶜym rqmh*
Jdg 5:30e *ṣbᶜ-rqmtym* lṣwʾry-šll

Here, two repeated terms occur in three out of five lines, and a third in two lines.

The trope of pick-up split repetition tropes itself in cases in which the pick-up split repetition picks up not one simple repetition but two.

Dt 33:13c *mmgd*-šmym mᶜl
Dt 33:13d wmthwm rbṣt tḥt
Dt 33:14a *mmgd*-tbwʾt-šmš
Dt 33:14b w*mmgd*-grš-yrḥ-m
Dt 33:15a wmrʾš-hrry-qdm
Dt 33:15b w*mmgd*-gbᶜwt-ᶜwlm
Dt 33:16a w*mmgd*-ʾrṣ-wmlʾh

In complex pick-up split repetition, there can be multiple repetitions on either side of the split; in Zph 1:14abcd 15abcde 16a, a repetition split (in 14abc) is split from a simple repetition (in 15abcde 16a).

### 4.5 *Juxtapositions*

The varieties of grammatical patterning discussed in the sections of this chapter need closer consideration and regrouping. The simplest and commonest form of repetition is by a factor of seven the best attested. It has three crucial features: continuity of form, continuity of grammatical function, and adjacency. Cases of the *figura etymologica* fail the first criterion, and those of buried simple repetition fail the second. Non-local repetition is the rubric under which we gather together lines which apparently do not fulfill the third criterion. The criterion of adjacency can be extended with the concept of common and restricted ground, to include instances of patterning which are, strictly speaking, non-local. There are two orders of repetition types: (I) simple repetition and non-local repetition and (II) buried simple repetition and the *figura etymologica*. The first type, we wish to suggest, constitutes the trope of repetition.

This suggestion leads to a prediction that if repetition were used several times over to give greater coherence to a short run of text, repetitions of Type I would be preferred to those of Type II. This is the case: all juxtapositions involve only Type I repetitions. Simple repetitions can occur in juxtaposed line braces.

Hab 3:2a *yhwh* šmᶜty šmᶜk
Hab 3:2b yrᵓty *yhwh* pᶜlk
Hab 3:2c *bqrb-šnym* ḥy yhw
Hab 3:2d *bqrb-šnym* twdyᶜ

There are other cases in Jdg 5:20ab 21ab; and Zph 1:5abcd. A repetition alternation, discussed in 4.1.5, precedes a case of non-local repetition without common ground, in Zph 2:2cdef 3abcde. A split repetition is split from a pick-up split repetition of three parts in Dt 33:12bcd 13bcd 14ab 15ab 16a. Two simple repetitions precede and follow non-local repetition, in Jdg 5:5bc 6abc 7abcd, as noted above. In Jdg 5:22bc 23abcde 24abc, two simple repetitions (in 22bc and 23de) alternate with two non-local repetitions without common ground, in 23abc and 24abc.

The complete predominance, in cases of juxtaposition, of Type I over II supports our hypothesis regarding the uses of the two types. Only Type I repetitions are noted in Chapter 2, and only they will be dealt with in Chapter 10; only they constitute the trope of repetition.

### *4.6 Summary*

A gross measure of the importance of repetition as a trope in organizing Hebrew poetry can be gotten simply by checking how many lines of the verse use it. A fifth of the lines in the corpus contain repetition tropes. One poem contains a remarkably high incidence of repetition, Judges 5. In complementation, the trope is virtually absent from Psalm 107 and nearly so from Psalm 78.

The poems in which repetition is clearly important are Judges 5, 2 Samuel 1, Zephaniah 1, Exodus 15, and Numbers 23-24. The poems which use it in only a minor way are Zephaniah 3, and Psalms 78 and 107. A remaining group is intermediate; it includes Genesis 49, Habaqquq 3, Deuteronomy 32 and 33, Psalm 106 and Zephaniah 2.

Two points require comment. The first is the inconsistent behavior of Zephaniah's three chapters; this is only surprising if we operate with them as separate entities, as we do for the moment. The three chapters balance together. The erratic distribution of the tropes through the book will be considered in Chapter 10. The second noteworthy fact is that in six of the poems, all or most of the repetitions are simple: Genesis 49, Exodus 15, 2 Samuel 1, Habaqquq 3, Psalm 78, Psalm 107; this is nearly true of Numbers 23-24. In the other texts, there are appreciable numbers of lines using complex forms of the trope. This suggests that in a finer analysis of Hebrew poetry than we are undertaking, the distinction among the types should be closely monitored.

# CHAPTER FIVE

# THE WORD-LEVEL TROPES OF COLORATION: BINOMINATION, COORDINATION AND COMBINATION

## *5.0 Introduction*

Like repetition, the tropes of coloration involve relations among words and phrases; the relations are not those of identity, but rather involve various kinds of difference, diversity in naming, and being, in syntactic and semantic structure. For some introductory remarks, see 1.5.4.

Words and phrases that perform the same grammatical function in associated lines (i.e., in lines that are grammatically of the same order, either verbal or verbless; exhibit the same degree of embedding; are adjacent; and anaphorically continuous) may themselves be related or not; the latter case is rare. The commonality of grammatical function refers to the categories outlined in the description of the constituency constraints (subject, object, prepositional object, focus marker, vocative, etc.); two prepositional objects have the same grammatical function only if they are governed by the same preposition.

Three types of relation concern us: binomination, coordination, and combination. The problems of exploration are those of reference and meaning and the limits, those to be anticipated in the study of written language, more like blinders than shackles. The notion of word-level relation is further restricted to nomina and noun phrases under shared verbal government. Virtually none of the regularities of relation occur in connection with verbs; given that the link between a verb and a clause is of an entirely different order than that of a clause and a noun phrase, this is not surprising. It may be that an approach to verb interrelations which transcends the obvious one of sequence is needed; the effort will not be taken up here. In instances in which phrases exhibit connections similar to relations, but fail to satisfy the criteria outlined here, the relation is buried.

## *5.1 Binomination*

Most of the basic questions involved in considering word relations reflect on meaning; they touch on matters internal to the sphere of language and indeed within that sphere to the lexicon. Binomination is chief among them in calling up extralinguistic considerations, questions of reference. It is not the case that binomination involves the most straightforward varieties of names, since the binomes of our texts refer to the divine and the divinizable realities of the ancient world, godheads, social leaders, social organizations and their homes, realities which are preeminently themselves (Hjelmslev 1970:135-36). In recognizing this category as it impinges on grammar, we do not mean to suggest that there necessarily existed a cultus of its particular members at any particular time, but only that cities, tribes, and important people were the sorts of things with which numina could be associated in the ancient world.

To use a name correctly, the user must be prepared to gloss it with an identifying description; but there are few functionally accurate descriptions of a divinizable reality, because theological language seeks to avoid controlling the reality it names as much as possible. Claiming that Ilimilku was the chief literary scribe of Ugarit around 1250 involves a much fuller description than the claims that God is God, Yahweh is God or God is Yahweh, do. If a personal name like Ilimilku serves to make possible reference to a person without coming to any agreement on a description of her or him, as Searle (1970:162-74) contends, how much more does the name of a divinizable reality serve to avoid description, and to force definite descriptions themselves toward use as names. English Christian usage of *the Lord* provides a convenient example; there is little to suggest that this has any descriptive force at all. Definite descriptions of divinizable entities generally have no greater information content, no closer connection with the properties of the thing described, than proper names do; in some cases, it may be impossible to distinguish the two. Given that we know nothing of Moabite laws of succession, can we determine whether Balaq was called "the child of Sippor" because Sippor was his biological father or because supposed descent from Sippor was responsible for his royal status?

Happily the vocabulary of divinizable realities has attracted enough attention that we can deal with these problems on an *ad hoc* basis in setting forth the data preliminary to a future evaluation of the relevant problems of reference. Five types of binomination are distinguished: divine (referring to high gods), numinous (referring to minor gods), personal, social, and geographical; divine and social binomes are the commonest.

### *5.1.1 Divine binomination*

Although we retain here the classification of names and definite descriptions argued for above, an interesting question as to its force is raised by the data. There are two major criteria for distinguishing names of God from definite descriptions of God and we retain, in correspondence with them, the customary terminology, divine names and divine epithets. The proper names of God cannot be inflected and they cannot be used in the indefinite: they are *yhwh* 'Yahweh,' (*ᵓl-*)*ᶜlywn* '(El-)Elyon,' *ᶜwlm* 'Olam,' and (*ᵓl*)*-šdy* '(El)-Shadday.' It is common to add to this list *ᵓl* 'God, god'; *ᵓlwh* 'God, god'; and *ᵓlhym* 'God, god, gods,' recognizing these words as both proper names *and* definite descriptions. Given that they fail to satisfy either criterion for the former, we reject this addition. The restricted list is to be preferred because it refers to the most basic grammatical distinctions between a definite description and a proper name, a differentiation hard enough to keep hold of in transcendental realms. This restriction entails that all divine binomes in our corpus contain no more than one name, a fact which cannot be explained adequately in a framework in which divine names and epithets are treated as roughly homogeneous categories. Having done no more than note this inadequacy and the reasons behind it, we may present the cases of divine binomination in the corpus.

In two cases, the plain prose order, divine name followed by an epithet, is found.

| | | |
|---|---|---|
| Ex 15:17bc | *yhwh-ʾdny* | Yahweh, my lord |
| Hab 3:18ab | *yhwh-ʾlhy-yšʿy* | Yahweh, the god of my salvation |

In some cases, the opposite order is found.

| | | |
|---|---|---|
| Gen 49:25ab | *ʾl-ʾbyk-ʾl-šdy* | the god of your father, El-Shadday |
| Num 23:8ab | *ʾl-yhwh* | the god, Yahweh |
| Num 24:4aa* | *ʾl-ʿlywn* | the god, Elyon |
| Dt 32:30cd | *ṣwrm-yhwh* | their rock, Yahweh |
| Dt 33:27ab | *ʾlhy-qdm-ʿwlm* | the eternal god, Olam |
| Ps 78:35ab | *ʾlhym-ʾl-ʿlywn* | the god, El-Elyon |
| Ps 107:11ab | *ʾl-ʿlywn* | the god, Elyon |

In six cases, epithets appear as both terms of the binome.

| | | |
|---|---|---|
| Dt 32:15cd | *ʾlwh-ṣwr-yšʿtw* | the god, the rock of its salvation |
| Dt 32:18ab | *ṣwr-ʾl* | the rock, the god |
| Dt 32:37ab | *ʾlhymw-ṣwr* | their god, the rock |
| Hab 3:3ab | *ʾlwh-qdwš* | the god, the holy one |
| Ps 78:22ab | *ʾlhym-yšwʿtw* | the god, its salvation |
| Ps 78:41ab | *ʾl-qdwš-yśrʾl* | the god, the holy one of Israel |
| Ps 78:59ab | *ʾlhym-mʾd* | the god, the almighty |

### *5.1.2 Numinous binomination*

References to minor deities, embodiments of numinous forces, are rare in the Hebrew Bible; and most of them treat the divine council en masse. Like Ugaritic minor deities, Yahweh's messengers and aides de camp, when they are named, are named in pairs. In some instances these pairs function conjointly, although it is impossible to say whether as one or two beings; plural agreement is hardly direct evidence of the manner in which the deities were conceived. Some examples of these numina are *ṭwb-wḥsd* 'Goodness-and-Kindness,' in Ps 23:6ab; *hwd-whdr* 'Honor-and-Majesty' and *ᶜz-wtpᵓrt* 'Strength-and-Glory,' in Ps 96:6. The most spectacular case is a coalescence in Ps 85:11-12 of *ḥsd-wᵓmt* 'Kindness-and-Truth,' and *ṣdq-wšlwm* 'Honesty-and-Peace' into the quadruple *ḥsd-wᵓmt-ṣdq-wšlwm*. The earthly and heavenly pairs first come together and then each pair strains out of its sphere of influence so that a daemonic rainbow is created. The monster of Kindness-and-Truth-and-Honesty-and-Peace is the most complex figuration of minor deities.

In the cases of numinous binomination in our corpus, we are hard pressed to determine the nature of the gods involved.

In Hab 3:5ab and Ps 78:48ab, we have *dbr-wršp* 'Pestilence-and-Firebolt,' the latter well-known as a Levantine deity. Despite our poor knowledge of ancient meteorology, it may be that we can recognize in Ps 78:26ab a binome *qdym-wtymn* 'Sirocco-and-Khamsin.' The geographical complexities involved in wind names are hinted at in the deceptive translation: an easterly wind by Arabic etymology and in Arab usage, the Sirocco is in Europe a southerly wind. From what perspective a poet living in Palestine would name the wind of the northern Arabian Shield or the Sinai is a mystery, but it would not be surprising to find an etymologically incoherent binome like Eastern-and-Southern. Neither is it inconceivable that the binome is to be read as a name for a non-quadrant direction, like sou'easter. Since the wind in question in the manna stories is generally recognized as having been European, i.e., northerly and westerly, the problem is irresolvable. The great heavenly numina of Hab 3:10d 11a present a simpler case, *šmš-wyrḥ* 'sun and moon.'

### *5.1.3 Personal binomination*

The naming and titling of public persons are inextricably bound together, in much the same way as the personal and the divinely endowed royal persons are in the English tradition of the King's Two Bodies, brought to bear on the problems of ancient royal ideology by Mendenhall (1973:32-66). Unlike Cromwell's parliament, we do not have to pull apart what resists separation and may fall back on intuitive distinctions between proper names and titles.

In five cases, the proper name precedes the title, which consists of a construct phrase. The proper name may appear first because it is shorter or because it is structurally simpler; either explanation comports well with the remaining case.

| | | |
|---|---|---|
| Gen 49:26de | *ywsp-nzyr-ᵓḥyw* | Joseph, Nazir of his "Brothers" |
| Num 23:7ab | *blq-mlk-mwᵓb* | Balaq, King of Moab |

| | | |
|---|---|---|
| Num 23:18ab | *blq-bnw-ṣpr* | Balaq, Sippor's child |
| Dt 33:16cd | *ywsp-nzyr-ʾḥyw* | Joseph, Nazir of his "Brothers" |
| Jdg 5:12de | *brq-bn-ʾbynʿm* | Baraq, Abinoam's child |

In the case of 2 S 1:26ab, in which the title precedes the proper name, the title's force can be overlooked easily: *ʾḥy-yhwntn* 'my "Brother," Jonathan.' The relationship between David and Jonathan warrants a technical reading of the term *ʾḥ* 'brother,' in view both of their covenanting and of David's later protection of Jonathan's son.

### *5.1.4 Social organization binomination*

The flexibility of the names of groups of people is a shadow of the groups' multifariousness: the referents of such names vary over time, through space and with regard to any outgroup involved in the discourse. Without historical and social information of subtlety and depth, such distinctions are easily lost.

The classic example of social organization binomination is the name of Yahweh's people, double as the eponymous father's name is double, Israel-Jacob. (The case of Gen 49:24cd is ambiguous: either patriarch or social organization could be meant; we assume the latter here.) Occurring 15 times in the corpus, the name provides an opportunity to check on the fixity of the order of the terms in binomes. In the eight cases in which the terms are governed directly by prepositions (Gen 49:7cd; Num 23:21ab, 23ab, 23cd; 24:17cd; Dt 33:10ab; Ps 78:5ab, 21bc), and in the two cases in which they are governed indirectly by prepositions (Gen 49:24cd; Ps 78:71bc), and in those in which they are governed by verbs, directly (Num 23:7cd) and indirectly (Num 23:10ab), and in which they are used as vocatives (Num 24:5ab), the order is the one recognized as canonical in the scholarly literature: *yʿqb-yśrʾl.* In the two instances in which the terms are used as sentential subjects, the order is the opposite: these are Num 24:18c 19a and Dt 33:28ab. This order, *yśrʾl-yʿqb(-ʾl)* is, however, the one that the prose would lead one to expect: Jacob is the commoner name for the patriarch, while Israel the more frequent designation of the social group. The deviant word order in one case may be the result of the preservation of the full name, Jacob-El. If it is not and if we assume that *yśrʾl-yʿqb* is the order for the two terms whenever they appear in subject position, two arguments could be put forth: a) the prose frequency indicates that the unmarked order should be *yśrʾl-yʿqb* and that order appears in poetic usage just in case the terms are sentential subjects; otherwise, it is reversed; or b) the prose usage itself is reversed in poetry in non-subject positions, and the subject use requires the special marking produced by "reverting" to "prose" order. To choose between these contentions we would need a clearer idea than we have of how much information is conveyed by the text about grammatical functions. A related binome, *(qhlt)-yʿqb-yšrwn* '(the congregation of) Jacob-Yeshurun' occurs in Dt 33:4b 5a.

Other cases of organization binomes push inquiry back to the frontiers of historical ignorance. In Dt 33:17ef, we may have the binome *ʾprym-mnšh* 'Ephraim-Manasseh.' The existence of a social entity composed of Ephraim, and Manasseh or at least the Cisjordanian half of Manasseh, is well known, but the actuality of the existence of the tribe of Joseph has never been clear. A fortiori, there is no clear answer to the question, was Joseph a functional entity at the time of the composition of Deuteronomy 33 or was Ephraim-Manasseh just a term of convenience?

A similar question poses itself apropos of Zph 2:9de in which *mwʾb* 'Moab,' and *bny-ʿmwn* 'the Ammonites' are mentioned. Moab and the Ammonites are far from and foreign to the homeland of our verse. The possibilities of political alliance and resultant, if temporary, merger, or plain confusion are complicated by the asymmetry in the naming of the south Levantine Iron Age nations. We have Israel, Judah, Edom, Moab, and the Ammonites; four simple names and one invariant covenantal designation.

### *5.1.5 Geographical binomination*

The last example cited above, Zph 2:9de, raises the pentapolis problem in mentioning *sdm-wʿmrh* 'Sodom-and-Gomorrah.' Are the five Cities of the Plain a single unit? Zephaniah's sense is plain. Both Sodom and Gomorrah suffered the desolation brought about by some severe crisis in the course of the demise of the Sea they bordered on; but so did the three other cities. Does the phrase *sdm-wʿmrh* designate the two cities separately, or conjointly, or all five cities and the land around and between them? What we know of volcanic and subvolcanic activity suggests that the last is the most likely answer. The binome is also used in Dt 32:32ab.

This solution may serve to clarify the enigma of the Philistine pentapolis posed by 2 S 1:20ab, which refers to *gt-ʾšqlwn* 'Gath-Ashqelon'; and Zph 2:4ab, which mentions *ʿzh-ʾšqlwn* 'Gaza-Ashqelon.' The bipartite titles refer to the whole geopolitical organization known as Philistia. The alternance in the titles themselves is probably conditioned historically.

The styling of these two pentapolises, distinguished among the geopolitical entities of the region by being located entirely on plains, by two-city titles is a reflex of Israelite recognition of variant political organization. What is striking about it is that it is shared between a government reasonably assumed to be indigenous to the Dead Sea region and one known to be foreign, on the coast.

There are too many cases in which our knowledge of ancient toponomy is too slight to permit any judgment of the relationship between place names. The hoary modern tradition that explains the dual ending of Heb *mṣrym* as referring to Upper and Lower Egypt suggests that the Israelites knew something of the whole of the country's structure; yet the tradition is not entirely plausible and one might wonder whether *śdh-ṣᶜn* and *mṣrym* function as a binome in Ps 78:43ab. Similarly the relationship between *ᵓrm* and *hrry qdm* in Num 23:7ab is obscure. The complexity of the orology of the northern Arabian Shield makes the relation of *hr prᵓn* and *tymn* in Hab 3:3ab equally dark.

### *5.2 Coordination*

In pairs of associated lines in our corpus two constituents of a single coordinate nominal phrase may appear in the same grammatical slot; presumably the absence of the phenomenon among triplets is an accident of the corpus. Since the data involved are few, the finer distinctions of pair types are best presented in conjunction with the cases at hand. There are a poulter's dozen of examples.

#### *5.2.1 Simple coordination*

There are few couples in Israelite story, the basic resources of which are geared to presenting the crowd and its lone leaders. Two of the few couples do appear as such in our texts. One includes *yhwntn-wšᵓwl*, the flower of the Saulide dynasty, father and son, spoken of by the dynasty's destroyer in 2 S 1:22cd. The second couple is the team of brothers that later Israelite tradition credited with the creation of its religious institution, *mšh-wᵓhrn*, Moses and Aaron, mentioned in Ps 106:16ab. Under this heading, we may also list the paired tribes *zbwln-wyśśkr*, of Dt 33:18bc; and the paired cult objects, Urim and Thummim, offered to Levi in Dt 33:8bc, *tmyk-wᵓryk*.

#### *5.2.2 Merismatic coordination*

Simple noun phrases are used *per merismum* to designate not merely the two extremes of a range but the whole of it. The phrase 'heaven and earth,' *hšmym-whᵓrṣ*, thus refers to the whole of creation in Dt 32:1ab and Hab 3:3cd. Brothers and sons mark off the whole generation of ego and the one after (which is contrasted to the generation before ego, which merits special mention) in Dt 33:9bc, *ᵓḥyw-wbnw* 'his sibs and children.' The personnel of civil life are comprehended by the merismus of high hereditary and elected officials in Zph 3:3ab, *śryh-wšpṭyh* 'its princes and magistrates.'

Prepositional noun phrases show similar diversity. Thus from morning to evening means all day; the activities described in Gen 49:27bc are opposed in the poem to hunting, which is a nighttime task, with the phrase *bbqr-lᶜrb* 'from morning to evening.' In the streets and inside the rooms marks off the whole of a city's structure in Dt 32:25ab, *mḥwṣ-wḥdrym* 'in the street and from rooms.' It need not be supposed that the bereaving sword hesitates on the threshold.

### *5.2.3 Emblematic coordination*

Two nouns which together suggest a class of phenomena without circumscribing it in any particular sense make up an emblem; the distinction between merismus and emblem is not always clear. We present three cases. The class of weaponry is signalled by arrow and sword in Dt 32:42ab, *ḥṣy-wḥrby* 'my arrows and my sword.' The emblem of food is bread and flesh in Ps 78:20de, *lḥm-wšʾr* 'bread and meat.' The class of domestic animals finds its emblem in what we might call an anti-merismus of small and large cattle, which are the middlemost terms of the class's size range, as well as the major terms of its economic import: larger animals, asses, horses and camels; and smaller ones, chiefly fowl and domesticated animals, are of marginal significance in the economy. The phrase, in Hab 3:17ef, is *ṣʾn-wbqr* 'small and large livestock.'

### *5.2.4 Numerical coordination*

The phenomenon of numerical climax may properly be a variety of pairing, although the sort of coordination underlying it is not obvious. Neither simple nor disjunctive, it may be closer to the latter, as in the rendering 'one, not to speak of two.' The advantage of classifying numerical climax as a kind of coordination is negative: for example, *ʾḥd* 'one' and *šnym* 'two' are clearly not synonymous and are entirely unlike the varieties of combination to be outlined below. In the corpus, two cases occur, both in a single verse, Dt 32:30ab: *ʾḥd-šnym* 'one, not to speak of two' and *ʾlp-rbbh* 'a thousand/company, not to speak of a myriad/battalion.'

## *5.3 Combination*

The elements of noun phrases bound by means more intimate than coordination can be distributed over pairs and triplets of associated lines. These means, construction and appositional and adjectival modification, are canonically regarded as constituting inviolable relations. No grammatical element, save members of the emphatic particle series, can separate two nomina in construction (NcN), a nomen from an adjective (NadjN), or a nomen from an appositive nomen (NappN). All the more clearly, nothing can divide a construct chain from a modifying nomen ([NcN]mN). All these grammatical relations are broken up in poetic usage, and the elements of the phrases appear over short stretches of discourse. In most cases, the usual markings of the relation are obliterated in the process of distribution: the phonological marking of the construct relation is generally lost, and definiteness and more importantly suffixation markings, which are ordinarily limited to unitary occurrences in a noun phrase, are often copied onto all the members of one that has been split up. (In the pages below, no special note of a few further definiteness problems is taken.)

### *5.3.1 Construct combination*

Most examples of construct combination are fairly straightforward, given the principle sketched above. The first order of complexity derives from word repetition: generally construct combination is a streamlining device but occasionally simple repetition overlaps with it. The number of elements in the construct chain is variable. The final variable is the order in which the elements of the chain are disposed. Most of the cases to be noted here present the simplest profile: a 2 element construct chain distributed over two lines without repetition. Examples in which construct combination is found with the same constituent as repetition and coordination are cited below; in these, the tropes interlock.

### *5.3.2 Construct combination without repetition. Two member construct chains*

This category is, as noted above, the best exemplified, comprehending most of the cases of construct combination. The two elements can appear in either of two orders. To streamline discussion we here introduce a simple formalism in which the posited "prose" order is represented on one side of an arrow and the attested poetic order on the other; the solidus marks the line break. The two possible orders are shown thus:

NcN
1c2 → 1/2
1c2 → 2/1

We will further simplify the formalism by omitting the top line of the description henceforth, given that only nomina are under discussion.

The variety of cases of the scheme 1c2 → 1/2 permits scrutiny of the treatment of the elements of a construct chain used in a combination. Working from the base of the consonantal text, we can set up a hierarchy of the degrees of adjustment away from the construct relation toward independent status. In some cases, there has been no adjustment: in the consonantal text, the first member of the construct chain is marked as being in the construct state. The perfect example of simple construct combination would have to show such marking; the elements of the chain would, further, have to be linearly non-contiguous, to insure against misdivision of lines, and the text would have to be free of emendation. There are no such examples; there is one which fails the second and third tests, but makes the essential point, at Jdg 5:22ab, *ᶜqby-swsm* 'heels of horses.'

In a substantial number of cases, the first member of the posited construct chain is not consonantally marked for state and insofar as the unvarnished example is of evidentiary value, these instances are of similar note.

| | | |
|---|---|---|
| Gen 49:10ab | *šbṭ-mḥqq* | the commander's staff |
| Gen 49:22bc | *ᶜyn-šwr* | the spring of Shur |
| Ex 15:17bc | *mkwn-mqdš* | sanctuary site |
| Num 24:4aa* | *ᵓmry-dᶜt* | the words of knowledge |
| Num 24:17cd | *kwkb-šbṭ* | 'star' of a tribe, tribal leader |
| Dt 32:23ab | *rᶜwt-ḥṣy* | the evils of my arrows |
| Dt 32:25ab | *ḥrb-ᵓymh* | the sword of terror |
| Dt 33:26bc | *ᶜz-gᵓwtw* | the strength of his majesty |
| Zph 2:3de | *ṣdq-ᶜnwh* | the rightness of humility |
| Ps 78:5ab | *ᶜdwt-twrh* | the witness of instruction |
| Ps 78:21bc | *ᵓš-ᵓp* | an angry fire |
| Ps 78:33ab | *hbl-bhlh* | a vapor of dismay |
| Ps 78:40ab | *mdbr-yšymwn* | the steppe of Jeshimon |
| Ps 106:14ab | *mdbr-yšymwn* | the steppe of Jeshimon |
| Ps 107:4ab | *mdbr-yšymwn* | the steppe of Jeshimon |
| Ps 107:11ab | *ᵓmry-ᶜṣt* | the words of counsel |
| Ps 107:25ab | *rwḥ-sᶜrh* | the wind of a storm |

It would be wrong to value too highly the testimony of these cases, since it is clear that often enough the members of the construct chain are adjusted to their independent existence. In some cases, the first member of the chain appears in the absolute state.

| | | |
|---|---|---|
| Ex 15:11ab | *ᵓly-qdš* | the holy gods |
| Num 24:6ab | *nḥly-gnt* | enclosured date-palms |
| Dt 33:10cd | *qṭwrt-klyl* | the smoke of a burnt offering |
| 2 S 1:22ab | *ḥlly-gbwrym* | wounded warriors |
| Hab 3:4ab | *nght-mdlw* | the radiance of his lightning |
| Zph 3:17cd | *śmḥt-ᵓhbtw* | the joy of his love |
| Ps 78:16ab | *nwzly-mym* | streams of water |

Even more frequent are the cases in which both terms of the chain are symmetrically inflected in the text.

| | | |
|---|---|---|
| Gen 49:6ab | *sd-qhlm* | the council of their congregation |
| Dt 33:7de | *ydy-ṣryw* | his enemies' hands |
| Dt 33:9de | *ᵓmrt-brytk* | the word of your covenant |
| Dt 33:10ab | *mšpṭy-twrtk* | the judgments of your instruction |
| Hab 3:2ab | *šmᶜ-pᶜlk* | report of your activity |
| Hab 3:13ab | *ᶜm-mšyḥk* | the people of your anointed |
| Zph 1:17de | *dm-lḥm-m* | the blood of their guts |
| Zph 3:15ab | *mšpṭy-ᵓybyk* | the judgments of your enemies |
| Ps 78:46ab | *ybwl-ygyᶜm* | the produce of their toil |
| Ps 78:50bc | *npš-ḥytm* | the life of their livestock |
| Ps 78:61ab | *ᶜz-tpᵓrtw* | the fortress of his glory |
| Ps 78:71bc | *ᶜm-nḥltw* | the people of his inherited land |
| Ps 106:5ab | *bḥyry-gwyk* | the chosen of your people |
| Ps 106:43bc | *ᶜṣt-ᶜwnm* | their iniquitous counsel |

Pairs of lines which contain cases of the scheme 1c2 ⟶ 2/1 exemplify some of the diversity just noted; there is a single "unvarnished" case, in which the first term of the construct chain appears in the construct state, in Dt 33:17ef, *ᵓlpy-rbbwt* 'the companies of battalions.' The concrete military rendering of these terms is somewhat misleading, since elsewhere they appear in numerical pairing with their technical senses; the reading of the pair as a construct combination is indicated by the fact that the numbers are in non-climactic sequence, a situation extremely rare in cases of numerical pairing.

Examples in which the first term of the posited underlying chain is consonantally unmarked for state occur also.

| | | |
|---|---|---|
| Gen 49:6cd | *šwr-ᵓyš* | an ox of a man, a warrior |
| Gen 49:15ab | *ᵓrṣ-mnḥh* | the land of rest |
| Num 23:10ab | *ᵓtrbᶜ-ᶜpr* | loose dirt corrals |
| Dt 32:16ab | *twᶜbt-zrym* | the horrors of strange ones |

| | | |
|---|---|---|
| Jdg 5:10bc | *drk-mdwn* | the realm of Madon |
| Jdg 5:28ab | *ʾšnb-hḥlwn* | the window lattice |
| Hab 3:2de | *rgz-šnym* | the upheaval of years |
| Hab 3:11bc | *ngh-ʾwr* | the radiance of light |
| Zph 1:10de | *gbʿwt-hmšnh* | the hills of the Mishneh |
| Ps 78:52ab | *ʿdr-ṣʾn* | a herd of small cattle |
| Ps 107:41ab | *mšpḥwt-ʾbywn* | the clans of the poor |

Some examples show the first term of the chain in the absolute state.

| | | |
|---|---|---|
| Gen 49:4bc | *yʿlt-ʾbyk* | your father's beloved |
| Ex 15:8ab | *nzly-mym* | streams of water |
| Dt 33:26bc | *šḥqy-šmym* | heavenly fine clouds |
| Jdg 5:4de | *ʿby-šmym* | heavenly clouds |
| Hab 3:4ab | *qrny-ʾwr* | beams of light |
| Hab 3:6ab | *gwy-ʾrṣ* | the peoples of the earth |
| Hab 3:12ab | *gwy-ʾrṣ* | the peoples of the earth |
| Zph 1:17de | *glly-ʿpr* | dusty dung |
| Zph 3:4bc | *twrt-qdš* | holy instruction |
| Ps 78:20bc | *nḥly-mym* | arroyos of water |

Sometimes the second term is inflected in anaphora to the first.

| | | |
|---|---|---|
| Gen 49:10ab | *rgly-yhwdh* | Judah's feet |
| Dt 32:9ab | *nḥlt-yhwh* | the heritage of Yahweh |
| Jdg 5:20ab | *mslwt-šmyhm* | their heavenly paths |
| Jdg 5:26cd | *rʾš-sysrʾ* | Sisera's skull |

Otherwise the possessive marking of the chain is extended to both members.

| | | |
|---|---|---|
| Hab 3:3cd | *thlt-hwdw* | praise of his glory |
| Hab 3:8de | *mrkbt-swsyk* | the chariots of your horses |
| Ps 78:36ab | *lšwn-pyhm* | the tongue of their mouths |
| Ps 78:44ab | *nzly-yʾryhm* | the streams of their rivers |
| Ps 78:58ab | *psyly-bmwtm* | the ikons of their high places |

*5.3.3 Construct combination without repetition. Three member construct chains*

In all 2 line combinations with more than two members in our corpus, the head of the underlying construct chain appears as the first element of the chain distributed in the lines. When 3 term chains are broken up, the heavier portion is more often in the second line, in the scheme 1c2c3 ⟶ 1/2c3. In three cases, the first member is consonantally unmarked for state.

| | | |
|---|---|---|
| Gen 49:22bc | *bn-bnwt-ṣᶜdh* | the colt of wild she-asses |
| Dt 33:21ab | *rʾšyt-ḥlqt-mḥqq* | the best of a commander's portion |
| Ps 78:27ab | *šʾr-ᶜwp-knp* | winged bird flesh |

In two others, the first term appears in the absolute state.

| | | |
|---|---|---|
| Dt 33:17cd | *ᶜmy-ʾpsy-ʾrṣ* | the peoples of the ends of the earth |
| Ps 106:16ab | *mḥnt-qdwš-yhwh* | the camp of Yahweh's shrine |

When a 3 term construct chain is broken with the heavier portion in the first line, it is the middle term which appears in the second, in the scheme 1c2c3 ⟶ 1c3/2.

| | | |
|---|---|---|
| Dt 33:21de | *ṣdqt-mšpṭ-yhwh* | the rightness of Yahweh's rule |

### *5.3.4 Construct combination with repetition*

Repetition in a 2 line distribution involves one member of a 3 term construct chain. The first term is the repeated element, in the scheme 1c2c3 ⟶ 1c3/1c2; the second term is inflected anaphorically from the third.

| | | |
|---|---|---|
| Jdg 5:11bc | *ṣdqwt-przn-yhwh* | the victories of Yahweh's peasantry |

### *5.3.5 Construct combination with coordination*

Having noted the remarkable range of coordinate and combinatory phenomena, we should not be astonished to find that the two classes overlap in braces of associated lines in which two construct chains are represented by a single chain and a single noun phrase distributed over the lines. Three schemata are attested in our corpus.

In two of these, the first term of the underlying construct chains is shared. One shows a heavy bottom, yielding the scheme (1c2)w(1c3) ⟶ 2/1c3; in the example, the common first term is unmarked for state.

| | | |
|---|---|---|
| Hab 3:11bc | *brq-ḥṣyk-wbrq-ḥnytk* | the flash of your arrows and the flash of your spear |

(Note also 2 S 1:20ab and Gen 49:24cd.) One example shows an expansion of this scheme: (1c2)w(1c3c4) ⟶ 2/1c3c4,

| | | |
|---|---|---|
| Dt 33:17ab | *qrny-rʾm-wqrny-bkwr-šwr* | the horns of an aurochs and the horns of an ox's firstborn. |

Another case in which the first term is common has a heavy top, i.e., (1c2)w(1c3) ⟶ 1c2/3; the first term is not marked for state.

| | | |
|---|---|---|
| Num 23:9ab | *rʾš-ṣrym-wrʾš-gbʿwt* | rock peaks and hill tops |

In the final attested case, it is the second term of the chains that is shared, i.e., (1c2)w(3c2) ⟶ 1/3c2; the free first term is consonantally unmarked for state.

| | | |
|---|---|---|
| Gen 49:10cd | *šy-ʿmym-wyqht-ʿmym* | the tribute and obedience of peoples |

*5.3.6 Adjectival combination*

Because the relationship between a nomen and its adjectival modifiers is not phonologically or morphologically marked, disruption in word order seems an even more drastic recasting in the case of adjectival modification than of construct relations. Simple noun-adjective modification is nonetheless among the grammatical processes subject to combination. Like the other forms of combination, the relevant types can be classified in terms of the contrast between the posited base order and the surface order. All examples are confined to two lines.

The ordinary word order, in which a noun is followed by the adjective it governs, is much commoner than the reverse. Thus examples of the scheme 1adj2 ⟶ 1/2 are half-a-dozen in number.

| | | |
|---|---|---|
| Gen 49:16ab | *dn-ʾḥd* | a single judgment |
| Dt 32:17bc | *ʾlhym-ḥdšym* | new gods |
| Dt 32:33ab | *yynm-ʾzkr* | their bitter wine |
| Dt 33:4b 5a | *mwršh-mlk* | a royal possessor |
| 2 S 1:20cd | *plštym-ʿrlym* | uncircumcised Philistines |
| Ps 107:33ab | *mdbr-ṣmʾwn* | a thirsty wilderness |

The reverse scheme, i.e., 1adj2 ⟶ 2/1, is uniquely exemplified.

| | | |
|---|---|---|
| Zph 2:4ab | *šmmh-ʿzwbh* | a ravaged wasteland |

### *5.3.7 Appositional combination*

The schemes noted above are applicable here, too. A non-restrictive apposition follows its noun once, according to the scheme 1app2 → 1/2.

| | | |
|---|---|---|
| Ps 78:26ab | *šmym-ᶜzw* | heaven, his stronghold |

Thrice the appositive precedes, in the scheme 1app2 → 2/1.

| | | |
|---|---|---|
| Gen 49:16ab | *yśrᵓl-ᶜmw* | Israel, his people |
| Dt 32:9ab | *yᶜqb-ᶜmw* | Jacob, his people |
| Dt 33:5bc | *yśrᵓl-ᶜm* | Israel, the people |

### *5.3.8 Construct-adjectival/appositional combination*

Just as coordination and construct combination cooccur, so do construct combination and the other kinds of combination, with the same number of terms as construct combination itself. The scheme 1c(2adj3) → 1/2adj3 is exemplified in one case.

| | | |
|---|---|---|
| Zph 1:10de | *yllh-šbr-gdwl* | a sound of great destruction |

In a second case, the scheme is 1c2c(3app4) → 1c4/2c3.

| | | |
|---|---|---|
| Ps 78:67ab | *ᵓhl-šbṭ-ᵓprym-ywsp* | the tent of the tribe of Ephraim-Joseph |

### *5.3.9 Patterns of combinations*

In the preceding paragraphs, the varieties of combination have proliferated to constitute a dense jungle which, it seems, would be impenetrable to the linguistically naive speaker. In fact, as we shall show now briefly, no more than three elements are ever in dislocation from their posited prose order, in conformity with Kiparsky's Rule, and all the types of combination together exhibit no more than a few basic patterns. To offer to view these patterns plain, we shall go from our already simple formalism to an even more reductionistic one: every stretch of elements in the base sequence which remains intact in the poetic one will be lettered and thus the schemes will be seen to fall together into a few patterns. Although most of the time we will be working with single word units, the operative unit in this paragraph is not a discrete or definable unit but one tracked down for the sake of the argument.

The most basic pattern without repetitions is the simple linear one, ab → ab, which includes five schemes.

| *a* | *b* | → | *a* | *b* | |
|---|---|---|---|---|---|
| 1 | c2 | | 1 | /2 | 5.3.2 |
| 1 | c2c3 | | 1 | /2c3 | 5.3.3 |

| *a* | *b* | → | *a* | *b* | |
|---|---|---|---|---|---|
| 1 | adj2 | | 1 | /2 | 5.3.6 |
| 1 | app2 | | 1 | /2 | 5.3.7 |
| 1 | c(2adj3) | | 1 | /2adj3 | 5.3.8 |

The reverse linear pattern ab → ba includes three schemes.

| *a* | *b* | → | *b* | *a* | |
|---|---|---|---|---|---|
| 1 | c2 | | 2 | /1 | 5.3.2 |
| 1 | adj2 | | 2 | /1 | 5.3.6 |
| 1 | app2 | | 2 | /1 | 5.3.7 |

In the remaining pattern without repetition, the first element of the base remains stable and the other two vary, i.e., abc → acb.

| *a* | *b* | *c* → | *a* | *c* | *b* | |
|---|---|---|---|---|---|---|
| 1 | c2 | c3 | 1 | c3 | /2 | 5.3.3 |
| 1 | c2c(3 | app4) | 1 | c4 | /2c3 | 5.3.8 |

Of the four patterns with repetition, three show repetition in the underlying form eliminated in the poetic form. The first maintains linearity, the rest do not.

| *a* | *b* | *a* | *c* → | *a* | *b* | *c* | |
|---|---|---|---|---|---|---|---|
| (1 | c2) | w(1 | c3) | 1 | c2 | /3 | 5.3.5 |

| *a* | *b* | *a* | *c* → | *b* | *a* | *c* | |
|---|---|---|---|---|---|---|---|
| (1 | c2) | w(1 | c3 | 2 | /1 | c3 | 5.3.5 |
| (1 | c2 | w(1 | c3c4) | 2 | /1 | c3c4 | 5.3.5 |

| *a* | *b* | *c* | *b* → | *a* | *c* | *b* | |
|---|---|---|---|---|---|---|---|
| (1 | c2) | w(3 | c2) | 1 | /3 | c2 | 5.3.5 |

In the remaining case, there is no repetition in the base form, but only in surface, poetic form; the pattern shows alternation.

| *a* | *b* | *c* → | *a* | *c* | *a* | *b* | |
|---|---|---|---|---|---|---|---|
| 1 | c2 | c3 | 1 | c3 | /1 | c2 | 5.3.4 |

Of these patterns, one is completely stable, i.e., the base order of the elements is unchanged; five involve one change from the base; and only one involves two changes. Never are more than two elements rearranged. The patterns follow.

| | | | |
|---|---|---|---|
| I | ab | → | ab |
| II | ab | → | ba |
| III | abc | → | acb |
| IV | abac | → | abc |
| V | abac | → | bac |
| VI | abcb | → | acb |
| VII | abc | → | acab |

The stable order requires no comment. The reversal of two elements takes two forms: in a pattern with two elements, II, the reversal is complete. In Pattern III, only two out of three elements are involved in flipping, while the first element remains stationary. Patterns IV, V and VI result from a simple deletion from the base order, with no change in element order. The last pattern involves two changes: flipping of the last two elements (abc ⟶ acb), followed by expansion with a second a element.

## *5.4 Burial*

The boundaries set to our inquiry above are broad but not vast enough to include all the words in any stretch of Hebrew poetic discourse which could be linked together. Two sets of circumstances are required of words and phrases to fit the categories above, one predicated of the lines in which they appear and the other of the words and phrases themselves. Cases which seem to present relations yet fail to meet these criteria seem to have been buried by our survey thus far; we shall exhume at least some of them for a brief postmortem.

The first requirements of relations are that the phrases involved occur over a number of lines which are adjacent, of the same grammatical order (i.e., either verbal or verbless and marked by the same degree of embedding) and anaphorically continuous. Connections which fail these criteria and are nonetheless patently similar to those within the pale do occur; they are not common enough to warrant recasting our descriptive framework, though it is not always obvious that they are of a completely different order than the phenomena subsumed within that framework.

Thus, double pairing over two construct chains occurs within a single line at e.g., Dt 32:14a; it is excluded from our corpus because of the restricted scope; the second pair is an emblem noted above (see 5.2.3 on Hab 3:17ef).

The second set of requirements used in judging word phrase relations refers to the phrases themselves: they must serve the same grammatical function in the clauses in which they occur, and they must be governed by the clause predicators of those clauses. The latter criterion is universally met by candidates for relations. The largest category of buried relations is tied to the second criterion, that they serve the same grammatical function. In the order of things under examination here, the two forms of verbal government, direct and prepositional, have been regarded as independent categories; and prepositions have been regarded as semantically distinct entities. These separations are not entirely clear cut. Some verbs, for example, can govern an object directly or through the *beth essentiae* with little variance in idiom. In Hebrew, further, it is not always possible to distinguish the preposition *ʾt* 'with' from the sign of the direct object *ʾt*; in the Phoenician dialects, the sign of the direct object *is* a preposition. Direct objects with *ʾyt* in Phoenician, that is, are in the "genitive" and those without the sign are in the "accusative." None of the buried relations in our corpus touches directly on these disputed points, yet they serve to show that the boundaries used here are open to question. The "mixing" of prepositions does occur, and connections exist between the objects of different prepositions. Again, our defense of the grammatical criteria used here must be largely methodological: they describe the largest area open to investigation which can be discretely defined.

A good starting point for a survey of connections buried by direct and prepositional object skew is afforded by a brace of lines in which a patent relationship lies alongside a buried connection; we noted above the construct combination in Ps 106:5ab; Ps 106:5c seems to enlarge the structure:

| | |
|---|---|
| Ps 106:5a | *lrʾwt bṭwbt-bḥyryk* |
| Ps 106:5b | *lśmḥ bśmḥt-gwyk* |
| Ps 106:5c | *lhthll ʿm-nḥltk* |

The plainest reading here is *bḥyry-gwy-nḥltk* 'the chosen ones of the people of your inheritance'; yet since the first two terms of the construct chain are indirectly governed by *b* and the last is governed directly by *ʿm*, there is no identity of grammatical function. One way in which the posited chain could be accounted for within the present grammatical framework would assume that *ʿm* governs all these terms of the chain and that the construct marking of *ṭwbt* and *śmḥt* is a product of the gapping of the preposition. The objection to this parsing arises from the construct marking of the two abstract nouns. We have assumed that in the surface form of a relation, a noun may appear in a less marked form (the absolute) than in the underlying form, since the intrinsic markedness of poetic discourse will serve to force the more marked reading. In this case, the reverse assumption, that a noun in the absolute state in the underlying form can appear on the surface in the more marked form, is demanded, and it is unlikely to be correct. The more complex reading of Ps 106:5abc remains possible, but it seems better to retain the simple reading of 5ab and assume that the connection with 5c is buried.

Other cases of burial induced by the direct and prepositional object skew can be listed in accord with the outline used in the first part of this chapter.

| | | |
|---|---|---|
| 5.1.1 | Divine Binomination | Dt 32:3ab |
| 5.2.1 | Simple Coordination | Ps 106:17bc (cf. 18a) |
| 5.2.2 | Merismatic Coordination | Jdg 5:17bc |
| 5.3.1 | Construct Combination | Ps 78:62ab; Ps 106:40ab |
| 5.3.7 | Appositional Combination | Dt 32:36ab |

Examples in which disparate prepositions govern items of what might be judged a relation are less frequent, though somewhat closer to meeting the criteria than those with the prepositional and direct object skew.

| | | |
|---|---|---|
| 5.1.1 | Divine Binomination | Zph 3:2cd |
| 5.1.5 | Geographical Binomination | Dt 33:8de |

Occasionally there are cases of burial with a double explanation. Skew in direct and prepositional object marking combines with a break in verbal government to bury a merismus in Dt 32:42ab.

In the remaining cases of disparate grammatical function, no obvious patterns appear; the scattering is wide and the burial of the connection is more or less complete. The words go together, but they cannot be put together. The structure of the first parts of this chapter will again serve as a framework.

| | | |
|---|---|---|
| 5.1.1 | Divine Binomination | Ps 78:7ab, 19ab, 56ab |
| 5.1.3 | Personal Binomination | Gen 49:2ab |
| 5.2.2 | Merismatic Coordination | Dt 33:13bc, 24bc |

In two instances, adjacent to one another in the text of Zephaniah 3, a buried merismus or emblem covering two lines shares one of them with a true trope. Thus, there is a true merismus in Zph 3:3ab and a buried one in 3bc; and there is a combination in 4bc and a buried merismus in 4ab. In Jdg 5:4cde, a merismus in 4cd seems to be blocked by the interfaces of a construct in 4de. It may be that both relations should be read here and that the sequential nature of the structure compensates for any possible conflict; the conflict in verbal government suggests that the form of description used here is better.

All these cases of burial seem to represent a different order of verbal patterning than that exhibited by the true relations, except perhaps those which differ from them only in the feature of prepositional consistency. It is possible that a scale of deviance from the norm of relation could be set up among these examples, with the cases of variant prepositions at their head as least variant. To do so would, however, press the descriptive vocabulary too far, and demand of it too much precision. Since our categories are makeshift, we must be content with makeshift classifications. The categories of burial, in serving to isolate the remarkable complexity of Jdg 5:4cde, Zph 3:3abc 4abc and Ps 106:5abc, have more than proven their usefulness, despite a makeshift origin.

## *5.5 Summary*

About one-fifth of the corpus uses the tropes of repetition and one-fifth uses the three color tropes, binomination, coordination and combination. The range of usage is smaller in the case of the color tropes than it is with repetition. There is no poem, that is, that uses the color tropes as extensively as Judges 5 uses repetition; and no text that uses them as rarely as Psalm 107 uses repetition. Still, the distribution is broader. Habaqquq 3 and Deuteronomy 33 use the trope most and Zephaniah's chapters and Psalm 106 use them least.

The tropes of Chapters 4 and 5 belong together; repetition, binomination, coordination and combination all involve word level textual turning. The number of lines involved in repetition or coloration or both is about one-third of the whole corpus. (A line is counted once no matter how many times it is troped.)

# CHAPTER SIX
# THE LINE-LEVEL TROPE OF MATCHING

## *6.0 Introduction*

One of the most basic forms of poetic discourse is the list: item after item fills, for example, the catalog of ships in the Second Book of the *Iliad* with units of approximately the same shape. The coherence of passages structured around the list derives from the predictability of the units with which the form is filled. In Hebrew verse, the predictability proper to the list often coincides with the basic integer of the verse, the line. One line of given constituent or unit structure is followed by one or more of identical structure. For some basic features of matching, see 1.5.6.

Matching, the identity of constituent or unit structure, is a device that holds together somewhat over a third of the lines in our corpus. Runs of between two and seven lines are created by the matching of line structure. Lines of every scope are held together in this way. The structures of the lines do not always exhibit the constituents or units in the same order: matches can show variation in the disposition of their components. In the following example, a line with the word order VS is followed by one with the opposite order.

Ps 78:20b *wyzwbw mym*
Ps 78:20c *wnḥlym yšṭpw*

Such alternance in word order is chiasm. If two elements are involved, the phenomenon is simple chiasm. Two lines of three elements can be chiastically arranged with respect to one another in six ways and three lines of three elements could lead to permutations of a complexity beyond facile calculation. Chiasm is constrained in a profound way by the word order demands of the language, but within its granted boundaries, it flourishes.

The difference emphasized throughout our report on Northwest Semitic poetic structure between nomina and verbs makes a difference with regard to matching. Gapping alters the structure of adjacent lines by removing a grammatical element which occurs in both. Sometimes, lines which have undergone gapping match one another except for the gapped constituent; these lines we consider with other matching lines. A gapped verb is generally missing from the second line of a brace of two lines.

Ps 78:33a *wykl bhbl ymyhm*
Ps 78:33b *wšnwtm bbhlh*

The order of constituents in the underlying 3 constituent form of Ps 78:33b is lost and therefore to the six possibilities of matching two 3 constituent lines, we must add the two possibilities in which the verb is gapped. The complexity of matching across more than two lines is such that few significant regularities would be turned up even by the most sophisticated attempts at characterization. All lines which have constituent structures match by them; lines which consist of only one constituent match by unit structure.

### *6.1 Two line matches*

The vast majority of line braces in which the lines have identical structures are two lines in length. The largest subgroup of those are simple verbal sentences with only two constituents. The braces are arranged according to the word order of the first line of the brace. The ranking follows the divisions used above: verb initial before verb medial sentences, etc.; sentences with subjects before those with direct objects, etc., in the series S-O-P-A. The achiastic precede the chiastic matches; chiasm is used here only as a device for sorting the examples and is not centrally tied to our description. It is only considered in connection with independent clause lines.

### *6.1.1 Independent verbal clause lines of two constituents*

Line braces in which two constituent single independent verbal clause lines match one another form the largest category of matches and the only one in which more than a few of the match types are exemplified more than once. In all but one case in which the chiastic match is attested, the achiastic one is also; chiastic matches occur only in the commoner types.

*VS:VS achiastic* 2 S 1:27ab; Hab 3:6cd.

2 S 1:27a *ʾyk-nplw gbwrym*

2 S 1:27b *wyʾbdw kly-mlḥmh*

*VS:SV chiastic* Ps 78:20bc.

*VO:VO achiastic* Gen 49:4bc; Num 23:8ab; Dt 32:7ab, 22cd; Jdg 5:26ed; Zph 1:3ab, 13de; 2:3de, 7e 8a; 3:13ab; Ps 106:35b 36a; 107:26ab.

*VO:OV chiastic* Num 23:24cd; Jdg 5:8ab; Ps 78:7bc; 107:11ab, 16ab.

*VP:VP achiastic* Gen 49:7cd; Num 23:23ab; Dt 33:2cd; 2 S 1:20ab; Zph 1:8ab; Ps 78:22ab; 106:10ab, 39ab; 107:20b 21a, 30b 31a.

*VP:PV chiastic* Ps 78:67ab, 72ab; 107:4ab, 32ab.

*VA:VA achiastic* Num 24:17ab.

*SV:SV achiastic* Dt 32:30cd; Jdg 5:4cd; Zph 2:9hi.

*OV:VO chiastic* Dt 33:11bc.

*PV:PV achiastic* Num 23:9ab; Zph 3:2cd.

*PV:VP chiastic* Ps 107:6b 7a, 13b 14a.

*PS:PS achiastic* Hab 3:8bc.

### *6.1.2 Independent verbal clause lines of three constituents*

The possibilities for chiastic arrangement of three constituents in two matching simple verbal sentence lines are five, if both lines have three constituents in their surface forms. There are six possibilities if account is taken of the chiastic arrangement after verb gapping; and since the second line of the brace can have the same constituent order as the first, with or without verb gapping, eight is the total number of word orders available for the second lines. These are listed below, for a first line with constituents 123.

(a) same order with verb gapping: 23
match: 123
23

(b) simple chiastic order with verb gapping: 32
match: 123
32

(c) same order: 123
match: 123
123

(d) front simple chiastic order: 213
match: 123
213

(e) back simple chiastic order: 132
match: 123
132

(f) back flip chiastic order: 231
match: 123
231

(g) front flip chiastic order: 312
match: 123
312

(h) mirror chiastic order: 321
match: 123
321

In (a) and (c), there is no chiasm. In (b), (d), and (e), there is a single chiastic crossing. In (f) and (g), there are two crossings. There is a triple crossing in (h).

There is a scale of complexity among matches.

| | | |
|---|---|---|
| 0. | no chiasm | (a), (c) |
| I. | simplest chiasm | (b), (d), (e) |

| | | |
|---|---|---|
| II. | intermediate chiasm | (f), (g) |
| III. | most complex chiasm | (h) |

With only forty-two examples in hand, it is hard to attribute significance to the ranking, but it is somewhat revealing.

| | | |
|---|---|---|
| 0. | no chiasm | 18 examples |
| I. | simplest chiasm | 15 examples |
| II. | intermediate chiasm | 9 examples |
| III. | most complex chiasm | ∅ |

The scale suggests that chiasm can be investigated on a larger scale, within the context of the trope of matching, in a way that provides interesting results. In the past students have frequently referred to the phenomenon but made no attempts at precise description. The tools are at hand now and the data plainly reveal an immense diversity of possibilities coupled with spareness of deployment. Why are there no mirror chiasms here, given that most handbook descriptions would lead one to expect nothing else? It would be rash to claim that mirror chiasms do not occur (cf. Jdg 5:25bc, in 6.3.2 and Hab 3:17ef 18a in 6.2.2), but it is likely that they are rare. The explanation will probably be found in connection with further study of Kiparsky's Rule.

*VSO:SVO front simple chiasm* Dt 32:30ab.
Dt 32:30a *ʾykh-yrdp ʾḥd ʾlp*
Dt 32:30b *wšnym ynysw rbbh*
*VSP:VSP same* Num 24:17cd.
*VSP:PVS front flip chiasm* Jdg 5:14bc.
*VSP:SP same with gapping* Zph 1:13ab.
*VSP:SPV back flip chiasm* Dt 33:29ef; 2 S 1:25ab; Zph 2:7ab.
*VSA:AVS front flip chiasm* Dt 33:28ab.
*VSO:SVO front flip chiasm* Hab 3:3cd.
*VPS:VPS same* Dt 32:2ab.
*VOP:OP same with verb gapping* Dt 32:13cd; Ps 107:33ab, 35ab.
*VOP:VOP same* Num 23:21ab.
*VOP:OVP front simple chiasm* Ps 78:5ab.
*VOP:VPO back simple chiasm* Dt 33:26bc; Hab 3:13d 14a; Ps 78:16ab, 26ab; 107:41ab.
*VPO:OP simple chiasm with verb gapping* Ps 78:33ab.
*VPO:OVP front flip chiasm* Dt 32:23ab.
*VPP:PP same with verb gapping* Ps 106:16ab.
*VPP:VPP same* Ps 106:23ab.

*VPP:PVP front simple chiasm* Jdg 5:13b 14a.

*VPA:AP simple chiasm with verb gapping* Ps 78:14ab.

*SVP:SVP same* Ps 78:21bc.

*SVA:SVA same* 2 S 1:22cd.

*PVS:VSP back flip chiasm* Hab 3:16bc.

*PVS:PS same with verb gapping* Dt 32:25ab.

*PVS:SP simple chiasm with verb gapping* Num 23:7ab.

*PVS:VSP back flip chiasm* Hab 3:5ab.

*PVO:PVO same* Gen 49:6cd, 16ab, 27bc; Hab 3:12ab.

*SPV:SP same with verb gapping* Hab 3:3ab; Zph 2:9de.

*SPV:PS simple chiasm with verb gapping* Hab 3:4ab.

*SPV:SVP back simple chiasm* Zph 2:14cd.

*PSV:PS same with verb gapping* Hab 3:11bc.

*SP:VPS simple chiasm with verb gapping* Dt 33:4b 5a.

### *6.1.3 Independent verbless clause lines*

Most matching verbless clause lines have single unit constituents. As in the case of two constituent simple verbal clause lines, the basic structure is simple and its instantiations often have several exemplifications. The chiastic arrangements are all simple. In only one instance is a match formed with two unit constituents; this is the concluding example given here. There is no chiasm in the case of the discontinuous predicate.

*SPred:SPred* Ex 15:3ab; Num 23:21cd, 24:9cd; Dt 33:17ef; Jdg 5:18ab.

Ex 15:3a *yhwh ᵓyš-mlḥmh*

Ex 15:3b *yhwh šmw*

*SPred:PredS* Gen 49:5ab; Dt 32:9ab.

*PredS:PredS* Dt 33:17ab, 27ab.

*PredS:SPred* Jdg 5:14d 15a.

*PredSPred′:PredSPred′* Gen 49:12ab.

### *6.1.4 Double clause lines with vocatives*

Lines which contain two clauses, one a main clause and the other represented by a vocative, are rarely matched. Some examples involve two constituent lines, others three constituent lines; some show verb gapping and some do not.

*VVoc:VVoc* Jdg 5:3ab; Zph 3:14ab.

*VocVO:VVocO* Hab 3:2ab.

*VVocP:VocP* Dt 33:18bc.

*PVVoc:PVVoc* Gen 49:6ab.

*VocPredS:SPredVoc* 2 S 1:21ab.

*SPredPred'Voc:SPredVocPred'* Ex 15:11ab.

### *6.1.5 Double clause lines with verbal coordination*

Braces of lines with two clauses in coordination can be matched.

*VV:VV* Hab 3:14bc.

*SVV:VSV* Dt 32:39de.

*VVO:VVO* Hab 3:6ab.

### *6.1.6 Double clause lines with verbal subordination*

In two cases, two lines with main and subordinate clauses are matched; the main clauses are verbal and verbless; the subordinate clauses are definite relative clauses. The examples are Dt 32:6cd, and 18ab.

### *6.1.7 Dependent verbal clause lines*

Matching among dependent verbal clause lines involves infinitive clauses, finite temporal clauses, exceptive clauses and relative clauses. In the infinitive clauses, there is no variation in word order; the examples are found at Dt 32:8ab; and Ps 106:26b 27a, and 47cd. Finite temporal clauses show gapping of the conjunctions *ʾšr* and *ʿd* in Ps 78:43ab and Gen 49:10cd, respectively. There is a pair of matching exceptive clauses in 2 S 1:20cd.

Relative clauses match on a constituent basis also. The examples in *ʾšr* show gapping of the relative pronoun.

*SVP:VP* Dt 33:8de.

Dt 33:8d *ʾšr nsytw bmsh*

Dt 33:8e *trybhw ʿl-my-mrybh*

*SVP:PV* Ps 107:2b 3a.

*SOV:VO* Dt 32:38ab.

There are some nonfinite examples in 2 S 1:24bc; Zph 1:12de; and 2:15bc.

### *6.1.8 Phrase-clause and phrase lines*

The two varieties of matching that belong under this head are notably different. Phrase-clause lines and two constituent phrase lines are matched by constituents, whereas single constituent phrase lines are matched by units. The disposition and nature of the single constituent phrase line matches may suggest that they are indeed pairs of a kind, but it is not obvious that it is the same kind as constituent matches. Since there is no obvious alternative description of the lines in question, we retain them here.

Only two pairs of phrase-clause lines match, Gen 49:3cd, and 25ab. Two constituent phrase line matches are more common.

Dt 32:2c *kśrᶜm ᶜly-dšʾ*
Dt 32:2d *wkrbybym ᶜly-ᶜśb*

There are other examples in Jdg 5:10bc; Ps 106:22ab; and 107:23ab. Two unit nominal phrases match once, in 2 S 1:22ab; and so do four unit nominal phrases, in Dt 32:24ab. Three unit phrases match more commonly.

Gen 49:26b *brkt-hrry-ᶜd*
Gen 49:26c *tʾwt-gbᶜt-ᶜwlm*

There are other examples in Dt 32:42cd; 33:5bc; Jdg 5:5bc; Ps 78:49bc; and 107:10ab.

## *6.2 Three line matches*

Line braces which include three lines match less often than shorter ones. With one exception, all the types of matches dealt with here are exemplified among the two line matching braces; the exception is the independent noun phrase match. Many of the more complex matches are not represented here. The diversity of chiasms on the two line level makes it certain that our corpus is too small to reveal any regularities in chiasm over a longer run.

### *6.2.1 Independent verbal clause lines of two constituents*

The following examples adumbrate the available diversity of three line matches in general. In the four patterns in which both possible arrangements of the two constituents occur within a line brace, all three possible positions of the line with the minority word order occur.

*VS:VS:VS* Zph 1:11abc.
Zph 1:11a *hylylw yšby-hmktš*
Zph 1:11b *ky-ndmh kl-ᶜm-knᶜn*
Zph 1:11c *nkrtw kl-nṭyly-ksp*
*VS:SV:VS* Jdg 5:22abc.
*VO:OV:OV* Num 24:8cde.
*VP:VP:PV* Zph 1:17abc; Ps 78:57b 58ab, 70ab 71a.
*VP:PV:VP* Dt 32:16ab 17a.
*PV:PV:PV* 2 S 1:23bcd.
*OV:OV:OV* Num 23:19d 20ab.

*6.2.2 Independent verbal clause lines of three constituents*

Complete continuity of constituent structure is uniquely exemplified below. In about half of the remaining cases, all three lines have different structures; the remaining examples are intermediate.

*VSO:VOS:SVO* Num 24:18abc.

Num 24:18a *whyh ᵓdwm yršh*

Num 24:18b *whyh yršh śᶜyr-ᵓybyw*

Num 24:18c *wyśrᵓl ᶜśh ḥyl*

*VSP:SP:SVP* Zph 1:17de 18a.

*VPS:VSP:SPV* Hab 3:17ef 18a.

*VOP:VPO:VOP* Ps 78:1b 2ab.

*VOP:VPO:OP* Hab 3:14d 15ab.

*VPO:OP:VPO* Ps 78:61ab 62a.

*VPO:VPO:VPO* Ps 78:55abc.

*SVO:SVO:VSO* Num 23:10abc.

*PVS:VPS:VSP* Ex 15:8abc.

*SPV:SP:SP* Gen 49:13abc.

*PSV:VSP:SP* Gen 49:9d 10ab.

*OPV:VPO:OP* Dt 33:7e 8bc.

*6.2.3 Independent verbless clause lines*

The few examples of three line matches of verbless sentences show both diversity and uniformity of constituent arrangement. They are Dt 32:35abc and 2 S 1:26cde.

*6.2.4 Dependent verbal clause lines*

A triply matching brace of infinitive clauses is the only example; it is Ps 106:5abc.

*6.2.5 Phrase lines*

There is only one 2 constituent phrase line match that extends over three lines, at Zph 1:10cde. There is a single 1 constituent phrase line match, at Dt 32:14bcd.

*6.3 Four line matches*

Matches extending over four lines of text make up the last well represented class of matches; other, longer forms are ill-attested. The range of scopes involved here is similar to that involved with three line matches, except that no phrase lines are represented.

### *6.3.1 Independent verbal clause lines of two constituents*

Two of the cases cited hère have consistent word orders; the one which does not, given last below, exhibits deviance in a middle position, in the third of four lines.

*VO:VO:VO:VO* Ps 107:36b 37abc.

Ps 107:36b *wykwnnw ᶜyr-mwšb*

Ps 107:37a *wyzrᶜw śdwt*

Ps 107:37b *wyṭᶜw krmym*

Ps 107:37c *wyᶜśw pry-tbwʾh*

*VP:VP:VP:VP* Ps 106:24ab 25ab.

*OV:OV:VO:OV* Dt 33:9bcde.

### *6.3.2 Independent verbal clause lines of three constituents*

The generally conservative handling of word order variation over four line braces is apparent here. In the first example, deviance from the order of the first line is confined to the third line of four; in the next two cases, non-gapped and gapped forms of a single word order alternate. The last example is more complex.

*VOP:VOP:VPO:VOP* Ps 106:14ab 15ab.

Ps 106:14a *wytʾww tʾwh bmdbr*

Ps 106:14b *wynsw ʾl byšymwn*

Ps 106:15a *wytn lhm šʾltm*

Ps 106:15b *wyšlḥ rzwn bnpšm*

*VOP:OP:VOP:OP* Dt 33:10abcd.

*VPO:PO:VPO:PO* Gen 49:11abcd.

*OVP:PVO:OPV:OP* Jdg 5:25bc 26ab.

### *6.3.3 Independent verbless clause lines*

Continuity of the word order subject-predicate is instanced in Jdg 5:30bcde.

## *6.4 Longer matches*

The rarity of matches longer than four lines is even greater than the scarceness of examples collected here would suggest, since two of the cases occur, as it were, back to back and form the core of a single poem. These seven and six line passages in Psalm 78 have the same constituent structure, VPO; the two sections of text are separated by only two lines. Despite their commonality and the fact that they both end with VPO lines, and the first of them begins with a VPO line, the two sections have independent structures. In the first, four VPO lines are separated from each other by OP lines.

| | | |
|---|---|---|
| Ps 78:46a | *wytn lḥsyl ybwlm* | VPO |
| Ps 78:46b | *wygyʿm lʾrbh* | OP |
| Ps 78:47a | *yhrg bbrd gpnm* | VPO |
| Ps 78:47b | *wšqmwtm bḥnml* | OP |
| Ps 78:48a | *wysgr ldbr bʿyrm* | VPO |
| Ps 78:48b | *wmqnyhm lršp-m* | OP |
| Ps 78:49a | *yšlḥ bm ḥrwn-ʾpw* | VPO |

In the second section, each of two 3 line parts contains a VPO line (50a, 51a), a VPO line (50b, 52a) and an OP(V) line (50c, 51b).

| | | |
|---|---|---|
| Ps 78:50a | *ypls ntyb lʾpw* | VOP |
| Ps 78:50b | *lʾ-ḥśk mmwt npšm* | VPO |
| Ps 78:50c | *wḥytm ldbr hsgyr* | OPV |
| Ps 78:51a | *wyk kl-bkwr bmṣrym* | VOP |
| Ps 78:51b | *rʾšyt-ʾwnym bʾhly-ḥm* | OP |
| Ps 78:52a | *wysʿ kṣʾn ʿmw* | VPO |

Dependent clauses alone figure in the five line match in Zph 1:5abcd 6a. The only extended series of verbless clauses includes the seven lines of Dt 32:31ab 32abc 33ab.

There are two passages of matching 1 constituent phrase lines. The first is six lines long and occurs in Dt 33:14ab 15ab 16ab. The second, Zph 1:15bcde 16a, is shorter, but more permanent.

### *6.5 Summary*

About one-third of the lines of the corpus match. There is an even distribution of the tropes over a fairly wide range of poems. One text, 2 Samuel 1, uses much more matching than the other poems; and two of them, Exodus 15 and Zephaniah 3, an erratic pair, use less. Matching is also important in Habaqquq 3, Zephaniah 1, Deuteronomy 33, Genesis 49, and Numbers 23-24, though less so than in David's Lament. Again, we note the raggedness of distribution of the trope over the Zephaniah book; as with repetition, the heaviest troping occurs in the first chapter and the third chapter is least troped.

# CHAPTER SEVEN

# THE LINE-LEVEL TROPE OF GAPPING AND RELATED PHENOMENA

## *7.0 Introduction*

The phenomenon of matching adjacent clauses against one another and deleting from all but either the first or the last some or all of the common elements is well-known in the languages of the world. It is scarcely in itself remarkable that the phenomenon is unknown in Hebrew prose. To ask why it is absent there is to formulate a question which, despite intensive study of syntactic patterns in recent years, historical and comparative linguistics is not prepared to answer; its rareness in contemporary English speech, in contrast to written prose usage, seems comparable. The reason gapping is of interest here is that it is a basic stylistic resource of Hebrew verse. For some introductory remarks on gapping, see 1.5.7.

The erratic recognition of gapping in Northwest Semitic languages has obscured a fundamental distinction in its varieties. Most instances of gapping involve major constituents, frequently the verb, which is usually gapped rightward. Subject gapping is impossible in languages like Hebrew in which finite verb forms are marked for subject categories, except in the case of the relative pronoun, and relatives are gapped in our corpus. The gapping of an independent constituent object of a transitive verb is rare, if it exists.

Particle gapping is the other major variety; it is difficult to describe because our understanding of the particle system is so primitive. The commonest form involves prepositions, although other particles are also involved. The particle gappings are not part of the body of troped lines as such. Particle gapping, that is, has the same relation to the trope of (constituent) gapping as the *figura etymologica* has to the trope of repetition.

## *7.1 Verb gapping*

The strategic use of verb gapping involves rightward gapping over two lines which pairs two underlying 3 constituent lines and results in a brace composed of a 3 constituent line followed by a 2 constituent line. In most cases, the underlying sentences match completely; after gapping, there are two common constituents in each of the lines. In case the common constituents appear in the same order, the lines are achiastic; if a structure like *Vab:ba* (in which *a* and *b* are nominal constituents) is noted, the lines are chiastic. Achiastic braces are more common. It is only in this largest class of verb gappings and in one smaller one that double clause lines occur; the less frequent types show largely simple sentences. Triplets of lines with verb gapping are not common; they are limited to simple sentences and are wholly achiastic. In a few cases, 4 constituent lines are gapped over two lines, paired with 2 constituent lines.

The two examples of leftward gapping, which are both located near the start of the texts they occur in, are the most highly marked instances of gapping behavior. Their disposition at poem openings may reveal the use made of such highly marked structures in overall verse structure.

### *7.1.1 Rightward verb gapping*

The major cluster of two line examples contains those with two matching clauses which are achiastic after gapping.

*VSP:SP* Gen 49:10ab; Zph 1:13ab.

Gen 49:10a *lʾ-yswr šbṭ myhwdh*

Gen 49:10b *wmḥqq mbyn-rglyw*

*VOP:OP* Dt 32:13cd; 33:10ab, 10cd; Zph 1:17de; Ps 78:51ab; 107:35ab.

*VPO:PO* Gen 49:11ab, 11cd.

*VPP:PP* Ps 106:16ab.

*PVS:PS* Dt 32:25ab.

*SPV:SP* Hab 3:3ab, 4ab; Zph 2:9de.

*PSV:PS* Hab 3:11bc.

*OPV:OP* Jdg 5:26ab.

Two line chiastic matching line braces which show a 3:2 constituency configuration are almost as diverse as the achiastic examples.

*VPO:OP* Dt 33:8bc; Hab 3:15ab; Ps 78:33ab, 46ab, 47ab, 48ab, 61ab.

Hab 3:15a *drkt bym swsyk*

Hab 3:15b *ḥmr mym-rbym*

*VPA:AP* Ps 78:14ab.

*PVS:SP* Num 23:7ab.

In only one case, matching is failed: Zph 2:4ab. Dependent verbal clauses show gapping in only two cases, Gen 49:10cd, and Ps 78:43ab.

We have, in classifying these examples, introduced the parameter of chiasm, which does not fall within the bounds of our investigation; even with this additional factor, it is possible at a glance to see that the patterns of gapping are elements of gross ordering in some texts. The most striking case is the run of six lines with chiastic verb gapping in the structure

VPO:OP at Ps 78:46ab 47ab 48ab. It is astonishing to remark that the other instances of the independent clause structure VPO:OP in that poem, Ps 78:33ab and 61ab, are virtually equidistant from this six line stretch: Ps 78:33ab precedes it by 27 lines and Ps 78:61ab follows it by 29 lines. A similar, achiastic structure, VPO:PO, is instantiated twice in sequence, in Gen 49:11abcd (note the achiastic VSP:SP frame in Gen 49:10ab, two lines above), and VOP:PO occurs in Dt 33:10abcd. The propinquous achiastic structures in Hab 3:3ab and Hab 3:4ab (both SPV:SP), and in Zph 2:4ab (SOV:SP) and 9de (SPV:SP) are also noteworthy. In only one case, Dt 33:18bc, does gapping occur in a double clause pair of lines; the non-gapped clause is a vocative.

The examples of verb gapping over two clauses, both with three constituents, show greater complexity of scope.

$V_1OV_2{:}OV_2P$
Dt 32:7c *š*ʾ*l* ʾ*byk wygdk*
Dt 32:7d *zqnyk wy*ʾ*mrw lk*
$V_1SV_1{:}SV_2O$
Dt 32:27c *pn-y*ʾ*mrw ydynw rmh*
Dt 32:27d *wl*ʾ*-yhwh p*ʿ*l kl-z*ʾ*t*

The patterning of the negative in the last example will be discussed further below. In both examples, the verb gapped is the leftmost in the structure, whether the first in a coordinate structure (in Dt 32:7cd) or the highest in a embedding structure (in Dt 32:27cd). Another example in which both lines contain three constituents is Hab 3:13ab; 13b includes a broken construct chain.

Of the last few cases, in which a 4 constituent line is gapped across a 2 constituent line, one is like the last two examples in that gapping takes place over a clause that is not involved in it.

Ps 78:45a *yšlḥ bhm* ʿ*rb wy*ʾ*klm*
Ps 78:45b *wṣprd*ʿ *wtšḥytm*

In the other examples, there is only one pair of clauses involved; these are Gen 49:17ab and Ps 78:27ab.

Rightward verb gapping over three lines results in a diversity of structures. In none of the cases are the constituents in the lines chiastically rearranged.

*SPV:SP:SP* Gen 49:13abc.
*PVVoc:PS:PS* Hab 3:8abc.
*VOP:OP:OP* Ps 107:33ab 34a.

### 7.1.2 *Leftward verb gapping*

There are only two cases of what appears to be leftward verb gapping. Although the lines do not present the structural description of ordinary, rightward gappings, there is no other way to account for their unusual shape than to suppose that leftward gapping has occurred.

Jdg 5:3c *ʾnky lyhwh*
Jdg 5:3d *ʾnky ʾšyrh*

The other example is Dt 33:4b 5a.

### 7.2 *Gapping of other constituents*

Next to verb gapping, the gapping of pronoun suffixes is the best known form of argument gapping. Both possessive and object pronouns are gapped in our corpus. Rightward gapping of possessive suffixes occurs across lines in Hab 3:9ab and 15ab and perhaps Ps 78:2ab; and within lines perhaps in Ex 15:2a; leftward gapping of such suffixes occurs in Dt 32:27ab. Rightward gapping of object suffixes occurs in the unemended text of Dt 32:13ab, and in Ps 107:20ab. (A cognate phenomenon of poetic diction, the omission of suffixes, can be seen in Ex 15:9b; Dt 32:19a; and Ps 78:15b.) Since these arguments are not constituents, however, these gappings are not examples of the trope.

The related process of relative gapping is represented. There are also cases of object gapping; these are difficult and though we cite them we do not regard them as examples of the trope. Since a verb's transitivity is a matter of degree, and not a present or absent feature, as we take it to be here for the sake of argument, it is possible that further cases of object gapping, associated with less obviously transitive verbs, are to be found in the corpus.

### 7.2.1 *Relative pronoun gapping*

The relative is only subject to constituent gapping in case it is used as a nomen, rather than as a temporal conjunction (as in, e.g., Ps 78:43ab). In two cases, the gapped lines match; these are Dt 32:38ab and Dt 33:8de. Some instances of relative gapping show no matching; these are Zph 2:8cd and Ps 78:3ab.

### 7.2.2 *Object gapping*

The eccentricity of independent constituent object gapping (if the phenomenon is to be so-called, rather than left dislocation) is plainest in the fact that it is always leftward. The examples are located close to the incipits of the texts they occur in. This may be sufficient excuse for their apparent oddness. Because there are so few examples, we only note them here and will not consider them in our overall evaluation of the texts' structure.

*SV:SVO*
Jdg 5:4d *gm-šmym nṭpw*
Jdg 5:4e *gm-ᶜbym nṭpw mym*
*PV:POV*
Hab 3:2d *bqrb-šnym twdyᶜ*
Hab 3:2e *brgz rḥm tzkwr*

## *7.3 Particle gapping*

The grammatical status and semantic load of the many particles of Northwest Semitic are the most problematic areas in current grammatical study and near chaos has replaced the irreal rigidity of received opinion. The most difficult subfield of study is poetic usage and progress is hardest there simply because the area is not adequately demarcated. The possibility that here the alphabet itself will need to be relearned leads us to prefix a particularly weighty warning to what follows: here, as nowhere else, is error on the side of omission likely to have occurred. The cases of particle gapping are not examples of the trope; they are noted here in order to direct attention to features they share with other forms of gapping.

### *7.3.1 Preposition gapping*

Despite difficulties in discriminating between prepositional objects the prepositions of which have been gapped out and simple adverbial usages, there are a few cases in which the process is not difficult to track. The examples show rightward gapping, with the exception of Gen 49:16ab and Dt 33:7de; the gapped preposition is shown in brackets below. The monographic prepositions predominate here, as elsewhere in the language.

*preposition b* Dt 33:5bc, 26bc; Hab 3:15ab; Ps 106:16ab.
Hab 3:15a *drkt bym swsyk*
Hab 3:15b *ḥmr [b]mym-rbym*
*preposition k* Gen 49:16ab; Hab 3:4ab.
*preposition m(n)* Dt 33:2cd, 7de, 16ab.

The independent prepositions, though not the denominatives, are also represented.

*preposition ᶜl* Hab 3:8de.

### *7.3.2 Negative gapping*

The rule that every verb must bear the burden of its own negation is rarely contravened by gapping and in our corpus there are no examples of negative gapping. It is possible that Dt 32:6cd should be so analyzed.

### *7.3.3 Gapping of other particles*

Marks of subordinate clauses are among the most regularly used particles in Hebrew. Their scope is limited to one clause in prose, in contrast to the coordinating conjunctions (including not only *w* but also *ky*), the domain and functioning of which is uncertain in prose and elastic in poetry.

In two cases of gapping, the subordinator introduces a temporal clause in *ᶜd*; these are Gen 49:10cd, and Num 23:24cd. A similar use of *ᵓšr* shows gapping in Ps 78:43ab.

The subordinator in Dt 32:27cd marks a negative purpose clause. The behavior of the negative *lᵓ* in Dt 32:27d is bizarre; it must modify *yᵓmrw*, the verb which has been gapped out, and not *yhwh*, since negative compounds are rare in the Semitic languages and negative compounds with proper names are unheard of. Further, if *lᵓ-yhwh* were the subject of the sentence, it would have to be the functional equivalent of *ydynw*, which seems wrong, since non-gods never do anything in Hebrew. The only rubric under which an explanation could be formulated would be conflict of negative scope; the underlying structure would be *wpn lᵓ yᵓmrw* 'in order that they not not say' and the collocation of *pn lᵓ*, which is in fact never attested in Hebrew, is probably impossible. The particle *pn* occurs in clauses below *ᵓl* ('do not do such-and-such, so that not such-and-such'), or above *lᵓ* ('so that not such-and such, and therefore not such-and-such'), but it is difficult to work out what sense it would have in the same clause as another negative. This conflict of scope would lead us at least to expect aberrant behavior, even if it does not provide a full explanation. The subordinator of exception, *ᵓm-lᵓ-(ky)*, is gapped in Dt 32:30cd.

The interrogative particle *h* can be gapped, as in Dt 32:6cd.

## *7.4 Summary*

Since most gapped lines match one another, the incidence of gapping over the corpus roughly corresponds to that of matching. The cases of constituent gapping which do not match are a mixed lot. They include cases in which the gapping is leftward (Jdg 5:3cd); in which the matching fails only because prepositional and unmediated objects do not match (Zph 2:4ab, 8cd); in which four constituent lines gap across to two constituent lines (Gen 49:17ab; Ps 78:27ab, 45ab); and those in which two clauses are involved in the gapping (Dt 32:7cd, 27cd; and Ps 78:45ab, again). All of these are areas which will need special treatment. In the first two groups of cases, it may be that our descriptive apparatus needs refining. In the second two, since we can already take account of the greater complexity of the lines, the definition of matching may need to be expanded to include them.

In most cases, particle gapping occurs in lines which match: such lines often also show constituent gapping. We may be tempted to include particle gapping as part of the trope of gapping. The strongest argument against doing so is the plainest: nowhere else in our description of the fine structure of the verse does particle activity take a central role and it should not do so here. Particle gapping, that is, belongs among phenomena like the *figura etymologica* and buried repetition. Though we are effectively including lines with particle gapping among troped lines (because most of them also match), we are not considering them as troped as such.

Constituent gapping occurs in under a tenth of the lines of the corpus. It is entirely absent from three texts, Exodus 15, 2 Samuel 1, and Zephaniah 3. The fact about the two archaic poems is striking, especially as Exodus 15 uses matching slightly, while there is no poem that uses it more than 2 Samuel 1. Gapping is commonest in Habaqquq 3 and Genesis 49. It is rare in Zephaniah 1, Judges 5, Numbers 23-24, and Psalms 106 and 107. The other poems, Deuteronomy 32 and 33, Psalm 78, and the middle chapter of Zephaniah, are intermediate.

# CHAPTER EIGHT

# THE SUPRALINEAR-LEVEL TROPE OF SYNTACTIC DEPENDENCY

## *8.0 Introduction*

The most unobtrusive and least remarked way of giving coherence to a passage of Hebrew poetic discourse is simple syntactic dependency. One main clause line is tied to lines around it because they consist of phrases or clauses dependent on it, or on its dependents. For some introductory remarks on the supralinear tropes, see 1.5.8.

One-third of the lines in our corpus are involved in syntactic dependency, in passages that range in length from two to two dozen lines. The bulk of these passages begin with the central, main clause, the core, and these passages are said to have an upfront core; less often, the core is postposed, i.e., appears at the end of the passage; and least often, the core occurs within the passage, encased.

There are two basic forms of dependency. One involves markers of quotation; the range over which they are active is probably always discernible in the full context of discourse but the extent to which range indicators penetrate the text itself in identifiable linguistic form is limited. The boundaries of a quotation marker are usually accessible, using the distribution of verb forms as a major criterion. There are, to be sure, some quotations which have no discernible lower limits, and an upper one which can be isolated only with difficulty is characteristic of others; these we point out briefly below, reserving our attention for quotations which can be demarcated clearly.

The second form of dependency involves the lower levels of sentential trees and the classification of these cases is based on the nature of the highest surface sentence. Passages with a core verbal sentence make up the largest group of syntactically dependent text cohesions. Implicit in the recognition of passages with distinct beginnings and ends is a principle of syntactic integrity, which requires that a line which contains one or more clause predicators cannot contain a nominal phrase not dependent on one of these. A minor extension of this principle requires that if a line contains an independent nominal phrase, it can contain nothing else.

## *8.1 Quotative passages*

Direct discourse is not consistently indicated in Classical Hebrew; shifts in and out of quotations are marked erratically in prose with *lʾmr* 'saying' and the like, and, if there is enough material, in both verse and prose, by alterations in the anaphora network. A further guiding principle, useful in the reading of prose, is that verbs which introduce direct discourse other than *ʾmr* are usually mediated by some form of it. The unspoken consensus has it that this principle fails for poetry, or at least that it is a less reliable guide; this consensus is reflected in any biblical translation, though not in systematic grammatical study. Before we examine the discrete sections of direct discourse that stretch over more than one line, which are our proper subject in this section, we must consider direct discourse marking more generally.

Lacking a study of the principles of direct discourse government and introduction, we must fall back on a rapid survey of our corpus. It is not obvious how to define the class of verbs which might govern discourse; let us devote our attention to the entire class of verbs that denote speech acts. Of these, most exemplified in our corpus are not used to introduce direct discourse; some may be so used; and several, besides *ʾmr*, are surely so used.

The speech act verbs which do not frame direct discourse require little comment. They are: *ʾrr* 'to curse,' *bwʿ* 'to speak,' *bṭy* 'to speak rashly,' *bśr* 'to announce,' *brk* 'to bless,' *zʿm* 'to denounce,' *z/ṣʿq* 'to scream,' *kzb* 'to lie,' *spr* 'to narrate,' *ʿny* 'to answer,' *pty* 'to deceive,' *pth* (*ph*) 'to speak,' *ṣwy* 'to command,' *qbb* 'to damn,' *rwʿ* 'to shout,' *šbḥ* 'to praise,' *šʾl* 'to ask,' *šbʿ* 'to swear,' *tny* 'to repeat.' Some of these words may not belong here, notably *zʿm*, *pty*, and *qbb*, which may not designate speech acts. Others, like *bṭy* and *tny*, are not sufficiently attested to warrant serious consideration. Still others present special ideological problems of performativity.

Before coming to terms with the direct discourse verbs of our corpus, we must distinguish three kinds of quotations. The primary distinction is between actual and global quotations, i.e., between quotations which the speaking voice of the poem identifies as proper to someone else's voice and which it uses as heterogeneous to itself; and quotations which the speaking voice allows to extend the force of its own reach, to enrich its intrinsic homogeneity. The latter, global quotations, are the result of the kind of sustained meditation on the poetic act that is essential to modern poetry; they are further at the core of the variety of speculations on the nature of verse that begins to appear in the late archaic poetry of Greece and reaches an initial flowering among the Hellenistic poets, speculations associated with the use of personae and the development of drama and with the modality generally called irony. Self-reflexiveness is not foreign to ancient Mediterranean poetry before the archaic age in Greece, however; it is the stuff of the *Odyssey* in the hero's constant deceptions and it achieves a negative clarity in 2 Samuel 1. A simple variety of self-reflexiveness frames the royal wedding psalm, Psalm 45. Although we cannot discuss this complex subject here, as any treatment of it would presuppose the elementary grammar we are tracing out in this essay, we will cite below passages that could be treated as introductions for global quotations; a fuller discussion of Northwest Semitic poetics will have to take them up.

The secondary distinction among quotations refers to the length of actual quotation: those that are contained within the line they are introduced by and those which are not must be separated. Those in the first group are necessarily short and are called here one liners, though that term is not strictly accurate. Those in the second category vary in length from a single phrase to a passage of discourse 17 lines long; these are called runovers. Because of indeterminacy of many of the cases, it is best to catalog all possible quotations by verb or idiom of introduction, with references to the major part of this section in which the runovers are treated in more detail. Also noted in the catalog are non-quotative uses of the speech act verbs.

*ᵓmr simplex. Note.* We exclude from consideration the prose rubrics of Deuteronomy 33 in 7a, 8a, 12a, 13a, 18a, 20a, 22a, 23a, and 24a. *Non-quotative uses,* i.e., *ᵓmr* 'to speak, give an order.' Num 23:19c; Ps 106:23a, 34b; 107:2a, 25a. *One liners.* Dt 32:26a, 26b; 33:9a, 27d; Ps 106:48c. *Runovers.* See 8.1.1 ad Ex 15:9a; Num 23:23c; Dt 32:19b, 26a, 27c, 37a, 40b; Jdg 5:23b; Zph 3:7a, 20f; and Ps 107:2a for active uses; Zph 3:16a for the passive; and 8.1.2 ad Zph 1:12e and Zph 2.15c; and *dbr + ᵓmr, ngd + ᵓmr* and *šwb ᵓmr* below. *Global quotations.* Ps 107:2a could be taken as quotative introduction to the rest of the poem.

*dbr simplex. Non-quotative uses.* Num 23:19d; Zph 3:13b; and Jdg 5:12c, the stimulus presumably for the traditional view of Deborah as the speaker of the poem; an accomodation of that view to recent study, suggesting that Deborah is the speaker of the lines from 13 to 21 or 22, is conceivable. *One liners.* None. *Runovers.* See *dbr + ᵓmr. Global quotations.* The opening of Deuteronomy 32, in 1a, may be intended as a frame over the whole poem.

*dbr + ᵓmr. Note.* The idiom is an instance of the usual prose pattern, in which a speech act verb is mediated by *ᵓmr. Non-quotative uses, one liners.* None. *Runovers.* See 8.1.1 ad Ps 78:19a. *Global quotations.* None.

*hll. Non-quotative uses.* Ps 106:5c, 47d; 107:32b. *One liners.* None. *Runovers, global quotations.* Ps 106:1a could be an introduction to 1b, or it could provide a cover for the entire poem. See *ydy.*

*ybb. Non-quotative uses, one liners.* None. *Runovers.* See 8.1.1 ad Jdg 5:28b. *Global quotations.* None.

*ydy. Non-quotative uses.* Gen 49:8a; Ps 106:47c; 107:8 = 15 = 21 = 31. *One liners, runovers.* In Ps 106:1b = 107:1b, the verb may introduce not only the ejaculation *ky-ṭwb*, but also the following line, Ps 106:1c = 107:1c. *Global quotations.* None.

*ngd simplex. Non-quotative uses.* 2 S 1:20a. *One liners, runovers, global quotations.* None, but see directly below.

*ngd* + *ʾmr* *Non-quotative uses, one liners, runovers.* None. *Global quotations.* The speech act idiom appears in Dt 32:7cd, directly after the introductory verses, and may serve as a frame for everything which follows it, i.e., Dt 32:8a *ad finem* could be a speech by the community elders. Observe that the idiom is spread over two lines. This suggestion need not conflict with the comparable one made above s.v. *dbr*, about Dt 32:1a.

*qrʾ*. *Non-quotative uses.* Dt 33:19a; Zph 3:9b. *One liners.* None. *Runovers.* Again, Deuteronomy 32 shows a notable usage. Dt 32:3b could be taken as the invocation promised in 3a. *Global quotations.* None.

*rnn*. *Non-quotative uses.* Zph 3:14a. *One liners.* None. *Runovers.* The closing of Deuteronomy 32 may contain a quotation, if Dt 32:43a introduces 43b; or it may be a quotation, if 43a governs 43bcd. *Global quotations.* None.

*šwb ʾmr*. *Non-quotative uses, ore liners.* None. *Runovers.* See 8.1.1 ad Jdg 5:29b. *Global quotations.* None.

*šyr, zmr*. *Non quotative uses/šyr.* Zph 2:14c; Ps 106:12b. *zmr*. None. *One liners.* None. *Runovers/šyr.* Ex 15:1a and its close parallel 21a could be taken as an introduction to the lines which follow them, Ex 15:1bc = 21bc. *amr*. None. *Global quotations.* The end of the introduction, in 3cde, to Judges 5, could be taken as a frame intended to include the rest of the poem.

These dozen verbs as they are used in our corpus make up a class too poorly attested to present the significant patterns that would surely emerge from a fuller study of speech act verbs in poetry. Two verbs introduce one liners, *ʾmr* and *ydy*. Of the runovers cited above, only those introduced by *ʾmr*, *dbr* + *ʾmr*, *ybb* and *šwb ʾmr* can be regarded as certain. Those prefaced by *hll*, *ydy*, *qrʾ*, *rnn* and *šyr* are not plain enough to warrant further discussion here. The leadins to what might be global quotations are *dbr*, *hll*, *ngd* + *ʾmr*, *šyr/zmr*.

### *8.1.1 Passages with a quotative frame*

The core clause of a passage which has a quotative frame is the indication of the act and circumstances of speaking. This clause may coincide with the line in which it occurs, as a clean core; or it may occupy only part of that line, in which case the core is mixed. Clean cores are about twice as common as mixed cores. Sometimes a clean core contains only an indication of speaker or speech act, and sometimes it presents further circumstances. About half the poems have quotations; Genesis 49, Deuteronomy 33, 2 Samuel 1, Habaqquq 3 and Psalm 106 are absent, while the first two chapters of Zephaniah are cited only in 8.1.2.

One of the most celebrated quotations in Hebrew poetry begins with an upfront clean core.

Ex 15:9a *ʾmr ʾwyb*
Ex 15:9b *ʾrdp ʾśyg*

Ex 15:9c *ʾḥlq šll*
Ex 15:9d tmlʾ*mw npšy*
Ex 15:9e *ʾryq ḥrby*
Ex 15:9f *twryšmw ydy*

The use of alliteration at the start of this passage is one of the few remarkable examples of the phenomenon in Classical Hebrew; equally noteworthy is the consistent 2 constituent line structure. The longest quotation in our corpus, which is 23 lines, begins with a core in Dt 32:19b which introduces the speech act and extends through Dt 32:19b 20abcd 21abcd 22abcd 23ab 24abcd 25abcd.

The conclusion of Judges 5 consists largely of a pair of quotations, a dialogue between Sisera's mother and one of her courtiers. In both, the speech act verbs are here uniquely so used in our corpus. The mordant irony of this section of the poem, created by the juxtaposition of the quotations, is also unique in our corpus and perhaps in Hebrew poetry. The first passage is Jdg 5:28bcd and the second, Jdg 5:29b 30abcde.

The conclusion of Zephaniah also involves a pair of quotations, the first with an upfront core, the second with a postposed core; the first with *ʾmr* in the passive (the only such usage in our texts), the second with that verb in the active. The thematic relation of the two quotations is even more shocking than the link just noted in Judges 5, though it is similarly skewed away from the principal argument of the whole poem. The first of the quotations is Zph 3:16abc 17abcde; the second is treated below, with the other examples of postposed cores.

The last example of an upfront clean core involves the speech act idiom *dbr* + *ʾmr* in a taunt song from the wilderness stories, given in Ps 78:19abc 20abcde.

The first example of a postposed clean core is the second of the Zephaniah 3 quotations mentioned above, at 18ab 19abcde 20abcdef. In this case, the postposition of the core, 20f, is not obscure because of the contrast between the end of the previous quotation, in 17e, and the start of the concluding one.

The other postposed clean core is a frame for lines containing a quotation which is at least a one liner (Ps 107:1a) and may be longer (Ps 107:1ab). The core is Ps 107:2ab 3ab. Double quotation is rare in Hebrew in any context and in a non-narrative situation, extremely infrequent.

In the only passage with an encased clean core, Jdg 5:23abcde, the problem of drawing together the two portions of direct discourse separated by the core, 23b, is solved by links of repetition and pronominal reference between them.

In every case in which the quotation is introduced and begun in the same line, the core is positioned upfront. An example of great complexity in Dt 32:26ab 27abcd has been cited earlier (7.3). The complexity revolves around the negative purpose clauses in the last two lines, with gapping of both *pn* and *y*ʾ*mrw* and retention of the *l*ʾ that stands between them in the underlying form of the sentence. The double quotations in both these lines are one liners.

In Deuteronomy 32, as in Judges 5 and Zephaniah 3, the poem's conclusion is concocted of two long quotations; here the second quotation occurs within the first. The first quotation's core is Dt 32:37a, and the quotation includes 37b 38abcd 39abcdef; then the core of the second quotation, 40ab, introduces the contained quotation of 41abcd 42abcd.

The two remaining examples of mixed cores are two lines each, the shortest of the passages with quotative frames. In Zph 3:7ab, the frame is limited to the first line, as in the cases above. In Num 23:23cd, the quotative frame extends into the second line, and the quotation itself is less than a line long.

Of these 13 examples, half present quoted texts in which there is some syntactic dependency within the quotation. In Dt 32:26a*ff*, the whole quotation is a single syntactic unit. In Jdg 5:23a*ff*, the only text with an encased core, the dependency within the text occurs at the end of it (23de). In both Dt 32:37a*ff* and Ps 78:19a*ff* the inner complexity follows the introduction directly (in 37a-38b and 19bc, respectively); in Zph 3:18a*ff*, a passage with a postponed core, the dependency precedes the core directly (20cde). In both Dt 32:19b*ff* and 40 b*ff*, the introduction stands foremost and the compounding is later (in 24abc and 42abcd, respectively). These dispositions evidently contribute to the markedness of these already marked passages, though how it is not clear. These examples of dependency in other forms are dealt with below.

### *8.1.2 Other quotative passages*

The bulk of the quotations which, with their introductions, are longer than one line are built around a simple core, a quotative frame, and extend outward, often including in the quotation further syntactic complexity. In two passages, the situation is reversed: the introduction and quotation are contained within a passage which is itself syntactically complex. Both are in Zephaniah's poem and both present emblematic utterances of the desperate, the first at Zph 1:12cdef and the second at Zph 2:15abcd. These will be dealt with further below (sub 8.2.3 and 8.3, respectively).

## *8.2 Passages with verbal clause cores*

The dependencies of an independent verbal clause line can be either phrases or subordinate clauses; they can be dependent directly on the independent clause or on its dependencies. These options create a field for great diversity. The three basic types of passages consist of independent clause lines and (a) phrase lines, (b) subordinate clause lines, and (c) both phrase and subordinate clause lines. This elementary typology gathers together the examples on the basis of the line shapes, not the overall structure of the superordinate sentence. It does reduce the complexity of syntactically dense passages to a single level; we shall try to make up for this reduction in discussing the examples.

### *8.2.1 Phrase lines*

In most cases, only one type of phrase line is dependent on a verbal sentence core; either unmarked noun phrases or prepositionally marked noun phrases are involved, more commonly the latter. If the dependent lines are unmarked, the core independent clause line is as commonly upfront as it is postposed. If they are prepositional phrases, the core is much more often upfront.

Upfront cores are more common overall, and most often the passages are two lines.

Num 24:6a *knḥlym nṭyw* core
Num 24:6b *kgnt ᶜly-nhr*

There are other examples in Gen 49:15ab; Num 24:4bc, 6cd, 17ef; Dt 32:5ab, 6ab, 10ab; 33:2de, 19cd, 21de, 28bc; Jdg 5:8cd, 11bc, 19bc, 23de, 24ab; Hab 3:6de; Zph 1:2ab, 4ab, 8bc, 18ab; 2:3fg, 6ab, 10bc, 11cd, 14ab; 3:12ab, 14cd, 19de; Ps 78:12ab; 106:20ab, 31ab; and 107:8ab, 34ab, and 39ab. There are 3 line examples in Jdg 5:5abc; Zph 1:3bcd; and Ps 78:49abc. Postposed cores are correspondingly less frequent.

Jdg 5:6a *bymy-šmgr-bn-ᶜnt*
Jdg 5:6b *bymy-yᶜl ḥdlw ᵓrḥwt*

There are other 2 line examples in Ex 15:4ab; Jdg 5:2ab; Zph 1:16b 17a, 18de; 2:5cd; 3:10ab; and Ps 107:17ab; there is a three line case in Ps 107:10ab 11a.

In only two cases do both prepositionally marked and unmarked noun phrase lines occur in apposition to a single core. Both texts are from Deuteronomy 32 and both involve a curious use of *ᶜm*, different from its usual sense of Arb *ᶜinda*, Latin *apud*, French *chez*, and not far from a conjunct sense 'and further, and in addition.' The longer of the two, Dt 32:13cd 14abcd, has an upfront core. The two phrases beginning with *ᶜm* in 14b and 14d break up lists; the first four objects of the main verb in 13c are enumerated in 13cd 14a and then the fifth is marked with *ᶜm*; four sources of milk are listed and the sixth object of the main verb of 13c is introduced with *ᶜm*. In a shorter passage from Deuteronomy 32, at 24abcd, *ᶜm* is also used to end a catalog, and to introduce its fifth member. The use of an encased core, at 24c, may be related to this usage of *ᶜm*.

In Ps 107:23ab 24ab, another example with an encased core (24b), there are three 2 constituent phrase lines, two before the core and one after it.

## *8.2.2 Phrase-clause and dependent clause lines*

Independent clause lines can have as dependent lines subordinate clauses formed with either finite or nonfinite verbs, but not, in our corpus, both. Usually only one functional category of clauses is involved in each superordinate sentence; in a few cases, however, several finite clause types occur together. In most cases, the independent clause, the core of the passage, is upfront and the subordinate clauses follow. Further, in most cases, the independent clauses occupy the whole of the line they occur in : mixed cores are found only in passages with nominal clauses. Encased clean cores are also rare, attested only among passages with two types of finite subordinate clauses.

All subordinate clauses with infinitives are deployed around clean cores. The passages with purpose clauses all have upfront cores.

| | | |
|---|---|---|
| Ps 78:18a | *wynsw ʾl blbbm* | core |
| Ps 78:18b | *lšʾl ʾkl lnpšm* | |

There are further 2 line examples in Jdg 5:16ab; Ps 78:17ab, 19bc; 106:8ab, 23bc; and 107:7ab. There are longer cases in Zph 3:9abc; and Ps 106:4b 5abc, and 26ab 27ab. Of the passages with temporal clause lines, most have upfront cores: Hab 3:16de; Zph 3:7cd, 20ab; Ps 78:42ab 43ab; and 106:44ab. Only one, Jdg 5:4abc, has a postposed core.

Relative clauses are formed with both finite and nonfinite verb forms. Of the five relative markers, four, *ʾšr* and *zw*, which govern finite verbs, and *h* and ∅, which govern nonfinite verbs, are attested in our corpus. Almost all the passages with relative clause dependencies have upfront cores. The standard marker *ʾšr* is attested in Zph 3:11ab; and Ps 78:11ab. In Dt 33:8cde 9a, two *ʾšr* relative clause lines are followed by a *h* relative clause line. The *h* marking is also exampled in the archaic verse of Gen 49:17abc and 2 S 1:24abc. The *zw* marking occurs in Ex 15:13ab. There are two passages with asyndetic relative clauses, Ps 78:60ab, and 107:40ab; the latter has a postposed core.

Other types of subordinate clauses formed with finite verbs are only sparsely attested. Nominal relative clauses occur in passages with a postposed core, at Ps 106:2ab; and 107:43ab. Nominal clauses uniformly occur in passages with upfront mixed cores. In two examples, with single embedding, both the nominal clauses are verbless, Ps 78:35ab, and 39ab. The only finite purpose clauses which are the sole dependents of an independent clause are the clauses of negative purpose in Dt 32:26b 27abcd. The concessive clause passage unique to our corpus, Ps 106:34ab, has a clean core. The only conditional clause in this group, at Dt 32:29ab, has a mixed postponed core.

In one passage, an independent clause line has as dependencies clauses of two different types of finite subordinate clauses. In Ex 15:16bcde, relative and temporal clauses occur together: the main clause, 16b, is upfront and two temporal clauses, 16cd, on the second of which is dependent a relative clause, 16e, follow. In Ps 78:5bcd 6a, three different clause types are represented: a relative clause, 5c, follows the core, 5b, and a nonfinite purpose clause, 5d, is followed by a finite one, 6a.

Ordinarily phrase-clause lines are dependent on independent clause lines along with phrase lines. In only one case does a phrase-clause line appear as the only dependent: Ps 78:68ab.

### *8.2.3 Phrase lines, phrase-clause lines and dependent clause lines*

The most complex superordinate sentences in our corpus contain independent and subordinate clauses, and appositional phrases. The pattern of decreasing dependency scope which would arrange the units in the order cited is not dominant. Rather, most passages which illustrate this degree of interlaced dependency consist of a core followed by appositives dependent on it, followed by or intermingled with relative clauses dependent on them. In an important variation of this scheme, the core is encased by the appositives and relative clauses. Other patterns show variant dispositions of the basic materials.

In the simplest form of the dominant pattern, an independent clause is followed by a noun phrase, on which a relative clause depends; in the example, there are two relative clauses.

| | | |
|---|---|---|
| Zph 2:8a | *šmʿty ḥrpt-mwʾb* | core |
| Zph 2:8b | *wgdwpy-bny-ʿmwn* | |
| Zph 2:8c | *ʾšr ḥrpw ʾt-ʿmy* | |
| Zph 2:8d | *wygydlw ʿl-gbwlm* | |

There are further examples in Ps 78:8abc; and 106:38abc. A pattern in which the phrase line is related to the core in a more complicated way is evidenced in Zph 1:9abc. Six dependent clause lines follow a single phrase line, dependent itself on the upfront core, in Zph 1:4cd 5abcd 6ab.

What we have characterized as the dominant pattern is varied in the blessing catalogues of Genesis 49 and Deuteronomy 33: the core appears encased, as the second last line of the superordinate sentence. The Deuteronomy 33 passage is the simpler. Of the 10 lines in the passage, eight contain phrase lines; the two which do not, a phrase-clause line and an independent clause, the core, are the second and the second-last lines, framing the six central lines.

Dt 33:13c *mmgd-šmym-mᶜl*

Dt 33:13d *wmthwm rbṣt tḥt*

Dt 33:14a *wmmgd-tbwʾt-šmš*

Dt 33:14b *wmmgd-grš-yrḥ-m*

Dt 33:15a *wmrʾš-hrry-qdm*

Dt 33:15b *wmmgd-gbᶜwt-ᶜwlm*

Dt 33:16a *wmmgd-ʾrṣ-wmlʾh*

Dt 33:16b *wrṣwn-škny-snh*

Dt 33:16c *tbwʾth lrʾš-ywsp* core

Dt 33:16d *wlqdqd-nzyr-ʾḥyw*

The passage in Genesis 49 at 24cd 25abcde 26abcde is similar but much more complicated. Of the 12 lines, six are phrase lines of one constituent; four of the others are phrase-clause lines (two of two constituents, two of three constituents); the remaining two are a two constituent phrase line and the core. There are two groups of five lines before the core in 26d. In the first (24c-25c), two of the phrase-clause lines (25ab) follow two of the phrase lines (24cd) and the group ends with the single 2 constituent phrase line (25c); in the second group (25d-26c), two phrase-clause lines (25d, 26a) alternate with phrase lines (25e, 26b), and the group ends with a phrase line (26c). The contrast between 24e-25b and 25d-26b in the use of phrase-clause and phrase lines is pointed. There is a pattern of alternating clause lines and phrase lines behind both these catalogues which the following diagram pictures; the leftmost column contain the highest clauses; the boxed unit is missing in Deuteronomy 33. The number of poetic lines involved is cited under the rubric of each line of the diagram.

| | | Gen 49 | Dt 33 |
|---|---|---|---|
| I. | Phrase | 2 | 1 |
| II. | Phrase-clause | 2 | 1 |
| III. | Phrase | 1 | 6 |
| | Phrase-clause | 1 | |
| | Phrase | 1 | |
| | Phrase-clause | 1 | |
| | Phrase | 2 | |
| IV. | Core | 1 | 1 |
| V. | Phrase | 1 | 1 |

The section labelled III, though it is variously arranged in the poems, is six lines long in each; the difference in the line length of the catalogs is the result of different instantiations of the first two sections.

A few minor patterns combining independent and subordinate clause lines and phrase lines remain. The first two illustrate the nesting effect alluded to several times above. In Ps 78:71abc, a purpose clause and a prepositional phrase line dependent on it follow a main clause. In Ps 106:21ab 22ab, a dependent clause which is in apposition to a constituent of the core line is glossed by two further phrase lines. A dependent clause follows a phrase line in Zph 3:20cde. A number of these patterns overlap in Zph 2:2cdef 3abc.

Sometimes the subordinate clauses and the phrase lines are distinct from one another. In Dt 32:8abcd, two clauses precede the core, 8c, and a prepositional phrase follows. In Ps 78:3ab 4abcd, the core is preceded by two dependent clause lines and followed by two phrase lines; the last line of the group is a phrase-clause line. The pattern is 2-1-2-1, perhaps in small a variant of the Blessing Catalog scheme discussed above.

We may include by way of coda to this section, two passages which contain dependent clauses and quotations. In Zph 1:12cdef, the quotation concludes the passage. The extended frame of the opening of Psalm 107, 1ab 2ab 3ab, comprehends two relative clauses dependent on the core, 2a, and a prepositional phrase which follows and qualifies the second relative clause.

## *8.3 Passages with verbless clause cores*

Just as the verbless clause is less common than the verbal, so extensions of it beyond the frame of one line are less frequent than passages built around a verbal core. Most often such extensions are expansions of the predicate of the core line, which is with few exceptions upfront. Sometimes other appositives appear with or without an extended predicate. Less frequently, clauses are subordinated to an independent verbless clause.

The simplest passages here contain a verbless clause line followed by lines containing extensions of the predicate. It is less common for the verbless clause to have the order subject-predicate, as in Dt 32:34ab, than the reverse, as in Gen 49:22abc; Num 24:5ab; Dt 32:4cd; and Zph 1:15abcde 16a. The phrase line contains an extension of the subject of the verbless core in Gen 49:7ab.

Appositional phrases which are not involved in the predication relationship of the verbless clause line can also be associated with such a line. An appositional noun phrase is used as a vocative in Ex 15:11bc. In Gen 49:3abcd, a vocative precedes the core and two lines of predicate extension follow it. In Dt 33:29bcd, an appositive follows a vocative.

An appositional prepositional phrase depends on a verbless clause in Ps 106:48ab. Both prepositionally marked and unmarked noun phrases are in apposition to an encased independent verbless clause in Zph 3:8cdefg.

The break in the sequence of prepositional phrases, created by the core clause, 8d, is bridged by the use of *l* before and after the core.

The only subordinate clause types dependent on verbless clauses are relative and nominal clauses. The independent clause line is clean of the relative clause, which follows in a separate line, in Gen 49:21ab. In both Ex 15:2cd and Num 23:19ab, the verbless clause adjoins a relative clause in the first of two lines, while in the second an extended predicate of the verbless clause adjoins another relative clause. A temporal clause precedes a verbless core in Zph 2:2ab.

A mix of appositives, largely extended predicates, and subordinate clauses, characterizes the remaining examples of syntactic dependency in passages with a verbless clause core. In Dt 32:37ab 38ab, the subordinate clauses are relatives which depend on the extended predicate, not the independent clause. In Zph 2:15abcd, the clause dependent on a predicate extension is a quotation, rather than a relative clause.

### *8.4 Independent noun phrases*

Syntactic dependency also associates phrase lines with independent noun phrases. In Num 24:3bc, the dependent is a relative clause. The dependent lines consist of further phrases in Num 24:4aa*; Zph 2:9bc; and Ps 106:3ab.

### *8.5 Summary*

The various forms of syntactic dependency unite over 400 lines of our corpus. Two texts use the trope most extensively, Deuteronomy 32 and Zephaniah; here the prophet's consistency is patent. Similarly, two texts use the trope almost not at all: 2 Samuel 1 and Habaqquq 3. The other texts use it in uniting about one-third of their lines.

# CHAPTER NINE

# THE SUPRALINEAR-LEVEL TROPE OF MIXING

## *9.0 Introduction*

There is a variety of syntactic dependency which is structurally distinct from the cases of the trope discussed above, mixing. In this trope, lines which are syntactically dependent on main clauses are not in direct contiguity with them. The domain is always four lines and there is only one break in the syntax: if *a* and *b* are main clauses and *c* and *d* are dependent line units, these form, from a pair of base sentences *acd* and *bcd*, a surface structure *abcd*; the *a* member is isolated from the line units dependent on it. For introductory remarks, see 1.5.8.

The elements involved in mixing can be either main and subordinate clauses or main clauses and phrase lines. The first and more common variety is clause mixing, the second, phrase mixing. The phenomenon is a rare one: with two exceptions, Deuteronomy 32 and 2 Samuel 1, no poem includes more than one example. There are no examples at all in Exodus 15, Habaqquq 3, and Psalms 78 and 107, and the first and third chapters of Zephaniah.

## *9.1 Clause mixing*

The basic form of clause mixing includes two main clauses and two subordinate clauses, in that order; both the subordinate clauses modify both the main clauses. Of the seven examples of this type, several involve temporal subordinate clauses. Two include clauses in *ᶜd* 'while'.

Gen 49:10a *lᵓ-yswr šbṭ myhwdh*
Gen 49:10b *wmḥqq mbyn-rglyw*
Gen 49:10c *ᶜd-ky-ybᵓ šy lh*
Gen 49:10d *wlw yqht-ᶜmym*

There is another case in Num 23:24abcd. Jdg 5:7abcd includes two clauses in *š* 'when.' In Dt 33:4b 5abc, the temporal clauses are infinitives; this example has bilateral symmetry in that gapping in the first two lines is leftward and in the second two is rightward. A further example, at Dt 32:30abcd, contains clauses of negative circumstance. The two remaining cases have subordinate clauses of purpose; those in Ps 106:47abcd are positive, and those in 2 S 1:20abcd negative.

### *9.2 Phrase mixing*

The mixing of phrase lines and main clauses presents the same basic shape as clause mixing: the independent sentence lines are followed by syntactically dependent lines. In the first two cases, from Deuteronomy 32, both the dependent members modify both the main clauses; these are Dt 32:2abcd and 25abcd. In the third, that is not so obviously the case.

Dt 32:42a *ᵓškyr ḥṣy mdm*
Dt 32:42b *wḥrby tᵓkl bśr*
Dt 32:42c *mdm-ḥll-wšbyh*
Dt 32:42d mrᵓ*š-prᶜwt-ᵓwyb*

Here it may be that the prepositional phrase of the *a* member finds an appositive in *c*; and the *b* member, with a gapped preposition, finds one in the *d* member. This alternating structure would be similar to another instance of mixing, involving the same martial imagery, in 2 S 1:22abcd. In Zph 2:9defg, as in the Dt 32:25 case, the phrase lines which follow the main clause are varied in structure: the first has one constituent and the second two. This passage occurs in the exact center of Zephaniah.

### *9.3 Summary*

Of the eight texts that have the trope of mixing, half-a-dozen only have a single example. Thus, in Genesis 49, Numbers 23-24, Deuteronomy 33, Judges 5, Zephaniah 2 and Psalm 106, the trope involves about a twentieth of the text. In 2 Samuel 1, the two examples make up a quarter of the text and in Deuteronomy 32, the four examples constitute a tenth of the text.

PART III: GROSS STRUCTURE

# CHAPTER TEN
# AN OVERVIEW

## *10.0 Introduction*

The linguistic features of Hebrew poetry that make it formally coherent and distinctive discourse fall into four classes. Two of these classes are primary: resources drawn from them characterize all poetic discourse. These are features of gross and fine structure, features that describe whole poems and those that describe the basic unit of verse, the line, in itself and in its interaction with contiguous lines. Fine structure features have been our chief concern in this essay; we have exhaustively characterized the syntactic varieties of lines and the troping devices that draw together and hold apart nearby lines. The twelve hundred lines treated here have so far been set all on a par: we have referred only in passing to their uses in the texts of our corpus. In turning now to gross structure, we turn to reexamine all the diversity of those lines in the context of the poulter's dozen poems at hand. In terms of lines, we have a large corpus; in terms of poems, it is small. We have to be as laboriously reticent here as we have been forthcoming above.

The other classes of linguistic features are secondary: figuration and ornamentation, often used as near synonyms in critical language, have been pressed into service here with distinct senses. Figuration refers to the features of coherence that have a domain less than that of gross structural features and greater than or equal to that of fine structural features. The stock of resources used to construct figures is vast; no figure is ever a necessary feature of poetic discourse. Some figures control the upper regions of the domain, others, the lower depths. Many have been tossed onto the great garbage heap of parallelism and left to rot there without any close consideration. A few of these we shall refer to here; figuration will not be a primary focus of our study and our final remarks will be inconclusive. The last class of linguistic features, ornamentation, has a domain equal to or less than that of fine structural features; its stock of resources is as vast as and probably not far different from that of figuration. Here, as elsewhere in this essay, ornamentation is the missing member of the party.

The four classes vary continuously in size and oppositionally in rank.

| *primary* | *secondary* |
|---|---|
| gross structural features | |
| | figuration |
| fine structural features | |
| | ornamentation |

The third level, fine structural features, we have laid out with as much clarity as possible. The first and peripherally the second levels shall concern us now. Some poems of our corpus are more approachable in these terms, because they have structural features that are evident and universally recognized. With these, the tribal testaments, the poems with repetition structures, and the Oracles of Balaam, we begin; then we consider the poems which lack such clues to structure.

We want to begin by taking firm hold of all that is clear about the gross structure of Hebrew verse; and so we begin empty handed. Nothing can have been finally ascertained in previous study because discussion of gross structure must rely on the basic unit; as long as the line remained undefined and undescribed, there was no foundation firm enough to support study of higher patterns. This is not to say that nothing has been done. Those commentators who have recognized that the integrity of a verse composition demands of them careful study have worked in directions we are pursuing. Much that is suggestive in the work of, for example, Alonso-Schökel, Freedman, Muilenburg, and Skehan has led us on in these areas.

We do not begin entirely empty handed, however. The core concept of Aristotelian rhetoric, which distinguishes beginnings, middles, and ends, we take as one formulation of a crucial structural principle. For a phenomenon to be discretely defined, its margins (beginning and end, temporally; edges, spatially) must be more marked than its middle. This concept is not merely Aristotelian, though its Aristotelian form has persisted through Carroll's Humpty-Dumpty into Bloom's antithetical, Kabbalistic criticism (Vendler 1976). It is also basic to gestalt psychology and descendant studies of pattern recognition; these have contributed the vocabulary of margins. Smith (1968) has studied poetic closure in European poetry and made specific reference to early 20th century work in psychology. The feature of poetic structure that in European poetry mates the closural phenomena Smith deals with is titling; there is no comparable study of it, though Howard (1976) is suggestive.

The difference between the often elaborate devices studied by Smith and titling, a relatively simple phenomenon, suggests that just as margins are different from middles, so beginnings are different from ends. Greenberg contends that there is a general tendency in the syntax of the languages of the world "to mark the end of units rather than the beginning. . . . This is probably related to the fact that we always know when someone has just begun speaking, but it is our sad experience that without some marker we don't know when the speaker will finish" (1963b:103). One of the most highly marked features of Latin public oratory are clausulae, ornate metrical patterns that are used at the *ends* of important passages or of whole speeches. Cicero says that a certain tribune won thunderous applause from his audience for ending a passage with a double trochee

(Pulgram 1975:264-71). Perhaps Cicero (or the audience) meant what Greenberg means. At any rate, we can accept Greenberg's observation that in speech the initial position is intrinsically emphatic, while final position must be specially marked. This is observed by O'Nolan (1969) in his study of Irish tales and doubtless by other linguists and readers. The circumstance is a consequence of the temporal organization of speech; and a corollary of the margins: middle opposition. We shall not deal with it explicitly, but only by indirection.

The vast amounts of data to be dealt with lead us to offer a few cautions. There are no discovery procedures involved here. If we begin with one group of facts about a phenomenon and present a summary note on it before going on to describe the whole, we are seeking only to orient the reader; such separations are heuristic and not substantive. We have tried at the same time to avoid tarting the facts up too much; indeed, to avoid directing the reader's attention anywhere but to the texts.

We would remind the reader also that our concern is with formal description. Thematic remarks are to be found but they are meant as digressions, to help focus the reader's attention, and not central parts of the argument. Our concern here is a single domain of linguistic texture; we have no illusions of presenting descriptions adequate to the texts themselves.

## *10.1 Poems with plain articulations*

The most plainly jointed poems in our corpus are the two tribal testaments attributed to Jacob and Moses, and the oracles ascribed to Balaam. (The tribal section of Judges 5 is only a small part of that poem and is therefore to be distinguished from the Testaments.) The joints in the Testaments are the result of the poems' shifts through the range of the tribes; the sections of the Oracles of Balaam are set off by title and invocation formulae. The Testaments are difficult poems. Indeed, the use of that term for the traditional "blessing" is a hedge which partially reflects their obscurity; some of the difficulty can be clarified, however, if close attention is paid to overall poetic structure.

The Oracles and Testaments are strikingly dissimilar poems and therefore provide a good base from which to begin an investigation of gross structural features which might describe a wide range of Hebrew poems. Further, the Testaments do not conform to any single formula, as is plain from differences in length and reference.

### *10.1.1 Genesis 49. The Testament of Jacob*

The Testament of Jacob has distributions of line types which are fairly typical of the corpus as a whole.

| | | | | |
|---|---|---|---|---|
| Class I | | 48 lines | 60% | |
| Class II | | 17 lines | 21% | 40% |
| Class III | | 12 lines | 15% | |
| Class IV | | 3 lines | 4% | |
| total | | 80 lines | 100% | |

The troping of the poem is above average. It is evenly distributed across the three levels.

| | | |
|---|---|---|
| word-level | 38 lines | 48% |
| repetition | 13 lines | 16% |
| coloration | 26 lines | 33% |
| line-level | 34 lines | 43% |
| matching | 34 lines | 43% |
| gapping | 13 lines | 16% |
| supralinear-level | 33 lines | 41% |
| dependency | 29 lines | 36% |
| mixing | 4 lines | 5% |
| total | 61 lines | 76% |

First, let us consider the order in which the tribes are presented. Among the primary determinants are order of birth and status. The six male offspring of the senior wife of Jacob, Leah, are mentioned first; the two children of Rachel appear last. The children of the slave wives occupy the middle range. Following the narrative of Genesis 29-30 and 35, we can compare this determinant with the text order.

| *text order* | *order of birth* | *mother* |
|---|---|---|
| Reuben | 1 | Leah |
| Simeon | 2 | |
| Levi | 3 | |
| Judah | 4 | |
| Zebulon | 10 | |
| Issachar | 9 | |
| Dan | 5 | Bilhah |
| Gad | 7 | Zilpah |
| Asher | 8 | |
| Naphtali | 6 | Bilhah |
| Joseph | 11 | Rachel |
| Benjamin | 12 | |

The plainest feature of the list is one which we may suspect was active throughout the formation of the Jacob saga. The senior party includes six members; the junior party, two; and the slave party, half of the sum of these, four. The pattern in Genesis 49 is 6:4:2, which complements the pattern in the stories themselves, which is 4:4:2:2. The first pattern presents a simple decrescendo and the second a sonnet-form decrescendo (cf. Petrarchan 4:4:3:3). The emphasis in both poem and story cycle is on the final "couplet," the Rachel children. (Without pausing to review the whole Jacob saga, we may remark on the stress in the narrative between the 4:4 set of children, all born with scarcely a pause for a pun, and the 2:2 set, born over much longer spaces of both real and narrated time. This stress is presented in the story about Reuben in Gen 30:14-18. The boy finds some mandragora and thereby supplies the aphrodisiac his mother barters for the use of his father in begetting Issachar. The first Leah child [the start of the 4:4 passage] is thus instrumental in the generation of the fifth, Issachar, who leads off the 2:2 movement. Finally, in the list above, we note that the Bilhah sons are split around the Zilpah sons. There is thus an overall alternation of rank: first, senior mother [the Leah sons], then junior mother [the first child of Bilhah, Rachel's slave]; then again, senior mother [the children of Zilpah, Leah's slave]; and finally, junior mother [the second Bilhah child and then Rachel's own children].)

The prose saga of Jacob is much later in date than the Testament and is not therefore an entirely independent witness to the tribal traditions. To understand fully the text's ordering and its evaluations of the tribes, we must look more closely at its structure. In addition to the individual testaments, the poem includes an opening invocation and two references to God, if the reading of 16ab argued for above is accepted. The two references to God frame and isolate the Dan testament. It is no coincidence that the first description (16ab) sounds like the Dan blessing it has always been taken for. The ring of the paronomasia so sharply swerved away from isolates Dan all the more forcefully.

The separation of Dan leaves two groups of tribes, dealt with in two passages of unequal length.

| *Set I* | | *Set II* | |
|---|---|---|---|
| A. | Reuben: 7 lines | A. | Gad: 2 lines |
| | Simeon & Levi: 10 lines | | Asher: 2 lines |
| | | | Naphtali: 2 lines |
| B. | Judah: 17 lines | B. | Joseph: 19 lines |
| C. | Zebulon: 3 lines | C. | Benjamin: 3 lines |
| | Issachar: 6 lines | | |
| Total: 43 lines | | Total: 28 lines | |

The balance of the sets is most obvious in the central positioning of the great exaltations of Judah and Joseph, the longest passages in the poem. Another feature is the relation of the A and C groups to each other, irrespective of the B groups: A is double C in length. There are two separate systems of length balance in covariance; if we call one member (the enveloping one) x, and the other (the core oracle) y, the sets each have the shape 2x-y-x. (This kind of covariance is similar to the system of tone balance described by Frankel 1972 in Chinese Regulated Verse.)

The meaning of the various sections of the poem is far from plain, so dense in every sense is the text. A grasp of the evaluation matrix in the poem will contribute greatly to our reading, so we may limn the matter.

Four of the tribes are plainly dealt with. The first two testaments are damnations of Reuben and his brothers, Simeon and Levi, who appear as a team. The two longest testaments are richly drafted praises of Judah and Joseph. Working from here, we can begin to trace the system of evaluation in the poetic structure. The traditional difficulty of the supposed double Dan blessing we have dissolved by associating the first of the two with Yahweh, leaving Dan as a snake in the grass. The figure matches across languages: Dan is condemned.

The remaining clue to the system lies in the Benjamin oracle. The pattern of animal metaphors in ancient Near Eastern thought is complex. Even in this poem, at least two different paradigms are operating. Judah, for example, is on the one hand a wild animal (9ab) and on the other a tender (rather than a ravager) of domesticated animals (11ab). No simple reading of the animal imagery will work in approaching the Benjamin oracle. Nonetheless, there seems to be a gradation across the three final oracles. Naphtali, the hind, Joseph, the wild ass, and Benjamin, the wolf, are all wild animals. Naphtali, who is here in female guise, is surrounded by her young: the situation is domestic stasis (in metaphoric extension of the Asher blessing). Joseph is harried by hunters, in a posture of defense, within a distinctly positive oracle. Benjamin, we suggest, is the last step in the sequence: ravenous attack, on the kind of stasis enjoyed by Naphtali, free of the oppression suffered by Joseph. Benjamin, that is, is condemned.

The evaluative structure of the poem is emerging roughly as follows.

| | | |
|---|---|---|
| I. | Reuben | condemnation |
| | Simeon & Levi | condemnation |
| | Judah | approbation |
| | Zebulon | |
| | Issachar | |
| * | Dan | condemnation |
| II. | Gad | |
| | Asher | |
| | Naphtali | |
| | Joseph | approbation |
| | Benjamin | condemnation |

The entries left unmarked are intermediate between condemnation and approbation: lukewarm or, perhaps better, loosely descriptive as far as we can tell. Jacob's patrimony has three parts: five tribes (the first five to disappear perhaps, or the least stable) are condemned, five are passed over with paternal indulgence, and two are powerfully blessed. The relation of these evaluations to the structure is simple: the marginal positions are reserved for strong comments and the inner positions for weak ones. Dan is the exception.

The isolated tribe stands at the structural core of the poem. It may be that a major point of this poem is the repudiation of Dan. To make the suggestion more forcefully we would have to read the whole of the poem and we lack the space here. Suffice it to make two observations. Of all the animals in the poem, the snake is the only one that lives alone; more strictly, Dan is associated with the only animals that are not noted for any social behavior. Further, Dan's victim is a horse, a member of the equid group associated in this poem with the most favored of the children, since Judah is pictured with his domestic ass and Joseph appears as a wild ass. Dan's midmost position in the poem has a telling link to the great blessings, as well as to the condemnations at the far margins.

The two tribal sets and the Dan blessing are not alone in the poem. The frame of the text consists of the opening 2 line invocation of the children, and of the section between Issachar and Gad. This opens with a 2 line description of Yahweh's dominion and closes with a prayer, enclosing the Dan condemnation.

With the two structural determinants we have considered we have been moving closer to the poem. The first, the ranking of the children in the saga, is alien to the text as such. The evaluations are less foreign: they are part of what the poem is "about." We can make a third attempt on the poem's structure, working from these two, and clarify the text further.

In Chapter 9, when we presented the trope of mixing, we noted that it is rare and its occurrences appear to be of overall structural importance. The beginning of the second tribal set occurs 28 lines from the end of the poem; the only occurrence of mixing in the poem begins at line 26. The text falls into thirds, which we may lay out thus.

*The First Third*

| | | | |
|---|---|---|---|
| 2a-9d | Invocation: 2ab: 2 lines | | |
| | The First Set: | Reuben: 3a-4c: 7 lines | Leah's Sons |
| | | Simeon & Levi: 5a-7d: 9 lines | |
| | | Judah's Origins: 8a-9d: 7 lines | |

*The Second Third*

| | | | |
|---|---|---|---|
| 10a-18 | | Judah's Dominion: 10a-12b: 10 lines | |

Zebulon: 13abc: 3 lines
Issachar: 14a-15d: 6 lines (Leah's Sons)

Yahweh's Rule: 16ab: 2 lines
Dan: 17a-d: 4 lines
Prayer: 18: 1 line

*The Third Third*

19a-27c The Second Set: Gad: 19ab: 2 lines
Asher: 20ab: 2 lines
Naphtali: 21ab: 2 lines (Slave Sons)
Joseph: 22a-26e: 19 lines
Benjamin: 27abc: 3 lines (Rachel's Sons)

We will try to show that one pattern, based on a unit of 26-28 lines, is used to elaborate another, more exigent one, isolating Dan and arraying the other tribes across a skein of maternal rank and filial conduct.

A further, crucial point is made by this arrangement. Judah and Joseph may match roughly; indeed, in size (both here and historically), Joseph may surpass Judah. But everlasting rule belongs to Judah, as the text asserts precisely at the transition from its first to its second section, in the unique use of the trope of mixing. The poem is balanced as carefully in Judah's favor as the commander's rod is positioned between his feet. The internal split of the Judah oracle into 7 and 10 line parts is reinforced by the pairing with the first two testaments: Reuben, and Judah's Origins take up seven lines; Simeon and Levi, and Judah's Dominion, 9 or 10 lines.

The small testaments are not either extensively troped or dominated by heavy line types, i.e., lines of Classes II, III and IV. The only three couplet oracles, those for Gad, Asher and Naphtali, are not troped at all, except for dependency in the last; each is homogeneous in the line type used. The sequence of the three, as they appear back to back, 19a-21b, is marked by variation: the first and third couplets have 2 Class I lines, while the middle member of the set has 2 Class II lines.

There is more troping in the two 3 line oracles. Both Zebulon, 13abc, and Benjamin, 27abc, open with a Class II line, followed by 2 Class I lines. Zebulon has repetition across its first two lines and matching and gapping across all three. A coordinated dyad and a match hold together the last two lines of Benjamin.

The Dan oracle, 17a-d, opens with one of the three Class IV lines in Genesis 49. Like the other Class IV lines (the first line of the poem and the first line of Judah oracle), the line marks a major juncture. The four lines of Dan are asymmetrically divided: the first two are gapped across, but their dependency extends to the third; the split by the dominant trope is 3:1. The lines after 17a, which is Class IV, are Class I; the split by line type is 1:3.

Class I lines make up the bulk of Issachar's oracle, which varies only in its fourth line, which is Class III. The troping in the oracle is limited to the middle, which shows both combination and dependency.

The Reuben oracle opens with 4 Class III lines (3abcd) and closes with 2 Class I lines (4bc), leaving only one unmatched, Class II line. The downshifting, III-II-I, and the predominance of rarer line types reflects the position of the oracle near the start of the poem. The opening four line passage has syntactic dependency and the last two lines of it (3cd) show both repetition and matching. Combination and matching occur in the final lines of the testament (4bc).

The Simeon and Levi oracle has a plain couplet form in its 10 lines.

| | | |
|---|---|---|
| 5ab | Class I | matching |
| 6ab | Class II | matching |
| 6cd | Class I | matching |
| 7ab | Classes I & II | |
| 7cd | Class I | matching |

The alternation of Class I and non-I pairs is undergirt by the use of couplet matching; 7ab shows syntactic dependency instead, as it were, of matching. There are color tropes in the second, third and fifth couplets.

The two part structure of the Judah oracle, suggested above as involved in gross structure, can be seen in fine. Judah's Origins, as we labelled 8a-9d, shows almost no troping while it does have variance in line types. Judah's Dominion, i.e., 10a-12b, is heavily troped and shows no variance in line types: 10 Class I lines occur in series. The oddity of this long run of Class I lines should not be missed: the second longest sequence of Class I lines in the poem is only half that long (13bc 14ab 15a). Thus the split between 8-9 and 10-12 appears on both the gross and fine levels, although after we look at the two sections separately, we shall note that there is a link across them. The oracle opens with a Class II line, 8a. The repetition of Judah's name in 8a and 9a may be a figure. The troping pattern of the next ten lines is best looked at in diagrammatic reduction. The superscripts show which lines are troped together.

10a combination combination matching[i] gapping mixing
10b combination combination matching[i] gapping mixing
10c repetition combination matching[j] gapping mixing
10d repetition combination matching[j] gapping mixing
11a matching[k] gapping
11b matching[k] gapping
11c matching[k] gapping
11d matching[k] gapping
12a matching[l]
12b matching[l]

The heaviest troping, fivefold, is in the first four lines. The four line domain of mixing, a crucial trope here, is "imitated" by matching in 11, which also extends over four lines. The passage has a 2x:2x:x structure (10abcd:11abcd:12ab). There is much more to read in this passage but we restrict ourselves to the bridge across the two sections. There is *almost* no troping in 8-9, we remarked. The only trope there is the matching of 9d with 10a(b), which serves to bind upward 10a, already firmly tied to what follows by mixing. The plain orientation of 10a is downward; the minor link to 9d contributes to the coherence of the Judah oracle as a whole.

Like Judah's, Joseph's testament can be split. A section of animal likenesses, 22a-24b, is followed by a 12 line blessing catalog, 24c-26e. A feature common to both parts is repetition, which opens the oracle in 22ab and blocks off the center of the catalog, at 25cde 26ab. The first section of the testament opens with a three line verbless clause (22abc) with both repetition and a pair of combinations; the rest of it (23-24) is untroped.

The longest sentence in our corpus in 24c-26e. Some features of it are discussed above in 8.2.3, but its tension of symmetry and asymmetry deserves further attention. The sense of the passage warrants three divisions: (a) the 4 lines that specify the sources of the blessings (24cd 25ab), (b) the 6 that refer to their character (25cde 26abc), and (c) the 2 that specify their destination, those with the main verb (26de). The troping in the first and third of these is symmetrical: binomination in all three couplets of (a) and (c), and matching in the second, 25ab. The section that lists the blessings is slightly skewed. Out of the six lines in it, five share the trope of repetition (25cde 26ab); these five do not match. The last line, which breaks the repetition trope, substitutes for it, as it were, matching with the line before, 26c. These six lines also show a 2 part split in terms of line types: twice over, a Class III line (25c, 26a) is followed by 2 Class II lines (25de, 26bc). (This arrangement throws into relief the structure of the sex roles involved. The referents of the Class III lines are masculine; those of the Class II lines are feminine and outnumbering, if second ranked.)

The frame of the poem remains, i.e., the lines which do not refer to particular tribes, 2ab, 16ab, and 18. The opening of the poem consists of a Class IV line followed by a Class I line; there is repetition in these lines. The description of Yahweh's rule in 16ab consists of 2 Class I lines, troped thrice over. The prayer of 18 is a Class II line, standing by itself.

The three part division of Genesis 49 described above suggests that the poem asserts the damnation of Dan and the eternal dominion of Judah. The distribution of the basic elements of the poetic system in part supports our division. Troped lines are spread evenly through the poem: 19 (troped lines):26 (total lines) (73%) in the section 2a-9d, 20:26 (77%) in 10a-18, and 19:28 (68%) in 19a-27c. Lines which vary from the norm of Class I are not spread so evenly. In the first section (2a-9d) and in the third (19a-27c), there are equal numbers of them: 13:26 (50%) for the first and 15:28 (54%)

for the third. In the middle section, lines of Class II-IV are few: 4:26 or 15%. This provides a further measure of support for a division we have shown to be operative on other textual levels; the distribution will be considered further below, at the end of 10.1.2.

### *10.1.2 Deuteronomy 33. The Testament of Moses*

The distribution of line types in the Testament of Moses is not remarkable.

| | | | |
|---|---|---|---|
| Class I | 67 lines | 69% | |
| Class II | 19 lines | 20% | 31% |
| Class III | 9 lines | 9% | |
| Class IV | 2 lines | 2% | |
| total | 97 lines | 100% | |

The troping is most pronounced on the word level and least so on the supralinear level.

| | | |
|---|---|---|
| word-level | 51 lines | 53% |
| repetition | 19 lines | 20% |
| coloration | 36 lines | 37% |
| line-level | 43 lines | 44% |
| matching | 43 lines | 44% |
| gapping | 12 lines | 12% |
| supralinear-level | 29 lines | 30% |
| dependency | 25 lines | 26% |
| mixing | 4 lines | 4% |
| total | 61 lines | 63% |

Several points of comparison with Genesis 49 will help to clear the way for our reading of Deuteronomy 33. The first is that despite textual difficulty, the testament ascribed to Moses is vastly more beneficent than that attributed to Jacob. The problems of evaluative sense which beset us above are gone and so is the help we derived from confronting them. The second point is that while the non-oracle material in Genesis 49 was restricted to 5 lines out of 80, here such material, though arrayed as there in three passages, is more extensive. One-third of the poem, 33 lines, refers in general to Israel and Yahweh; the oracles make up the remaining two-thirds.

The textual state is good but some points require attention. The ten prose rubrics we deleted in Chapter 2 we continue to set aside, mentioning them here only to note that there is no *syntactic* reason for their exclusion. The argument to follow would be unaffected in substance by their restoration. Some long range tropes would be knocked askew and a few, new short range ones would be introduced. The feature of the poem often supposed to be a major textual problem, the absence of Simeon, is no problem at all, since we are describing the received text and not some unavailable alternative. Freedman (p.c.) notes the paronomasia of 7b in suggesting that Judah's oracle may originally have been Simeon's; nonetheless the received text is not in doubt at this point. In support of the text, we note that in both Testaments there is one less oracle than there are tribes. In Genesis 49, twelve tribes receive eleven acknowledgments and in Deuteronomy 33, eleven receive ten; in the first, Simeon and Levi pattern together, while in the second, Zebulon and Issachar do so. This is basically true even though Joseph shows signs of mitosis in that Ephraim and Manasseh are mentioned in Dt 33:17ef. For the breaks between individual testaments which are obscured by our deletions (those before and after the Benjamin testament), we follow the received text.

Mother's state and time of birth here, as in Genesis 49, are partial determinants of the tribal ordering. Status has the priority in this poem that seniority of birth has in that one. The first six testaments, which run to 49 lines (three-quarters of the oracles' length), go to the children of the free wives; the last four, 15 lines in length (one-quarter), refer to the slave wives' children. In both groups, the children pertaining to the senior wife surround those associated with the junior wife. Given this framework the birth order of the prose saga is followed, with two exceptions: Judah precedes his older brother Levi, and Benjamin his older brother Joseph.

The pattern here is the following. Mother's name follows order of birth.

| *free wife* | *slave wife* | |
|---|---|---|
| *Reuben:1:Leah* | *Gad:7:Zilpah for Leah* | *senior wife* |
| *Judah:4:Leah* | | |
| *Levi:3:Leah* | | |
| *Benjamin:12:Rachel* | *Dan:5:Bilhah for Rachel* | *junior wife* |
| *Joseph:11:Rachel* | *Naphtali:6:Bilhah for Rachel* | |
| *Zebulon & Issachar:9-10:Leah* | *Asher:8:Zilpah for Leah* | *senior wife* |

The senior wife entries (i.e., those associated with both the senior wife and her surrogate) in both columns not only surround those for the junior wife (Rachel and her surrogate); they are also more extensive. The Leah oracles in the first column are 29 lines long, while the Rachel oracles there are 20 lines long. Similarly, the Zilpah tribes get 10 lines and the Bilhah tribes, 5 lines.

One feature of the left column deserves further attention. The two superoracles, for Levi and Joseph, are the final entries in the first two groups: Levi is the last of Leah's first brood mentioned and Joseph the last of Rachel's children. These are the two exceptions to the pattern of ordering by time of birth. Now we can hear the last of Simeon: this ordering exception in the two groups is the counterargument to any allegation that Judah has usurped his older brother's place. (We shall not discuss the possibility that the Judah oracle sounds like a Simeon oracle precisely because it is supposed to sound like a Simeon oracle, i.e., to reflect the fact that Judah absorbed Simeon.)

The linear ordering of the tribes breaks down into three groups in terms of length. The first two groups include the two major oracles and the major tribes; this division explains any slight that might be thought to be directed against Judah. The first group includes Leah's first brood (minus Simeon): Reuben, Judah and Levi together get 23 lines. The second set, which comprehends the beloved children, Joseph and Benjamin, is dealt with in 20 lines. The last group, Leah's second brood and the slave children, gets 21 lines.

These two ordering determinants in hand, we can turn to the whole text of the poem and extend our consideration to the one-third of the text that deals with supratribal affairs. The three passages are not balanced in themselves in length nor is their locale structurally easy to understand. The opening and closing passages are rounded out by a short one, near the end of the poem, 21cde. The number of lines between that passage and the poem's close is 27, a block of lines with a length familiar to us from Genesis 49. The breakdown of these 27 lines into four subject parts, and the breakdown of the rest of the poem into nine parts are related circumstances. The last 84 lines of the poem fall into three units of roughly the same length, each with four subject parts. The first of these units includes four oracles, Reuben, Judah, Levi, and Benjamin, over 26 lines; and the second and third of them include three oracles and a general passage over 31 and 27 lines, respectively. This leaves the introduction to the poem standing by itself, a 13 line section, which we can call a half-unit. The breakdown looks like this.

| | | | | |
|---|---|---|---|---|
| Half Unit | Introduction | 2a-5c | 13 lines | |
| First Unit | Reuben | 6ab | 2 lines | |
| | Judah | 7b-e | 4 lines | |
| | Levi | 8b-11d | 17 lines | |
| | Benjamin | 12bcd | 3 lines: | 26 lines |
| Second Unit | Joseph | 13b-17f | 17 lines | |
| | Zebulon-Issachar | 18b-19d | 6 lines | |
| | Gad | 20b-21b | 5 lines | |
| | General | 21cde | 3 lines: | 31 lines |
| Third Unit | Dan | 22bc | 2 lines | |
| | Naphtali | 23bcd | 3 lines | |

| | | |
|---|---|---|
| Asher | 24b-25b | 5 lines |
| General | 26a-29f | 17 lines: 27 lines |

The range of the operating unit which is emerging is enlarged from 26-28 to 26-31 lines.

The analysis recognizes an inverted sonnet form poem of one half-unit followed by three full units. Some properties of the three units can be seen in the following scheme.

| *First* | *Second* | *Third* |
|---|---|---|
| *Reuben* | **Joseph* | *Dan* |
| *Judah* | *Zebulon-Issachar* | *Naphtali* |
| **Levi* | *Gad* | *Asher* |
| *Benjamin* | *General* | **General* |

The starred entry in each group is the 17 line group. In the first, it is positioned centrally; thereafter, marginally, first initially, then finally. This switching is complemented by the relative sizes, within each unit, of the non-starred entries. In the first unit, there is this size grouping (the short units are in lower case): little (2 lines), big (4 lines), LEVI (17 lines), medium (3 lines). Thus the oracles which are big are together in the middle; and the little ones are on the margins. In the other two blocks, the grouping of the four parts follows size, first down, then up. In the second unit, we have: JOSEPH (17 lines), big (6 lines), medium (5 lines), little (3 lines). In the third, the plan is: little (2 lines), medium (3 lines), big (5 lines), CODA (17 lines).

There is an overall thematic pattern of the four units (the three full and the half) which we may note in conclusion to our first discussion of the poem's overall structure. The half-unit is entirely general material; the first full unit is entirely testamentary. The third unit (the second full unit) is 90% oracles and 10% general. The last block is one-third oracles and two-thirds general material. The thematic focus of the poem is the coherence of the tribes, and so the supratribal dominance of the opening, followed by tribal dominance of the First Unit, captures the poem's tension. The rest of the text seeks resolution of that tension.

We turn to the individual sections' structures now. The short oracles are only slightly troped and include few rare line types. Neither Reuben (6ab), a sequence of Class II and I lines, nor Dan (22bc), 2 Class I's, is troped. The first 3 line testament, Benjamin (13bcd), includes a repetition trope and is part of a further repetition trope that includes the first half of the Joseph oracle (13b-16a). (The latter would be broken if 13a were considered integral to the text.) The line types of Benjamin are II-IV-I. The occurrence of a Class IV line here is somewhat surprising. It may serve as an anticipatory marking of the close of the Reuben-Benjamin unit. The other 3 line oracle, for Naphtali, presents a mild contrast: it is untroped and includes only Class I lines.

Judah's oracle opens with a Class III line and closes with a doubly troped couplet: 7de include a combination and a gapping. We noted earlier that 7e matches 8bc, the first two lines of the Levi oracles; this is probably a mistake, a sign that our descriptive devices are too strong. The difficulty could be averted by reintroducing 8a. It may, however, not be an error, since 8bc are also troped downward and the dubious match may be a transsectional link like the match across the two parts of the Judah oracles in Genesis 49 (i.e., the match of 9d and 10a).

The Gad oracle, 20b-21b, includes only Class I lines and a single trope, the combination in the final two lines, 21ab. The other 5 line oracle, for Asher, 24b-25b, is not troped and has only Class I lines, except for 25b, which is Class III.

The only 6 line oracle, for Zebulon and Issachar, 18b-19d, is more complex. The first two lines, 18bc, are triply troped, with coordination, matching and gapping; these two lines are Classes II and III respectively. The last two lines, 19cd, are also troped, with dependency. The middle two lines are, like the last two lines, of Classes I and II. Thus the troping is marginal while the Class II lines tie the margins to the center.

| | | | |
|---|---|---|---|
| 18b | trope | Class II | |
| 18c | trope | | Class III |
| 19a | | | Class I |
| 19b | | Class II | |
| 19c | trope | | Class I |
| 19d | trope | Class II | |

The two remaining oracles are both 17 lines long. The Levi oracle alternates blocks of matching lines with single non-matching lines.

| | | |
|---|---|---|
| 8bc | 2 line match } | 4 lines |
| 8de | 2 line match } | |
| 9a | | |
| 9b-e | 4 line match } | 8 lines |
| 10a-d | 4 line match } | |
| 11a | | |
| 11bc | 2 line match | 2 lines |
| 11d | | |

This intricate byplay furnishes a clear illustration of our contention that the bicolon, i.e., the couplet, is not a primary unit, but a secondary one available for all variety of use in creating structure on levels beyond the line. The first pair of lines, 8bc, are further troped by combination and gapping. The second, 8de, is marked by gapping. Each of the four pairs in

9 and 10 has at least one color trope: coordination in 9bc, combinations in 9de and 10cd; and binomination and combination in 10ab. Further, both parts of 10 show gapping. The first line isolated in the matching scheme above, 9a, is joined to 8cde by syntactic dependency. The entire Levi oracle consists of Class I lines, except for the first and second of the non-matching lines, 9a and 11a, which are of Classes III and II respectively.

These two lines provide a clue to the typological breakdown of the oracle, which cuts across the pattern established by matching.

| | | | | | |
|---|---|---|---|---|---|
| I | 8bcde | 4 lines | I | 9de 10abcd | 6 lines |
| III | 9a | 1 line | II | 11a | 1 line |
| I | 9bc | 2 lines | I | 11bcd | 3 lines |

The breakdown is based on two parts, arranged around a non-Class I line with a distribution of Class I lines before and after in the proportion 2:1. All but the last of the Class I lines match, so troping supports this pattern. The 7 line section (on the left) is bounded by two coordination couplets, 8bc at the start and 9bc at the close. The 10 line section (on the right) opens with three combination couplets, the middle one of which also has a binomination. The division is also thematically grounded: the 7 line section refers to Levi's origins and family, the 10 line section to his work and his future.

The Joseph oracle we have met before. The ten line blessing catalog, 13c-16d, which opens it, appears before the animal parade, 17abcd; the arrangement in Genesis 49 is reversed. The first 7 lines of the catalog show a repetition trope which is joined to another in the Benjamin oracle as we noted above; the blessing catalog constitutes the second longest sentence in our corpus, treated in 8.2.3. As in the Genesis 49 Joseph oracle, repetiton is not limited to the catalog; it also occurs in 17ef, the last lines of the testament. Each of the couplets 17ab, 17cd, and 17ef contains a combination. The first and last are internally matching. The last also includes a binomination, as do the last lines of the catalog, 16cd. These binominations are complementary: the one in 16cd refers to Joseph in his own person and the one in 17ef to him in his dual tribal identity. The two cases of two tropes within the whole oracle span its length (save for the isolated first line) to hold it together.

| | |
|---|---|
| repetition | 13c-16a |
| binomination | 16cd |
| repetition<br>binomination | 17ef |

The alternance of line types within the catalog 13c-16d is dealt with above, in 8.2.3. All the other lines in the oracle are Class I. The Class I lines, which number 9, frame the other types, of which there are 8, in alternating groups.

| | Class I | Class II | Class III |
|---|---|---|---|
| 13b | 1 | | |
| 13c | | | 1 |
| 13d | 1 | | |
| 14a-16b | | 6 | |
| 16c | 1 | | |
| 16d | | 1 | |
| 17a-f | 6 | | |

The odd line out, the single Class III, serves to start off the catalog; the two 6 line bunches balance each other.

The opening lines of the poem, 2a-5c, have always been regarded as odd, most notably in the reference to the prophet. Students have often tried to work out the problem by excising Moses, and, understandably missing the leftward verb gapping of 4b 5a, have frequently jettisoned 4b as well. What does such an operation yield? No easy text, at any rate, since Yahweh the theophanic storm deity rising mighty from the Arabian Shield is not entirely at home with Yahweh the Palestinian amphictiarch. In fact, in the received text there are two oddities: the two pictures of Yahweh *and* the reference to Moses. But one hand washes its partner.

Moses is mentioned here in his basic historical role: he is the mediator between the storm god and the amphictiarch. Yahweh is only comprehensible as a covenant deity in Israelite ideology through the instruction given Moses, which he gave his followers. We are glad to frame this explanation without direct reference to the lines 3abc, but they are not beyond our grasp. The movement of 2a-e presents the deity alone. In 4ab 5abc, he is surrounded by his covenanters. The lines of 3, which are imagistically continuous with those of 2, introduce the divine council, the heavenly counterpart of the people of Moses.

In the opening passage, the only Class III line, 2e, is joined by a repetition trope to 2b; these surround 2cd, which match; the 4 lines before 2e are Class I. A Class I line, 3a, precedes a Class II line, 3b; and another, 3c, precedes a Class IV line, 4a, the Moses line. The last 4 lines of the passage are two Class I lines, 4b and 5a, and two Class II lines, 5bc, held together by the trope of mixing. The first two lines of the four, 4b 5a, are matching and gap across each other. The second two are only half so troped, with combination and matching. The last five lines are formally and thematically distinct from the opening lines.

The second supratribal passage, 21cde, returns to the tribal gathering and reintroduces the figure of Moses, for such, as Freedman (p.c.) points out, must be the subject of *ᶜśy* ‘to do, make’ in 21d. The last two of these three lines have a combination and show dependency; the last one is a Class III, while the others are Class I.

The most explicit thematic tie across the three general passages is an attempt to draw together cosmic and covenantal Yahweh ideologies. This tie is formally grounded in the sequencing of names for Moses' people; two split binominations are used with two other name sequences interspersed.

| | | | | |
|---|---|---|---|---|
| 4b | *yʿqb* | | | |
| 5a | | *yšrwn* | | |
| 5c | *yśrʾl* | | | |
| 21e | | | *yśrʾl* | |
| 26a | | *yšrwn* | | |
| 28a | | | *yśrʾl* | |
| 28b | | | | *yʿqb-ʾl* |
| 29a | | | | *yśrʾl* |

The chief subject of the passages is Yahweh; only the last lines concern his people. In the eight lines of 2a-3c, Yahweh is a storm deity, while in the eight lines of 4a-5c and 21cde, Yahweh is the god of Moses. In the concluding 17 lines of the poem, Yahweh is both. He is first considered as a cosmic deity (26bc 27ab) and then as a historical actor (27cd). Then Israel is discussed and Yahweh reappears in the guise of its chief beneficiary. (We ignore the reference to *ʾl* in 26a for the sake of this quick graph.)

The couplet 26bc is one of the most heavily troped in our corpus, with repetition, two combinations, and matching. The following couplet, 27ab and another below, 28ab, have binominations and match. The concluding lines of the poem also match. Syntactic dependency joins 28bc and 29cd.

The opening Class I line joins with the Class III line, 27d, to set off the treatment of Yahweh. The matches in 28ab and 29ef demarcate the Israel passage, within which the non-Class I lines are entirely contained; both the Class II lines (28bc) and the Class III line (29d) are located near or interlock with the matches.

In our concluding remarks on Genesis 49, we noted that the heavy lines of that poem are concentrated in the first and third blocks; the middle block has few heavy lines. This pattern is easy to comprehend and we cite it in preparation for a glance at the more complex pattern of Deuteronomy 33. The most highly marked units in Genesis 49 are the marginal ones, the first and last. The middle unit, which is insulated, as it were, from other discourse and which will be perceived as poetic in part because of what goes before and after it, is less marked as verse. This is an easy solution to the problems of setting off any patch of discourse: where does it start and stop, and how is it different? The answers are: it is different because it is more patterned than other speech; and it starts and stops just where the differences most plainly start and stop.

One way to measure the differentness of verse across a text would be by using the percentage of the text which has features peculiar to verse and which we have seen are used to mark portions as distinctive. These are troping and line typology. There are several ways of using these materials.

It is possible to consider, for example, the number of lines which are both troped and non-Class I as opposed to the number of lines which are neither troped nor non-Class I. That is, we can take the conjunct of two marked sets and oppose to it the number of lines in neither set (the complement of the dual set). We can further take the ratio of these groups as percentages, to balance off differences in size of the groups. Here are the figures for Genesis 49.

| *unit* | *troped lines* | | *non-Class I lines* | | *conjunct: remainder* | *percent-ages* |
|---|---|---|---|---|---|---|
| I:2a-9d 26 lines | 19 | 73% | 13 | 50% | 8:3 | 73%:27% |
| II:10a-18 26 lines | 20 | 77% | 4 | 15% | 3:5 | 37%:63% |
| III:19a-27c 28 lines | 19 | 68% | 15 | 54% | 11:5 | 69%:31% |

Let us call the proportion of lines marked for *both* troping and line type to those marked for *neither*, the *weight* of a section. Further, taking the even weight of 50%:50% to indicate a base level of poetic markedness (a level at which all marked lines are fully marked and balance all unmarked lines), let us arbitrarily call a block of lines with a higher conjunct percentage than 50% (an) overweight and one with a lower conjunct percentage than 50% (an) underweight. Thus the structure of Genesis 49 is two overweights holding in an underweight. The overall weight of the poem is 22:13 lines, 63:37%.

The physiognomy behind a weight may also prove to be useful; this is the ratio of troped lines to heavy lines, which we may take together in the form of percentages, calling this the T(roping-) H(eavy lines) ratio. The outer units of Genesis 49 have similar TH ratios, 59:41% and 56:44%; the inner section has a TH ratio of 84:16%. The overall TH ratio is 61:32 lines, 66:44%.

With this fairly simple case in mind, we can try weighing up Deuteronomy 33. The usefulness of weighing becomes clear when we note that the numbers of troped lines and of non-Class I lines are irregular across the sections of the poem and that the irregularities do not coincide in a simple and obvious way. The highest level for troping is in the Second Unit, 13b-21e, at 25:31, 81%. The lowest is little less than half, 44% (12:27 lines), in the Third Unit, 22b-29g. The First Unit (6a-12d) is almost as high as the Second, 20:26, 77%. The Half-Unit, 2a-5c, is intermediate, 8:13 or 62%. If we, for the nonce, call 62% medium (the average for the poem is 67%), 44% low and 77-81% high, the gradient across the poem is medium-high-high-low.

The distribution of non-Class I lines is a little more regular. The First and Third Units (6a-12d and 22b-29g) are about one-quarter non-Class I: 6:26 (23%) and 6:27 (22%), respectively. The Half-Unit (2a-5c) and the Second Unit (13b-21e) are closer to half non-Class I: 5:13 (38%) and 13:31 (42%), respectively. The poem as a whole has 30 non-Class I lines, 31%. These two factors vary over different spans: troping over three levels (ca. 40-60-80%) and rare line types over two (ca. 25-40%). Weighting will help to focus the data.

| *unit* | *troped lines %* | *non-Class I lines %* | *weight percentages* |
|---|---|---|---|
| Half | 62% | 38% | 50:50% |
| First | 77% | 23% | 50:50% |
| Second | 81% | 42% | 71:29% |
| Third | 44% | 22% | 21:79% |
| Total | 67% | 37% | 48:52% |

The first two parts of Deuteronomy 33 are apparently in excellent physical shape, neither overweight nor underweight. Further, they correspond closely to the average for the poem. The last two parts are complementarily overweight and underweight. The strategy seems, then, to be that a normal weight is established in the first two units and then the basic deviations from it (and there are only two) are deployed.

The T(roping-) H(eavy or non-Class I lines) ratios of Deuteronomy 33 are also interesting.

| | *TH ratio* |
|---|---|
| Half-Unit | 62:38% |
| First Unit | 77:23% |
| Second Unit | 66:34% |
| Third Unit | 67:33% |
| Average | 66:34% |

The First Unit has a 3/4:1/4 ratio of troped lines to heavy lines; all the others have a markedly different balance, averaging out at 65%:35%, two-thirds to one-third. If we call this a norm for the poem, we can use this designation to gain further leverage in putting together the features of the text. Consider the following.

| | *weight* | *TH ratio* |
|---|---|---|
| Half-Unit | even | 2/3:1/3 |
| First Unit | even | 3/4:1/4 |
| Second Unit | overweight | 2/3:1/3 |
| Third Unit | underweight | 2/3:1/3 |

Using normal to mean normal for this text, we can simplify the above diagram further.

| | *weight* | *TH ratio* |
|---|---|---|
| Half-Unit | normal | normal |
| First Unit | normal | deviant |
| Second Unit | deviant (high) | normal |
| Third Unit | deviant (low) | normal |

The three major units are all deviant from a norm, which can be extrapolated from the initial Half-Unit and specifies both weight and TH ratio. If we note that the Half-Unit is itself deviant in length, we can see that the poem has a standard shape unit and each of its parts deviates from that shape in one respect.

### *10.1.3 Numbers 23-24. The Oracles of Balaam*

The heterogeneity of Numbers 21-27 (to fix on a somewhat arbitrary block of material as a starting point) is astonishing. The victory over Arad is followed by a journey in the neighborhood of Moab which is studded with special effects in both prose and verse. One of the rare references in Scripture to a precanonical source, the Book of Yahweh's Wars, introduces a four line poem in 21:14-15, which is followed after a prose interlude by a five line poem, the Song of the Well, in 21:17-18. The chapter, after recounting the fall of Sihon, presents the Song of Heshbon (Stuart 1976: 93-95). The Balaam cycle follows, introducing in prose first a rather serious North Syrian prophet and then a comical counterpart who derives guidance from his talking ass in Chapter 22. Chapters 23 and 24 include seven difficult poems interspersed through a narrative which is at least partly comical. The whole is followed by the decimation of the Baal Beth Peor plague in Chapter 25 (Mendenhall 1973:105-122) and, in bizarre complementation, the record of the second census of the Israelites in Chapters 26 and 27. The ensemble is among the most mixed sections of the Torah and students have been much exercised in sorting out the material.

We are concerned with one feature of this part of Numbers only but the pervasive complexity is good to keep in mind. Seven poems are attributed to Balaam; we have considered only the first four in Parts I and II. We noted in Chapter 2 that others have excluded the last three poems from consideration, but we wish to make something more of that exclusion than they did, so we must examine it.

The first four Oracles of Balaam are eighty lines long; the last three are ten. That fact alone provides some warrant for separating the two groups of poems. The texts of the last three do not mention Jacob-Israel or Yahweh, the principal subjects of the first four poems. (The reference to *ʾl* in 24:23 almost certainly cannot stand.) And the little oracles of 24:20-24 are almost illegible. (Such is probably the main reason behind their exclusion by others; and it is not a bad reason for us to exclude them.) Where they are intelligible, they seem to refer to historical entities removed from those treated in the first four poems. There are reasons, then, for suggesting that the Oracles "proper" (in some sense or other) stop in 24:19.

We need not, however, take up so radical a hypothesis. The facts mentioned above also warrant us in saying that the first four oracles should be separated as Balaam's Oracles over Jacob-Israel. Tradition also took them this way, and it referred the other three poems to other entities, plainly in 24:20 and 24:21 and probably in 24:23, where the introductory formula is incomplete. Thus we can take up the substantial part of Balaam's Oracles as a unit without slighting the minor verses that follow.

What kind of unit? We shall formulate our argument as if the four oracles made up a single poem. Nothing in our discussion will rule out the obvious alternative formulation, that they make up a sequence or set of poems with a fixed order. Given our ignorance about Hebrew poetry, it would be silly to quibble over the difference between calling the Oracles one poem, or a sequence of four; and there is no reason to question the order of the four. The integrity and ordering of the texts remain, to be sure, in the realm of assumptions. The problems of judging the integrity of the great late sixteenth-century English sonnet sequences (how many people did Shakespeare love, how?); and the fact that most of them break from the sonnet form occasionally into related but distinct forms, the double and triplet sonnet; these and other comparative considerations would argue caution here anyway.

The Oracles of Balaam over Israel is a poem in four parts, marked off by indisputable boundaries. (In what follows, by Oracles we mean the whole poem, and by oracle one of the parts of the whole.) The text is 80 lines long, the same length as Genesis 49. One passage is repeated in the third and fourth parts, the 7 line introduction to each, 24:3a-4c=24:15a-16d. Another is nearly repeated in the second and third parts, 23:22ab=24:8ab; there is a difference of a pronoun between 23:22a and 24:8a.

The boundaries between the parts are established by the prose tradition, by the integrity of the parts, and by the referents of the openings of each. The first two poems refer to the silent partner in the interchange described, Balaq, who commissioned the cursing. Balaam, the sorcerer, is mentioned at the start of the last two. The superficial evidence of repetition and name usage provides a network of links among the parts. (The parts of the poem are designated with Roman numerals.)

| | *names* | *repetitions* | |
|---|---|---|---|
| I | ] | | |
| II | ] | ] | |
| III | ] | ] | ] |
| IV | ] | | ] |

This much is clear without any consideration of poetic structure.

The distribution of line classes for the poem show an equal concentration of Classes II and III, which is unusual; but neither figure departs far from its mean for the corpus as a whole.

| | *lines* | *percentages* | |
|---|---|---|---|
| Class I | 50 | 63% | |
| Class II | 14 | 17% | |
| Class III | 13 | 16% | 37% |
| Class IV | 3 | 4% | |
| total | 80 lines | 100% | |

The trope distributions show a low incidence of gapping, a circumstance to which we shall return directly.

| | | |
|---|---|---|
| word-level | 39 lines | 49% |
| repetition | 18 lines | 23% |
| coloration | 24 lines | 30% |
| line-level | 32 lines | 40% |
| matching | 32 lines | 40% |
| gapping | 2 lines | 3% |
| supralinear-level | 28 lines | 35% |
| dependency | 24 lines | 30% |
| mixing | 4 lines | 5% |
| total | 67 lines | 84% |

The troping is highest on the word level, involving half the lines, and lowest on the supralinear level, involving a third; the line-level troping is intermediate. The weight of the poem is 26:9 lines or 74:26% and the TH ratio is 69:31%.

The trope of mixing sometimes serves to mark a major textual cut, as we have seen, and it does so here. The only case of mixing occurs at 23:24abcd, the boundary between Parts II and III. There is only one case of gapping in the Oracles and it, too, marks a boundary: it occurs in the first two lines of the poem, 23:7ab. The use of Class IV lines to mark emphatic positions in verse partially "follows" these trope usages. The first Class IV line, 23:7c, immediately follows the gapping in 23:7ab and the third, 23:23d, immediately precedes the mixing in 23:24abcd. The other Class IV line is 23:18a, at the start of the second oracle.

Each of the parts is a different length.

| | | |
|---|---|---|
| Part I | 23:7a-10d | 14 lines |
| Part II | 23:18a-24d | 22 lines |
| Part III | 24:3a-9d | 26 lines |
| Part IV | 24:15a-19b | 18 lines |

The 80 line length hints that the Oracles has something in common with Genesis 49, also 80 lines. And the occurrence here of a 26 line unit suggests the same, as Genesis 49 has three sections of 26-28 lines. The Testament, however, is a poem of three stanzas and the Oracles has four parts. The half-unit of Deuteronomy 33 is 13 lines long and we can call Part I here a similar half-unit.

Parts I and III are a half-unit and a unit then; together they make up half the poem, 40 lines. The other half of the poem, Parts II and IV, is also 40 lines and thus a unit and a half in length. But that half is split up differently, so that IV is four-sixths of a unit and II is five-sixths. More simply, II is III minus 4 lines; IV is III minus 8; and I is III minus 12.

If we for the moment set aside speculations on the unit and consider the line numbers in themselves, a sense of the poem's structure emerges. The part lengths are related to each other in a simple way. Letting *a* stand for the shortest and *d* for the longest part, the pattern is *acdb*. The splitting of one pair (*ad*) in a 4 unit series (*abcd*) by another pair (*bc*) can be considered in a variety of ways to suggest the symmetry further. There are only three ways to divide a sequence *abcd* into pairs: by simple pairing (*ab*/*cd*), by alternation (*ac*/*bd*), and by splitting the margins from the middle (*ad*/*bc*). The second is the base for the ordering of stanza lengths in the Oracles, but all three of these possibilities are highlighted in the actual ordering, which results from one of two possible permutations of the alternating pattern, i.e., *ac*/*bd* ⟶ *ac*/*db*.

*partners by alternation* *partners by pairing* *partners by splitting*

These remarks should establish something of the character of the pattern in Numbers 23-24. They are not meant to explain either the pattern or the poem, but to refer the poem to an entity that can be considered in the realm of patterning.

Let us return to the half-unit and unit observation. Since these unit phenomena have proved useful thus far, we should try to associate them with this poem, along lines necessarily distinct from characterizing its intrinsic structure. Let us try a fudge-finger exercise. We assume that an available unit length is 26-28 lines and that it is fissionable, allowing half-units of 13-14 lines. Given these, we can regard the text as the result of an attempt to write a four-part poem in a three-unit form.

Three full units would not, plainly, fit the four-part requirement, although the length would be right. Two units and two half-units would yield the same length and would have greater flexibility. There are a number of obvious structures, which we need not detail; they have in common that they are all symmetrical. Let us stipulate that what is needed is an *asymmetrical* four-part 80 line poem. Of the symmetrical solutions available, the two with mirror symmetry are the "least" symmetrical. These are the following.

| | | |
|---|---|---|
| I | half-unit | unit |
| II | unit | half-unit |
| III | unit | half-unit |
| IV | half-unit | unit |

The structure on the left has something in common with our text; positions I and III correspond. All we need do is vary two of the entries away from their present values, which support the symmetry. Let us vary the second and fourth toward one another by the same amount; let the variation be by a unit x.

| | |
|---|---|
| I | half-unit |
| II | unit minus x |
| III | unit |
| IV | half-unit plus x |

This pattern is essentially our text's.

We have not described why our text is as it is; let us say *that* before trying to say what we have done. We have shown that *if* our text's prime features are regarded as (a) its length, (b) its four-part structure, and (c) its asymmetry, *then* its structure can be understood in a poetic system that favors a fissionable 26-28 line block.

A consideration of couplets will help us round out this attempt to see Numbers 23-24 both in its own right and in the light of the Testaments. The couplet *as a formal unit* is non-existent in our description. It has no definition beyond its plainest one, a pair of lines. We use the term to refer to pairs of lines in case they have something in common. In this broad sense of couplet, the Oracles has an astonishingly high number of couplets. Let us illustrate the informal sense of couplet we will use here. In the first part of the poem, 23:7a-10d, every line is part of a couplet. Troping is the basis of the first four couplets and non-troping for the next (that is, the lines before and after 23:9cd are parts of other couplets). On the word troping level, 23:10ab form a couplet and 10cd are a couplet by non-troping. (The situation is complicated by the match of 23:10abc which breaks the couplet structure.) In this sense of couplet, which has no unitary linguistic referent or base, the poem has 30 couplets in 80 lines, 75%. (The exact specification is not crucial here; we include in that figure no overlapping couplets.)

The asymmetry in the overall shape of the poem is a clear complement to this trend toward symmetry on the level of line pairs. In the Testaments, there is little uniformity in small and thus (we reason) some regularity in gross structure is necessary. The opposite situation obtains here.

We have shown thus far that the section pattern of Numbers 23-24 is comprehensible both in its own right and in relation to the unit lengths we used in describing Genesis 49 and Deuteronomy 33. Both those poems join small scale variations in large units. We have seen evidence, and will see more, that suggests that Numbers 23-24 does the opposite.

The individual sections of the poem can be considered in their turn. The first part, 23:7a-10d, has the weight 6:3 lines, 67:33%. The TH ratio is 65:35% and the first, troping figure is lower than the poem's average probably because there is no syntactic dependency troping in the section. Color tropes and matching occur in the first (23:7ab), second (23:7cd), third (23:8ab), fourth (23:9ab) and sixth couplets (23:10ab). Repetition occurs in the second (23.7cd) and sixth (23:10ab). The matching mentioned in 23:10ab extends to 10c and thus a 3 line group jangles the couplet pattern. This same 3 line group appears in the diagram of the distribution of line types.

| | *lines* | *line classes* |
|---|---|---|
| 23:7a | 1 | I |
| 23:7bcd | 3 | III-IV-II |
| 23:8a-9d | 6 | I |
| 23:10abc | 3 | II-II-II |
| 23:10d | 1 | I |

This reveals that there are two 3 line groups amidst the two-line braces of this section.

The second unit, 23:18a-23:24d, has the weight 5:1, or 83:17% and a TH ratio of 73:27%, with a slightly higher troping figure than the rest of the poem. The distribution of the troped lines among the varieties of troping is ordinary for this poem. We have already cited the mix that concludes the part (23:24abcd). The mix is preceded immediately by two lines in syntactic dependency, 23:23cd. The only other lines so troped are on the far side of the oracle, 23:19ab. The last two lines of the mix contain a match in 23:24cd; there are others in 23:19d 20ab (three lines), 21ab, 21cd (thus there are seven lines with matching, in sequence), and in 23:23cd.

Repetition occurs in 23:20ab and binomination in 23:18ab, 21ab, 23ab, and 23cd. In the first five lines of the section, 18a-19c, there are four non-Class I lines, 23:18ab 19ac. In the last seventeen, there are only three, 23:22a, 23d, and 24b. This oracle opens with greater line type markedness and closes with greater troping markedness.

The third part of the Oracles, 24:3a-9d, contains 26 lines of arguments in favor of descriptive devices we have adopted. The weight is 8:4 or 67:33%, identical to that of the other well-formed chunk of this poem, Part I; Part III like Part I also has a lower troping level than the rest of the poem; the TH ratio is 69:31%. A partial explanation in both cases is plain: avoidance of certain tropes. In Part I, the supralinear-level tropes are not used. In Part III, the line-level tropes are little used and, as we shall see, that slight use is peculiar.

The opening 7 lines of Part III, 24:3a-4c, are the lines which appear at the start of Part IV. Five of them are non-Class I lines. There are only 5 other non-Class I lines in the oracle and their distribution forms a gradient which, if we can anticipate further discussion, we can set up like this.

| | I | non-I | total |
|---|---|---|---|
| IIIa. 3a-4c | 5 lines | 2 lines | 7 lines |
| IIIb. 5a-6d | 3 lines | 3 lines | 6 lines |
| IIIc. 7a-8b | 1 line | 5 lines | 6 lines |
| IIId. 8c-9d | 1 line | 6 lines | 7 lines |

The sixes and sevens into which the oracle is subdivided are easier to see in connection with the tropes. The first two subdivisions are entirely troped; the last two together are about half-troped. In the first subdivision, IIIa, the tropes are repetition (24:3ab, 3abc 4a), binomination and combination (both in 24:4aa*), and dependency (in 24:3bc, 4aa*, and 4bc; note that 24:3ab is a repetition couplet and 24:3bc is a dependency couplet). In the second subdivision, IIIb, the last three of these occur (binomination in 24:5ab; combination in 24:6ab; dependency in 24:5ab, 6ab, 6cd), while in the third, IIIc, only the first occurs (in 24:7ab). The only trope in the last subdivision is matching and all the matches of Part III occur there (in 24:8cde and 9cd). The scheme is the following.

| | *non-Class I:* | *word-level* | | *line-level* | *supralinear-level* |
|---|---|---|---|---|---|
| | *total lines* | *rep* | *color* | *match* | *depend* |
| IIIa | 5:7 | x | x | | x |
| IIIb | 3:6 | | x | | x |

| | | | |
|---|---|---|---|
| IIIc | 1:6 | x | |
| IIId | 1:7 | | x |

The distribution of tropes follows a clear pattern. The sequestration of matching and dependency is unquestionable. Setting this factor aside, we can simplify the diagram; the percentages of lines are rounded to the tens, as they are percentages of small numbers.

| | *troping* | *non-class I* |
|---|---|---|
| IIIa | 100% | 70% |
| IIIb | 100% | 50% |
| IIIc | 30% | 20% |
| IIId | 70% | 10% |

The oracle begins with lines heavily marked in both tropological and line typological terms. The line class markedness declines across the poem consistently, though with a sharp break between IIIb and IIIc. The troping declines sharply after the same point, in IIIc, but is greater in the final subdivision, IIId. The part's least marked subdivision, IIIc, is thus entirely contained within it.

The concluding part of the Oracles, 24:15a-19b, is less evidently complex. The weight of this part is somewhat higher than that of the poem as a whole, 7:1, 88:12%; the TH ratio, 70:30%, is not remarkable. The repetition of 24:3a-4c as 24:15a-16d insures an opening in which 5 out of 7 lines are of Classes III (24:15ab, 16ab) and II (24:16d) and all the lines are troped with repetition (24:15ab, 15abc 16a) or dependency (24:15bc, 16ab, 16cd), or both. In the eleven lines which follow the introduction, 24:17a-19b, there are only 1 Class III line (24:17f) and 1 Class II line (24:18b). The first 10 of those 11 lines are troped; only the last line, 24:19b, is not. Repetition occurs in 24:18ab; and binomination in 24:17cd and 18c 19a, in the former case cooccurring with combination, and matching. The two lines before 24:17cd, 24:17ab, also match. The doubly repetitive pair 24:18ab is the first part of a 3 line match, 24:18abc; the last matching line is tied to the following line by binomination. Dependency is limited to 24:17ef.

The weighting of the four parts of the Oracles is not uniform throughout. The first and third parts are weighted at 67:33% (6:3 and 8:4, respectively), underweight for the poem, 26:9 lines, or 74:26%; the other parts are compensatorily overweight, the second at 5:1 lines or 83:17% and the last at 7:1 or 88:12%. The distribution of tropes is also not uniform. The supralinear-level tropes are entirely missing in Part I, 23:7a-10d, and the line-level tropes are infrequent in Part III, 24:3a-9d. Of the four parts of the poem, these two are precisely the two which seem, in the context of our readings of Genesis 49 and Deuteronomy 33, to have regular unit shapes. It is the rigidity that results from these regular unit shapes that makes possible the underweighting and the variation in trope usages in these parts.

### *10.1.4 Summary*

In the course of studying Genesis 49, Deuteronomy 33, and Numbers 23-24, we have had recourse to a wide variety of explanatory hard- and software. Concentrating on the texts and approaching them without any notions of gross structures has led to a bewildering array of parts, sets, sections, divisions, units and the like. This array can be replaced by two simpler tools which perform the services of the larger troop. Before this replacement, a central piece of software, the notion of symmetry, needs a little polishing.

All discussions of art objects refer to notions of symmetry, recurrence, and pattern, usually without qualification or apology. Both are needed and neither is possible. What is possible is limitation of the discussion and recognition of the varieties of arguments to be accepted. This can be done conveniently by illustration.

The sound of the sibilant *s* can be described in terms of the frequencies of its components. The frequency representation is a complex curve, which reveals in an accurate way the physical properties of the signal; the sound wave is shown in Ladefoged (1962:29). This sound can be distinguished from what acousticians call white noise, "a sound with an equal amount of power at every component frequency over the audible range" (Ladefoged 1962:114). But it cannot be distinguished easily or clearly, so that it is not far from sounding like radio static, a closer approximation of white noise.

Let us suppose that a student of an art object—a poem or a rug, it does not matter—were to isolate a variable in that object which varies in a way that could be represented in a curve identical to the frequencies of *s*. It is conceivable that this student could point to the curve and claim that the likeness is meaningful, observing that the curve of an *s* can be perceived by the human sensory apparatus and processed as information bearing; that is, *s*'s can be heard. We would surely reject the claim.

Why? First, because the *s* curve is almost a random signal, almost white noise; patterns that approach randomness lose their status as patterns. This is the simplest reason and it would probably work for this example. There are, however, other reasons to regard the claim as suspect. Chief among these is context. The sound *s* is perceived only in the context of speech. The low incidence of patterning within the *s* sound sets it off from, say, a preceding or following vowel, since all vowels have fairly simple frequency patterns. What is perceived about an *s* is not only its low patterning, but its contrast to a neighboring segment's high degree of patterning.

The category speech is a rough approximation of the lowest order of context, the acoustic phonetic level. There are other orders. Any use of *s* occurs within a language and languages only use sounds in highly patterned ways. Any speaker of English who perceives an initial 3 consonant cluster need not perceive *s* within it at all. She or he knows that the phonological organization of English stipulates that the first consonant must be *s*. There can be no doubt that such a speaker is processing information about overall word structure simultaneous with individual segment structure (if we suppose that the latter is processed in any independent way). She or he can suppress the processing of the low patterning *s* as soon as the clustering is recognized. This order of context, the phonological, also includes other features of word structure; the speaker need not consider the voicing or the manner of articulation of the next two consonants in our example. The second consonant must be a voiceless stop, like *t*, and the third must be a voiced continuant, like *r*.

Further levels of context can be perceived all the way up a complex hierarchy of speech organization. On every one there are additional factors which make hearing the noise of an *s* easier. They make it so easy in fact that it may make sense linguistically to say that the low patterning is not perceived as patterning at all.

The notions of context and redundancy are only understood in rudimentary form in linguistics. They are not understood at all for art objects. The more or less that a beholder expects cannot be defined or described in any generalized way. Yet patterns are referred to in connection with art objects. The implicit controls on the argumentation are various. The most obvious confines the student to a tradition and yields statements like the following. "For a piece of Chinese calligraphy, that's a good piece. We who know Chinese calligraphy know that the best of it has feature x and we see it here; feature y, abundantly shown in this piece; and feature z, which is plainly everywhere in the piece at hand." These are usually satisfactory and often interesting statements. A major problem is that x, y and z often cannot be specified with enough precision to convey information; but that is not always the case. Any reader familiar with the canons of rhyme in Pope could read the heroic couplets of his immediate contemporaries and judge their rhymes by Pope's in a clear and pertinent way. Pope never rhymes by eye alone, so any eye rhyme would be rejected. He never rhymes against stress, masculine on feminine. Any such rhyme would be found a fault, though probably a less severe fault than an eye rhyme.

(We are assuming the existence of a hermeneutic circle beyond which appeal is not allowed, since in some sense everything can be used to prove something else. It is all very well to propose that a supposed structure is a functional pattern and apply an adjective indicating approbation; such application does not prove anything about the structure but that the student likes it, unless it is stated in terms of factors the existence of which can be demonstrated or at least suggested on other grounds. In fact, such application does not even provide much of a handle to use in considering plausibility. Arguments about the pleasure structures probably gave to their originators are also useless. Similarly, to refer to the effectiveness of patterns in preserving things in the memory short-circuits the fact that we really do not know much about how memory works. Most of the time such arguments also sidestep the fact that people of our culture at the present time have a relation to information intake which is entirely unlike any that has obtained in human history. Our problems in even talking sense about memory are astounding and we shall not try to do so here. We have seen arguments to the effect that supposed poetic patterns are such because they helped the author remember the poems he had composed during the twenty years before they were written down. This is no argument at all. And again, to judge that a pattern usable in argumentation or liturgy is a pattern in poetry is to ignore the fact that poetry has not been dominant in the courtrooms, councils, or worship chambers of many cultures. This is not to say the arguments are useless, but merely that they are not arguments about the structure of poems as such. We only mention these excluded arguments because they turn up often; all of them occur frequently, e.g., in Lundbom 1975.)

The problem of defining criteria already in use is a major problem but it is not our primary problem. We are faced, as are all students of ancient literatures from Sievers to Karlgren, with a closed corpus. This fact stimulated Albright's famous taxonomic approach to poetry, modelled on his parallel studies in ceramics; such inductive study supposes uncontrollable and undescribable changes over a limited range of entities. Thus Albright focused on describing a loosely characterized system of changes. We have shown that the entities themselves can be described and are now seeking to discover whether the particularities of description add up to a larger particularity. (We are not at the moment interested in constructing a historical taxonomy, but the task is now reconceivable.)

The first condition on a symmetry description for a closed corpus is that the feature for which symmetry is alleged be independent of other features. The only feature of Hebrew poetry for which such independence is obvious is length. Let us examine the three major length patterns we have found.

The first poem we considered was Genesis 49, which we described as containing three units of equal length. Virtually without comment we offered this as a symmetrical structure. There is no comment: three units measured with the same measure must be symmetrical. If the units are cut off in a meaningful way, then the poem is symmetrical. The arguments about whether the divisions are meaningful are presented above and taken up again below. The point here concerns the symmetry.

Deuteronomy 33 we characterized as having three units and one half-unit, positioned initially. The symmetry of this pattern, 1/2x-x-x-x, we attempted to capture with the term inverted Shakespearian sonnet. This is roughly accurate: the pattern is the same as that of a Shakespearian sonnet except for the position of the half-unit. We implicitly suggested further that this naming is easier and more useful than specifying a pattern in which (a) two units, related in length in a simple way, are used; (b) the occurrences of the smaller unit are not intermixed with those of the larger (thus far the sonnet is general); and (c) the units occur in a 3:1 ratio favoring the larger. The simple statement is plainly easier. A few observations can be made in defense of its greater usefulness. The first involves the term itself. The sonnet recommends itself for use here first of all because it designates a common Euroamerican poetic form. It is a crude but not luniacal assumption that what is a pattern in one sort of poetry may turn out to be a pattern in another.

The second defense of the term's use we owe to Gene Schramm, who has observed that the Book of Lamentations is organized in sonnet form. The first three chapters have 22 stanzas of six lines, roughly 132 lines (we ignore minor deviations here); the fourth has 22 stanzas of four lines and the fifth, 22 stanzas of two lines. Overall this yields 132-132-132-88-44. This scheme meets the (b) requirement noted above; the (a) stipulation is extended to three units and the (c) ratio to 3:1:1; Lamentations also meets the decrescendo requirement. (We have simplified Schramm's argument by omitting reference to the acrostic form.) The existence of another not-quite sonnet, representing a different level of poetic organization in Hebrew, is a striking piece of support for the usage.

Neither of these supposed defenses is strong in itself and they are so different they scarcely reinforce each other. We are driven back to the case itself: even if there were no name for it, we would want to call 1/2x-x-x-x a pattern. If the measure has any significant organizing power (and since it is repeated three times over it must), then it must also be strong enough to be halved.

The surge back to the case was our immediate response in Numbers 23-24. We argued there that the structure 1/2x-(x-y)-x-(x-2y) was a pattern on the basis of a rearrangement of a series of lengths *abcd* in the order *acdb*. This ordering of the lengths (14 lines - 22 - 26 - 18) can be taken as a case of the permutation *acdb*, itself the result of picking alternating pairs from the set. All three schemes for picking pairs from the set of four are visible in the arrangement *acdb*. The alternating pairs (*abcd*/*ac* and *bd*) are simple linear pairs in *acdb*. The simple linear pairs (*abcd*/*ab* and *cd*) are the margins and the middle of the pattern *acdb*. The pairs found by splitting the basic margins off the middle (*abcd*/*ad* and *bc*) are the alternating pairs in *acdb*. This is the least obvious pattern of length we have seen but it is far indeed from white noise. This, too, is the sort of thing we will call a pattern.

A final point in connection with the pattern of the Oracles involves a reference not yet explicitly made. In the series *acdb*, there is a crescendo in size, rounded off with a decrescendo. This property suggests a name for the pattern (and since we shall see it again, it needs a name): swell. The musical analogy is slightly confusing since musicians and musicologists are not consistent in their use of the term. We will use the term to mean a pattern of rising length followed by declining length, in which the crescendo is fuller.

We have three patterns in three poems; the simple pattern of Genesis 49, x-x-x; the inverted sonnet of Deuteronomy 33, 1/2x-x-x-x; and the swell of Numbers 23-24, 1/2x-(x-y)-x-(x-2y), where x is 26-28 and y is 4. Let us find a better name for x.

We have been erratic in designating the 26-28 block of lines which is a structural factor in the poems we have discussed. Most of the terms we have used are unsatisfactory: block, section, and so on. Stanza seems appropriate but the term in modern usage refers to a smaller grouping which is more consistent in shape. Strophe avoids these problems but introduces the problem of approximating the Alexandrian rhetoricians which has been the Charybdis of so many students of poetics, including whole fleets of Semitists, some still spinning. We would like to revitalize for our description a little used English term for a section of a poem, stave. The word is a back formation from staves, the plural of staff, which is also used in this sense. The use of stave for part of a poem seems distinct from both the Old Norse term *stef* 'refrain' and English *stave* 'a member of an alliterative pattern,' used of Old English verse, cf. German *stabreimender Vers*.

The facts about staves can be summarized. The stave is a unit of variable length; the basic range is 26-28 or -31 lines. The seven staves we have discussed are the following:

| | |
|---|---|
| 26 line staves | Gen 49:2a-9d |
| | Gen 49:10a-18 |
| | Dt 33:6a-12d |
| | Num 24:3a-9d |
| 27 line stave | Dt 33:22b-29f |
| 28 line stave | Gen 29:19a-27c |
| 31 line stave | Dt 33:13b-21e |

The last named is an irregularity if we retain the range 26-28 lines.

The stave can also be divided. We have noted two semi-staves, one of 13 lines, Dt 33:2a-5c; the other of 14 lines, Num 23:7a-10d. Further, the stave can be varied, under fairly special circumstances, as we saw in an 18 line stave, Num 24:15a-19b, and a 22 line stave, Num 23:18a-24d. The special circumstances in the Oracles of Balaam are that the poem has clearly demarcated sections and that it displays a tendency to fall into a couplet structure. The argument is that the stave, a high level organizational device, can be made free if there are major devices operating on other levels to support the overall organization of the text. The phenomena are all ways of holding lines together, so some sort of tradeoff is plausible.

The strongest feature of our demonstration of the stave's existence so far is that it has proved useful in talking about some poems that are not obviously similar. We can strengthen that demonstration if we can show that all the poems in our corpus are written in staves. As a first step, we will show that it is plausible that all of them can be divided into staves. (The approach to Zephaniah will be justified below.)

| | *26-28 line staves* | *poem: length* |
|---|---|---|
| 2 | 52-56 | Ex 15: 56 lines |
| 3 | 78-84 | Gen 49: 80 lines |
| | | Num 23-24: 80 lines |
| | | Zph 3: 79 lines |
| 4 | 104-112 | Jdg 5: 106 lines |
| | | Ps 106: 106 lines |
| 5 | 130-140 | Dt 32: 140 lines |
| 6 | 156-168 | Ps 78: 163 lines |
| 8 | 182-224 | Zph (total): 213 lines |

Of the fifteen poetic units under examination (taking Zph 1, 2, 3, and total as separate units), nine can be accounted for with regular distribution of staves. (We know that in the case of Num 23-24 the accounting requires some modification.) Allowing for the semi-stave, we can extend the list.

| | *26-28 line stave* | *poem: length* |
|---|---|---|
| 2 1/2 | 65-70 | Hab 3: 65 lines |
| | | Zph 1: 69 lines |
| | | Zph 2: 65 lines |
| 3 1/2 | 91-98 | Dt 33: 97 lines |

Two poems remain. 2 Samuel 1 is 30 lines, a single long stave evidently; Psalm 107 is 89 lines long, either slightly short of 3 1/2 26-28 line staves or 3 long (30 line) staves. Both these poems have refrain groups or burdens, so we have reason to be reluctant about squeezing them into the system.

The stave is a hefty unit of verse. In the course of discussing the Testaments we had occasion to discuss small areas of discourse. Essentially these were the individual oracles themselves, although the longest of these, 17-19 lines long, tended to break into subsections. These sections are often arrayed in distinctive patterns. Further, the third stave of Numbers 23-24 showed strong sectional patterning, in units of 6-7 lines. This suggests that there is another poetic unit to be ferreted out. The investigation will need to be careful because the unit seems to have a broad range of activity. This unit too needs a name; let us revitalize another largely dormant English word for a section of a poem, batch.

The facts about the batch are rather dark. We will need to establish the range of batch sizes and see whether there is a mean range. The easy end of the range first: the shortest batch is the prayer in Gen 49:18, 1 line. The far upper limit must be the semi-stave range, 13-14 lines.

There are some long oracles and other units in the Testaments: one 17 and one 19 line oracle in Genesis 49, and three 17 line passages in Deuteronomy 33. There are also 10, 11, 12 and possibly 13 line sections in these poems. No section of either poem is 14, 15, 16 or 18 lines long. This suggests a need to reexamine all five 17-19 line passages.

We already know that such reexamination is necessary: the Judah oracle in Genesis 49 has to be split into Gen 49:8a-9d, Judah's Origins (7 lines), and Gen 49:10a-12d, Judah's Dominion (10 lines). The split is necessary on other grounds and the distribution of troping and heavy lines supports the division. The Joseph oracle in Jacob's Testament is easily split: the 12 lines of the blessing proper, Gen 49:24c-26e, are all troped together and thus set off from the 7 lines describing Joseph among the animals, Gen 49:22a-24b. The other Joseph oracle splits in roughly the same way, with the blessing first, grouped with an introductory line, Dt 33:13b-16d (11 lines); followed by an animal passage, Dt 33:17a-f (6 lines). Three easy divisions, supported by usage of supralinear tropes.

The division of the two remaining 17 line passages is more complex. The Levi oracle in Deuteronomy 33 can be cut across the overall matching arrangement into two sections on the basis of word trope array and non-Class I line distribution. The first subsection refers to Levi's family relations in 7 lines, Dt 33:8b-9c; the second devotes ten lines to his work and its upshot, Dt 33:9d-11d. The Coda to Deuteronomy 33 treats first of Yahweh, in 7 lines, Dt 33:26a-27d; this section is bounded by non-Class I lines. Yahweh's people occupy the rest of the Coda, Dt 33:28a-29f (10 lines).

Of the five 17-19 line oracles, three split off initial units of 7 lines and final sets of 10 or (in one case) 12 lines. The Deuteronomy Coda and Joseph oracle begin with a large unit, and follow with a smaller.

Having cut down the range of the batch from 1-17 lines to 1-13, we may go further. The only 13 line unit, the initial section of Deuteronomy 33, is formally and thematically bipartite. The opening passage, Dt 33:2a-3c (8 lines), is transhistorical; the next, Dt 33:4a-5c (5 lines), historical. The range of the batch is, then, 1-12 lines in the testamentary poems. There are no obviously coherent longer passages in the Oracles of Balaam, but except for the third stave of the poem, Num 24:3a-9d, we have not inquired about batch lengths. In that stave, the divisions are as follows: 24:3a-4c (7 lines); 5a-6d (6 lines); 7a-8b (6 lines); and 8c-9d (7 lines). These batches are differentiated on the basis of troping distribution.

The last stave can be cut on the same basis. The syntactic dependency of Num 24:16cd and 17ef is of the same variety and these set the bounds of the first two of three batches. The last line of the poem, 24:19b, is made distinctive by the fact that it is the only one in the stave that is not troped. The three batches of the fourth stave are then 24:15a-16d (7 lines), the repeated section; 24:17a-f (6 lines); and 24:18a-19b (5 lines). The second batch begins with two 2 line matches, 24:17ab and 17cd; and the third begins with one 3 line match, 18abc; these are the only matches in the stave. In the last of these matches, the last line, 18c, is the first line of a binomination couplet, 18c 19a.

The first two staves are harder to divide into batches. The second, Num 23:18a-24d, should probably be cut after 20ab, which lines contain the only repetition figure in the stave, and thus after 19d 20ab, the only 3 line match in it; and before 23cd, a couplet with dependency. The third batch, 23:23c-24d, is heavily marked, as it contains a trope of mixing in 24abcd, and a Class IV line, 23d. It also contains the remarkable use of the poem's commonest binomination in 23:23cd. The same binomination is used immediately before, in 23ab, in a much more standard way and with 21ab forms a ring around the second batch, 21a-23b. Both pairs of lines are passives, both either singular or plural. The first batch is left, by default, as it were. Thematic correlations of these batch divisions are obvious (as they are in the batch divisions of the other staves) and support our parsing. Although not proper to our concerns, we may mention the inside-outside figuration in the stave, crucial to a poem which is about putting Israel together and putting Yahweh together with Israel.

The first and shortest stave, Num 23:7a-10d, is the hardest to divide. The most striking formal criterion involves the lack of troping: 23:9cd and 10d are untroped Class I lines and their plainness (i.e., the interruption of the heavy troping of the previous lines) sets off 23:9c-10d as a 6 line batch. The remaining batch is the opening of the poem, 23:7a-9b, 8 lines.

In the three poems, there are 45 batches of between one and twelve lines; there are 257 lines all told, so the average length is 6 lines. Two dozen are between 5 and 8 lines long; half a dozen are longer; and 15 are shorter. The longer and shorter all occur in the Testaments.

The distribution of short batches is summarized below, followed by the data on long batches.

| *lines* | *Gen 49* | *Dt 33* | *total occ* | *total lines* |
|---|---|---|---|---|
| 1 | 1 | ∅ | 1: 2% | 1: — |
| 2 | 5 | 2 | 7: 15% | 14: 5% |
| 3 | 2 | 3 | 5: 11% | 15: 6% |

| | | | | |
|---|---|---|---|---|
| 4 | 1 | 1 | 2: 4% | 8: 3% |
| | | | *15: 33%* | *38: 15%* |
| 9 | ∅ | ∅ | ∅ | ∅ |
| 10 | 2 | 2 | 4: 9% | 40: 16% |
| 11 | ∅ | 1 | 1: 2% | 11: 4% |
| 12 | 1 | ∅ | 1: 2% | 12: 5% |
| | | | *6: 13%* | *63: 25%* |

The data suggest that batches of 1-4 lines and those of 9-12 lines constitute a balanced group. The former are shorter and therefore there are more of them; one-third of the batches are in the small batch group. The large batch group accounts for far fewer batches, but, since its members are larger, it accounts for substantially more lines, one-quarter. The balance is not perfect. That it comes as close as it does is surprising given that other factors seem to be at work. The obvious one is the use of the couplet form, a basic domain of troping; an available resource is being marshalled into service here.

The middle range of the batch sizes is 5-8 lines. Over half the batches, including all those of Numbers 23-24, fall in this range; and well over half of the 257 lines occur in middle size batches.

| *lines* | *Gen 49* | *Dt 33* | *Num 23-24* | *total occ* | *total lines* |
|---|---|---|---|---|---|
| 5 | ∅ | 3 | 1 | 4: 9% | 20: 8% |
| 6 | 1 | 2 | 5 | 8: 18% | 48: 19% |
| 7 | 3 | 2 | 3 | 8: 18% | 56: 22% |
| 8 | ∅ | 1 | 3 | 4: 9% | 32: 12% |
| | | | | *24: 54%* | *156: 61%* |

The mean range of batch size is not only dominant, but also has its own mean, 6-7 lines. One-third of the middle range batches are 5 *or* 8 lines, one-third are 6 lines and one-third are 7.

The range of the batch is 1-12 lines, the mean range is 5-8 lines, and the mean of the mean is 6-7 lines. This seems a vague refinement of a descriptive tool, but it is vague for particular reasons. Recall our intimations about where and why the two extremes of the range are used. The Testaments use batch sizes of more than usual diversity because in them the batch is not the only factor supporting the poetic structure on the level below the stave. The subject shifts completely and often in these poems, and in them there is thus less need for predictability on the stave level. The reader will note that this argument has a family relationship to the one used earlier in proposing that Numbers 23-24 has irregular staves.

This consideration allows us to approach the definition of the batch again. It is a poetic unit with boundaries marked by troping or, less often, non-Class I lines, which is usually between 5 and 8 lines long, frequently 6 or 7 lines. In poems with other overall structuring devices relevant to the sub-stave domain, it may vary more widely, between 1 and 12 lines.

The relation of the stave and the batch may be discussed. The data thus far suggest that they are not necessarily features of a single simple system. The groups of batches within a stave (since all batches are contained within staves) may vary not only over that stave; it may also be involved in other patterns that cut across staves. Similarly, in a Petrarchan sonnet, the quatrains are not controlled by the octet they compose nor the triplets (or couplets) by the sestet. There may be an octet-sestet relation along with relations between either quatrain, and either triplet or any of the couplets.

### *10.1.5 Reconsideration*

Beginning with three texts, we have gathered together materials for a consideration of gross poetic structure. Having put all those materials in a heap, we sorted through them. We ended with three usable items: a general notion of symmetry and definitions of two poetic units, the stave (26-28 lines) and the batch (5-8 lines, rarely 1-12 lines). We have constantly appealed to various features of the poems to broaden the gate of acceptability for the definitions. Let us repeat the diverse appeals all at once.

The poetic units stave and batch show gross variation only in case they are used to match the subject sections of the texts. In the Testaments, the oracles or parts of them correspond to batches, and batch size varies. In the Oracles of Balaam, the four individual oracles correspond to staves, and stave size varies. The subject sections themselves correspond to what we might call genre features. This denomination explains nothing intrinsically because if the poems under discussion constitute examples of two genres, they also exhaust our reserves of those genres. It is theoretically useful to refer to genre, however, because subject sectioning is expected in genre definition. An archaic Greek victory ode, for example, must include reference to the victor's situation, his family and his family's mythohistorical situation, in that order. We need not press the genre point too far, however, because the subject sections are recognized as a working base of study by all students. Given these, we can say that the poetic unit that coincides with the subject section most closely is most amenable to the pressure of reshaping.

One way in which our conception of batches and staves as poetic units could be strengthened is a demonstration that they vary independently in similar ways. This demonstration would also support the correlation of poetic unit and subject section, which we shall call the genre correlation. The opportunity to combine the results of the first three parts of this section, 10.1.1-3, with the fourth, 10.1.4, in an orderly way will be seized.

Before that overview, we must supplement our remarks on symmetry. To be worth noticing, we suggested, a figure claimed to pattern symmetrically should be independent. Length is the prime candidate for status as an independent feature and we have reviewed the length symmetries of the simple symmetry, inverted sonnet and swell patterns. To this feature, we will add two others, troping and non-Class I lines, in the guise of two phenomenal measures extracted and found useful earlier. These are weight, the percentage ratio of troped and non-Class I lines to unmarked lines; and the TH ratio, the percentage ratio of troped lines to non-Class I lines. Weight and TH ratio approximate the independence of the factors involved (or of what they have in common), in a way that is different from separate measures of the factors because TH ratio and weight reflect the interdependence of the classes of lines involved. This is because most troped lines are Class I lines; non-Class I lines are troped less often.

We have not tried to show the independence of weight and the TH ratio. This is because the question of their independence in the whole poetic system is the same as the question of the correctness of our definition of the fine structure of Hebrew verse. Arguments for independence would be complex restatements of Part II. Instead of undertaking these, we will remind the reader that accepting the full form of any discussion here requires accepting the bulk of the earlier discussion. The dependence relation however is unidirectional. Nothing in Part II depends on anything here. Further, many of the facts observed here will need some accounting in any serious description of Hebrew verse; the reader should be capable of reading at once both our description and the facts behind it with no more than occasional eyestrain.

The simple symmetry of Genesis 49 consists in the even lengths of its three units: Stave I, 2a-9d, 26 lines; Stave II, 10a-18, 26 lines; and Stave III, 19a-27c, 28 lines. This pattern is complicated by variations in weight and TH ratios, which result largely from irregular distribution of non-Class I lines. The first and last staves are overweight and have ca. 60:40% TH ratios. The middle stave is underweight and has an 84:16% TH ratio. The outer staves form a ring around the middle one and we shall call Genesis 49's overall structure a ring. In our usage of the term ring we suppose a situation of simple symmetry and we shall treat ring structures as a subspecies of simple symmetry.

The first and last staves have a common batch structure which is of some interest. Stave I contains four batches and Stave III, six. (Batches are signalled with lower case letters.)

| | *Stave I* | *Stave III* |
|---|---|---|
| P. | a. Invocation. 2ab: 2 lines | a. Gad. 19ab: 2 lines |
| | b. Reuben. 3a-4c: 7 lines | b. Asher. 20ab: 2 lines |

| | | |
|---|---|---|
| | c. Simeon & Levi. 5a-7d: 10 lines | c. Naphtali. 21ab: 2 lines |
| | | d. Joseph-Animals. 22a-24b: 7 lines |
| | | e. Joseph-Blessings. 24c-26e: 12 lines |
| Q. | d. Judah's Origins. 8a-9d: 7 lines | f. Benjamin. 27abc: 3 lines |

Through the first three batches of Stave I and the first five of Stave III, the region labelled P, the batch lengths increase. In the last batch of each, labelled Q, they decline. This pattern looks familiar: it is, on the batch level, the pattern which we have named a swell on the stave level.

The middle stave of Genesis 49 has a different structure.

*Stave II*

a. Judah's Dominion. 10a-12b: 10 lines
b. Zebulon. 13abc: 3 lines
c. Issachar. 14a-15d: 6 lines
d. Yahweh's Rule. 16ab: 2 lines
e. Dan. 17a-d: 4 lines
f. Prayer. 18: 1 line

The overall length movement is from 10 lines to 1 line, a decrescendo, but it is a complex one because the descent takes place on two levels. There is a descent *within pairs*: a is longer than b, c than d, e than f. There is also a descent *by pairs*: ab is longer than cd, which is longer than ef. The latter pattern is played out on two planes: a is longer than c, which is longer than e; and b is longer than d, which is longer than f. (Further, e is larger than b!)

The ensemble could be described, using traditional metrical language, as three trochees arranged roughly as a dactyl (the trochee-measured unit is the batch, and the dactyl-measured unit is two batches). The "roughness" of the dactyl may be specified. The length of a and b (13 lines) is the sum of the lengths of c and d (8 lines) and of e and f (5 lines). That is, the pattern is not a dactyl made up of three trochees so much as one trochee, with resolution, made up of three smaller trochees. This naming approach is likely to prove confusing and we shall abandon it and look elsewhere for a name for this pattern. Let us call this type of decrescendo pattern, a double decrescendo; double decker for short.

The overall structure of Genesis 49 described above is a ring structure. Let us summarize, adding the information about batch structures.

| *Stave* | *length* | *weight* | *TH ratio* | *batch structure* |
|---|---|---|---|---|
| I | 26 lines | 72:27% | 59:41% | swell |
| II | 26 | 37:63 | 84:16 | double decker |
| III | 28 | 69:31 | 56:44 | swell |

The batch configurations of Staves I and III support the ring structure overall. Perhaps the underweightiness of Stave II is compensated for by the more complex batch structure.

Deuteronomy 33 is structurally more dense everywhere. The length pattern, the inverted sonnet, marks out as deviant the first stave (a half-unit, henceforth numbered continuously with the full staves). The TH ratio of the poem is stable across the staves except for the second stave. The weight of the first two staves is even; the third is overweight and the fourth under. The term inverted sonnet is unequal to the task of describing these three patterns. Each stave is deviant in one respect: I, 2a-5c, in length; II, 6a-12d, in TH ratio; III, 13b-21e, in being overweight; and the last, 22b-29f, in being underweight.

In considering the batch structure of Deuteronomy 33, we will need to backtrack considerably. Earlier, we noted that each full stave contains four subject sections. With the reanalysis of the 17-19 line passages, we can say that each has five batches. The reanalysis also allows us to return to some patterns noted earlier within staves. Consider the batches of the last two staves.

| | *Stave III* | *Stave IV* |
|---|---|---|
| a. | Joseph's Blessings. 13b-16d: 11 lines | Dan. 22bc: 2 lines |
| b. | Joseph-Animals. 17a-f: 6 lines | Naphtali. 23bcd: 3 lines |
| c. | Zebulon-Issachar. 18b-19d: 6 lines | Asher. 24b-25b: 5 lines |
| d. | Gad. 20b-21b: 5 lines | Coda: Yahweh. 26a-27d: 7 lines |
| e. | General. 21cde: 3 lines | Coda: Israel. 28a-29f 10 lines |

The third stave shows a constant decrescendo (except at Batches b and c), and the fourth a constant crescendo. These are the first two staves we have seen with a single movement in batch size variation (i.e., the size changes, but only in one direction). The opening stave of Deuteronomy 33 is another simple decrescendo.

| | *Stave I* |
|---|---|
| a. | Theophany. 2a-3c: 8 lines |
| b. | Revelation. 4a-5c: 5 lines |

The batches of the second stave of Deuteronomy 33 are arranged in a familiar pattern.

| | *Stave II* |
|---|---|
| a. | Reuben. 6ab: 2 lines |
| b. | Judah. 7b-e: 4 lines |
| c. | Levi's family. 8b-9c: 7 lines |
| d. | Levi's work. 9d-11d: 10 lines |
| e. | Benjamin. 12bcd: 3 lines |

This is another swell. The important feature of its presence here (in contrast to such shapes in Genesis 49) is that here it is the most complex batch structure in the poem; in Genesis 49, it is the simplest.

The denomination of Deuteronomy 33 as an inverted sonnet can be further supported now. To the three varying dimensions, length, weight, and TH ratio, let us add a fourth. Three of the four staves have only one direction of batch size change: Staves I and III decline and Stave IV rises. Only Stave II has two directions, in swell form; thus it has the greatest complexity of directionality. Let us suppose that variance in weight, TH ratio, batch directionality, and length all serve to render a poetic text complex and that the last is first among equals. The least marked staves are the last two, deviant only in weight; the next least deviant is the first, deviant only in length; and the most deviant is the second, singular in TH ratio and directionality. The convergence point of deviance is the transition between Staves I and II; the best way to highlight that convergence is the term inverted sonnet.

The swell of staves in Numbers 23-24 has been amply discussed. The batches within the staves are distributed according to easily discernible patterns. The first two and the last vary in line length in decrescendi.

| | *Stave I* | | *Stave II* | | *Stave IV* |
|---|---|---|---|---|---|
| | ch 23 | | ch 23 | | ch 24 |
| a. | 7a-9b.<br>8 lines | a. | 18a-20b.<br>8 lines | a. | 15a-16d.<br>7 lines |
| b. | 9c-10d.<br>6 lines | b. | 21a-23b.<br>8 lines | b. | 17a-f.<br>6 lines |
| | | c. | 23c-24d.<br>6 lines | c. | 18a-19b.<br>5 lines |

The third stave's batches form a ring.

| | *Stave III* |
|---|---|
| | ch 24 |
| a. | 3a-4c. 7 lines |
| b. | 5a-6d. 6 lines |

c. 7a-8b. 6 lines
d. 8c-9d. 7 lines

We point these out in part because batch size has been important above, and in part because they are obvious. They are, on any level of working interest, trivial. The pitch is too small to be noteworthy; this is plain from the greater range of variation used in the Testaments. There is no point to be made by denying these patterns, but there is also no point to be made by taking them as significant. In fact, all the batch length patterns of Numbers 23-24 are simply symmetrical.

There are some features of the batches which are of interest. The first is that the two staves with deviant lengths, II and IV, though those lengths are different, have the same number of batches. The three-fold batch structure serves to reinforce their common feature, irregular stave lengths. The other noteworthy feature of the batches of Numbers 23-24 is that, of all the staves the batches of which we have surveyed, only the two of "regular" length in the Oracles, I and III, have erratic distribution of troping. In these staves, there is a marked decline in the extent of troping overall; the situation is more complex in the third stave, since there is also a reverse swell of troping, i.e., troping declines across the first three batches and then rises in the fourth. This is the only occasion on which we have noted the structure of troping within a stave on the batch level. This is probably because Stave III of this poem is the only stave worked on so fine a level. A general compensation is at work here again: the most regular stave in the poem's overall structure has the most complex internal structure.

Let us return to what we called the genre correlation, relying on the factor of length only to summarize our reconsideration. The lengths of staves can vary over poems and the lengths of batches can vary over staves. If the genre correlation were valid, we would expect that the variations in stave size in Numbers 23-24 would be of the same sort as the variations of batch size in the Testaments. That is, we would expect (a) that stable stave size, resulting from a correlation between subject section and batch size, would be associated with the Testaments; (b) that their batch sizes would vary; (c) that the opposite would be true of the Oracles; and (d) the kinds of variations involved would be the same. We may lay out the facts for inspection, with attention to the number of changes in direction of size variation within the units.

| *changes in size variation* | *stave size* | *batch size* |
|---|---|---|
| no changes: simple symmetry | Gen 49 | Num 23-24, St. I, II, III, IV |

| | | |
|---|---|---|
| one change: | | |
| crescendo | Dt 33 | Dt 33, St. IV |
| decrescendo | | Dt 33, St. I, III |
| two changes: | | |
| swell | Num 23-24 | Gen 49, St. I, III |
| | | Dt 33, St. II |
| three changes: | | |
| double decker | | Gen 49, St. II |

There are no directionalities of stave size variation not exemplified in batch size change except for the most complex, the double decker. This directionality occurs in the poem with the simplest stave structure, the one with no change in stave size. The third line of the chart reveals that the swell pattern, which looked eccentric when we first saw it, is ordinary. The poem with the widest variation in stave size is Numbers 23-24 and this is the poem with the least variation in batch size.

We have commented on Genesis 49 and Numbers 23-24; they occupy the extreme ranks of the chart. Unlike Deuteronomy 33, they vary only one of the two basic poetic units. In Deuteronomy 33, both vary, though in different ways. Because both vary, each varies less than in the other poems.

We have not exhausted in these remarks the complexities of even the facts mentioned in our reconsideration. The small number of non-Class I lines in the middle stave of Genesis 49 and the decline in troping over the first and third staves of the Oracles of Balaam are only the most obvious facts set aside in these paragraphs. Further, we have not taken into account the fact that both Genesis 49 and Deuteronomy 33 have a section of general material immediately before the beginning of the last stave which circles back to the opening material. We have, however, begun to indicate the seriousness with which the gross structure of Hebrew verse must be studied and we are ready to look at more texts.

### *10.2 Poems with burdens*

Four poems in our corpus have complexes of repeated lines. Only one text, however, contains extensive simple repetition of whole lines, Numbers 23-24. In our treatment of that text, we found a passage of 6 lines given twice (Num 24:3a-4c=24:15a-16d); we restored one line to the first passage to make a total of 7 lines in perfect repetition. In addition, there are in that text two shorter passages, one of the two lines in them identical, the other nearly so (Num 23:22ab=24:8ab). The nearly identical passages present the commoner situation in our corpus: verbatim repetition of whole lines is rare. We shall study the phenomenon of long distance line repetition in the other three poems before we circle back to reconsider the repetitions of the Oracles of Balaam.

In the other texts, the repeated lines vary and the context of the repetition schematically alters. The combination of repetition and context is the burden, a unit smaller than or equal to the batch. The burden in 2 Samuel 1 is 2 lines long; in Exodus 15, 3 lines; and in Psalm 107, it is between 6 and 8 lines. The term burden allows for this large-scale phenomenon more clearly than the term refrain.

The second line of David's Lament is repeated as the second last line of the poem. A similar line, sometimes taken as a refrain, occurs near the end of the poem, at 2 S 1:25a; this line has a peculiar function in the poem's order but it is not part of the repetition structure. Rather, the burdens consist of the duplicate lines, and their mates, which are not at all alike.

| | |
|---|---|
| 2 S 1:19a | *hṣby yśrʾl ʿl-bmwtyk ḥll* |
| 2 S 1:19b | *ʾyk-nplw gbwrym* |
| 2 S 1:27a | *ʾyk-nplw gbwrym* |
| 2 S 1:27b | *wyʾbdw kly-mlḥmh* |

The reasons for separating off both these lines as the burden will be clearer after we look at the other poems. Suffice it to note that, granted that these are the burdens, they have a structure of one fixed line (the inner line) and one free line (the outer line).

The burdens of Exodus 15, which are 3 lines long, occupy the same positions as the Lament's: the first and last lines. A combination of fixed and free lines is used there, too: the first line is somewhat free (1a=21a), and the last two are fixed (1bc=21bc). The analogy of marginal positioning and of fixed and free makeup bolsters the reading of these sets of burdens.

The burdens of Psalm 107 are not located at the extreme ends of the poem; they do have the feature of fixed and free composition. The fixed lines are arranged so as to give the impression of two independent refrains; a schematic reading reveals the interdependence of the sets. The first two lines of the burden are somewhat fixed; the first line is more fixed than the second. The first line has two forms. One is used in 6a and 28a, the first and last burdens; the other occurs in 13a and 19a. The lines differ only in using variant forms of the root *z/ṣʿq* 'to cry out.' The second line of the burden has three forms, which differ more substantially, in the verb used. The middle burdens, 13b and 19b, both use forms of *yšʿ* 'to save'; the first burden has a form of *nṣl* 'to pluck' in 6b, the last a form of *yṣʾ* 'to go out' in 28b. The modulations involving the crucial sibilant in the lines are subtle enough to warrant a summary.

| *lines* | *sibilant* |
|---|---|
| 6a/b | *ṣ / ṣ* |
| 13a/b | *z / š* |

19a/b *z* / *š*
28a/b *ṣ* / *ṣ*

This neat spread is the result of two varying factors, one scarcely distinctive (in *z*/*ṣ*ᶜ*q*), the other amply so (*nṣl-yšᶜ-yṣ*ᵓ). The combination of sibilants varies independently of thematic development. In the latter, if we may digress, the point is made that people are unchangingly unsteady, while Yahweh is constantly various in answering their cries. The three verbs follow a progression from the one that expresses most immediate agency (*nṣl* 'to pluck') to the one that expresses most distant agency (*yṣ*ᵓ 'to go out'; here, 'to cause to go out').

The lines after the first two in each burden in Psalm 107 are entirely free. In three burdens, there are 2 free lines: in the first, 7ab; in the second, 14ab; and in the third, 20ab. In the fourth and last burden, there are 4 free lines, 29ab 30ab. The last 2 lines of each burden are entirely fixed: 8ab=15ab=21ab=31ab.

The complex burden structure of Psalm 107 makes its overall shape less accessible than that of the other poems. Let us turn first to the poems with marginal burdens.

### *10.2.1 2 Samuel 1. David's Lament*

The single stave of David's Lament can be treated as a somewhat long stave (30 lines as opposed to the normal range, 26-28 lines); if the burdens, 19ab and 27ab, are excluded from the stave proper, it falls within the standard range. The distribution of tropes suggests that the exclusion may be meaningful, since the only two lines in the text which are not troped are those of the first burden. We shall draft our arguments assuming the exclusion.

Although troping is most extensive on the line level, it is limited there to matching; gapping is absent.

| | | | | |
|---|---|---|---|---|
| word-level | 15 lines | | 50% | |
| repetition | | 9 lines | | 30% |
| coloration | | 10 lines | | 33% |
| line-level | 22 lines | | 73% | |
| matching | | 22 lines | | 73% |
| gapping | | ∅ lines | | |
| supralinear-level | 11 lines | | 37% | |
| dependency | | 3 lines | | 10% |
| mixing | | 8 lines | | 27% |
| total | 28 lines | | 93% | |

Although there are more non-Class I lines in total here than is usual in our corpus, the distribution of line types is not remarkable.

| | | | |
|---|---|---|---|
| Class I | 16 lines | 54% | |
| Class II | 7 lines | 23% | |
| Class III | 4 lines | 13% | 46% |
| Class IV | 3 lines | 10% | |
| total | 30 lines | 100% | |

The weight of the poem is 13:1 or 93:7% and the TH ratio is 67:33%.

The substructure of the single stave of 2 Samuel 1 is clearly marked off by both troping and the deployment of non-Class I lines. Indeed, this text provides one of the clearest examples of collaboration between these features. The tropes involved are three supralinear tropes: one case of clause mixing, 20abcd, another of phrase mixing, 22abcd, and yet another of dependency, 24abc. The heavy lines are the 3 Class IV lines, 19a and 26ab. The three tropes mark the beginnings of the first three batches; the Class IV lines start off the poem and the fourth batch.

The four batches are arranged within the envelope of the two burdens in descending order of length. The first two batches, 20a-21d and 22a-23d, are both 8 lines long. The last two are 5 lines long, 24a-25b and 26a-e. The decrescendo in the form of a Petrarchan sonnet (in triplets) is unmistakable; the proportions of the sonnet's 4:3 and the Lament's 8:5 are not merely numerically close, but arithmetically similar. Both proportions are balanced, even over odd, and in both, half of the first unit's length would be the unit after the second, were the series to be continued, i. e., 4:3 (: 2) and 8:5(: 4). (The speculation on continuation arises from the fact that poetic texts tend, while they are going on, to seem as if they are going to go on forever.)

The patterning alleged here, of batch size within a stave, is of the type referred to as trivial in connection with the Oracles of Balaam in 10.1.5. There are two differences between the cases. The first is that since 2 Samuel 1 is a single stave poem, it is *a priori* more likely to put the onus of poetic structure on the substave level. The second difference is the use of the median range of batch length, 5-8 lines. In Numbers 23-24, all the terms of the range are used: there are 5, 6, 7 and 8 line batches. In David's Lament, in contrast, only the extremes of the range, 5 and 8 line batches, occur.

The two batches which are even in line length tend to form couplets. The first batch, 20a-21d, is entirely coupleted, except that the trope of mixing breaks the single couplet pattern by coupling two couplets. The second batch is ordered away from coupling in a more complex way, although it, too contains a couplet of couplets in mixing. The royal names which occur within the mixed lines 22cd also occur in 23a and thus a repetition trope creates a 5 line unit to weigh against the 3 line match, 23bcd.

In the first batch, there are word-level tropes and line-level tropes in 6 of the 8 lines: both color troping and matching in the two couplets of the mix, 20ab and 20cd; matching in 21ab; and repetition in 21cd. The same cooccurrence of color tropes and matching characterizes the second batch's first 4 lines, 22ab and 22cd. The second couplet is joined to 23a, as we have noted, by a repetition trope. The last 3 lines of the batch, 23bcd, match.

The third batch begins with, and the fourth batch ends with, a 3 line group containing a 2 line group. The dependency group, 24abc, contains the match of 24bc; the match of 26cde includes the repetition of 26de. The third batch, then, opens with a step from supralinear- to line-level tropes and the fourth closes with a step from line- to word-level troping. The last lines of the third batch, 25ab, match, while the first lines of the fourth batch, 26ab, contain both a repetition and a coordination trope. The lines of the second burden match each other.

The distribution of line types is not as crucial here as troping. The first batch contains only Class I lines in the mix 20abcd and only Class II lines thereafter. The last batch opens with the 2 Class IV lines cited earlier and contains only Class I lines thereafter, 26cde. This means that after the initial Class IV line, there are five Class I lines, 19b-20d; and after the final Class IV lines, there are also 5 Class I lines, 26c-27b. This patterning across the batch-burden divide (if there is such; our argument does not depend on it) yields a set of Class IV lines plus Class I lines at the start and finish of the poem.

This phenomenon directs our attention again to the lines 25ab. The first of these includes the words of the fixed line of the burden, with a further phrase. The second is similar to the opening line of the poem, 19a: the vocative is dropped and the epithet 'the Gazelle' is either replaced by its referent (if Freedman is correct in taking Jonathan as the Gazelle, as we believe) or by another noun (if Cross is right in tying the epithet to Saul).

To describe this relation and the phenomenon of the Class IV lines followed by Class I lines at the extremes of the poem, we need to turn back to a point noted in connection with the Testaments. The second last stave of each Testament contains a batch of general import which can be tied back to the opening of the poems. In David's Lament, too, the second last poetic unit (a batch rather than a stave) has important links to the poem's opening, links underscored by the last unit itself. What is involved here is a kind of *trompe l'oeil* in the realm of figuration; these three poems have in common a false bottom, a trick conclusion which serves to refocus attention on the actual concluding poetic unit. There are both formal and thematic grounds for alleging the same phenomenon in Numbers 23-24. First, the three initial staves of the poem build up to a level of what we have argued is normality, the 26 line stave; the achievement of this normality could well be taken as a signal of conclusion. Further, the last lines of the third stave, Num 24:9cd, refer to blessings and cursings, the canonical concluding elements of ancient Near Eastern documents.

Let us consider several further points about these pseudoendings. The fake end of Genesis 49 does not correspond to the real end: although we have not said so explicitly, we trust it is clear that nothing can be thought to have been lost at the end of the poem; there is no general conclusion, only ravenous Benjamin. In other words, the fake ending satisfies expectations based on a genre feature (if we may resort to that term again) which will ultimately be disappointed. (The recognition of the genre feature hangs on Deuteronomy 33 only in strict terms; a ring structure is in general the sort of unifying device expected in a poem with many diverse subjects.) Further, note that we have no calculus to express the link between 2 S 1:19ab and 25ab. This lack is an important gap in our description because the fact that our four examples of the false coda have nothing in common suggests that we should not be able to describe the phenomenon on a simple linguistic level. This plain and simple *trompe* belongs to the order of poetic structure we call figuration; the phenomenon itself we call the fake coda.

A note on thematic concerns may be appended. There is no structural reading of the Lament based on linguistic criteria which will resolve the tension of reference in the poem, because it is a genuine tension; similarly, some doubt will always attach to the explication of the epithet 'the Gazelle'. The poem is about Saul and Jonathan; and, further, it is more about Jonathan. The treatment of Saul is split over two loci, 21cd and 24abc. The split has the effect of setting Saul up as dominant over the whole poem. In contrast, six of the seven or six lines treating Jonathan occur together. These six (despite their blocking) balance Saul's five because they include the last batch of the poem. Further, Jonathan is treated in the fake coda, 25b. The reading of the first line is not crucial in working out Jonathan's place in the poem's scheme, because even if it refers to Saul, Jonathan's lines still have greater structural prominence. The poem is diverse in its use of resources: it does not slight Saul, while giving prominence to Jonathan.

### *10.2.2 Exodus 15. The Song at the Sea*

The Song at the Sea and David's Lament are the two shortest poems in the corpus. They are further the only two with burdens positioned first and last, and the only two without gapping. These similarities notwithstanding, the poems are remarkably different. The Lament is overweight (13:1 lines, 93:7%), while the Song is even weight (15:15 lines, 50:50%). The Lament has a TH ratio of 67:33%, as opposed to the Song's, which is 51:49%. One superficial source of these differences is mixing; there are two mixes in the Lament and none here. The tropes are not otherwise remarkable in distribution.

| | | |
|---|---|---|
| word-level | 14 lines | 25% |
| repetition | 10 lines | 18% |
| coloration | 6 lines | 11% |
| line-level | 7 lines | 13% |
| matching | 7 lines | 13% |
| gapping | ∅ lines | |
| supralinear-level | 18 lines | 32% |
| dependency | 18 lines | 32% |
| mixing | ∅ lines | |
| total | 28 lines | 50% |

Line typologies are similar to those of the Lament; Class III is outnumbered by Class IV.

| | | | |
|---|---|---|---|
| Class I | 29 lines | 52% | |
| Class II | 16 lines | 29% | 48% |
| Class III | 4 lines | 7% | |
| Class IV | 7 lines | 12% | |
| total | 56 lines | 100% | |

The two staves of the Song are both 28 lines, if we include the burdens, or 25, if not; let us follow our practice with the Lament and exclude them here. There are six supralinear tropes, only two extending over more than 2 lines. The first is the enemy speech, 9a-f, and the second the falling silent of the enemy, 16b-e. The end of the first of these coincides with the end of the first stave, at the exact midpoint of the poem. The second is positioned near the end of the second stave. The weights of the two staves are nearly identical: Stave I, 8:6 lines, 57:43%; Stave II, 7:5 lines, 58:42%.

Since the significance of the median break in the poem does not seem to have been noted before, a brief thematic digression may be helpful. The structure we have presented highlights the orality that is the subject of the poem. The poem opens and closes with the speaker's hortation to song. The first stave ends with one enemy boasting and the second with another enemy being silenced. With these features in mind, the distinctiveness of the opening of the second stave, 10a, emerges. The central feature is the use of *nšp* 'to blow.' Only here is Yahweh's deed defined without the periphrases of hand actions. All other references to it are metalepses, tropes of the central metaphor of *nšp*. The pivot of the poem is the contrast of the enemy's long speech and Yahweh's single gesture, unarticulated non-speech to which the Song itself is a response.

The batches of Exodus 15 are sometimes difficult to isolate precisely; for one separation here we shall rely on the definition of the median range, 5-8 lines. The concluding batches of both staves are easily isolable. The last batch of Stave I, 9a-f (6 lines), is troped throughout with syntactic dependency and thus set off clearly. The second stave's last batch, 16b-18 (8 lines), is also heavily troped. The batch before the last in the second stave, 14a-16a (6 lines), is distinguished by a complete absence of troping. The third and first batches of the first stave, 7a-8c (6 lines) and 2a-3b (6 lines), both end with troping; the batch between them, 4a-6b (7 lines), begins and ends with troping. Final troping is also characteristic of the first batch of Stave II, 10a-11c. The second stave's second batch, 12a-13c (5 lines), is the plainest in the poem; the troping in it is internal. The boundary between it and the next batch, 14a-16a, is determined as much by the desirability of five line lengths as by the batches themselves. We may summarize the batch structure of the Song before we rehearse it further.

Burden I. 1abc

| | | |
|---|---|---|
| Stave I. | Batch a. | 2a-3b: 6 lines |
| | b. | 4a-6b: 7 lines |
| | c. | 7a-8c: 6 lines |
| | d. | 9a-f: 6 lines |
| Stave II. | Batch a. | 10a-11c: 6 lines |
| | b. | 12a-13c: 5 lines |
| | c. | 14a-16a: 6 lines |
| | d. | 16b-18: 8 lines |

Burden II. 21abc

Though the batch divisions have been described on the basis of troping, there is more troping in the first stave than the second. There are some patterned dispositions of non-Class I lines in both staves, but the staves do not show comparable numbers of such lines: there are more in the second stave than the first.

| | *troped lines* | *heavy lines* | *TH ratio* |
|---|---|---|---|
| Stave I 25 lines | 18 lines/72% | 9 lines/36% | 67:33% |
| Stave II 25 lines | 11 lines/44% | 16 lines/64% | 40:60% |

There are few non-Class I lines in Ia and d; and more in the middle batches of the first stave. In the second stave, only the second batch has a restricted number of heavy lines; all the rest are well-endowed.

The first three batches of Stave I, since they are only partially troped, contrast with the last, which is fully troped. Batch Ia ends with repetition and matching; Ib ends (as it begins) with repetition; and Ic ends with matching. The second and fourth batches begin with tropes of dependency (and the fourth continues with it throughout). The tropes of repetition, color and dependency which cooccur and interlock at the end of Batch IIa are the tropes which are spread across Batch IId.

There are four descriptions of Yahweh which invoke the divine name. The first two are positioned at the end of the first two batches of the first stave, 3ab and 6ab; in these, the name Yahweh is repeated. In the two descriptions of the second stave, the name Yahweh is followed by a title: near the end of the first batch, the title is *nᵓdr* 'Glorious One,' and near the end of the last batch, 17bc, it is *ᵓdny* 'Lord.' Of these four descriptions, the first and third (3ab and 11ab) involve verbless clauses, and the second and fourth (6ab and 17bc) are verbal clauses; the last three, but not the fourth (17c), include a vocative.

As in the other poems, so in Exodus 15, there are figures at work. Both figures to be presented here are more amenable to presentation in terms we have been using than the fake coda seems to be.

In defining the trope of matching, we restricted it to contiguous lines in order to reflect the fact that in most cases, matching is so limited. Rarely there appear patterns of matching within short groups of lines which involve no contiguity; and these we shall refer to the figure of matching. (The reader will recall that we break with traditional rhetorical usage in using trope and figure as exclusive rather than overlapping terms.) The matching figure has a much smaller domain than the fake coda figure. The batch in which it is plainest is the last of the first stave, 9a-f; here there is a double matching figure, one half the match of three VS lines, the other the match of two VO lines.

| | *VS figure* | *VO figure* | *non-figured lines* |
|---|---|---|---|
| 9a | VS | | |
| 9b | | | VV |
| 9c | | VO | |
| 9d | VS | | |
| 9e | | VO | |
| 9f | VS | | |

The batch with no troping, IIc, 14a-16a, contains a double matching figure which, rather than spanning the batch, is enclosed within it.

| | *VSO figure* | *VS figure* | *non-figured lines* |
|---|---|---|---|
| 14a | | | VSV |
| 14b | SVO | | |
| 15a | | VS | |
| 15b | OVS | | |
| 15c | | VS | |
| 16a | | | VPS |

The matching of 14b and 15b is especially interesting because it gives an example of mirror chiasm, a phenomenon unattested among matching tropes. The third example of matching figuration is the simplest; the first batch, 2a-3b, begins and ends with simple verbless clauses. The figure is chiastic, since 2a has the word order PredS and 3ab the reverse.

The second figure which occurs in Exodus 15 involves contiguous lines of which one has three constituents *abc*, while two have two constituents, one *ab* and the other *ac*. Neither the ordering of the constituents nor that of the lines is relevant to the definition. It seems, however, that (on the line level), *a* must be a finite verb and that the domain is three lines. We can think of *abc* as a putting together of *ab* and *ac*, and call this the recombinant figure. The burdens of the Song both have this figuration, with the longest line last.

| | | | |
|---|---|---|---|
| 1a=21a | | V | P |
| 1b=21b | O | V | |
| 1c=21c | O | V | P |

In another case, in the middle of Batch Ib, the long line is medial.

| | | | |
|---|---|---|---|
| 4b | | V | P |
| 4c | S | V | P |
| 5a | S | V | |

In the following batch, Ic, the three constituent line is initial.

| | | | | |
|---|---|---|---|---|
| 7a | P | V | O | |
| 7b | | V | O | |
| 7c | | V | | P |

This recombinant figure is followed within the batch by a 3 line match, 8abc; the figure and the trope cover the batch.

These figures help to round out the structural image of Exodus 15. Despite the complementation noted within Batch Ic, the exact relation of troping and figuration cannot be specified until the extent of figuration is clearer.

### *10.2.3 Psalm 107*

Numbers 23-24, though three staves in length, is not structured as three staves, but as four. Because of the clarity of its sectional structure and its tendency to coupleting, the Oracles can "afford" to vary the stave length without losing its coherence. Such is the essence of the account we gave earlier and it affords a useful model in considering Psalm 107. A quick glance at the burdens of Psalm 107 reveals that they are not positioned in any simple way. The plainness of the burden may take up part of the structural task usually borne by regular stave lengths, in a tradeoff like the one we argued for in Numbers 23-24. We have already noted that Psalm 107 is the only poem in our corpus of a length which is not factorable to an obvious number of staves. At 89 lines, it is too long for 3 staves of 26-28 lines and too short for 3 1/2 such staves.

The line typology of the poem is normal.

| | | | |
|---|---|---|---|
| Class I | 56 lines | 63% | |
| Class II | 16 lines | 18% | |
| Class III | 12 lines | 13% | 37% |
| Class IV | 5 lines | 6% | |
| total | 89 lines | 100% | |

Repetition and gapping are rare and there is no mixing. Line-level and supralinear-level troping are more common than troping on the word level.

| | | | | |
|---|---|---|---|---|
| word-level | 10 lines | | 11% | |
| repetition | | 2 lines | | 2% |
| coloration | | 8 lines | | 9% |
| line-level | 33 lines | | 37% | |
| matching | | 30 lines | | 34% |
| gapping | | 5 lines | | 6% |
| supralinear-level | 35 lines | | 39% | |
| dependency | | 35 lines | | 39% |
| mixing | | ∅ lines | | |
| total | 59 lines | | 66% | |

The weight of the poem is 19:16 lines or 54:46%, nearly even weight. The TH ratio is 64:36%.

The stave structure of the poem is best gotten at backwards. The distance from the last burden to the end of the poem is 26 lines, a normal stave length. This fact suggests that the burden in this poem is not, as we supposed (tentatively) in the cases of the Song of the Sea and David's Lament, extrinsic to the staves, but integral. Allowing irregular stave lengths, the distribution of burdens can be taken to coincide with that of the staves: the last stave is left unburdened, as it were. (Lamentations makes a similar use of the acrostic pattern: of five units, five poems, the first four are acrostics, while the last is not.)

The designation of the last 26 lines of the poem as a stave is not accurate, however, as is apparent from an inspection of the distribution of the trope of dependency in the rest of the poem. There are nine occurrences of this trope in the poem. Four are internal to burdens: 7ab and 8ab in the first, 21ab in the third, and 31ab in the fourth. The first dependency is the opening of the poem, 1a-3b, and the next 3 occur just two lines after the burdens: 10a-11a, 17ab, 23a-24b, and 33a-34b. The use of dependency at the start of the poem makes it clear that the trope and not the burden marks the stave breaks. This is supported on thematic grounds. The subject of the first stave is concluded in 9ab; of the second, in 16ab; of the third, in 22ab; and of the last, in 32ab.

Let us examine the five staves we have isolated.

| | | |
|---|---|---|
| Stave I | 1a-9b | 18 lines |
| Stave II | 10a-16b | 14 lines |
| Stave III | 17a-22b | 12 lines |
| Stave IV | 23a-32b | 21 lines |
| Stave V | 33a-43c | 24 lines |
| total | | 89 lines |

The regularity of the final stave postulated at the outset has been sacrificed, but there is a regularity of overall pattern which is much more striking. The pattern of line lengths in the stave is a 3 part decrescendo followed by a 2 part crescendo, the reverse of the swell pattern of Numbers 23-24 and of a number of staves in the Testaments. Let us call this a reverse swell.

The five irregular staves of Psalm 107 have characterizable lengths. The last is close enough to the normal length to pass as standard. The second and third are semi-staves; the range previously defined can be extended to 12-14 lines. The lengths of the first and fourth staves, 18 and 21 lines, are comparable to those of the second and fourth staves of Numbers 23-24, 18 and 22 lines. These resemblances will be reexamined after we work out the batch structure of the staves.

In the four staves with burdens, the final batch consists of the burden and the next two lines. In Staves I, II, and III, the final batch is 8 lines long, 6a-9b, 13a-16b, and 19a-22b. In the fourth stave, the last unit is 10 lines long, 28a-32b. The second and third staves each have only one other batch; in the second, it is 10a-12b, 6 lines and in the third, 17a-18b, 4 lines. The first ten lines of the first stave contain two batches; the first consists of the six lines troped with dependency, 1a-3b; and the second, of the next four lines, 4a-5, a passage with the only match in the stave not internal to the burden or the dependency passage, 4ab. The use of dependency and then matching to mark the first two batches is also found in the fourth stave; there, too, the only match not internal to the last batch or the opening dependency passage, 26ab, is the start of the second batch. The first batch is thus 6 lines long, 23a-25b, and the second, 5 lines, 26a-27b.

The last stave is more difficult to divide but here too the marking of batches first with dependency and then with matching appears. Since matching is more common in this stave, it is not simply an otherwise unbound use of it that separates the first two staves, but an especially long match, 36b-37c. The first batch begins with dependency and is 7 lines long, 33a-36a; and the second starts with matching and is 6 lines long, 36b-38b. The third batch begins with dependency again, although since both 39ab and 40ab show dependency, the second batch could be taken to include 39ab. There are two arguments against this: (a) other things being equal, 6 lines is a batch length preferable to 8 lines; and (b) the two verb forms in

38b and 39a. These two verbs are not a case of the repetition trope, since they are of different stems, one *Hip*ᶜ*il*, the other *Qal*, and such diversity is not permitted the trope. The repetition is unmistakable, however, and we would like to suggest that this is a case of a figure of repetition. This figure would include the phenomenon of variant stems of the same root; we would like to suggest that the figure has an effect directly opposed to that of the trope. The figure, that is, does not draw lines together but sets a boundary between them. The boundary is clear from the completely different character of the verbs' case frames: the verb in 38b has an animate subject and object, the verb in 39a, abstract subjects. The third batch, 39a-41b, is 6 lines long and the last, 42a-43c, 5 lines. This division is supported by the disposition of non-Class I lines: these begin the last two batches, in 39ab and 42ab, and occur nowhere else in them.

The batch structure of the poem can be summarized.

| | | | | |
|---|---|---|---|---|
| Stave I | Batch | a. | 1a-3b | 6 lines |
| | | b. | 4a-5 | 4 lines |
| | | c. | 6a-9b | 8 lines |
| Stave II | Batch | a. | 10a-12b | 6 lines |
| | | b. | 13a-16b | 8 lines |
| Stave III | Batch | a. | 17a-18b | 4 lines |
| | | b. | 19a-22b | 8 lines |
| Stave IV | Batch | a. | 23a-25b | 6 lines |
| | | b. | 26a-27b | 5 lines |
| | | c. | 28a-32b | 10 lines |
| Stave V | Batch | a. | 33a-36a | 7 lines |
| | | b. | 36b-38b | 6 lines |
| | | c. | 39a-41b | 6 lines |
| | | d. | 42a-43c | 5 lines |

The median range of the batch size is 5-8 lines, and we have just proposed to use this fact (or more strictly, a fact dependent upon it) in dividing the batches of the last stave. Yet among these 14 batches, there are three of a length outside the range: Ib and IIIa are four lines and IVc is ten lines. Given the integrity of the burden and of the first dependency passage of the poem, there are no alternative analyses of the three staves.

Although we cannot alter our analyses, we can gloss them. The first three staves use batches of only three lengths, 4, 6 and 8 lines. Stave I uses all three lengths, the second stave uses the last two lengths, and the third the 4 and 8 line length. The deployment of constituent structures in the recombinant figure in Exodus 15 (of the form VSO-VS-VO) is a comparable phenomenon in a different dimension. The batch sizes of these staves form a recombinant figure. The case of the single 10 line batch is easier to comprehend. The last in the series of four burdens is the most highly marked, since it rounds off the sequence, while clarifying the fact that the primary definitional parameter of the burden is not the proportion of lines but the degrees of fixity they exhibit.

The batch analysis enables us to clarify two further points. We begin by recalling that we have not contended that the numerical factoring of a poem's length into stave lengths has any importance apart from a stave breakdown. If it is worth noting the factoring in cases in which it differs from the breakdown, then Psalm 107 is a 3 1/2 stave poem. This follows from the fact that the normative batch:stave ratio is 4:1.

The second point clarified by the batch analysis is the relation of the various batch lengths to each other. In Numbers 23-24, the second and fourth staves have different lengths but both are composed of three batches. In Psalm 107, all the line lengths are different, but the batch analyses are not.

| | *length* | *batches* |
|---|---|---|
| Stave I | 18 lines | 3 batches |
| Stave II | 14 lines | 2 batches |
| Stave III | 12 lines | 2 batches |
| Stave IV | 21 lines | 3 batches |
| Stave V | 24 lines | 4 batches |

Thus I and IV are different in length but both have three batches; and II and III differ in length but are both bipartite. The reverse swell of length in this poem is the only swell noted so far in which the last movement (here, the crescendo) involves two poetic units, rather than one. This fact is related to the ring structure of the first four staves. The repetition of a 3 batch stave as the fourth poetic unit (combined with the variant shape of the burden) makes the fourth stave seem like a closing complementary to the first stave. This is another case of the fake coda figure. The final stave is highlighted by the false expectations of conclusion created by the similarity in shape of the first and fourth staves.

(The thematic correlations of this structure may be outlined. The four depravities of the first four staves, enforced steppe wandering, imprisonment, starvation, and seafaring, and their reversals, form an exemplary catalog. The fifth stave spins off in treating first the reversibility of all things—if geology is reversible, how much more easily are human situations reversed?—and then the byproduct of depravity's absence, civilization. The uncivilizable places par excellence are the steppe, the high seas, prison, and anywhere people are starving.)

Many of the major tropological and typological features of the staves have already been touched on; a brief review will suffice. In the first stave, the first 8 and the last 7 lines are troped; the middle three are not. The dependency trope, 1a-3b, is supplemented by a match, 2b 3a. The beginning of the second batch includes both a combination and a match in 4ab. The first dependency, within the burden, 7ab, overlaps with a match of a relatively fixed line and a free line, 6b 7a. The second dependency is 8ab. The two lines after the burden, 9ab, have a repetition.

At the start of the second stave, the dependency trope of 10a-11a includes one match, 10ab, and overlaps with another, 11ab; the latter couplet also includes two color tropes. As in the first burden, the second relatively fixed line matches a free line in 13b 14a; and the 2 lines after the burden match each other, 16ab. The last 2 lines of the burden, 15ab, are dependent. The dependencies at the start of the third stave, 17ab, and at the end of its burden, 21ab, are the only tropes here, save for the match of the last free line of the burden and the first fixed one, 20b 21a. (Compare, then, 6b 7ab and 20b 21ab.) After the initial dependency of the fourth stave, 23a-24b, which includes the match of 23ab, there follow directly a combination in 25ab and a match in 26ab. As in the previous stave, the dependency of the burden, 31ab, overlaps with a match, 30b 31a.

The final stave begins with a complex overlap of tropes; a 4 line dependency, 33a-34b, includes a 3 line gap, 33a-34a, which includes 2 matching lines which contain a combination, 33ab. This is followed by 2 lines which match and are gapped, 35ab. The last line of the first batch, 36a, is not troped. The second batch contains only the long match of 36b-37c. Like the first batch, the third opens with 4 lines of dependency, albeit in two tropes rather than one, 39ab and 40ab. The next 2 lines match and contain a combination, 41ab. The last batch is untroped save for the dependency of 43ab.

The Class IV lines of the poem are the opening lines of the four burdens, 6a, 13a, 19a, 28a; and the line directly before the first burden, 5. The first four staves begin with either Class II (1a, 10ab) or Class III lines (17a, 23ab). The last line of the first batch of Stave I, 3b, is Class III and the line one line before it, 2b, is Class II; the last line of the third batch is Class II, 9b, and the line one line before it is Class III, 8b (the last line of the burden).

Just as the second stave's first batch starts with Class II lines, 10ab, so it ends with such, 12b. The remaining non-Class I line is the last line of the burden, 15b. The third stave has two Class III lines, 17a and 21b (the last line of the burden) and within them, 2 Class II lines, 18a and 20a. The first 2 lines of Stave IV, of Class III, 23ab, are followed by 24a, Class II, 24b, Class III, and 25a, Class II. The untroped portion of Batch IVb contain a Class II line, 27a; and there are 2 Class III lines in the burden, 30a and 31b (the last line of the burden). The heavy lines of the first 2 batches of Stave V occur directly before the end of the batches: 35a, Class II; 35b, Class III; and 38a, Class II. As noted, the heavy lines of the last two batches occur at the onset of the batches, 39a, Class III; 39b, Class II; and 42ab, Class II.

The three lines of the last stave which are neither troped nor heavy, 36a, 38b, and 43c, are all batch final.

The weights of the five staves of Psalm 107 show an interesting distribution.

| | *lines* | *weight/lines* | *weight/percentages* |
|---|---|---|---|
| Stave I | 18 | 5:1 | 83:17% |
| Stave II | 14 | 2:3 | 40:60% |
| Stave III | 12 | 2:4 | 33:67% |
| Stave IV | 21 | 6:5 | 55:45% |
| Stave V | 24 | 4:3 | 57:43% |
| total | 89 | 19:16 | 54:46% |

The weights of the staves decrease and increase (recall that these expressions refer to relative changes in the first number) just as the line lengths decrease and increase. In other words, the poem is a two-dimensional reverse swell, which, while it has important resemblances to the Oracles of Balaam, has independent complexities.

### *10.2.4 Summary*

As in 10.1, so in 10.2 we have looked cursorily at three poems and found two to be more similar to each other than to the third. In this case, two of the poems have external burdens. The unresolved question is the relation of the burden to the stave. In treating the Song and the Lament, we separated stave and burden; in the Psalm we did not. There are two approaches to the problem. We can either suppose that the poems are of two different types or we can adjust the staves of the Song and the Lament to include the burdens (and adjust the batches correspondingly). The crucial point involves the range of the stave and it seems best to suppress the question of the burden/stave relation until we can reassess the stave range, and consider in particular whether 30 line staves should fit within the normal range, or, failing that, whether the irregularity is of a describable type.

Another outstanding problem is the character of the repetition in Numbers 23-24. Are the two repeated passages there burdens? It is clear they are not, since they are not symmetrically arranged and have little variable composition. Whether the repetition in the Oracles is *sui generis* and if so, whether it is related to the Oracles' possible status as a sequence of poems rather than one—these are questions that can only be considered in relation to other poems with similar repetition. That there are other forms of long distance repetition is plain from the distribution of the *n*ᵓ*m yhwh* formula in prophetic poetry, which has nothing in common with burdens.

In the preceding paragraphs we have begun to flesh out the concept of figuration. We have identified four figures. Two involve the same sort of phenomena as the tropes do: the matching figure, which operates within a single batch, and the repetition figure, meagerly exemplified, which apparently ranges within a stave. The false coda figure appears in five of the six poems treated thus far and is remarkably diverse. The simple functional explanation given for the figure is broad enough to encompass this diversity. That is, the need to set off the final poetic unit can easily be thought of as motivating a wide range of strategies for its implementation. What these strategies have in common is that they all resist reduction to the terms in which we have studied troping. This resistance, as we have noted, supports the distinction between troping and figuration. The recombinant figure we have seen operating on the level of constituency structure.

### *10.3 Other individual poems*

Five individual poems in our corpus lack plainly articulated or burdened structures; they make up about half the corpus in size. The three chapters of Zephaniah and the Book as a whole we reserve for separate treatment. There is no summary for this section; the drawing of conclusions is best deferred to the end of the chapter. The five poems are treated here in order of length: Habaqquq 3 (65 lines), Judges 5 (106 lines), Psalm 106 (106 lines), Deuteronomy 32 (140 lines), and Psalm 78 (163 lines).

### *10.3.1 Habaqquq 3. The Psalm of Habaqquq*

The psalm that concludes the Book of Habaqquq is one of the most variously singular poems in the corpus. It has nearly the greatest percentage of Class I lines of any poem under study; only Psalm 106 has a greater concentration..

| | | | |
|---|---|---|---|
| Class I | 50 lines | 77% | |
| Class II | 8 lines | 12% | 23% (Classes II–IV) |
| Class III | 5 lines | 8% | |
| Class IV | 2 lines | 3% | |
| total | 65 lines | 100% | |

The troping is almost entirely confined to the word and line levels. Dependency is limited to two cases and there is no mixing.

| | | |
|---|---|---|
| word-level | 33 lines | 51% |
| repetition | 10 lines | 15% |
| coloration | 28 lines | 43% |
| line-level | 39 lines | 60% |
| matching | 32 lines | 49% |
| gapping | 17 lines | 26% |

| | | | |
|---|---|---|---|
| supralinear-level | 4 lines | 6% | |
| dependency | 4 lines | | 6% |
| mixing | ∅ lines | | |
| total | 46 lines | 71% | |

The TH ratio is 46:15 lines, 75:25%; the weight is 10:14 lines, 42:58%.

The troping and heavy lines are not distributed evenly in the poem and their positioning provides major clues to the stave structure of the poem. The length, 65 lines, suggests a 2 1/2 stave analysis and in fact the two staves and single semi-stave are easily isolable. There are only three places at which more than two lines together are not troped: 9abc, 16f 17abcd, and 19abc. The last of these is the poem's conclusion, while the first two mark the stave breaks. The second break we position after 16f on the grounds of batch structure; thematic considerations also support this division. The staves are, then, as follows.

| | | |
|---|---|---|
| Stave I | 2a-8e | 26 lines |
| Stave II | 9a-16f | 28 lines |
| Stave III | 17a-19c | 11 lines |

The form is another of those with a single change in size, a decrescendo after two equivalent units; it is, in fact, another pseudo-sonnet. The unusual array of troping and heavy lines across the staves will be easier to see after we review the batch structure.

The batches of the second stave are marked by both troping and heavy lines. The first batch is entirely untroped, 9a-10c, 6 lines; and the second, entirely troped, 10d-13b, 8 lines. The next two batches begin with 1 line breaks in troping. The first line of the third batch, 13c, though untroped, is a Class IV line, like the first line of the second, 10d; the third batch includes 13c-15d, 8 lines. The last and first lines of the last batch in the stave are untroped; the first is a Class II line, the only heavy line in the batch, which is thus 16a-f, 6 lines.

The two batches of the semi-stave can be separated before or after the single block of troping within it, 17a-18b. We locate the break after the troping, yielding an initial 8 line batch, 17a-18b, and a final 3 line batch, 19a-c. The division could be set before the troping; since either division creates an irregular batch size, the case is indeterminate; other cases to be treated below suggest that the order larger-smaller is more common in this situation.

Just as the last two batches of this text and the first two of Psalm 107 are hard to separate, so the first two batches of the first stave, to which we now turn, can only be picked out with difficulty. The last batch of the stave is set off by a brief break in troping in 7ab; the batch is 7a-8e, 7 lines. The third batch begins with a pair of Class II lines after a long stretch of Class I lines; and it ends with a heavy line; it is thus 6a-e, 5 lines. The best division of the first two batches is after 3b, i.e., after an overlapping 4 line repetition trope, and 4 lines of gapping, and after a gap in gapping, and a change from single to double coloration. The first batch is 2a-3b, 7 lines, and the second, 3c-5b, also 7 lines. The stave and batch breakdown can be summarized.

| | | | | |
|---|---|---|---|---|
| Stave I. | Batch | a. | 2a-3b. | 7 lines |
| | | b. | 3c-5b. | 7 lines |
| | | c. | 6a-e. | 5 lines |
| | | d. | 7a-8e. | 7 lines |
| Stave II. | Batch | a. | 9a-10c. | 6 lines |
| | | b. | 10d-13b. | 8 lines |
| | | c. | 13c-15d. | 8 lines |
| | | d. | 16a-f. | 6 lines |
| Stave III. | Batch | a. | 17a-18b. | 8 lines |
| | | b. | 19a-c. | 3 lines |

This onceover has suggested some of the irregularity of the placement of marked elements. Let us reconsider the phenomena. In the first stave, the troping is heaviest, and is interrupted only twice, once at the start of Batch Id and once within Ib. The batch beginnings do not seem to have anything in common, but there is one line (and in one case, there are two lines) with less troping than the others. In Ib, it is 4c; in Ic and Id, the lines are 6c and 8c, while in Ia, the lines are 2c and 2e. This arrangement of weakness within strength probably belongs to the realm of figuration. It is the result of couplets and triplets of tropes overlapping with one another; cases of such overlapping are absent only in the second batch. The heavy lines in the stave have all been noted; we need only add that the span of twelve Class I lines from 2c to 5b, across most of the first and all of the second stave, is one of the longest stretches of such lines in our corpus; there is another such stretch from Batch IId, 16b-f, through Stave III, 17a-19c, which is 16 lines, also preceded by a Class II line, 16a. (The third longest stretch here is 11a-13b, 7 lines.) If we compare the Batches Ia and IId, we find a sequence of one or two Class II lines (2ab, 16a) and five Class I lines (2c-3b, 16b-f), another instance of a resumptive fake coda. The instance is apparently underscored by the use of further Class I lines in the following batches. The weight of the first stave is 6:1 lines or 86:14%; the TH ratio is 23:8 lines or 74:26%.

The troping of the second stave is simpler to read. The first batch has no tropes; the second is troped throughout. The third batch begins with an untroped line; the fourth batch begins and ends with an untroped line. The stave, then, as a whole begins and ends with untroped lines, and both 9a and 16f are Class I lines. In contrast to the abundant overlapping troped braces in the first stave, there is only one case of overlapping tropes in the second. The second batch begins with a singly troped couplet, 10d 11a; 11bc is quadruply troped; the third couplet, 12ab, is doubly troped; and the fourth is triply troped. The third batch is singly troped throughout except for the last two lines, 15ab, the lines with the overlapping tropes, which are doubly troped. The troping in the last batch is single. The heavy lines of the stave are either batch initial, in the last three batches, as recorded above; or batch medial, in the second and fourth batches, i.e., 10a in IIa and 14abc in IIc. The weight of the stave is 4:6 lines or 40:60%. The six lines which are neither troped nor heavy are located marginally here, at the stave's start (9abc, 10bc) and end (16f); the one such line in the first stave is, in contrast, located medially (4c). The TH ratio of the second stave is like that of the first, 19:7, or 73:27%.

The final stave, since it has no non-Class I lines, and medial troping (17e-18b), also has marginal lines which are untroped Class I lines. The three tropes in the stave are overlapping: the match of 17ef 18a includes the coordination of 17ef and part of the binomination in 18ab. The weight of the stave is Ø:7, or Ø:100%; the TH ratio is 4:Ø, 100:Ø%.

Three important features of the poem's markedness present a simple decline from the first stave through the second to the end. In each case, the middle stave is most like the poem overall.

| | *troping* | *heavy lines* | *weight* |
|---|---|---|---|
| Stave I | 23 lines 88% | 8 lines 31% | 6:1 lines 86: 14% |
| Stave II | 19 lines 68% | 7 lines 25% | 4:6 lines 40: 60% |
| Stave III | 4 lines 36% | Ø lines | Ø:7 lines Ø:100% |
| total | 46 lines 71% | 15 lines 23% | 10:14 lines 42: 58% |

The decrescendo length pattern is complemented by this more complex pattern of continuous decline. The first and second staves correspond not just in length, however, but also in TH ratio.

| | *length* | *TH ratio* |
|---|---|---|
| Stave I | 26 lines | 23:8 lines 74:26% |
| Stave II | 28 lines | 19:7 lines 73:27% |
| Stave III | 11 lines | 4:Ø lines 100: Ø% |
| total | 65 lines | 46:15 lines 75:25% |

With regard to both these features, it is clear that the normative force of the first two staves coexists with great differences between them.

The fake coda of Habaqquq 3 was cited earlier. Among other figures in the poem, we note first an example of inclusion, a figure in which a poetic unit opens and closes either with the same word or with two words with the same reference serving the same grammatical function. (Here, too, our appropriation of a term in current usage is accompanied by restriction in application.) The inclusion spans the first stave, from the vocative 'Yahweh' in 2a to the vocative 'Saviour' at the end of 8e.

The matching figure occurs in 7 of the 10 batches of Habaqquq 3 and the cases extend our conception of the phenomenon based on the Exodus 15 examples. In 2 of the 3 batches involved there, single lines match each other; and in the same 2 cases, there are 2 different matching figures in a batch. In the remaining case, there is only one matching figure, but it involves a matching trope: that is, the lines Ex 15:3ab match each other in a trope and they match 2a in a figure. There are, then, single and double matching figures within a batch; and matching figures of line on line, and line on trope. There is a third possibility in the latter dimension, in which a trope forms a matching figure with another trope. All these possibilities occur in Habaqquq 3; there is little evidence that the domain of the matching figure extends beyond the batch. In every example here (save the last) and in Exodus 15, one of the lines involved is either the last or first of the batch.

The simplest matching figure involves 2 lines in a batch which match over a distance; this is the case of the first and last lines of Batch IIa, 9a (OVS) and 10c (VSO). The other line on line matching figure cooccurs with a second figure and so we reserve treatment of it.

Figures involving a line and a matching trope occur in the first batch, Ia (2c, PSV, matches 3a, SPV, and 3b, SP); and in the second batch of the second stave, IIb (11b, PSV, and 11c, PS, match 13b, PS) and in the fourth, IId (16b, PVS, and 16c, VSP, match 16f, PSV). Matching figures involving two tropes occur in Batches Ib and IIc.

| *Ib* | | *IIc* | |
|---|---|---|---|
| 3c | | 13c | |
| 3d | | 13d | VOP |
| 4a | SPV | 14a | VPO |
| 4b | PS | 14b | |
| 4c | | 14c | |
| 5a | PSV | 14d | VOP |
| 5b | VSP | 15a | VPO |
| | | 15b | OP |

A double matching figure, one line on line figure and one line on trope figure, is found in the last stave's first batch.

| | *figure I* | *figure II* |
|---|---|---|
| 17a | SV ┐ | |
| 17b | │ | VSP ┐ |
| 17c | VS ┘ | │ |
| 17d | | │ |
| 17e | | VPS ⎫ │ |
| 17f | | VPS ⎬ ┘ |
| 18a | | SPV ⎭ |
| 18b | | |

We hinted above that there may exist some evidence for extending the domain of the matching figure beyond the batch but since there is no simple overall pattern it would be futile to try to tie the examples together here.

### *10.3.2 Judges 5. The Song of Deborah*

No trope orders more of any of our texts than repetition does the Song of Deborah: over half of the lines of the text contain repetition tropes, which are themselves often arranged in complex ways. The description of the higher order repetition tropes in Chapter 4, though intrinsically strong, seems only slightly too powerful from the evidence of this poem. There is one case here (and another in Deuteronomy 33, cited there), in which the highest orders of repetition troping operate too forcefully. The correction required in Chapter 4 is not obvious from the two putative counterexamples; we note the possibility in order to remind the reader that some of the crucial evidence for refining the description of fine level structure may have to come from gross structure study.

The summative line typology of Judges 5 is not remarkable in itself, save in that Class III is better represented than Class II.

| | | | |
|---|---|---|---|
| Class I | 56 lines | 53% | |
| Class II | 19 lines | 18% | 47% (Classes II–IV) |
| Class III | 21 lines | 20% | |
| Class IV | 10 lines | 9% | |
| total | 106 lines | 100% | |

Word-level troping is most abundant; supralinear-level troping is somewhat more common than troping on the line level. This is one of the few texts in which repetition is more important than coloration. Gapping is rare; there is one case of mixing and it is not as structurally functional as the other examples we have noted.

| | | |
|---|---|---|
| word-level | 66 lines | 62% |
| repetition | 57 lines | 54% |
| coloration | 14 lines | 13% |

| | | |
|---|---|---|
| line-level | 31 lines | 29% |
| matching | 29 lines | 27% |
| gapping | 4 lines | 4% |
| supralinear-level | 38 lines | 36% |
| dependency | 34 lines | 32% |
| mixing | 4 lines | 4% |
| total | 87 lines | 82% |

The TH ratio is thus 87:50 lines, 64:36%; the weight is 38:7 lines, 83:17%.

Judges 5 is the first of the two 4 stave poems in our corpus to be considered. Both it and Psalm 106 are 106 lines long. The staves do not clarify any of the obscure subject transitions in the poem, but the light shed by the divisions to be proposed does not blot out what little other light there is. The first and last staves begin with troped lines and end with untroped lines, while the middle staves end with troped lines and begin with untroped ones. The division is as below.

| | | |
|---|---|---|
| Stave I | 2a-9b. | 28 lines |
| Stave II | 10a-16c. | 25 lines |
| Stave III | 17a-23e. | 24 lines |
| Stave IV | 24a-31b. | 29 lines |

The problematic division is the one between III and IV, since it requires breaking a repetition trope, alleged in 4.5 to extend from 22b to 24c. If we do break the trope, as the stave evidence argues we must, no structural feature beyond the counter-indicated one will be lost, since the lines on both sides of the division are involved in other repetition tropes.

The batches of the first stave are marked off by their use of supralinear troping: the first three begin with dependencies and the last begins after the mixing trope of 7abcd.

| | | |
|---|---|---|
| Stave I Batch a. | 2a-3e. | 7 lines |
| b. | 4a-5c. | 8 lines |
| c. | 6a-7d. | 7 lines |
| d. | 8a-9b. | 6 lines |

Both word and supralinear troping involve 16 lines here; troping on the line level, only half that number. The troping in Batch Ic is uniform and uses both repetition and dependency, but not line-level troping. In contrast, in both Ia and Id, and in the first part of Ib, the troping moves gradually, with only partial, never complete, overlap. In Ia and b, the first trope used is dependency (2ab, 4abc), followed by matching (3ab, 4cd), and gapping (3cd), and concluding in repetition (3cde, 4de) and combination (4de). In the second part of Batch Ib, the sequence is repeated with the middle term omitted: dependency (5abc) is followed by repetition (5bc). In the last batch, matching (8ab) precedes dependency (8cd); repetition still follows. Heavy lines in the first three batches are only marginal. In Ia, they are initial (2ab 3ab) and final (3e); so also in Ib, initial (4a) and final (5bc); and Ic, only initial (6abc). In the last batch, there is, beside the concluding Class IV line, 9b, one medial, Class III line, 8d.

The close relation between the pairs of lines 2ab and 9ab is not to be expressed in any simple way. Note that the lines of 2ab are troped together, while 9a is troped by repetition to 8d and 9b is untroped; and note further that 9a is Class I, 2b is Class II, 2a is Class III, and 9b is Class IV. This is not the result of textual disarray or trampled tropes, but of *tromp l'oeil*; let us call this the figure of the fake burden.

In the second stave, supralinear troping is little used. There are some striking correlations of heavy lines and tropes. The heavy line pattern is similar to that in the previous stave: the first, second, and here, the fourth batches end with heavy lines and all the batches start off with them.

| | | | |
|---|---|---|---|
| Stave II Batch | a. | 10a-11c. | 6 lines |
| | b. | 11d-12e. | 6 lines |
| | c. | 13a-14c. | 5 lines |
| | d. | 14d-16c. | 8 lines |

The third batch is entirely troped, with both repetition and matching; the troping in IIb is limited to repetition and coloration. Dependency in the second stave occurs only in the first and last batches, in which all three trope levels are represented. Batches IIa and IIb each contain a pair of sequences of the shape 1 untroped line plus 2 troped lines; if we mark troped and untroped lines with t and u, we obtain the following.

| *Batch IIa* | | *Batch IIb* | |
|---|---|---|---|
| 10a u | 11a u | 11d u | 12c u |
| 10b t | 11b t | 12a t | 12d t |
| 10c t | 11c t | 12b t | 12e t |

The final batch, IId, opens with a match, 14d 15a, and closes with a repetition, 15d-16c, encircling a dependency, 16ab. The balance of trope levels in the first two staves can be examined in terms of percentages of lines involved; we can compare the percentages if we set the lowest in each case as an arbitrary variable.

| | *Stave I* | | *Stave II* | |
|---|---|---|---|---|
| word-level | 57% | 2x | 68% | 4y |
| line-level | 29% | x | 32% | 2y |
| supralinear-level | 57% | 2x | 16% | y |

The relationship between the word-level and line-level troping is constant in both cases; it is the distribution of supralinear-level tropes that makes the difference.

Another factor which distinguishes the first two staves is the greater number of heavy lines in the second, most of them concentrated in the first batch, which includes only heavy lines, and the second batch, which encompasses only one Class I line, 12c (the line is also untroped). Batch IIc has one heavy line, the initial line, 13a; and IId begins and ends with heavy lines, 14c and 16c; the latter's repetition mate, 15d, is also a non-Class I line.

The third stave is the shortest of the poem, 24 lines. Like the other staves, over half of its lines contain repetition tropes but this distribution is here obtained along with the inclusion of a 7 line stretch without repetition, 17a-18c; this we take to be the initial batch. The second and third batches can be divided before the 2 line interruption in repetition in 21c 22a. The last batch is troped together as a quotation. The divisions are thus the following.

| | | | |
|---|---|---|---|
| Stave III Batch | a. | 17a-18c. | 7 lines |
| | b. | 19a-21b. | 8 lines |
| | c. | 21c-22c. | 4 lines |
| | d. | 23a-e. | 5 lines |

The first batch not only contains no repetition; it is troped lightly in general, by the match in 18ab. The only other match in the stave is in the third batch, 22abc. Just as the matches alternate in the first and third batches, so the dependencies alternate in the second (19bc) and fourth batches (throughout). Coloration is limited to the third batch, 22ab. The repetition in IIId is thorough; in IIIc, it is final, 22bc; and in IIIb, it is initial, 19ab, and final, 20a-21b. The troping levels are used in the following way.

| | *word-level* | *line-level* | *supralinear-level* |
|---|---|---|---|
| Batch III a. | | x | |
| b. | x | | x |
| c. | x | x | |
| d. | x | | x |

The word-level troping is twice as frequent as supralinear troping, 58% over 29%; the line-level troping is less common than either, 21%.

The first two batches of Stave III begin (17abc, 19a) and end (18c, 21b) with non-Class I lines. The second batch is like the first in having as its third line a heavy line, 19c, but the second line of the batch, 19b, is not heavy. The third batch starts with, and the fourth ends with, the only other heavy lines in the stave.

The fourth stave, the story of the women besides Deborah who were concerned with the battle, is transparent in its divisions. The breaks between the second and third, and the third and fourth batches can be seen in the interruption of the repetitions, at 28ab and 29ab. The transition across the first two batches is marked at the change in matching after the four line match of 25bc 26ab. The units are these, then.

| | | | |
|---|---|---|---|
| Stave IV Batch | a. 24a-26b. | 8 lines |
| | b. 26c-27e. | 8 lines |
| | c. 28a-28d. | 4 lines |
| | d. 29a-31b. | 9 lines |

The apportionment of the stave between the two active women, Yael and the loquacious courtier, and the reserved members of the Sisera clan, mother and son; and the ironies of drawing together silence and speech, simple food and luxurious clothing, wives and mothers, queens and courtiers; all of these thematic features of the poem's conclusion are handled economically in the framework given above.

The repetition tropes of the first and third batches, 24abc and 28cd, are straightforward cases. We have already seen that the tropes of the second batch, 27abcde, and of the fourth, 30abcde, are among the densest we have; most of the repeated elements in IVb are verbs, in verbal clauses, while all of them in IVd are nomina, in verbless clauses. Tropes of combination begin the two middle batches at 26cd and 28ab and occur nowhere else in the stave.

There are two 4 line matches in the stave, one in the first batch (25bc 26ab) and one in the last (30bcde); the only other match is at the start of the second batch. Gapping is restricted to the last 2 lines of the first batch, 26ab. The use of the various levels in the stave is roughly the same as in Stave III: word-level troping is twice as common as both line-level and supralinear-level troping, in the percentages 66%, 34% and 38%.

The non-Class I lines increase across the batches. All in the first two batches are medial: in IVa, 24b and in IVb, 26e and 27bc. Those in IVc are final, 28bcd, while in the last batch, heavy lines begin (30abc) and end (30e 31ab) the group. We have assumed that the last 2 lines of the poem are not set off in any particular way, but that assumption seems intuitively dubious. Certainly the distinctions noted—that neither is troped and both are heavy lines (31a is Class IV, 31b is Class II)—are relevant.

The structure of the poem is determined by the simple symmetry of the stave lengths and by the wildly divergent distributions of heavy, troped and unmarked lines among the staves. Further, the staves differ in the use they make of individual troping levels in a way not remarked for any other poem. We can recapitulate this point in a diagram, again using arbitrary variables for the lowest level within the staves.

| | *Stave I* | | *Stave II* | | *Stave III* | | *Stave IV* | |
|---|---|---|---|---|---|---|---|---|
| word-level | 57% | 2x | 68% | 4y | 58% | 2z | 66% | 2z |
| line-level | 29% | x | 32% | 2y | 21% | z | 34% | z |
| supralinear-level | 57% | 2x | 16% | y | 29% | z | 38% | z |

The third and fourth staves are slightly out of line with our abstraction, notably the third stave's figure for line-level troping; for the sake of argument, let us ignore this. The pattern that emerges is essentially that the extent of line-level and supralinear-level troping are equal in the last two staves, and equal to about half the word-level troping. In the first two staves, this relation is skewed; supralinear troping is avoided, as it were, in the second stave and sought after in the first. The second half of the poem provides a norm for the first to deviate from; the point of this norm is the word-level troping, which is consistently dominant: the norm seems to be a consequence of the crucial role of repetition in the poem. This arrangement does not provide us with any direct measure of the staves' differentiae, but is an introduction to them.

Let us return to the factors we have noted in previous treatments, in particular the relationship between the text as a whole and the fourth stave. The percentage of heavy lines in both is the same (47%, 45%, respectively); the percentage of troped lines is the same (87%, 83%); the TH ratio is the same (64:36%, 65:35%); and the weight is the same (84:16%, 83:17%). All the other staves vary from the poem's overall set of features. The TH ratio is the most uniform; normal, here as elsewhere, refers to the poem's average and not to an outside measure.

| | | |
|---|---|---|
| Stave I | 68:32% | normal |
| Stave II | 56:44% | |
| Stave III | 65:35% | normal |
| Stave IV | 64:36% | normal |
| total | 64:36% | normal |

With regard to the percentage of heavy lines and weight, two staves fit the average and two do not.

| | *heavy line* | | *weight* | |
|---|---|---|---|---|
| Stave I | 46% | normal | 100:∅% | |
| Stave II | 60% | | 80:20% | normal |
| Stave III | 37% | | 67:33% | |
| Stave IV | 45% | normal | 83:17% | normal |

The number of troped lines is normal only for stave IV.

| | | |
|---|---|---|
| Stave I | 96% | |
| Stave II | 76% | |
| Stave III | 71% | |
| Stave IV | 83% | normal |
| total | 87% | normal |

The first three staves vary from the norm in different ways. The first differs in only two features, troping and weight; both are higher than normal figures. The next two differ from the norm in three out of four ways. The second stave is high on heavy lines, and low on troping and the TH ratio. The third stave is low throughout: heavy lines, troping and weight. We can read off these modulations as indicating, first, that the poem ends with its norms, with overall reconciliation. (On the use of the norms in poetic closure, see Smith 1968:158-66.) It begins with half-normal configurations *and* half-high ones, as if to establish the features' presence by overemphasis. The staves of the middle of the poem are homogeneous in encasing an equal amount of deviance, and linear in progressing toward the negative features of the third stave through the mixed features of the second.

### *10.3.3 Psalm 106*

Unlike its immediate companion in the Psalter, Psalm 107, Psalm 106 is wholly historical recitation. The core of the poem, which begins at 7a and ends at 46 (the only two Class IV lines in the text), proceeds in roughly chronological order. The stages of Israelite history as they are reviewed are not treated discretely but are allowed to fuse under the pressure of the poem's thesis of historical cyclicity, of people being pulled out of impossible positions gratuitously. The stages do not therefore create any clear articulations within the text, and in identifying the poetic structure, they do not provide great help. The prayers which precede and follow the historical core are similarly not major structural determinants.

There is a clear articulation at the margins of the text, however, in the first and last pairs of lines. The first and last lines are identical; and the lines paired with them, 1b and 48c, both contains quotations which are in the nature of liturgical rubrics. There is, then, no reason that we should hesitate to call these pairs marginal burdens, save the text critical one. The line *hllw yh* is used so often at the interstices of texts in this region of the Psalter that it seems dangerous to put much confidence in these points of our text. Let us say only that it is probable that Psalm 106 is a poem with marginal burdens.

Like Judges 5, the Psalm is a 4 stave poem of 106 lines. This major common feature accentuates the immense differences between the poems. It is hardly surprising to compare the amount of repetition in the poems and note that the Psalm has only one-third as much as the Song. But further dissimilarities occur at every turn, except, rather remarkably, at the highest level, at which the texts have certain similarities beyond the 4 stave analysis.

The distribution of line classes in the poem emphasizes Class I; the two Class IV lines have already been cited. Classes II and III are equally represented.

| | | | |
|---|---|---|---|
| Class I | 83 lines | 78% | |
| Class II | 10 lines | 10% | 22% |
| Class III | 11 lines | 10% | |
| Class IV | 2 lines | 2% | |
| total | 106 lines | 100% | |

The Psalm is like Judges 5 in using more repetition than coloration. The extent of supralinear-level troping in both poems is about the same, but that troping level is major here and secondary there. Both gapping and mixing occur once only.

| | | |
|---|---|---|
| word-level | 23 lines | 22% |
| repetition | 17 lines | 16% |
| coloration | 6 lines | 6% |
| line-level | 25 lines | 24% |
| matching | 25 lines | 24% |
| gapping | 2 lines | 2% |
| supralinear-level | 37 lines | 35% |
| dependency | 33 lines | 31% |
| mixing | 4 lines | 4% |
| total | 62 lines | 58% |

The TH ratio of the poem is 62:23 lines, 73:27%. The poem is remarkably underweight with 40 lines which are neither troped nor non-Class I lines; the weight is 15:40, 27:73%.

The first and last staves close without troping; the first stave opens in that way, while the last begins with a match; the first and last lines of each are Class I lines. The middle staves begin and end with troping: the second with matches and the third with both repetition and dependency. Thus all three levels of troping serve to mark off these two staves. The divisions we propose are these.

| | | |
|---|---|---|
| Stave I | 1a-13b. | 29 lines |
| Stave II | 14a-25b. | 25 lines |
| Stave III | 26a-38d. | 27 lines |
| Stave IV | 39a-48d. | 24 lines |

The single gapping occurs in the second stave, at 16ab; and the only mix is positioned near the end of the poem, at 47abcd. The first and last staves embody the cyclic theory at greatest length, while the middle two rehearse the cycles of the cycle. The second stave puts greatest emphasis on one, positive way out of the cycle, the chance that Moses the intercessor could permanently turn away the consequences of violent misconduct; a chance that fails. The third stave emphasized the one, negative way out of the cycle, the one sin of such great moral degeneracy that no redemption is conceivable, the sin of religiously sanctioned infanticide. One of the contentions of the poem is that if the first way out failed, it is plausible to hope that the second will fail in turn.

The first stave, as we have noted, begins and ends with untroped lines. This array is not unlike the array of the batches within the stave. The first batch begins and the last batch ends without troping; and conversely, the first batch ends with and the last batch begins with troping. The middle batches begin and end without troping and both are troped internally. The batches are the following.

| | | | |
|---|---|---|---|
| Stave I. Batch | a. | 1a-3b. | 7 lines |
| | b. | 4a-6b. | 7 lines |
| | c. | 7a-9b. | 7 lines |
| | d. | 10a-13b. | 8 lines |

The first batch ends with two dependencies, 2ab and 3ab. The opening of Id is marked by repetition and matching in 10ab. The 4 line dependency in Ib, 4b-5c, includes a 3 line match, 5abc, which in turn encompasses a 2 line combination, 5ab. The troping in the third batch similarly is limited to one multiply troped passage: the repetition in 7c-9a contains a dependency in 8ab. Batches Ia, Ib, and Ic begin with heavy lines (1a, 4a, 7a) and Ia and Ib end with such (3b, 6b). The first batch includes two more non-Class I lines, 2a and 3a. The second batch includes no more. The last two batches have as their second-last lines, Class II lines, 9a and 13a; the latter is the only heavy line in Id.

The second stave includes one group of 7 lines which are untroped Class I lines, the second batch. The other batches are troped in toto. The end of the third batch is marked by a 4 line dependency. These batches are the following.

| | | | |
|---|---|---|---|
| Stave II. Batch | a. | 14a-16b. | 6 lines |
| | b. | 17a-19b. | 7 lines |
| | c. | 20a-22b. | 6 lines |
| | d. | 23a-25b. | 7 lines |

The stave opens and closes with 4 line matches. The first, 14a-15b, which includes a combination in 14ab, is followed by a two line match, 16ab, which is gapped and contains both a binomination and a combination. The concluding long match, 24a-25b, is preceded by 3 lines, the first two of which match (23ab) and the second two of which are dependent (23bc). (Dependent here means troped with syntactic dependency and thus grammatically interdependent.) The third batch begins with a 2 line dependency, 20ab, followed by a 4 line dependency, 21a-22b, which includes the match of 22ab. There are no non-Class I lines in either of the first two batches. The three in Ic include one medial line, 20b, and the last 2 lines, 22ab. The only heavy line in the last batch is the first one, 23a. No repetition is used in the second stave.

Repetition and dependency cooccur at the margins of the third stave. The internal batches are marked, in one case, by a heavy line, and in the other, by dependency. The batches proposed are, then, the following.

| | | | |
|---|---|---|---|
| Stave III. Batch | a. | 26a-29b. | 8 lines |
| | b. | 30a-33b. | 8 lines |
| | c. | 34a-36b. | 6 lines |
| | d. | 37-38d. | 5 lines |

The first batch opens with a 4 line dependency, 26a-27b, which includes a match with repetition in 26b 27a. The rest of the first batch is untroped; the second is troped only medially, in the dependency in 31ab; the third is so troped initially, in 34ab, and by matching medially at 35b 36a. The last batch is entirely troped. The repetition trope of blood, children and ritual slaughter covers the batch, 37-38d, and includes a dependency, 38abc. This batch and the second of the stave are the only ones with heavy lines; both use them initially, 30a and 37, and medially, 31b and 38bc.

The last stave's first batch begins with a 2 line match; the last batch is untroped finally; the margins of both have 4 line tropes. The middle batches are more difficult to separate, but if division is warranted it must be based on the contrast of the use of troping in the second and neglect of it in the third batch. These batches are proposed.

| | | | |
|---|---|---|---|
| Stave IV Batch | a. | 39a-42b. | 8 lines |
| | b. | 43a-44b. | 5 lines |
| | c. | 45a-46. | 3 lines |
| | d. | 47a-48d. | 8 lines |

The opening two lines of IVa, 39ab, match; the closing 4 lines contain a repetition trope, 41a-42b. The second batch encompasses a combination in 43bc and a dependency in 44ab. The third, small batch is untroped. The mix at the start of the last batch, 47abcd, includes a match, 47cd, and is followed by a dependency, 48ab. There are no heavy lines in the first two batches and only one in the third, 46, a Class IV line. The last batch is half heavy lines: 47a and 48abc.

The staves of Psalm 106 present structural profiles of less diversity than those of Judges 5, but the gestalt the profiles compose is similar. The last stave here has percentages of troped and heavy lines, a TH ratio and a weight, all similar to the poem's average. The third stave of Psalm 106 is not, however, as in Judges 5, least like the norm; it is as nearly like it as the fourth, and the second stave is the most deviant. The percentages of troped and heavy lines, and the TH ratios follow.

| | *troping* | *heavy lines* | *TH ratios* |
|---|---|---|---|
| Stave I | 48% | 30% | 61:39% |
| Stave II | 73% | 15% | 83:17% |
| Stave III | 56% | 19% | 75:25% |
| Stave IV | 58% | 21% | 74:26% |
| total | 59% | 22% | 73:27% |

The total figures compare closely with those for Staves III and IV. Stave I, in contrast, is low on troping and high on heavy lines; the opposite is true of Stave II. The weights of the five entities serve to diversify the picture.

| | *weight* |
|---|---|
| Stave I | 29:71% |
| Stave II | 36:64% |
| Stave III | 21:79% |
| Stave IV | 27:73% |
| total | 27:73% |

Here the first and last staves agree with the average and the middle staves differ. The last stave is the consistent norm or base line, while the second last is close to it; the first stave agrees with the average in the only features in which the third stave differs from it. Of the three long poems we have considered which have simple symmetry, only Genesis 49 is a ring composition; Judges 5, however, is closer to being such than our text. In the structure of Psalm 106, closure takes precedence over inclusion.

Only some of the figures in Psalm 106 will be noted: 7 matching figures and 1 recombinant figure. The 8 batches involved are not symmetrically distributed: three are in the first and third staves and only one occurs in each of the others. There are 3 line on line matching figures. In the first batch of the poem, 1a and 2b match (VO); the first of these is marginal. (In Psalm 106, the matching figure clearly serves to tie the margins and middles of batches together.) In the second batches of both middle staves, there are figures: in IIb, 17c-19b (final line of batch) (VP) and in IIIb, 32a-33b (final line of batch ) (VO). In the last batch of the first stave, there is a three part matching figure which includes a trope of matching: 10a (initial line of batch)-10b-12a-13b (final line of batch) (VP). The line on trope matching figure of IIIc is in two parts: 34a (initial line of batch)-35b 36a (VO). There is a double line on line matching figure in Batch IIIa and another one in IVa.

| | | *VOP figure* | *VP figure* | *(trope)* |
|---|---|---|---|---|
| IIIa. | 26a | VOP | | |
| | 26b | | | x |
| | 27a | | | x |
| | 27b | | | |
| | 28a | | VP | |
| | 28b | | | |
| | 29a | | VP | |
| | 29b | VOP | | |

| | | *VP figure* | *VSP figure* |
|---|---|---|---|
| IVa. | 39a | VP | |
| | 39b | | |
| | 40a | | VSP |
| | 40b | | |
| | 41a | VP | |
| | 41b | | VPS |
| | 42a | | |
| | 42b | VP | |

The single case of the recombinant figure occurs in Batch Ic: 7b (VO)-7c (VOP)-8a (VP). Here, the three constituent line is central.

### *10.3.4 Deuteronomy 32. The Song of Moses*

The Song ascribed to Moses on his death bed stands out among the Pentateuchal poems for its great reliance on supralinear troping. The poem's 140 lines fall into five staves, the last three of which open with lengthy quotations. It is not surprising to find that one of the longest poems in our corpus, though it lacks any overall structural devices, does make use of such a partial ordering schema.

The line typology reveals a sharp split between Class I and heavy lines.

| | | | |
|---|---|---|---|
| Class I | 84 lines | 60% | |
| Class II | 33 lines | 23% | 40% (Classes II–IV) |
| Class III | 18 lines | 13% | |
| Class IV | 5 lines | 4% | |
| total | 140 lines | 100% | |

The troping levels decline in importance as their domain declines.

| | | |
|---|---|---|
| word-level | 45 lines | 32% |
| repetition | 20 lines | 14% |
| coloration | 26 lines | 19% |

| | | | | |
|---|---|---|---|---|
| line-level | 54 lines | | 39% | |
| matching | | 50 lines | | 36% |
| gapping | | 10 lines | | 7% |
| supralinear-level | 81 lines | | 59% | |
| dependency | | 73 lines | | 52% |
| mixing | | 12 lines | | 9% |
| total | 114 lines | | 81% | |

The TH ratio is 114:56 lines, or 67:33%. The weight is 49:19 lines, or 72:28%.

The concluding stave of the poem consists of a 22 line quotation and a 4 line coda. The two preceding staves are also quotative, the fourth only in small part and the third almost entirely. The second stave opens with a minor, 2 line dependency. These divisions are proposed.

| | | |
|---|---|---|
| Stave I | 1a-9b | 28 lines |
| Stave II | 10a-18b | 31 lines |
| Stave III | 19a-25d | 24 lines |
| Stave IV | 26a-36d | 31 lines |
| Stave V | 37a-43d | 26 lines |

There are five Class IV lines in the poem and four instances of mixing. One of each occurs in Staves I (which includes a further Class IV line), IV and V; there is, of the two phenomena, only a Class IV line in Stave II; and a mix alone in Stave III. The Stave II line in question is 15b, the only line in our corpus with three finite verbs.

The first stave opens and closes with the only combinations in it. There is only one break in troping, at the start of the second batch; and only one 4 line dependency, at the start of the fourth. The break between the second and third batches comes after the dependency containing the Class IV line, 5ab. The batches offered are the following.

| | | | |
|---|---|---|---|
| Stave I Batch | a. | 1a-2d. | 6 lines |
| | b. | 3a-5b. | 8 lines |
| | c. | 6a-7d. | 8 lines |
| | d. | 8a-9b. | 6 lines |

The 6 line batches have at their outer limits couplets, 1ab and 9ab, and within, 4 line supralinear tropes, the mix 2abcd and the dependency 8abcd. Four lines of these batches contain matches: both halves of the mix, 2ab and 2cd; and the first and last couplets of Id, 8ab and 9ab. The third batch also contains two 2 line matches, 6cd and 7ab; the former occurs with a repetition. The batch opens with a dependency couplet, 6ab, and closes with the gapping in 7cd. The second batch is half untroped, 3ab 4ab; and half troped with dependency, 4cd and 5ab.

The third batch has the greatest number of heavy lines, 6 out of 8; twice over, one Class I line (6a, 7a) is followed by three non-Class I lines (6bcd, 7bcd). The last batch has only 1 heavy line, 8d. The first two batches each have 4 heavy lines. In the first, these are initial (lab) and final (2cd); and include the Class IV line which opens the poem. In the second, the heavy lines are medial (4a, c) and final (5ab), and include another Class IV line, 5a. Without digressing far on thematic grounds, we can bring up the vexed question of covert quotations; this passage contains three candidates. The first is the recitation by parents and elders mentioned in 7cd: is that recitation the batch that follows, or the dependency which starts the batch? Or is the recitation the rest of the poem? A second covert quotation may be introduced by *šm . . .ʾqrʾ* 'I will recite/rehearse the name/glory': is the rehearsal contained in the rest of the batch, i.e., is *šm* here simply 'name' or is it to be taken more broadly as 'glory,' which would suggest that the glory rehearsal is the rest of the poem? Finally, are the words of the speaker offered to heaven and earth simply the prayer for the words' efficacy (thus, the rest of the batch)? Or are those words the rest of the poem? The correct answers to these questions cannot be adduced on formal grounds; our purpose here is served if it is observed that some of the alternatives refer to units of the poem we have proposed on other grounds. To play out an overloaded hand, we can answer the three questions: in every case, both alternatives are correct. The alternatives that refer to the rest of the text are important because they point up how the poem defines its own territory using the fictions of speaker and audience. The poem is, first of all, the words spoken. It is further asserted to be the *šm yhwh* 'the name/glory rehearsal of Yahweh,' since one major step in the legitimation of the text consists in tying it to the divine realm. Finally, the poem is said to be what the hearers' parents and elders would tell them if they asked: the rest of the legitimation involves bringing the text into the community. The fiction of the speaker which is prominent at the start of the stave, in the phrase 'my mouth,' is completely abolished by the end of the stave.

The second stave is structurally like the first. In both, the marginal batches are similar. Here, the first and last batch are only troped marginally, i.e., at the start and finish respectively. The second batch is not troped initially and the third is troped in toto, in both the first and second staves. The batches here are these.

| | | | |
|---|---|---|---|
| Stave II. | Batch a. | 10a-12b. | 10 lines |
| | b. | 13a-14e. | 9 lines |
| | c. | 15a-17a. | 7 lines |
| | d. | 17b-18b. | 5 lines |

Troping in the first batch is confined to the dependency in 10ab; in the last batch it is limited to the combination of 17bc and the combination and match of 18ab. The second batch is not troped initially or finally; the one passage with troping is the food catalog, 13c-14d, which contains two matches. The first of these, 13cd, is also gapped; the second is a 3 line match, 14bcd. (This catalog is structured on a scale from most to least luxurious or rare: cooking and sweetening media, dairy products, cereal. The ranking also determines the order of honey over oil and obliquely, the isolation of the last item, since there is nothing like grain among foods. Drink is a separate category in 14e. Another paradigm intervenes in 14a: grossvieh over kleinvieh. The original paradigm takes up again in the specification of kleinvieh, since lambs are rarer than rams, 14b, and Bashanite kleinvieh, whatever they are, are rarer than male kleinvieh, 14c.) The third batch is troped first on the line level by repetition in 15ab, by combinations in 15cd and 16ab, and by matching in 16ab 17a.

Heavy lines are concentrated in the middle of the stave. There is only one in the last batch, 18a; 3 are spread over the first batch, 10bc and 11c. Eight heavy lines occur in sequence at the end of the second batch, 14abcde, and at the start of the third, 15abc. The second in the latter group, 15b, is a Class IV line; its non-initial position is the result apparently of its inclusion within a repetition couplet.

In the third stave, we come to the first of the marked quotations in the poem, a series of three prepared for by the three false quotations in the first stave. The quote extends from 19b to 25d and necessarily, the batches fall within it. The first batch is troped only by the quotation; the second begins with repetition and ends with matching, but is otherwise not secondarily troped (i.e., troped beyond the embracing dependency of the quote). The last two batches are troped in toto, the third by combination initially and dependency finally and the last by mixing. These divisions can be set out.

| | | | |
|---|---|---|---|
| Stave III. Batch | a. | 19a-20d. | 6 lines |
| | b. | 21a-22d. | 8 lines |
| | c. | 23a-24d. | 6 lines |
| | d. | 25a-d. | 4 lines |

The first batch is not secondarily troped. Four of its 6 lines are heavy: 19ab, 20bd. The second starts with the repetition of 21abcd and concludes with the match of 22cd; it includes only Class I lines. The combination and match of 23ab overlaps with the repetition of 23b 24abc, which in turn overlaps with the dependency of 24abcd. This dependency includes the match of 24ab. (We note that of the four monsters the first in each line, *r*$^{c}$*b* and *qṭb*, are relatively unknown, while the second, *ršp* and *bhmwt*, are well-attested superstars of the Canaanite infernal gallery.) Heavy lines conclude both the third and fourth batches, 24d and 25cd, and are used medially in the third batch, 24ab. The last batch is not only coextensive with a mix, but inclusive of the double combination, matching, and gapping of 25ab.

The fourth stave also opens with a quotation, which we have taken to be rather short. There is some evidence that we have cut it too short, in fact, and that this whole stave is also quotative, i.e., 34ab and 35ab. The question is simply whether it is more likely that the speaker of the stave-opening quote, 26a-27d, would refer to himself in the third person while using an inclusive first person suffix in 30cd and 31ab; or that the speaker of the poem is likely to use an unsignalled quotation, as we suppose, in 34ab and 35ab. We regard the first person inclusive use as diagnostic but the matter is plainly open for consideration. (Quotations in Hebrew verse seem to be more or less homogeneous with their contexts [in contrast to prose]; if further study reveals that speakers in verse have unusual grammar, the whole matter would be simplified.) The middle batches of the stave are troped throughout and can be separated on the basis of a 7 line match at the start of the third batch. The first and fourth batches end without troping and start with it; the third and fourth batches can be separated at the 3 line match at the latter's head. The divisions are thus the following.

| | | | |
|---|---|---|---|
| Stave IV. Batch | a. | 26a-28b. | 8 lines |
| | b. | 29a-30d. | 6 lines |
| | c. | 31a-34b. | 9 lines |
| | d. | 35a-36d. | 8 lines |

The first batch includes within the quotation 26a-27d, the dependency 26b-27d with the complex chain of exceptive and negative purpose clauses which culminates in the gapping of 27cd. The last 2 lines of the batch are not troped. The second batch opens with the dependency of 29ab and is filled out with the mix of 30abcd; both couplets of the mix, 30ab and 30cd, include both combination and matching tropes. Just as the second batch begins with a 2 line dependency and ends with a larger trope, so the third batch ends with a 2 line dependency, 34ab, and starts with a larger trope. The sequence of 7 bipartite verbless clauses in 31a-33b is punctuated by two color tropes in 32ab and 33ab. The last batch opens with a 3 line match of bipartite verbless clauses, 35abc (this may constitute a transbatch matching figure with 31a-33b), which contains the repetition of 35ab. The batch is otherwise untroped.

Non-Class I lines open the first two batches, 26a and 29a; the second batch contains no others, but the first does, viz., 27cd 28a. The third batch ends with a Class III line, 34b, and includes a Class IV line, 32b, at the center of the 7 line match. The 2 heavy lines in the last batch are the second and second last, 35b and 36c.

The last stave includes the third quotation and the division between it and the coda is also the separating point for the last two batches. The other three batches are within the quote. The third comprehends the oath quote within the larger quote. The first 2 batches can be separated within an area in which there is little secondary troping on the basis of a break from a pattern of alternating non-Class I and Class I lines in the first batch. The batches are the following.

| | | | |
|---|---|---|---|
| Stave V. Batch | a. | 37a-38d. | 6 lines |
| | b. | 39a-f. | 6 lines |
| | c. | 40a-42d. | 10 lines |
| | d. | 43a-d. | 4 lines |

The quotation opens and closes with a sequence of a color trope (37ab, 42ab) and a matching trope (38ab, 42cd); the first of these matching tropes, 38ab, is also gapped. The sequence in the third batch coincides with the mix, 42abcd, as in the first it coincides with the dependency 37ab 38ab. The first batch of the stave is not otherwise troped. The third batch is troped with this sequence and with the two quotations; thus, 42d is the last line of 4 troped passages, one 22 lines long, another 9 lines long, a third 4 lines long, and the last, 2 lines long. The last batch has only the repetition trope, 43abcd, already noted.

The heavy lines in the first batch, 37a, 38a, and 38c, alternate with Class I lines. There are 3 Class II lines in the second batch, one isolated, 39b, and the rest together, 39def. The second line of Vc, which opens the inner quote, is Class IV; the last 2 lines of the third and the first line of the fourth batch are Class II.

The simple symmetry of the staves in the Song of Moses is complicated by the staves' great diversity. In trying to approach this complexity, we can look first at the ratio of lines with troping to heavy lines.

| | |
|---|---|
| Stave I | 62:38% |
| Stave II | 59:41% |
| Stave III | 72:28% |
| Stave IV | 58:42% |
| Stave V | 70:30% |
| total | 67:33% |

Although there is some variation in these data, it is not considerable in light of the extensive fluctuation we noted in other poems. The TH ratio is more or less steady throughout the text. The same cannot be said of the components of the ratio or their relation to the stave size, i.e., weight. In all three of these features, there are broad divergences as well as some agreement with the poem average, here noted by n, or normal.

| | troping | | heavy lines | | weight | |
|---|---|---|---|---|---|---|
| Stave I | 86% | n | 54% | | 82:18% | n |
| Stave II | 55% | | 38% | n | 45:55% | |
| Stave III | 96% | | 38% | n | 100:∅ % | |
| Stave IV | 77% | n | 29% | | 58:42% | |
| Stave V | 100% | | 42% | n | 100:∅ % | |
| total | 81% | n | 40% | n | 72:38% | n |

The percentage of heavy lines is closest to being constant; Staves II, III and V are close to the norm of the text. The percentage of heavy lines is high in the first and low in the fourth staves. Exactly the staves normal in this respect are deviant in extent of troping, as we would expect from the constancy of the TH ratio; it is the first and fourth staves which fit the poem's total gestalt. The first stave but not the fourth is normal for weight; all others are, alternately, deviant under the poem's weight (II, IV) or over it (III, V). If we consider these three factors together, we note that the first stave deviates in only one respect: its percentage of heavy lines is greater than the poem's. The other 4 staves vary from the norm more. The second and fourth staves have two features lower than the poem on the whole, though a different two. The second stave has fewer troped lines and a lower weight; the fourth also has a lower weight, and it has fewer heavy lines. The third and fifth staves use two features more than the whole poem; and they use the same two in this way: the percentage of troped lines and the weight. Thus II and III, and IV and V constitute pairs which balance each other in the direction of the whole poem, while the first stave, the least deviant from the poem's norm, opens the text in a close imitation of its overall shape. The anchor function which the closing staves of the four stave poems perform seems in this text to be assigned to the first stave. Within this array, the recapitulation of the weights of II and III in IV and V suggests that the text has a false bottom, which occurs not at the end of the second last poetic unit, but before it. It is at the end of the third stave, 25abcd, that we find the only case of mixing that is not stave medial in the poem. Given that mixes elsewhere mark major breaks, it may be that this arrangement is also part of the fake coda figure.

### *10.3.5 Psalm 78*

The longest unitary poem in our corpus is the great historical recitation, Psalm 78. Its 163 lines fall into 6 staves, and the stave divisions reveal the structural basis of what many have recognized as a hidden thesis of the poem, and suggest an odd hypothesis about its origins. The larger line classes occur in the text in their ordinary proportions; Class IV is, however, more heavily and, as we shall see, more remarkably used here than elsewhere.

| | | | |
|---|---|---|---|
| Class I | 111 lines | 68% | |
| Class II | 38 lines | 23% | 32% |
| Class III | 6 lines | 4% | |
| Class IV | 8 lines | 5% | |
| total | 163 lines | 100% | |

The three troping levels are exploited to about the same degree in the text, but not in any simple or homogeneous way. Mixing is absent.

| | | | | |
|---|---|---|---|---|
| word-level | 51 lines | | 31% | |
| repetition | | 6 lines | | 4% |
| coloration | | 46 lines | | 28% |
| line-level | 56 lines | | 34% | |
| matching | | 52 lines | | 32% |
| gapping | | 20 lines | | 12% |
| supralinear-level | 47 lines | | 29% | |
| dependency | | 47 lines | | 29% |
| mixing | | ∅ lines | | |
| total | 107 lines | | 66% | |

The TH ratio in the poem is 107:52 lines, 67:33%. The weight is 26:30 lines, 46:54%.

The stave analysis of the poem is straightforward. The first and third staves begin and end without troping; the second is framed by dependency; the fourth by gapping; the fifth by matching; and the last by a cooccurrence of coloration, matching, and dependency. The staves hereby demarcated are the following.

| | | |
|---|---|---|
| Stave I | 1a-10b. | 28 lines |
| Stave II | 11a-20e. | 24 lines |
| Stave III | 21a-32b. | 25 lines |
| Stave IV | 33a-45b. | 28 lines |
| Stave V | 46a-58b. | 29 lines |
| Stave VI | 59a-72b. | 29 lines |

The importance of the preference of Judah over Joseph in Stave VI is obvious, as is the censure of Joseph at the end of the first stave (9a-10b). Less obvious is the link of the ends of the first and fifth staves, which are joined by references to treacherous archery (9a, 57b). Although the first person inclusive and third person usages of the poem elaborate a maze all their own, the common features of the first and fifth stave endings suggest that the inclusion of the first person here is not all Israel and certainly not Judah, but Joseph. The honor paid Judah and David, if this is true, would be the tribute of a defeated rival, offered doubtless by a speaker who knew the wisdom of diplomacy over patriotism better than his auditors.

The three quotations in Deuteronomy 32 provide an undergirding for the stave structure in its extension over so large a domain. There is no single comparable feature in Psalm 78, but there are several features which might do such duty. Among these are the heavy concentration of Class IV lines in stave III (5 of the 8 in the poem); the quotations at the end of the second stave; and the matches at the head of the fifth; both these troping clusters cover about half of the staves they occur in.

The first stave closes its first two batches with dependencies in 3a-4d and 5b-6a and similarly opens its fourth, in 8abc. The first and last batches have untroped outer margins and the third is untroped initially; the second is, in toto, troped. The batches are thus the following.

| | | | |
|---|---|---|---|
| Stave I. Batch | a. | 1a-4d. | 10 lines |
| | b. | 5a-6a. | 5 lines |
| | c. | 6b-7c. | 5 lines |
| | d. | 8a-10b. | 8 lines |

The repetition that opens the first batch, 1b 2a, is contained within the match of 1b 2ab. The repetition that opens the last batch, 8bc, is included within the dependency of 8abc. The first batch is further troped by the 6 line dependency of 3a-4d, which includes the gapping of 3ab. The last batch is not otherwise troped. The second batch opens with a couplet of binomination, combination, and matching, 5ab, the last line of which opens the dependency of 5bcd 6a. The third batch is troped only with the matching of 7bc.

The middle batches have few heavy lines; indeed, the second has none at all, while the third has only one, 6b, the opening line. There are 5 Class II lines in the first batch: one pair, 1ab, is followed by a pair of Class I lines and a single Class II line, 3a; the pattern is then reversed and a pair of Class I lines is followed by 2 Class II lines, 4bc, and 1 Class I line. In the last batch, there are 2 Class II lines together, 8bc; 9a is a Class IV line.

The last 2 batches of the second stave are completely troped by dependency and are distinguished by opening with heavy lines. The break between the first 2 batches follows a break in troping. These divisions yield the following arrangement.

| | | | |
|---|---|---|---|
| Stave II. Batch | a. | 11a-13b. | 6 lines |
| | b. | 14a-16b. | 6 lines |
| | c. | 17a-18b. | 4 lines |
| | d. | 19a-20e. | 8 lines |

The first 2 couplets of IIa are dependent, 11ab and 12ab; the first and last couplets of IIb are matching; the first of these is gapped and the second has a combination. The two couplets of the third batch, 17ab and 18ab, are both dependent. The 8 line dependency which covers the final batch, 19a-20e, includes within it, a dependency, 19bc; one couplet, which includes a combination and a match, 20bc; and another which has a coordination, 20de.

There are 2 heavy lines in the first and last batches, 12b 13a, and 19a (which is batch initial) and 20d. There is only one heavy line in each of the middle batches, 14b and 17a, the latter a Class IV line at the start of a batch.

Class IV lines are almost commonplace in the third stave: there are five in 25 lines, and three of them head off the first three batches. The last batch begins after a run of 5 heavy lines. These batches can be set forth.

| | | | |
|---|---|---|---|
| Stave III. Batch | a. | 21a-23b. | 7 lines |
| | b. | 24a-26b. | 6 lines |
| | c. | 27a-29b. | 5 lines |
| | d. | 30a-32b. | 7 lines |

The 8 troped lines of the stave occur in 2 groups. The first is in the first batch: the double coloration and matching of 21bc is followed by the single coloration, also accompanied by matching, of 22ab. The second group is like the first but is split across the middle batches. The second batch ends with the double coloration and matching of 26ab, while the third opens with the single coloration and gapping without matching in 27ab. The areas of untroped lines across the stave increase from 1 (21a) through 6 (23a-25b) up to 10 (28-32b).

The splitting of the block of troped lines, 26a-27b, is necessary in light of the heavy line patterns in the stave. There are two Class IV lines in Batches IIIb and IIIc, one initial (24a, 27a) and one medial (25b, 28). The only heavy line in the first batch is the initial Class IV line. The last batch has no Class IV lines; it has three Class II lines, 31a, and 31c 32a. The first 4 of the 6 lines of Batch IIIb are heavy, 24ab 25ab; and all 5 lines of Batch IIIc are heavy. The first lines of IIIb and IIIc match and partially repeat each other in describing the two alimentary precipitates of manna and quail flesh; the repetition is more significant than the matching and presents a variety of inclusion we have not seen before. That this is not a case of a matching figure exceeding what seems to be its proper domain is underscored by the fact that no other two lines in the batches match.

The fourth stave begins and ends with gapping. The first and third batches end with coloration, while the third and fourth begin with dependency. The second batch is untroped. The batches thus divided are herewith specified.

| | | | |
|---|---|---|---|
| Stave IV. Batch | a. | 33a-36b. | 8 lines |
| | b. | 37a-38d. | 6 lines |
| | c. | 39a-41b. | 6 lines |
| | d. | 42a-45b. | 8 lines |

These divisions also reflect the action/reaction balance of this segment of the narration. Yahweh acts at the start of IVa and c, and at the end of IVb and IVd; the Israelites act at the start of IVb and IVd and at the end of IVa and IVc. Thus there is one oscillation between God and people in each batch.

The first batch opens (after the 10 line hiatus in troping at the end of Stave III) with a triply troped couplet, 33ab, a gapped matching with a combination. The last couplet of the batch, 36ab, also has a combination; the couplet before, 35ab, has a binomination with a dependency. The first batch's range of tropes is used in the fourth. The opening 4 line dependency, 42ab 43ab, includes a gapped matching, 43ab. The next 2 lines, 44ab, have a combination, and the last 2 are gapped.

The last lines of the last batch, 45ab, are also heavy lines, Classes IV and III, the only such in the batch. There are also only 2 heavy lines in Batches IVb and IVc, viz., 38bc, and 39a (a batch initial line) and 41a. The 3 heavy lines in the first batch, 34ab 35a, occur between the 2 troped groups in the batch.

The fifth stave is dominated by matching, which covers the whole of the first, most of the second, and the ends of the third and fourth batches. The conclusion of the first batch is signalled by a break in a dependency trope, and the ends of the next two by a break in troping. These batches are thus arranged.

| | | | |
|---|---|---|---|
| Stave V. Batch | a. | 46a-49c. | 9 lines |
| | b. | 50a-52b. | 7 lines |
| | c. | 53a-55c. | 7 lines |
| | d. | 56a-58b. | 6 lines |

There are 2 matches in the first batch, the first one 7 lines long, 46a-49a, and the second, 2 lines, 49bc; each line is also troped in at least one other way. The last line of the long match, 49a, has as its dependencies the two lines of the short match. All of the lines of the long match but the last fall into gapping couplets, 46ab, 47ab, and 48ab. The first of these, 46ab, contains a combination and the third, 48ab, a binomination. The first line of the second batch is not secondarily troped and its last line is troped, but as part of a combination only, not as part of a match. The sequence of coloration-gapping-coloration that undergirds the first batch is also present in the second, without the instances of gapping alongside the colorations. Thus, 50bc and 52ab contain combinations and 51ab is gapped. The match of 55abc concludes the third batch and that of 57b 58ab, the fourth; the latter overlaps with the combination of 58ab. There are 2 heavy lines in each of the first two batches, both juxtaposed; the lines 49bc end the first batch and 51ab occur within the second. The 3 heavy lines in the third batch are spaced at 2 line intervals: 53a, 54b, and 55c. The three in the last batch are initial, 56ab 57a.

The sixth stave concludes with a batch troped in toto; the first batch is almost so treated. The second batch is untroped and the transition from it to the third is marked by a resumption of troping. These batches are proposed.

| | | | |
|---|---|---|---|
| Stave VI. Batch | a. | 59a-62b. | 8 lines |
| | b. | 63a-66b. | 8 lines |
| | c. | 67a-69b. | 6 lines |
| | d. | 70a-72b. | 7 lines |

The binomination that opens the first batch, 59ab, is followed, after the dependency of 60ab, by another color trope; 61ab, which contain this combination, are also gapped and constitute the first 2 lines of a 3 line match, 61ab 62a. After the untroped second batch, the third batch begins with further overlapping. The repetition trope, 67b 68a, includes part of the matching couplet, 67ab (which also contains a combination), and part of the dependency, 68ab.

Each of the troped batches of the stave has only one heavy line: 59a, which is batch initial, 68b, and 71c. The second, untroped batch has two, 65b, and 66b, which is batch final.

The overall structure of the longest unitary poem in our corpus is not easy to get at. We have noted Josephite references which are explicit in the first and last staves; the covert one at the end of the fifth stave may constitute a thematic false coda. Another link across the poem is the reference to Yahweh hearing in the first lines of the third and last staves, 21a, and 59a. There is other evidence that the poem breaks, as this fact suggests, in half; we shall continue to refer to formal criteria only.

The fourth stave in the poem exhibits the striking resemblance to the poem's overall shape that we saw previously reserved for marginal staves. The fourth corresponds closely to the whole poem in the use of troping (71% for Stave IV, 66% for the poem) and heavy lines (32% for both), and in TH ratio (51:40%, 49:51%) and weight (56:44%, 46:54%). Only the fourth stave so corresponds. All the others vary between one and four of these features. Heavy line distribution varies least.

| | | |
|---|---|---|
| Stave I | 32% | normal |
| Stave II | 25% | normal |
| Stave III | 52% | |
| Stave IV | 32% | normal |
| Stave V | 34% | normal |
| Stave VI | 17% | |
| total | 32% | normal |

Only the third and sixth differ much from the norm, the third being higher and the last lower. Troping is normal as often as not; the TH ratio is rarely so.

| | *troping* | *TH ratio* |
|---|---|---|
| Stave I | 68% normal | 68:32% normal |
| Stave II | 83% | 53:47% |
| Stave III | 32% | 38:62% |
| Stave IV | 71% normal | 51:49% |
| Stave V | 76% | 54:46% |
| Stave VI | 62% normal | 78:22% |
| total | 66% normal | 67:33% normal |

The deviances here do not correspond across the poem except in the first stave, but it is evident from the heavy line use that the relationship is not a simple complementation. Weight is the least regular feature.

| | |
|---|---|
| Stave I | 50:50% normal |
| Stave II | 62:38% |
| Stave III | 25:75% |
| Stave IV | 56:44% normal |
| Stave V | 71:29% |
| Stave VI | 25:75% |
| total | 46:54% normal |

The sequences from I to III and from IV to VI are identical: from normal to overweight to under. Let us combine these four features in a single table, letting *n* stand for normal, *plus* for a higher than normal value and *minus* for the opposite.

| | n | + | - |
|---|---|---|---|
| I | 4 | ∅ | ∅ |
| II | 1 | 2 | 1 |
| III | ∅ | 1 | 3 |
| IV | 3 | ∅ | 1 |
| V | 1 | 2 | 1 |
| VI | 1 | 1 | 2 |

The most evident features of the table are the correspondence of Staves II and V, and the perfect normality of Stave I. Stave IV comes closest to reproducing perfect normality. The text traces one movement away from normality in Staves I-II-III and repeats it in Staves IV-V-VI. At the same time, the normality declines across the three pairs of staves: Staves I-II have five normal features, III-IV have three, and V-VI have two. The gap in these pairings is greatest for the middle staves. Thus, the shift away from the well-wrought initial stave is most pronounced in the center of the text.

### *10.4 The Book of Zephaniah*

The essential integrity of Zephaniah is unquestioned. Though it is not in any simple sense homogeneous, the only portions of the text which have been consistently treated as extrinsic are the few that refer to theologoumena judged to be of later date, usually on problematic grounds. While the fall of Jerusalem is not an event that can be regarded as other than epochal, historians of Israelite ideology must reckon with the fact that it was not hard to see the destruction coming. The last quarter of the seventh century is obscure to modern historians because those were confused years to contemporary observers; the major realignments in the Mesopotamian sphere, however, were clear all round and Levantine consequences were to be expected. Further, to deny Zephaniah insights afforded to his younger pre-exilic and exilic contemporaries is to miss the central assertion of the seventh and sixth century prophets: the destruction of Jerusalem should have surprised no one. Most of the questions put to the text by previous students can only be answered in favor of textual excision in defiance of structural factors. The most obvious case involves the conclusion of the book: deletion of the supposed universalist references there would destroy the back to back double quotation, discussed in 8.1.1.

It is not only the integrity of the text we shall assume, but also that of the chapter divisions in the received form of the text. The relative status of the accidents in the Massoretic text is unclear but there is virtually universal agreement that the chapter divisions are both old and valuable. In the case of Zephaniah, we shall go further and assume that they reflect major divisions in the text. This happens not to be a radical assumption in this case.

The integrity of the third chapter of the book is commonly accepted. The barrier between the first two chapters is as often rejected. The standard division is at Zph 2:4: it is argued that the oracles against foreign nations form a unit distinct from the treatment of Judah in Zph 1-2:3. A close look at the text reveals the superiority of the Massoretic division.

The subject of Chapter 1 is Judah, that of Chapter 3, Jerusalem. The relation of these entities is that of container to contained. In Chapter 1, that is, the speaker isolates the field of his concern, and in the conclusion he deals with the portion of it he regards as critical. With this relation in mind, we can define the subject matter of Chapter 2: it is Judah as a nation (here, the contained) among the nations (here, the container). The progression among the chapters is from medium focus (Judah), to broad focus (Judah among the nations), to close-up (Jerusalem within Judah).

This reading is easily confirmed by a consideration of the beginning and end of Chapter 2. In 2:1, one of the rare applications of *gwy* 'nation' to a group of Yahwists occurs. There could be no better leveling of Judah with the rest of the nations than to swerve from the standard designation for groups of Yahwists, ᶜ*m* 'people,' to *gwy*. The reference to the exultant city that opens the final section of the chapter has been tied back to Nineveh in 2:13c and forward to Jerusalem in Chapter 3; the prospective tie is correct. The reference to Nineveh is structurally functional but is no more a sign of thematic concerns than the rest of the nations mentioned. The chapter opens with the nation of Judah and follows with other nations referred to as such; the last of these is Assyria, in 2:13b. The capital of the country is mentioned in the next line, 2:13c and thus the shift from country to capital is made in fine in 2:13bc, just as the same shift is made on a large scale from Chapter 1 to Chapter 3. The Assyria-Nineveh paradigm, which is cited while Judah is being considered amidst the nations, modulates the transition within the Judah-Jerusalem instance of the same paradigm. (This transition is effected within the context of the geographical progression of the oracles from the near west to the near east, followed by the distant southeast and the distant northwest.)

This discussion of Chapter 2 is offered as a rough defense of an assumption. Our formal analysis of the Book of Zephaniah will yield much evidence to support the assumption; since we are not presenting a full reading of the book, we need not defend the assumption further. In such a reading, the circles of argumentation regarding formal structure would have to be closer. We would need to say that our analysis warrants our assumptions, but we could only do so in a context fitted out with other, distinct forms of argumentation. The thematic sketch above adumbrates one of them.

In analyzing the Poem of Zephaniah, we shall be working with not two, but three levels of poetic organization: the batch, the stave and the chapter. The last could be called a poem, by analogy with individual texts we have already looked at, but it seems better to reserve the term generally for the whole book. The fact that no theory of prophetic activity can encompass the notion that the whole book is one poem (and thus presumably, one "utterance") is no obstacle to our work. In the first place, we are making no claims at all about the prophet, only the book. If we discuss only the internal evidence about the relation of the two, we shall say nothing. Further, standard notions of prophetic activity are too deeply influenced by misconceptions about the nature of culture to be taken too seriously. We have in mind particularly ultimately contradictory notions about memory and originality among "primitive peoples" which so often lurk behind discussions of prophecy.

The text of Zephaniah is 213 lines, or roughly 8 (26-27) line staves. The three chapters are of unequal lengths. The last is 79 lines, a 3 stave text like Genesis 49 and Numbers 23-24 (both 80 lines). The first two chapters are 69 and 65 lines, respectively, 2 1/2 stave texts, like Habaqquq 3 (65 lines). The basic structure is then one of rising length: two (roughly) equal units, followed by a somewhat longer one. Before we consider other features of the whole text, we shall review the chapters severally.

### *10.4.1 Zephaniah 1*

The staves of the first chapter can be recognized with little difficulty once it is realized that the repetition trope of 1:9bc 10a must either be ignored or overriden. The line typology shows more heavy lines than Class I lines; and more Class III lines than even Classes II and IV combined.

| | | | |
|---|---|---|---|
| Class I | 32 lines | 46% | |
| Class II | 12 lines | 17% | |
| Class III | 21 lines | 31% | 54% |
| Class IV | 4 lines | 6% | |
| total | 69 lines | 100% | |

The trope levels increase in frequency as their domains broaden; mixing is absent.

| | | | | |
|---|---|---|---|---|
| word-level | 26 lines | | 38% | |
| repetition | | 22 lines | | 32% |
| coloration | | 4 lines | | 6% |
| line-level | 32 lines | | 46% | |
| matching | | 32 lines | | 46% |
| gapping | | 4 lines | | 6% |
| supralinear-level | 36 lines | | 52% | |
| dependency | | 36 lines | | 52% |
| mixing | | ∅ lines | | |
| total | 58 lines | | 84% | |

The TH ratio is 58:37 lines, 61:39%. The weight is 33:7 lines, or 83:17%.

The chapter begins and ends with cooccurrences of repetition and dependency, and all three staves end with dependency tropes. The second stave begins with a break in troping and the third after a break in the 5 line matching trope of the *Dies irae* catalog. The staves are thus.

| | | |
|---|---|---|
| Stave 1/I | 2a-9c | 29 lines |
| Stave 1/II | 10a-16a | 29 lines |
| Stave 1/III | 16b-18e | 11 lines |

We have already alluded to the major thematic correlation of this analysis, the position of the catalog at the end of Stave 1/II. Batch analysis will facilitate further examination.

There are two breaks in troping in Stave 1/I, at the end of the first batch, and throughout the third. All but the last batch open with Class I lines. These are the batches proposed.

| | | | |
|---|---|---|---|
| Stave 1/I Batch | a. | 2a-3f | 9 lines |
| | b. | 4a-6b | 10 lines |
| | c. | 7a-d | 4 lines |
| | d. | 8a-9c | 6 lines |

The first batch begins with the repetition trope of 2a-3b, which includes the smaller repetition and match of 3ab and the dependency of 2ab. This initial repetition overlaps with the dependency of 3bcd. There are also two dependencies in the second batch, which together cover the batch, one of 2 lines, 4ab, and another of 8 lines, 4c-6b. The long dependency includes a 5 line match, 5a-6a, which in turn envelops the two 2 line repetitions of 5ab and 5cd. The third batch is entirely untroped. The fourth is troped in toto like the second; and it is troped with overlapping and sequent, rather than inclusive, troping. The match of 8ab overlaps with the dependency of 8bc; the latter is followed by the dependency of 9abc.

Only the third batch is free of heavy lines. Class IV lines conclude the second (6b) and fourth (9c) batches, and there is another (4c) in a group of heavy lines near the start of the second batch (4bcd). The first batch opens with a Class I line, 2a; after 2 heavy lines, 2bc, and 2 Class I lines, 3ab, there are 4 further heavy lines. Only one line in 1/Id is Class I, 9a; the other 5 lines are heavy; four belong to Class III (8abc, 9b) and the last, 9c, is, as noted, from Class IV.

The first two batches of the second stave are marked by breaks in troping. The second batch ends after, and fourth begins with, a major dependency; the first and third batches have no supralinear-level tropes. The division between the third and fourth batches is bridged by a higher order repetition trope. The batches are these.

| | | | |
|---|---|---|---|
| Stave 1/II Batch | a. | 10a-11c | 8 lines |
| | b. | 12a-f | 6 lines |
| | c. | 13a-14d | 9 lines |
| | d. | 15a-16a | 6 lines |

Batch 1/IIa includes two 3 line matches, 10cde and 11abc; the former encompasses the 2 combinations of 10de. The second batch also has inclusive troping: the dependency of 12c-f includes the match of 12de. Matching and gapping open the third batch, in 13ab, and there is another match in 13de. The conclusion of the batch shows repetition troping in 14abc and in 14d, if the trope of *ywm* repetitions from 14a-16a is allowed to stand despite the batch division. The last batch, the *Dies irae* catalog, is troped throughout with dependency and repetition; and the last 5 of the 6 lines, 15b-16a, match.

Every line of the last batch is heavy; all but 2 of the first batch, i.e., 10b-e and 11bc, are also. Only the last line of the second batch, 12f, is heavy and only 3 of the 9 lines of the third, viz., 13c, 14a and 14c, are heavy.

The last stave, 11 lines in length, is troped throughout; the break between the batches is set at the point at which troping increases most sharply. The batches are these.

| | | | |
|---|---|---|---|
| Stave 1/III | Batch a. | 16b-17c | 4 lines |
| | b. | 17d-18e | 7 lines |

There are dependencies at the start of the first batch, 16b 17a, and at the end of the second, 18de. Interlocking with the opening dependency is a 3 line match, 17abc. The first 2 lines of the 3 line match that opens the second batch, 17de, contain 2 combinations and show gapping. The last line of that match, 18a, is the first line of a dependency, 18ab. The 3 line repetition trope that follows in 18cde includes the final dependency.

Line typology and TH ratio are constant across the staves of the chapter. The point can be made adequately by looking at only the Class I: Class II-IV balance.

| | *Class I: heavy lines* | |
|---|---|---|
| Stave I | 14:15 lines | 48:52% |
| Stave II | 13:16 lines | 45:55% |
| Stave III | 5:6 lines | 45:55% |
| total | 32:37 lines | 46:54% |

| | *TH ratio* | |
|---|---|---|
| Stave I | 23:15 lines | 61:39% |
| Stave II | 24:16 lines | 60:40% |
| Stave III | 11:6 lines | 65:35% |
| total | 58:37 lines | 61:39% |

The troping and weight both increase slightly through the staves.

| | *troping* | | *weight* | |
|---|---|---|---|---|
| Stave I | 23 lines | 79% | 13:4 lines | 76:24% |
| Stave II | 24 lines | 83% | 14:3 lines | 82:18% |
| Stave III | 11 lines | 100% | 6:∅ lines | 100:∅ % |
| total | 58 lines | 84% | 33:7 lines | 83:7 % |

Less impressive in both cases than the increase in itself is the agreement between the middle stave and the average. The use of trope level is a more evident source of differentiation among the staves.

| | *word-level* | *line-level* | *supralinear-level* |
|---|---|---|---|
| Stave I | 9 lines 31% | 9 lines 31% | 20 lines 69% |
| Stave II | 12 lines 41% | 17 lines 59% | 10 lines 34% |
| Stave III | 5 lines 45% | 6 lines 55% | 6 lines 55% |
| total | 26 lines 38% | 32 lines 46% | 36 lines 52% |

Word-level troping increases rather uniformly but the others do not. The lowest point of line-level troping is in the first stave; thereafter, the use rises and then falls somewhat. On the supralinear level, the use starts out at its highest point in the first stave, falls to the lowest and then rises somewhat. Because the changes in these two levels are complementary, the total troping pattern corresponds to the pattern of word-level troping.

### *10.4.2 Zephaniah 2*

The chapter opens and closes with untroped lines. The distinction noted earlier between the oracles against the nations proper and the Judah-Jerusalem portions of the chapter is undergirt by the distribution of heavy lines. The largest blocks of Class I lines in the chapter occur at the start of the second two staves, 4abcd and 9hi 10a. The first stave is thus the opening address to Judah. The line typology is the following.

| | | | |
|---|---|---|---|
| Class I | 35 lines | 54% | |
| Class II | 13 lines | 20% | 46% |
| Class III | 11 lines | 17% | |
| Class IV | 6 lines | 9% | |
| total | 65 lines | 100% | |

The only mix in the book occurs at the end of the second stave, 9defg; this is also the midpoint of the book, after three full staves and two semi-staves and before the four remaining staves; more strictly, 105 lines precede the mix and 104 lines follow. The Cities of the Plain and the incestuous offspring of Noah are center stage in the text; and, we can add, cities balance nations in the trope just as a nation, Judah, opens the whole poem, and a city, Jerusalem, closes it. The troping as a whole is structured like this.

| | | | | |
|---|---|---|---|---|
| word-level | 16 lines | | 25% | |
| repetition | | 12 lines | | 18% |
| coloration | | 6 lines | | 9% |
| line-level | 18 lines | | 28% | |
| matching | | 14 lines | | 22% |
| gapping | | 6 lines | | 9% |

| | | |
|---|---|---|
| supralinear-level | 34 lines | 52% |
| dependency | 30 lines | 46% |
| mixing | 4 lines | 6% |
| total | 46 lines | 71% |

The TH ratio of the chapter is 46:30 lines, 61:39%. The weight is 21:10 lines, 68:32%. The staves of Chapter 2 are these.

| | | |
|---|---|---|
| Stave 2/I | 1-3g | 14 lines |
| Stave 2/II | 4a-9g | 26 lines |
| Stave 2/III | 9h-15g | 25 lines |

Like the poem's first line, the first line of Chapter 2 contains a *figura etymologica*; and like 3:2, 2:1 is a Class IV line.

The first stave, at half size, contains only two batches. To isolate these, we must cross over the repetition trope formed by *bqšw* in 3a and 3de. The batches are these.

| | | | |
|---|---|---|---|
| Stave 2/I Batch | a. | 1-3c | 10 lines |
| | b. | 3d-g | 4 lines |

The first dependency in Batch 2/Ia is 2 lines, 2ab; the next is seven lines. The first four lines of the second dependency, 2c-f, have a repetition trope; and if the *bqšw* trope stands, so do the last 3, 3abc. At any rate, the first two lines of the second batch, 3de, have a lower order repetition trope, coincident with a combination and a match. The last lines of the stave, 3fg, are dependent.

The first two lines of stave 2/Ia, 1 and 2a, and the last one, 3g, are heavy. The other three heavy lines, 2df and 3b, are separated from each other by one line; from the first two heavy lines by two Class I lines; and from the last, heavy line by four Class I lines.

The first two batches of the second stave open with troping and close without it, while the last two open without it and close with it. The break between the middle staves is assured by a break in heavy lines. The batches are proposed to lie like so.

| | | | |
|---|---|---|---|
| Stave 2/II Batch | a. | 4a-5b | 6 lines |
| | b. | 5c-7c | 7 lines |
| | c. | 7d-8d | 6 lines |
| | d. | 9a-g | 7 lines |

The only troped lines in batch 2/IIa are the first two, 4ab, which contain a binomination, a combination and are gapped. Two two-line dependencies open the second batch in 5cd and 6ab. A match follows in 7ab; a trope of repetition, 6ab 7a, overlaps with both the second dependency and the match. The first trope in the third batch is the match of 7e 8a and the last is the gapping of 8cd; the dependency of 8abcd overlaps both of these. Of the seven lines of batch 2/IId, the first, 9a, is untroped. The next two, 9bc, are dependent; and the last four, 9defg, are in a mix. The first two lines of the mix match and are gapped and house the binominations cited above.

The last stave of the second chapter confirms expectations of irregular troping levels rather plainly: word-level troping is entirely absent as are gapping and mixing. Matching opens the first batch and closes the third and dependency closes the first and opens the third and fourth. The batches are the following.

| | | | |
|---|---|---|---|
| Stave 2/III Batch | a. | 9h-10c | 5 lines |
| | b. | 11a-13c | 8 lines |
| | c. | 14a-e | 5 lines |
| | d. | 15a-g | 7 lines |

Only in the last batch do the two tropes represented overlap. In the first three batches, the two 2 line matches of 9hi and 14cd frame the three 2 line dependencies of 10bc, 11cd and 14ab; 11cd is batch medial. This is the sequence.

| | | |
|---|---|---|
| Batch a. | match 9hi | |
| | | dependency 10bc |
| Batch b. | | dependency 11cd |
| Batch c. | | dependency 14ab |
| | match 14cd | |

In the last batch, the enclosing relation is flipped and condensed into a single troped passage: the dependency of 15abcd contains the match of 15bc.

No batch opens with heavy lines; all batches but the last close with them, in 10bc, 13c and 14e, the last two being Class IV lines. There are four medial heavy lines in sequence in Batch 2/IIIb, at 11bcd 12; and there are two in sequence in both the last two batches, 14bc and 15de.

The line typology of Chapter 2 is stable in the staves, as the ratio of lines in Class I to those in Classes II-IV shows.

| | *Class I: heavy lines* | |
|---|---|---|
| Stave I | 8:6 lines | 57:43% |
| Stave II | 14:12 lines | 54:46% |
| Stave III | 13:12 lines | 52:48% |
| total | 35:30 lines | 54:46% |

Not only is the balance here stable, but despite its closeness to even balance, it is consistently tipped away from the comparable ratio of Chapter 1, which is the flip of the average here, 46:54%.

The consistent decline noted in the other gross features of Chapter 1 is mirrored here in an equally gradual and consistent rise. The rise shows up not only in connection with troping and weight but also TH ratio.

| | *troping* | | | *TH ratio* | | | *weight* | | |
|---|---|---|---|---|---|---|---|---|---|
| Stave I | 13 | lines | 93% | 13:6 | lines | 68:32% | 5:∅ | lines | 100:∅% |
| Stave II | 19 | lines | 73% | 19:12 | lines | 61:39% | 9:4 | lines | 69:31% |
| Stave III | 14 | lines | 56% | 14:12 | lines | 54:46% | 7:6 | lines | 54:46% |
| total | 46 | lines | 71% | 46:30 | lines | 61:39% | 21:10 | lines | 68:32% |

The chapter averages show close similarities to the second stave's features. The decline is least apparent in the TH ratio. Troping levels also vary: word-level and supralinear-level troping decline consistently; the line-level troping is more complex.

| | *word-level* | | | *line-level* | | | *supralinear-level* | | |
|---|---|---|---|---|---|---|---|---|---|
| Stave I | 9 | lines | 64% | 2 | lines | 14% | 10 | lines | 71% |
| Stave II | 7 | lines | 27% | 10 | lines | 38% | 14 | lines | 54% |
| Stave III | ∅ | lines | | 6 | lines | 24% | 10 | lines | 40% |
| total | 16 | lines | 25% | 18 | lines | 28% | 34 | lines | 52% |

The line troping reaches a maximum in the second stave after a low point in the first, before declining further in the last.

### *10.4.3 Zephaniah 3*

The concluding chapter, 79 lines in length, is composed of 3 standard staves. The line typology is similar to that of the poem as a whole.

| | | | | |
|---|---|---|---|---|
| Class I | 44 | lines | 56% | |
| Class II | 15 | lines | 19% | 44% |
| Class III | 12 | lines | 15% | |
| Class IV | 8 | lines | 10% | |
| total | 79 | lines | 100% | |

The troping levels are more striking in themselves.

| | | | | |
|---|---|---|---|---|
| word-level | 14 lines | | 18% | |
| repetition | | 8 lines | | 10% |
| coloration | | 6 lines | | 8% |
| line-level | 6 lines | | 8% | |
| matching | | 6 lines | | 8% |
| gapping | | ∅ lines | | |

| | | |
|---|---|---|
| supralinear-level | 39 lines | 49% |
| dependency | 39 lines | 49% |
| mixing | ∅ | |
| total | 52 lines | 66% |

The TH ratio is 52:35 lines, 60:40%; the weight is 20:12 lines, 62:38%.

The first two staves end without troping, as the chapter itself begins. The second begins with the first dependency longer than 2 lines in the chapter; and the third with the last match of the poem. The staves are the following.

| | | |
|---|---|---|
| Stave 3/I | 1-8b | 27 lines |
| Stave 3/II | 8c-13e | 23 lines |
| Stave 3/II | 14a-20f | 29 lines |

The troping plainly increases through the staves, a progress we shall note in detail in the batch analyses.

The batches of Stave 3/I are sparely marked. The first trope closes the first batch and the last troped passage opens the last batch. The other two troped passages are almost back to back in the middle. These batches are the following.

| | | | |
|---|---|---|---|
| Stave 3/I Batch | a. | 1-2d | 5 lines |
| | b. | 3a-5a | 7 lines |
| | c. | 5b-6d | 8 lines |
| | d. | 7a-8b | 7 lines |

The match of 2cd closes Batch 3/Ia and the coordination of 3ab opens 3/Ib. The combination of 4bc occurs directly before the end of Batch 3/Ib. The repetition of 5bc opens Batch 3/Ic. Two sequent dependencies open the last batch in 7ab and 7cd.

Heavy lines open Batches 3/Ia, 3/Ib, and 3/Id, at 1, 3a, and 7a; and close Batches 3/Ic and 3/Id, at 6d and 8b. There are medial heavy lines in Batches 3/Ib and 3/Id, at 4a and 7e.

In Stave 3/II, as in 2/III, there are only two tropes represented, matching and dependency; word-level troping is not present. Further, there is little matching. The second batch is fully troped, separated from what precedes and follows by untroped lines. Like its beginning, the end of the third batch is untroped. The last batch opens with a trope. These batches are the following.

| | | | |
|---|---|---|---|
| Stave 3/II Batch | a. | 8c-h | 6 lines |
| | b. | 9a-11b | 7 lines |
| | c. | 11c-12c | 5 lines |
| | d. | 13a-e | 5 lines |

As in Stave 3/I, no line here is troped more than once. The five dependencies in the stave are arranged in order of descending size. The first, which is the only trope in the first batch, is 5 lines long, 8c-g. The next dependency, the first of three in Batch 3/IIb, is 3 lines, 9abc; the next two are 2 lines, 10ab and 11ab, as is the dependency of the third batch, 12ab, the only trope there. The match of 13ab is the only trope in Batch 3/IId.

The first and third batches close with heavy lines, at 8gh and 12bc. The second and third open with them, at 9a and 11cd. The first, second, and fourth batches have medial heavy lines, at 8d, 10ab 11a, and 13cd.

The last stave of the poem reveals a conclusive efflorescence of troping. The concluding quotation straddles two batches, separable at the point at which second order dependency begins. The first batch ends after a break in troping. The repetition trope of 15d 16ab must be overridden. The second batch starts with and ends with the first quotation, that of the divine counselor. These batches follow.

| | | | |
|---|---|---|---|
| Stave 3/III Batch | a. | 14a-15d | 8 lines |
| | b. | 16a-17e | 8 lines |
| | c. | 18a-19c | 5 lines |
| | d. | 19d-20f | 8 lines |

The match that starts off the first batch, 14ab, is followed by a dependency in 14cd; there is a combination in 15ab. The second batch is troped throughout with the quotative dependency and otherwise only with combination of 17cd. The third batch is only dependent. The last batch contains three smaller dependencies, two 2 lines long, in 19de and 20ab, and one 3 lines, at 20cde. The repetition of 20abc straddles the last two of these.

No batch in this stave ends with heavy lines. The first and third start off with sequences of four, 14abcd and 18ab 19ab. There is a single medial heavy line in the first batch, at 15c; one medial pair of heavy lines in the second batch, at 16bc; and two medial pairs in the last batch, at 19e 20a and 20cd.

The gross structural features of Chapter 3 do not fulfill the easiest predictions to be extrapolated from Chapters 1 and 2. That is, having risen in Chapter 1 and declined in Chapter 2, the features do not stabilize in the last chapter. Nor do the features pattern in ways divergent from one another. As in the other chapters, there is a feature which is stable; here, it is the TH ratio.

| | | |
|---|---|---|
| Stave I | 10:7 lines | 59:41% |
| Stave II | 16:13 lines | 55:45% |
| Stave III | 26:15 lines | 63:37% |
| total | 52:35 lines | 60:40% |

There is some divergence, to be sure; and it is the first stave that agrees with the average, in so far as the others differ from it. The variations in the extent to which troping and heavy lines are used separately and in the weights are much greater.

| | *troping* | *heavy lines* | *weight* |
|---|---|---|---|
| Stave I | 10 lines 37% | 7 lines 26% | 1:11 lines 8:92% |
| Stave II | 16 lines 70% | 13 lines 57% | 7:1 lines 88:12% |
| Stave III | 26 lines 90% | 15 lines 52% | 12:∅ lines 100:∅ % |
| total | 52 lines 66% | 35 lines 44% | 20:12 lines 62:38% |

The troping rises gradually through the staves and the middle stave is close to the average. The heavy line percentage and weight rise abruptly after the first stave. After the second, the weight rises further, while the number of heavy lines declines slightly.

Two of the troping levels vary and one level is steady; here it is the line-level troping that is steady, while the other two rise, after a fashion.

| | *word-level* | *line-level* | *supralinear-level* |
|---|---|---|---|
| Stave I | 4 lines 15% | 2 lines 7% | 4 lines 15% |
| Stave II | ∅ lines | 2 lines 9% | 14 lines 61% |
| Stave III | 10 lines 34% | 2 lines 7% | 21 lines 72% |
| total | 14 lines 18% | 6 lines 8% | 39 lines 49% |

The curious mode of the word-level rise involves complete disappearance in the middle; supralinear-level troping rises more consistently.

### *10.4.4 The Poem of Zephaniah*

The formal devices we have proposed and used in describing individual poems and chapters of Zephaniah are also appropriate to the Book of Zephaniah. The concision and abstractness of such description reaches an apogee here and the phenomena as discussed on this level demand great concentration. As in Psalm 78 and Deuteronomy 32, however, the demand is partially met in advance. There are plainly perceptible patterns of various and considerable markedness in the poem. Most obvious among these is the only mix in the book, at its center, 2:9defg. Also noteworthy are the victim catalog, 1:4a-6b and the *Dies irae* catalog, 1:15a-16a; and the two depraved boasts of 1:12cdef and 2:15abcd, which are counterbalanced by the final quotations of 3:16a-17e and 3:18a-20f. The gross structural features we shall be talking about below are in part the result of these, and their presence should aid the reader in following our argument as it follows the poem.

We begin with the three chapters of the poem, ignoring for the moment the three component staves of each. How do the gross structural features of the whole poem behave in its major units? Length, as we have noted, increases: the last chapter is 3 staves, while the first two are 2 1/2 staves. The ratio of troped to heavy lines is constant.

| | | |
|---|---|---|
| Zph 1 | 58:37 lines | 61:39% |
| Zph 2 | 46:30 lines | 61:39% |
| Zph 3 | 52:35 lines | 60:40% |
| total | 156:102 lines | 60:40% |

The components of the ratio both decline across the poem.

| | *troping* | *heavy lines* |
|---|---|---|
| Zph 1 | 58 lines 84% | 37 lines 54% |
| Zph 2 | 46 lines 71% | 30 lines 46% |
| Zph 3 | 52 lines 66% | 35 lines 44% |
| total | 156 lines 73% | 102 lines 48% |

Since both decreases are of roughly equal degree, though over different ranges, the ratio is kept constant. Because of both these decreases, the weight also decreases.

| | | |
|---|---|---|
| Zph 1 | 33:7 lines | 76:24% |
| Zph 2 | 21:10 lines | 68:32% |
| Zph 3 | 20:12 lines | 62:38% |
| total | 74:29 lines | 72:28% |

In each of these cases of decreasing gross features, the average for the poem overall falls between the figures for the first and second chapters.

With this overall decrease in gross structural features in mind, we can recapitulate the patterns of these features within the chapters, across their staves. In Chapter 1, the line distribution and TH ratio are constant, while troping and weight rise. Line distribution is constant in the second chapter, and troping, TH ratio, and weight decline. In the final chapter TH ratio is constant, while troping, weight and heavy line use rise. The overall movement of decreased reliance on poetic markedness features in the whole poem correlates with the decrease in the second chapter and is in conflict with the increases in the first and third chapters. If we consider troping alone among the staves of the poem, the tension will be plainer.

| | | | | |
|---|---|---|---|---|
| Chapter 1 | Stave I | 23 lines | 79% | |
| | Stave II | 24 lines | 83% | |
| | Stave III | 11 lines | 100% | |
| | average | 58 lines | | 84% |
| Chapter 2 | Stave I | 13 lines | 93% | |
| | Stave II | 19 lines | 73% | |
| | Stave III | 14 lines | 56% | |
| | average | 46 lines | | 71% |

| | | | | | |
|---|---|---|---|---|---|
| Chapter 3 | Stave I | 10 lines | 37% | | |
| | Stave II | 16 lines | 70% | | |
| | Stave III | 26 lines | 90% | | |
| | average | 52 lines | | 66% | |
| total | | 156 lines | | | 73% |

Roughly the same array is associated with weighting, and partial forms of it with both heavy line distribution and TH ratio. We note again that in each case, the average figure for the chapter is closest to the figure for the central stave; and that overall the second chapter is most like the poem. The patterns of decrease and increase in gross features also reflect the correspondence of the middle to the whole, the mean to the median. The correspondence is not so simple, however. Although Chapter 2 is closest to the poem overall in gross features, in each case, the average figure falls between those for Chapters 1 and 2. This slight skewing arises from the length discrepancies in the chapters: attention is focused here on the border between the two short chapters, and the third serves as an anchor, with its normative length.

The troping levels are used erratically in the poem. The decline in troping is the result of gradual decrease in word-level troping, and abrupt decline in line-level troping.

| | *word-level* | | *line-level* | |
|---|---|---|---|---|
| Zph 1 | 26 lines | 38% | 32 lines | 46% |
| Zph 2 | 16 lines | 25% | 18 lines | 28% |
| Zph 3 | 14 lines | 18% | 6 lines | 8% |
| total | 56 lines | 26% | 56 lines | 26% |

In both cases, the second chapter is closest to the poem overall. Supralinear-level troping does not decline significantly across the poem.

| | | |
|---|---|---|
| Zph 1 | 36 lines | 52% |
| Zph 2 | 34 lines | 52% |
| Zph 3 | 39 lines | 49% |
| total | 109 lines | 51% |

Thus, this troping level is, along with the constant TH ratio, a stabilizing factor which serves to forge the unity of the three chapters.

There is one further complexity we need to work out: the variation in the use of trope levels within chapters. Such variation does exist, and yet we have just seen that the overall movement of trope level usage across the chapters is consistent. Rather than construct the 27 token matrix needed to visualize the resolutions of tensions which leads to this consistency, we can review the facts more simply. Line-level troping in Chapter 3 gives an initial pointer to stability, since of the three levels in the three chapters, it is the only one without significant variation (St. I: 7%; St. II: 9%; St. III: 7%; average: 8%). Line-level troping in the first two chapters varies identically.

| | *Zph 1* | *Zph 2* |
|---|---|---|
| Stave I | 31% | 14% |
| Stave II | 59% | 38% |
| Stave III | 55% | 24% |
| average | 46% | 28% |

The difference between the first two staves in each chapter is a considerable increase; the difference between the second two, a less considerable decrease. The increase-decrease pattern does not occur elsewhere, but the opposite does. Supralinear-level troping for the first chapter declines and then rises; and word-level troping does the same in the third chapter.

| | *Zph 1* *supralinear troping* | *Zph 3* *word-level troping* |
|---|---|---|
| Stave I | 69% | 15% |
| Stave II | 34% | ∅ |
| Stave III | 55% | 34% |
| average | 52% | 18% |

It is true the patterns are less comparable than those cited above because the high levels are in different places; the resemblance is plain nonetheless.

Two chapters have troping levels that rise consistently; the word-level troping of Chapter 1 rises, as does the supralinear-level troping of Chapter 3.

| | *Zph 1* *word-level troping* | *Zph 3* *supralinear-level troping* |
|---|---|---|
| Stave I | 31% | 15% |
| Stave II | 41% | 61% |
| Stave III | 45% | 72% |
| average | 38% | 49% |

The increases are not closely correspondent, but they are clear. So also are the decreases in word-level and supralinear-level troping in the second chapter.

| | *Zph 2* *word-level troping* | *Zph 2* *supralinear-level troping* |
|---|---|---|
| Stave I | 64% | 71% |
| Stave II | 27% | 54% |

| | | |
|---|---|---|
| Stave III | ∅ | 40% |
| average | 25% | 52% |

Let us put these modulations into a matrix of nine slots, marking a rise in trope usage within a chapter with *r* and a fall with *f*, and where both rise and fall occur, marking both in appropriate sequence.

| | *word-level* | *line-level* | *supralinear-level* |
|---|---|---|---|
| Zph 1 | *r* | *rf* | *fr* |
| Zph 2 | *f* | *rf* | *f* |
| Zph 3 | *fr* | — | *r* |

Observe that in each column, there are two rises and two falls, four alterations in each troping level. Word-level and supralinear-level troping present mirror image developments, symmetrical around the second chapter. Line-level troping is initially the most variable but ultimately the only resolved level. The numbers of changes in Chapter 1 (reading across the diagram) is 5; in the second chapter, it is 4; and in the last, it is three. The equilibrium of the second chapter is revealed again in the number of troping level changes, which is average for the poem.

### *10.5 Summary*

We have undertaken to characterize the rudiments of the gross structure of our corpus of poems and to point out a few examples of poetic figurations previously overlooked or not clearly recognized. The second effort is incomplete, much more than stipulated even by the subject itself, and requires only a few words of summary. The first effort commands our first attention.

The gross structure of Hebrew verse is determined by the disposition of the elements of its fine structure. These elements are the six trope classes and the four classes of lines. There must be troping and variation of line types for discourse to be poetic: this our corpus shows, since in twelve hundred lines, there is no single passage of more than two dozen untroped Class I lines. Tropological and typological variation are required in order to create gross structure, but there is no simple mapping from variation to structure.

In examining the tropes and heavy lines, we have been able to discern poetic units which they mark out. We were guided at first by the inherently strong frameworks of the Testaments and the Oracles of Balaam; having worked out the parameters of the poetic units, we went on without external supports. The marked features of troping and heavy lines do not set off the poetic units in any consistent way. Argumentation proceeds from the whole of a unit to its parts with a view to the constituent elements, but the argumentation takes a different form each time. That this approach is not "subjective" is obvious from its bases. The tropes and line types are defined; the possibilities of their cooccurrences are finite; and the density of each line can be characterized in a simple way. Errors of description there may be, but such errors would make little difference in a corpus our size. The poetic system described here, then, is "objectively" available.

Three levels of poetic units are recognized: chapters, which compose a book length poem; staves, which constitute chapters or poems; and batches, which make up staves. The chapters of Zephaniah need no review here. The way in which a further element of gross structure, the burden, is related to the others, is not clear.

We have adduced four measures of poetic markedness in a poetic unit and examined those measures, troping, heavy line use, TH ratio and weight, within individual texts. In summary here, we shall discuss whole texts in relation to the corpus averages. The further variations of troping level use will also be presented. One salutary effect of this rehearsal will be a demonstration that the poems considered here are all remarkably distinct.

A final word. We have assigned prime evidentiary value to blocks of lines created by troping and yet on several occasions we have set poetic divisions within or across such blocks. In some cases, there is no conflict. The quotations in Staves III and V of Deuteronomy 33 and in Stave III of Zephaniah 3 correspond to groups of batches and it is not implausible to separate units within the quotes. In most of the remaining cases, it seems that our description of troping is at fault. The highest orders of repetition troping (4.4-4.5) may belong to the realm of figuration. Sometimes, cases of these repetition tropes violate both stave and batch divisions (in Dt 33:12b-16a, Jdg 5:22b-24c, Zph 1:9bc-10a) and sometimes batch divisions only (in Zph 1:14a-16a, Zph 2:3a-3e, Zph 3:15d-16d). All six of these cases constitute evidence that Chapter 4 requires revision, though what sort we cannot tell. Finally, there are two other cases in which the troping is correctly described but it nonetheless does not comport well with the batch divisions, at Gen 49:9d 10ab and Dt 33:7e 8bc. For both we have noted avenues for ad hoc explanations and have nothing further to advance. *If* this description of the conflicts is correct, and *if* the gross structural reconstruction is a measure of the accuracy of fine structural description, then the margin of error in the latter is under 3 1/2%.

### *10.5.1 Staves*

The stave is a descriptive approximation of a poetic unit which can take two forms. The more common is the standard stave, which is between 23 and 31 lines long, generally between 26 and 29 lines long. The less common form is the half-size stave, which is between 11 and 14 lines long. Under unusual circumstances, irregular stave sizes occur; staves 18, 21 and

22 lines in length are attested in our corpus. (Since the burden-stave relation in poems with external burdens is unclear, we will not separate the burdens here; this reverses our treatment above.)

We have examined 50 staves; all but four fit the definition; the four irregular staves occur in Numbers 23-24 and Psalm 107, poems with other structural factors which serve to compensate for the irregularity. Of the 50, 39 staves are standard, i.e., between 23 and 31 lines; and 25 staves fall in the mean of the standard range, 26-29 lines. There are 7 semi-staves.

The usefulness of the mean of the standard range is rather dubious: it suggests that there are poems which use that mean range only or in a special way. The first suggestion is true but only for two poems, Genesis 49 and Exodus 15; and the second is false. The value of noting the mean is heuristic. The dividing line between irregular and standard staves, at 22-23 lines, is close; it is the clarity of the case of Numbers 23-24 that leads us to regard 22 lines as an irregular length.

In the list that follows, we enter only the roman numeral for the stave; the verse numeration is given above, and in the Appendix.

*Standard Staves. Mean Sizes* (26-29 lines). *26 lines* (7 exx): Gen 49 I, II; Num 23-24 III; Dt 32 V; Dt 33 II; Hab 3 I; Zph 2/II. *27 lines* (3 exx): Dt 33 IV; Zph 3/I; Ps 106 III. *28 lines* (8 exx): Gen 49 III; Ex 15 I, II; Dt 32 I; Jdg 5 I; Hab 3 II; Ps 78 I, IV. *29 lines* (7 exx): Jdg 5 IV; Zph 1/I, 1/II, 3/III; Ps 78 V, VI; Ps 106 I.

*Standard Staves. Other Sizes* (23-25, 30-31 lines). *23 lines* (1 ex): Zph 3/II. *24 lines* (5 exx): Dt 32 III; Jdg 5 III; Ps 78 II; Ps 106 IV, Ps 107 V. *25 lines* (4 exx): Jdg 5 II; Zph 2/III; Ps 78 III; Ps 106 II. *30 lines* (1 ex): 2 S 1. *31 lines* (3 exx): Dt 32 II, IV; Dt 33 III.

*Semi-staves* (11-14 lines). *11 lines* (2 exx): Hab 3 III; Zph 1/III. *12 lines* (1 ex): Ps 107 III. *13 lines* (1 ex): Dt 33 I. *14 lines* (3 exx): Num 23-24 I; Zph 2/I; Ps 107 II.

*Irregular Staves. 18 lines* (2 exx): Num 23-24 IV; Ps 107 I. *21 lines* (1 ex): Ps 107 IV. *22 lines* (1 ex): Num 23-24 II.

In all the individual poems, save 2 Samuel 1, and in the chapters of Zephaniah, stave size is available for variation. Seven poems show no such variation; there is, then, simple symmetry in Genesis 49, Exodus 15, Deuteronomy 32, Judges 5, Zephaniah 3, and Psalms 78, and 106. The slight variations in the actual size of the stave are trivial. In four poems, all the staves are symmetrical but for the semi-stave; this is positioned initially in Deuteronomy 33 and Zephaniah 2, and finally in Habaqquq 3 and Zephaniah 1. The staves in Numbers 23-24 form a swell (crescendo, followed by diminuendo); those in Psalm 107, a reverse swell.

*10.5.2 Batches*

The batch is a descriptive approximation of a poetic unit of between 5 and 8 lines in general. Under unusual circumstances, it can vary much more widely, between 1 and 12 lines. There are 193 batches in our corpus and 144 of them, 75%, are between 5 and 8 lines long. For the purposes of these remarks, we count the external burdens as if they were batches; the alternative would be to count them as part of contiguous batches. (The batch seems identical to the rhyme unit used in the Mactar Neo-Punic poems, which is 6 lines; Krahmalkov 1975.)

Of the remaining batches, there are more shorter than normal than longer than normal; 31 batches are 1-4 lines and 18 batches are 9-12 lines. Fewer than half the irregular batch lengths occur in the Testaments, 15/31 short batches (i.e., 1-4 lines) and 6/18 long batches (i.e., 9-12 lines). The presence of irregular lengths in those poems has already been attributed to the strong organizational frame of such poems. We can extend "unusual circumstances" further, to encompass the external burdens, accounting in some sense for 4 more short batches; 25 out of 49 irregular batches are covered easily by the phrase. Among these 25 are all batches of 1, 2, 11 and 12 lines lengths. Half-a-dozen 9 line batches, the same number of 10 line batches, ten 4 line batches and a pair of 3 line batches remain: 12 are shorter and 12 are longer than the standard range's 144. This suggests another length formulation: a batch is between 5 and 8 lines in length; rarely, the range extends from 3 to 10 lines; and under unusual circumstances, 1, 2, 11 and 12 line batches occur. The first clause covers 144 out of 193 batches (75%); the second, 181 out of 193 (94%); the last clause covers all. (It is possible that all longer batches could be factored down; that area of inquiry need not be treated here, but note that the 11 and 12 line examples would always resist such treatment.)

*Standard Size Range* (5-8 lines). *5 lines* (24 exx): Ex 15 IIb; Num 23-24 IVc; Dt 32 IId; Dt 33 Ib, IIId, IVc; Jdg 5 IIc, IIId; 2 S 1 c, d; Hab 3 Ic; Zph 2/IIIa, 2/IIIc, 3/Ia, 3/IIc, 3/IId, 3/IIIc; Ps 78 Ib, Ic, IIIc; Ps 106 IIId, IVb; Ps 107 IVb, Vd.

*6 lines* (46 exx): Gen 49 IIc; Ex 15 Ia, Ic, Id, IIa, IIc; Num 23-24 Ib, IIc, IIIb, IIIc, IVb; Dt 32 Ia, Id, IIIa, IIIc, IVb, Va, Vb; Dt 33 IIIb, IIIc; Jdg 5 Id, IIa, IIb; Hab 3 IIa, IId; Zph 1/Id, 1/IIb, 1/IId, 2/IIa, 2/IIc, 3/IIa; Ps 78 IIa, IIb, IIIb, IVb, IVc, Vd, VIc; Ps 106 IIa, IIc, IIIc; Ps 107 Ia, IIa, IVa, Vb, Vc.

*7 lines* (33 exx): Gen 49 Ib, Id, IIId; Ex 15 Ib; Num 23-24 IIIa, IIId, IVa; Dt 32 IIc; Dt 33 IIc, IVd; Jdg 5 Ia, IIIa; Hab 3 Ia, Ib, Id; Zph 1/IIIb, 2/IIb, 2/IId, 3/Ib, 3/Id, 3/IIb; Ps 78 IIIa, IIId, Vb, Vc, VId; Ps 106 Ia, Ib, Ic, IIb, IId, Va.

*8 lines* (41 exx): Ex 15 IId; Num 23-24 Ia, IIa, IIb; Dt 32 Ib, Ic, IIIb, IVa, IVd; Dt 33 Ia; Jdg 5 Ib, Ic, IId, IIIb, IVa, IVb; 2 S 1 a, b; Hab 3 IIb, IIc, IIIa; Zph 1/IIa, 2/IIIb, 3/Ic, 3/IIIa, 3/IIIb, 3/IIId; Ps 78 Id, IId, IVa, IVd, VIa, VIb; Ps 106 Id, IIIa, IIIb, IVa, IVd; Ps 107 Ic, IIb, IIIb.

*Rare Size Ranges. Shorter than Standard Size* (3-4 lines). *3 lines* (9 exx): Gen 49 IIb, IIIf; Dt 33 IIe, IIIe, IVb; Hab 3 IIIb; Ps 106 IVc; and the burdens of Ex 15 I, II. *4 lines* (12 exx): Gen 49 IIe; Dt 32 IIId, Vd; Dt 33 IIb; Jdg 5 IIIc, IVc; Zph 1/Ic, 1/IIIa, 2/Ib; Ps 78 IIc; Ps 107 Ib, IIIa.

*Longer than Standard Size* (9-10 lines). *9 lines* (6 exx): Dt 32 IIb, IVc; Jdg 5 IVd; Zph I/Ia, 1/IIc; Ps 78 Va. *10 lines* (10 exx): Gen 49 Ic, IIa; Dt 32 IIa, Vc; Dt 33 IId, IVe; Zph 1/Ib, 2/Ia; Ps 78 Ia; Ps 107 IVc.

*Unusual Size Ranges. Shorter than Standard Size* (1-2 lines). *1 line* (1 ex): Gen 49 IIf. *2 lines* (9 exx): Gen 49 Ia, IId, IIIa, IIIb, IIIc; Dt 33 IIa, IVa; and the burdens of 2 S 1 I, II. *Longer than Standard Size* (11-12 lines). *11 lines* (1 ex): Dt 33 IIIa. *12 lines* (1 ex): Gen 49 IIIe.

In discussing stave size, we noted that variations within the standard size are not significant. The same is essentially true of variations in batch size over a poem, but it is less obviously and uniformly so. In staves with regular batches, it is possible for the batches to be of uniform size, but this never is the case. It is possible for the direction of size variation to change not at all (in constant crescendo or diminuendo); or once (either falling, then rising, in a reverse swell; or rising, then falling, in a swell): or twice (the only cases show rising, then falling, then rising). All these possibilities occur but none often enough to give a clue to any broader arrays across the corpus. It is true that decrease in batch size is more common than increase. One rule of thumb that emerges is that it is more common for batch size to decrease than increase across a stave of 2 or 3 batches. There are seven relevant cases: three 2 batch staves show a decrease (Num 23-24 I: 8 lines-6 lines; Dt 33 I: 8-5; Hab 3 III: 8-3): and so do two 3 batch staves (Num 23-24 II: 8-8-6; IV: 7-6-5). The two semi-staves with a rise are, morever, in Psalm 107, and their structure must be related to the burden they bear (Ps 107 II: 6-8; III: 4-8). Of the regular staves, three decrease (2 S 1: [2]-8-8-5-5-[2]; Ps 106 III: 8-8-6-5; Ps 107 V: 7-6-6-5); one increases (Ps 106 I: 7-7-7-8). The first of these is exceptional because in 2 Samuel 1, the stave and the poem are coextensive.

Among the staves with two directions of batch size variation, we count a group of double rings, which perhaps deserve separate consideration; they are double starred below. The single ring is single starred. The analyses given of Exodus 15 are based on a separation of burden from contiguous batch; contrary analyses are given below.

*reverse swell (decrease: increase)*

| | |
|---|---|
| Ex 15 II | 6-5-6-8-[3] |
| **Num 23-24 III | 7-6-6-7 |
| Jdg 5 II | 6-6-5-8 |
| Hab 3 I | 7-7-5-7 |
| Zph 3/III | 8-8-5-8 |
| Ps 78 II | 6-6-4-8 |
| Ps 78 III | 7-6-5-7 |
| **Ps 78 IV | 8-6-6-8 |
| Ps 78 VI | 8-8-6-7 |
| *Ps 107 I | 6-4-8 |

*swell (increase: decrease)*

| | |
|---|---|
| Ex 15 I | [3]-6-7-6-6 |
| **Dt 32 I | 6-8-8-6 |
| Dt 32 III | 6-8-6-4 |
| Jdg 5 I | 7-8-8-6 |
| **Hab 3 II | 6-8-8-6 |
| Zph 3/I | 5-7-8-7 |
| Zph 3/II | 6-7-5-5 |

The clustering of Psalm 78 examples here is curious.

In the three remaining cases, the batch size rises, then falls, and then rises again. In two of them, there is an alternation of the two sizes used: Zph 2/II (6-7-6-7), Ps 106 II (6-7-6-7). In the last, one of the sizes alternates: Zph 2/III (5-8-5-7).

Much the same picture appears when we look at staves with irregular batch lengths. A third of the examples have either consistent decrease or increase. These include two semi-staves (decrease in Zph 2/I: 10:4; increase in Zph 1/III: 4:7) and the two movements already noted in Deuteronomy 33 (decrease in III: 11-6-6-5-3; increase in IV: 2-3-5-7-10). Some remaining examples decrease (Dt 32 II: 10-9-7-5; Ps 78 V: 9-7-7-6; and, if the first burden of Exodus 15 is joined to the following batch, Ex 15 I: 9-7-6-6).

There are more examples of swell and reverse swell than of single movement; though they are about equally represented all told, three of the four swell cases belong among the tribal oracles. The analyses of Exodus 15 Stave II and 2 Samuel 1 are based on counting the burdens as part of the contiguous batches.

*reverse swell (decrease: increase)*

| | |
|---|---|
| Ex 15 II | 6-5-6-11 |
| Jdg 5 IV | 8-8-4-9 |
| 2 S 1 | 10-8-5-7 |
| Ps 78 I | 10-5-5-8 |
| Ps 106 IV | 8-5-3-8 |
| Ps 107 IV | 6-5-10 |

*swell (increase: decrease)*

| | |
|---|---|
| Gen 49 I | 2-7-10-7 |
| Gen 49 III | 2-2-2-7-12-3 |
| Dt 32 V | 6-6-10-4 |
| Dt 33 II | 2-4-7-10-3 |

There are four further cases, in which the direction of batch variation changes twice: twice a decrease is followed by an increase, which is followed by a decrease (Dt 32 IV: 8-6-9-8; Zph 1/II: 8-6-9-6); and twice the reverse happens (Jdg 5 III: 7-8-4-5; Zph 1/I: 9-10-4-6). Once only are there more changes in directions in batch size, in the double decker of Genesis 49 (Stave II: 10-3-6-2-4-1).

There are no simple or consistent patterns here. We have argued that there are three poems in which batch size varies in a significant way: 2 Samuel 1, in which although the batches are of standard size, they form a pattern based on the extremes of that size range (8-8-5-5; we set aside the burdens); and the tribal testaments (Gen 49 I, a swell; II, a doubler decker; III, another swell; Dt 33 I and III decrescendi; II, a swell; IV crescendo). It is possible to come up with some regularity of variations in other poems. The most striking case is Psalm 78 in which every stave, except Stave V, has a reverse swell; Stave V has a simple decrease in batch size and it could be argued that this forms a prospect of conclusion. In Habaqquq 3, the two full staves are reverse swells followed by a swell; the semi-stave is a decrescendo. Exodus 15, burdens aside, consists of a swell followed by a reverse swell. All three non-standard staves of Numbers 23-24 show a decrease in batch size; Stave III is a reverse swell and a double ring. Psalm 107 has a reverse swell in both 3 batch staves (I and IV), simple rise in the 2 batch staves (II and IV) and simple decline in the 4 batch stave (V). Zephaniah presents this picture.

| | |
|---|---|
| 1/I | increase-decrease-increase } |
| 1/II | decrease-increase-decrease } |
| 1/III | increase (2 batches) } |
| 2/I | decrease (2 batches) } |
| 2/II | increase-decrease-increase } |
| 2/III | increase-decrease-increase } |

3/I increase-decrease }
3/II increase-decrease }
3/III decrease-increase

It is no task at all to read off the pairs of staves here (with an odd man out) and link them to the poem's structure. Three other poems are less amenable to this treatment; Judges 5 (I: inc-dec; II: dec-inc; III: inc-dec-inc; IV: dec-inc), Deuteronomy 32 (I: inc-dec; II: dec; III: inc-dec; IV: dec-inc-dec; V: inc-dec), and Psalm 106 (I: inc; II: inc-dec-inc; III: dec; IV: dec-inc).

It is, we said, possible to see something in this mass of data but it would be wrong or at least premature to regard as reliably discerned anything except in case (a) the batch size varies between the *extremes* only of the standard range (2 Samuel 1), (b) it varies over the entire range, from 1 to 12 lines (Genesis 49, Deuteronomy 33), or (c) the stave is shorter than four batches, in which case decrease in batch size may be expected.

### *10.5.3 Burdens*

The burden is a refrain structure which contains fixed and free lines; it varies in length between 2 and 8 lines. If it is contained within the poem, as in Psalm 107, it is reckoned part of a batch. If it occurs at the start and finish of the poem, as in Exodus 15 and 2 Samuel 1 and perhaps Psalm 106, its relation to batch structure is unclear.

### *10.5.4 Line typology*

We have at numerous points in our analyses called attention to patterning of lines of Classes II, III and IV, notably the last, yet this preliminary survey has not revealed any consistent significant variation among the heavy line classes. This may be because the classes are of such disproportionate size. We may take all the heavy lines together. The distribution of Class I lines and heavy lines varies widely through the corpus. There are 761 Class I lines (62%) and 464 heavy lines (38%). For the sake of simplicity, we will refer to heavy lines in what follows; the corresponding figure for Class I lines will be obvious.

The range of heavy lineation is between 54% in Zephaniah 1 and 22% in Psalm 106. We can sort the poems into groups within this range. Let us call the poems closest to the average *the 5 point range*, arbitrarily taking as limits 5 percentage points above and below the average, in this case 43-33%. Another group we shall call *the 10 point range above* (44-48%) and *below* (28-32%). The remaining texts we shall call *out of range above* (i.e., 49% heavy lines or more) and *below* (i.e., 27% or less).

*Five point range* (43-33%): Gen 49 (40%), Dt 32 (40%), Ps 107 (37%), Num 23-24 (37%).

*Ten point range above* (44-48%): Ex 15 (48%), Zph total (48%), Jdg 5 (47%), 2 S 1 (46%), Zph 2 (46%), Zph 3 (44%).
*Ten point range below* (28-32%): Ps 78 (32%), Dt 33 (31%).
*Out of range above* (49% or more): Zph 1 (54%).
*Out of range below* (27% or less): Hab 3 (23%), Ps 106 (22%).

### *10.5.5 Troping*

The number of troped lines in the corpus is another gross structural feature we have discerned. Of the corpus, more than two-thirds of the lines are troped: 876 lines, 72%. Troping varies more widely than heavy line distribution, from 93% in David's Lament to 50% in the Song at the Sea; the two poems with external burdens are not at all homogeneous in this respect.

*Five point range* (77-67%): Gen 49 (76%), Zph total (73%), Hab 3 (71%), Zph 2 (66%).
*Ten point range above* (82-78%): Jdg 5 (82%), Dt 32 (81%).
*Ten point range below* (66-62%): Zph 3 (66%), Ps 78 (66%), Ps 107 (66%), Dt 33 (63%).
*Out of range above* (83% or more): 2 S 1 (93%), Num 23-24 (84%), Zph 1 (84%).
*Out of range below* (61% or less): Ps 106 (58%), Ex 15 (50%).

### *10.5.6 TH ratio*

The ratio of lines in a text which are troped to those which are drawn from Classes II, III, and IV is another gross structural feature; it varies independently of its two components because there is no necessary relation between them. There are 876 troped lines in the corpus and 464 heavy lines, so the overall TH ratio is 65:35%. Its range of variation is smaller than the range of either of its components' variation: troping is most dominant in Habaqquq 3 (ratio 75:25%) and the two factors are nearly balanced in Exodus 15.

*Five point range* (70:30%-60:40%): Num 23-24 (69:31%), 2 S 1 (67:33%), Dt 32 (67:33%), Ps 78 (67:33%), Gen 49 (66:34%), Dt 33 (66:34%), Ps 107 (64:36%), Jdg 5 (64:36%), Zph 1 (61:39%), Zph 2 (61:39%), Zph 3 (60:40%), Zph total (60:40%).
*Ten point range above* (75:25%-71:29%): Hab 3 (75:25%), Ps 106 (73:27%).
*Out of range below* (54:46% or less): Ex 15 (51:49%).

### *10.5.7 Weight*

In every poem there are some troped, heavy lines and at least one line which is neither troped nor heavy (2 Samuel 1 is the case with only one such). The ratio of doubly marked to unmarked lines is weight. A poem with an equal number of each (or none of either), we have called even weight. Exodus 15 is the only text which fits this description. The corpus as a whole is overweight, more doubly marked than unmarked. There are 393 troped heavy lines (32% of the corpus) and 278 untroped Class I lines (23%). The overall weight is 59:41%. Of the four structural features, weight is the most widely varying: the weight of David's Lament is 93:7%, that of Psalm 106, 27:73%.

*Five point range* (64:36%-54:46%): Gen 49 (63:37%), Zph 3 (62:38%), Ps 107 (54:46%).

*Ten point range above* (69:31%-65:35%): Zph 2 (68:32%).

*Ten point range below* (49:51-53:47%): Ex 15 (50:50%).

*Out of range above* (70:30% or above): 2 S 1 (93:7%), Jdg 5 (83:17%), Zph 1 (83:17%), Num 23-24 (74:26%), Dt 32 (72:28%), Zph total (72:28%).

*Out of range below* (48:52% or less): Dt 33 (48:53%), Ps 78 (46:54%), Hab 3 (42:58%), Ps 106 (27:73%).

### *10.5.8 Troping levels*

In contrast to the three classes of heavy lines, the three varieties of troping do vary in significant ways which we have noted. The three levels are about equally represented in the corpus, each accounting for slightly more than a third of the corpus. Each varies across the corpus more than troping itself, which occurs in two-thirds of the corpus' lines. None of the three varies as widely as weight.

Word-level troping, repetition and coloration, occur in 441 lines of the corpus, 36%; we have seen evidence that our description of repetition may require qualification, which would reduce this figure slightly. The greatest extent of word-level troping is in Judges 5 (62%); it is rarest in Ps 107 (11%).

*Five point range* (41-31%): Zph 1 (38%), Dt 32 (32%), Ps 78 (31%).

*Ten point below* (30-26%): Zph total (26%).

*Out of range above* (42% or more): Jdg 5 (62%), Dt 33 (53%), Hab 3 (51%), 2 S 1 (50%), Num 23-24 (49%), Gen 49 (48%).

*Out of range below* (25% or less): Ex 15 (25%), Zph 2 (25%), Ps 106 (22%), Zph 3 (18%), Ps 107 (11%).

Line-level troping, matching and gapping, characterize 432 lines of the corpus, 35%; gapping is much rarer than matching. Line-level troping varies between 73% in 2 Samuel 1 and 8% in the last chapter of Zephaniah.

*Five point range* (40-30%): Num 23-24 (40%), Dt 32 (39%), Ps 107 (37%), Ps 78 (34%).

*Ten point range above* (45-41%): Dt 33 (44%), Gen 49 (43%).

*Ten point range below* (25-29%): Jdg 5 (29%), Zph 2 (28%), Zph total (26%).

*Out of range above* (46% or more): 2 S 1 (73%), Hab 3 (60%), Zph 1 (46%).

*Out of range below* (24% or less): Ps 106 (24%), Ex 15 (13%), Zph 3 (8%).

The various forms of syntactic dependency and mixing are found in 470 lines of the corpus, 39%. They are commonest in Deuteronomy 32 and almost non-existent in Habaqquq 3. Deuteronomy 32, the three chapters of Zephaniah and the book as a whole are all troped supralinearly between 49% and 59%. This is a formal description of the "prosiness" often referred to in connection with these poems; whether it is related to their prophetic *or* expository nature is a point for future consideration.

*Five point range* (44-34%): Gen 49 (41%), Ps 107 (39%), 2 S 1 (37%), Jdg 5 (36%), Num 23-24 (35%), Ps 106 (35%).

*Ten point range above* (49-45%): Zph 3 (49%).

*Ten point range below* (29-33%): Ex 15 (32%), Dt 33 (30%), Ps 78 (29%).

*Out of range above* (50% or more): Zph 1 (52%), Zph 2 (52%), Dt 33 (59%).

*Out of range below* (28% or less): Hab 3 (6%).

### *10.5.9 Figuration*

The domain bordering that of gross structural features and overlapping with that of fine structural features is a large one. The few cases of figuration we have discussed fall into categories distinguished largely by their subdomains.

The largest subdomain is controlled by the most protean figure, that of the fake coda, in which the second last poetic unit is associated with the poem's opening. Even if this phenomenon is unitary, it does not admit of simple characterization. Related phenomena of foreclosure and anticlimax (Smith 1968:222-24, cf. 59-60, 64-66, 67-70) are even more complex. The figuration in some cases is structural, involving whole staves. In Psalm 107, the second last stave forms a ring with the first in size; in the Oracles of

Balaam, the second last stave is a standard size unit, apparently rounding out a growing set.

The fake coda is also instantiated through partial repetition of a line, in 2 Samuel 1; and by etymological figuration in Psalm 78. Clusters of Class II and Class I lines in sequence serve to figure the start of the first and the end of the second stave of Habaqquq 3. In the Testaments, the fake coda is the thematic tie of supratribal references to the start of the poem.

Sometimes the phenomenon is even more remote, as in part in the Oracles of Balaam, in which the reference to curses and blessings at the end of Stave III may be a false ending. The fake coda we suggested in Deuteronomy 32 comes at the end of the third last, not the second last, unit. Many of these codas involve the grammatical phenomena we have described, but in radically distinctive ways.

The fake burden of the first stave of Judges 5 in 2ab and 9ab is similar to the fake coda but is more discrete in domain, as are some similar figures. The prime example is the verbal repetition in Psalm 78, at the opening of Batches IIIb and IIIc. The case of Ps 107:38b 39a differs in being etymological repetition; and the two *yhwdh*'s of Gen 49:8a and 9a are contained within a batch. The inclusion of Habaqquq 3, in Stave I, shares the domain of these repetition figures, as does the putative figure of weakness within strength we noted in that poem.

The clearest figure involves the matching of non-contiguous lines (or braces of lines) within batches. The matching figure is noted in three batches of Exodus 15 and seven each in Habaqquq 3 and Psalm 106. There is only slight evidence that it extends beyond the batch level. The recombinant figure joins the constituent structures of three contiguous lines of the form AB-AC-ABC; this figure is found in Exodus 15 and Psalm 106; no more than one example occurs per batch.

### *10.5.10 A last word*

The character of the gross structural units we have described in a preliminary way is in the first instance a function of the component fine structural features. Our exposition here is designed in part to show that the congeries of phenomena we treated in Part II can orient readers to features of the text beyond themselves; having demonstrated that all of *that* can add up to *this*, it remains to turn around and, having seen that *this* is a summative byproduct of *that*, inquire further about the relation of lines and clauses, parallelistic and cognate phenomena.

In the second instance, the units must be correlated with other slightly variable entities in other poetic systems. The "paragraphs in Chinese and Russian parallelistic poetry" Jakobson (1966:406) mentions are most likely to be bound in ways similar to those we have seen; the theme and episode units of long verse forms can also be considered. How are these units shaped? How are the ends and beginnings marked? Are marked phenomena definable in simple ways? In ways that are related to other features of the verse?

The first great obstacle to the work will arise from a refusal to read without psychological supports, i.e., to study a text in itself, abandoning however briefly the calculus of second guessing the supposed author. The reader will have noticed that the major gross structural units we recognize have numerically potent bases. The commonest batch size is 7 lines and 7 is a prime number; the commonest stave size is 28 lines and 28 is a perfect number, the sum of its divisors (1+2+4+7+14). We did not formulate our description with a view to getting these numbers, but we suspect that the generalized distrust of highly symmetrical systems will focus on those numbers in framing accusations of numerological mystificationalism.

An initial correction can be derived from the demonstration of Peterson (1976) that classical Greek and Roman theories of symmetry were never extended into literature. Numerological and symmetrical patternings have been shown to exist in the art objects of that world but the considerable body of critical writing it produced knows nothing of them. Indeed, even the term chiasmus is post-classical, occurring first in Hermogenes. There are classical notions of symmetry and numerical order but they are never applied to literature explicitly. The patterns are, like the circulation of the blood, "no less real for having been long undiscovered" (Peterson 1976:373). A more general corrective can be derived from the intellectual historiography of Ong, whose work shows clearly that whatever psychological supports we might rig up, they can only be effective on local ground. From ancient oral through medieval chirographic and Renaissance typographic into modern and post-modern electronic cultures, modalities change in ways that cannot be seen through since they are what we see through. If the range of culture and not just our ridiculous village customs are to see us through, then we must yield to being seen through. In a word, if what we have seen here cannot be seen simply, that is because it is looking at us.

The second great obstacle to the work derives from an approach to Hebrew poetry which regards it as weak verse. It is all one whether a modern midrashist reads biblical verse verbatim or a literary critic intimates that it is formless. We can for the moment set aside attempts to explain the diversity of responses and frame a single explanation. Hebrew verse is so insistently treated as weak because it is too strong even at an underestimate. The form of the poetry provides two historical arguments, from the translatability of the verse and from the loanableness of the verse form, as into the Greek Christian scriptures. To grasp more plainly the verse itself, we must put it in the context of oral, as well as of written, literatures. This context is itself a new thing because literature is in our time passing beyond writing. It is a real loss to limit oneself to written traditions but the loss is compensated for since the reader is spared the anxieties of our culture. The need for reading is an invention of those anxieties nonetheless and it is better to greet the shades as they come for us.

# APPENDIX: THE TEXTS

## Genesis 49. The Testament of Jacob

| | | | |
|---|---|---|---|
| 2a | *hqbṣw wšmʿw bny-yʿqb* | batch Ia | stave I |
| 2b | *wšmʿw ʾl-yśrʾl-ʾbykm* | 2ab | 2a-9d |
| | | 2 lines | 26 lines |
| 3a | *rʾwbn-bkry* | batch Ib | |
| 3b | *ʾth kḥy-wrʾšyt-ʾwny* | 3a-4c | |
| 3c | *ytr-śʾt* | 7 lines | |
| 3d | *wytr-ʿz* | | |
| 4a | *pḥz kmym ʾl-twtr* | | |
| 4b | *ky-ʿlyt mškby-ʾbyk* | | |
| 4c | *ʾz-ḥllt yṣwʿ-yʿlh* | | |
| 5a | *šmʿwn-wlwy ʾḥym* | batch Ic | |
| 5b | *kly-ḥms mkrtyhm* | 5a-7d | |
| 6a | *bsdm ʾl-tbʾ npšy* | 10 lines | |
| 6b | *bqhm ʾl-tḥd kbdy* | | |
| 6c | *ky-bʾpm hrgw ʾyš* | | |
| 6d | *wbrṣnm ʿqrw šwr* | | |
| 7a | *ʾrwr ʾpm-ky-ʿz* | | |
| 7b | *wʿbrtm-ky-qšth* | | |
| 7c | *ʾḥlqm byʿqb* | | |
| 7d | *wʾpyṣm byśrʾl* | | |
| 8a | *yhwdh ʾth ywdwk ʾḥyk* | batch Id | |
| 8b | *ydk bʿrp ʾybyk* | 8a-9d | |
| 8c | *yštḥww lk bny-ʾbyk* | 7 lines | |
| 9a | *gwr-ʾryh yhwdh* | | |
| 9b | *mṭrp bny ʿlyt* | | |
| 9c | *krʿ rbṣ kʾryh* | | |
| 9d | *wklbyʾ my yqymnw* | | |
| 10a | *lʾ-yswr šbṭ myhwdh* | batch IIa | stave II |
| 10b | *wmḥqq mbyn-rglyw* | 10a-12b | 10a-18 |
| 10c | *ʿd-ky-ybʾ šy lh* | 10 lines | 26 lines |
| 10d | *wlw yqht-ʿmym* | | |
| 11a | *ʾsry lgpn ʿyrh* | | |
| 11b | *wlśrqh bny-ʾtnw* | | |
| 11c | *kbs byyn lbšw* | | |
| 11d | *wbdm-ʿnbym swth* | | |
| 12a | *ḥklyly ʿynym myyn* | | |
| 12b | *wlbn šnym mḥlb* | | |

| | | | |
|---|---|---|---|
| 13a | *zbwln lḥwp-ymym yškn* | batch IIb | |
| 13b | *whwʾ lḥwp-ʾnywt* | 13abc | |
| 13c | *wyrktw ʿl-ṣydn* | 3 lines | |
| 14a | *yśśkr ḥmr-grm* | batch IIc | |
| 14b | *rbṣ byn-hmšptym* | 14a-15d | |
| 15a | *wyrʾ mnḥh-ky-ṭwb* | 6 lines | |
| 15b | *wʾt-hʾrṣ-ky-nʿmh* | | |
| 15c | *wyṭ škmw lsbl* | | |
| 15d | *wyhy lms-ʿbd* | | |
| 16a | *dn ydyn ʿmw* | batch IId | |
| 16b | *kʾḥd šbṭ yśrʾl* | 16ab | |
| | | 2 lines | |
| 17a | *yhy dn nḥš ʿly-drk* | batch IIe | |
| 17b | *špypn ʿly-ʾrḥ* | 17a-d | |
| 17c | *hnšk ʿqby-sws* | 4 lines | |
| 17d | *wypl rkbw ʾḥwr* | | |
| 18 | *lyšwʿtk qwyty yhwh* | batch IIf | |
| | | 18 | |
| | | 1 line | |
| 19a | *gd gdwd ygwdnw* | batch IIIa | stave III |
| 19b | *whwʾ ygd ʿqb-m* | 19ab | 19a-27c |
| | | 2 lines | 28 lines |
| 20a | *ʾšr šmnh lḥmw* | batch IIIb | |
| 20b | *whwʾ ytn mʿdny-mlk* | 20ab | |
| | | 2 lines | |
| 21a | *nptly ʾylh-šlḥh* | batch IIIc | |
| 21b | *hntn ʾmry-špr* | 21ab | |
| | | 2 lines | |
| 22a | *bn-prt ywsp* | batch IIId | |
| 22b | *bn-prt ʿly-ʿyn* | 22a-24b | |
| 22c | *bnwt-ṣʿdh ʿly-šwr* | 7 lines | |
| 23a | *wymrrhw wyrbhw* | | |
| 23b | *wyśṭmhw bʿly-ḥṣym* | | |
| 24a | *wtšb bʾytn qštw* | | |
| 24b | *wypzw zrʿy-ydyw* | | |
| 24c | *mydy-ʾbyr-yʿqb* | batch IIIe | |
| 24d | *mšm-rʿh-ʾbn-yśrʾl* | 24c-26e | |
| 25a | *mʾl-ʾbyk wyʿzrk* | 12 lines | |
| 25b | *wʾl-šdy wybrkk* | | |
| 25c | *brkt-šmym mʿl* | | |

| | | |
|---|---|---|
| 25d | *brkt-thwm rbṣt tḥt* | |
| 25e | *brkt-šdym-wrḥm* | |
| 26a | *brkt-ʾbyk gbr-wʿl* | |
| 26b | *brkt-hrry-ʿd* | |
| 26c | *tʾwt-gbʿt-ʿwlm* | |
| 26d | *thyyn lrʾš-ywsp* | |
| 26e | *wlqdqd-nzyr-ʾḥyw* | |
| 27a | *bnymyn zʾb yṭrp* | batch IIIf |
| 27b | *bbqr yʾkl ʿd* | 27abc |
| 27c | *wlʿrb yḥlq šll* | 3 lines |

## Exodus 15. The Song at the Sea

| | | | |
|---|---|---|---|
| 1a | *ʾšyrh lyhwh* | **burden I** | stave I |
| 1b | *ky-gʾh gʾh* | **1abc** | 1a-9f |
| 1c | *sws-wrkb rmh bym* | **3 lines** | 28 lines |
| 2a | *ʿzy-wzmrt yh* | batch Ia | |
| 2b | *wyhy ly lyšwʿh* | 2a-3b | |
| 2c | *zh ʾly wʾnwhw* | 6 lines | |
| 2d | *ʾlhy-ʾby wʾrmmnhw* | | |
| 3a | *yhwh ʾyš-mlḥmh* | | |
| 3b | *yhwh šmw* | | |
| 4a | *mrkbt-prʿh-wḥylw* | batch Ib | |
| 4b | *yrh bym* | 4a-6b | |
| 4c | *wmbḥr-šlšyw ṭbʿw bym-swp* | 7 lines | |
| 5a | *thmt yksymw* | | |
| 5b | *yrdw bmṣwlt kmw-ʾbn* | | |
| 6a | *ymynk yhwh nʾdry bkḥ* | | |
| 6b | *ymynk yhwh trʿṣ ʾwyb* | | |
| 7a | *wbrb-gʾwnk thrs qmyk* | batch Ic | |
| 7b | *tšlḥ ḥrnk* | 7a-8c | |
| 7c | *yʾklmw kqš* | 6 lines | |
| 8a | *wbrwḥ-ʾpyk nʿrmw mym* | | |
| 8b | *nṣbw kmw-nd nzlym* | | |
| 8c | *qpʾw thmt blb-ym* | | |
| 9a | *ʾmr ʾwyb* | batch Id | |
| 9b | *ʾrdp ʾśyg* | 9a-f | |
| 9c | *ʾḥlq šll* | 6 lines | |
| 9d | *tmlʾmw npšy* | | |
| 9e | *ʾryq ḥrby* | | |
| 9f | *twryšmw ydy* | | |

| | | | |
|---|---|---|---|
| 10a | *nšpt brwḥk* | batch IIa | stave II |
| 10b | *ksmw ym* | 10a-11c | 10a-21c |
| 10c | *ṣllw kʿwprt bmym-ʾdyrym* | 6 lines | 28 lines |
| 11a | *my kmkh bʾlm yhwh* | | |
| 11b | *my kmkh nʾdr bqdš* | | |
| 11c | *nwrʾ-thlt-ʿśh-plʾ* | | |
| 12a | *nṭyt ymynk* | batch IIb | |
| 12b | *tblʿmw ʾrṣ* | 12a-13c | |
| 13a | *nḥyt bḥsdk ʿm* | 5 lines | |
| 13b | *zw gʾlt* | | |
| 13c | *nhlt bʿzk ʾl-nwh-qdšk* | | |
| 14a | *šmʿw ʿmym yrgzwn* | batch IIc | |
| 14b | *ḥyl ʾḥz yšby-plšt* | 14a-16a | |
| 15a | *ʾz-nbhlw ʾlwpy-ʾdwm* | 6 lines | |
| 15b | *ʾyly-mwʾb yʾḥzmw rʿd* | | |
| 15c | *nmgw kl-yšby-knʿn* | | |
| 16a | *tpl ʿlyhm ʾymth-wpḥd* | | |
| 16b | *bgdl-zrwʿk ydmw kʾbn* | batch IId | |
| 16c | *ʿd-yʿbr ʿmk yhwh* | 16b-18 | |
| 16d | *ʿd-yʿbr ʿm* | 8 lines | |
| 16e | *zw qnyt* | | |
| 17a | *tbʾmw wtṭʿmw bhr-nḥltk* | | |
| 17b | *mkwn lšbtk pʿlt yhwh* | | |
| 17c | *mqdš ʾdny kwnnw ydyk* | | |
| 18 | *yhwh ymlk lʿlm-wʿd* | | |
| 21a | *šyrw lyhwh* | **burden II** | |
| 21b | *ky-gʾh gʾh* | **21abc** | |
| 21c | *sws-wrkb rmh bym* | **3 lines** | |

## Numbers 23-24. The Oracles of Balaam

*Chapter 23*

| | | | |
|---|---|---|---|
| 7a | *mn-ʾrm ynḥny blq* | batch Ia | stave I |
| 7b | *mlk-mwʾb mhrry-qdm* | 23:7a-9b | 23:7a-10d |
| 7c | *lkh ʾrh ly yʿqb* | 8 lines | 14 lines |
| 7d | *wlkh zʿmh yśrʾl* | | |
| 8a | *mh-ʾqb lʾ-qbh-ʾl* | | |
| 8b | *wmh-ʾzʿm lʾ-zʿm-yhwh* | | |
| 9a | *ky-mrʾš-ṣrym ʾrʾnw* | | |
| 9b | *wmgbʿwt ʾšwrnw* | | |

| | | | |
|---|---|---|---|
| 9c | *hn-ʿm lbdd yškn* | batch Ib | |
| 9d | *wbgwym lʾ-ytḥšb* | 23:9c-10d | |
| 10a | *my mnh ʿpr-yʿqb* | 6 lines | |
| 10b | *wm spr ʾtrbʿ-yśrʾl* | | |
| 10c | *tmt npšy mwt-yšr-m* | | |
| 10d | *wthy ʾḥryty kmhw* | | |
| 18a | *qwm blq wšmʿ* | batch IIa | stave II |
| 18b | *hʾzynh ʿdy bnw-ṣpr* | 23:18a-20b | 23:18a-24d |
| 19a | *lʾ-ʾyš ʾl wykzb* | 8 lines | 22 lines |
| 19b | *wbn-ʾdm wytnḥm* | | |
| 19c | *hhwʾ ʾmr wlʾ-yʿśh* | | |
| 19d | *wdbrw wlʾ-yqymnh* | | |
| 20a | *hnh-brk lqḥty* | | |
| 20b | *wbrk wlʾ-ʾšybnh* | | |
| 21a | *lʾ-hbyṭ ʾwn byʿqb* | batch IIb | |
| 21b | *wlʾ-rʾh ʿml byśrʾl* | 23:21a-23b | |
| 21c | *yhwh-ʾlhyw ʿmw* | 8 lines | |
| 21d | *wtrʿt-mlk bw* | | |
| 22a | *ʾl mwṣyʾm mmṣrym* | | |
| 22b | *k-twʿpt-rʾm lw* | | |
| 23a | *ky-lʾ-nḥš byʿqb* | | |
| 23b | *wlʾ-qsm byśrʾl* | | |
| 23c | *kʿt yʾmr lyʿqb* | batch IIc | |
| 23d | *wlyśrʾl mh pʿl ʾl* | 23:23c-24d | |
| 24a | *hn-ʿm klbyʾ yqwm* | 6 lines | |
| 24b | *wkʾry ytnśʾ lʾ-yškb* | | |
| 24c | *ʿd-yʾkl ṭrp* | | |
| 24d | *wdm-ḥllym yšth* | | |

*Chapter 24*

| | | | |
|---|---|---|---|
| 3a | *nʾm-blʿm-bnw-bʿr* | batch IIIa | stave III |
| 3b | *wnʾm-hgbr* | 24:3a-4c | 24:3a-9d |
| 3c | *š tm hʿyn* | 7 lines | 26 lines |
| 4a | *nʾm-šmʿ-ʾmry-ʾl* | | |
| 4a* | *wydʿ-dʿt-ʿlywn* | | |
| 4b | *mḥzh-šdy yḥzh* | | |
| 4c | *npl-wglwy-ʿynym* | | |
| 5a | *mh-ṭbw ʾhlyk yʿqb* | batch IIIb | |
| 5b | *mškntyk yśrʾl* | 24:5a-6d | |
| 6a | *knḥlym nṭyw* | 6 lines | |
| 6b | *kgnt ʿly-nhr* | | |

| | | | |
|---|---|---|---|
| 6c | *kᵓhlym nṭᶜ yhwh* | | |
| 6d | *kᵓrzym ᶜly-mym* | | |
| 7a | *yzl mym mmdlyw* | batch IIIc | |
| 7b | *wzr ᶜwb mym-rbym* | 7a-8b | |
| 7c | *wyrm mᵓgg mlkw* | 6 lines | |
| 7d | *wtnśᵓ mlktw* | | |
| 8a | *ᵓl mwṣyᵓw mmṣrym* | | |
| 8b | *k-twᶜpt-rᵓm lw* | | |
| 8c | *yᵓkl gwy-m-ṣryw* | batch IIId | |
| 8d | *wᶜṣmtyhm ygrm* | 24:8c-9d | |
| 8e | *wḥṣyw ymḥṣ* | 7 lines | |
| 9a | *krᶜ škb kᵓry* | | |
| 9b | *wklbyᵓ my yqymnw* | | |
| 9c | *mbrkyk brwk* | | |
| 9d | *wᵓrryk ᵓrwr* | | |
| 15a | *nᵓm-blᶜm-bnw-bᶜr* | batch IVa | stave IV |
| 15b | *wnᵓm-hgbr* | 24:15a-16d | 24:15a-19b |
| 15c | *š tm hᶜyn* | 7 lines | 18 lines |
| 16a | *nᵓm-šmᶜ-ᵓmry-ᵓl* | | |
| 16b | *wydᶜ-dᶜt-ᶜlywn* | | |
| 16c | *mḥzh-šdy yḥzh* | | |
| 16d | *npl-wglwy-ᶜynym* | | |
| 17a | *ᵓrᵓnw wlᵓ-ᶜth* | batch IVb | |
| 17b | *ᵓšwrnw wlᵓ-qrwb* | 24:17a-f | |
| 17c | *drk kwkb myᶜqb* | 6 lines | |
| 17d | *wqm šbṭ myśrᵓl* | | |
| 17e | *wmḥṣ pᵓty-mwᵓb* | | |
| 17f | *wqdqd-kl-bny-št* | | |
| 18a | *whyh ᵓdwm yršh* | batch IVc | |
| 18b | *whyh yršh śᶜyr-ᵓybyw* | 28:18a-19b | |
| 18c | *wyśrᵓl ᶜśh ḥyl* | 5 lines | |
| 19a | *wyrdm yᶜqb* | | |
| 19b | *whᵓbyd śryd mᶜyr* | | |

## Deuteronomy 32. The Song of Moses

| | | | |
|---|---|---|---|
| 1a | *hᵓzynw hšmym wᵓdbrh* | batch Ia | stave I |
| 1b | *wtšmᶜ hᵓrṣ ᵓmry-py* | 1a-2d | 1a-9b |
| 2a | *yᶜrp kmṭr lqḥy* | 6 lines | 28 lines |
| 2b | *tzl kṭl ᵓmrty* | | |
| 2c | *kśrᶜm ᶜly-dšᵓ* | | |
| 2d | *wkrbybym ᶜly-ᶜśb* | | |

| | | | |
|---|---|---|---|
| 3a | *ky-šm-yhwh ʾqrʾ* | batch Ib | |
| 3b | *hbw gdl lʾlhynw* | 3a-5b | |
| 4a | *hṣwr tmym pʿlw* | 8 lines | |
| 4b | *ky-kl-drkyw mšpṭ* | | |
| 4c | *ʾl-ʾmwnh-wʾyn-ʿwl* | | |
| 4d | *ṣdyq-wyšr hwʾ* | | |
| 5a | *šḥt lw lʾ-bnyw mwmm* | | |
| 5b | *dwr-ʿqš-wptltl* | | |
| 6a | *h-lyhwh tgmlw zʾt* | batch Ic | |
| 6b | *ʿm-nbl-wlʾ-ḥkm* | 6a-7d | |
| 6c | *hlwʾ-hwʾ ʾbyk qnk* | 8 lines | |
| 6d | *hwʾ ʿśk wyknnk* | | |
| 7a | *zkr ymwt-ʿwlm* | | |
| 7b | *bynw šnwt-dwr-wdwr* | | |
| 7c | *šʾl ʾbyk wygdk* | | |
| 7d | *zqnyk wyʾmrw lk* | | |
| 8a | *bhnḥl-ʿlywn gwym* | batch Id | |
| 8b | *bhprydw bny-ʾdm* | 8a-9b | |
| 8c | *yṣb gblt-ʿmym* | 6 lines | |
| 8d | *lmspr-bny-ʾlhym* | | |
| 9a | *ky-ḥlq-yhwh ʿmw* | | |
| 9b | *yʿqb ḥbl-nḥltw* | | |
| 10a | *ymṣʾhw bʾrṣ-mdbr* | batch IIa | stave II |
| 10b | *wbthw-yll-yšmn* | 10a-12b | 10a-18b |
| 10c | *ysbbnhw ybwnnhw* | 10 lines | 31 lines |
| 10d | *yṣrnhw kʾyšwn-ʿynw* | | |
| 11a | *knšr yʿyr qnw* | | |
| 11b | *ʿl-gwzlyw yrḥp* | | |
| 11c | *yprś knpyw yqḥhw* | | |
| 11d | *yśʾhw ʿl-ʾbrtw* | | |
| 12a | *yhwh bdd ynḥnw* | | |
| 12b | *wʾyn ʿmw ʾl-nkr* | | |
| 13a | *yrkbhw ʿl-bmwty-ʾrṣ* | batch IIb | |
| 13b | *wyʾkylhw tnwbt-śdy* | 13a-14e | |
| 13c | *wynqhw dbš mslʿ* | 9 lines | |
| 13d | *wšmn mḥlmyš-ṣwr* | | |
| 14a | *ḥmʾt-bqr-wḥlb-ṣʾn* | | |
| 14b | *ʿm-ḥlb-krym-wʾylym* | | |
| 14c | *bny-bšn-wʿtwdym* | | |
| 14d | *ʿm-ḥlb-klywt-ḥṭh* | | |
| 14e | *wdm-ʿnb tšth ḥmr* | | |

| | | | |
|---|---|---|---|
| 15a | *wyšmn yšrwn wybʿṭ* | batch IIc | |
| 15b | *šmnt ʿbyt kśyt* | 15a-17a | |
| 15c | *wyṭš ʾlwh ʿśhw* | 7 lines | |
| 15d | *wynbl ṣwr-yšʿtw* | | |
| 16a | *yqnʾhw bzrym* | | |
| 16b | *btwʿbt ykʿyshw* | | |
| 17a | *yzbḥw lšdym-lʾ-ʾlh* | | |
| 17b | *ʾlhym lʾ-ydʿwm* | batch IId | |
| 17c | *ḥdšym mqrb bʾw* | 17b-18b | |
| 17d | *lʾ-śʿrwm ʾbtykm* | 5 lines | |
| 18a | *ṣwr yldk tšy* | | |
| 18b | *wtškḥ ʾl-mḥllk* | | |
| 19a | *wyrʾ yhwh wynʾṣ* | batch IIIa | stave III |
| 19b | *mkʿs-bnyw-wbntyw wyʾmr* | 19a-20d | 19a-25d |
| 20a | *ʾstyrh pny mhm* | 6 lines | 24 lines |
| 20b | *ʾrʾh mh ʾḥrytm* | | |
| 20c | *ky-dwr-thpkt hmh* | | |
| 20d | *bnym lʾ-ʾmn bm* | | |
| 21a | *hm qnʾwny blʾ-ʾl* | batch IIIb | |
| 21b | *kʿswny bhblyhm* | 21a-22d | |
| 21c | *wʾny ʾqnyʾm blʾ-ʿm* | 8 lines | |
| 21d | *bgwy-nbl ʾkʿysm* | | |
| 22a | *ky-ʾš qdḥh bʾpy* | | |
| 22b | *wtyqd ʿd-šʾwl-tḥtyt* | | |
| 22c | *wtʾkl ʾrṣ-wyblh* | | |
| 22d | *wtlhṭ mwsdy-hrym* | | |
| 23a | *ʾsph ʿlymw rʿwt* | batch IIIc | |
| 23b | *ḥṣy ʾklh bm* | 23a-24d | |
| 24a | *mzy-rʿb-wlḥmy-ršp* | 6 lines | |
| 24b | *wqṭb-mryry-wšn-bhmwt* | | |
| 24c | *ʾšlḥ bm* | | |
| 24d | *ʿm-ḥmt-zḥly-ʿpr* | | |
| 25a | *mḥwṣ tškl ḥrb* | batch IIId | |
| 25b | *wmḥdrym ʾymh* | 25a-d | |
| 25c | *gm-bḥwr-gm-btwlh* | 4 lines | |
| 25d | *ywnq ʿm-ʾyš-śybh* | | |
| 26a | *ʾmrty ʾpʾyhm* | batch IVa | stave IV |
| 26b | *ʾšbyth mʾnwš zkrm* | 26a-28b | 26a-36d |
| 27a | *lwly-kʿs-ʾwyb ʾgwr* | 8 lines | 31 lines |
| 27b | *pn-ynkrw ṣrymw* | | |
| 27c | *pn-yʾmrw ydynw rmh* | | |

| | | | |
|---|---|---|---|
| 27d | *wlʾ-yhwh pʿl kl-zʾt* | | |
| 28a | *ky-gwy-ʾbd-ʿṣwt hmh* | | |
| 28b | *wʾyn bhm tbwnh* | | |
| 29a | *lw-ḥkmw yśkylw zʾt* | batch IVb | |
| 29b | *ybynw lʾḥrytm* | 29a-30d | |
| 30a | *ʾykh-yrdp ʾḥd ʾlp* | 6 lines | |
| 30b | *wšnym ynysw rbbh* | | |
| 30c | *ʾm-lʾ-ky-ṣwrm mkrm* | | |
| 30d | *wyhwh hsgyrm* | | |
| 31a | *ky-lʾ-kṣwrnw ṣwrm* | batch IVc | |
| 31b | *wʾybynw plylym* | 31a-34b | |
| 32a | *ky-mgpn-sdm gpnm* | 9 lines | |
| 32b | *wmšdmt-ʿmrh ʿnbmw-ʿnby-rwš* | | |
| 32c | *ʾšklt-mrrt lmw* | | |
| 33a | *ḥmt-tnynm yynm* | | |
| 33b | *wrʾš-ptnym ʾkzr* | | |
| 34a | *hlʾ-hwʾ kms ʿmdy* | | |
| 34b | *ḥtm bʾwṣrty* | | |
| 35a | *ly nqm-wšlm* | batch IVd | |
| 35b | *ly ʿt-tmwṭ-rglm* | 35a-36d | |
| 35c | *ky-qrwb ywm-ʾydm* | 8 lines | |
| 35d | *wḥš ʿtdt lmw* | | |
| 36a | *ky-ydyn yhwh ʿmw* | | |
| 36b | *wʿl-ʿbdyw ytnḥm* | | |
| 36c | *ky-yrʾh ky-ʾzlt yd* | | |
| 36d | *wʾps ʿṣwr-wʿzwb* | | |
| 37a | *ʾmr ʾy ʾlhymw* | batch Va | stave V |
| 37b | *ṣwr ḥsyw bw* | 37a-38d | 37a-43d |
| 38a | *ʾšr ḥlb-zbḥymw yʾklw* | 6 lines | 26 lines |
| 38b | *yštw yyn-nsykm* | | |
| 38c | *yqwmw wyʿzrkm* | | |
| 38d | *yhyw ʿlykm strh* | | |
| 39a | *rʾw ʿth* | batch Vb | |
| 39b | *ky-ʾny ʾny hwʾ* | 39a-f | |
| 39c | *wʾyn ʾlhym ʿmdy* | 6 lines | |
| 39d | *ʾny ʾmyt wʾḥyh* | | |
| 39e | *mḥṣty wʾny ʾrpʾ* | | |
| 39f | *wʾyn mydy mṣyl* | | |
| 40a | *ky-ʾśʾ ʾl-šmym ydy* | batch Vc | |
| 40b | *wʾmrty ḥy ʾnky lʿwlm* | 40a-42d | |
| 41a | *ʾm-šnwty brq-ḥrby* | 10 lines | |

| | | |
|---|---|---|
| 41b | *wtᵓḥz bmšpṭ ydy* | |
| 41c | *ᵓšyb nqm lṣry* | |
| 41d | *wlmśnᵓy ᵓšlm* | |
| 42a | *ᵓškyr ḥṣy mdm* | |
| 42b | *wḥrby tᵓkl bśr* | |
| 42c | *mdm-ḥll-wšbyh* | |
| 42d | *mrᵓš-prᶜwt-ᵓwyb* | |
| 43a | *hrnynw gwym ᶜmw* | batch Vd |
| 43b | *ky-dm-ᶜbdyw yqwm* | 43a-d |
| 43c | *wnqm yšyb lṣryw* | 4 lines |
| 43d | *wkpr ᵓdmt-wᶜmw* | |

## Deuteronomy 33. The Testament of Moses

| | | | |
|---|---|---|---|
| 2a | *yhwh msyny bᵓ* | batch Ia | stave I |
| 2b | *wzrḥ mśᶜyr lmw* | 2a-3c | 2a-5c |
| 2c | *hwpyᶜ mhr-pᵓrn* | 8 lines | 13 lines |
| 2d | *wᵓth mrbt-qdš* | | |
| 2e | *mymynw-ᵓšdt lmw* | | |
| 3a | *ᵓp ḥbb-ᶜmym* | | |
| 3b | *kl-qdšyw bydk whmtkw* | | |
| 3c | *lrglk yśᵓ-m dbrtyk* | | |
| 4a | *twrh ṣwh lnw mšh* | batch Ib | |
| 4b | *mwršh qhlt-yᶜqb* | 4a-5c | |
| 5a | *wyhy byšrwn mlk* | 5 lines | |
| 5b | *bhtᵓsp-rᵓšy-ᶜm* | | |
| 5c | *yḥd-šbṭy-yśrᵓl* | | |
| 6a | *yḥy rᵓwbn wᵓl-ymt* | batch IIa | stave II |
| 6b | *wyhy mtyw mspr* | 6ab | 6a-12d |
| | | 2 lines | 26 lines |
| 7b | *šmᶜ yhwh qwl-yhwdh* | batch IIb | |
| 7c | *wᵓl-ᶜmw tbyᵓnw* | 7b-e | |
| 7d | *ydyw rb lw* | 4 lines | |
| 7e | *wᶜzr mṣryw thyh* | | |
| 8b | *hbw llwy tmyk* | batch IIc | |
| 8c | *wᵓryk lᵓyš-ḥsdk* | 8b-9c | |
| 8d | *ᵓšr nsytw bmsh* | 7 lines | |
| 8e | *trybhw ᶜl-my-mrybh* | | |
| 9a | *hᵓmr lᵓbyw-wlᵓmw lᵓ-rᵓyty* | | |
| 9b | *wᵓt-ᵓḥyw lᵓ-hkyr* | | |
| 9c | *wᵓt-bnw lᵓ-ydᶜ* | | |

| | | | |
|---|---|---|---|
| 9d | *ky-šmrw ʾmrtk* | batch IId | |
| 9e | *wbrytk ynṣrw* | 9d-11d | |
| 10a | *ywrw mšpṭyk lyʿqb* | 10 lines | |
| 10b | *wtwrtk lyśrʾl* | | |
| 10c | *yśymw qṭwrh bʾpk* | | |
| 10d | *wklyl ʿl-mzbḥk* | | |
| 11a | *brk yhwh ḥylw* | | |
| 11b | *wpʿl-ydyw trṣh* | | |
| 11c | *mḥṣ mtny-m-qmyw* | | |
| 11d | *wmśnʾyw mn yqwmwn* | | |
| 12b | *ydyd-yhwh yškn lbṭḥ* | batch IIe | |
| 12c | *ʿly ḥpp ʿlyw kl-hywm* | 12b-12d | |
| 12d | *wbyn-ktypyw škn* | 3 lines | |
| 13b | *mbrkt-yhwh ʾrṣw* | batch IIIa | stave III |
| 13c | *mmgd-šmym mʿl* | 13b-16d | 13b-21e |
| 13d | *wmthwm rbṣt tḥt* | 11 lines | 31 lines |
| 14a | *wmmgd-tbwʾt-šmš* | | |
| 14b | *wmmgd-grš-yrḥ-m* | | |
| 15a | *wmrʾš-hrry-qdm* | | |
| 15b | *wmmgd-gbʿwt-ʿwlm* | | |
| 16a | *wmmgd-ʾrṣ-wmlʾh* | | |
| 16b | *wrṣwn-škny-snh* | | |
| 16c | *tbwʾ-th lrʾš-ywsp* | | |
| 16d | *wlqdqd-nzyr-ʾḥyw* | | |
| 17a | *bkwr-šwr whdr* | batch IIIb | |
| 17b | *lw-wqrny-rʾm qrnyw* | 17a-f | |
| 17c | *bhm ʿmym yngḥ* | 6 lines | |
| 17d | *yḥd ʾpsy-ʾrṣ* | | |
| 17e | *whm rbbwt-ʾprym* | | |
| 17f | *whm ʾlpy-mnšh* | | |
| 18b | *śmḥ zbwln bṣʾtk* | batch IIIc | |
| 18c | *wyśśkr bʾhlyk* | 18b-19d | |
| 19a | *ʿmym hr yqrʾw* | 6 lines | |
| 19b | *šm yzbḥw zbḥy-ṣdq* | | |
| 19c | *ky-špʿ-ymym yynqw* | | |
| 19d | *wśpwny-ṭmwny-ḥwl* | | |
| 20b | *brwk mrḥyb-gd* | batch IIId | |
| 20c | *klbyʾ škn* | 20b-21b | |
| 20d | *wṭrp zrwʿ-ʾp-qdqd* | 5 lines | |
| 21a | *wyrʾ rʾšyt lw* | | |
| 21b | *k-yšm ḥlqt-mḥqq* | | |

| | | | |
|---|---|---|---|
| 21c | *wytʾspwn rʾšy-ʿm* | batch IIIe | |
| 21d | *ṣdqt-yhwh ʿśh* | 21cde | |
| 21e | *wmšpṭyw ʿm-yśrʾl* | 3 lines | |
| 22b | *dn gwr-ʾryh* | batch IVa | stave IV |
| 22c | *ynzq mn-hbšn* | 22bc | 22b-29f |
| | | 2 lines | 27 lines |
| 23b | *nptly śbʿ-rṣwn* | batch IVb | |
| 23c | *wmlʾ brkt-yhwh* | 23bcd | |
| 23d | *ym-wdrwm yršh* | 3 lines | |
| 24b | *brwk mbnym ʾšr* | batch IVc | |
| 24c | *yhy rṣwy-ʾḥyw* | 24b-25b | |
| 24d | *wṭbl bšmn rglw* | 5 lines | |
| 25a | *brzl-wnḥšt mnʿlyk* | | |
| 25b | *wk-ymyk-dbʾk* | | |
| 26a | *ʾyn kʾl yšrwn* | batch IVd | |
| 26b | *rkb šmym bʿz* | 26a-27d | |
| 26c | *rkb gʾwtw šḥqym* | 7 lines | |
| 27a | *mʿnh ʾlhy-qdm* | | |
| 27b | *wmtḥt zrʿt-ʿwlm* | | |
| 27c | *wygrš mpnyk ʾwyb* | | |
| 27d | *wyʾmr hšmd* | | |
| 28a | *wyškn yśrʾl bṭḥ* | batch IVe | |
| 28b | *bdd ʿwn yʿqb-ʾl* | 28a-29f | |
| 28c | *ʾrṣ-dgn-wtyrwš* | 10 lines | |
| 28d | *ʾp-šmyw yʿrpw ṭl* | | |
| 29a | *ʾšryk yśrʾl* | | |
| 29b | *my kmwk* | | |
| 29c | *ʿm nwšʿ byhwh* | | |
| 29d | *mgn-ʿzrk-wḥrb-gʾwth* | | |
| 29e | *wykḥšw ʾybyk lk* | | |
| 29f | *wʾth ʿl-bmwtymw tdrk* | | |

## Judges 5. The Song of Deborah

| | | | |
|---|---|---|---|
| 2a | *bprʿ-prʿwt byśrʾl* | batch Ia | stave I |
| 2b | *bhtndb-ʿm brkw yhwh* | 2a-3e | 2a-9b |
| 3a | *šmʿw mlkym* | 7 lines | 28 lines |
| 3b | *hʾzynw rznym* | | |
| 3c | *ʾnky lyhwh* | | |
| 3d | *ʾnky ʾšyrh* | | |
| 3e | *ʾzmr lyhwh-ʾlhy-yśrʾl* | | |

| | | | |
|---|---|---|---|
| 4a | *yhwh bṣʾtk mśʿyr* | batch Ib | |
| 4b | *bṣʿdk mśdh-ʾdwm* | 4a-5c | |
| 4c | *ʾrṣ rʿšh* | 8 lines | |
| 4d | *gm-šmym nṭpw* | | |
| 4e | *gm-ʿbym nṭpw mym* | | |
| 5a | *hrym nzlw* | | |
| 5b | *mpny-yhwh-zh-syny* | | |
| 5c | *mpny-yhwh-ʾlhy-yśrʾl* | | |
| 6a | *bymy-šmgr-bn-ʿnt* | batch Ic | |
| 6b | *bymy-yʿl ḥdlw ʾrḥwt* | 6a-7d | |
| 6c | *whlky-ntybwt ylkw ʾrḥwt-ʿqlqlwt* | 7 lines | |
| 7a | *ḥdlw przwn byśrʾl* | | |
| 7b | *ḥdlw ʿd* | | |
| 7c | *šqmty dbwrh* | | |
| 7d | *šqmty ʾm byśrʾl* | | |
| 8a | *ybḥr ʾlhym-ḥdšym* | batch Id | |
| 8b | *ʾz-lḥm śʿrm* | 8a-9b | |
| 8c | *mgn ʾm-yrʾh wrmḥ* | 6 lines | |
| 8d | *bʾrbʿym-ʾlp byśrʾl* | | |
| 9a | *lby lḥwqqy-ysrʾl* | | |
| 9b | *hmtndbym bʿm brkw yhwh* | | |
| 10a | *rkby-ʾtnwt-ṣḥrwt* | batch IIa | stave II |
| 10b | *yšby ʿl-mdwn* | 10a-11c | 10a-16c |
| 10c | *whlky ʿl-drk* | 6 lines | 25 lines |
| 11a | *śyḥw-m qwl-mḥṣṣym byn-mšʾbym* | | |
| 11b | *šm ytnw ṣdqwt-yhwh* | | |
| 11c | *ṣdqt-prznw byśrʾl* | | |
| 11d | *ʾz-yrdw lšʿrym ʿm-yhwh* | batch IIb | |
| 12a | *ʿwry ʿwry dbwrh* | 11d-12e | |
| 12b | *ʿwry ʿwry* | 6 lines | |
| 12c | *dbry šyr* | | |
| 12d | *qwm brq* | | |
| 12e | *wšbh šbyk bn-ʾbynʿm* | | |
| 13a | *ʾz-yrd śryd lʾdyrym ʿm-yhwh* | batch IIc | |
| 13b | *yrd ly bgbwrym* | 13a-14c | |
| 14a | *mny-ʾprym šršm bʿmlq* | 5 lines | |
| 14b | *ʾḥrk bnymyn bʿmmyk* | | |
| 14c | *mny-mkyr yrdw mḥqqym* | | |
| 14d | *wmzbwln mškym bšbṭ-spr* | batch IId | |
| 15a | *wśry byśśkr ʿm-dbrh* | 14d-16c | |
| 15b | *wyśśkr kn-brq* | 8 lines | |

| | | | |
|---|---|---|---|
| 15c | *bᶜmq šlḥ brglyw* | | |
| 15d | *bplgwt-rᵓwbn gdlym ḥqqy-lb* | | |
| 16a | *lmh yšbt byn-hmšptym* | | |
| 16b | *lšmᶜ šrqwt-ᶜdrym* | | |
| 16c | *lplgwt-rᵓwbn gdwlym ḥqry-lb* | | |
| 17a | *glᶜd bᶜbr-hyrdn škn* | batch IIIa | stave III |
| 17b | *wdn lmh ygwr ᵓnywt* | 17a-18c | 17a-23e |
| 17c | *ᵓšr yšb lḥwp-ymym* | 7 lines | 24 lines |
| 17d | *wᶜl-mprṣyw yškwn* | | |
| 18a | *zblwn ᶜm-ḥrp* | | |
| 18b | *npšw lmwt* | | |
| 18c | *wnptly ᶜl mrwmy-śdh* | | |
| 19a | *bᵓw mlkym nlḥmw* | batch IIIb | |
| 19b | *ᵓz-nlḥmw mlky-knᶜn* | 19a-21b | |
| 19c | *btᶜnk ᶜl-my-mgdw* | 8 lines | |
| 19d | *bṣᶜ-ksp lᵓ-lqḥw* | | |
| 20a | *mn-šmym nlḥmw hkwkbym* | | |
| 20b | *mmslwtm nlḥmw ᶜm-sysrᵓ* | | |
| 21a | *nḥl-qyšwn grpm* | | |
| 21b | *nḥl-qdwmym nḥl-qyšwn* | | |
| 21c | *tdrky npšy ᶜz* | batch IIIc | |
| 22a | *ᵓz-hlmw ᶜqby* | 21c-22c | |
| 22b | *swsm dhrwt* | 4 lines | |
| 22c | *dhrwt ᵓbyryw* | | |
| 23a | *ᵓwrw mrwz* | batch IIId | |
| 23b | *ᵓmr mlᵓk-yhwh* | 23a-23e | |
| 23c | *ᵓrw ᵓrwr yšbyh* | 5 lines | |
| 23d | *ky-lᵓ-bᵓw lᶜzrt-yhwh* | | |
| 23e | *lᶜzrt-yhwh bgbwrym* | | |
| 24a | *tbrk mnšym yᶜl* | batch IVa | stave IV |
| 24b | *ᵓšt-ḥbr-hqyny* | 24a-26b | 24a-31b |
| 24c | *mnšym bᵓhl tbrk* | 8 lines | 29 lines |
| 25a | *mym šᵓl* | | |
| 25b | *ḥlb ntnh bspl* | | |
| 25c | *lᵓdyr-m hqrybh ḥmᵓh* | | |
| 26a | *ydh lytd tšlḥnh* | | |
| 26b | *wymynh lhlmwt-ᶜmlym* | | |
| 26c | *whlmh sysrᵓ* | batch IVb | |
| 26d | *mḥqh rᵓšw* | 26c-27e | |
| 26e | *wmḥṣh wḥlph rqtw* | 8 lines | |

| | | |
|---|---|---|
| 27a | *byn-rglyh krʿ* | |
| 27b | *npl škb* | |
| 27c | *byn-rglyh krʿ npl* | |
| 27d | *bʾšr krʿ* | |
| 27e | *šm npl šdwd* | |
| | | |
| 28a | *bʿd-hḥlwn nšqph* | batch IVc |
| 28b | *wtybb ʾm-sysrʾ bʿd-hʾšnb* | 28a-d |
| 28c | *mdwʿ bšš rkbw lbwʾ* | 4 lines |
| 28d | *mdwʿ ʾḥrw pʿmy-mrkbwtyw* | |
| | | |
| 29a | *ḥkmwt-śrwtyh tʿnynh* | batch IVd |
| 29b | *ʾp-hyʾ tšyb ʾmryh lh* | 29a-31b |
| 30a | *hlʾ-ymṣʾw yḥlqw šll* | 9 lines |
| 30b | *rḥm-rḥmtym lrʾš-gbr* | |
| 30c | *šll-ṣbʿym lsysrʾ* | |
| 30d | *šll-ṣbʿym rqmh* | |
| 30e | *ṣbʿ-rqmtym lṣwʾry-šll* | |
| 31a | *kn yʾbdw kl-ʾwybyk yhwh* | |
| 31b | *wʾhbyw kṣʾt-hšmš bgbrtw* | |

## 2 Samuel 1. The Lament of David

| | | | |
|---|---|---|---|
| 19a | *hṣby yśrʾl ʿl-bmwtyk ḥll* | **burden I** | stave |
| 19b | *ʾyk-nplw gbwrym* | **19ab** | 19a-27b |
| | | **2 lines** | 30 lines |
| | | | |
| 20a | *ʾl-tgydw bgt* | batch a | |
| 20b | *ʾl-tbśrw bḥwṣt-ʾšqlwn* | 20a-21d | |
| 20c | *pn-tśmḥnh bnwt-plštym* | 8 lines | |
| 20d | *pn-tʿlznh bnwt-hʿrlym* | | |
| 21a | *hry bglbʿ ʾl-ṭl* | | |
| 21b | *wʾl-mṭr ʿlykm wśdy-trwmt* | | |
| 21c | *ky-šm ngʿl mgn-gbwrym* | | |
| 21d | *mgn-šʾwl bly-mšyḥ bšmn* | | |
| | | | |
| 22a | *mdm-ḥllym* | batch b | |
| 22b | *mḥlb-gbwrym* | 22a-23d | |
| 22c | *qšt-yhwntn lʾ-nśwg ʾḥwr* | 8 lines | |
| 22d | *wḥrb-šʾwl lʾ-tšwb ryqm* | | |
| 23a | *šʾwl-wyhwntn hnʾhbym-whnʿymm* | | |
| 23b | *bḥyyhm-wbmwtm lʾ-nprdw* | | |
| 23c | *mnšrym qlw* | | |
| 23d | *mʾrywt gbrw* | | |

| | | |
|---|---|---|
| 24a | *bnwt-yśrʾl ʾl-šʾwl bkynh* | batch c |
| 24b | *hmlbškm šny ʿm-ʿdnym* | 24a-25b |
| 24c | *hmʿlh ʿdy-zhb ʿl-lbwškn* | 5 lines |
| 25a | *ʾyk-nplw gbrym btwk-hmlḥmh* | |
| 25b | *yhwntn ʿl-bmwtyk ḥll* | |
| 26a | *ṣr ly ʿlyk ʾḥy* | batch d |
| 26b | *yhwntn nʿmt ly mʾd* | 26a-e |
| 26c | *nplʾ ʾth* | 5 lines |
| 26d | *ʾhbtk ly* | |
| 26e | *m ʾhbt-nšym* | |
| 27a | *ʾyk-nplw gbwrym* | **burden II** |
| 27b | *wyʾbdw kly-mlḥmh* | **27ab** |
| | | **2 lines** |

## Habaqquq 3. The Psalm of Habaqquq

| | | | |
|---|---|---|---|
| 2a | *yhwh šmʿty šmʿk* | batch Ia | stave I |
| 2b | *yrʾty yhwh pʿlk* | 2a-3b | 2a-8e |
| 2c | *bqrb-šnym ḥy yhw* | 7 lines | 26 lines |
| 2d | *bqrb-šnym twdyʿ* | | |
| 2e | *brgz rḥm tzkwr* | | |
| 3a | *ʾlwh mtymn ybwʾ* | | |
| 3b | *wqdwš mhr-pʾrn* | | |
| 3c | *ksh šmym hwdw* | batch Ib | |
| 3d | *wthltw mlʾh hʾrṣ* | 3c-5b | |
| 4a | *wnghh kʾwr thyh* | 7 lines | |
| 4b | *qrnym mdlw* | | |
| 4c | *wšm-ḥbywn ʿzh* | | |
| 5a | *lpnyw ylk dbr* | | |
| 5b | *wyṣʾ ršp lrglyw* | | |
| 6a | *ʿmd wymdd ʾrṣ* | batch Ic | |
| 6b | *rʾh wytr gwym* | 6a-e | |
| 6c | *wytpṣṣw hrry-ʿd* | 5 lines | |
| 6d | *šḥw gbʿwt-ʿwlm* | | |
| 6e | *hlykwt-ʿwlm lw* | | |
| 7a | *tḥtʾwn rʾyty ʾhly-kwšn* | batch Id | |
| 7b | *yrgzwn yryʿwt-ʾrṣ-mdyn* | 7a-8e | |
| 8a | *hbnhr-m ḥrh yhwh* | 7 lines | |
| 8b | *ʾm-bnhr-m ʾpk* | | |
| 8c | *ʾm-bym ʿbrtk* | | |

| | | | |
|---|---|---|---|
| 8d | *ky-trkb ʿl-swsyk* | | |
| 8e | *mrkbtyk yšwʿh* | | |
| 9a | *ʿryh tʿwr qštk* | batch IIa | stave II |
| 9b | *šbʿt-mṭwt ʾmr* | 9a-10c | 9a-16f |
| 9c | *nhrwt tbqʿ ʾrṣ* | 6 lines | 28 lines |
| 10a | *rʾwk yḥylw hrym* | | |
| 10b | *zrm-mym ʿbr* | | |
| 10c | *ntn thwm qwlw* | | |
| 10d | *rwm ydyhw nśʾ šmš* | batch IIb | |
| 11a | *yrḥ ʿmd zblh* | 10d-13b | |
| 11b | *lʾwr ḥṣyk yhlkw* | 8 lines | |
| 11c | *lngh brq-ḥnytk* | | |
| 12a | *bzʿm tṣʿd ʾrṣ* | | |
| 12b | *bʾp tdwš gwym* | | |
| 13a | *yṣʾt lyšʿ-ʿmk* | | |
| 13b | *lyšʿ ʾt mšyḥk* | | |
| 13c | *mḥṣt rʾš mbyt ršʿ* | batch IIc | |
| 13d | *ʿrt yswd ʿd-ṣwʾr* | 13c-15d | |
| 14a | *nqbt bmṭyw rʾš-przw* | 8 lines | |
| 14b | *ysʿrw l-hpyṣn* | | |
| 14c | *yʿlṣw tmk-m* | | |
| 14d | *l-ʾklw ʿny bmstr* | | |
| 15a | *drkt bym swsyk* | | |
| 15b | *ḥmr mym-rbym* | | |
| 16a | *šmʿty wtrgz bṭny* | batch IId | |
| 16b | *lqwl ṣllw śpty* | 16a-f | |
| 16c | *ybwʾ rqb bʿṣmy* | 6 lines | |
| 16d | *wtḥty ʾrgz* | | |
| 16e | *ʾšr-ʾnwḥ lywm-ṣrh* | | |
| 16f | *lʿlwt l-ʿm ygwdnw* | | |
| 17a | *ky-tʾnh lʾ-tprḥ* | batch IIIa | stave III |
| 17b | *wʾyn ybwl bgpnym* | 17a-18b | 17a-19c |
| 17c | *kḥš mʿśh-zyt* | 8 lines | 11 lines |
| 17d | *wšdmwt lʾ-ʿśh ʾkl* | | |
| 17e | *gzr mmklh ṣʾn* | | |
| 17f | *wʾyn bqr brptym* | | |
| 18a | *wʾny byhwh ʾʿlwzh* | | |
| 18b | *ʾgylh bʾlhy-yšʿy* | | |
| 19a | *yhwh-ʾdny ḥyly* | batch IIIb | |
| 19b | *wyśm rgly kʾylwt* | 19abc | |
| 19c | *wʿl-bmwty ydrkny* | 3 lines | |

## Zephaniah 1

| | | | |
|---|---|---|---|
| 2a | *ʾsp ʾsp kl* | batch 1/Ia | stave 1/I |
| 2b | *mʿl-pny-hʾdmh* | 2a-3f | 2a-9c |
| 2c | *nʾm-yhwh* | 9 lines | 29 lines |
| 3a | *ʾsp ʾdm-wbhmh* | | |
| 3b | *ʾsp ʿwp-hšmym* | | |
| 3c | *wdgy-hym* | | |
| 3d | *whmkšlwt ʾt-hršʿym* | | |
| 3e | *whkrty ʾt-hʾdm mʿl-pny-hʾdmh* | | |
| 3f | *nʾm-yhwh* | | |
| 4a | *nṭyty ydy ʿl-yhwdh* | batch 1/Ib | |
| 4b | *wʿl-kl-ywšby-yrwšlm* | 4a-6b | |
| 4c | *whkrty mn-hmqwm-hzh ʾt-šʾr-hbʿl* | 10 lines | |
| 4d | *ʾt-šm-hkmrym ʿm-hkhnym* | | |
| 5a | *wʾt-hmštḥwym ʿl-hggwt* | | |
| 5b | *lṣbʾ-hšmym wʾt-hmštḥwym* | | |
| 5c | *hnšbʿym lyhwh* | | |
| 5d | *whnšbʿym bmlkm* | | |
| 6a | *wʾt-hnswgym mʾḥry-yhwh* | | |
| 6b | *wʾšr lʾ-bqšw ʾt-yhwh wlʾ-dršhw* | | |
| 7a | *hs mpny-ʾdny-yhwh* | batch 1/Ic | |
| 7b | *ky-qrwb ywm-yhwh* | 7a-d | |
| 7c | *ky-hkyn yhwh zbḥ* | 4 lines | |
| 7d | *hqdyš qrʾyw* | | |
| 8a | *whyh bywm-zbḥ-yhwh* | batch 1/Id | |
| 8b | *wpqdty ʿl-hśrym-wʿl-bny-hmlk* | 8a-9c | |
| 8c | *wʿl-kl-hlbšym mlbwš-nkry* | 6 lines | |
| 9a | *wpqdty ʿl-kl-hdwlg* | | |
| 9b | *ʿl-hmptn bywm-hhwʾ* | | |
| 9c | *hmmlʾym byt-ʾdnyhm ḥms-wmrmh* | | |
| 10a | *whyh bywm-hhwʾ* | batch 1/IIa | stave 1/II |
| 10b | *nʾm-yhwh* | 10a-11c | 10a-16a |
| 10c | *qwl-ṣʿqh mšʿr-hdgym* | 8 lines | 29 lines |
| 10d | *wyllh mn-hmšnh* | | |
| 10e | *wšbr-gdwl mhgbʿwt* | | |
| 11a | *hylylw yšby-hmktš* | | |
| 11b | *ky-ndmh kl-ʿm-knʿn* | | |
| 11c | *nkrtw kl-nṭyly-ksp* | | |
| 12a | *whyh bʿt-hhyʾ* | batch 1/IIb | |
| 12b | *ʾḥpś ʾt-yrwšlm bnrwt* | 12a-f | |
| 12c | *wpqdty ʿl-hʾnšym* | 6 lines | |

| | | | |
|---|---|---|---|
| 12d | *hqpʾym ʿl-šmryhm* | | |
| 12e | *hʾmrym blbbm* | | |
| 12f | *lʾ-yyṭyb yhwh wlʾ-yrʿ* | | |
| 13a | *whyh ḥylm lmšsh* | batch 1/IIc | |
| 13b | *wbtyhm lšmmh* | 13a-14d | |
| 13c | *wbnw btym wlʾ-yšbw* | 9 lines | |
| 13d | *wnṭʿw krmym* | | |
| 13e | *wlʾ-yštw ʾt-yynm* | | |
| 14a | *qrwb ywm-yhwh-hgdwl* | | |
| 14b | *qrwb wmhr mʾd* | | |
| 14c | *qwl-ywm-yhwh mr* | | |
| 14d | *ṣrḥ šm gbwr* | | |
| 15a | *ywm-ʿbrh hywm-hhwʾ* | batch 1/IId | |
| 15b | *ywm-ṣrh-wmṣwqh* | 15a-16a | |
| 15c | *ywm-šʾh-wmšwʾh* | 6 lines | |
| 15d | *ywm-ḥšk-wʾplh* | | |
| 15e | *ywm-ʿnn-wʿrpl* | | |
| 16a | *ywm-šwpr-wtrwʿh* | | |
| 16b | *ʿl-hʿrym-hbṣrwt-wʿl-hpnwt-hgbhwt* | batch 1/IIa | stave III |
| 17a | *whṣrty lʾdm* | 16b-17c | 16b-18e |
| 17b | *whlkw kʿwrym* | 4 lines | 11 lines |
| 17c | *ky-lyhwh ḥṭʾw* | | |
| 17d | *wšpk dmm kʿpr* | batch 1/IIIb | |
| 17e | *wlḥm-m kgllym* | 17d-18e | |
| 18a | *gm-kspm-gm-zhbm lʾ-ywkl lhṣylm* | 7 lines | |
| 18b | *bywm-ʿbrt-yhwh* | | |
| 18c | *wbʾš-qnʾtw tʾkl kl-hʾrṣ* | | |
| 18d | *ky-klh-ʾk-nbhlh* | | |
| 18e | *yʿśh ʾt-kl-yšby-hʾrṣ* | | |

## Zephaniah 2

| | | | |
|---|---|---|---|
| 1 | *htqwššw wqwšw hgwy-lʾ-nksp* | batch 2/Ia | stave 2/I |
| 2a | *bṭrm-ldt ḥq* | 1-3c | 1-3g |
| 2b | *k-mṣ-ʿbr ywm* | 10 lines | 14 lines |
| 2c | *bṭrm-lʾ-ybwʾ ʿlykm* | | |
| 2d | *ḥrwn-ʾp-yhwh* | | |
| 2e | *bṭrm-lʾ-ybwʾ ʿlykm* | | |
| 2f | *ywm-ʾp-yhwh* | | |
| 3a | *bqšw ʾt-yhwh* | | |
| 3b | *kl-ʿnwy-hʾrṣ* | | |
| 3c | *ʾšr mšpṭw pʿlw* | | |

| | | | |
|---|---|---|---|
| 3d | *bqšw ṣdq* | batch 2/Ib | |
| 3e | *bqšw ᶜnwh* | 3d-g | |
| 3f | *ᵓwly tstrw* | 4 lines | |
| 3g | *bywm-ᵓp-yhwh* | | |
| 4a | *ky-ᶜzh ᶜzwbh thyh* | batch 2/IIa | stave 2/II |
| 4b | *wᵓšqlwn lšmmh* | 4a-5b | 4a-9g |
| 4c | *ᵓšdwd bṣhrym ygršwh* | 6 lines | 26 lines |
| 4d | *wᶜqrwn tᶜqr* | | |
| 5a | *hwy yšby-ḥbl-hym* | | |
| 5b | *gwy-krtym dbr-yhwh ᶜlykm* | | |
| 5c | *knᶜn-ᵓrṣ-plštym* | batch 2/IIb | |
| 5d | *whᵓbdtyk mᵓyn-ywšb* | 5c-7c | |
| 6a | *whyth ḥbl-hym-nwt* | 7 lines | |
| 6b | *krt-rᶜym-wgdrwt-ṣᵓn* | | |
| 7a | *whyh ḥbl lšᵓryt* | | |
| 7b | *byt-yhwdh ᶜlyhm yrᶜwn* | | |
| 7c | *bbty-ᵓšqlwn bᶜrb yrbṣwn* | | |
| 7d | *ky-ypqdm yhwh-ᵓlhyhm* | batch 2/IIc | |
| 7e | *wšb šbwtm* | 7d-8d | |
| 8a | *šmᶜty ḥrpt-mwᵓb* | 6 lines | |
| 8b | *wgdwpy-bny-ᶜmwn* | | |
| 8c | *ᵓšr ḥrpw ᵓt-ᶜmy* | | |
| 8d | *wygdylw ᶜl-gbwlm* | | |
| 9a | *lkn ḥy ᵓny* | batch 2/IId | |
| 9b | *nᵓm-yhwh-ṣbᵓwt* | 9a-g | |
| 9c | *ᵓlhy-yśrᵓl* | 7 lines | |
| 9d | *ky-mwᵓb ksdm thyh* | | |
| 9e | *wbny-ᶜmwn kᶜmrh* | | |
| 9f | *mmšq-ḥrwl-wmkrh-mlḥ* | | |
| 9g | *wšmmh ᶜd-ᶜwlm* | | |
| 9h | *šᵓryt-ᶜmy ybzwm* | batch 2/IIIa | stave 2/III |
| 9i | *wytr-gwyy ynḥlwm* | 9h-10c | 9h-15g |
| 10a | *zᵓt lhm tḥt-gᵓwnm* | 5 lines | 25 lines |
| 10b | *ky-ḥrpw wygdlw* | | |
| 10c | *ᶜl-ᶜm-yhwh-ṣbᵓwt* | | |
| 11a | *nwrᵓ yhwh ᶜlyhm* | batch 2/IIIb | |
| 11b | *ky-rzh ᵓt-kl-ᵓlhy-hᵓrṣ* | 11a-13c | |
| 11c | *wyštḥww lw ᵓyš mmqwmw* | 8 lines | |
| 11d | *kl-ᵓyy-hgwym* | | |
| 12 | *gm-ᵓtm kwšym ḥlly-ḥrby hmh* | | |

| | | |
|---|---|---|
| 13a | *wyṭ ydw ʿl-ṣpwn* | |
| 13b | *wyʾbd ʾt-ʾšwr* | |
| 13c | *wyśm ʾt-nynwh lšmmh-ṣyh kmdbr* | |
| 14a | *wrbṣw btwkh ʿdrym* | batch 2/IIIc |
| 14b | *kl-ḥytw-gwy* | 14a-e |
| 14c | *gm-qʾt-gm-qpd bkptryh ylynw* | 5 lines |
| 14d | *qwl yšwrr bḥlwn* | |
| 14e | *ḥrb bsp ky-ʾrzh ʿrh* | |
| 15a | *zʾt hʿyr-hʿlyzh* | batch 2/IIId |
| 15b | *hywšbt lbṭḥ* | 15a-g |
| 15c | *hʾmrh blbbh* | 7 lines |
| 15d | *ʾny wʾpsy ʿwd* | |
| 15e | *ʾyk-hyth lšmh-mrbṣ lḥyh* | |
| 15f | *kl-ʿwbr ʿlyh yšrq* | |
| 15g | *ynyʿ ydw* | |

## Zephaniah 3

| | | | |
|---|---|---|---|
| 1 | *hwy mrʾh-wngʾlh hʿyr-hywnh* | batch 3/Ia | stave 3/I |
| 2a | *lʾ-šmʿh bqwl* | 1-2d | 1-8b |
| 2b | *lʾ-lqḥh mwsr* | 5 lines | 27 lines |
| 2c | *byhwh lʾ-bṭḥh* | | |
| 2d | *ʾl-ʾlhyh lʾ-qrbh* | | |
| 3a | *śryh bqrbh ʾrywt-šʾgym* | batch 3/Ib | |
| 3b | *špṭyh zʾby-ʿrb* | 3a-5a | |
| 3c | *lʾ-grmw lbqr* | 7 lines | |
| 4a | *nbyʾyh pḥzym-ʾnšy-bgdwt* | | |
| 4b | *khnyh ḥllw qdš* | | |
| 4c | *ḥmsw twrh* | | |
| 5a | *yhwh-ṣdyq bqrbh* | | |
| 5b | *lʾ-yʿśh ʿwlh bbqr* | batch 3/Ic | |
| 5c | *bbqr mšpṭw ytn* | 5b-6d | |
| 5d | *lʾwr lʾ-nʿdr* | 8 lines | |
| 5e | *wlʾ-ydʿ ʿwl bšt* | | |
| 6a | *hkrty gwym* | | |
| 6b | *nšmw pnwtm* | | |
| 6c | *hḥrbty ḥwṣwtm mbly-ʿwbr* | | |
| 6d | *nṣdw ʿryhm mbly-ʾyš mʾyn-ywšb* | | |
| 7a | *ʾmrty ʾk-tyrʾy ʾwty* | batch 3/Id | |
| 7b | *tqḥy mwsr* | 7a-8b | |
| 7c | *wlʾ-ykrt mʿwnh kl* | 7 lines | |

| | | | |
|---|---|---|---|
| 7d | *ʾšr-pqdty ʿlyh* | | |
| 7e | *ʾkn-hškymw hšḥytw kl-ʿlylwtm* | | |
| 8a | *lkn ḥkw ly* | | |
| 8b | *nʾm-yhwh* | | |
| 8c | *lywm-qwmy lʿd* | batch 3/IIa | stave 3/II |
| 8d | *ky-mšpṭy lʾsp gwym* | 8c-h | 8c-13e |
| 8e | *lqbṣy mmlkwt* | 6 lines | 23 lines |
| 8f | *lšpk ʿlyhm zʿmy* | | |
| 8g | *kl-ḥrwn-ʾpy* | | |
| 8h | *ky-bʾš-qnʾty tʾkl kl-hʾrṣ* | | |
| 9a | *ky-ʾz-ʾhpk ʾl-ʿmym śph-brwrh* | batch 3/IIb | |
| 9b | *lqrʾ-klm bšm-yhwh* | 9a-11b | |
| 9c | *lʿbdw škm-ʾḥd* | 7 lines | |
| 10a | *mʿbr lnhry-kwš ʿtry* | | |
| 10b | *bt-pwṣy ywblwn mnḥty* | | |
| 11a | *bywm-hhwʾ lʾ-tbwšy mkl-ʿlyltyk* | | |
| 11b | *ʾšr pšʿt by* | | |
| 11c | *ky-ʾz-ʾsyr mqrbk ʿlyzy-gʾwtk* | batch 3/IIc | |
| 11d | *wlʾ-twspy lgbhh ʿwd bhr-qdšy* | 11c-12c | |
| 12a | *whšʾrty bqrbk* | 5 lines | |
| 12b | *ʿm-ʿny-wdl* | | |
| 12c | *wḥsw bšm-yhwh šʾryt-yśrʾl* | | |
| 13a | *lʾ-yʿśw ʿwlh* | batch 3/IId | |
| 13b | *wlʾ-ydbrw kzb* | 13a-e | |
| 13c | *wlʾ-ymṣʾ bpyhm lšwn-trmyt* | 5 lines | |
| 13d | *ky-hmh yrʿw wrbṣw* | | |
| 13e | *wʾyn mḥryd* | | |
| 14a | *rny bt-ṣywn* | batch 3/IIIa | stave 3/III |
| 14b | *hryʿw yśrʾl* | 14a-15d | 14a-20f |
| 14c | *śmḥy wʿlzy* | 8 lines | 29 lines |
| 14d | *bkl-lb bt-yrwšlm* | | |
| 15a | *hsyr yhwh mšpṭyk* | | |
| 15b | *pnh ʾybyk* | | |
| 15c | *mlk-yśrʾl-yhwh bqrbk* | | |
| 15d | *lʾ-tyrʾy rʿ ʿwd* | | |
| 16a | *bywm-hhwʾ yʾmr* | batch 3/IIIb | |
| 16b | *lyrwšlm ʾl-tyrʾy* | 16a-17e | |
| 16c | *ṣywn ʾl-yrpw ydyk* | 8 lines | |
| 17a | *yhwh-ʾlhyk bqrbk* | | |
| 17b | *gbwr ywšyʿ* | | |
| 17c | *yśyś ʿlyk bśmḥh* | | |

| | | |
|---|---|---|
| 17d | *yḥryš bʾhbtw* | |
| 17e | *ygyl ʿlyk brnh* | |
| 18a | *nwgy mmwʿd ʾspty mmk* | batch 3/IIIc |
| 18b | *hyw mśʾt ʿlyh ḥrph* | 18a-19c |
| 19a | *hnny ʿśh ʾt-kl-mʿnyk* | 5 lines |
| 19b | *bʿt-hhyʾ whwšʿty ʾt-hṣlʿh* | |
| 19c | *whndḥh ʾqbṣ* | |
| 19d | *wśmty-m lthlh-wlšm* | batch 3/IIId |
| 19e | *bkl-hʾrṣ bštm* | 19d-20f |
| 20a | *bʿt-hhyʾ ʾbyʾ ʾtkm* | 8 lines |
| 20b | *wbʿt-qbṣy ʾtkm* | |
| 20c | *ky-ʾtn ʾtkm lšm-wlthlh* | |
| 20d | *bkl-ʿmy-hʾrṣ* | |
| 20e | *bšwby ʾt-šbwtykm lʿynykm* | |
| 20f | *ʾmr yhwh* | |

## Psalm 78

| | | | |
|---|---|---|---|
| 1a | *hʾzynh ʿmy twrty* | batch Ia | stave I |
| 1b | *hṭw ʾznkm lʾmry-py* | 1a-4d | 1a-10b |
| 2a | *ʾptḥh bmšl py* | 10 lines | 28 lines |
| 2b | *ʾbyʿh ḥydwt mny-qdm* | | |
| 3a | *ʾšr šmʿnw wndʿm* | | |
| 3b | *wʾbwtynw sprw lnw* | | |
| 4a | *lʾ-nkḥd mbnyhm* | | |
| 4b | *ldwr-ʾḥrwn-msprym* | | |
| 4c | *thlwt-yhwh-wʿzwzw* | | |
| 4d | *wnplʾwtyw ʾšr ʿśh* | | |
| 5a | *wyqm ʿdwt byʿqb* | batch Ib | |
| 5b | *wtwrh śm byśrʾl* | 5a-6a | |
| 5c | *ʾšr ṣwh ʾt-ʾbwtynw* | 5 lines | |
| 5d | *lhwdyʿm lbnyhm* | | |
| 6a | *lmʿn-ydʿw dwr-ʾḥrwn* | | |
| 6b | *bnym ywldw yqmw* | batch Ic | |
| 6c | *wysprw lbnyhm* | 6b-7c | |
| 7a | *wyśymw bʾlhym kslm* | 5 lines | |
| 7b | *wlʾ-yškḥw mʿlly-ʾl* | | |
| 7c | *wmṣwtyw ynṣrw* | | |
| 8a | *wlʾ-yhyw kʾbwtm* | batch Id | |
| 8b | *dwr-swrr-wmrh* | 8a-10b | |
| 8c | *dwr lʾ-hkyn lbw* | 8 lines | |
| 8d | *wlʾ-nʾmnh ʾt-ʾl rwḥw* | | |

| | | | |
|---|---|---|---|
| 9a | *bny-ʾprym nwšqy-rwmy-qšt* | | |
| 9b | *hpkw bywm-qrb* | | |
| 10a | *lʾ-šmrw bryt-ʾlhym* | | |
| 10b | *wbtwrtw mʾnw llkt* | | |
| 11a | *wyškḥw ʿlylwtyw-wnplʾwtyw* | batch IIa | stave II |
| 11b | *ʾšr hrʾm* | 11a-13b | 11a-20e |
| 12a | *ngd-ʾbwtm ʿśh plʾ* | 6 lines | 24 lines |
| 12b | *bʾrṣ-mṣrym-śdh-ṣʿn* | | |
| 13a | *bqʿ ym wyʿbyrm* | | |
| 13b | *wyṣb mym kmw-nd* | | |
| 14a | *wynḥm bʿnn ywmm* | batch IIb | |
| 14b | *wkl-hlylh bʾwr-ʾš* | 14a-16b | |
| 15a | *ybqʿ ṣr-m bmdbr* | 6 lines | |
| 15b | *wyšq kthmwt-rbh* | | |
| 16a | *wywṣʾ nwzlym mslʿ* | | |
| 16b | *wywrd knhrwt mym* | | |
| 17a | *wywsypw ʿwd lḥṭʾ lw* | batch IIc | |
| 17b | *lmrwt ʿlywn bṣyh* | 17a-18b | |
| 18a | *wynsw ʾl blbbm* | 4 lines | |
| 18b | *lšʾl ʾkl lnpšm* | | |
| 19a | *wydbrw bʾlhym ʾmrw* | batch IId | |
| 19b | *hywkl ʾl* | 19a-20e | |
| 19c | *lʿrk šlḥn bmdbr* | 8 lines | |
| 20a | *hn-hkh ṣwr* | | |
| 20b | *wyzwbw mym* | | |
| 20c | *wnḥlym yšṭpw* | | |
| 20d | *hgm-lḥm ywkl tt* | | |
| 20e | *ʾm-ykyn šʾr lʿmw* | | |
| 21a | *lkn šmʿ yhwh wytʿbr* | batch IIIa | stave III |
| 21b | *wʾš nśqh byʿqb* | 21a-23b | 21a-32b |
| 21c | *wgm-ʾp ʿlh byśrʾl* | 7 lines | 25 lines |
| 22a | *ky-lʾ-hʾmynw bʾlhym* | | |
| 22b | *wlʾ-bṭḥw byšwʿtw* | | |
| 23a | *wyṣw šḥqym mmʿl* | | |
| 23b | *wdlty-šmym ptḥ* | | |
| 24a | *wymṭr ʿlyhm mn lʾkl* | batch IIIb | |
| 24b | *wdgn-šmym ntn lmw* | 24a-26b | |
| 25a | *lḥm-ʾbyrym ʾkl ʾyš* | 6 lines | |
| 25b | *ṣydh šlḥ lhm lśbʿ* | | |
| 26a | *ysʿ qdym bšmym* | | |
| 26b | *wynhg bʿzw tymn* | | |

| | | | |
|---|---|---|---|
| 27a | *wymṭr ᶜlyhm kᶜpr šᵓr* | batch IIIc | |
| 27b | *wkḥwl-ymym ᶜwp-knp* | 27a-29b | |
| 28 | *wypl bqrb-mḥnhw sbyb lmškntyw* | 5 lines | |
| 29a | *wyᵓlkw wyśbᶜw mᵓd* | | |
| 29b | *wtᵓwtm ybᵓ lhm* | | |
| | | | |
| 30a | *lᵓ-zrw mtᵓwtm* | batch IIId | |
| 30b | *ᶜwd ᵓklm bpyhm* | 30a-32b | |
| 31a | *wᵓp-ᵓlhym ᶜlh bhm* | 7 lines | |
| 31b | *wyhrg bmšmnyhm* | | |
| 31c | *wbḥwry-yśrᵓl hkryᶜ* | | |
| 32a | *bkl-zᵓt ḥṭᵓw ᶜwd* | | |
| 32b | *wlᵓ-hᵓmynw bnplᵓwtyw* | | |
| | | | |
| 33a | *wykl bhbl ymyhm* | batch IVa | stave IV |
| 33b | *wšnwtm bbhlh* | 33a-36b | 33a-45b |
| 34a | *ᵓm-hrgm wdršwhw* | 8 lines | 28 lines |
| 34b | *wšbw wšḥrw ᵓl* | | |
| 35a | *wyzkrw ky-ᵓlhym ṣwrm* | | |
| 35b | *wᵓl-ᶜlywn gᵓlm* | | |
| 36a | *wyptwhw bpyhm* | | |
| 36b | *wblšwnm ykzbw lw* | | |
| | | | |
| 37a | *wlbm lᵓ-nkwn ᶜmw* | batch IVb | |
| 37b | *wlᵓ-nᵓmnw bbrytw* | 37a-38d | |
| 38a | *whwᵓ rḥwm* | 6 lines | |
| 38b | *ykpr ᶜwn wlᵓ-yšḥyt* | | |
| 38c | *whrbh lhšyb ᵓpw* | | |
| 38d | *wlᵓ-yᶜyr kl-ḥmtw* | | |
| | | | |
| 39a | *wyzkr ky-bśr hmh* | batch IVc | |
| 39b | *rwḥ-hwlk wlᵓ-yšwb* | 39a-41b | |
| 40a | *kmh ymrwhw bmdbr* | 6 lines | |
| 40b | *yᶜṣybwhw byšymwn* | | |
| 41a | *wyšwbw wynsw ᵓl* | | |
| 41b | *wqdwš-yśrᵓl htww* | | |
| | | | |
| 42a | *lᵓ-zkrw ᵓt-ydw ywm* | batch IVd | |
| 42b | *ᵓšr-pdm mny-ṣr* | 42a-45b | |
| 43a | *ᵓšr-śm bmṣrym ᵓtwtyw* | 8 lines | |
| 43b | *wmwptyw bśdh-ṣᶜn* | | |
| 44a | *wyhpk ldm yᵓryhm* | | |
| 44b | *wnzlyhm bl-yštywn* | | |
| 45a | *yšlḥ bhm ᶜrb wyᵓklm* | | |
| 45b | *wṣprdᶜ wtšḥytm* | | |

| | | | |
|---|---|---|---|
| 46a | *wytn lḥsyl ybwlm* | batch Va | stave V |
| 46b | *wygyʿm lʾrbh* | 46a-49c | 46a-58b |
| 47a | *yhrg bbrd gpnm* | 9 lines | 29 lines |
| 47b | *wšqmwtm bḥnml* | | |
| 48a | *wysgr ldbr bʿyrm* | | |
| 48b | *wmqnyhm lršp-m* | | |
| 49a | *yšlḥ bm ḥrwn-ʾpw* | | |
| 49b | *ʿbrh-wzʿm-wṣrh* | | |
| 49c | *mšlḥt-mlʾky-rʿym* | | |
| 50a | *ypls ntyb lʾpw* | batch Vb | |
| 50b | *lʾ-ḥśk mmwt npšm* | 50a-52b | |
| 50c | *wḥytm ldbr hsgyr* | 7 lines | |
| 51a | *wyk kl-bkwr bmṣrym* | | |
| 51b | *rʾšyt-ʾwnym bʾhly-ḥm* | | |
| 52a | *wysʿ kṣʾn ʿmw* | | |
| 52b | *wynhgm kʿdr bmdbr* | | |
| 53a | *wynḥm lbṭḥ wlʾ-pḥdw* | batch Vc | |
| 53b | *wʾt-ʾwybyhm ksh hym* | 53a-55c | |
| 54a | *wybyʾm ʾl-gbwl-qdšw* | 7 lines | |
| 54b | *hr-zh qnth ymynw* | | |
| 55a | *wygrš mpnyhm gwym* | | |
| 55b | *wypylm bḥbl nḥlh* | | |
| 55c | *wyškn bʾhlyhm šbṭy-yśrʾl* | | |
| 56a | *wynsw wymrw ʾt-ʾlhym* | batch Vd | |
| 56b | *ʿlywn wʿdwtyw lʾ-šmrw* | 56a-58b | |
| 57a | *wysgw wybgdw kʾbwtm* | 6 lines | |
| 57b | *nhpkw kqšt-rmyh* | | |
| 58a | *wykʿyswhw bbmwtm* | | |
| 58b | *wbpsylyhm yqnyʾwhw* | | |
| 59a | *šmʿ ʾlhym wytʿbr* | batch VIa | stave VI |
| 59b | *wymʾs mʾd byśrʾl* | 59a-62b | 59a-72b |
| 60a | *wyṭš mškn-šlw* | 8 lines | 29 lines |
| 60b | *ʾhl škn bʾdm* | | |
| 61a | *wytn lšby ʿzw* | | |
| 61b | *wtpʾrtw byd-ṣr* | | |
| 62a | *wysgr lḥrb ʿmw* | | |
| 62b | *wbnḥltw htʿbr* | | |
| 63a | *bḥwryw ʾklh ʾš* | batch VIb | |
| 63b | *wbtwltyw lʾ-hlylw* | 63a-66b | |
| 64a | *khnyw bḥrb nplw* | 8 lines | |
| 64b | *wʾlmntyw lʾ-tbkynh* | | |
| 65a | *wyqṣ kyšn ʾdny* | | |

| | | | |
|---|---|---|---|
| 65b | *kgbwr mtrwnn myyn* | | |
| 66a | *wyk ṣryw ʾḥwr* | | |
| 66b | *ḥrpt-ʿwlm ntn lmw* | | |
| 67a | *wymʾs bʾhl-ywsp* | batch VIc | |
| 67b | *wbšbṭ-ʾprym lʾ-bḥr* | 67a-69b | |
| 68a | *wybḥr ʾt-šbṭ-yhwdh* | 6 lines | |
| 68b | *ʾt-hr-ṣywn ʾšr ʾhb* | | |
| 69a | *wybn kmw-rmym mqdšw* | | |
| 69b | *kʾrṣ ysdh lʿwlm* | | |
| 70a | *wybḥr bdwd-ʿbdw* | batch VId | |
| 70b | *wyqḥhw mmklʾt-ṣʾn* | 70a-72b | |
| 71a | *mʾḥr-ʿlwt hbyʾw* | 7 lines | |
| 71b | *lrʿwt byʿqb-ʿmw* | | |
| 71c | *wbyśrʾl-nḥltw* | | |
| 72a | *wyrʿm ktm-lbbw* | | |
| 72b | *wbtbwnwt-kpyw ynḥm* | | |

## Psalm 106

| | | | |
|---|---|---|---|
| 1a | *hllw yh* | batch Ia | stave I |
| 1b | *hwdw lyhwh ky-ṭwb* | 1a-3b | 1a-13b |
| 1c | *ky-lʿwlm ḥsdw* | 7 lines | 29 lines |
| 2a | *my ymll gbwrwt-yhwh* | | |
| 2b | *yšmyʿ kl-thltw* | | |
| 3a | *ʾšry-šmry-mšpṭ* | | |
| 3b | *ʿśy-ṣdqh bkl-ʿt* | | |
| 4a | *zkrny yhwh brṣwn-ʿmk* | batch Ib | |
| 4b | *pqdny byšwʿtk* | 4a-6b | |
| 5a | *lrʾwt bṭwbt-bḥyryk* | 7 lines | |
| 5b | *lśmḥ bśmḥt-gwyk* | | |
| 5c | *lhthll ʿm-nḥltk* | | |
| 6a | *ḥṭʾnw ʿm-ʾbwtynw* | | |
| 6b | *hʿwynw hršʿnw* | | |
| 7a | *ʾbwtynw bmṣrym lʾ-hśkylw nplʾwtyk* | batch Ic | |
| | | 7a-9b | |
| 7b | *lʾ-zkrw ʾt-rb-ḥsdyk* | 7 lines | |
| 7c | *wymrw ʿly-m bym-swp* | | |
| 8a | *wywšyʿm lmʿn-šmw* | | |
| 8b | *lhwdyʿ ʾt-gbwrtw* | | |
| 9a | *wygʿr bym-swp wyḥrb* | | |
| 9b | *wywkylm bthmwt kmdbr* | | |

| | | | |
|---|---|---|---|
| 10a | *wywšyᶜm myd-śwnᵓ* | batch Id | |
| 10b | *wygᵓlm myd-ᵓwyb* | 10a-13b | |
| 11a | *wyksw mym ṣryhm* | 8 lines | |
| 11b | *ᵓḥd mhm lᵓ-nwtr* | | |
| 12a | *wyᵓmynw bdbryw* | | |
| 12b | *yšyrw thltw* | | |
| 13a | *mhrw škḥw mᶜśyw* | | |
| 13b | *lᵓ-ḥkw lᶜṣtw* | | |
| 14a | *wytᵓww tᵓwh bmdbr* | batch IIa | stave II |
| 14b | *wynsw ᵓl byšymwn* | 14a-16b | 14a-25b |
| 15a | *wytn lhm šᵓltm* | 6 lines | 26 lines |
| 15b | *wyšlḥ rzwn bnpšm* | | |
| 16a | *wyqnᵓw lmšh bmḥnh* | | |
| 16b | *lᵓhrn qdwš-yhwh* | | |
| 17a | *tptḥ ᵓrṣ* | batch IIb | |
| 17b | *wtblᶜ dtn* | 17a-19b | |
| 17c | *wtks ᶜl-ᶜdt-ᵓbyrm* | 7 lines | |
| 18a | *wtbᶜr ᵓš bᶜdtm* | | |
| 18b | *lhbh tlhṭ ršᶜym* | | |
| 19a | *yᶜśw ᶜgl bḥrb* | | |
| 19b | *wyštḥww lmskh* | | |
| 20a | *wymyrw ᵓt-kbwdm btbnyt* | batch IIc | |
| 20b | *šwr-ᵓkl-ᶜśb* | 20a-22b | |
| 21a | *škḥw ᵓl-mwšyᶜm* | 6 lines | |
| 21b | *ᶜśh-gdlwt bmṣrym* | | |
| 22a | *nplᵓwt bᵓrṣ-ḥm* | | |
| 22b | *nwrᵓwt ᶜl-ym-swp* | | |
| 23a | *wyᵓmr lhšmydm lwly-mšh-bḥyrw* | batch IId | |
| 23b | *ᵓmd bprṣ lpnyw* | 23a-25b | |
| 23c | *lhšyb ḥmtw mhšḥyt* | 7 lines | |
| 24a | *wymᵓsw bᵓrṣ-ḥmdh* | | |
| 24b | *lᵓ-hᵓmynw ldbrw* | | |
| 25a | *wyrgnw bᵓhlyhm* | | |
| 25b | *lᵓ-šmᶜw bqwl-yhwh* | | |
| 26a | *wyśᵓ ydw lhm* | batch IIIa | stave III |
| 26b | *lhpyl ᵓwtm bmdbr* | 26a-29b | 26a-38d |
| 27a | *wlhpyl zrᶜm bgwym* | 8 lines | 27 lines |
| 27b | *wlzrwtm bᵓrṣwt* | | |
| 28a | *wyṣmdw lbᶜl-pᶜwr* | | |
| 28b | *wyᵓklw zbḥy-mtym* | | |

| | | | |
|---|---|---|---|
| 29a | *wykʿysw bmʿllyhm* | | |
| 29b | *wtprṣ bm mgph* | | |
| 30a | *wyʿmd pynḥs wypll* | batch IIIb | |
| 30b | *wtʿṣr hmgph* | 30a-33b | |
| 31a | *wtḥšb lw lṣdqh* | 8 lines | |
| 31b | *ldr-wdr ʿd-ʿwlm* | | |
| 32a | *wyqṣypw ʿl-my-mrybh* | | |
| 32b | *wyrʿ lmšh bʿbwrm* | | |
| 33a | *ky-hmrw ʾt-rwḥw* | | |
| 33b | *wybṭʾ bśptyw* | | |
| 34a | *lʾ-hšmydw ʾt-hʿmym* | batch IIIc | |
| 34b | *ʾšr-ʾmr yhwh lhm* | 34a-36b | |
| 35a | *wytʿrbw bgwym* | 6 lines | |
| 35b | *wylmdw mʿśyhm* | | |
| 36a | *wyʿbdw ʾt-ʿṣbyhm* | | |
| 36b | *wyhyw lhm lmwqš* | | |
| 37 | *wyzbḥw ʾt-bnyhm-wʾt-bnwtyhm lšdym* | batch IIId<br>37-38d | |
| 38a | *wyšpkw dm-nqy* | 5 lines | |
| 38b | *dm-bnyhm-wbnwtyhm* | | |
| 38c | *ʾšr zbḥw lʿṣby-knʿn* | | |
| 38d | *wtḥnp hʾrṣ bdmym* | | |
| 39a | *wyṭmʾw bmʿśyhm* | batch IVa | stave IV |
| 39b | *wyznw bmʿllyhm* | 39a-42b | 39a-48d |
| 40a | *wyḥr ʾp-yhwh bʿmw* | 8 lines | 24 lines |
| 40b | *wytʿb ʾt-nḥltw* | | |
| 41a | *wytnm byd-gwym* | | |
| 41b | *wymšlw bhm śnʾyhm* | | |
| 42a | *wylḥṣwm ʾwybyhm* | | |
| 42b | *wyknʿw tḥt-ydm* | | |
| 43a | *pʿmym-rbwt yṣylm* | batch IVb | |
| 43b | *whmh ymrw bʿṣtm* | 43a-44b | |
| 43c | *wymkw bʿwnm* | 5 lines | |
| 44a | *wyrʾ bṣr lhm* | | |
| 44b | *bšmʿw ʾt-rntm* | | |
| 45a | *wyzkr lhm brytw* | batch IVc | |
| 45b | *wynḥm krb-ḥsdw* | 45a-46 | |
| 46 | *wytn ʾwtm lrḥmym lpny-kl-šwbyhm* | 3 lines | |

| | | | |
|---|---|---|---|
| 47a | *hwšyʿnw yhwh-ʾlhynw* | batch IVd | |
| 47b | *wqbṣnw mn-hgwym* | 47a-48d | |
| 47c | *lhdwt lšm-qdšk* | 8 lines | |
| 47d | *lhštbḥ bthltk* | | |
| 48a | *brwk yhwh-ʾlhy-yśrʾl* | | |
| 48b | *mn-hʿwlm wʿd-hʿwlm* | | |
| 48c | *wʾmr kl-hʿm ʾmn* | | |
| 48d | *hllw yh* | | |

## Psalm 107

| | | | |
|---|---|---|---|
| 1a | *hdw lyhwh ky-ṭwb* | batch Ia | stave I |
| 1b | *ky-lʿwlm ḥsdw* | 1a-3b | 1a-9b |
| 2a | *yʾmrw gʾwly-yhwh* | 6 lines | 18 lines |
| 2b | *ʾšr gʾlm myd-ṣr* | | |
| 3a | *wmʾrṣwt qbṣm* | | |
| 3b | *mmzrḥ-wmmʿrb-mṣpwn-wmym* | | |
| 4a | *tʿw bmdbr* | batch Ib | |
| 4b | *byšymwn drk* | 4a-5 | |
| 4c | *ʿyr-mwšb lʾ-mṣʾw* | 4 lines | |
| 5 | *rʿbym-gm-ṣmʾym npšm bhm ttʿṭp* | | |
| 6a | *wyṣʿqw ʾl-yhwh bṣr lhm* | batch Ic | |
| 6b | *mmṣwqwtyhm yṣylm* | 6a-9b | |
| 7a | *wydrykm bdrk-yšrh* | 8 lines | |
| 7b | *llkt ʾl-ʿyr-mwšb* | | |
| 8a | *ywdw lyhwh* | **burden I** | |
| 8b | *ḥsdw-wnplʾwtyw lbny-ʾdm* | **6a-8b** | |
| 9a | *ky-hšbyʿ npš-šqqh* | **6 lines** | |
| 9b | *wnpš-rʿbh mlʾ ṭwb* | | |
| 10a | *yšby-ḥšk-wṣlmwt* | batch IIa | stave II |
| 10b | *ʾsyry-ʿny-wbrzl* | 10a-12b | 10a-16b |
| 11a | *ky-hmrw ʾmry-ʾl* | 6 lines | 14 lines |
| 11b | *wʿṣt-ʿlywn nʾṣw* | | |
| 12a | *wyknʿ bʿml lbm* | | |
| 12b | *kšlw wʾyn ʿzr* | | |
| 13a | *wyzʿqw ʾl-yhwh bṣr lhm* | batch IIb | |
| 13b | *mmṣqwtyhm ywšyʿm* | 13a-16b | |
| 14a | *ywṣʾm mḥšk-wṣlmwt* | 8 lines | |
| 14b | *wmwsrwtyhm yntq* | | |
| 15a | *ywdw lyhwh* | **burden II** | |
| 15b | *ḥsdw-wnplʾwtyw lbny-ʾdm* | **13a-15b** | |
| 16a | *ky-šbr dltwt-nḥšt* | **6 lines** | |
| 16b | *wbryḥy-brzl gdʿ* | | |

| | | | |
|---|---|---|---|
| 17a | *ʾwlym mdrk-pšʿm* | batch IIIa | stave III |
| 17b | *wmʿwntyhm ytʿnw* | 17a-18b | 17a-22b |
| 18a | *kl-ʾkl ttʿb npšm* | 4 lines | 12 lines |
| 18b | *wygyʿw ʿd-šʿry-mwt* | | |
| 19a | *wyzʿqw ʾl-yhwh bṣr lhm* | batch IIIb | |
| 19b | *mmṣqwtyhm ywšyʿm* | 19a-22b | |
| 20a | *yšlḥ dbrw wyrpʾm* | 8 lines | |
| 20b | *wymlṭ mšḥytwtm* | | |
| 21a | *ywdw lyhwh* | **burden III** | |
| 21b | *ḥsdw-wnplʾwtyw lbny-ʾdm* | **19a-21b** | |
| 22a | *wyzbḥw zbḥy-twdh* | **6 lines** | |
| 22b | *wysprw mʿśyw brnh* | | |
| 23a | *ywrdy-hym bʾnywt* | batch IVa | stave IV |
| 23b | *ʿśy-mlʾkh bmym-rbym* | 23a-25b | 23a-32b |
| 24a | *hmh rʾw mʿśy-yhwh* | 6 lines | 21 lines |
| 24b | *wnplʾwtyw bmṣwlh* | | |
| 25a | *wyʾmr wyʿmd rwḥ* | | |
| 25b | *sʿrh wtrwmm glyw* | | |
| 26a | *yʿlw šmym* | batch IVb | |
| 26b | *yrdw thwmwt* | 26a-27b | |
| 26c | *npšm brʿh ttmwgg* | 5 lines | |
| 27a | *yḥwgw wynwʿw kškwr* | | |
| 27b | *wkl-ḥkmtm ttblʿ* | | |
| 28a | *wyṣʿqw ʾl-yhwh bṣr lhm* | batch IVc | |
| 28b | *wmmṣwqtyhm ywṣyʾm* | 28a-32b | |
| 29a | *yqm sʿrh ldmmh* | 10 lines | |
| 29b | *wyḥšw glyhm* | | |
| 30a | *wyśmḥw ky-yštqw* | **burden IV** | |
| 30b | *wynḥm ʾl-mḥwz-ḥpṣm* | **28a-31b** | |
| 31a | *ywdw lyhwh* | **8 lines** | |
| 31b | *ḥsdw-wnplʾwtyw lbny-ʾdm* | | |
| 32a | *wyrmmwhw bqhl-ʿm* | | |
| 32b | *wbmwšb-zqnym yhllwhw* | | |
| 33a | *yśm nhrwt lmdbr* | batch Va | stave V |
| 33b | *wmṣʾy-mym lṣmʾwn* | 33a-36a | 33a-43c |
| 34a | *ʾrṣ-pry lmlḥh* | 7 lines | 24 lines |
| 34b | *mrʿt-yšby bh* | | |
| 35a | *yśm mdbr lʾgm-mym* | | |
| 35b | *wʾrṣ-ṣyh lmṣʾy-mym* | | |
| 36a | *wywšb šm rʿbym* | | |

| | | |
|---|---|---|
| 36b | *wykwnnw ᶜyr-mwšb* | batch Vb |
| 37a | *wyzrᶜw śdwt* | 36b-38b |
| 37b | *wyṭᶜw krmym* | 6 lines |
| 37c | *wyᶜśw pry-tbwᵓh* | |
| 38a | *wybrkm wyrbw mᵓd* | |
| 38b | *wbhmtm lᵓ-ymᶜyṭ* | |
| 39a | *wymᶜṭw wyšḥwm* | batch Vc |
| 39b | *ᶜṣr-rᶜh-wygwn* | 39a-41b |
| 40a | *špk-bwz ᶜl-ndybym* | 6 lines |
| 40b | *wytᶜm bthw-lᵓ-drk* | |
| 41a | *wyśgb ᵓbywn mᶜwny* | |
| 41b | *wyśm kṣᵓn mšpḥwt* | |
| 42a | *yrᵓw yšrym wyśmḥw* | batch Vd |
| 42b | *wkl-ᶜwlh qpṣh pyh* | 42a-43c |
| 43a | *my ḥkm* | 5 lines |
| 43b | *wyšmr ᵓlh* | |
| 43c | *wytbwnnw ḥsdy-yhwh* | |

# BIBLIOGRAPHY

Except for editions and translations of the Bible, which are listed in the first section, all references are given by author, in the second section. Starred items are difficult of access and distributors' addresses are given at the end of the section.


BFBS N. H. Snaith, ed. 1962. *Spr twrh nby$^{\circ}$ym wktwbym*. London: British and Foreign Bible Society.

BH3 R. Kittel, P. Kahle, A. Alt and O. Eissfeldt *et al.* 1937. *Biblia Hebraica*. Stuttgart: Württembergische Bibelanstalt.

BHS K. Elliger, W. Rudolph, H. P. Rüger and G. Weil, eds. 1968-. *Biblia Hebraica Stuttgartensia*. Stuttgart: Württembergische Bibelanstalt.

BJ *La Sainte Bible traduite en Français sous la direction de l'École Biblique de Jérusalem*. 1961. Paris: Éditions du Cerf.

JPS *The Torah. The Five Books of Moses*. 1962. Philadelphia: The Jewish Publication Society.

NAB *The New American Bible translated . . . by members of the Catholic Biblical Association of America*. 1970. New York: P. J. Kenedy. Apparatus cited from *Textual Notes on the New American Bible: Textual Notes on Old Testament Readings*. n. d. Paterson: St. Anthony's Guild.

NEB *The New English Bible with the Apocrypha*. 1970. Oxford and Cambridge: Oxford and Cambridge University Presses. Apparatus cited from Brockington 1973.

RSV H. G. May and B. M. Metzger, eds. 1965. *The Oxford Annotated Bible with the Apocrypha: Revised Standard Version*. New York: Oxford University Press.

---

Aartun, K.
1974 *Die Partikeln des Ugaritischen 1. Adverbien, Verneinungspartikeln, Bekräftigungspartikeln, Hervorhebungspartikeln*. Alter Orient und Altes Testament 21/1. Kevelaer and Neukirchen-Vluyn: Verlag Butzon und Bercker and Neukirchener Verlag.

Abu-Deeb, K.
1975 Toward a Structural Analysis of Pre-Islamic Poetry. *International Journal of Middle East Studies* 6: 148-84.

Ackroyd, P. R., and Lindars, B., eds.
1968 *Words and Meanings: Essays Presented to David Winton Thomas*. Cambridge: Cambridge University Press.

Adams, P. G.
1973 The Historical Importance of Assonance to Poets. *Publications of the Modern Language Association of America* 88: 8-18.

Albright, W. F.
1944 The Oracles of Balaam. *Journal of Biblical Literature* 63: 207-33.

1950 The Psalm of Habakkuk. Pp. 1-18 in H. H. Rowley, ed. *Studies in Old Testament Prophecy Presented to Theodore H. Robinson*. Edinburgh: Clark.

1959 Some Remarks on the Song of Moses in Deuteronomy XXXII. *Vetus Testamentum* 9: 339-46.

1969 *Yahweh and the Gods of Canaan*. Garden City: Doubleday.

Alonso-Schökel, L.

1959 Is 10, 28-32: Análisis Estilístico. *Biblica* 40: 230-36.

1963 *Estudios de poética hebrea*. Barcelona: Juan Flors.

Alonso-Schökel, A. [sic]

1975 Hermeneutical Problems of a Literary Study of the Bible. *Supplements to Vetus Testamentum* 28: 1-15.

Andersen, F. I.

1966 A Lexicographical Note on Exodus XXXII 18. *Vetus Testamentum* 16: 108-12.

1969a A Short Note on Construct *k* in Hebrew. *Biblica* 50: 68-69.

1969b Note on Genesis 30:8. *Journal of Biblical Literature* 88: 200.

1970a *The Hebrew Verbless Clause in the Pentateuch*. Journal of Biblical Literature Monograph Series 14. Nashville: Abingdon.

1970b Orthography in Repetitive Parallelism. *Journal of Biblical Literature* 89: 343-44.

1970c Biconsonantal Byforms of Weak Hebrew Roots. *Zeitschrift für die Alttestamentliche Wissenschaft* 82: 270-74.

1971 Passive and Ergative in Hebrew. Pp. 1-15 in Goedicke 1971.

1974 *The Sentence in Biblical Hebrew*. Janua Linguarum Series Practica 231. The Hague: Mouton.

1976 Rev. Kuhnigk 1974. *Biblica* 57: 573-75.

Anderson, S. R.

1973 *u*-Umlaut and Skaldic Verse. Pp. 3-13 in Anderson and Kiparsky 1973.

Anderson, S. R., and Kiparsky, P., eds.

1973 *A Festschrift for Morris Halle*. New York: Holt, Rinehart and Winston.

Andrews, W. G.

1973 A Critical-Interpretive Approach to the Ottoman Turkish Ġazel. *International Journal of Middle East Studies* 4: 97-111.

1976 *An Introduction to Ottoman Poetry*. Studies in Middle Eastern Literatures 7. Minneapolis: Bibliotheca Islamica.

Andrzejewski, B. W., and Lewis, I. M.

1964 *Somali Poetry: An Introduction*. Oxford: Clarendon.

Antilla, R.

1975 Linguistics and Philology. Pp. 145-55 in R. Bartsch and T. Vennemann, eds. *Linguistics and Neighboring Disciplines*. North-Holland Linguistic Series 14. Amsterdam: North-Holland Publishing Company.

Arberry, A. J.

1970 *The Koran Interpreted*. New York: Macmillan.

Auffret, P.
1977 Note sur la structure littéraire du Psaume cxxxvi. *Vetus Testamentum* 27: 1-12.

Austerlitz, R.
1958 *Ob-Ugric Metrics: The Metrical Structure of Ostyak and Vogul Folk-Poetry.* Folklore Fellows Communications 174. Helsinki: Academia Scientiarum Fennica.
1975 Literary and Folklore—Philology and Linguistics: Sacred Eurasian Antiquity and Profane Worldwide Modernity. Pp. 3-17 in Paper 1975.
1976 Author/Reader and Performer/Listener. Pp. 286-88 in Stolz and Shannon 1976.

Avishur, Y.
1971-72 Pairs of Synonymous Words in the Construct State (and in Appositional Hendiadys) in Biblical Hebrew. *Semitics* 2: 17-81.
1972 Addenda to the Expanded Colon in Ugaritic and Biblical Verse. *Ugarit-Forschungen* 4: 1-10.
1975 Word Pairs Common to Phoenician and Biblical Hebrew. *Ugarit-Forschungen* 7: 13-47.

Awoyale, Y.
1974 Yoruba Gerundive Structures and the Notion of 'Target Structures'. *Studies in the Linguistic Sciences* 4: 1-31.

ᶜAysa, ᶜAbd al-Jalīl
1385 *Al-Muṣḥaf al-Muyassar.* Cairo: Dār al-Qām.

Baisas, B. Q.
1973 Ugaritic *ᶜdr* and Hebrew *ᶜzr* I. *Ugarit-Forschungen* 5: 41-52.

Baker, A.
1973 Parallelism: England's Contribution to Biblical Studies. *Catholic Biblical Quarterly* 35: 429-40.

Barr, J.
1975 The Nature of Linguistic Evidence in the Text of the Bible. Pp. 35-57 in Paper 1975.

Batto, B. F.
1974 *Studies on Women at Mari.* Baltimore: Johns Hopkins University Press.

Bauman, R., and Sherzer, J., eds.
1974a *Explorations in the Ethnography of Speaking.* Cambridge: Cambridge University Press.
1974b Introduction. Pp. 6-12 in Bauman and Sherzer 1974a.

Beardsley, M. C.
1972 Verse and Music. Pp. 238-52 in Wimsatt 1972.

*Bell, A.
1975 *If speakers can't count syllables, what can they do?* Bloomington: Indiana University Linguistics Club.

Bencheikh, J. E.
1975 *Poétique Arabe.* Paris: Anthropos.

Benz, F. L.

1972 *Personal Names in the Phoenician and Punic Inscriptions*. Studia Pohl 8. Rome: Pontifical Biblical Institute.

Bierwisch, M., and Heidolph, K. E., eds.

1970 *Progress in Linguistics*. The Hague: Mouton.

Bishop, J. L., ed.

1966 *Studies in Chinese Literature*. Cambridge: Harvard University Press.

Blachère, R., ed.

1947-51 *Le Coran*. Paris: Maisonneuve.

Blommerde, A. C. M.

1969 *Northwest Semitic Grammar and Job*. Biblica et Orientalia 22. Rome: Pontifical Biblical Institute.

Bloomfield, L.

1933 *Language*. New York: Holt.

Bloomfield, M., and Haugen, E., eds.

1974 *Language as a Human Problem*. New York: Norton.

Boadt, L.

1975 The A:B:B:A Chiasm of Identical Roots in Ezekiel. *Vetus Testamentum* 25: 693-99.

Boling, R. G.

1960 "Synonymous" Parallelism in the Psalms. *Journal of Semitic Studies* 5: 221-55.

1975 *Judges*. Anchor Bible 6A. Garden City: Doubleday.

Boomslitter, P. C., Creel, W., and Hastings, G. S.

1973 Perception and English Poetic Meter. *Publications of the Modern Language Association of America* 88: 200-8.

Borowski, O.

1975 Notes on the Song of Deborah. *Rackham Literary Studies* 4: 97-101.

Bowler, P. J.

1977 *Fossils and Progress*. New York: Science History Publications.

Bream, H. N., Heim, R. D., and Moore, C. A., eds.

1974 *A Light Unto My Path: Old Testament Studies in Honor of Jacob M. Myers*. Gettysburg Theological Studies IV. Pittsburgh: Temple University Press.

Brickner, V. R.

1974 The Ethnographic Context of Some Traditional Mayan Speech Genres. Pp. 368-88 in Bauman and Sherzer 1974a.

Brockington, L. H.

1973 *The Hebrew Text of the Old Testament: The Readings Adopted by the Translators of the New English Bible*. Oxford and Cambridge: Oxford and Cambridge University Presses.

Brower, R. H.

1972 Japanese. Pp. 38-51 in Wimsatt 1972.

Brown, F., Driver, S. R., and Briggs, C. A.

1907 *A Hebrew and English Lexicon of the Old Testament*. Oxford: Clarendon.

Buttenweiser, M.
1938 *The Psalms*. Chicago: University of Chicago Press.
Cagni, L.
1969 *L'epopea di Erra*. Studi Semitici 34. Roma: Istituto di Studi del Vicino Oriente, Università di Roma.
1977 *The Poem of Erra*. Sources and Monographs/Sources from the Ancient Near East 1.3. Malibu: Undena.
Campbell, E. F., Jr.
1975 *Ruth*. Anchor Bible 7. Garden City: Doubleday.
Cantarino, V.
1975 *Arabic Poetics in the Golden Age*. Leiden: Brill.
Carroll, R. P.
1971 Psalm LXXVIII: Vestiges of a Tribal Polemic. *Vetus Testamentum* 21: 133-50.
Cathcart, K. J.
1973 *Nahum in the Light of Northwest Semitic*. Biblica et Orientalia 26. Rome: Pontifical Biblical Institute.
Ceresko, A. R.
1975 The A:B:B:A Word Pattern in Hebrew and Northwest Semitic, with Special Reference to the Book of Job. *Ugarit-Forschungen* 7: 73-88.
1976 The Chiastic Word Pattern in Hebrew. *Catholic Biblical Quarterly* 38: 303-11.
Chaney, M. L.
1976a *ḤDL-II and the 'Song of Deborah'.* Harvard Dissertation. Not seen.
1976b The Song of Deborah and Peasants' War. Unpublished paper.
Chatman, S., and Levin, S. R., eds.
1967 *Essays on the Language of Literature*. Boston: Houghton Mifflin.
Chelhod, J.
1973 A Contribution to the Problem of the Pre-eminence of the Right, Based upon Arabic Evidence. Pp. 239-62 in Needham 1973.
Chomsky, N.
1966 *Cartesian Linguistics: A Chapter in the History of Rationalist Thought*. New York: Harper and Row.
Chomsky, N., and Halle, M.
1968 *The Sound Pattern of English*. New York: Harper and Row.
Christensen, D. L.
1974 The Prosodic Structure of Amos 1-2. *Harvard Theological Review* 67: 427-36.
1975 The Acrostic of Nahum Reconsidered. *Zeitschrift für die Alttestamentliche Wissenschaft* 87: 17-30.
Clifford, R. J.
1972 *The Cosmic Mountain in Canaan and the Old Testament*. Cambridge: Harvard University Press.
1977 Rev. Fisher 1975. *Catholic Biblical Quarterly* 39: 112-13.
Coats, G. W.
1969 The Song of the Sea. *Catholic Biblical Quarterly* 31: 1-17.

Cogan, M.

1974 *Imperialism and Religion: Assyria, Judah and Israel in the Eighth and Seventh Centuries* B.C.E. Society of Biblical Literature Monograph Series 19. Missoula: Scholars Press.

Cole, P., and Morgan, J. L., eds.

1975 *Syntax and Semantics Volume 3: Speech Acts*. New York: Academic Press.

Collins, T.

1971 The Kilamuwa Inscription—A Phoenician Poem. *Welt des Orients* 6: 183-88.

Cooper, A. M.

1976 *Biblical Poetics: A Linguistic Approach*. Yale Dissertation. Quoted with permission of the author.

*Cooper, W. E., and Ross, J. R.

1975 World Order. Pp. 63-111 in R. E. Grossman, L. J. San, and T. J. Vance. 1975a. *Papers from the Eleventh Regional Meeting*. Chicago: Chicago Linguistic Society.

Coote, R. B.

1976 Oral Tradition, Old Testament. Pp. 914-16 in Crim *et al.* 1976.

Corcoran, D. W. J.

1971 *Pattern Recognition*. Harmondsworth: Penguin.

Crim, K. *et al.*

1976 *The Interpreter's Dictionary of the Bible: Supplementary Volume*. Nashville: Abingdon.

Cross, F. M.

1973a *Canaanite Myth and Hebrew Epic: Essays in the History of the Religion of Israel*. Cambridge: Harvard University Press.

1973b Notes on the Ammonite Inscription. *Bulletin of the American Schools of Oriental Research* 212: 12-15.

1974a Leaves from an Epigraphist's Notebook. *Catholic Biblical Quarterly* 36: 486-94.

1974b Prose and Poetry in the Mythic and Epic Texts from Ugarit. *Harvard Theological Review* 67: 1-15.

Cross, F. M., and Freedman, D. N.

1948 The Blessing of Moses. *Journal of Biblical Literature* 67: 191-210.

1955 The Song of Miriam. *Journal of Near Eastern Studies* 14: 237-50.

1972 Some Observations on Early Hebrew. *Biblica* 53: 413-20.

1975 *Studies in Ancient Yahwistic Poetry*. Society of Biblical Literature Dissertation Series 21. Missoula: Scholars Press.

Cross, F. M., and Saley, R. J.

1970 Phoenician Incantations on a Plaque of the Seventh Century B.C. from Arslan Tash in Upper Syria. *Bulletin of American Schools of Oriental Research* 197: 42-49.

Cross, F. M., and Talmon, S.

1975 *Qumran and the History of the Biblical Text*. Cambridge: Harvard University Press.

Culley, R. C.

1967 *Oral Formulaic Language in the Biblical Psalms*. Toronto: University of Toronto Press.

1970 Metrical Analysis of Classical Hebrew Poetry. Pp. 12-28 in Wevers and Redford 1970.

Dahood, M.

1954 Ugaritic *DRKT* and Biblical DEREK. *Theological Studies* 15: 627-31.

1955 A New Translation of Gen. 49, 6a. *Biblica* 36: 229.

1958 Ancient Semitic Deities in Syria and Palestine. Pp. 64-95 in S. Moscati, ed. *Le antiche divinità semitiche*. Studi Semitici 1. Roma: Centro di Studi Semitici.

1959a The Linguistic Position of Ugaritic in Light of Recent Discoveries. Vol. 1, pp. 267-79 in J. Coppens *et al.*, eds. *Sacra Pagina*. Gembloux: Duculot.

1959b The Value of Ugaritic for Textual Criticism. *Biblica* 40: 160-70.

1959c Is *ʾEben Yiśrāʾēl* a Divine Title (Gen 49, 24)? *Biblica* 40: 1002-7.

1960 Textual Problems in Isaia. *Catholic Biblical Quarterly* 22: 400-9.

1961 MKRTYHM in Genesis 49, 5. *Catholic Biblical Quarterly* 23: 54-56.

1962a Northwest Semitic Philology and Job. Pp. 55-74 in J. L. McKenzie, ed. *The Bible in Current Catholic Thought*. St. Mary's Theology Series 1. New York: Herder and Herder.

1962b *Nādâ* 'To Hurl' in Ex 15, 16. *Biblica* 43: 248-49.

1962c Ugaritic Studies and the Bible. *Gregorianum* 43: 55-79.

1963a *Proverbs and Northwest Semitic Philology*. Scripta Pontificii Instituti Biblici. Rome: Pontifical Biblical Institute.

1963b Hebrew-Ugaritic Lexicography I. *Biblica* 44: 289-303.

1964a Ugaritic Lexicography. Pp. 81-104 in *Mélanges Eugéne Tisserant*. Studi e Testi 231. Città del Vaticano.

1964b Rev. JPS. *Biblica* 45: 281-83.

1964c Hebrew-Ugaritic Lexicography II. *Biblica* 45: 393-412.

1965a *Ugaritic-Hebrew Philology: Marginal Notes on Recent Publications*. Biblica et Orientalia 17. Rome: Pontifical Biblical Institute.

1965b Hebrew-Ugaritic Lexicography III. *Biblica* 46: 311-32.

1966a *Psalms I. 1-50*. Anchor Bible 16. Garden City: Doubleday.

1966b Hebrew-Ugaritic Lexicography IV. *Biblica* 47: 403-19.

1967a Hebrew-Ugaritic Lexicography V. *Biblica* 48: 421-33.

1967b Nest and Phoenix in Job 29, 18. *Biblica* 48: 542-44.

1967c Ś$^{c}$RT "Storm" in Job 4, 15. *Biblica* 48: 544-45.

1967d A New Metrical Pattern in Biblical Poetry. *Catholic Biblical Quarterly* 29: 574-79.

1967e Congruity of Metaphors. *Supplements to Vetus Testamentum* 16: 40-49.
1968a *Psalms II. 51-100.* Anchor Bible 17. Garden City: Doubleday.
1968b The Phoenician Contribution to Biblical Wisdom Literature. Pp. 123-48 in W. Ward, ed. *The Role of the Phoenicians in the Interaction of Mediterranean Civilizations.* Beirut: American University Centennial Publications.
1968c The Name *yiśmā*$^{c\supset}$*ēl* in Genesis 16, 11. *Biblica* 49: 87-88.
1968d G. R. Driver and the Enclitic *mem* in Phoenician. *Biblica* 49: 89-90.
1968e Scriptio Defectiva in Qoheleth 4, 10a. *Biblica* 49: 243.
1968f Hebrew-Ugaritic Lexicography VI. *Biblica* 49: 355-69.
1968g HDK in Job 40, 12. *Biblica* 49: 509-10.
1968h Proverbs 8, 23-31. Translation and Commentary. *Catholic Biblical Quarterly* 30: 512-21.
1968j Ugaritic and the Old Testament. *Ephemerides Theologicae Lovanienses* 44: 35-54.
1969a Accusative $^{c}$*ēṣāh*, "Wood," in Isaiah 30, 1b. *Biblica* 50: 57-58.
1969b Comparative Philology Yesterday and Today. *Biblica* 50: 70-79.
1969c Hebrew-Ugaritic Lexicography VII. *Biblica* 50: 337-56.
1969d Rev. Ackroyd and Lindars 1968. *Catholic Biblical Quarterly* 31: 394-95.
1969e Ugaritic-Hebrew Syntax and Style. *Ugarit-Forschungen* 1: 15-36.
1970a *Psalms III. 101-150.* Anchor Bible 17a. Garden City: Doubleday.
1970b Hebrew-Ugaritic Lexicography VIII. *Biblica* 51: 391-404.
1970c The Independent Personal Pronoun in the Oblique Case in Hebrew. *Catholic Biblical Quarterly* 32: 86-90.
1971a Phoenician Elements in Isaiah 52:13-53:12. Pp. 63-73 in Goedicke 1971.
1971b Hebrew-Ugaritic Lexicography IX. *Biblica* 52: 337-56.
1972 Hebrew-Ugaritic Lexicography X. *Biblica* 53: 386-403.
1973a Some Rare Parallel Word Pairs in Job and in Ugaritic. Pp. 19-34 in R. J. Clifford and G. W. MacRae, eds. *The Word in the World: Essays in Honor of Frederick L. Moriarty, S. J.* Cambridge: Weston College Press.
1973b Ugaritic and Phoenician or Qumran and the Versions. Pp. 53-58 in H. A. Hoffner, ed. *Orient and Occident: Essays Presented to Cyrus H. Gordon on the Occasion of his Sixty-fifth Birthday.* Alter Orient und Altes Testament 22. Kevelaer and Neukirchen-Vluyn: Verlag Butzon und Bercker and Neukirchener Verlag.
1973c Honey that Drips: Notes on Proverbs 5, 2-3. *Biblica* 54: 65-66.
1973d Hebrew-Ugaritic Lexicography XI. *Biblica* 54: 351-66.
1973e A Note on *ṭôb* "Rain." *Biblica* 54: 404.
1973f Northwest Semitic Notes on Dt 32, 20. *Biblica* 54: 405-6.
1973g Vocative Lamedh in 1 Kings 19, 10.14. *Biblica* 54: 407-8.
1973h The Breakup of Two Composite Phrases in Isaiah 40, 13. *Biblica* 54: 537-38.

1973j The Breakup of Stereotyped Phrases: Some New Examples. *Journal of the Ancient Near East Society of Columbia University* 5: 83-89.
1974a Chiasmus in Job: A Text-Critical and Philological Criterion. Pp. 119-30 in Bream *et al.* 1974.
1974b Northwest Semitic Notes on Genesis. *Biblica* 55: 76-82.
1974c Hebrew-Ugaritic Lexicography XII. *Biblica* 55: 381-93.
1974d *ḤÔL* "Phoenix" in Job 29:18 and in Ugaritic. *Catholic Biblical Quarterly* 36: 85-88.
1974e The Verb *ʾĀRĀH*, "To Pick Clean," in Ps. XXII 17. *Vetus Testamentum* 24: 370-71.
1975a Phoenician-Hebrew Philology. Pp. 5-8 in A. Caquot, ed. *Études sémitiques: Actes du XXIXe congrès international des orientalistes, section sémitique*. Paris: L'Asiathèque.
1975b Ugaritic-Hebrew Parallel Pairs. Pp. 1-39 in Fisher 1975.
1975c Isaiah 51, 19 and Sefîre III 22. *Biblica* 56: 94-95.
1975d Ezekiel 19, 10 and Relative *kî*. *Biblica* 56: 96-99.
1975e The Archaic Genitive Ending in Proverbs 31, 6. *Biblica* 56: 241.
1975f Emphatic *Lamedh* in Jer 14:21 and Ezek 34:29. *Catholic Biblical Quarterly* 37: 341-42.
1975g The *aleph* in Psalm CXXVII 2 *šēnāʾ*. *Orientalia* 44: 103-5.
1975h *UT*, 128 *IV* 6-7, 17-18 and Isaiah 23:8-9. *Orientalia* 44: 439-41.
1976a Chiasmus. P. 145 in Crim *et al.* 1976.
1976b Hebrew Poetry. Pp. 669-72 in Crim *et al.* 1976.
1976c The Chiastic Breakup in Isaiah 58, 7. *Biblica* 57: 105.
1976d Jeremiah 5, 31 and *UT* 127:32. *Biblica* 57: 106-8.
1976e Canticle 7, 9 and *UT* 52, 61: A Question of Method. *Biblica* 57: 109-110.
1976f The Conjunction *pa* in Hosea 7, 1. *Biblica* 57: 247-48.

Dahood, M., and Penar, T.
1970 The Grammar of the Psalter. Pp. 361-456 in Dahood 1970a.
1972 Ugaritic-Hebrew Parallel Paris. Pp. 71-382 in Fisher 1972.

Davidson, D., and Harman, G., eds.
1972 *Semantics of Natural Language*. Dordrecht: Reidel.

Dietrich, M., and Loretz, O.
1972 Zur ugaritischen Lexikographie (V). *Ugarit-Forschungen* 4: 27-35.
1975 Kollationen zum Musiktext aus Ugarit. *Ugarit-Forschungen* 7: 521-22.

Dijk, H. J. van
1968 *Ezekiel's Prophecy on Tyre (Ez. 26, 1-28, 19): A New Approach.* Biblica et Orientalia 20. Rome: Pontifical Biblical Institute.

Driver, G. R.
1953 Hebrew Poetic Diction. *Supplements to Vetus Testamentum* 1: 26-39.
1960 Abbreviations in the Massoretic Text. *Textus* 1: 112-31.
1962 Problems in Judges Newly Discussed. *Annual of the Leeds University Oriental Society* 4: 6-25.

1964 Once again Abbreviations. *Textus* 4: 76-94.

Duchesne-Guillemin, M.

1975 Les problèmes de la notation hourrite. *Revue d'Assyriologie* 69: 159-73.

Eissfeldt, O.

1958 Das Lied Moses Deuteronomium 32. 1-43 und das Lehrgedicht Asaphs Psalm 78 samt einer Analyse der Umgebung des Moses-Leides. *Berichte über die Verhandlungen der sächischen Akademie der Wissenschaften zu Leipzig* 104 #15: 1-54.

Emeneau, M. B.

1966 Style and Meaning in an Oral Literature. *Language* 42: 323-45.

1971 *Toda Songs*. Oxford: Clarendon.

1974 *Ritual Structure and Language Structure of the Todas.* Transactions of the American Philosophical Society N. S. 64.6. Philadelphia: The American Philosophical Society.

Emerton, J. A.

1977 A Textual Problem in Isaiah 24.2. *Zeitschrift für die Alttestamentliche Wissenschaft* 89: 64-73.

Fearey, M. S.

1977 *Navaʾi's Turkic and Persian Quatrains: Discourse Typology and the Bilingual Poet*. University of Michigan Dissertation.

Feldman, B.

1972 Introduction to Robert Lowth. Pp. 144-46 in B. Feldman and R. D. Richardson, eds. *The Rise of Modern Mythology, 1680-1860*. Bloomington: Indiana University Press.

Fensham, F. C.

1976 Book of Zephaniah. Pp. 983-84 in Crim *et al.* 1976.

Finnegan, R.

1967 *Limba Stories and Story-Telling*. Oxford: Clarendon.

1970 *Oral Literature in Africa*. Oxford: Clarendon.

1973 Literacy versus Non-Literacy: The Great Divide? Some Comments on the Significance of 'Literature' in Non-Literate Cultures. Pp. 112-44 in R. Horton and R. Finnegan, eds. *Modes of Thought: Essays on Thinking in Western and Non-Western Societies*. London: Faber and Faber.

1976a *Oral Poetry: Its Nature, Significance and Social Context*. Oxford: Clarendon.

1976b What is Oral Literature Anyway? Comments in the Light of Some African and Other Comparative Materials. Pp. 127-66 in Stolz and Shannon 1976.

Fisher, L. R., ed.

1972 *Ras Shamra Parallels I*. Analecta Orientalia 49. Rome: Pontifical Biblical Institute.

1975 *Ras Shamra Parallels II*. Analecta Orientalia 50. Rome: Pontifical Biblical Institute.

Flanagan, J. W., and Robinson, A., eds.

1975 *No Famine in the Land: Studies in Honor of John L. McKenzie*. Missoula: Scholars Press.

Flescher, J.
1972 French. Pp. 177-90 in Wimsatt 1972.
Foley, J. M.
1976 Formula and Theme in Old English Poetry. Pp. 207-32 in Stolz and Shannon 1976.
Fox, J. J.
1971a A Rotinese Dynastic Genealogy: Structure and Event. Pp. 37-77 in T. O. Beidelman, ed. *The Translation of Culture: Essays to E. E. Evans-Pritchard*. London: Tavistock.
1971b Sister's Child as Plant: Metaphors in the Idiom of Consanguinity. Pp. 219-52 in R. Needham, ed. *Rethinking Kinship and Marriage*. Association of Social Anthropologists Monograph 11. London: Tavistock.
1971c Semantic Parallelism in Rotinese Ritual Language. *Bijdragen tot de Taal-, Land- en Volkenkunde* 127: 215-55.
1973 On Bad Death and the Left Hand: A Study of Rotinese Symbolic Inversions. Pp. 342-86 in Needham 1973.
1974 'Our Ancestors Spoke in Pairs': Rotinese Views of Language, Dialect and Code. Pp. 65-85 in Bauman and Sherzer 1974a.
Frankel, H. H.
1972 Classical Chinese. Pp. 22-37 in Wimsatt 1972.
1976 *The Flowering Plum and the Palace Lady: Interpretations of Chinese Poetry*. New Haven: Yale University Press.
*Frantz, D. G.
1974 *Generative Semantics: An Introduction, with Bibliography*. Bloomington: Indiana University Linguistics Club.
Freedman, D. N.
1955 PŠTY in Hosea 2:7. *Journal of Biblical Literature* 74: 275.
1960 Archaic Forms in Early Hebrew Poetry. *Zeitschrift für die Alttestamentliche Wissenschaft*. 72:101-7.
1963 The Original Name of Jacob. *Israel Exploration Journal*. 13: 125-26.
1968a The Structure of Job 3. *Biblica* 49: 503-8.
1968b Isaiah 42:13. *Catholic Biblical Quarterly* 30: 225-26.
1969 The Burning Bush. *Biblica* 50: 245-46.
1970 "Mistress Forever." A Note on Isaiah 47, 7. *Biblica* 51: 538.
1971a The Structure of Psalm 137. Pp. 131-41 in Goedicke 1971.
1971b Is Justice Blind? (Is 11, 3f). *Biblica* 52: 536.
1971c II Samuel 23:4. *Journal of Biblical Literature* 90: 329-30.
1972a The Refrain in David's Lament over Saul and Jonathan. Pp. 115-26 in C. J. Bleeker *et al.*, eds. *Ex Orbe Religionum: Studia Geo Widengren Oblata*. Studies in the History of Religions/Supplements to Numen 21. Leiden: Brill.
1972b Prolegomenon. Pp. vii-lvi in Gray 1915, rpt. 1972.
1972c The Broken Construct Chain. *Biblica* 53: 534-36.
1972d Acrostics and Metrics in Hebrew Poetry. *Harvard Theological Review* 65: 367-92.

1973 God Almighty in Psalm 78, 59. *Biblica* 54: 268.

1974 Strophe and Meter in Exodus 15. Pp. 163-203 in Bream *et al.* 1975.

1975a The Aaronic Benediction (Numbers 6: 24-26). pp. 35-48 in Flanagan and Robinson 1975.

1975b Early Israelite History in the Light of Early Israelite Poetry. Pp. 3-35 in H. Goedicke and J. J. M. Roberts, eds. *Unity and Diversity: Essays in the History, Literature, and Religion of the Ancient Near East.* Baltimore: John Hopkins University Press.

1976a Divine Names and Titles in Early Hebrew Poetry. Pp. 55-107 in F. M. Cross, W. E. Lembke, and P. D. Miller, eds. *Magnalia Dei: The Mighty Acts of God: Essays on the Bible and Archaeology in Memory of G. Ernest Wright.* Garden City: Doubleday.

1976b The Twenty-Third Psalm. Pp. 139-66 in Orlin *et al.* 1976.

1977 Pottery, Poetry, and Prophecy: An Essay on Biblical Poetry. *Journal of Biblical Literature* 96: 5-26.

Freedman, D. N., and Hyland, C. F.

1973 Psalm 29: A Structural Analysis. *Harvard Theological Review* 66: 237-56.

Freedman, D. N., and Lundbom, J. R.

1975 *ḥdl.* Vol. 2, sp. 748-55 in G. J. Botterweck and H. Ringgren, eds. *Theologisches Wōrterbuch zum Alten Testament.* Stuttgart: Kohlhammer.

Freeman, D. C., ed.

1970 *Linguistics and Literary Style.* New York: Holt, Rinehart and Winston.

Friedrich, P.

1975 *Proto-Indo-European Syntax: The Order of Meaningful Elements.* Journal of Indo-European Studies Monographs 1. Butte: Montana College of Mineral Science and Technology.

Fussell, P.

1965 Meter. Pp. 496-99 in Preminger *et al.* 1965.

1972 English I. Historical. Pp. 191-203 in Wimsatt 1972.

Gardiner, A.

1957 *Egygtian Grammar.* London: Oxford University Press.

Gefter, I.

1977 Previously Unrecognized Examples of the Break-Up of Stereo-type Expressions. Paper read at the American Academy of Religion/ Society of Biblical Literature Pacific Northwest Joint Meeting, 5-7 May. Not heard.

Gevirtz, S.

1971 The Reprimand of Reuben. *Journal of Near Eastern Studies* 30: 87-98.

1973 On Canaanite Rhetoric: The Evidence of the Amarna Letters from Tyre. *Orientalia* 42: 162-77.

1975 Of Patriarchs and Puns. Joseph at the Fountain, Jacob at the Ford. *Hebrew Union College Annual* 46: 33-54.

Ginsberg, H. L.
1950 Interpreting Ugaritic Texts. *Journal of the American Oriental Society* 70: 156-60.
Ginsburg, C. D.
1897 Reprint, 1966. *Introduction to the Massoretico-Critical Edition of the Hebrew Bible.* Prolegomenon by Harry M. Orlinsky. New York: Ktav.
Globe, A.
1974 The Text and Literary Structure of Judges 5, 4-5. *Biblica* 55: 168-78.
1975a Judges V 27. *Vetus Testamentum* 25: 362-67.
1975b The Muster of the Tribes in Judges 5: 11e-18. *Zeitschrift für die Alttestamentliche Wissenschaft* 87: 169-83.
Glück, J.
1970 Paronomasia in Biblical Literature. *Semitics* 1:50-78.
Goedicke, H., ed.
1971 *Near Eastern Studies in Honor of William Foxwell Albright.* Baltimore: Johns Hopkins Press.
Goldsmith, U. K.
1965 Alliteration. Pp. 15-16 in Preminger *et al.* 1965.
Goodwin, D. W.
1969 *Text-Restoration Methods in Contemporary U.S.A. Biblical Scholarship.* Pubblicazioni del Seminario di Semitistica 5. Naples: Istituto Orientale di Napoli.
Gordon, C. H.
1965 *Ugaritic Textbook.* Analecta Orientalia 38. Rome: Pontifical Biblical Institute.
1976 Hebrew Language. Pp. 392-94 in Crim *et al.* 1976.
Gossen, G. H.
1974 To Speak With a Heated Heart: Chamula Canons of Style and Good Performance. Pp. 389-413 in Bauman and Sherzer 1947a.
Gottwald, N. K.
1962 Hebrew Poetry. Vol. 3, pp. 829-38 in G. Buttrick *et al.*, eds. *The Interpreter's Dictionary of the Bible.* Nashville: Abingdon.
Gray, G. B.
1915 Reprint, 1972. *The Forms of Hebrew Poetry.* Prolegomenon by D. N. Freedman. New York: Ktav.
*Green, G. M.
1970 How Abstract is Surface Structure? Pp. 270-81 in L. Campbell *et al.* *Papers from the Sixth Regional Meeting.* Chicago: Chicago Linguistic Society.
Greenberg, J. H.
1963a *Universals of Language.* Cambridge: M.I.T. Press.
1963b Some Universals of Grammar with Particular Reference to the Order of Meaningful Elements. Pp. 73-113 in Greenberg 1963a.
Greenfield, J. C.
1965a Stylistic Aspects of the Sefire Treaty Inscriptions. *Acta Orientalia* 1: 1-18.

1965b Three Notes on the Sefire Inscriptions. *Journal of Semitic Studies* 11: 98-105.

1971 Scripture and Inscription: The Literary and Rhetorical Elements in Some Early Phoenician Inscriptions. Pp. 253-68 in Goedicke 1971.

1974 Standard Literary Aramaic. Pp. 280-89 in A. Caquot and D. Cohen, eds. *Actes du premier congrès international de linguistique sémitique et chamito-sémitique*. The Hague: Mouton.

Greenfield, S. B.

1967 Grammar and Meaning in Poetry. *Publications of the Modern Language Association of America* 82: 377-87.

Greenstein, E. L.

1974 Two Variations of Grammatical Parallelism in Canaanite Poetry and their Psycholinguistic Background. *Journal of the Ancient Near Eastern Society of Columbia University* 6: 87-105.

Gröndahl, F.

1967 *Die Personennamen der Texte aus Ugarit*. Studia Pohl 1. Rome: Pontifical Biblical Institute.

Guillaume, A.

1964 Paronomasia in the Old Testament. *Journal of Semitic Studies* 9: 282-90.

Gunn, D. M.

1974 Narrative Patterns and Oral Tradition in Judges and Samuel. *Vetus Testamentum* 24: 286-317.

Güterbock, H. G.

1970 Musical Notation in Ugarit. *Revue d'Assyriologie* 64: 45-52.

Halle, M.

1970a On Meter and Prosody. Pp. 64-80 in Bierwisch and Heidolph 1970.

1970b Is Kabardian a Vowel-less Language? *Foundations of Language* 6: 95-103.

Halle, M., and Keyser, S. J.

1972a *English Stress: Its Form, Its Growth and Its Role in Verse*. New York: Harper and Row.

1972b English III. The Iambic Pentameter. Pp. 217-37 in Wimsatt 1972.

*Hamp, E. P.

1974 Reassignment of Nasality in Early Irish. Pp. 127-30 in A. Bruck, R. A. Fox, and M. W. LaGaly, eds. *Papers from the Parasession on Natural Phonology*. Chicago: Chicago Linguistic Society.

Hanson, P. D.

1968 The Song of Heshbon and David's NÎR. *Harvard Theological Review* 61: 297-320.

1973 Zechariah 9 and the Recapitulation of an Ancient Ritual Pattern. *Journal of Biblical Literature* 92: 37-59.

1975 *The Dawn of Apocalyptic*. Philadelphia: Fortress Press.

Harris, Z. S.

1939 *Development of the Canaanite Dialects*. American Oriental Series 16. New Haven: American Oriental Society.

1970 *Papers in Structural and Transformational Linguistics.* Formal Linguistics Series 1. Dordrecht: Reidel.

Hart, G. L., III

1975 *The Poems of Ancient Tamil. Their Milieu and Their Sanskrit Counterparts.* Berkeley: University of California Press.

Hartmann, B.

1967 "Mögen die Götter dich behüten und unversehrt bewahren." *Supplements to Vetus Testamentum* 16: 102-5.

Hawkes, D.

1959 *Chʾu Tzʾŭ: The Songs of the South.* Oxford: Clarendon.

Held, M.

1959 *mḫṣ/*mḫš* in Ugaritic and Other Semitic Languages (A Study in Comparative Lexicography). *Journal of the American Oriental Society* 79: 169-76.

1965a Studies in Comparative Semitic Lexicography. Pp. 395-406 in *Studies in Honor of Benno Landsberger on his Seventy-fifth Birthday, April 21, 1965.* Assyriological Studies 16. Chicago: University of Chicago Press.

1965b The Action-Result (Factitive-Passive) Sequence of Identical Verbs in Biblical Hebrew and Ugaritic. *Journal of Biblical Literature* 84: 272-82.

1968 The Root ZBL/SBL in Akkadian, Ugaritic and Biblical Hebrew. *Journal of the American Oriental Society* 88:90-96.

1969 Rhetorical Questions in Ugaritic and Biblical Hebrew. *Eretz-Israel* 9: 71-79.

1973 Pits and Pitfalls in Akkadian and Biblical Hebrew. *Journal of the Ancient Near Eastern Society of Columbia University* 5: 173-90.

1974 Hebrew *maᶜgāl*: A Study in Lexical Parallelism. *Journal of the Ancient Near Eastern Society of Columbia University* 6: 107-16.

1976 Two Philological Notes on *Enûma eliš.* Pp. 231-39 in B. L. Eichler *et al.*, eds. *Kramer Anniversary Volume: Cuneiform Studies in Honor of Samuel Noah Kramer.* Alter Orient und Altes Testament 25. Kevelaer and Neukirchen-Vluyn: Verlag Butzon und Bercker and Neukirchener Verlag.

Hightower, J. R.

1966 Some Characteristics of Parallel Prose. Pp. 60-91 in Bishop 1966.

Hillers, D. R.

1965 A Note on Judges 5, 8a. *Catholic Biblical Quarterly* 27: 124-26.

1972 *Lamentations.* Anchor Bible 15. Garden City: Doubleday.

1974 Observations on Syntax and Meter in Lamentations. Pp. 265-70 in Bream *et al.* 1974.

Hillers, D. R., and McCall, M. H.

1976 Homeric Dictated Texts: A Reexamination of Some Near Eastern Evidence. *Harvard Studies in Classical Philology* 80: 19-23.

Hjelmslev, L.

1970 *Language: An Introduction.* Trans. F. J. Whitfield. Madison: University of Wisconsin Press.

Hock, H. H.
1977 Archaisms, Morphophonemic Metrics, or Variable Rules in the Rig-Veda? Paper read at the Spring 1977 American Oriental Society Meeting, Ithaca, New York. Courtesy of the author.
Hockett, C. F.
1977 Rev. Sebeok *et al.* 1974. *Current Anthropology* 18: 78-82.
Hoftijzer, J.
1973 The Nominal Clause Reconsidered. *Vetus Testamentum* 23: 446-510.
Holladay, J. S.
1968 The Day(s) the *Moon* Stood Still. *Journal of Biblical Literature* 87: 166-78.
Hopper, P. J.
1971 The Free Word Order Languages: A Fourth Category in the Greenberg Syntactic Typology? Pp. 115-19 in F. Ingemann, ed. *Papers from the Fifth Kansas Linguistics Conference*. Lawrence: The Linguistics Department, University of Kansas.
Horwitz, W. J.
1973 A Study of Ugaritic Scribal Practices and Prosody in CTA 2:4. *Ugarit-Forschungen* 5: 165-73.
Howard, R.
1976 On the Naming of Poems. *Antaeus* 21/22: 89-91.
*Hudson, R. A.
1975 *Conjunction Reduction, Gapping, Hacking and the Preservation of Surface Structure*. Bloomington: Indiana University Linguistics Club.
Huffmon, H. B.
1965 *Amorite Personal Names in the Mari Texts*. Baltimore: Johns Hopkins Press.
1976 Religious Significance of Names. Pp. 619-21 in Crim *et al.* 1976.
Jackson, J. J., and Kessler, M., eds.
1974 *Rhetorical Criticism: Essays in Honor of James Muilenburg*. Pittsburgh Theological Monograph Series 1. Pittsburgh: Pickwick Press.
Jacobson, S.
1971 *Studies in English Transformational Grammar*. Stockholm: Almqvist and Wiksells.
Jakobson, R.
1963 Implications of Language Universals for Linguistics. Pp. 263-78 in Greenberg 1963a.
1966 Grammatical Parallelism and its Russian Facet. *Language* 42: 399-429.
1967 Linguistics and Poetics. Pp. 296-322 in Chatman and Levin 1967.
Johnson, D. E.
1974 Adjective Flipping and the Notion of Target Structure. *Studies in the Linguistic Sciences* 4: 59-79.
Jongeling, B.
1971 Jeux de mots en Sophonie III 1 et 3? *Vetus Testamentum* 21: 541-47.
Kaddari, M. Z.
1973 A Semantic Approach to Biblical Parallelism. *Journal of Jewish Studies* 24: 167-75.

Kapelrud, A. S.
1975 *The Message of the Prophet Zephaniah: Morphology and Ideas.* Oslo: Universitetsforlaget.

Keenan, E. L.
1974 Logic and Language. Pp. 187-96 in Bloomfield and Haugen 1974.

Kessler, M.
1973 Rhetoric in Jeremiah 50 and 51. *Semitics* 3: 18-35.
1974 A Methodological Setting for Rhetorical Criticism. *Semitics* 4: 22-36.

Kilmer, A. D.
1971 The Discovery of an Ancient Mesopotamian Theory of Music. *Proceedings of the American Philosophical Society* 115: 131-49.
1974 The Cult Song with Music from Ancient Ugarit: Another Interpretation. *Revue d'Assyriologie* 68: 69-82.
1976 Music. Pp. 610-12 in Crim *et al.* 1976.

Kinnier Wilson, J. V.
1968 "Desonance" in Accadian. *Journal of Semitic Studies* 13: 93-103.

Kiparsky, P.
1970 Metrics and Morphophonemics in the Kalevala. Pp. 165-81 in Freeman 1970.
1972 Metrics and Morphophonemics in the Rigveda. Pp. 171-200 in M. K. Brame, ed. *Contributions to Generative Phonology.* Austin: University of Texas Press.
1973 The Linguistic Basis of Literary Form. Lecture at the Summer Linguistic Society of America.
1973-74 Commentary. *New Literary History* 5: 177-85.
1974 The Role of Linguistics in a Theory of Poetry. Pp. 233-46 in Bloomfield and Haugen 1974.
1975 Stress, Syntax and Meter. *Language* 51: 576-616.
1976 Oral Poetry: Some Linguistic and Typological Considerations. Pp. 73-106 in Stolz and Shannon 1976.
1977 The Rhythmic Structure of English Verse. *Linguistic Inquiry* 8: 189-247.

Kosmala, H.
1964 Form and Structure in Ancient Hebrew Poetry (A New Approach). *Vetus Testamentum* 14: 423-45.
1966 Form and Structure in Ancient Hebrew Poetry. *Vetus Testamentum* 16: 152-80.

Krahmalkov, C. R.
1965 *Studies in Amorite Grammar.* Harvard Dissertation.
1969 The Amorite Enclitic Particle *TA/I. Journal of Semitic Studies* 14: 201-4.
1970 The Enclitic Particle TA/I in Hebrew. *Journal of Biblical Literature* 89: 218-19.
1974 A Carthaginian Report of the Battle of Agrigentum 406 B.C. (*CIS I,* 5510. 9-11). *Rivista di studi fenici* 2: 171-77.
1975 Two Neo-Punic Poems in Rhymed Verse. *Rivista di studi fenici* 3: 169-205.

1976 An Ammonite Lyric Poem. *Bulletin of the American Schools of Oriental Research* 223: 55-57.

Krenkow, F.

1934 *Sadj*[c]. Vol. 4, pp. 43-44 in M. Th. Houtsma *et al.* 1913-1934. *The Encyclopaedia of Islam*. Leyden: Brill.

Kselman, J. S.

1970 A Note on Jer 49, 20 and Ze 2, 6-7. *Catholic Biblical Quarterly* 32: 579-81.

1973 A Note on Gen 7:11. *Catholic Biblical Quarterly* 35: 491-93.

1977 A Note on Ps 51:6. *Catholic Biblical Quarterly* 39: 251-53.

Kuhnigk, W.

1974 *Nordwest-semitische Studien zum Hoseabuch*. Biblica et Orientalia 27. Rome: Pontifical Biblical Institute.

Kurylowicz, J.

1972 *Studies in Semitic Grammar and Metrics*. Prace Jezykoznawze 67. Wroclaw: Polska Akademia Nauk.

1973 Verbal Aspect in Semitic. *Orientalia* 42: 114-20.

Lack, R.

1973 *La Symbolique du Livre d'Isaïe: Essai sur l'image littéraire comme élément de structuration*. Analecta Biblica 59. Rome: Biblical Institute Press.

1977 Le psaume 1—Une analyse structurale. *Biblica* 57: 154-67.

Ladefoged, P.

1962 *Elements of Acoustic Phonetics*. Chicago: University of Chicago Press.

1967 *Three Areas of Experimental Phonetics*. London: Oxford University Press.

1971 *Preliminaries to Linguistic Phonetics*. Chicago: University of Chicago Press.

LaDrière, C.

1965 Prosody. Pp. 669-77 in Preminger *et al.* 1965.

Lakoff, G.

1970a *Irregularity in Syntax*. New York: Holt, Rinehart and Winston.

1970b Repartee. *Foundations of Language* 6: 389-422.

1972 Linguistics and Natural Logic. Pp. 545-665 in Davidson and Harman 1972.

Lambert, W. G.

1971 The Converse Tablet: A Litany with Musical Instructions. Pp. 335-53 in Goedicke 1971.

Lass, R.

1977 Rev. Emeneau 1974. *Journal of the American Oriental Society* 97: 251-53.

Legge, J.

1960 *The Chinese Classics III. The Shoo King*. Hong Kong: Hong Kong University Press.

Lehmann, W. P.

1972 Contemporary Linguistics and Indo-European Studies. *Publications of the Modern Language Association of America* 87: 976-93.

Liu, W-c. and Lo, I.
1975 *Sunflower Splendor*. Bloomington: Indiana University Press.
Loewenstamm, S. E.
1969 The Expanded Colon in Ugaritic and Biblical Verse. *Journal of Semitic Studies* 14: 176-96.
1975a Ugarit and the Bible. I. Rev. Fisher 1972. *Biblica* 56: 103-19.
1975b The Expanded Colon, Reconsidered. *Ugarit-Forschungen* 7: 261-64.
Lonergan, B. J. F.
1972 *Method in Theology*. New York: Herder and Herder.
Long, B. O.
1976 Recent Field Studies in Oral Literature and Their Bearing on Old Testament Criticism. *Vetus Testamentum* 26: 187-98.
Lord, A. B.
1965 *The Singer of Tales*. New York: Atheneum.
1976 The Traditional Song. Pp. 1-15 in Stolz and Shannon 1976.
Lord, A. B. and Bynum, D. E.
1974 *Serbo-Croatian Heroic Songs Collected by Milman Parry III. The Wedding of Smailagić Meho by Avdo Medodović*. Publications of the Milman Parry Collection. Texts and Translations Series I. Cambridge: Harvard University Press.
Loretz, O.
1973 Textologie des Zephanja-Buches: Bemerkungen zu einem Missverständnis. *Ugarit-Forschungen* 5: 219-28.
1975 Die Analyse der Ugartischen und Hebräischen Poesie Mittels Stichometrie und Konsonantenerzählung. *Ugarit-Forschungen* 7: 265-69.
Lotz, J.
1972a Elements of Versification. Pp. 1-21 in Wimsatt 1972.
1972b Uralic. Pp. 100-21 in Wimsatt 1972.
Lowth, Robert
1762 Reprint, 1967. *A Short Introduction to English Grammar*. Menston, U. K.: Scolar Press.
1829 *Lectures on the Sacred Poetry of the Hebrews*. Trans. G. Gregory. Boston: Crocker and Brewster.
Lundbom, J. R.
1975 *Jeremiah: A Study in Ancient Hebrew Rhetoric*. Society for Biblical Literature Dissertation Series 18. Missoula: Scholars Press.
Maas, P.
1962 *Greek Metre*. Trans. H. Lloyd-Jones. Oxford: Clarendon.
McCarus, E. N.
1976 A Semantic Analysis of Arabic Verbs. Pp. 3-28 in Orlin *et al.* 1976.
McCawley, J. D.
1970 English as a VSO Language. *Language* 46: 286-99.
1972 A Program for Logic. Pp. 498-544 in Davidson and Harman 1972.
Magoun, F. P., Jr., trans.
1963 *The Kalevala, or Poems of the Kaleva District Compiled by Elias Lönnrot*. Cambridge: Harvard University Press.

1969 *The Old Kalevala and Certain Antecedents Compiled by Elias Lönnrot*. Cambridge: Harvard University Press.

Maling, J. M.
1973 *The Theory of Classical Arabic Metrics*. Massachusetts Institute of Technology Dissertation. Courtesy of the author.

Margalit, B.
1975 Studia Ugaritica I. Introduction to Ugaritic Prosody. *Ugarit-Forschungen* 7: 289-314.

Martinez, E. R.
1967 *Hebrew-Ugaritic Index to the Writings of Mitchell J. Dahood*. Rome: Pontifical Biblical Institute.

Melamed, E. Z.
1961 Breakup of Stereotype Phrases as an Artistic Device in Biblical Poetry. Pp. 115-53 in Rabin 1961.

Mendenhall, G. E.
1973 *The Tenth Generation*. Baltimore: John Hopkins Press.
1975 Samuel's "Broken Rîb": Deuteronomy 32. Pp. 63-74 in Flanagan and Robinson 1975.

Merwin, W. S.
1959 *Poem of the Cid*. New York: New American Library.

Milik, J. T.
1957 Deux documents inédits du désert de Juda. *Biblica* 38: 245-68.

Miller, P. D.
1970 Ugaritic ǴZR and Hebrew ᶜZR II. *Ugarit-Forschungen* 2: 159-75.

Molière, J. B. P.
1856 *Oeuvres Complètes*. Paris: Firmin Didot.

deMoor, J. C.
1971 *The Seasonal Pattern in the Ugaritic Myth of Baᶜlu According to the Version of Ilimilku*. Alter Orient und Altes Testament 16. Kevelaer and Neukirchen-Vluyn: Verlag Butzon und Bercker and Neukirchener Verlag.

Moore, Marianne
1967 *The Complete Poems*. New York: Macmillan/Viking.

Moran, W. L.
1958 Gen 49:10 and Its Use in Ez 21:32. *Biblica* 39: 405-25.
1961 The Hebrew Language in its Northwest Semitic Background. Pp. 59-84 in G. E. Wright, ed. *The Bible and the Ancient Near East: Essays In Honor of William Foxwell Albright*. Garden City: Doubleday.
1962 Some Remarks on the Song of Moses. *Biblica* 43: 317-27.
1969 New Evidence from Mari on the History of Prophecy. *Biblica* 50: 15-56.

Mowinckel, S.
1930 Der Ursprung des Bilᶜamsage. *Zeitschrift für die Alttestamentliche Wissenschaft* 42: 233-71.

Muilenburg, J.
1953 A Study in Hebrew Rhetoric: Repetition and Style. *Supplements to Vetus Testamentum* 1: 97-111.
1961 The Linguistic and Rhetorical Usages of the Particle *ky* in the Old Testament. *Hebrew Union College Annual* 32: 135-60.
1966 A Liturgy on the Triumphs of Yahweh. Pp. 233-51 in van Unnik and van der Woude 1966.
1969 Form Criticism and Beyond. *Journal of Biblical Literature* 89: 1-18.

Murphy, R. T. A.
1968 Zephaniah. Vol. 1, pp. 290-93 in R. E. Brown, J. A. Fitzmyer and R. E. Murphy, eds. *Jerome Biblical Commentary*. Englewood Cliffs: Prentice-Hall.

Nabokov, V.
1964 *Notes on Prosody and Abram Gannibal From the Commentary to the Author's Translation of Pushkin's Eugene Onegin*. Princeton: Princeton University Press.

Nagy, G.
1974 *Comparative Studies in Greek and Indic Meter*. Harvard Studies in Comparative Literature 33. Cambridge: Harvard University Press.
1976 Formula and Meter. Pp. 239-60 in Stolz and Shannon 1976.

Needham, J. and Wang, L.
1959 *Science and Civilisation in China. 3. Mathematics and the Sciences of the Heavens and the Earth*. Cambridge: Cambridge University Press.
1965 *Science and Civilisation in China. 4. Physics and Physical Technology. II. Mechanical Engineering*. Cambridge: Cambridge University Press.

Needham, R., ed.
1973 *Right and Left: Essays on Dual Symbolic Classification*. Chicago: University of Chicago Press.

Nelson, L.
1972 Spanish. Pp. 165-76 in Wimsatt 1972.

Newman, L. I.
1918 *Studies in Biblical Parallelism 1. Parallelism in Amos*. University of California Publications in Semitic Philology 1. Berkeley: University of California.

O'Connor, M.
1977 The Rhetoric of the Kilamuwa Inscription. *Bulletin of the American Schools of Oriental Research* 226: 15-29.

Olmo Lete, G. del
1973 El libro de Sofonías y la filología semitica nor-occidental. *Estudios Biblicos* 32: 291-303. Not seen.

Ong, W. J., ed.
1960a *Darwin's Vision and Christian Perspectives*. New York: Macmillan.
1960b Evolution and Cyclism in Our Time. Pp. 125-48 in Ong 1960a.
1962 *The Barbarian Within and Other Fugitive Essays and Studies*. New York: Macmillan.

O'Nolan, K.
1969 Homer and Irish Heroic Narrative. *Classical Quarterly* 19: 1-19.
Opland, J.
1975 *Imbongi Nezibongo*: The Xhosa Tribal Poet and the Contemporary Poetic Tradition. *Publications of the Modern Language Association of America* 90: 185-208.
1976 Huso and Mqhayi: Notes on the Southslavic and Xhosa Traditions of Oral Poetry. Pp. 120-24 in Stolz and Shannon 1976.
*Orlin, L. L., *et al.*
1976 *Michigan Oriental Studies in Honor of George G. Cameron*. Ann Arbor: Department of Near Eastern Studies, The University of Michigan.
Palacas, A. L.
1971 The Higher Predicate Status of Modals. *Glossa* 5: 31-46.
*Paper, H. H., ed.
1975 *Language and Texts: The Nature of Linguistic Evidence*. Ann Arbor: Center for Coordination of Ancient and Modern Study, The University of Michigan.
Pardee, D. G.
1974 Rev. Sabottka 1972 and Cathcart 1973. *Journal of the American Oriental Society* 94: 506-9.
1975 The Preposition in Ugaritic I. *Ugarit-Forschungen* 7: 329-78.
1977 Rev. Fisher 1972. *Journal of Near Eastern Studies* 36: 65-68.
Parry, M.
1930 Studies in the Epic Technique of Oral Verse-Making. I. Homer and Homeric Style. *Harvard Studies in Classical Philology* 41: 73-147.
Paul, S. M.
1976 Mnemonic Devices. Pp. 600-2 in Crim *et al.* 1976.
Payne, D. F.
1967 Characteristic Word-play in "Second Isaiah." A Reappraisal. *Journal of Semitic Studies* 12: 207-29.
Peabody, B.
1976 *The Winged Word*. Albany: State University of New York Press.
Penar, T.
1975 *Northwest Semitic Philology and the Hebrew Fragments of Ben Sira*. Biblica et Orientalia 28. Rome: Pontifical Biblical Institute.
Peterson, D. J.
1974 *Noun Phrase Specificity*. University of Michigan Dissertation.
Peterson, R. G.
1976 Critical Calculations: Measure and Symmetry in Literature. *Publications of the Modern Language Society of America* 97: 367-75.
Pike, K.
1967 *Language in Relation to a Unified Theory of Human Behavior*. The Hague: Mouton.
Pope, M. H.
1971 The Scene on the Drinking Mug from Ugarit. Pp. 393-405 in Goedicke 1971.

Popper, W.
1918 *Studies in Biblical Parallelism 2. Parallelism in Isaiah, chaps. 1-10.* University of California Publications in Semitic Philology 1. Berkeley: University of California.

Postal, P. M.
1971 *Cross-Over Phenomena.* New York: Rinehart and Winston.

Smith, J. M. Powis
1911 Zephaniah. Pp. 157-263 in J. M. Powis Smith, W. H. Ward, and J. A. Bewer. *A Critical and Exegetical Commentary on Micah, Zephaniah, Nahum, Habakkuk, Obadiah and Joel.* Edinburgh: Clark.

Preminger, A., Warnke, F. J., and Hardison, O. B.
1965 *Princeton Encylopaedia of Poetry and Poetics.* Princeton: Princeton University Press.

Pulgram, E.
1975 *Latin-Romance Phonology: Prosodics and Metrics.* Ars Grammatica 4. München: Wilhelm Fink.

Pulte, W.
1973 Some Claims Regarding Gapping: The Evidence from Cherokee. Pp. 256-60 in J. Battle and J. Schweitzer, eds. *Mid-America Linguistics Conference Papers.* Stillwater: Oklahoma State University.

Rabin, C.
1955 Judges V, 2 and the "Ideology" of Deborah's War. *Journal of Jewish Studies* 6: 125-34.
1961 *Studies in the Bible.* Scripta Hierosolymitana 8. Jerusalem: Magnes.

Reichardt, K.
1928 *Studien zu Skalden des 9. und 10. Jahrhunderts.* Palaestra 159. Leipzig: Mayer und Müller.

Reid, P. V.
1975 *Šbṭy* in 2 Samuel 7:7. *Catholic Biblical Quarterly* 37: 17-20.

Riding, C. B.
1976 Psalm 95:1-7c as a Large Chiasm. *Zeitschrift für die Alttestamentliche Wissenschaft* 88: 418.

Roberts, J. J. M.
1971-72 Erra, Scorched Earth. *Journal of Cuneiform Studies* 24: 11-16.

Robertson, D. A.
1972 *Linguistic Evidence in Dating Early Hebrew Poetry.* Society of Biblical Literature Dissertation Series 3. Missoula: Society of Biblical Literature.
1976 The Bible as Literature. Pp. 547-51 in Crim *et al.* 1976.

Robinson, T. H.
1950 Basic Principles of Hebrew Poetic Form. Pp. 438-50 in W. Baumgartner *et al.*, eds. *Festschrift Alfred Bertholet.* Tübingen: J. C. B. Mohr.
1953 Hebrew Poetic Form. *Supplements to Vetus Testamentum* 1: 128-49.

*Ross, J. R.
1967 *Constraints on Variables in Syntax.* Bloomington: Indiana University Linguistics Club.

1969 Adjectives as Noun Phrases. Pp. 353-60 in D. A. Reibel and S. A. Schane, eds. *Modern Studies in English*. Englewood Cliffs: Prentice-Hall.
1970a Gapping and the Order of Constituents. Pp. 249-59 in Bierwisch and Heidolph 1970.
1970b On Declarative Sentences. Pp. 222-72 in R. Jacobs and P. S. Rosenbaum, eds. *Readings in English Transformational Grammar*. Waltham: Ginn.
1972 Act. Pp. 70-126 in Davidson and Harman 1972.
1975 Where to Do Things With Words. Pp. 233-56 in Cole and Morgan 1975.

Russo, J. A.
1976 Is "Oral" or "Aural" Composition the Cause of Homer's Formulaic Style? Pp. 31-54 in Stolz and Shannon 1976.

Sabottka, L.
1972 *Zephanja: Versuch einer Neuübersetzung mit philologischem Kommentar*. Biblica et Orientalia 25. Rome: Pontifical Biblical Institute.

Sadock, J. M.
1975 The Soft, Interpretive Underbelly of Generative Semantics. Pp. 383-96 in Cole and Morgan 1975.

Sasson, J. M.
1976 Wordplay in the Old Testament. Pp. 968-70 in Crim *et al.* 1976.

*Sanders, G. A.
1976 *A Functional Typology of Elliptical Coordinations*. Bloomington: Indiana University Linguistics Club.

Schmerling, S. F.
1975 Asymmetric Conjunction and Rules of Conversation. Pp. 211-31 in Cole and Morgan 1975.

Schramm, G. M.
1976 Poetic Patterning in Biblical Hebrew. Pp. 167-91 in Orlin *et al.* 1976.

Searle, J. R.
1970 *Speech Acts: An Essay in the Philosophy of Language*. Cambridge: Cambridge University Press.

Sebeok, T. A. *et al.*
1974 *Current Trends in Linguistics 12*. The Hague: Mouton.

Segert, S.
1960 Problems of Hebrew Prosody. *Supplements to Vetus Testamentum* 7: 283-91.

Shea, W. H.
1976 David's Lament. *Bulletin of the American Schools of Oriental Research* 221: 141-44.
1978 The Siran Inscription: Amminadab's Drinking Song. *Palestine Exploration Quarterly* 110: 107-12.

Sherzer, J.
1974 *Namakke, sunmakke, kormakke:* Three Types of Cuña Speech Event. Pp. 263-82 in Bauman and Sherzer 1974a

Sinclair, C.
1976 Deep Structure, Elision and the Distribution of Grammatical Phenomena in Hebrew Poetry. Paper read at the Society of Biblical Literature Annual Meeting, St. Louis, Missouri. Not heard.
Skehan, P. W.
1951 The Structure of the Song of Moses in Deuteronomy (Dt 32: 1-43). *Catholic Biblical Quarterly* 13: 153-63.
1954 A Fragment of the "Song of Moses" (Deut. 32) from Qumran. *Bulletin of the American Schools of Oriental Research* 136: 12-15.
1957 The Qumran Manuscripts and Textual Criticism. *Supplements to Vetus Testamentum* 4: 148-60. Reprinted in Cross and Talmon 1975.
1959 Qumran and the Present State of Old Testament Text Studies: The Masoretic Text. *Journal of Biblical Literature* 78: 21-25.
1971 *Studies in Israelite Poetry and Wisdom.* Catholic Biblical Quarterly Monograph Series I. Washington: Catholic Biblical Association of America.
Smith, B. H.
1968 *Poetic Closure: A Study of How Poems End.* Chicago: University of Chicago Press.
Speiser, E. A.
1963 The Stem PLL in Hebrew. *Journal of Biblical Literature* 82: 301-6.
1964 *Genesis.* The Anchor Bible 1. Garden City: Doubleday.
Stek, J. H.
1974 The Stylistics of Hebrew Poetry. *Calvin Theological Journal* 9: 15-30.
*Stolz, B. A., and R. S. Shannon, eds.
1976 *Oral Literature and the Formula.* Ann Arbor: Center for the Coordination of Ancient and Modern Studies, The University of Michigan.
Strugnell, J.
1974 A Plea for Conjectural Emendation in the New Testament, with a Coda on 1 Cor. 4:6. *Catholic Biblical Quarterly* 36: 543-58.
Stuart, D. K.
1976 *Studies in Early Hebrew Meter*, Harvard Semitic Monograph Series 13. Missoula: Scholars Press/Harvard Semitic Museum.
Suárez, P.
1964 Praepositio $^{c}l$ = coram in Litteratura Ugaritica et Hebraica-Biblica. *Verbum Domini* 42: 71-80.
Taber, C. R.
1964 Semantics. Pp. 800-7 in Crim *et al.* 1976.
Talmon, S.
1961 Synonymous Readings in the Textual Traditions of the Old Testament. Pp. 335-83 in Rabin 1961.
1975 The Textual Study of the Bible—A New Outlook. Pp. 321-400 in Cross and Talmon 1975.
1976 Conflate Readings. Pp. 170-73 in Crim *et al.* 1976.
Tawil, H.
1974 Some Literary Elements in the Opening Sections of the Hadad, Zākir,

and the Nērab II Inscriptions in the Light of East and West Semitic Royal Inscriptions. *Orientalia* 43: 40-65.

Thompson, J. M.
1974 *The Form and Function of Proverbs in Ancient Israel.* Studia Judaica 1. The Hague: Mouton.

*Thráinsson, H.
1975 Gapping in Icelandic: Functional Explanation and the No-Ambiguity Condition. Pp. 604-14 in R. E. Grossman, L. J. San, and T. J. Vance. 1975b. *Papers From the Parasession on Functionalism.* Chicago: Chicago Linguistic Society.

Tromp, N. J.
1969 *Primitive Conceptions of Death and the Nether World in the Old Testament.* Biblica et Orientalia 21. Rome: Pontifical Biblical Institute.

Unnik, W. C. van and Woude, A. S. van der, eds.
1966 *Studia Biblica et Semitica Theodoro Christians Vriezen . . . Dedicata.* Wageningen: Veenman.

Vendler, H.
1976 Defensive Harmonics. *The Times Literary Supplement* 775-76 (25 June 1976).

Watkins, C.
1963 Indo-European Metrics and Archaic Irish Verse. *Celtica* 6: 194-249.
1974 Language and its History. Pp. 85-97 in Bloomfield and Haugen 1974.

Watson, B.
1971 *Chinese Rhyme-Prose.* New York: Columbia University Press.

Watson, W. G. E.
1969 Shared Consonants in Northwest Semitic. *Biblica* 50: 525-33.
1971 More on Shared Consonants. *Biblica* 52: 44-50.
1975 Verse-Patterns in Ugaritic, Akkadian, and Hebrew Poetry. *Ugarit-Forschungen* 7: 483-92.
1977 Rev. Sabottka 1972. *Biblica* 57: 270-71.

Watters, W. R.
1976 *Formula Criticism and the Poetry of the Old Testament.* Beiheft zur Zeitschrift für die Alttestamentliche Wissenschaft 138. Berlin: de Gruyter.

Weiden, W. A. van der
1970 *Le Livre des Proverbs: Notes philologiques.* Biblica et Orientalia 23. Rome: Pontifical Biblical Institute.

Weinfeld, M.
1972 The Worship of Molech and of the Queen of Heaven and Its Background. *Ugarit-Forschungen* 4: 133-54.

Welch, J. W.
1974 Chiasmus in Ugaritic. *Ugarit-Forschungen* 6: 421-36.

Wevers, J. W. and Redford, D. B.
1970 *Essays on the Ancient Semitic World.* Toronto: University of Toronto.

Whallon, W.
1969 *Formula, Character and Context: Studies in Homeric, Old English and Old Testament Poetry.* Washington: Center for Hellenic Studies.

Whitley, C. F.
1974 Has the Particle *šm* an Asseverative Force? *Biblica* 55: 394-98.
1975 Some Aspects of Hebrew Poetic Diction. *Ugarit-Forschungen* 7: 493-502.
Widengren, G.
1959 Oral Traditions and Written Literature Among the Hebrews in the Light of Arabic Evidence, with Special Regard to Prose Narrative. *Acta Orientalia* 23: 201-62.
Wilkinson, L. P.
1963 *Golden Latin Artistry*. Cambridge: Cambridge University Press.
Williams, D. L.
1963 The Date of Zephaniah. *Journal of Biblical Literature* 82: 77-88.
Williams, G.
1968 *Tradition and Originality in Roman Poetry*. Oxford: Clarendon.
Williams, R. J.
1970 The Passive Qal Theme in Hebrew. Pp. 43-50 in Wevers and Redford 1970.
Wimsatt, W. K., ed.
1972 *Versification: Major Language Types*. New York: Modern Language Association/New York University Press.
Wolsky, A.
1960 A Hundred Years of Darwinism in Biology. Pp. 9-32 in Ong 1960a.
Wright, G. T.
1974 The Lyric Present: Single Present Verbs in English Poems. *Publications of the Modern Language Association of America* 89: 563-79.
Wulstan, D.
1971 The Earliest Musical Notation. *Music and Letters* 52: 365-82.
1974 Music from Ancient Ugarit. *Revue d'Assyriologie* 68: 125-28.
Yoder, P. B.
1971 A-B Pairs and Oral Composition in Hebrew Poetry. *Vetus Testamentum* 21: 470-89.
1972 Biblical Hebrew. Pp. 52-65 in Wimsatt 1972.
Young, A. M.
1931-32 Schematized Word Order in Vergil. *Classical Journal* 27: 515-22.
Young, G. D.
1950 Ugaritic Prosody. *Journal of Near Eastern Studies* 9: 124-33.
Zeps, V. J.
1973 Latvian Folk Meters and Styles. Pp. 207-11 in Anderson and Kiparsky 1973.
*Zwicky, A. M.
1974 Hey, Whatsyourname! Pp. 787-801 in M. W. LaGaly, R. A. Fox, and A. Bruck, eds. *Papers from the Tenth Regional Meeting*. Chicago: Chicago Linguistic Society.

The publications of the Chicago Linguistic Society (Bruck *et al.* 1974, Campbell *et al.* 1970, Corum *et al.* 1973, Grossman *et al.* 1975a and 1975b, LaGaly *et al.* 1974, and Peranteau *et al.* 1972) are available from the Society, Goodspeed 205, 1050

East 59th Street, Chicago, Illinois 60637. The publications of the Indiana University Linguistics Club (Bell 1975, Frantz 1974, Hudson 1975, Ross 1967, and Sanders 1976) are available from the Club, 310 Lindley, Bloomington, Indiana 47401. The publications of the Department of Near East Studies of The University of Michigan (Orlin *et al.* 1976) and the Center for the Coordination of Ancient and Modern Studies of The University of Michigan (Paper 1975 and Stolz and Shannon 1976) are available from Eisenbrauns, P.O.B. 275, Winona Lake, Indiana 46590.

# INDEXES

In the subject index, (Heb) indicates references to the Hebrew language and (HV) to Hebrew verse in particular; the separation could hardly be clearcut. In the scripture index, the poems under study are indexed only for Part I; the references in Chapter 2 and in the Table of Contents will guide the reader to further discussions. The indexes were compiled by William Barrick.

## SUBJECT INDEX


Aaron 114, 377
abbreviation 253
absolute (state) 224, 231, 261, 306, 311, 312, 380, 382, 383, 388
accentuation 22-23, 97, 150
accusative case 301, 304, 311, 388
achiastic 392, 401, 402, 403
acoustics 451
acrostic poems 39, 142, 152, 454, 476
action/reaction 508
addressee 80
*adhalhending* (Old Norse) 59
adjacency 366, 369, 371, 387
adjective 62, 68, 79, 90, 91, 99, 104, 116, 117, 118, 134
—(HV) (*see also* combination) 67, 68, 174, 248, 308, 309, 310, 312, 378, 384
adverb 62, 93, 126, 147, 235, 299
adverbial (HV) 68, 82, 83, 121, 299, 300, **300-03**, 308, 313, 334-43, 405
——accusative 299, 301, 302
——deverbative 301
——memized 301, 302
aesthetics 20, 40
affixation 362
Afroasiatic 90, **117-18**
agent 86, 311, 312, 468
agreement 124
Ahiram Text 27
Akkadian 22, 26, 40-41, 118, 121, 126, 161, 162
—cognates 186, 187, 192
—musical texts 40-41
—verse 33, 38, 107, 125-26, 143
alliteration 15, **57-58**, 61, 140, 455
—(HV) 10, 141, 143, 413
alternation 386, 438, 446
ambiguity 48, 71, 143
Ammonite 26
Ammonites 376, 516
Amorite 161, 220
anadiplosis 144
analogy 96
anapest 64
anaphora 144, 365, 371, 382, 383, 387, 410
anchor function 504, 524
animals 378, 428-30, 438, 470
antecedent, dummy 303
anticlimax 536
anti-merismus 378
antonymy 57
aphrodisiac 427
aposiopesis 219
apothegm 28
apposition (*see also* combination) 91, 92
apposition (HV) 74, 84, 85, 92, 131, 181, 184, 308, 309, 310, 356, 378, 415, 417, 419, 420, 422
Aqhat 231
Aquila 254
Ar 193
Arab grammarians, the 4, 13, 68, 297
Arabic 121, 124, 145, 297, 299, 303
—cognates 176, 186, 187, 214, 215
—proverbs 7
—verse 7, 24, 33, 61, 135, 142, 146, 159
Aramaic, Old 27, 101
Aramaic cognates 186, 187

# AUTHOR INDEX

## SCRIPTURE INDEX

## WORD INDEX

**Hebrew**

*qnʾ* 200
*qny* 185
*qrʾ* 412
*qsm* 189
*qrwb* 302
*qštw* 177

*rʾb* 201
*rʾy* 215
—*rʾy b* 279
*rb* 210
*rbṣ* 186
*rglw* 216
*rwḥw* 285
*rwm* 237, 302
*rwʿ* 410
*rzh* 253
*rāzôn* 253
*ryqm* 302
*rkb* 197, 216
*rekeb* 179
*rkbw* 179
*rmym* 277
*rnn* 412
*rʿ* 260

*śbʿ* 242
*śdy* 198
*śʿr/šʿr* 199, 222
*śry* 224
*śrym* 243
*śrʿ/šrʿ* 194

*š* 168, 300, 323, 421
*šʾl* 410
*šʾr-hbʿl* 243
*šbb* 177
*šbḥ* 410
*šbṭ* 175
*šbṭy* 175
*šbʿ* 242, 410
—*hnšbʿym* 242
*šbʿwt* 236
*šgʿ* 154
*šdy* 372
*šwb ʾmr* 412
*šwr* 171
*šḥḥ* 295
*šḥn-šḥnt-šḥt* 292
*šay lōh* 172-73
*šyr* 412
*škm* 303
*škm-ʾḥd* 303

*šm* (adv.) 235, 301, 302
*šm* (n.) 177, 235, 242, 500
*špṭ* 175
*špk* 247
*špr* 176
*šršm* 224

*tbʾ* 171
*thwmwt* 266, 293
*twr* 235
*twryšmw* 182
*tḥt* 239, 298, 300, 302
*tkw* 209
*tkk* 209
*tm* 190
*tmwṭ* 204
*tmk* 238
*tmlʾmw* 182
*tny* 410
*trbʿ* 187
*trwmt* 231
*trʿt* 188

**Phoenician**

*ʾyt* 388

*kn* 303

**Ugaritic**

*ʾaḥ* 101
*ʾary* 101

*bl* 231
*bn-ʾum* 101
*bṯn* 215
*bt* 101, 103

*hyn* 113
*hkl* 101, 103
*ḥẓr* 101, 103

*kṯr-wḫss* 113

*mdl* 191, 235
*mṯb* 101

*ʿl-ʾumt* 101

*ġry* 197

*šrʿ* 194

*trbṣ* 187

**Arabic**